Middle East

March 30, 1996

To Princetta ~

At Your Own Risk

With our love and
best wishes ~

Tom
and Jean Sutherland

At Your Own Risk

An American Chronicle of
Crisis and Captivity in the Middle East

Tom and Jean Sutherland

Fulcrum Publishing
Golden, Colorado

Book design by Deborah Rich

Library of Congress Cataloging-in-Publication Data

Sutherland, Tom, 1931–
    At your own risk : an American chronicle of crisis and captivity in the Middle East / Tom and Jean Sutherland.
        p.   cm.
    Includes index.
    ISBN 1-55591-255-9 (alk. paper)
    1. Sutherland, Tom, 1931—Captivity, 1983–1993.   2. Sutherland, Jean.   3. Hostages—Lebanon—Biography.   4. Hostages—United States— Biography.   I. Sutherland, Jean.   II. Title.
DS87.2.S87A3   1996
956.9204'4'092—dc20   95-49855
[B]   CIP

Printed in the United States of America

0 9 8 7 6 5 4 3 2 1

Fulcrum Publishing
350 Indiana Street, Suite 350
Golden, Colorado 80401-5093
(800) 992-2908

Contract understood with the American University of Beirut

*There is a job here at AUB for you, but the
situation in Beirut is very bad.
If you come, you come at your own risk.
Do you still wish the job?*

Yes.

See there a spectacle worthy of God's regard ...
a man pitted against hard fate—
and doubly so if his was the choice to challenge it.

*—Seneca, "On Providence"
(Translated from the Latin)*

Tom Sutherland is a true American hero. ... He was a hostage, yes; but he never felt sorry for himself nor did he complain of his situation. He inspired us all with his grit and his unfailing faith in his God and his country.

—George Bush

Contents

Preface

1983 to 1993. Definitely an American encounter with crisis and captivity in the Middle East, that decade. For us, personally, yes, as we went to live and work in strife-torn Lebanon as educators at the American University of Beirut with captivity becoming part of that work through our decision to stay against all warnings.

But the American encounters proliferated. The American University of Beirut itself was caught up and involved in its own as well as the larger Lebanese conflict, incorporating the American, Palestinian, Christian, Druze, Sunni, Shiite, Israeli, Syrian, Libyan, Iranian, British, French, German, and other national-international struggles for power and hegemony. As anarchy and chaos took over, shells and bullets rained in, car bombs obliterated buildings, cars, and people, and Americans and other westerners were kidnapped, held hostage, or killed, the American institution on Lebanese soil hung on and struggled to redefine its mission in the face of all odds.

On another plane, many saw the American government in its turn held hostage by Shiite fundamentalists and Iran's Ayatollah Khomeini, plagued as the government was in the early years by the Iran-Contra Affair that seemed to exemplify the ignorance, false dealing, and sheer powerlessness of an American administration without firm and legitimate rationale in its dealing with a Middle East crisis. With all the force at its command to be shown so graphically in the Gulf War, the United States appeared to have no real or positive way to deal with religious extremists in Lebanon. As an instrument of their war, these Shiite fundamentalists picked up hostages and held them for nearly seven years just as the Palestinians in the Intifada of the Left Bank and Gaza picked up stones and, throwing them at Israelis for over two years, successfully challenged that government, pushing it into wrong and unethical retaliation. Lessons for governments that could lead to straight dealing and peace processes.

Perhaps, however, the most important American encounter through it all was that of the American people themselves who engaged in the hostage crisis, hanging on, caring, praying, frustrated, wondering, yet so rightly demanding answers, resolution, and individual Americans home.

Indeed it was a multilevel American encounter. We here do what we can to chronicle the momentous happenings, motives, rumors, opinions, and feelings as we lived and experienced them through the years in Lebanon, hoping to find meaning in it all.

Our book has found its final form in the Year of the Family. This is, for us, a powerful symbol of what we discovered as individuals caught in the web of international affairs for those years. We had taken the risk and were paying the price while trying to take responsibility for our choice to be and to stay in Lebanon during that focal period. If we should ask or cry for help, we felt the integrity of that choice to be subverted. So we just couldn't ask or cry. But like a miracle, the people came forward and held firm in their support, their caring, their prayers. With these gifts, they became our immediate and extended Family and we love them for it.

Thus, we dedicate this book to Family: to our close kin in America and Scotland who felt and did so much for us, including especially Dad, dying 39 hours before the freedom; to those wonderful Friends of Tom Sutherland who didn't know it couldn't be done and so did it every year and for homecoming and afterward; to our close, dear friends whose love was a tangible; to professional colleagues in all countries who didn't let down; to our loving communities and the media who bridged the years with continuous observance and welcomed us home; to our acquaintances and other Americans and people worldwide who didn't know us personally yet understood, those who can't be named yet know who they are. All of you are integral to our text, made the difference, and have a special piece in that release and our life now and afterward.

Particular members of this Family helped us turn a rough manuscript into a finished book, and we acknowledge their special efforts—Jacques Rieux, John Pratt, Bill Griswold, Bob Baron and his staff at Fulcrum Publishing, and Adib Saad who helped us with Arabic transliteration.

And last but first:

to our precious daughters, so "true, fair, and kind"
and of whom we are so proud,
Ann, Kit, and Joan,
and their husbands, their children, and their children's children to come,
we dedicate this book.

PART I

Beirut Balcony
1983–1985

Part I part page—Jean on the balcony of their home at AUB with its cherished view of the university Green Field and the Mediterranean Sea.

Tom

1   Assassination

January 18, 1984. I stood over the pool of blood that was Malcolm Kerr's, there in the hall outside his office as president of the American University of Beirut, and I was sick—sick in mind and heart and stomach. Why? Why and how could someone shoot down in the coldest of blood a man so sharp, so dynamic, so right for the university at this time and place—at least the kind of university I understood with a dedication to the education of young people of all religions and a chance for positive dialogue among them? But, as he stepped out of the elevator on the third floor, two professional assassins in black jackets were there to put two bullets through silencers into the back of his head at point-blank range. By the time anyone got there, Malcolm was down and dead and the assassins had disappeared by the stairs, into the crowd, out of College Hall and presumably the Main Gate, perhaps brushing right past Malcolm's wife Ann who was standing in the rain there, reading a book as she waited for a friend—"If I hadn't been reading I must have seen them."

As dean of the Faculty of Agricultural and Food Sciences at the university, I had gotten the news quickly. Fadi, a new young professor, had come running into my office very scared and distraught—"Someone's been shot!" "What?! Who?" "I don't know." "It was not President Kerr?" "Maybe. I am not sure. It was on the third floor of College Hall." Oh, my God, I thought. Surely not Malcolm! Impossible. So I immediately tried to call Annie Baasiri—trusted, efficient Annie who had just gone from being my secretary to being Malcolm's because he needed her. I knew I would get the straight scoop from her. Her line was busy; I tried again. Still busy. Again. Same story. So I tried calling another office on the second floor and got the secretary there. She confirmed my worst fears. It was indeed President Kerr.

I went directly to the office of Dr. Abed Saghir just down the hall from mine and gave him the terrible news. He reacted immediately: "You must stay here, in case they are on their way down here. You could be next!" That thought hadn't occurred to me, but I could see the logic of it; perhaps "they" wanted to make a clean sweep of all the American administrators on campus. But soon there was Annie on the phone, "Can you come up to an emergency meeting of the Board of Deans in the president's office in College Hall?" "Is it safe for me to come up there?" "I think so. I think they have left now." Saghir insisted that I take a bodyguard, so we got mighty Hassan from the greenhouses to go with me. A huge man of impeccable integrity, he was, as Jean put it in loving description, "enormous ... chews nails, breaks bricks with his hands, and lifts 500-pound weights." We set off up the hill.

The American University Hospital people (AUH) had already come, leaving the blood but removing Malcolm's body to their facility and shortly thereafter pronouncing him dead. I went from that blood to the meeting—an ordeal for me. The reality had set in, and I found myself unable to speak in the meeting. *By God, some son of a bitch killed him. Some son of a bitch ... .* The academic vice president was in charge and was trying to keep an air of calm in a roomful of distraught administrators—all of them were there, down to the level of directors. My friend Radwan Mawlawi, Director of Information, became concerned about my silence, "Are you feeling okay?" "I'm all right," I mumbled, "I'll join in the discussion in a few minutes." But I never was able to do it, and afterward in a daze, I returned to my office. *Some son of a bitch killed him!* Hassan, my new "guard," ceremoniously gave me the great Luger-type pistol he was carrying, no English necessary for his message, and I held it, heavy and ugly in my hand, wondering where on earth it came from, knowing I wouldn't know what to do with it. Nevertheless, it went into my desk drawer and stayed. Hassan "stayed" also, to accompany me whenever I left the office. Loyalty. All those hours are graphic in my memory, the words of my diary seeming only to touch the surface of my emotion:

> ... Rest of day was with a heavy heart... . Jean, Kit, and Joan and I went upstairs to Marquand House at 1:00 or so and hugged Ann Kerr, who was strong and said, "We had planned to make such beautiful music together ... . How can I live without Malcolm?" Touching. She is a marvelous lady, Ann ... . In the evening we talked and Muin and Annie came by to talk and grieve. Recorded a BBC statement on Malcolm. Kit and Joan went to Marine House—all there are confined now ... .

President Malcolm Kerr of the American University of Beirut, our beloved AUB, assassinated. Who could, who would have done it? Speculation was rife. It reportedly was the day before he was to get bodyguards—who knew that? Who would be threatened by him and want him out of the way? To whose advantage was his death? Islamic Jihad who had claimed responsibility for the U.S. Embassy and U.S. Marine barracks bombings? The Christian Phalangists at the other end of the spectrum who saw Malcolm as a renowned Arabic-speaking Arabist scholar/president too fair to the Moslems and Palestinians? The Israelis? A personal enemy? As usual it might have been to anyone's or three groups' advantage and it would be, as with most murders in Beirut then, an unsolved mystery. To this day there has been no official definitive answer to Malcolm's murder and more telling perhaps is that no one expects it. How easy in chaos to get away with murder.

The only truth I knew that day, sick with shock and horror at that dark pool of blood, was that if there were a Hit List for Americans at AUB I could very well be the next one on it. That night, January 18, 1984, is one of the clearest memories I have, of lying in bed next to Jean, both of us still in shock and nearly paralyzed with the need for decision—Malcolm Kerr brought us here to do a job, he's been assassinated, do we cut and run or do we stay and face the bullets and do the job he hired us for? And the answer was there almost without our having to argue or debate alternatives although we did that and kept doing that—it was, however, there in the choice we had made to come. We could not let Malcolm's assassins get away with it nor could we let his trust in us be dishonored. So be it. We would stay and do the job. To this it had come in six months: from my arrival with ordinary hopes and dedication to do an administrator's job in the faculty of agriculture at this most prestigious of Middle East universities, dealing with personnel and budgets, with students and faculty and staff, getting grants and establishing extension programs, making this unique-among-private-regional-universities' agriculture program shine—to now, my life on the line. I wrote home:

> You are no doubt all convinced that we are totally crazy to be still here .... We have, however, discussed all the options and have decided to stay and give it our best for Malcolm and AUB; ... we realized it was risky when we came and to "cut and run" now would be a serious blow in many directions—to AUB, to the Agriculture Faculty especially, and to the reputation of Americans in general, to say nothing of our own self-respect and feeling of responsibility—it's amazing how one's determination hardens against assassins ....

The Lebanese tradition of holding a three-day public reception for people to present their condolences was maintained for Malcolm Kerr. Thousands came from all walks of life, and I stood in the receiving line for the entire three days, watching. I saw the Moslems openly grieving; stricken, even, were the student leaders of Amal, the secular Shiite militia, who had been a real bane of Malcolm's existence all the time I had been there. By contrast, there were those among the Lebanese Christian administrators dry-eyed or even smug, and I thought, is this the Christian way? Was there any truth in the circulating rumor that the Lebanese President Amin Gemayel had said, "Well, I wasn't going to renew his visa anyway"? I asked one of the senior administrators, "*Why* would anyone have done such a horrible deed?" He smiled and said, "Someone is sending a message to the United States," and shrugged his shoulders. I was horrified, and demanded, "Why did they have to do this? Don't they know that there are telephones and mail service to send messages?" It seems I was slow in learning the truth about Beirut Rumor and Beirut Messages.

Ann Kerr was an exemplar along with their family—Jean recorded our feelings in her letter to friends a week later:

> I spent most of two to three days at Marquand House helping receive, answer phones, etc. and cannot describe my admiration for Ann—stricken as she was, she received people, talked with reporters, got her family gathered and set the pattern for all of them with strength and determination, met her English Class at 8 A.M. Monday and Tuesday ... and then she went to the Memorial Service yesterday and spoke to all there at the end of the service. What an example she gave—the Lebanese women mourn by letting go and people were overcome by "the American way" of stalwart public composure—what it did for AUB was to bridge the week and get the University started again by providing a strong central presidential presence in Marquand House—she'll never be forgotten here nor of course will Malcolm ... .
>
> When the family left this morning the students in her class and close friends followed the family to the ground in front of the chapel where a plaque was set on a piece of Roman pillar—we read it as the family placed the flowers on it: "In memory of Malcolm Hooper Kerr, who lived his life abundantly ... we are proud our dad and husband came to AUB ... Ann, Susan, John, Stephen, Andrew," a beautifully ironic complement to the words carved in stone over Main Gate—"That they may have life and have it more abundantly"—AUB's motto since its founding ... .

I was given two M-16–toting military bodyguards and a rotating set of AUB guards for the house and Agriculture Building, and I did my job for the next year and a half shackled by a couple of bodyguards trailing along behind me everywhere: a year and a half that brought the kidnappings of Jerry Levin, Ben Weir, Father Jenco, Peter Kilburn, Marcel Carton, Marcel Fontaine, Michel Seurat, Jean-Paul Kauffmann, Terry Anderson, David Jacobsen, and the killing of Dennis Hill. And then would come my return on June 9, 1985, when there would be no AUB bodyguard—indeed, by my own decision, no Amal militiamen either.

Jean

2   Hello to Lebanon

Was I responsible? Soon after Tom's kidnapping, a radio talk show host in Denver took me to task, accusing me almost belligerently, "Why didn't you keep your husband from going back to Beirut? From going there at all? It was clearly dangerous—why did you let him go?" I was nonplused: "It wasn't a question of 'let'—we made the decision together." And so we did.

I remember well the fall of 1982, the day and the scene—even to what I was wearing: a silk blouse, brown plaid skirt, and boots. Tom had brought the chairman of AUB's Board of Trustees, Najeeb Halaby, to meet me and they were standing together in the front hall of our home. I came down the stairs, turned the bottom curve of the banister, and shook hands. A fine man, Najeeb Halaby. After the exchange of greetings, he looked at me and said, "Tom wants to come to AUB—do *you?*" As if by reflex my answer was there, so straight, decisive, and vehement that I think it startled us all—"Yes." That was it, there it was.

Where does a choice begin? Not for me on that day in the fall of '82, not for me even a year and a half before that when Tom had gone to interview for the position of dean of agriculture and had come back so fired up about AUB. He'd given his own "Yes" then and there, but three days later, war breaking out in Zahle in the Bekaa and the resignation of the university president put Tom's decision into limbo until Malcolm Kerr became the new president. For me—well, perhaps my choice began long before with my two Uncle Eds. Mother's older brother Edgar had gone in 1911 to AUB, then the Syrian Protestant College, in Beirut, Lebanon, to serve a three-year contract before coming back and ending up as provost at Yale. As for me, I grew up knowing extremely little about Yale but much about Beirut, that wonderful, exotic, storied place. Tales came down to me of Uncle Edgar being called on the carpet by President Bliss for leading the students astray by playing pool and drinking wine in downtown Beirut, of hikes and picnics in the mountains in the moonlight, of pre–World War I Turkish and Italian gunboats in St. Charles Bay. My other Uncle Ed was Dad's younger brother Edward, a doctor who didn't get married until he was 50 because he was busy traveling all over the world working on trachoma and, as we grew up, sending back from far-flung places things such as gourd lamps, Egyptian wall hangings, Turkish peasant utensils, ostrich eggs, and diverse small objects that were displayed for our wonder and delight in a special glass cabinet at Grandma and Grandpa's house in Cedar Rapids, Iowa. Most exotic of all was the story of Uncle Edward's being lost in the Gobi Desert for most of a year, unable to get proper papers to leave Mongolia until President Franklin Roosevelt was informed and got him out by negotiating a Russian visa. It turned out that after nearly getting wiped out by a rebellion, he used his time profitably by spending the summer with a desert nomadic tribe, publishing his experience in the January 1936 issue of *National Geographic*.

But then, perhaps, there was no choice for either Tom or me—perhaps it was meant that we go to Beirut and stay in Beirut.

Tom was due to go to AUB and take up his duties as dean of the Faculty of Agricultural and Food Sciences (FAFS) in May. On April 18, 1983, at 1:05 P.M. their time, the American embassy next to AUB was blown up by a truck bomb. We sat before the TV in our living room that evening aghast at the news but we didn't call to resign. May duly came, and Tom's visa got held up and held up. Thinking that it had to come any day and that he could leave from there, he went off to Washington to make useful contacts with the U.S. Agency for International Development (USAID) and talk over the upcoming job with Dr. Jim Cowen, a former agriculture dean at AUB. Tom stayed as long as was feasible, but no visa appearing even yet he was obliged to return to Colorado. In Beirut, Malcolm was angry and frustrated. He told Tom in one of their many telephone conversations, "You are a guinea pig of sorts, for there is strong political pressure to block your coming at all. The Christians have a Lebanese candidate for the dean's job."

In this struggle, AUB was simply reflecting the country's political struggle: For 40 years the Maronite Christians had been in charge of the country, the 1943 French Mandate on Independence setting out that the president would be a Christian, the prime minister a Sunni Moslem, and the speaker of the house a Shiite. For us, it was our first brush with this sort of national, sectarian, political struggle for the university: a battle enjoined as to who had control of hiring, of who had control of all. It would be, and will be still more in the future, the crux of an American institution on Lebanese soil. Tom said to Malcolm, "Can't you go to the American ambassador and put some pressure on them?" "Well," he replied, "I would rather save that big gun for more serious issues that are liable to come up. I think I can get this one done on my own. In the meantime, hang on." Tom began thus to discover Malcolm's continuing conflict with the Lebanese Maronite Christians both in the government of President Amin Gemayel and the AUB administration over the assertion of his authority as president of the university, meeting with obstruction of programs at every turn. The Christian government of Lebanon might court and welcome American support in its war against Moslems, but it would use all ways and means to control the American university.

How could we understand this? We had to understand this. Asking people we could find and reading all we could find, in the definitive works from Philip Hitti to AUB's own Kamal Salibi, we began to glean the simple outlines of Lebanon's complex historical past so important as the backdrop for understanding what we were going into in 1983. Sectarianism, human migrations, Western intervention, and war seemed almost to define Lebanon—reaching far back into the ancient shifting history of the past and forward into the likewise shifting history of the present.

The old Phoenician city-states of Trablus (Tripoli), Jbeil (Byblos), Sida (Sidon), and Tyre, whose people looked back perhaps to an origin in the Persian Gulf, were independent, competitive centers trading throughout the Mediterranean, thriving back to some 3,000 years B.C. on the coastal plain backdropped by the high, rugged cedar-forested mountains. Through Assyro-Babylonian, Persian, Greek, and Roman domination they maintained their importance along the ancient trade routes through which East met West, the city of Heliopolis (Baalbek) with its great temples to Jupiter and Bacchus and the city of Berytus (Beirut) coming to importance in the Roman period during the first centuries A.D.

Although there are Lebanese who claim to go back to the original Phoenicians, most scholars would trace their ancestries back to peoples who migrated from the Arabian south coast and inland regions and developed the Christian Maronite and Greek Orthodox and early Moslem Shiite and Sunni identities in the seventh century A.D. The Maronite Christians, named after one of their early leaders, St. Maroun, members of a sect who would later identify themselves with Rome and with Catholic France, found their early home in the northern mountain region of the Orontes River. The Shiites dominated Kisrawan below and also east to the Bekaa Valley and south to the Jabil Amil area east and south of Tyre. By the time of the Crusades in the 11th and 12th centuries, the Druze, named after their early leader al-Darazi, had separated themselves from the Ismaili Shiites to become a separate, cohesive, closed, and secret sect of mountain fighters centered in the Shouf Mountains. They squared off early with Moslem allies against the European crusading armies with whom the Maronite Christians had joined forces. For us, it wouldn't take too much juggling of the mind to telescope 800 years and understand the Druze shelling of American Marine positions in 1983–1984 when the American government took sides with the Maronite Christian government in their war with the Druze and Shiites.

In the 13th century, the Shiites were driven from Kisrawan to consolidate their regions in the eastern Bekaa and South Lebanon (the two places outside the southern suburbs of Beirut where Tom would be taken and held) while the Maronites became dominant in the country, migrating south not only into Kisrawan, the Metn, and the Shouf Mountains where they developed intersectarian control with the Druze, but also into South Lebanon itself among the Shiites. Six hundred years later they would become a central force of the South Lebanon Army to ally with Israel and fight for her interests and theirs in the border zone. Then in 1516 the Sunni Ottomans of Turkey captured and set up control over the entire area we know as the Middle East, holding sway until 1918. The Sunnite populations were thus underwritten in Lebanon for 400 years, populations that had, in contrast to the mountain-dwelling Maronites and Druze and the farming Shiites of the plains areas, predominantly gone into the urban coastal cities, becoming traders and businesspeople. As much as possible they would—as a dispersed minority—remain neutral in the Lebanese civil war of the last decades of our century.

In the 1850s and 1860s, war erupted in Mount Lebanon, ending in massacre and persecution of the Maronites by the Druze. The resolution came in 1861 with a new administration of Mount Lebanon (excluding Tripoli, Beirut, Sidon, the Bekaa, and the south) under Ottoman rule with an international guarantee from Europe. A notable and able administration responsible for progressive policies and technical improvements in the country, it set the pattern for 20th-century sectarian Lebanese government, the head of government from 1861–1915 answerable to Istanbul being a Catholic Christian with a council of 12 comprising 4 Maronites, 3 Druze, 2 Greek Orthodox, 1 Greek Catholic, 1 Sunnite, 1 Shiite. It was into this situation that the founding fathers of AUB came in 1862 to deal with the Turkish pashas in establishing their Syrian Protestant College on the Ras Beirut headland. Although feudalism was officially abolished with the new regime in Mount Lebanon, the concept of personal leadership with attendant follower allegiance surely persisted, producing the warlords of the 1970s and 1980s. The conflict we went into centered around particular people—Amin

Gemayel, Camille Chamoun, Suleiman Franjieh, Walid Jumblatt, Nabih Berri, Muhammad Hussein Fadlallah, Hafiz al-Assad, and others.

It would be seen over the next century, however, that it is easier to make decrees fixing boundaries and nominating nations and governments than truly to establish national identities. After World War I, in the juggling and manipulation by the British and the French of the old, now-defeated Ottoman Empire of the Middle East, the French received the mandate for Mount Lebanon, extended the boundaries to include the Bekaa, the coastal cities, and the south, and declared the state of Greater Lebanon in 1920 with a Republic of Lebanon announced in 1926 and an independent Lebanon in 1943. As established in 1861 and true to the centuries-old rapprochement between the French and the Maronite Christians, the head of government for Lebanon would be Maronite Christian. In addition, for this new government the prime minister would be Sunni and the speaker of the house Shiite. The Druze would figure in the cabinet. That the state of Syria was designated also in 1920 and its boundaries fixed with those of the new Lebanon, Iraq, Iran, Saudi Arabia, Jordan, and Palestine (some say by a woman in the British War Office drawing lines) did not mean that Syria was in accord. Syria still felt that the whole area was "Greater Syria" out of past centuries. The creation of Israel in 1948 completed the setup and became the catalyst for the Lebanese conflagration to come. Meanwhile, the migrations of peoples had continued—the Maronites especially to Beirut and to foreign shores.

Lebanon had thus been an independent state for only 40 years when we arrived there. In those years, the Maronite Christian-Sunni hegemony and entrepreneurialism had established a Western-oriented "Paris of the Middle East," or "Switzerland of the Middle East," with French the mandated second language and economic prosperity entrenched in their international banking centers and luxury hotels. As such, however, it was only a surface to a cauldron of pan-Arabism, Syrian claims, strong Druze and Shiite sectarian solidarities, Palestinian refugee camps, and the Palestine Liberation Organization (PLO) waiting to contest and challenge that hegemony. The Nasserite pan-Arab challenge to Maronite Chamoun rule broke out in 1958, drawing in American Marines. The Israeli Six-Day War of 1967 and follow-up war of 1973 upset the Arab-Israeli balance of power and the Palestinian influx from Jordan, following its "Black October" massacre of Palestinians in 1973, gave final challenge to Christian leadership in Lebanon. In 1975 the Lebanese civil war erupted.

That many other countries in the Middle East and the West were involved was a historical given; that the Israeli invasion of Lebanon in 1982 to "cleanse" its "border" of Palestinian threat was a massive incendiary that awoke the Shiite "sleeping giant" in the south of Lebanon triggering their migrations to Baalbek and to Beirut and the building of the southern suburbs was an additional given; and that the Maronite Christian community had a mandate to control Lebanon and its institutions of power including the American University of Beirut was a final given. And thus war itself became the ultimate given—war for land, for power, for control, war between Christians and Palestinians, Christians and Druze and Moslems, Shiite extremists and Shiite moderates, Druze and Americans, Shiites and westerners, Christians and Syrians, Christians and Christians … . Macrocosmic in the country and the region, microcosmic at AUB, war was what we walked into as fresh Americans in 1983 to start a job we saw as ordinary. There was no other way than to become part of it all.

It was on June 12 that Tom's visa materialized as a three-month, single-entry visa—not much use for a dean on a three-year contract, but he accepted it and left immediately for Lebanon. I went to work packing up and renting the house and making the myriad of arrangements including reservations on Pan Am to fly into Beirut on September 3 with our two younger daughters, Kit and Joan. Our oldest daughter, Ann, had been offered a position teaching anatomy in the Medical School at AUB but was well into her studies at the University of California at San Francisco by this time and couldn't leave to come. In Beirut, even after the embassy bombing, hope was high for AUB and Beirutis alike that summer of 1983—"now that the Israeli War is over and the Palestinians are 'out,' things can 'get back to normal' and go forward." Tom, indeed, wrote us glowing letters from Lebanon that first month he was there:

JUNE 21— It is now 11 P.M. and I have just come up to my room in Marquand House after a delightful and enjoyable reception … . I have sure been working hard at this. 12–13 hour days solid … listening, listening, listening, and exuding optimism and confidence with lots of understanding and charity thrown in—but I am standing firm on doing things straight and openly in the good of AUB … . You are going to enjoy this place so much you won't even believe it!! Lots of organizations for Joan to work in … . Kit will like this place I think—smaller, personal, international, neat campus, exotic environment—and BEAUTIFUL!! … Had a nice long chat with Malcolm after the party and find I really like and respect him—he is SHARP and a super straight shooter with a delightful sense of humor … . He is totally sincere and upright … unflagging dedication to the "right cause in the right way" … . And he is really a fun guy to be around—I am sure that we are in for a few interesting and exciting years, sweetheart— and this sure has been a right choice for us at this time … . If all goes well, it will launch us on a new life of adventure and fun—and Lord knows it has been fun to now, huh?!!

… The tour of the old "Downtown Beirut" was an incredible experience—like the Grand Canyon it defies description. When you and the girls arrive, we will go back, and you will see for yourselves what war can do. Horrible desecration, to say the least; … had lunch with 4 marines—Big Guys … .

JULY 10—I am sitting now in the final session of the AUB Board of Trustees—and it has been three pretty solid days.… We had a marvelous dinner here at Marquand House on Friday night, with all the power of Beirut here—U.S. ambassador, colonel of Marines, USAID representative, Foreign Secretary Eli Salem, ministers from the Lebanese government—you name 'em, they were here on the lawn of Marquand House!! … Malcolm says he will tell me about housing arrangements tomorrow! I surely hope we come up with a house, and I have in fact heard by a very obscure grapevine that he may put us in the David Dodge home … it's a year on July 19 since he was kidnapped, and a prayer gathering will be held in the chapel at 11:00 on that day for David and his well-being [and as though in answer to prayer David was released the very next day] … . The house is marvelously situated—next door practically to the tennis courts, steps to the beach are only a skip away, and it is 2 minutes walk to the dean's office— and 2 minutes the other way to Marquand House. So it would be ideal if he does indeed assign it to us!! Keep your fingers crossed!! …

JULY 11—Well—it's true!! We get to live in the Dodge House! Malcolm describes it as having 2 bedrooms, a third room, a maid's quarters up in a garret arrangement, … then a huge living room and dining room and kitchen—with also an enormous balcony overlooking the Med Sea!! And a gorgeous yard … (our telephone number will be Beirut 353-081) … . Went to dinner at a mansion—I simply can't describe it to you—enormous, stone, decorated to the last degree, with special "collection" rooms and halls and stairs like you see in the movies, … way up in the hills of East Beirut—and interestingly, East and West Beirut are like night and day—with the West being crowded, narrow streets, relatively dirty but with lots of atmosphere and seething with life—East is cleaner, crisper, wider streets, newer buildings, wealthy—and Christian, while West is Moslem … . The Maronites are far right; … was they and the Palestinians who started the civil war in 1975 that created the "Green Line" which no one dared cross for 7 years, but which now is relatively seething with traffic—and the destruction along that two-three block wide strip is incredible! Wait till you see it—gutted buildings of all sizes and shapes stand like gruesome skeletons. Hardly a building that doesn't have bullet marks all over it, or worse, huge holes where bigger stuff had hit it—diminishes as you get farther from the "epicenter" … . Actually, last night at the mansion, we heard rockets being fired farther up in the hills, reportedly at the Druze Moslems up there—quite a few bangs which visibly scared quite a few of the guests, especially the women! I wasn't scared, but then they have been through eight years of it up close and are pretty much "gun shy" … .

Thus did the Summer of Hope show signs of its real nature. The "glow" dimmed as the ominous warnings of the war to come in September began to crop up in Tom's August letters—life at AUB, however, was still full of activity and fascination and learning experience and the anticipation of our coming together there on September 3:

AUG. 7—Yesterday was quite a day—too bad you couldn't have been here to get in on it—Larry Parker took me to the Marine headquarters which is right by the airport, and there was a young lieutenant waiting for me with his jeep—drove me down to where a lieutenant commander was waiting with Dr. Acra of health sciences and about 30-plus AUB students; walked out to the landing strip to 2 waiting helicopters (monsters), got life jackets, earmuffs/helmet combination, strapped in and up and away we went—in minutes we were touching down on board the *U.S.S. Portland* ... . Apparently, they are glad to have visitors—it brightens the days of the sailors, who on this mission are not allowed ashore, poor guys!! And boy were their tongues all hanging out at the sight of these AUB students!! The girls, that is!! The captain had asked that the girls spread around 2 per table "and give the sailors a chance to talk to you ladies." They were a very nice bunch of young men, the sailors. And the officers were really quite high class I thought; ... they have invited us back when you all get here—and we should invite the officers to dinner some evening too ... . The "helios" came back at 15:30 and presto we were back in Marine-land, and proceeded to meet some of the real "pros" of the Marines—tough-looking sons of guns every one—the kind that would inspire some real confidence in you for defense!! ... Then off back to AUB! Quite an experience really; ... the Marine camp is a fascinating sight, how they have it all put together ... .

AUG. 11—Had a very interesting experience last week—I bid on a bunch of the air conditioners in the blown-up American embassy—they took it, but said we had to remove them at our own risk—so I lined up a group, 2 students, two tough laborers, 70-year-old Larry Parker from Wyoming, and me. And among us we carted 23 air conditioner units out of that ruin. An experience I will never forget. Eerie, in many ways—concrete walls cracked and falling, broken glass shattered everywhere—a beautiful building with three marble staircases, beautiful doors and walls, and furnishings, and blown to smithereens—you could not believe that one single explosion from a car could wreak such horrendous damage! But it did, no doubt about it. We recovered a few souvenirs, Larry and I—a photo of President Ford, a U.S. Marine Corps insignia, a bottle of bitters left on the floor of the bar on the very top floor, some books scattered around, a map of Beirut ... . [Tom proudly and perhaps somewhat superstitiously carried the leather Marine insignia in his briefcase till the day he was kidnapped, when he lost everything. He told me on his release that, along with the paper on Islam, it had aroused enormous suspicion among the Islamic Jihad guards and their bosses, and reinforced their belief that he was some sort of secret agent for someone, leading to lots of threats and harassment.] 5:00 P.M. The "rat race" began early today and I have been going at 90 mph all day—but maybe now I can catch my breath—Mahmud Solh is coming by at 6:00 to pick this up, but in fact I do not believe he will get out tomorrow, for the airport is closed and during the Board of Deans meeting from 10:30–1:00 there were horrendous explosions for over an hour, away to the south and east—I have not heard what it was all about, but presumably more shelling by the Druze, perhaps into the airport (I hope not!) or perhaps into Christian areas!!

AUG. 26—Boy it will be fun to have you here, sweetheart!! I have really missed you more than I even realized—I buried myself in work, and did not allow myself to think too much about being all alone here—but now that you will be here in 7 short days, my anticipation is skyrocketing … .

As it turned out in the end, Kit and Joan and I didn't make our scheduled flight to Beirut—the September War of 1983 erupted there instead. We waited and hung on with what news we could get with intermittent phone calls from Tom. Things were savage—the mainly Christian Lebanese Army at this time controlling mainly Moslem West Beirut had decided to go into the Shouf Mountains to take them as well from the Druze. The Israelis pulled out from the area leaving a vacuum into which the war poured, setting Christians and Druze into mortal conflict. The century of "peaceful coexistence" between the two sects there following after the massacre of 1860 was as if it had never been and bloody massacres on both sides ensued in the Shouf while at the airport below the "peacekeeping" Marines became more and more vulnerable to Druze attack as American policy took sides with Lebanese President Amin Gemayel and the Christians. Tom described it vividly for us:

SEPT. 6—Tis 5:55 P.M. and just a few hours over a week since this real hullabaloo started—though in fact the actual outset in the south of Beirut was on August 28, the result of "someone" firing shots from a car at a Shiite group who were hanging posters near the airport in commemoration of the "Imam Musa Sadr" who was abducted in Libya—the Shiites got in their car and gave chase, in the process going through a checkpoint—the Army fired at them for that, they fired back at the Army and the Marines really opened up on them and I believe, killed most of them in an instant—from there it went from bad to worse. The Shiite militia came out of the woodwork, and went wild, moving all the way up into West Beirut, and took it over, essentially, from the Army—the Army retreated from all its posts to its barracks to regroup, armed militia were everywhere on the streets, and it was apparently back to the "bad old days" of militia control of the city—even the gates of AUB were left unattended except for the AUB guards … . Thus Monday and Tuesday were tense all over—then on Tuesday P.M. and all day Wednesday the Army came back in force, organized for business and went systematically through West Beirut to clean up the militia men and restore order—so we had two days and nights of block-by-block fighting, sniper fire rat-a-tat-tatting all day and all night in the most vigorous and crisp and eerie way; … but the biggest horror by far was the apparently random shelling of all of West Beirut at the rate of 1 to 2 shells per minute as far as we could determine, which landed all over the place including the previously relatively in-violate AUB!! About 10 fell across the campus on Wednesday, including the one on Samir's lab in biology, which he had just left 15–30 minutes before. I was in my office here and heard a couple of shells whistle overhead, pretty loudly, and decided that maybe I ought to get out of here in case one fell outside—so I went out into the hallway—another one whistled over and exploded rather close—and then another one whistled in very close and BANG! It was the biggest bang I have ever been exposed to, at 50 meters distance—with fortunately the Agriculture Wing between it and me … . The lesson I learned is that the danger from these things (outside of a direct hit!) is the shrapnel which sprays everywhere—you will see it when you come—one piece drilled a six-inch hole through a concrete block wall and into the library next door; … well needless to say I was fairly well shaken up … . I decided that perhaps discretion really is the better part of valor—recalled friend Sandy Black's advice, "Think chicken shit, Tom!" and moved with cautious alacrity to the basement of the faculty apartments next door—not a very pleasant place, could surely have been fixed up by now, and a rather discouraging scene, with lots of young kids, and mothers everywhere, and people at loose ends … . Finally by 8:00 or so, it subsided and the army seemed to have gained control of most of the city … . The weekend was a bit quieter until the Israelis withdrew from the Shouf and Aley on Sunday—and since then, all hell has been loose down there—instead of 1–2 shells per minute, it has been 10–20 or more per minute, like thunder rolling in the dis-tance—and it has gone on almost without ceasing for nearly three days now!! Vir-tually everyone has agreed that the past ten days have been every bit as bad as the worst times of either the civil war or the Israeli invasion—and as far as the AUB is concerned, worse than either one.

SUNDAY, SEPT. 11—Hi Again Lasses! Greetings from a still war-torn Lebanon! By now you would have been 8 days in Beirut and we could have been sitting on the balcony up the hill a little watching a tranquil Mediterranean Sea … . Alas, here I am alone … . Have been reading *The Battle of Beirut*, a documentation of the Israeli invasion of Lebanon, which is shattering—the force that they employed against Sidon, Tyre, and Beirut is totally beyond belief, Jean—you too will be shocked and horrified at what apparently took place. However, at this moment, things almost as horrible and inhuman are apparently going on less than 25 miles from here between the "phalangists" or "Lebanese forces" and the Druze of Walid Jumblatt. This whole bit has now been going for 8 days and shows little hope of resolution—so it may be quite some time before the airport opens.

Resolution of the Lebanese kind did come, however, in the form of a victory for the Druze. By October 3, the Christians had been driven back and out of the mountains and the Druze had taken charge there; the inevitable shelling on Marine targets had sent American Marine bodies back to the States for burial; and the airport had reopened. That day I flew into Beirut via TWA (Pan Am never went back to Beirut), without daughter Ann, but with daughters Kit and Joan, Kit's Siamese cat, 20 cartons of household goods, and lots of hope. It was on a wonderful evening that we saw for the first time our AUB home with the cool north wind blowing off the sea and through the balcony doors. The top half of an early twentieth-century house, "Dodge House," as we named it, perched on a hill, hovering as it were between upper and lower campus and from its Arabic-arched balcony looking out over the AUB playing field to the Mediterranean Sea.

And so we settled in. I met Tom's faculty and administrative colleagues, and accustomed myself to shopping and to the environs of Ras Beirut. Life was full, exciting, and fascinating—not a moment of culture shock or feeling of alienation. I turned down a chance the first week to go on a trip to the south of Lebanon and have regretted it ever since, for it was the last chance there was to see it before the Israelis closed it off. Kit registered for her junior year abroad at AUB in psychology and Joan found friends and looked for jobs. Two teenage daughters meant that we soon made the acquaintance of a number of Marine embassy guards, a buildingful of them being at one corner of the AUB compound to serve the American embassy being housed temporarily since the destruction of their quarters in the Duraffourd Building of the Buckleys at the other corner of AUB along the Corniche or sea road. Although, according to custom, AUB kept itself quite separate from the American embassy for the purposes of staying apolitical and clearly nongovernmental, the university administration had offered unofficial hospitality to the Marine guards when they were off-duty, allowing them to run on the track around the Green Field, to use the outdoor basketball courts, and to play a hot game of softball with the AUB faculty team on Sundays.

Thus it was, on October 23, 1983, less than three weeks after our arrival, that we were personally involved in that horrendous 6:00 A.M. double blast at the airport Marine barracks and the French military compound. Kit and Joan got the news right away through the embassy guards who were shattered by the word that came about their Marine buddies at the airport. It was unbelievable that that smiling driver and the truck loaded with explosives had gotten through into the center of that building; it was unbelievable that President Ronald Reagan and General P. X. Kelley had set up our men to be so vulnerable despite the strong pleas from the front; it was, however, all very believable to our girls who went to visit the injured at AUH. Kit describes their experience today as though it had happened yesterday:

The Marine barracks blast. I remember so clearly that Sunday morning of October 23 and Joanie and I getting ready to go to the embassy guard-AUB baseball game— we had gotten up early to get our hair done and our makeup on—they were Marines after all—we'd met them the week before. The radio was on but all of a sudden over the music came the sound of that blast! My friend Russ from the Marine House came up in shock a little later: "250 were in that building ... 250 were in that building!!" He left and then came back and asked me if I'd go with him to the American University Hospital to see the guys that had been brought there. Terry Valour was one, not hurt the worst, but the one we got to know the best and who told us all about what he saw from his room at the airport barracks: he'd gotten up early to get dressed for his assignment, and he was standing there in his skivvies, he said, and getting out a cigarette when he looked out the window and saw the truck come in and he yelled, "Truck Bomb, Truck Bomb" but it was in and done and there was this fireball coming up and a rebar went through his leg and he was burned. When we saw him in the hospital he looked just like a burned log, a stump ... .You couldn't make out eyes or nose or mouth—he was really in bad shape. I had to put on a mask and it was so horrible and so close in there and he was too bad to travel .... . He stayed for weeks, but he really survived. Russ showed me a picture of Terry years later when he came for Dad's 1,000th day commemoration in March of 1988 and it's just amazing how he has recovered. But he still has a lot of trauma and he walks with a cane and he can't really work so he was trying to get some disability payment and having a really hard time collecting—how could that be? A guy who survived??! I remember too the gunnie who was so bad and in a coma—he'd been hit and laid down by the truck coming in—he was evidently trying to do something and none of them had loaded weapons—I'll never forget the stuffed animals that someone had put next to him—I just thought what an ugly thing had happened to him and how out of place those animals were ... he died. And then there was Rodney, little Rodney—he was so cute, so young .... . We kept going to the hospital because we felt we needed to go there and say "We're here, we're American, we want to connect, we care."

Thus Kit and Joan have never forgotten nor been the same—nor have we. It was our introduction to the truism—that governments and military establishments "do as they do do"—and we would not later be surprised or shocked by the Iran-Contra Affair. What we now heard by the grapevine was that the Brits said that American intelligence in Lebanon being sent back was impeccable—"wish we had the like of it"—but was being systematically ignored in Washington.

It was a subdued family Thanksgiving next month. Kit's embassy guard friend Russ came for dinner and afterward took platefuls of food back to those embassy guards on duty. But by Christmas we were exerting a positive life force again with festive gatherings at our home. As we wrote to our friends:

> We gave four parties in six days over Christmas and couldn't believe it—Friday the 23rd we had a wonderful "Olde Fashioned Christmas Social" for about 75 people young and old from the AUB and Ras Beirut community, and had all sorts of toasts … and the young Marines and girls and even oldies like us cranked up the music and danced until 11 P.M. It was tremendous fun and everyone said it set off the season for them—on Christmas Day it turned out that no one had invited the Marine embassy guards for dinner (I think mainly because since the Pickwick Bar blast the week before when the staff sergeant had barely escaped with his life they were restricted to their house and embassy and AUB), so we had 12 for dinner with turkey and all the trimmings—All of this is to show you the schizophrenic life we lead here because while all this was going on, the shops were being blown up, the embassy was receiving daily threats, periodic shelling was going on—ka-whoom, ka-whoom—and the Israelis were fighting it out in the south … . But it's a new year now, 1984.

We made plans for a big entertainment at our house on January 25, the birthday of Robert Burns, the eighteenth-century Scottish national poet whom all Scots love and memorialize with a great dinner, haggis, the poetry, and song—and, of course, Scotch whisky. But it was not to be. That last week of January was instead a time of grieving for our friend and president, Malcolm Kerr. Life at AUB was not, could not, be the same after that 18th of January. Definitive was the death knell to the old, gracious times with promise of new American possibilities. Definitive also was the death knell to our personal collegiality. No more would we go up for a barbecue in the Marquand House garden, no more call out greetings to Malcolm and Ann as they came up the stairs by our house from an early morning swim at AUB beach, no more for Tom the objective debating of AUB policies with Malcolm and colleagues in the board of deans' meetings or over coffee, no more for me the discussing of English teaching and ideas with Ann and friends. I took over Ann's freshman composition class for her when she and the family left campus after the memorial service and I'll never forget finishing Somerset Maugham's *The Moon and Sixpence* with her students, the book

Ann was reading when Malcolm was assassinated. Together we recognized the symbolic meaning of the closing images of the Tahitian, Gauguinesque Garden and its Fruit—for it was AUB:

> It was beautiful and obscene … . It was enchanted fruit, to taste which might open the gateway to God knows what secrets of the soul and to mysterious palaces of the imagination. They were sullen with unawaited dangers, and to eat them might turn a man to beast or god. All that was healthy and natural, all that clung to happy relationships and the simple joys of simple men shrank from them in dismay; and yet a fearful attraction was in them, and, like the fruit on the Tree of the Knowledge of Good and Evil they were terrible with the possibilities of the unknown.[1]

Tom

3   Work and War

It was with mixed feelings that I went to AUB to interview for the job of dean of agriculture, for I was very happy at Colorado State University (CSU). But I discovered in the AUB a fascinating and attractive place. Well over 100 years old, it had maintained the highest standards for both students and faculty, the latter having been trained in all the best American institutions—Harvard, Princeton, Berkeley and Davis, California, Texas, Wisconsin—and the former selected from as many as 20 or more applicants for each place. In its heyday, the students had come from all over the Middle East, but, of late, parents had understandably been reluctant to send their progeny to such a dangerous place as Beirut, the AUB's reputation notwithstanding, so that on my arrival I found that the vast majority of the students were now Lebanese. And, frankly, most of the renowned American faculty members had fled the scene for fresh fields and pastures new and safer, where they could ply their trade without constant threats of bombs, shells, and bullets. Some of my colleagues with characteristic frankness suggested that that was the only reason I could have been hired, and they may well have been right. In any case, graduates of the AUB had always had, and still did have, first choice of almost any job in the entire Middle East.

AUB had always been renowned for its open education—for being, like any other true American university, a place where one could learn to think objectively, to dialogue, to question, to solve problems. Chartered in the state of New York, AUB was indeed an American university in the fullest sense, with a strong history of interrelationship with other American institutions—students could transfer back and forth with ease; faculty were always welcome on sabbaticals and special leaves at such venerable institutions as Harvard, Princeton, and Cornell; and medical graduates were accepted at all the top U.S. institutions for internships and residencies. That the makeup of the student body was "open" as well was evidenced by the spectrum of its graduates—from George Habash, the Palestinian "terrorist," and the numerous others likewise using violence in the fight against the political status quo in the Middle East, to such brilliant and distinguished people as Hanan Ashrawi, leading the Palestinian delegation to the peace process. These graduates are part of AUB's history as described in John Munro's *A Mutual Concern,* in which he quotes an article from *Newsweek* of October 5, 1970, the heyday of Palestinian terrorism. Under the title of "Guerrilla U.," the article reported,

> Politics at AUB today is tied directly to the Palestinian guerrilla movement. Many students belong to one of the guerrilla groups, mainly to the Popular Front for the Liberation of Palestine (PFLP) or Al-Fateh, and often spend their summers or weekends in commando training camps. Some students have even been accused of stealing chemicals from university laboratories to use in making explosives … . The aggressive young men and women who spring from AUB appear torn between admiration for their American-style education and distrust of the country that offers it. "Of course we reject American foreign policy and the capitalist mentality of most Americans," an AUB student who doubles as a guerrilla group leader said recently. "But we have also learned to respect a culture that gives rebels even the right to think and say what they want. If there should be a Palestinian state run by us, it would be anti-imperialist, anti-Washington and anti-bourgeois. But I don't think it would be truly anti-American." [2]

I was later to hear very similar statements from my Shiite fundamentalist kidnappers.

The Palestinian connection had persisted. My mind went back to February 1981, when I had come to interview. President Hal Holscher had made no bones about the fact that he had lunch once a week with none other than Yasser Arafat! When I expressed amazement, he smiled and said, "Why not? He is our protection. No one dares to touch AUB while we have the protection of these tough Palestinian fighters." This whole admission took me by complete surprise, but I could readily see the logic in it. His camaraderie with Arafat was at least in part responsible for his demise from the presidency. The Christians did not like his hobnobbing with their archenemy at all, and although the official reason for his being let go was that he had proven unable to make his budget, I always had a very strong suspicion that his politics had played a strong role.

So if truly American, AUB was at the same time truly Middle Eastern, proof that higher education is an international process transcending national boundaries and self-interests. Thus the title of Munro's history of the institution is most ap-propos—*A Mutual Concern*. I bought a copy shortly after my arrival to learn where the university had come from. First established in 1866 as the Syrian Protestant College with Daniel Bliss, a Congregational missionary from New England, as its first president, it added a medical school the next year and later a college of arts and sciences. In the 1920s, a faculty of engineering was added, in the 1950s, a faculty of agriculture. In the 1970s, a faculty of health sciences completed AUB's growth, by which time the student body had reached almost 5,000 students. At the time of my arrival, the vast majority were in the arts and sciences, most of them hoping to be accepted into the medical school. This college had the small-est enrollment, but a faculty roughly equal to that of arts and sciences, and had also the lion's share of the budget—in every sense it was "the tail that wagged the dog," for it took vast sums to run a 400-bed hospital, which in these war years was subsidizing virtually every militia in town, receiving in return constant protection.

I quickly learned about Middle Eastern educational priorities. Almost no-body wanted anything to do with agriculture—that education is for Bedouins. Everyone wanted his son or daughter to be a doctor, and failing that, at least an engineer. I delighted in teasing the dean of medicine that "Agriculture, you know, is much more important than your medical college." He would smile disdain-fully. But I pushed it. "You don't believe me, do you?" "No." He was still smiling indulgently. "Then tell me, what about the starving millions in Ethiopia? How much have you been able to do for them lately?" The smile faded as he realized that I wasn't joking. I doubt if he had ever thought of things in that way. That the country that can't feed itself is in dire straits for which medicine has no answers. But that didn't lower the applications for the medical school, nor raise ours in agriculture above two or three for each of the 500 places in our college; and as at CSU, 50 percent of these were men and 50 percent women.

Despite the hard times that had befallen the university, the struggle to keep it apolitical, and the greatly reduced amount of aid being received from the USAID in comparison to its heyday, AUB by its very nature could not escape having a role in overall American foreign policy in the Middle East. From AUB's graduates came many of the movers and shakers of Middle Eastern governments: ministers of the economy, of defense, of state, even prime ministers and busi-nessmen, none of whom ever lost appreciation for American–style education. As Robert Kaplan said in his book, *The Arabists*, honestly if cynically, "The Syr-ian Protestant College, Daniel Bliss's brainchild, was probably the most inspired idea in the history of foreign aid. Not only was it a quintessential cottage industry project for filtering Western values into the Arab world over time, but it also provided a permanent aesthetic monument to America in the region."[3] And the ideals of Bliss were there to provide the high-minded aspirations for the place: AUB as "A Mutual Concern"—the Middle East and America working together for education in the best sense, at the highest standard. All very fascinating.

I went at my new job as dean with enthusiasm and joy. The faculty had been without a full-time dean for some time, and there was a vacuum in leadership. One of the first things I had to do was to infuse a spirit of optimism into both the students and the faculty. They were all ready for it. I immediately, in American style, drew up a detailed list of the specific projects that needed funding and submitted it to our Sunni Vice President for External Programs, Dr. Abdul Hamid Hallab. He used my list of projects as a prototype for the other deans to follow, a move not designed to enhance my popularity among that group, but one typical of Hallab, a "go-getter" par excellence. Malcolm Kerr had recognized Hallab's qualities right away and promoted him to vice president—again to the displeasure of the Lebanese Christians, who had never had a Moslem in a vice president's chair. I used to describe Hallab as a fellow who had ten solutions for every problem—as opposed to another senior administrator, George Sayegh, a Christian who always seemed to have ten problems for every solution. Presidents Kerr and Calvin Plimpton got a chuckle out of that designation, for they both had had exactly my experience with Sayegh. Malcolm asked me one day very early on, "Do you have any problems dealing with this man?" "Not really," I answered, "but I haven't actually had much to do with him yet." "Well," said Malcolm, "I can't get a thing out of Sayegh. I am completely frustrated." "Fire him," I suggested, in my naïveté. But Malcolm was either too much of a gentleman or too wise in the ways of Lebanese politics to take such drastic action. Later, I too would try to fire a Shiite faculty member and get into deep problems, for the realities of campus and Lebanese politics did not allow that to be done either. And it was only shortly after my conversation with Malcolm that my own problems with George Sayegh began—our permission to purchase computers. A telephone conversation ended so acrimoniously that our relationship was permanently soured. I did, however, get the computers.

In July, barely a month after my arrival, I began to realize the degree of obfuscation Malcolm was facing. He had just left for California to attend his daughter's wedding and to help his wife Ann pack for Beirut. At the meeting of the Board of Deans prior to his departure, he announced this very clearly and appointed the Academic Vice President Samir Thabet as acting president. A few days later, David Dodge was released, and the president's office was besieged by the media of Beirut and the world in a huge press conference. I was there. "Where is the president?" asked one of the journalists. "I don't know," said Thabet, sitting in Malcolm's chair. "Why don't you ask him?" I was stunned. Why should he lie? This was betrayal of President Kerr. And it wasn't over yet. Through the duration of the conference, Vice President Thabet was very obviously in his element with all the attention. I turned to a colleague, Landry Slade, a long-time faculty member at AUB. "I have a strong suspicion that this guy likes sitting in that chair. Does he have ambitions to fill it?" He looked at me incredulously. "Sutherland, you catch on fast!"

My suspicions only grew over the ensuing months, as I saw Malcolm face obstruction at every turn. Every time he left campus, I was shocked anew at the blatant attempts by all the Christians in the Board of Deans to undercut his authority and to defame him. And not only *I* knew that Malcolm was aware of this and puzzled and bothered by it. Ann Kerr writes in her book, *Come with Me from Lebanon*, "During our weekend in Aqaba, Malcolm for the first time told me in other than a joking or offhand manner that he believed he was being personally singled out by the Gemayel government as an enemy. He had been told by trusted friends, that one, if not more, administrators and former administrators within AUB were involved in whispering in the ear of the president and his supporters to plant or reinforce the idea that Malcolm was against the Phalangist regime."[4] Even those who had hired Malcolm showed their awareness of the obvious campaign to force Malcolm out of the presidency, for we had a visit from the chairman of the Board of Trustees himself, Najeeb Halaby, who warned the Board of Deans, "And if you get rid of this man, we will put another American into his place immediately. Fuck you!" For emphasis, he bent his right arm at the elbow over his left fist in the traditional show of defiance and his tone, angry and ominous, left the entire Board of Deans quivering. After his exit, the meeting broke into chaos, with declarations of shock and dismay at the allegations of the chairman, and especially at the strong language he had just used! The chairman, however, was familiar with the ways of the Middle East and of AUB, and was, in retrospect, prescient.

Several of the projects in the list I gave to Hallab concerned upgrading the farm in the Bekaa, the 250-acre Agricultural Research and Extension Center (AREC). We had drawn up the list of needs following a visit to the farm by some of the senior faculty, the budget officer, and the head of the physical plant. The office and laboratory building was in serious need of renovation. The steam boiler house had been blown to bits by an Israeli bomb during one of their raids. The dormitories needed complete revamping, especially the bathrooms, which had likewise suffered from a bomb and were no longer usable. The dairy was decades old and had had no maintenance. In fact, just about the whole farmstead needed serious upgrading even to approach what any reputable American university would require to carry out its program. All of this involved some millions of dollars, but I was fairly confident that we could get this donated from several of the large foundations who knew of AUB's long and prestigious record of American-style training and education.

On campus, too, there had been a long-standing plan to add a third floor to wing B of the agriculture complex, and indeed several hundred thousand dollars were already sitting in the bank to undertake this. But something had always come up to put the project on the back burner, with resultant erosion of faculty morale. I appointed yet another committee to draw up a valid set of plans and to make recommendations on the allocation of the space. On the supposition and premise that a new broom sweeps clean, and since everyone seemed willing to go along with my desires, I began pushing for these projects soon after my arrival, going after them with American optimism and spirit. I would take nine projects in my briefcase in May of 1985 to pursue funding in the States. Indeed, among the last things I did in the United States before my final and fateful trip back on June 8, 1985, was to send a letter to the Ford Foundation asking permission to redirect funds from South Lebanon (where we could no longer work due to the Israeli invasion) and another proposal requesting support for a nutrition project proposed by Professor Nahla Baba. I am sad to say that to this day, none of them has been initiated, such have been the prevailing conditions over the intervening years during which survival took precedence over optimization, and American foundation monies dried up or were diverted for the time being. The need is simply greater now than ever.

My personal involvement in the American-Lebanese tension reflected itself not only in visa granting but also on the ground throughout, and my education in cultural differences proceeded apace. At my first faculty meeting, I was amazed to discover that faculty members had been in the habit of speaking whenever they wished, regardless of whether someone was already holding the floor. There might be three or four competing to be heard and it was a circus, almost as bad as the British houses of Parliament, though that's hardly possible. I rectified that right away, changing the rules so that no one could speak without first being recognized, and amazingly, most everyone agreed that it was a great improvement, since it meant that we could get through meetings in about half the time.

I wasn't long on campus, however, before doing things American-style got me into intercultural trouble. In a discussion of how Malcolm was doing as president, I casually suggested at a dinner party that "Once he has all his deans installed, he will really be able to move forward." My remarks were made out of the American context I knew, because a number of the deans were "acting," and every university president, like a football coach, builds his or her administrative team. If it meant hiring, however, it surely didn't to me mean firing. But immediately these remarks were misinterpreted to mean that Malcolm was going to replace all deans currently in office. Thus he no doubt intended to fire Dr. Raja Khouri, the dean of medicine, who it transpired was a kind of cousin to Samir, the husband of Roseanne Khalaff, the woman I had been speaking to! This got back to Dr. Nicholas Khouri, Raja's brother who was on the Board of Trustees, and who in the next board meeting grilled Malcolm about why he wanted to fire the dean of medicine! Malcolm was thunderstruck, and asked me if I had ever suggested such a thing. I was totally nonplused, so together we set ourselves to unravel the devious paths of this particular rumor. It took hours. And it was a lesson to me to be super careful about saying *anything* that could in any way be misconstrued or misinterpreted.

Tension, moreover, was not only in the Lebanese-American sphere. The intra-Lebanese conflicts were ever present. Our faculty was roughly half Christian and half Moslem, and being highly educated and in an academic environment, they strove to and by and large managed to keep their differences submerged. But these invariably surfaced. A position came open—should it be filled by a Christian or by a Moslem? I got lots of pressure from both groups every time. We lost a secretary, and Annie, my own, who had had much experience with everything that had gone on in the past, advised me to get a woman from West Beirut. "If you take someone from the east side, the first outburst of violence means that you will be without her for days or weeks on end, for they simply cannot come across during periods of shelling and war." We found a marvelous young woman who was Druze. But the director of personnel (appointed by Malcolm shortly before his assassination) was Christian—one of my American colleagues had even told me bluntly, "There are no Moslems on campus who can fill administrative positions"—and the director put up every excuse one could think of to keep this young Druze from being appointed. Even with fragile traditions of and lip service given to peaceful coexistence, there are of course ancient enmities between the Christians and the Druze, centuries-old, basic, and bitter. This was perhaps my first encounter with such rivalries, and it frankly aroused my strong feelings of fair play. I fought like hell, and finally hired the woman. She turned out to be the smartest secretary we had, next to Annie, an Armenian. We had no Sunni and certainly no Shiite secretaries, for parents of these groups do not customarily allow their daughters to work. The pool therefore came from the Maronites, the Druze, the Protestants, and the Armenians, plus the odd foreigner who had married a Lebanese man and wanted to augment the family income. In the course of time, I hired as administrative assistant a sharp British young woman, and found myself of course as a bad guy by all the Lebanese staff, no matter what the sect. Whatever troubles they might have among themselves, they maintained a united front against the foreigners. I came to appreciate that if the university was a microcosm of the Lebanese scene as was so often recognized, my office was certainly a mini-microcosm of it.

I kept on putting my American foot in it and thus kept learning fast. One of my very first tasks was to evaluate my faculty for salary increases. I learned that my predecessor, John Fisher, had insisted on taking "student evaluations," much to the horror of all the Lebanese faculty—the very idea of students passing opinions on them was anathema; it simply wasn't done in the Middle East. But having been long used to the system at CSU and feeling that it was valuable, I began to inquire as to the status of these evaluations. They had never been analyzed, but a senior faculty member was in charge of having this done. I asked him about the status. "Oh," said he, "they are up at the computer center to be punched on cards and processed." Fine. So I asked my secretary, "Annie, why don't you call up the computer center and find out when we can have their analysis of the student evaluations?" "Student evaluations?" said Annie. "They are not up at the computer center. They are all lying in our closet. And I can tell you that the faculty don't want to have them analyzed. No way." I was furious, and in the next faculty meeting I took to task the senior faculty member for having deliberately deceived and misled me on the matter. Afterward, another colleague took me aside and explained that one must never cause an Arab to lose face in front of his colleagues, on penalty of making a lifelong enemy. One must always do such things in the privacy of one's office. I can see from this distance that even if one is angry as hops, as I was in this particular case, it's a good idea to do so for an administrator in general, even in American situations. But there and then in Lebanese cultural conditions, it was essential.

I did use as much input as possible in preparing my recommendations for faculty salary increases. But I was totally unprepared for the reactions to my evaluations—a general dissatisfaction of the faculty. Malcolm Kerr had persuaded the Board of Trustees to authorize an average salary increase of some 25 percent, a figure unheard of in Stateside institutions. After ranking the faculty on their performance, I awarded the top people some 40 percent, while those less highly recommended got from 15–20 percent. Even those were raises that as far as I knew no one in the United States had ever heard of. But within a few days, the procession of faculty to my office began. The lower end had of course learned that they were below average, were unhappy about it, and did not hesitate to let me know. I stood my ground, for I had worked for enough department heads who had not been willing to tell me straight to my face how they had arrived at decisions that I had long ago resolved to be firm and straight, and to defend my decisions, at least until I had been reasoned out of it by superior logic. I found the friendly confrontations stimulating, and since I kept an open-door policy, all the complainers could at least feel that they had had a hearing—sometimes several.

And then there were the students. Except for their strong cultural belief in *wasta* (influence) to get them admitted or better grades, they loved the American way and I loved them. Tradition ruled that the dean's position was full-time administrative, with no teaching duties. Eventually, after getting things set up, I believe I would have gone back into the classroom for at least one course, but in the first two years my contact with the students was restricted to the odd guest lecture in a class, and informal discussions with the bevy of them who seemed always to be holding forth at the green picnic table located just at the entry to the Agriculture Building. It was a veritable court where all issues and concerns were hotly debated, and I had to pass this table every morning and every evening, plus every time I exited to attend a meeting in College Hall. The students quickly realized that I was interested and willing to listen to them, and I had many a late arrival at meetings of the Board of Deans on the upper campus. But with an open-door policy for the students also, I felt that I could keep abreast of their worries and concerns—and there were many during these troubled times in Lebanon. I learned, for example, of the financial difficulties of one student; due to the war, his father had harvested not one bushel of apples while the previous year he had sold many thousands. The student thus would not possibly be able to continue his studies. I listened, went to bat, and was able to arrange some financial aid for him. At least some of my predecessors had apparently kept very much aloof from all such contacts with the students, academic hierarchy and the position of dean in the Lebanese culture being sacrosanct, but I was fresh out of the classroom at Colorado State, where I had maintained a sign-up sheet for students to make appointments to talk with me. There was no way I was going to deny contact with our agriculture students—their presence after all being the principal reason for my position—and these students were all very highly selected and bright. I could learn from them.

And in and around all the work, the tension, and the crisis were the beautiful extracurricular times: a visit with the Slades to the Nahr Ibrahim, a spectacularly beautiful valley just north of Beirut; a visit to Byblos with the Abi Saabs after a very special breakfast at their home above the town; elegant and extravagant dinner parties at the homes of faculty members and other AUB friends—the Saghirs, the Saouds, the El-Zeins, the Saads, the Daghirs, the Larsons, the Dodds, the Franks, and so many others. Not bombs nor threats nor administrative problems could keep us from enjoying this ancient and famous corner of the world so full of history, culture, good food, and good people.

Two weeks after Malcolm's death, on February 5, 1984, I left for Saudi Arabia not knowing that the next day the Christian-Moslem antagonisms would take on a completely new dimension, at least compared to anything I had yet seen, in what would become known as the February 6th War. The Moslem forces would retake West Beirut from the Christian army and again change radically the political reality of Beirut, sending the Christians back to East Beirut and reinstituting the Green Line between Christian and Moslem sectors (the "Green Line" was seemingly a Western term, the Lebanese calling it the "Red Line," which more nearly connoted the actual area of firing and blood that it was). While I was away, Joan left Beirut to go back home and Jean and Kit evacuated to Cyprus—Jean kept a running diary of the events of those fateful weeks:

SUNDAY, FEB. 5—Tom left with Daghir and Moussa for Ryadh ... were to have gone yesterday but Daghir advised against it because the security of the road to the airport very questionable with the shelling in southern suburbs .... Sharif the driver came to take Tom today and was stricken because his nephew had been killed by shrapnel in the shelling.

MONDAY, FEB. 6—Took Joan to airport with her two big boxes—Sharif came with Haj Omar [the wonderful AUB man who arranged travel and went everywhere fearlessly to effect it—tragically killed by a sniper on the Green Line in 1985, breaking our hearts] to accompany her at 6:30 A.M. ... today Sharif's news was that his sister's husband had been killed—son and husband gone in two days .... Haj Omar pointed out the Amal and Lebanese army sites on the way to the airport—the road we were on was the neutral strip between the two and Sharif was making the tires squeal on the trip out and back. Joan got off OK—turned out to be about last flight out .... AUB closed for day .... About 1 P.M. Kit and I walked up to Fisk Hall to get mail from English Department and heard shooting start up in the streets—didn't know what was going on but a woman came by and said American Community School [ACS] children being kept in the school basement because streets unsafe—she was dashing home ... we went back to the house, sat on porch listening to all the artillery fire ... curfew called and traffic jam resulted ... could hear the horns honking ... . At night we had a fire and sat inside in the living room ... people called to see if we were all right … news came over that army was disintegrating and West Beirut being taken by Amal militia … . Went to bed and awoke at 11 P.M. with whine of shell overhead and blast nearby … ? "It's time to go to the basement, Kit" … We sat in the basement until 1 A.M. under intermittent shelling—tried sleeping upstairs again until 2:30 but the shelling got worse again so went to the basement until 3 A.M.—it was so uncomfortable [a derelict privy next to the boiler room] that we came up again and sat in the hall—about 5:30 A.M. a call on the phone that school buses by the dorms were on fire and then shells started coming in about every 5 minutes … . [Kit and I learned well the harsh Beirut lesson of the sounds that shells make and how to differentiate between "outgoing" and "incoming." Also how it was lucky if you heard the whistle of the shell for it meant that that shell was not falling on you.]

TUESDAY, FEB. 7—Shelling stopped mid-morning but everyone was tense and news of damage in dorms and West Beirut was bad … could smell the gun powder … stayed in all day—lots of rain which seems to be customary after heavy shelling because of the powder in the air … .

WEDNESDAY, FEB. 8—Went up to the dorms and down to the ACS [next door to AUB] to take pictures of the shell damage—Awful. Muin and Annie in charge of 500 displaced students—had organized them into 4 committees: bread, food, clean up, control … students to spend next two nights in corridors of Basic Sciences building—they took Kit and me to visit the students in Basic Sciences building—impressively orderly and clean … . The battleship *New Jersey* firing started up while we were there—enormous bangs [this was the American government still taking sides and supporting President Gemayel and the Christians against the Moslems]. Had thought we'd go out into West Beirut and take pictures today but didn't after all—stayed in and cleaned house and listened to news … 300 shells from the *New Jersey* … call came about possible evacuation next day … .

THURSDAY, FEB. 9—Went to see the evacuation on the Corniche below us—had decided to stay so said good-bye to all the people we knew—spoke to Frank Regier about 11:30 A.M. and he said how he'd not been able to get over Malcolm Kerr's death—at 2:00 P.M. Virginia Slade called me over on the Corniche to say he'd been kidnapped as he was talking to the travel agent on Jeanne d'Arc Street. Talked to Ellises and Virginia Slade that evening—still thought we'd stay until about 10 P.M. when all of a sudden machine gunfire, RPG [rocket-propelled grenade] blast very close, and bullet whined past my ear when I crawled on hands and knees out onto front porch—more fell in the yard after another burst of machine gunfire … "Kit, we're being attacked … back to the basement again." Later, we went back to bed, firing seemed to have gone off but we talked about leaving—Ann called at 1:30 A.M.

and we had her phone Tom in Riyadh who said, "Tell them to get the hell out of there." … So we worked the rest of the night packing and getting ready to leave … .

FRIDAY, FEB. 10—Left at 9 A.M. to evacuate from Corniche—4 RPGs were fired at distant helicopter so we were ushered back to British embassy while Marines and security men went up to clear AUB—RPGs evidently fired from tennis court by our house (last night a target practice??) … . Marine contingent from airport brought in on first two choppers to come in—they helped us all evacuate—we were with group of 12 on about the 4th helicopter to go out—landed on the *Fort Snelling* and were taken down to the sleeping quarters with our luggage—sailors making up beds—then up for a great lunch in the mess room—went out on front bridge—met and talked to the editor of the *Daily Star* newspaper [American-owned Beirut daily] who had decided to leave—didn't think prognosis good—went to bed at 6 P.M. and slept all night—felt great to sleep safely if not most sumptuously—amazed how many Lebanese people evacuating in an American evacuation—seems families evacuating on passport of baby born in America—many AUH doctors someone said … .

SATURDAY, FEB. 11—Ship docked about 4 or 5 A.M.—absolutely great breakfast—Kit with 2 or 3 sailors around her—she then got tour of ship and baggage carried and explanation of how everything worked and ended up with 2 tee shirts, a sailor hat, and four addresses to write to—finally ushered on landing craft and taken into dock—Kit interviewed by NBC on the landing craft—met at dock by American embassy people who helped us through customs, etc. and onto bus to Carpassiana Beach Hotel where we had room along with lots of others—people began to disperse to other destinations and make travel arrangements … talked to Tom … .

SUNDAY, FEB. 12—Went into Larnaca and talked with travel agent to make arrangements to go to Scotland to meet up with Tom and wait for Lebanon developments—Kit called Russ and he said all was quiet in Beirut… .

FEB. 14–15—To Scotland—met by Tom and Peter—Scotland green, beautiful, and peaceful … quiet day, great salmon dinner … .

FEB. 15–24—Days have run together—News confirms solidification of Moslem gains, obvious that Gemayel and Americans lose—Reagan has announced that Marines will be pulled out and brought home … . Hallab called and Russ and Adib Saad—Hallabs will go back Sunday I believe—all is "quiet" there—this morning news of new cease-fire to go into effect today—we'll see how things go over the weekend and especially if the airport will open … .

The airport didn't open, but we went back to Beirut by boat from Cyprus and made it home to AUB—everything quiet and the same as before. Thus were we poorer by $3,000 for having evacuated when we could have stayed and been safe as ever. Our good friend Jean-Marie Cook of the English Department, a seasoned American Beiruti, told us blithely, "Yes, we evacuated in 1967, others did in 1975 ... guess everyone does it once and then never again." As with those other years and other evacuations, however, many who went away didn't return. The need for teacher replacements was critical, so Jean went to work, taking on two English composition classes at AUB and a senior American literature course at ACS. A new dimension was thus added to our lives as she brought home the experiences of her days. The AUB freshmen learning how to define terms *(Green Line: where life is absent and destroying occurs ... Lebanon as a hole* [sic!] *is a Green Line. Cease-Fire: the time when two enemies decide to stop a war. In Lebanon this word is announced daily but it brings with it a hard explosion in the situation. It must be said as "declaration of firing."),* and the ACS seniors reading *Catch 22* and getting their own introduction to the truism that governments and military establishments "do as they do do" and the individual caught in the process must try to "do" as he or she can. Jean was therefore busy but absolutely loving the teaching and her students.

The general life of Beirut and AUB along with the work of our FAFS went forward that spring and summer in the usual round of what we came to call "Beirut Normal," a state perhaps well defined in my letter of March 24, 1984, back to friends in the United States:

An absolutely beautiful morning—sunshine and nearly 70 degrees again. Things are gradually coming back to normal after two days of extremely intense fighting in West Beirut between two rival militias ... the machine guns were rattling and the rocket-propelled grenades were booming and blasting in what can only be described as fearsome fashion. One grenade hit a building on campus at 5 P.M. (Bliss Hall, in the corner classroom where Jean teaches at 8 A.M.), so we're not completely immune to the "spillover" (the new term in Beirut to indicate everything which comes into the residential area from Green Line shelling), although we are much more protected (so the AUB rationale for mental health goes) than the rest of West Beirut I suppose! The town has been seething so they say with armed militiamen for the last two days ... we have no firsthand proof of this for we stayed tightly on campus, and indeed I have not been off it in the three weeks since our return to AUB. All Americans are cautioned to stay low—our Professor Regier has not been heard of and William Buckley, the first secretary of the embassy, was kidnapped last week, so the American picture is quite grim and tense. Yesterday we almost had a violent clash among student members of two factions—the Murabitoun (Sunni Moslem) wanted the university to close while the Progressive Socialist Party (Druze) wanted it to stay open—all very complex, but it was tense for an hour or so; finally it was resolved without resort to violence or shooting. And last night a "high level conference among the religious and political leaders" arrived at some kind of solution to their differences and declared a cease-fire (the 181st or 182nd or ??) and by 8:30 it was quiet. But two cats took up where the militia left off, and their screeching echoed over the campus in apropos fashion. This morning the birds were singing and children laughing and the cats still fighting and it seemed hard to believe that 18 hours ago all hell was raging around us! Tis a crazy place to be sure—and that's literal since Beirut defines schizophrenia for the modern world .... .

There was lots of work for me. For one thing, the reestablished Green Line meant that once again Christian students living in the East were kept from crossing into West Beirut to the campus; to enable them to work toward graduation, classes and programs in agriculture were set up for them in the Off-Campus Program (OCP) in East Beirut. In a Board of Deans meeting, I announced, "Our faculty is prepared to offer a whole array of courses on the East Side so that the presently enrolled Christian students there can graduate." Afterward Landry Slade, a long-time faculty member and currently acting dean of the Faculty of Arts and Sciences, told me, "You realize, of course, that you have just established a faculty of agriculture on the East Side?" "No way," I replied. "We can't justify that in any way." "You wait," said he, and he was right: I had long and intense battles with the Christians in charge of things on the East Side, notably the director of the OCP, Dr. George Frayha, a tough and capable administrator. In retrospect one cannot blame them for wanting a campus over there, for there had been many young men in years past, both Christian and Moslem, abducted while trying to cross the Green Line and never heard of again. But it was the subterfuges and implied threats from the radical Christian element ("Where would you like the shell?!") used in order to get what they wanted that incensed me, and while I empathized with and tried to help the Christian students to graduate, I hardened my resolve against permitting the establishment of a permanent East Side Campus.

The second major concern for me was that all the students East and West needed to get back to the farm or AREC in the Bekaa Valley (some 20 miles southwest of Baalbek) for their practical work, a part of their education that had been suspended for some years due to the war in Lebanon and the Israeli invasion of 1982. The director of the farm, a faculty member who came from one of the major Shiite families in the Bekaa, had kept the farm at least intact and nominally AUB's, not only by working deals but also by hiring great numbers of laborers and putting them to work on guard duty—nevertheless, to persuade parents to allow their sons and daughters to go off to the wild Bekaa Valley ("the situation being what it is in Lebanon" and the stronghold of the Iranian Revolutionary Guards just 20 miles away in Baalbek) was sure to be a monumental task. But necessary. Almost all of our agriculture students were from towns and cities and had spent their lives in apartments with balconies—how could we logically give them a degree in agriculture without knowledge of farmwork?! And the students desperately wanted it. So we planned and in the meantime we developed a "Mini-AREC" on campus with greenhouses and had students driving a tractor around campus for their practical training in mechanization: Thus was added alternative programming to crisis management in the addenda to my job description.

The Mini-AREC was a space of about two acres behind the Chemistry Building, which had never been put to any use to that point—fallow in the true sense. Malcolm Kerr gave me permission to "occupy" it, and our other faculty members lost no time in putting it to good use. Bob Rice, hired for us by the Near East Foundation, was instrumental in designing the layout. First we moved the greenhouses from their original position, on which was scheduled to be built "Faculty Four," a new high-rise apartment building that was being donated completely by Mr. Rafiq Hariri (now prime minister of Lebanon, and a great benefactor both to Lebanon and to AUB), onto the new site and laid out plots for more to be constructed. Soon plants were growing in abundance inside, and dozens of research plots were cultivated and sown all over Mini-AREC. Even flowers were grown and sold as horticultural projects. Hardly a day passed without a dozen graduate students working assiduously on their research—they were like coiled-up springs being suddenly and finally able to get back to their thesis projects in earnest. And all over the campus, people were noticing the diligence and the buzz of activity on the formerly waste ground. I think that agriculture assumed from that time a much more prominent and even respectable role in the social hierarchy of AUB; certainly the wonder of all the city-raised kids grew along with the plants at what could be done with a little work and imagination. The project was a huge success all around, my one regret being that Malcolm did not live to see the fruits of what he had authorized. Spurred by our success, we tried to find other pieces of land we could cultivate—the head of grounds and of the physical plant drew the line, however, when it came to the softball outfield! We ended up with more greenhouses on the flat top of the Agriculture Building.

And then there was computerization! What a thrill to win out over George Sayegh, introduce the computers, create a center, and participate in the education of all to the "new learning," even if all the computers were to be stolen after my kidnapping.

May was an interesting month. Jean accompanied me on a trip with other faculty members to Aleppo, Syria, to see the International Center for Research in Dry Areas—a most impressive place. Although they brought me home by the more secure coast road, Jean was able to travel in another car down through the Bekaa Valley, past Baalbek and the AUB farm, and through a Druze Progressive Socialist Party (PSP) militia interaction on the mountain road to Beirut. Back on campus, the "Aggie Olympics" took place one Saturday/Sunday on the Green Field. In track, field, and court sports, each class plus the graduate students fielded a team; the faculty team made six. I emerged stiff, sore, and sunburned from an active two days of participation. I threw the javelin, pulled in the tug-of-war (the faculty won—much fatter and heavier!), and ran the first leg of the 4 by 100 yards relay—in the outside lane, I had a long start on the others, but was chagrined to have them all catch up and pass me before we got near the baton change (we lost heavily!). I was, however, also a winner in the tennis doubles tournament. Following the finals, we had a four-hour gala session with a band, dancing, and singing in our garden. The whole affair generated a wonderful spirit .... Later, a three-day Student Festival culminated in a Miss AUB Competition held on the upper campus oval (Kit had a great time participating—made the finals!). And finally, a great event for us at the end of the month—an old-fashioned American barbecue for FAFS faculty and friends in our garden in the midst of which arrived a missive (brought by the now assistant-to-the-president, Landry Slade):

> Hizbollah will execute kidnapping operation at American University of Beirut and the U.S. Embassy. The targets will have American identities. Have prepared 100 people for the operation, from which 20 are inside the university. These elements are afraid of the PSP and Amal because the PSP and Amal have provided some of their people as guards for the embassy. Will execute operation on the occasion of the celebration. Some of the elements will have explosives wrapped around them. In case these elements are hit by fire they and the people they have kidnapped both will be killed by the explosion. Hizbollah is watching all movements and are waiting for Zero Hour. The plan is prepared and its execution is soon ... First axis is from inside AUB. The second axis is from the Corniche. The third axis is from a civilian building which overlooks the new embassy... .

Our letters home to family and friends in the next two weeks made comment:

You would no doubt have heard of the big scare from the Hizbollah threat, which indeed shook up the campus and especially the Americans. You will see from the enclosed xerox that Hizbollah deny any part of the threat, and there are strong suspicions everywhere that it originated with the Deuxieme Bureau [the Lebanese Secret Police] or some such, as part of a long-range coordinated plan to get all the important institutions such as embassies, businesses, AUB, and the like to move to the East Side! All sounds incredible, but credible and the Moslems are strongly convinced of it all!! Seem to be no proof of course, so it slides into the past of Lebanon like all the other murky doings … . God, what a place! … the *Daily Star* keeps reporting that the cabinet is giving high priority to 1) getting the Israelis out of the South—which is a futile hope I suspect; 2) reuniting the Army (which has of course split into Christian and Moslem contingents)—but nothing happens for they can't agree on how it should be controlled; 3) restoring security conditions in Beirut—but reportedly there are dozens of small militia all over West Beirut so that it is still close to anarchy … . Yesterday's paper had reports of all the extortion rackets hitting the merchants … so apparently it is still a jungle out there; 4) political reform—ho, ho, huh? See how cynical I have become … . Jean, however, professes no serious regrets about having come! She is even more determinedly committed than I, has lots of courage, and stays cool at all times. She even went out on our porch during the February barrage when shells were falling every 2–5 minutes … more threatening to me is the kidnap business—that would be no fun at all, and there do seem to be some idiots out there who are determined to get Americans whether the Hizbollah deny the threats or not!! Regier and Dodge both said they were in the hands of Moslems (radical, with pictures of Khomeini, etc.—presumably Iranian, or at least pro-Iranian) … . AUB had to take the latest threat seriously and greatly beefed up the security around the campus and especially the faculty apartments where most Americans are now living. Kit's Marine friend Russell tells us that the embassy and the Marines get this kind of threat daily and nothing usually happens—when the disasters have struck, there has been zero warning and wham, out of the blue it comes leaving everyone stunned … . The embassy has just announced its intent to move virtually everyone over to the Christian East Side where they have of course been guaranteed more security—we think that this is in one sense a cop-out and a capitulation to pressure from the Christians and the Israelis, but on the other hand it may mean a clear recognition that the East is where the threat came from and the announcement will keep more from coming and take the pressure off AUB at the same time that the embassy takes its time moving. In any case, the poor embassy has been in a most untenable position, and if they can get a little peace to operate in over on the other side, more power to them—and we'll miss the helicopters that whirr in from the sea umpteen times a day to bring and take Marines and embassy personnel and supplies—they're fascinating to watch, but the residents in the faculty apartments and the biology department [located right on the Corniche] both will be happy, for each enormous twin-bladed chopper relocates about half an inch of red dust into kitchens, bedrooms, and laboratories with ruthless regularity!

Since we last wrote, Professor Frank Regier has been released through the Amal, but another American long-time missionary Ben Weir has been kidnapped, perhaps in retaliation for Frank's forced release? So West Beirut, although supposedly under the control of Nabih Berri's Shiite Amal militia and Walid Jumblatt's Druze PSP militia, still has oodles of minor "gangs," "parties," "militias," "movements" roaming around loose, and while it is probably no more dangerous really than New York or Chicago and less so perhaps than Miami or Los Angeles (in fact the brother of one of our AUB Lebanese friends died in a Florida car crash and they're having the body returned this week to Beirut—ironic twist indeed), still most of us Americans are taking few chances and we are "circulating" little and carefully in West Beirut these days … . There is also a thriving debate on how far the Moslem community wishes to push the "Islamification" of West Beirut: threats appear regularly against bars, night clubs, Westerners, Americans, private swimming beaches, grocery stores that sell booze, etc.—but they are systematically denied by the Moslem parties who attribute them to the Phalangists from the East Side or their allies the Israelis who wish to scare the Westerners and businesses into coming to the East Side and damage the "reputation" of the Moslems. Ramadan began last week so the tensions are higher—most bars have closed for the one-month religious fasting and festival, rather than risk that the rumors are real, and have their places blown up—which again might be done by any one of the parties and not necessarily the fundamental Moslems who would get the blame or might take the blame!

Meantime on campus, events have been swinging to a glorious climax—one more week of class then a reading period and finals and the semester may even end on time and exams completed for the first time in years (that is, if the June 15 rumors stay rumors and unprepared students don't blow the place up so they don't have to take finals—we've had a couple of warning shots in a fire bomb in the library that didn't go off and dynamite in an empty physics classroom which did) …

Jean

4   Keeping in at AUB

Classes finished, grades got sent in, and Graduation 1984 for AUB did indeed come July 15. Tom and I had a party for all the FAFS graduates and their families in our home and garden with food, fun, laughter, and celebration and only a hint of security in the form of guards who also ate and enjoyed themselves. Leaving right afterward, we went to the States for summer vacation, and the American embassy left West Beirut for East Beirut—"too soon" some said prophetically, for their protection was not fully in place. I got to stay on at our cabin in the Rockies for an extended "home leave" to work on my Ph.D. dissertation for the University of Colorado while Tom returned in late August to AUB. His copious letters filled us in on all the details of his September round of Beirut Normal along with his deanly activities, which included time as acting president:

SEPT. 2—As such, I "led" a delegation of the acting deans of engineering and of arts and sciences to Bikfaya today to present official AUB condolences to the president of the Republic of Lebanon, Mr. Amin Gemayel, on the death of his father Pierre. So I have once again shaken the hand that is trying to steady things in Lebanon and guide the state to peace and harmony!! … The pomp and circumstance was heavy and thick; … literally thousands streaming through. As the official AUB delegation, we were invited to sit in the front row facing, 6 feet away, all the Gemayel family, including Amin and his wife; his mother, the bereaved widow, who was physically and emotionally strong; and the brother of Sheikh Pierre who resembled him strongly!! Most people were not seated, but simply ushered on through, and it was only a selective few who were singled out and ushered to the chairs. Likewise with the guest book—most were not invited to sign, but I did as acting president of AUB …. I can report, however, that our "delegation's" visit was never reported in either the newspapers, the radio, or the TV!! They snubbed us completely in that regard, presumably because of the ongoing hullabaloo about closing AUB's OCP on the East Side, etc.!! ... Today I had another presidential duty—to call on Salim Hoss in the American University Hospital where he was recovering from a narrow escape! Someone set off a 75 kilogram car bomb at 6:20 A.M. yesterday to get both him and Grand Mufti Khaled who were going together to prayers for the Feast. It was on the Corniche near Raouche, and it shook our house like blazes!! I thought it was College Hall for sure and it turned out to be over a mile away by God. What a bang! He had not gotten back into his car, but was still in the Mufti's courtyard, and the driver backed out of the gate, and BANG—they detonated the bomb—blew his car to hell and the driver and several others were killed, many wounded, etc.—but they escaped, Hoss and Khaled, with minor burns!! ... I suspect it was because of the accusations that he is behind "closing" OCP—you will see in the clippings, etc. I am enclosing that the Phalangists are blaming him heavily for the decision to phase it out—I don't know how big a role if any he may have played in it! But I suspect only a minor one at best so it may be an excuse to get rid of one more sane head who represents the Moslems well and rationally?? Gad, what a place?!! So now, when do they decide that I should go?? Maybe I should decide that first??! ...

SEPT. 9—The most recent disaster in Lebanon, the bombing again of the embassy, this time in East Beirut. I predicted that that would happen in one form or another since the Moslem community was incensed at the decision to move the embassy over to the East Side; ... after the Moslems got control of the West Side, they were actually protecting the embassy themselves, ... and you note that the guards at the new location were mainly Lebanese Forces .... Now, we have had lots of discussions with Lebanese about who could have blown up the original building in April of '83 ... and lots of scenarios have been proposed, including the Israelis who then blame it on the Moslems, or the Phalangists who also immediately call up and claim it for the Islamic Jihad and of course get all Americans angry against all Moslems, and reinforce the U.S. determination to support Israel and thus indirectly the Phalangists here .... Many are likewise convinced that most if not all of the threats that were being received by AUB and the embassy were not originating in West Beirut but from the East Side to hasten the decision of the embassy to move their headquarters over there. Thus the incentive to the Moslems to hit the place on that side, right??? There was of course a double incentive this time, too, in the form of the U.S. veto of the Lebanese complaint to the UN two weeks ago .... I will make a prediction here and now, that there will be more attacks on U.S. installations around the world; this is only the first, and of course appropriately in Lebanon. But there will be others, for the depth of feeling about that veto is great, I can assure you. First, however, you have to understand a little about what the Israelis are in fact doing in the south of Lebanon, and I am fairly sure that no newspaper in the U.S. is carrying any news on that. But I hear it all the time from our students and workers from the south, who have to get in and out of the area from time to time. Without doubt it is inhuman, and the Israelis should get all that would be coming to them for it, including cutting out of all U.S. aid until they get out. Instead what happens?? The U.S. vetos the relatively mild complaint, made mild at the request of the Brits and the French, who then deserted the U.S. position and voted for the resolution, which made a vote of 14 to 1 ... the one being the U.S. veto!! The moment I heard that one, I felt like clearing out of Lebanon myself ... and am still not sure that I should stay in fact!! This sort of stuff, however, is not for quotation, at least as far as blaming things on the Israelis and especially the Phalangists is concerned, for it could well cost me my life, and I am perfectly serious about that. Remember Malcolm Kerr .... And I have already been labeled as a Moslem sympathizer simply for trying to be objective and do my job as fairly as I can!! Some groups of course have not been used to having to submit to objectivity and impartial treatment, and take to it very reluctantly to say the least, and try to remove the perpetrator of same!! 'Nuff said.

I look back on this now and cannot see Tom as anything but objective; yet he absolutely reacted to *people*. Those who were genuine and dedicated to AUB were alike in his book no matter the religion or political orientation. He can name the people he liked and respected, and they were of all persuasions: Maronite, Greek Orthodox, Protestant, Sunni, Druze, Shiite, Western, Lebanese, or other. Those of whatever religion or nationality, East or West, however, who were devious, self-aggrandizing, intolerant, corrupt, he could not respect. The students, well, he liked all of them, as did I. May they keep their openness and tolerance; the country has such great need of them.

Tom's letters continued on into September:

Yesterday I was invited to go into the Shouf Mountains by a Druze family .... The boyfriend of one of the daughters had arranged to get us into the "castle" of Walid Jumblatt for the grand tour; ... it is hundreds of years old and was a fascinating place!! ... It is located in the small town of Mukhtara, which is a few miles southeast of Beiteddine and of Dar Al Qamar, the latter of which is in fact a Christian town and the one where several thousands of Christians were surrounded by the Druzes for many months last fall, from September till just before Xmas in fact, at which time the Druzes relented and let them go free .... The most impressive thing to me of the whole day ... was the fantastic dedication of all of them, young and old alike, to the Jumblatt family!!! They literally worship the man ....

SEPT. 13—Hi Sweetheart!! Enjoyed talking to you this morning! And I am delighted that you are coming! That will be very nice to have you here again, and we can be "fulfilled" again!! I think we both feel like half a person when we are apart, though I was and am willing to sacrifice to get you over that thesis ....

SEPT. 16—Friday I went to the farm in the Bekaa! ... The students went up there last Sunday, and I was up to check on how they were getting along and to put in a first appearance as dean of the faculty ... . There is a lot to be done, but it is really a super place for training students and doing research, and it is easy to see why all former students have such fond memories of the place and consider it the highlight of their stay at the AUB ... . The trip there was a beautiful one to begin with, through some beautiful mountain scenery that would have to be considered a serious rival even to Colorado; ... since the Damascus highway is still closed, we had to do the usual and go by some terribly circuitous roads, that is for sure. It is really incredible how the Lebanese keep roads closed all over the place, and force everyone to go all around Robin Hood's barn to get to anywhere ... .

October 9. For my own part, I had thoroughly enjoyed my summer/fall sojourn in the Rockies. Refreshed and inspirited, I got the cabin all winterized, took a last look at that wonderful land—felt the cold moving in among the bare aspen and decided it was probably the right time to leave for Beirut. Tom was off at a meeting in Amman, Jordan, so on my return I settled back into our AUB home on my own, writing to the family to let them know I was safe:

Interesting my reaction on being back—everything strange again yet the same— funny feeling. Reminded me of our coming in last year except for being alone this time!! They are beginning to clean up some of the building rubble on the way from the airport to AUB which looks promising ... . Anyway the house was so welcoming and nice and I just prowled around looking at everything again—went out on the balcony and sniffed the sea breeze and sat and absorbed it all—then went to bed and woke up not knowing for a minute where I was! ... Tom got back that morning and had great stories to tell about Jordan: he'd given a good speech, lots of high Middle East brass were there so he'd made some good contacts and had good discussions, then he'd had a day out sightseeing in the Jordan Valley at the Dead Sea, West Bank, Jurash, etc. He was full of it and really glad he'd gone ... . Our days are now fitting into routine—this morning we jogged on the Green Field from 6:30 to 7:00 to get much-needed exercise and decided we'd do that two or three times a week at least. Tonight we go to Saghirs in the department to have dinner with the Lebanese ambassador to China (a relative) who is here, and tomorrow we go somewhere else I'm not sure where. I hadn't been 10 minutes in the house than Al Buckley called and invited us to a "sundowner" in their fourth floor apartment and we got a chance last Friday to see all the American set there ... . Other small happenings have been the first big rain of the season the last two days with a big surf, sheeting rain, and a break in the hot weather—a faculty reception on the lawn at Marquand House notable for the small number of people, lack of alcohol and Kerrs, and thoughts of last year and what might have been—the death of Pauline's father from an automobile hitting him (she's Tom's secretary)—the Lebanese pound has gone down from 6–1 to 8–1 on the dollar which is causing a big stramash on campus on the part of those paid in Lebanese pounds—and it's a gorgeous day today with the sea blue, the sun out, and a view all the way up the Lebanese coast to the headland, especially clear after the rain—and of course our hot water cut off because of a break in the city water main (responsibility not claimed) and so our reserves are "at one-third capacity until October 18 (yesterday)" and that shower was cold again—the news is slightly ominous that Berri and Jumblatt are rumbling resignation although that is probably the normal way of dealing with Christian intractability in order to call in Syrian support again—the Israelis are discussing withdrawal which amazingly seems to be a mixed blessing because of the vacuum created again. Have to say I really miss the Marines and the American embassy .... So strange to walk down the road that used to be all secured up—past the British embassy (still with its netting against suicide planes—and the paper said that they'd netted their new one also!)—down to the Corniche—no razor wire or barricades, just a dead rat and garbage now down the AUB wall, and people and cars galore on the seaside; ... even the dogs are gone—taken by the dogcatcher, all except Spot who was too smart for him I guess .... All I saw left were a few broken sandbags piled where the Marine gate used to be by the old faculty gate. But amazingly the life and the view are the same—I've made two trips to Smith's Grocery—cars and people everywhere. I am trying to keep your dad safe and he's under pressure right now with the OCP on the East Side wanting more courses for their agriculture students .... But things seem OK if a bit uneasy ....

The following weeks of the fall/winter semester seemed to speed by and we kept the home fronts filled in on the details of our lives, often with joint letters:

NOV. 8—[Jean at the office computer] Not much has happened on the political front here—a couple of anonymous explosions somewhere this morning as there were last week but one never seems to hear anything more about them. One bad outbreak a week ago tonight—between PSP and PPS [Syrian Progressive Party]—if it's not out-fighting it's in-fighting. In fact with this one on Bliss Street, a stray bullet went through a dorm window and wounded a student (he evidently was a member of one of the above militias and so there was a question about the strayness of the bullet) .... But otherwise things are quiet and beautiful here—the weather has been just out of this world, 72 degrees and only an occasional rain to keep the dust down. Tom and I have been keeping to our 8 to 8 work schedule .... My thesis is going very well but still so much work to do .... Tom has been inundated with work and some very hairy problems; his honeymoon here administratively seems to be well over, if it ever began! But I must tell you all that he is really reveling in it! He's getting the experience in spades and ought to be ready to tackle anything after this .... We did have some social life over the weekend—went out for dinner all three nights .... [Later] Went out for a walk to get some exercise and a few things from the store … first to Smith's for good bread, dodging cars all the while, then down to the Corniche to see what was going on there— it's a man's world during the day down there—some fishermen out, some in their boats dynamiting and picking up the fish that then float to the surface—other men sitting by the snack and beer vans on little stools, doing their worry beads, chatting, and drinking beer and coffee—so much garbage on the inner rocks of the beach it is unbelievable—to Washington's store and his tale of woe about how bad it is in this country and how he was in the U.S. with his sons this summer (little tiny shop you wouldn't think he'd have the plane fare—all his children are engineers or Ph.D.'s of some kind) … .

NOV. 10—[Tom to his family in Scotland] It is finally a little quieter than it has been for a couple of days now, and you will see from the letter that I wrote to the American side of the ocean, that when I was sitting down in the office, the most recent outbreak of Beirut madness occurred! It is still a bit obscure why it ever happened at all, but it did; I may stick in a copy of the paper article about the scene, along with one on the latest threats to Americans!! We have a hard time frankly deciding on whether these are for real or not, and it seems that most of the time they are not at all, but I am being careful nonetheless, believe me! I do not want to end up a kidnap victim!! 'Nuff on that mournful subject … . We have just returned from a very nice trip up to the Shouf Mountains past Aley to see an advanced system of hydroponics, a setup of plastic tunnel greenhouses in which the plants are grown in a rock base with water pumped through them containing all the necessary ingredients for growth, correct pH, and the works … it was impressive … . The fellow who had invited us is the manager who had graduated in agriculture from the AUB some years ago … . The owner is the brother-in-law of Walid Jumblatt, the leader of the Druze people here in Lebanon, and so they arranged for an armed escort for us … . It was certainly interesting to see how they operate in such a situation—the guards, two of them were in a jeep, sitting in the back with their submachine guns pointing conspicuously up in the air and sometimes back toward the people (lots of them) that we were passing, and they had a siren on their vehicle which they arrogantly blew a lot to warn the folk out of their way, then as they passed the cars, they would wave the car aside to let us follow on, … which quite frankly I found a bit embarrassing … .

NOV. 17—[Tom to Ann, Kit, and Joan] Yesterday, we had the whole faculty up here at the house for a big fall welcoming party, and it was a rip-roaring success. Your mother had really worked on the food and the house; she got many compliments on it in fact. There were about 50 people here, I suppose; the Christians from the East Side did not come, for they had to get back over the Green Line before dark so they all gave their apologies … but the West-Siders, Christian and Moslem, were here in force and stayed for about four hours … . Still have my bodyguard all day;

am now on my third one I think, or maybe my fourth?? On the first day that I was acting president, there was an announcement in the morning paper that Sheikh Shaaban from Tripoli, a rabid anti-American fundamentalist, was to speak on the AUB campus!! That afternoon, no less, without any permission or anything. Promptly at three, he arrived with about two or three hundred armed men of his Tawheed militiamen, swarmed onto campus, and proceeded to speak to a huge audience!! Your mother asked later if I should have allowed them, and how did they get on campus anyway? I told her that what let them on here to AUB were known by their common names as M-16s!!! Since I had not my militia quite ready at that point, I stayed discreetly in my office although did duly notify the Board of Trustees that it had happened. Nice first day on the job, huh?? I enclose a cutting reporting his speech from which you will see that he even had the gall to throw brickbats at the AUB while on the campus itself!! Most people were really quite incensed about it, but said he is really a nobody anyway, who is trying to drum up support in West Beirut … . Ignoring him thus sent the right message!?

NOV. 23—[Jean] It does look as if Tom's second week of acting president could end quietly and safely—knock on wood, we've still got two hours to go! Things were surely exciting over the weekend though with the American student John Cronin kidnapped and Tom going to Amal headquarters to try to get the hunt going—then the call Tuesday evening at 10 P.M. that he was being released and brought back which took Tom and the dean of students to the AUB hospital at the dead of night … . Then another trip to see Nabih Berri this time on Wednesday evening to thank him for their efforts in releasing John. They were sent home from Amal headquarters with armed guards and sirens, etc. [Berri was quite angry that Tom and Fawzi Hajj had come to his office without armed guards—I can imagine what he thought when he heard of Tom's kidnapping after turning down three of his Amal militiamen.] … Fascinating but Tom will be happy when someone else comes to be president!! The word is that Dr. Plimpton comes December 1st as president—he's been giving news conferences in the U.S. so it seems assured that he will come although people here have been getting antsy about him—"Why isn't he here?" Especially have the West Beirutis been concerned lest the Christian administrators at AUB get all sorts of new appointments and legislation through before he comes … . Word from the Board of Trustees however says that everything has been tabled for Plimpton … .

DEC. 14—These last two weeks have been Christmas letter and shopping weeks; … we've tried to send something to you all in small packets … . I had a good time shopping this year—it's been awhile since I've been up and down Hamra Street and I found everything going strong in Beirut Normal style—electric generators going to get lighting in the stores (the power plant in Jiyeh was hit again!), prices higher "because of the increase in the dollar you know," and everything from New York to

Paris to Hong Kong being offered. Amazing how they do it .... I must tell you frankly I am already very sad about our being parted for Christmas! But I am going to get it out of my system this week, and then start looking ahead! Tom goes to Athens the 18th–20th for an FAO [Food and Agriculture Organization]-Saudi meeting and while he's gone I will put up Dodges' artificial tree ... and the crèche that Kit and Russ gave us last year, and wreaths on the door, and get Tom some little things to put under the tree ... and I will sit in the evening and look at the lights and think of you all ... .

JAN. 2, 1985—HAPPY NEW YEAR ... . Can't believe the time and the season has just about gone! We thought about you all especially on Christmas Eve and Christmas Day; ... then the next week collapsed into thesis and word processor and before we knew it New Year's Eve was here—we took a nice long walk on the Corniche in the evening—all the vendors were out, but not so many people until midnight when we were well ensconced back at home—all Hell broke loose as usual with guns and RPGs and cannons being shot off—the sky was full of tracer bullets and what a din!! And probably hundreds of people in the hospital with stray bullets in arms and legs and backs, etc. These are their celebrations here! In the meantime the kidnap relatives (of people kidnapped by both sides during the last 10 years and never seen again—they figure maybe 2,000 of whom 200 might still be alive??) had closed the crossings between East and West with burning tires and buses and lines of angry women—until today when the cabinet meets I guess. Also in the meantime, Calvin Plimpton arrived to take up the big job of presidency of AUB—came incognito on the 31st and has quietly started to work ... . I saw the Marquand House servant Hassan this morning and he was wearing broad smiles—"We have a president!" he said ... .

JAN. 3—[to good friends John and Dorcas Murray in Boulder] Meanwhile on the AUB front, things are on an upswing for 1985 with Cal Plimpton coming in to assume the presidency—we're invited to dinner there tonight for the Van Arsdales, an American couple who are interviewing for the vice president of business affairs—a critical step to get things on the road here again—he's "90 percent convinced and she's 75 percent convinced" so we'll see what we can do. What a difference it would make to get some more American presence and administrative expertise here—it's been a long year downhill since Malcolm's death. Agriculture is swinging and keeping Tom head over heels busy, so along with his new computer studies he's fully occupied ... . The political situation has continued tense and up and down; ... the latest has been the closing of all the crossings (although not the airport, thank God) ... . South Lebanon is still a mess, and hundreds of robberies, etc., all over West Beirut show that army control on this side of the city is very minimal—you probably read about the journalists stumbling into a restaurant robbery and being abducted and robbed themselves—the 16-year-old son of one of Tom's faculty members was abducted on the street outside of AUB, held for 6 hours, robbed of what money he had and then released; then the wife of a bursary officer here had her purse snatched also, and they have instituted a guard service for AUB people going to their banks … . This really is about as close to anarchy as one could live in and still move and have being!! Bombings continue—the latest development has been a refocusing of the battle between Christian and Druze sects—the Druze shell East Beirut from the mountains, and the East retaliates with bombs planted in garbage dumps outside Druze temples and schools to hit them where they would most care I guess. One bomb in West Beirut went off minutes before a school was scheduled to let out—a bomb in a mountain village got the school and killed several children and wounded others. It's not a nice war—but then it never has been!

I got 8.8 to 1 on my dollar exchange yesterday … . Some people even predict a further increase—perhaps up to 10 or even 12 … .

JAN. 8–9—[From Enclosures: *Daily Star* clippings] "AMERICAN PRIEST AB-DUCTED IN W. BEIRUT STREET" … According to police sources, Jenco's Pontiac was stopped by gunmen at 7:30 A.M., just one block from the Hobeish Police Station … . "EXPLOSIVE CHARGE TEARS THROUGH SMUGGLERS' INN, LEAVES 4 DEAD" … Eyewitnesses said that as the subsequent series of gas explosions occurred, Smugglers' Inn owner, George Zeini, screamed: "I have built this place with my life, all my life and now it is destroyed for what?" … Zeini's restaurant, a favorite gathering place of West Beirut artists, writers, and university professors, has been robbed by gunmen six times in the past three months (marginal comment: Heard the blast in the office—couldn't believe it—some say he didn't pay his extortion money) … .

January 18, 1985. One year since Malcolm Kerr was assassinated. The Assembly Hall was full for the memorial service and it was a Sunni Moslem woman student who gave the student address, letting us have a copy of it afterward:

"Mrs. Kerr, Mr. President, honored guests, fellow students. Here we are today to honor Dr. Malcolm Kerr … . The beginning of our relationship with Dr. Kerr started during the Israeli invasion of Beirut, when Dr. Kerr stood at the AUB Main Gate and insisted on the refusal of the entry of the Israeli Army to the campus. From that day on we were intimately in relation with Dr. Kerr who showed deep understanding of the circumstances we, students, were passing through during his presidency.

One of his most appreciated positions was his attitude toward the problems of the Lebanese south. Moreover, Dr. Kerr was the first AUB president who started a serious investigation concerning the employing system at AUB for he asked for honest statistics about the employees at AUB and the way they are assigned for their jobs.

Another contribution of his was his deep well understanding to all our problems. He was always with us, listening to our problems and taking our opinion concerning all issues. One of the most important issue was our everlasting demand of having a student-council.

In addition, his ultimate goal at AUB was to attain a high academic level which AUB used to have 10 years ago, when students from AUB were welcomed all over the world from the most important universities to continue their higher studies even without an entrance exam.

Suddenly, on January 18, 1984, Dr. Kerr was shot. He wanted to fulfill democracy at AUB but there are people who have planned for something else and Dr. Kerr stood an obstacle in the way of their scheme, so he was shot.

After his death, these people took the opportunity and tried their best to fulfill their scheme. Yet we students have always refused to surrender and we have worked as best as we can to stop these people. By this assassination, we lost Dr. Kerr, the man who wanted an ideal university with complete cooperation between students and administration."

JAN. 29—[Jean] Dr. Plimpton ... named Tom as acting president while he was gone the last ten days .... Tom's almost swamped with things and the two jobs together are a bit of a pressure. Only one incident really while Plimpton was in the gulf; ... the head of the physical plant got roughed up by a couple of guys in his office, ostensibly after him to give them jobs, but perhaps a vindictive return for not paying someone who had been off the job for a half year or so; ... hard to sort out all the reasons. But they scraped through it .... Things are organized to send students back to the farm in the Bekaa starting next semester—they stay February to September for their practical training and it will be a good sign if this one pulls off. Tom even had two students from the East Side program come to sign up for the farm and they said more were going to come .... We had a great Rabbie Burns Night last Friday—about 75 people and it was fantastic—people really raved and are still raving about it—they were ready for a party!! It was my last effort before the final setting in to ultimate seclusion for my thesis—the writing part has turned out to be a lot harder than I thought—there's so much to say and I feel the pressure of doing justice to two such great authors as Seneca and Shakespeare ....

Seneca, the Roman tragedian-philosopher-moralist-politician, whose life spanned that of Christ and 30 years beyond, tutor of Nero and credited with postponing for 5 years at least the worst of his excesses, committing suicide by order, but giving the early Christian Fathers his ethics, the martyrs his stoicism, and bequeathing the Renaissance World 1,500 years later his stoic philosophy, his tragedies, his letters, and his moral essays. And Shakespeare, in his consummate genius, using this Senecan "language" transmitted to him and his world to create "a symbolic language for tragedy." Mythic, archetypal images and symbols came from the Greeks and Romans through Seneca to Shakespeare, and there in Beirut I was to find them current and vital. Especially was the sign of the North Star embedded in the classical and Renaissance plays as the symbol of ultimate power, the heavenly reflected so dramatically and horrendously in the earthly power. How many nights with Tom "somewhere out there" would I sit on my Beirut balcony in the years to come, drawing on Senecan stoicism, Shakespearean neo-stoicism, Senecan ancient blood-filled tragedy, Shakespearean English Renaissance tragedy, and looking north over the AUB Green Field and the Mediterranean Sea to a heaven laid out with the Great Bear and Cassiopeia wheeling around their and our center—the North Star—and contemplating, as I looked, on the multiple faces of power. Contemplating also, and getting strength from Seneca's stoic principles from his *On Steadfastness:*

> *The wise man can lose nothing … .*
> *The good man can receive neither injury nor insult … .*
> *Freedom is having a mind that rises above injury.*

FEB. 2—[Tom] Dear Dad and Alice/Ann, Kit, Joan/Peter, Elizabeth, et al./Others … This is Tom and Jean at the word processor doing a joint effort to get a letter off to you with a man who is leaving for the U.S. tomorrow … . We got your letter the other day and we are glad that you approved of our hanging in there tough, even though it is really quite dicey these days, I would say. We have, though, put in about 21 months of the 36 that we had contracted for and by this time I am getting really familiar with the job here. It is in fact a very complex one, not because of the mechanics of the thing but rather because of the politics of the place and the complex nature of the culture; … one cannot do things in the way that they are done in the good ole U.S. of A. … One can't go around saying just what is on one's mind, or even expressing anything very candidly … egos are very fragile, and courtesy must rule at all times it seems … . But then there is lots of downright deception and corruption that goes on and quite accepted … and indeed I sometimes wonder if I will have an easy transition back to a similar post in the U.S. … Overall, however, I must admit that I have enjoyed this experience a great deal, and have few regrets at coming … . I can assure you though that we have been keeping a rather low profile for these last few weeks. I used not to worry at all about going out in the car, feeling that they can't quite force you to get out and stick you in another one, etc.; you could always, I thought, rev it up, and be off … . But no sir; … they took Rev. Jenco of the Catholic Relief Services by blocking his way with cars both in front of and behind his, and ten (no less!) armed men held him up and forced him to get into their car and off they went, and he has not been seen since, though the word is that he is OK. Since then, I have not been out without quite a bit of "protection"!! There do seem to be some bad boys out there who are indeed intent on getting all Americans out of Lebanon … .

Lo and behold came three explosions right after noon; … at the El-Zein household where we were not long after we heard that the explosions had been at three banks, those which had had the finger pointed at them the other day as being those allegedly involved in playing with the dollar/Lebanese pound exchange rate, and causing it to bounce around and mainly go up and up and up … . In fact there is a really serious erosion of the pound now, and it has gone from 4.5 to the dollar when we came here to a low of 12.5 to the dollar yesterday!! The average guy in the street is horrified at all this, for the Lebanese pound has traditionally been one of the world's most stable currencies for decades … .

[Jean] Right now it's Friday night about a week after Tom started this letter to you—we had another nice evening out last Sunday with a great artist, Martin Giesen, and his wife … in a little hole in the wall near AUB where a German Nazi (he thinks Hitler was great and Winston Churchill a baddie) gave us good food and lots of wine … . Things still remain tense here with the Israeli withdrawal not going easily … . Keep praying for us—right now it's quiet … . Sunday a trip to Byblos—the oldest continually inhabited city in the world!

The week before, I had contracted with Joana, the Ghanaian woman who was working with the Giesens, to come in every other day to look after the house and do things for Tom while I was gone. I didn't know it then, but Joana would become my mainstay in the six and a half years to come—loyalty doesn't come stronger than hers! For now I was just happy to know that Tom would have a clean house and shirts. And so I left Beirut for Colorado on March 14. Two days later, Terry Anderson was kidnapped in Ain el Mreisse and a week later Marcel Fontaine and Marcel Carton from the French embassy. Tom's letter in late March was full of foreboding:

MARCH 20—Just about everyone is fighting everyone else, it seems, and by now anarchy is just about complete, I believe. The Hizbollah are also kidnapping every foreigner in sight, it seems, not only the Americans these days (they have sent out a "final warning" to all "foreign agents" to get out of Lebanon, and that masquerading as journalist, scientist, diplomat, cleric, or businessman will be no cover; they know us all, they say!!). Needless to say, many have taken the warning and gone, but not from AUB, fortunately. That vote in the Security Council really made the fundamentalists mad, I can tell you … . The Israelis in the south of Lebanon are creating a lifetime of enemies … and of course, the backlash against all of that which is perceived as having full U.S. backing and support really descends on us in spades; hence all the threats and kidnappings … . I have not, frankly, felt ever very much threatened, and people like Radwan Mawlawi have always said that I of all people was not at risk to any degree; however, I had a talk with him today and he advised me to take it easy for the next few days or so and not to go out into the town … . But I dare not say that things cannot possibly get worse, for if I say that, they will; … they always do … .

On the home front, with our house in Fort Collins still rented out, I holed up with Joan and her roommate Jeannie in their apartment and worked nonstop to try to get my dissertation done so Kit and I could graduate from the University of Colorado together May 23, when Tom, Ann, and Joan would be here. That was not to be, however, for my rented word processor kept eating up words and spitting them out in every which order—perhaps because the disks from Lebanon couldn't be read properly in the United States—was that symbolic? Whatever, completely frustrated, I returned to my typewriter and a postponed graduation. Tom, in the meantime, kept writing from Lebanon—I remember so graphically the first week of May when he sent to me his graduation remarks to his students—to be published, no less. I couldn't believe he would speak out against the Israelis in South Lebanon in print like that—fear for him hit me in the pit of my stomach.

Tom

5   Two Farewells

The agriculture students asked me to write a message for the graduating class to put into the 1985 yearbook with my picture. "Be sure to say something about the south," they begged. I complied, not knowing that when it was published, I'd be kidnapped. This became, thus, my final farewell to AUB and my students:

On behalf of all the members of our faculty, may I take this opportunity to congratulate the class of 1985 on reaching your goal of graduation. At the end of my second year as Dean of the Faculty, I am happy to say that I have come to know many of you quite well and that in common with all of your professors, I will miss you, a class with great spirit, a willingness to work and an obvious commitment to your chosen professions in agriculture and the food sciences. In my admittedly biased view, you have chosen wisely, for agriculture and the production and processing of foods are the most vital industries in any nation. In the midst of modern opulence, some are inclined to forget the basic importance of food production, and it takes a disaster such as we are still witnessing in sub-Saharan Africa to remind them of the facts—that a well-fed nation is a healthy nation and that agriculture may well have a more fundamental role in preserving that health than does any other profession. Or that a well-fed nation is a nation at peace; hunger on the other hand frequently leads to social upheavals and violence. As graduates of our faculty therefore, you have a very important role to play, not only in Lebanon, whose bounteous agriculture has sustained you so well in the past years, but in the entire region. Everywhere I have gone in the past two years—to Bahrain, to Cyprus, to Greece, to Jordan, to Saudi Arabia, to Syria, to the U.K. and to the U.S.A.—everywhere our graduates are at work and recall with obvious pleasure their experiences at the AUB and at the AREC. I saw too in September last year your obvious joy in your reunion with the farm in the Bekaa, and will long remember the evening of music, dancing and discussion we shared on the lawn. A moving experience. And I know that similar experiences were shared by all the students who went to Jordan instead of AREC. You will all treasure these memories.

To the Lebanese I say—go forth therefore and strive to restore Lebanon's agriculture, and particularly in the South which has suffered so drastically from a wanton, destructive, and murderous occupying force. Restore it to its former productivity, and to all of you I say, revive the region to its former glory. And remember to come back and see us frequently; we will follow your careers with interest and pride. Good Luck!

—Thomas M. Sutherland, Dean of Agriculture

May 19, 1985, I left for the States myself—in the next week Kit duly graduated with the whole family in attendance and we had a splendid time together! Afterward there was for me a conference on African famine in California at Pepperdine University where my role was to give the Middle East desert experiences to see if there would be purposeful application to Africa's situation. I came back to Jean on June 5 full of excitement at the kind of people in the voluntary humanitarian nongovernmental organizations who were doing so much out in the world. The next three days we spent at our cabin in the Rockies, and thus I had the memories of three perfect mountain days to carry back with me to Beirut when Jean took me to the airport on June 8. Did I have a presentiment or a worry on that journey back? I recall that I was disturbed, but I don't remember fear. I had given an interview to our Fort Collins newspaper on May 31, which highlighted my statement, "I'm not scared. I would not go back if I had to go back with constant fear." I got no negative feedback or warning from the AUB New York office through my daily calls that last week, so Friday I sent the telex to AUB, not even regarding that it was an open line: "Returning Sunday June 9 MEA [Middle East Airlines] from London—can Sharif meet me?"

On Saturday, as we left the cabin for the airport, I said to Jean, "I'll always remember these days in the mountains"—almost, as we both thought afterward, as though I wouldn't be back. I called Jean from New York and told her that an airport rendezvous with two Christian Lebanese colleagues from AUB reassured me that Dave Jacobsen's kidnapping was personal and the dean of medicine was assured of having him out shortly. My brothers, however, tried to dissuade me from going back when I called them from London on June 9: "You ought to be going back home to look after your family, man!"—but I had no feeling of personal threat against me. I do remember being surprised, however, that AUB President Calvin Plimpton was not in the boarding area at Heathrow on June 9 for he had been scheduled to return to Beirut on that same flight. I duly boarded the plane for Beirut without fear, however, and enjoyed the trip. I recall visiting with Dr. Ayash, an AUH medical faculty physician, and with his wife and their young daughter sitting beside me. It was a pleasant trip.

Part I photo collage (clockwise from top left)—AUB's famed College Hall with its clock and bell tower, a symbol for over a century of the university's presence on the Ras Beirut headland (courtesy Robert Rice); Tom wears a fez for his agriculture students in a happy moment during the last year at AUB before his kidnapping; Looking up from the Green Field to the Sutherland's AUB home with its balconies; Just after his arrival in Beirut in June 1983, Tom is photographed by a new friend as he stands on the Corniche in front of AUB with the Beirut coastal skyline behind him; The Sutherland cabin in the Rocky Mountains, family home and retreat—Tom carried this in his mind as the last picture of home before his fateful trip back to Beirut and captivity, Jean here received the news of his kidnapping June 9, 1985; Tom with U.S. marines in Beirut's Martyr Square, July 1983; Kit with U.S. marines before boarding the incoming helicopter during the evacuation of February 1984; Tom is accompanied everywhere by a bodyguard after the assassination of Malcolm Kerr, January 1984—Jean took this shot of him as he left home for the dean's office in the agriculture building at AUB in the spring of 1984.

Part II photo collage (clockwise from top left)—Jean is greeted by Vice President George Bush as she and Kit arrive for his meeting with the hostage families following Ben Weir's release, September 1985; Muhammad Hussein Fadlallah, publicly known as the spiritual guide for Hizbollah, at his home in Bir Al Abed (courtesy *Middle East Insight*); Kit and Jean join with Fort Collins' Boltz Junior High students as they release yellow balloons in a fervent show of support for Tom, October 1986 (courtesy *Fort Collins Coloradoan*); Jean walks with reporters at Beirut International Airport, leaving Beirut for Washington, D.C., and the meeting with President Reagan after mediation offer to Islamic Jihad, October 1986; UN Secretary-General Pérez de Cuéllar receives from Kit and Joan the petitions with more than 18,000 signatures of Coloradoans in support of UN efforts to free the hostages in Lebanon, February 26, 1990 (courtesy *Associated Press*/Mario Cabrera); Jean and daughters Ann, Kit, and Joan in a photograph taken for the first anniversary observance in Fort Collins, June 8, 1986 (courtesy *Fort Collins Coloradoan*); The Northern Colorado Pipe Band opens with Scottish spirit an anniversary observance for Tom as the CSU and Fort Collins communities gathered on the CSU campus—observances were held by this loyal community throughout the years of Tom's captivity and this pipe band massed with others to welcome him home December 1, 1991 (courtesy *Fort Collins Coloradoan*/Joseph DeVera); This November 1985 polaroid photo of Tom holding a *Wall Street Journal* signed by Terry Waite was given to Terry Waite by Islamic Jihad as proof of their holding of him—it is the only photo to have come out of him in captivity (courtesy Terry Waite and Harcourt Brace).

PART II

Captivity
1985–1991

Part II part page—Tom in captivity, November 1985. The polaroid shot by Islamic Jihad (see previous photo page).

6 Kidnapped: Or Brown Simca and Baseball Cap

The MEA jet drifted lazily toward Beirut Airport and I could see the city laid out to the east of us as we reached the end of the Mediterranean Sea. But funny, I thought. We are approaching from a strange angle. Always before when I had arrived in Beirut, it had been from the north, directly over the campus of the AUB (which meant that every instructor stopped teaching for a few seconds of deafening jet roar) and straight south onto the north-south runway, touching down just abreast of the terminal. This time we were approaching from the southwest, obviously giving me my first landing ever on the southwest-northeast runway. Strange.

Soon we were parked at the terminal, and I descended the steps to be met by a young woman who said she was representing Mr. Husni Serhal, the vice president for passenger relations of MEA, and by Sharif, my driver. Sharif had been at the AUB College of Agriculture since its origin way back in 1952, and now gave me, his latest boss, the traditional warm Lebanese greeting, kissing me three times on alternate cheeks. No bodyguard. Sharif had been unable to locate Mehdi all day despite fervent attempts. But the young woman adding her welcome said that Mr. Serhal had sent her to offer three body-guards from the Amal militia to escort me from the airport to the campus. I smiled; Mr. Serhal always had my best interests in mind. But, I thought, it's only six miles up to campus, and Sharif would have his nice new Chevrolet Caprice (a gift to the AUB from a generous Arab friend of the university, orchestrated by Hallab); surely it wouldn't be necessary to take three young men far out of their way simply to escort me. So I declined. "We don't need a bodyguard, do we Sharif? Tell you what; *you* be my bodyguard, okay?" "Okay, Dean," he beamed half delighted, half apprehensive. "I be your body-guard." The young woman was obviously a bit taken back. "Yánee (the Arabic catch-all term: "I mean," "You know," etc.) … it's up to you, yánee, but Mr. Serhal wanted you to have them." I insisted that it was not necessary.

So Sharif and I went to pick up my bags, after passing through immigration. Sharif disappeared for a few minutes, leaving me in the Caprice just outside of the terminal. The three Amal militiamen passed me in their beat-up, little car, smiling and waving as they drove off. Soon Sharif reappeared and two other cars lined up alongside. In one was Nazih Zaidan, the director of development at AUB, a Shiite with powerful political connections who was always immaculately dressed with shirt sleeves exactly the correct length below the cuff, and collar and tie perfect; he ranged in behind our Caprice. Ahead of us went Dr. Ayash, the Christian doctor, and his family, with whom I had had the very pleasant conversation on the plane coming in. Obviously, Sharif wanted to have a little support in his guard duties or they had insisted, being nervous. I remember nervousness. We took off.

A mile or so north on the main road from the airport to downtown, our caravan suddenly did a U-turn, and a few yards south turned into a narrow westbound road toward the coast. A little apologetically, Sharif explained that we could not go any farther north on the main road—the Amal militia was attacking the two Palestinian camps, Sabra and Shatila. These "camps" were so labeled not because they were made up of tents but because 40 years ago that was the name applied to ill-constructed concrete buildings supposedly temporary. These very same camps had suffered a devastating massacre at the hands of the Christian Lebanese Forces militia only three years before with the Israeli army looking on—now it was the Shiite militia's turn to devastate the Palestinians. Good Lord, I thought. Nobody wants the Palestinians. What's to become of them? Sure enough, from where we turned, we could hear the shells and rocket-propelled grenades pounding, pounding, pounding; I knew now the reason for our plane's landing from the south.

West we went, into the sunset, Sharif and I eagerly exchanging respective news. Suddenly I became conscious of a little brown Simca drawn alongside of us, uncomfortably close, windows rolled down and four young men staring ominously at us. "Who are you?" barked a little fellow in the right rear seat, wearing a baseball cap turned backward like a catcher. Strange. Never seen these characters in my life before. Why should he want to know who I am? *CRASH.* Sideswiped, by God! Then *CRASH.* Sideswiped again! I should have smelled a rat when they first approached and ordered Sharif, "Go—go. Get out of here!" His powerful Caprice could easily have outrun that clunker little Simca. Too late. They darted in front of us, cut us off, Sharif jammed on the brakes and we all came to a dead stop, including Dr. Ayash ahead and Nazih Zaidan behind. The four young men poured out of the Simca. Another four appeared from a second car behind it. Eight men in their late teens/early twenties, each carrying a submachine gun he promptly started to use. *What a bloody racket!* Bullets flying everywhere, spewing onto the tar of the road and into our car—ricocheting in all directions as the men danced excitedly around our car. "Good Lord, what's going on, Sharif?" I muttered in disbelief. Eyes dilated, obviously nervous and hyped-up—so were we by this time. "Get out of the car," ordered young Baseball Cap, appearing at my side and pulling open the door of the Caprice. I didn't argue with him. He still had a red-hot machine gun in his hands, and the words of advice from the American embassy suddenly flooded my mind, "Don't be a hero. Don't resist. Do what they say and maybe you'll live."

Kidnapped! Can't be true! Must be dreaming. But Baseball Cap was dragging me out of the car and his pushing and exhortation seemed real enough—no dream. There to my left was Sharif wrestling with three of them. Good Lord, Sharif, don't fight with them. They'll shoot you. But there he was, valiant little fellow, wrestling away, trying to get to me. The vision is still clear in my mind, and bothered me for my entire captivity. I had really been joking with Sharif about being my bodyguard. But one didn't joke about such matters in Beirut. He had taken me literally. To the rear, I could see Nazih vehemently arguing with his fellow Shiites. To no avail. I was pushed into the passenger's seat of the Simca—the four others bundled in and zoom—we sped west. Vaguely I was aware of Dr. Ayash's car in front speeding off into the sunset.

I was off at high speed the mile to the coast road, then off south for a while—"Give me everything," Baseball Cap was demanding. I started to give them all I had in my pockets, but kept my knife and a CSU pin. They had just taken my briefcase, and were all rummaging through it like a pack of dogs at the kill—looking for money, no doubt. Suddenly, the driver pulled up in the median, took a walkie-talkie from under his seat, and started talking excitedly into it. A few moments and turning the car around, he was off again, now northward, toward Beirut—high speed. Eyes still flashing, one hand on the wheel, and one on the horn, the driver roared north in the southbound lanes—70 miles an hour, while any southbound vehicles scattered out of his way. The two northbound lanes were clogged with Beirutis returning from a pleasant weekend in southern Lebanon or maybe from the Shouf Mountains to the southeast of Beirut—all favorite and pleasant spots, I knew from experience—from a Sunday outing even in these troubled times. By now my abductors had relieved me of my pen, my knife, my billfold, my comb, my change, my handkerchief—everything except, amazingly, my watch. Suddenly the driver spotted that on my wrist—a nice Seiko from my wife for our 25th wedding anniversary almost three years before. "Give me watch," he shouted menacingly. "You can't have it," I answered coldly, "It's a present from my wife for our 25th wedding anniversary." That watch meant a lot to me—it was the nicest I'd ever owned. Damned if I was going to give it up! "Give me watch," he repeated even more threateningly. "No," I replied, still coldly determined. "Give me watch," he barked loudly. "No. It's from my wife." He leered at me and, changing his tone, suggested, "Tell her you give it to a friend." I gave him the watch.

We raced past the Summerland Hotel at breakneck speed, through all the intervening checkpoints manned by militias of diverse stripes; seeing startled expressions on dozens of Lebanese faces, I wondered almost idly if they realized that yet another westerner was in the process of disappearing into the dungeons of the southern suburbs. I kept looking back at the men in the backseat, still eagerly rummaging in my briefcase, which looked by now as if it had been stirred by a stick. The immaculate order—papers, passport, Minox camera, documents case—was now in unholy disarray. "Hey, quit messing up my briefcase, dammit." Engrossed in my briefcase, they only hissed at me, but Baseball Cap snarled, "Why you looking? No looking—*we blow you head off!*" He kept repeating the threat; it apparently didn't register as urgent with me, for I continued to look in dismay at the incredible rubble they were creating with *my* stuff. Terry Anderson was later to be astonished at my naïveté concerning the immediate danger I was in—"You dummy! They *would* have blown your head off!"

Just north of the Summerland Hotel they cut through the northbound lanes and off to the east, stopped briefly to change drivers for some reason, then we were off again, this time ending up in a blind alley, where we sat for a minute or two while the original driver quizzed me about my salary—"How many dollar you get for one year?" "Maybe fifty thousand dollars," I ventured. "Fifty thousand! Dollar?" he asked incredulously (I learned later they were being paid somewhere between $75 and $300 a month, so it must have seemed like a fortune to him). But all four now got out and ordered me to get out; not possible, for the door on my side had jammed completely, no doubt a result of their sideswiping. So I struggled across the tiny car, and out the driver's side, only to be pushed into the trunk, which was predictably filthy. "There go my slacks!" The fumes were also coming into the trunk with me, until we got moving. They drove around for five or ten minutes, probably to disorient me. A waste of time, for I had zero idea of where we were. In my two years at AUB, I had spent very little time in the southern suburbs; those were effectively off-limits to westerners, particularly Americans who were looked upon with hostility by the majority of the residents there who had been pushed out of South Lebanon by the Israelis during their invasion some three years earlier. These southern suburbs were a mass of narrow canyons between rows of quickly, cheaply, and poorly constructed cinder-block high-rises, up to 12 stories above ground, put up in an effort to house the masses of poor Shia refugees who had arrived with no money, no job, no home, no decent prospects—nothing save the clothes they stood in. They had one thing in common—their fear and their hatred of Israel, the Archenemy, and of its American supporter, the Great Satan.

The car stopped, and they pulled me out of my cramped quarters onto a big slab of concrete in front of one of the 10- to 12-story buildings with a mob of some 30–40 young men milling around and jabbering away excitedly in Arabic—they had after all, another new trophy. I didn't have time to more than quickly take in much of the surroundings before one young fellow cried out (in English, amazingly), "The eyes; the eyes. Cover the eyes!" And immediately one of them produced a regular blindfold (the kind one gets for sleeping on an airplane) and tied it around my head. Another young man then produced what turned out to be, when I examined it later, the cover for a front seat headrest of a car. He pulled this too over my head for good measure—and, though I blessedly didn't know it then, *that was the last time I would see the sun for the next six and a half years.*

Someone then led me thus blindfolded down two flights of stairs, and I was locked in a small cell of some sort—I didn't raise the covers over my eyes so I wasn't sure of my exact surroundings—only that there was a steel door, and considerable comings and goings while I sat on a chair. After a half hour or so, a "boss" of some kind arrived with a young interpreter and proceeded to interrogate me. He spoke only in Arabic, but with a deeper, more mature voice than any of my abductors, and with an obvious authority and crispness, meaning business with no nonsense, I decided. It was quickly obvious that they had no idea of who I was. More questions: "Why you coming Beirut?" I answered honestly. "What you do AUB?" Again straight. "How long you there?" "Maybe you CIA?" ("Oh God, I thought—not that!") "You know about Green Berets who helping Lebanese Army on Christian side?" "No. I don't know anything at all about Green Berets, either in Lebanon or in America." And I really didn't, but he apparently didn't believe me. "You lie! How many Americans at AUB now?" By this time, I was thinking a little more clearly and had collected myself a little. In truth, I wasn't afraid, nor had I experienced real fear during the whole episode so far; a little shock, yes, and disbelief for sure. This was the sort of thing that only happens to others, right? So how could I be here, two floors down in a strange building, sitting blindfolded on a chair being questioned by two complete strangers, about relatively personal matters concerning my job and my family—really none of their damn business! Back came the advice of the embassy again: Play it safe, cooperate within reason, and survive! So I did, and tried to answer them with reasonable honesty. But the question about the other Americans at the AUB put me on guard. How could I betray good friends like Bob and Laura Rice, Landry and Virginia Slade, Peter and Erica Dodd? Suddenly I thought of all the recent retirees. And of those who had become discouraged with the chaos and anarchy in Beirut and had decided there were safer and quieter places in which to pursue academic excellence. That was it: Harry Henderson had just retired from agriculture. Bob Cook from chemistry had gone to Canada. The Scotts had retired to Pennsylvania after many years at AUB, and so on. "What are their addresses?" "I don't know." This truthfully. I hadn't known exactly where most of them had lived at AUB much less where they were now, thousands of miles safely away from these types. It felt good and righteous! Finally, the "boss man" seemed satisfied, and they both left.

Some time later, several more young men came, and escorted me to a new cell. "Is there a bed?" I asked, for by this time I was becoming a little tired. "Yes, bed for you." Arrived, some bed! A narrow roll-away too long to go down flat—with the cell barely six feet long, the roll-away stuck partially down at about a 30-degree angle. But at least it was a bed … *Clang!* went the steel door behind me. And there I was, locked in, securely and unforgivingly. Not a pleasant thought. But curiously for me, there was at the same time a feeling of exhilaration. "I've been kidnapped, by God." Not many people have *that* happen to them. And absurdly, as it turned out, I was not even terribly worried about it. After all, I reasoned, I was a dean at the American University of Beirut, the most prestigious university in the Arab Middle East. The Board of Trustees was such a powerful group of men and women that they would soon get me out of here! And they would, of course, have the backing of the Lebanese government who had always resisted any efforts to remove AUB to another location. Bahrain, Cyprus, Jordan would all have loved to be the home of the famous AUB. In Bahrain, they had argued, it would not even have had to change initials.

AUB, so powerful and important, thought I, will have me out in a matter of days—or in at most a few weeks, I'll be homeward bound, restored to my family and friends, and back in my beloved position as dean of the Faculty of Agricultural and Food Sciences. And back to our nice home, overlooking the Green Field with its soccer field and running track where I had jogged so freely and so happily for the previous two years, and the Mediterranean Sea beyond the palm trees—away from this hellhole where I now find myself. Still not unduly afraid, nor yet even worried. But the clang of that door shutting on me still rang in my ears.

The night progressed. No toilet, not even a hole in the floor in this cell. I rattled the door. No response. More loudly. No response. Only the roar of the air conditioning blasting into my cell. Soon I became more desperate. "Hey," I shouted, "I need to go to the bathroom." No response. More loudly yet. Still no response. What the hell! What does one do?! Isn't anyone listening? Obviously not. Whir went the air-conditioning blowers. I became absolutely desperate—to the point where there is nothing else in the universe. There was the dirt floor of my cell. Nothing for it, no matter how irreconcilable to my upbringing or to my position as a dean in a prestigious university. I used the corner. Thus irrevocable, my initiation into hostageship.

Morning. After what seemed like an age, a young man I hadn't met up to this point appeared. "My name Bassam. You want food?" He offered me some breakfast of bread and processed cheese, from France no less: "La Vache Qui Rit," which our daughters had loved so much the year we spent near Paris. And a *glass* of tea, not a cup. It was hot and sweet, in the typical Lebanese style. After another long time, Bassam returned to take me to the toilet—out my cell door, along the short piece of corridor, through an enormous steel door while going up one step, across a short space, and voila, the bathroom. What a place! In the corner to the left of the door was a plastic bag, in which as I discovered later, other prisoners were supposed to empty their food bowls. Only, they did not make a very good job of it, for much of the food ended up on the floor. Most of it looked as if it had been there for some time, never tidied, and beginning to smell—but the flies liked it! Hundreds of them sticking to the wall, not moving, of a species that I had not ever seen before but was to see much more of in the months to come, with wide bodies, fairly flat, and a kind of dirty brown color, not the blue black that we normally associate with flies. The toilet itself was the Arabic style, a hole in the floor more or less, but somewhat more complicated—a porcelain unit, shiny and smooth, and fitted into the plumbing system, two ribbed feet marks for a person to plant the feet. Probably considered uptown, European, the kind we used to see all over France in the sixties. (We discovered over the years as hostages that these toilets were not such a bad idea, in fact, for squatting makes things easier and with always a very limited time in the toilet, every little help in this department was more than welcome!) Up in the top corner of the small room (only about five feet by five feet) was a big electric water heater, but not on at that time. All the galvanized-style water pipes were out in the open, not a very neat job. I have done a fair bit of plumbing myself in my time, and I sure could have improved on that lot! Some copper pipe, a bit of solder, some salve, and a blow torch and I could soon have it done right. What futile thoughts. The water heater was a powerful job though, about four kilowatts, I figured.

Soon Bassam was at the door tapping lightly, "*Vite*"—they all knew that word, I was to discover. So I hastened my ablutions at a piece of pipe sticking out from the wall with a faucet on it—primitive stuff. No towel—"Damn." So I used my undershirt. Back to the cell, bang went that huge steel door again.

I sat back on the bed and reflected for a long time. In my head I went over the things I should be getting done: This was Monday morning, lots of things waiting at my office at the AUB; reports to write to the Ford Foundation, who had given us a cool $100,000 to support our teaching program, and to the Near East Foundation, who had given us $50,000 to support the students' practical work on the farm in the Bekaa, besides travel to Jordan for those students who for security reasons couldn't go to the Bekaa. I had been mulling them over in my head for days before leaving for Beirut—they would be easy. Then salary increase recommendations for all of the faculty. I already had two experiences doing that, too, so not difficult either. But I could expect plenty of complaints again. So now in my cell, I went over the case to be made for each one and how I would defend it. And also how to handle the case of a cantankerous and paranoid Irishman who was giving me fits with his claims and his complaints. I was sick to the teeth with the guy, and I resolved that when I got out, I would start proceedings to fire him. And how to replace the IBM correcting Selectric typewriters that had been stolen out of our secretarial pool; there had been an epidemic of thefts in all the buildings around ours, and we had been the latest to get "hit." So the hours passed. Lunch arrived, a gooey mess of vegetable stew, floating in olive oil; it was mainly eggplant, but diverse other unrecognizable types of vegetables, it seemed. Amazingly, it tasted not too bad—luckily, for it was not the last time I was to have it. It was so caloric, though, that by evening, I was not the least bit hungry, and told Bassam that I didn't care for any more food. He spoke little or no English, so I used my little Arabic: "Mabiddee" ("I do not want"). So he went on to the next cell.

The days passed. Bassam came daily, both to feed me and to take me to the toilet—reasonably pleasant fellow—but I had a run-in with him on only my second day in captivity. Feeling sticky and sweaty, I had started to take a shower—even cold water felt great—but Bassam burst into the bathroom, allowing me even to see him full face, and called angrily, "No douche," insisted that I get out of the bathroom immediately, and hustled me back to my cell dripping wet. A few minutes later he reappeared with a note written in poor English that I assume he had had one of his buddies write up for him; it had a list of instructions for me to follow:

"No take shower. We tell you."

"No look me any time. This very bad."

"No speak any time."

"No make any noise."

"Wash your bowl each day."

Interestingly, this was one of the few times in all of my captivity that I was ever given explicit instructions on how to behave or to proceed. We were supposed to deduce from their actions and verbal commands what they expected of us. But he was obviously scared about my looking at him, which I did fairly brazenly at first.

Another young fellow appeared about the second or third day, and came in and sat beside me on my bed. He introduced himself: "My name is 'Jameel.' You know what that mean?" "Yes," I replied, "Beautiful." He chuckled. "That not my real name," he explained. "Then what is your real one?" "Not your business!" he said. But he had no qualms about asking me all kinds of questions: "How many children you have? How old are they? Where they live? How much money you paid?" And my private life, "How many times you have sex with your wife?" Whether he wanted the answer to this question by the day, week, month, or year I didn't ask! He soon explained his real purpose: "I want to learn English better. You will teach me, yes?" His English in truth was not bad, and he understood almost everything I told him. He came back almost every evening, and we got to know each other fairly well. He knew a lot about me, it seemed, and eventually admitted that he had learned much of it from the newspapers and the radio. "Many people talking about you. Many stories in papers and on TV. Many, many people want you to be free." Well, that was comforting, and reinforced my conviction that I would not be here long anyway. So, drawing short of my sex life, I told him all about my family and my own history; after all, I would never see him again after I got out. But when I in turn asked him about himself, it was "not your business." But, "I have job," he admitted. "In the day I work with computers, and I very good. I knowing all how to make bombs," he boasted, "even big ones." He said that with a good deal of emotion in his voice, and later told me, "CIA not able to catch *me!* I too clever!" Bassam was still taking me to the toilet by myself. But I began to peek through the small cracks along the side of the steel door, and each morning I could hear him pouring out the tea and stirring in all that sugar. He did about seven or eight glassfuls—must be at least that many others here with me, I thought. Later each morning, another guard, older by the sound of his voice, was taking others to the toilet; as I peered through the crack, I saw six or seven men being driven like cattle along the hallway, all of them blindfolded, and each with his hand on the shoulder of the man in front of him. "My God! How humiliating!" At least I was not being subjected to *that* kind of treatment. Adding insult to injury, the older guy following them was whapping a stick on the floor and crying "Yellah" ("Let's go" or "Hurry up"). They were traipsing along as fast as they could blindfolded, not saying a word—they must all be Lebanese, since he would also say a few words to them from time to time in Arabic. Two years later I learned from Jean-Paul Kauffmann that he and three other French-men who had been kidnapped just before me were in this group. Generally about a half hour later, they would reappear, and the stick would crack on the floor, and the "Yellahs" would resound again along the hallway.

Evenings often brought through the big outside door some of the guards or militiamen to try out guns. With no warning, they would open up, sometimes single rounds, sometimes a sequence of volleys, *right outside my door*—scared the living daylights out of me! Gradually I got used to it, but setting off a gun in closed quarters like that makes one *hell* of a racket! They were shooting down the hallway, presumably at some kind of target stuck on the wall at the end. Actually, I had no way of verifying these hypotheses; my small cracks at the side of the door didn't permit my seeing even remotely down that hall. But I did discover that it was quite long, with lots of cells along it, with even a right-angle corridor running off it.

All of this I found out from complaining about the fact that my cell was too short to allow my bed to go all the way down—eventually Jameel took me on a tour of the vacant cells, and offered me my choice of any of these. Some of them were much bigger than my little one, but most had water standing on the floor. Surely didn't want to get moved into that kind of mess. Then too, they were far away from the big steel door to the outside, and I could sort of monitor what was happening, the comings and goings of the guards, and the number of cups of tea that Bassam was pouring morning and evening. Much more isolated away down there. Jameel also told me that others were much more cramped than I, and let me look in the cell adjacent to mine. Hot in there too. It was occupied by a young man in his early twenties, who of course put his blindfold down the moment Jameel began to open his door. I could not see his whole face for his blindfold, but saw enough to think he was Lebanese, fairly light-skinned, wearing shorts. He was busy with books around him, writing on pads of paper. Lots of Christians had been kidnapped by the Moslems in the past years (and vice versa, it should be added) and most of them never had been seen again. I wondered if this was one of the luckier ones who at least was still alive. Again no proof of my theory, and Jameel was no help—"Not your business!"

Frightening was the nightly beating of someone down the hall; it seemed to be coming from a distance, but the screams were so piercing that it was almost as though it were next door. In this case when I asked Jameel one night when he was in my cell for his English lesson, he volunteered, "This *very* bad man, one of men caught trying to blow up Sheikh Fadlallah's house. Did you know they try to kill Sheikh?" "Yes, of course," I replied, "it was in all the papers some months before I was kidnapped." "That very bad," said Jameel, "was CIA did it!" Here we go again; the CIA is blamed for everything bad that happens around here. I thought it very unlikely that the CIA had had anything to do with this operation in the southern suburbs of Beirut, since Americans of any stripe would scarcely venture down there among a seething mass of Shia. But that only reflected my naïveté concerning the CIA and their ventures under Bill Casey. I learned later that although it had been Lebanese who had perpetrated that terrible bombing, killing many innocent citizens, they had apparently all been trained by the CIA. The rumor ran that this was the "American" retaliation for the Marine barracks bombing. Fadlallah was suspected and Fadlallah would get it. Thus the definition of "war" for the Lebanese Shiites and the definition of "terrorism" for the United States.

On the fourth day of my captivity, I had a visit from a big man, both physically and politically, a man different from my original interrogator who sat on my rollaway bed with Jameel and talked to me for some time, in French, telling me that indeed they had had no idea who I was, and that at first they had decided to let me go. "But now we decide to keep you—you are unlucky." What could I say but a very facetious, "Merci beaucoup. Vous êtes très gentil!" He confirmed that lots of people had been calling for my release, which prompted me to think that by causing a fuss, perhaps the citizens of Beirut and AUB had unknowingly rendered me valuable to the kidnappers, who had decided that I might be of some importance after all. I was at least getting them a little publicity, and I soon learned that this was very important to them. But perhaps most important of all was the fact of the TWA hijacking, which had taken place that very day. The "boss man" told me all about the hijacking, was very excited about it, and was of the opinion that they would be able to lump us in with all the airplane hostages and thus finally get their demands—he did not elaborate on exactly what these were, but said jubilantly, "They have to give in to us now—we have so many!" It would be some months later, at Ben Weir's release, before I learned what they wanted—their "brothers" out of prison in Kuwait. Seventeen Shia had been caught trying to blow up the American and French embassies in Kuwait, had been tried in court, and imprisoned; three were actually sentenced to death, but that was never carried out. Freedom for their "brothers" was the primary demand, as we learned, of the Lebanese group involved in the kidnapping of westerners. The Ayatollah Khomeini had much wider objectives—to rid the Middle East of all westerners. By this time, they had some dozen hostages, including the four Frenchmen kidnapped just prior to me. The demands, however, were very much public knowledge long before this, for the *New York Times,* unbeknownst to me, had been reporting regularly on the whole affair:

> MAY 17, 1985—"Aidan Walsh, UN Relief and Works Agency, is freed un-harmed 36 hours after being kidnapped by gunmen in Moslem West Beirut: Islamic Holy War says it will free at least six American and French hostages kidnapped in Beirut if Kuwait releases the men convicted of bombing United States and French Embassies there in December 1983. They threaten to ter-rorize the U.S. and France forever if the men are not freed."

It was apparently common knowledge that Walsh had been deliberately kid-napped and released to bring out this message from Islamic Jihad. At that time, I had not even departed Lebanon for the United States on my recruit-ing and conference trip, but regrettably, neither was I reading the *New York Times!*

In retrospect, it seems amazing that we had not been apprised of these spe-cific warnings and threats—by friends, by the embassy, or by the Board of AUB—surely some of them must have been reading the *Times?!* As it was, I recall several discussions with Professor Landry Slade, a longtime AUB faculty member, in which we puzzled over the reasons behind the kidnapping of westerners, and the best we could come up with was that Iran probably wanted spare parts for its war effort against Iraq.

My French-speaking friend was rather nice to me, in fact, and sympathetic—he took me for a shower, after giving me a big bar of soap, a toothbrush, and a huge tube of toothpaste. That shower sure felt good!

The next evening, Jameel invited me upstairs into their room to have some fruit and watch TV. So upstairs I traipsed, two whole flights, and into a room where evidently several guards were busy lounging, their favorite occupation as I was to learn! From time to time, someone would come to the door of this room, which seemed to open straight to the outside. Knock, knock. "Meen?" they would ask, Arabic for "Who's there?" Some reply would come, which I could not follow, but evidently was satisfactory, for the visitors were always allowed in, stayed a few minutes, then left. The fruit was bing cherries. A whole big bowlful of them. Delicious. But to go with them, a glass of water! What would I have given for an old-fashioned, or maybe even better yet, some liqueur? Maybe chocolate brandy? Obviously, having this kind of delusion I was not yet into Islamic fundamentalism!

But worse than the austerity of the water was the nature of the film they showed me. Never in my life had I seen such gory scenes—men would burst out of trees with submachine guns blaring and literally massacre tens of people sitting around a swimming pool—blood and guts everywhere. I was completely nauseated, but the guards sitting behind me were fascinated and cheering on the action! I asked to go back to my "own room." Ungrateful wretch that I was, I was never again asked to partake of their "hospitality"!

Meantime, Bassam continued to show irritation and even anger when I would try to peek at him. But my curiosity generally got the better of me, and I would tilt my head backward to get a look at him. He was about five feet six, fairly stocky or even slightly fat—unusual for most young Lebanese men—with the obligatory beard and moustache. He was usually well dressed and fairly pleasant, though not too eager to give me a shower! Once or twice, a very young boy appeared who didn't at all seem worried about being seen; in fact he was *very* friendly, so I always took the chance to ask *him* for a shower. On one of these occasions, he was with a second youngster, both of them fairly fluent in English to boot, and they again gave me permission to shower. But there was no soap. "Wait few minutes," they said. Sure enough, they returned with a nice bar of Dove soap, handed it to me, still naked in the bathroom, and smiled. I thought to myself "How young. What do they think about what they're doing?" When I complained to Jameel about the shortage of showers, he chuckled, "You not working. You not needing many showers."

In the toilet, I had discovered a four-inch-diameter pipe leading up through the ceiling, to allow air to be drawn out of the bathroom—this was a technique that they employed quite a lot, I found—and when I put my head and ear up next to it, I could hear distant muffled noises of children laughing and screaming. Intriguing yet sad to know that I was *so close to freedom and civilization,* but so confined and unable to be any part of it. I was envious of those free little kids, and they made me think of my own carefree, happy childhood. I began to recount to myself some of my childhood memories, and dwelt at length on these. Amazingly, things from my past popped up that I hadn't thought about for well over 45 years, such as my first day going into the local village school with my mother and finding under the stair by the entryway a little red tricycle parked. How I longed to have it. I coveted that thing for years. It belonged to a boy about five years older than I who had contracted polio at an early age, and this little trike was his means of getting around, pedaling it with his hands, while he crouched in the body of the thing. While I felt terribly sorry for him, I still wanted his trike. There in a cell many years later I felt guilty about that.

Many other episodes from my life passed before me, to my constant astonishment. The names of just about every one of my classmates, admittedly not a formidable task for there were only a dozen of us. My sixth-grade afternoons of working in the school garden for the headmaster, since I was generally a bit ahead of the rest of the class, and he could do some catching up with the others while I toiled; besides I was farm-fed, stronger, and more used to working than were the village kids, who were all existing on war-time diets.

So, as I learned afterward, I was normal—for I went through the classic symptoms of the first days of a hostage in captivity: Phase One, denial of the event: "This isn't really happening, not to me!" Then Phase Two: "I won't be in here very long; the police will have me out in no time!" In my case, not the Lebanese police, but surely the Lebanese government, the American government, and the AUB? The Board of Trustees after all is made up of very powerful and generally rich men and women from both the United States and the Middle East who have *influence,* or as the Arabs say "*wasta.*" So I knew for sure that my circumstances were temporary.

Phase Three, "Taking Stock," I also went through, reviewing my life and all the experiences that I could recall from earliest times up to Kit's graduation from the University of Colorado. Amazing how such diverse people in such completely different hostage situations, in totally different regions of the world, all go through such similar stages of a captivity. Then comes the vow to "be a better person." Not only I—all of us went through that phase too. Pledging to God that if only He would let us out of this hellish situation, we would *never again* do such and such. We would all be model citizens, God-fearing, loving, respectful, considerate, and kind.

Then Phase Four: "Antagonism-Hostility" toward the captors. I became so angry at them for taking me away from my career, and I had had *so much* to get done back in my office, and I knew that I was only a few miles from it. I became frustrated beyond any kind of frustration I had ever known, and it lasted for a very long time, years in fact, until it was obviously so long since my kidnapping that my life would simply have to be completely changed, and all the subverted plans were by then long out-of-date and useless. After this, Phase Five and "Self-Blame." I went through that too. I had stupidly turned down the three bodyguards that Husni Serhal had offered me at the airport, after Kit had warned me to be very careful. "How dumb" I kept thinking, for if I had taken them, there would have been no attempt to kidnap me; these guys were not very brave, and despite their frequently expressed desires to "meet my God," they wouldn't remotely have come after me with three armed men sitting in my car. Surprisingly, however, I never once gave a thought to blaming myself for having come to Beirut and the AUB. I had really enjoyed that experience, and was only frustrated that these guys had cut me off from the job.

Many hostages apparently go through a final phase, after a longer period I presume, which I never experienced. This phase has come to be known as "The Stockholm Syndrome," after a case in Sweden in which a girl fell in love with the captor who raped her. In this syndrome as it has been generalized today, the hostage identifies with the cause of the captors instead of with one's government or formerly held ideals. Patty Hearst is the American exemplar. *Never*, however, did *any* of us, American or British hostages, come even remotely close to entering that phase. Instead, we kept telling them: "You should not be doing this, you know. You will never be able to push the American government to give you anything for us. You are only getting a bad name for the Shia people, and for all the Lebanese, and indeed all of the Arab world. You should all of you go back to school and get an education and learn to do something worthwhile for Lebanon instead of all this nonsense." "But what can we do," they would reply, "America will not listen to us." "They certainly will not listen to you when you are blowing up their embassies, and hijacking their airplanes, and kidnapping their citizens." "Oh, don't worry," they would claim optimistically, "America will deal!" "No they won't," we would counter. And of course we did not know what they knew and we wouldn't know it for another year—that Oliver North was dealing—unconstitutionally—not only giving arms for hostages, but selling second-rate arms for hostages, charging an inflated price to make money for subsidizing Contras, then on the side giving intelligence about Iran to Iraq, the mortal enemy. Ollie would sum it all up in his "A neat idea," which in the end, I guess, sums up Ollie North and his approach to foreign and domestic policy.

About two weeks after arriving in this sub-Hilton, the toilet apparently started acting up, so that some "workers" had to start digging up the floor. This meant that all of us on the "second floor down" had to be traipsed up two flights of stairs to where there were two more toilets. They still took me alone, but up there it was a regular Times Square. Every time I arrived there were all sorts of people waiting to use the toilets, and when I was inside, there were constant demands of "*Vite*." The stairs up to these were steep, concrete, and not well made. But it gave a *little* bit of exercise going up and down them. And out of my tiny cell, every little bit helped. But the pressure to get into the toilet and out again in a hurry made the daily trip even less satisfying. The bed being at an angle was still bothering me, so that I asked Jameel for a hammer and a chisel to let me bash out a piece of the wall at the top of the bed. I could have done that in a few minutes, for at that time I was still strong enough that I could easily have wielded a hammer. But reflecting on how paranoid they were about all of us, and our superior size, I have to chuckle at the naive image of me asking for a hammer, which they would be sure would be wielded against them. I continued to complain about the bed, though, even after my guided tour of the prison by Jameel, when I turned down all of the other cells that he showed me, and made him quite exasperated; but next night, he took me out of my cell, made me sit on the table where Bassam routinely fixed the cups of tea, and proceeded to move a whole arsenal of rocket launchers, which look like the cardboard tubes that westerners mail posters in. There must have been hundreds of the things, for the entire cell, number one in the row, somewhat bigger than mine, was stuffed full of them. He carried them into cell two, my former cell, and eventually locked me into cell number one. Wonder of wonders, the bed now went down flat, and I was finally able to lie level.

But there were other problems. I couldn't reach the light bulb in this cell, which had been easy in my first cell, cell two, where I could turn out the light by unscrewing the bulb a little. The bulb in this cell was higher wattage, and blazed on me day and night. I felt I was getting dehydrated and disoriented. Or perhaps I had just been in isolation for close to a month and that was beginning to work on me? How can I be sure? In any case, I became irritable and spent a lot of time complaining, and if I recall correctly, even whining in the most unbrave and undeanlike manner. Jameel soon tired of this and began to berate me. The end result was a move away from the prison altogether. On the 28th day in that place, Jameel came down late in the evening and told me, "Bring your 'things'." Accordingly I picked up my Freeman shoes, a shirt, pants, towel, toothbrush, a couple of razors they had given me, and the few odds and ends that I had accumulated by this time—a plastic spoon, a bowl, and an old pair of shoes that I had found under the bed. "*At last,*" I thought, "I'm going home!" I posed the question to Jameel, as he waited for me to stuff my junk into a plastic bag. "Am I going home?" "Maybe," he replied, "I don't know." The standard reply, that we were to get hundreds of times in the coming months and years. I was led out of the cell and up the two flights of stairs that by now I had become used to, and arrived in some kind of outer room where I had never been. Jameel made me sit on the concrete floor, hard and cold, but at least it was cooler up here than it had been down below, with lots of good fresh air. So cool and fresh, I breathed deeply and long until I felt almost light-headed!

I sat there a long time, almost an hour it felt like, but of course when one has absolutely nothing to do except sit, time really does seem to drag! Eventually, an engine sound appeared, and along with it, loads of guards; all sorts of commotion, argumentation, and shouting. I hadn't heard that kind of bustle in a month, since my kidnapping experience. I was hauled roughly to my feet and hustled into a van in which I could easily stand up. It sounded as though there were four or five young men in it. "Don't afraid," one of them said to me, in an attempt to reassure me. "I'm not afraid," I told him. After all, I was on my way out to freedom. July 7, 1985.

It took a long time for them to get everything sorted out, but finally we were on our way in the rattling old van, which sounded as though its differential was about to fall out any minute. The driver drove furiously for about 15 minutes, erratically accelerating and then braking in turns. When he stopped, I was hustled out of the van and given over to another young man. The truck crew, however, insisted on getting their blindfold back. "Close eyes, okay?" Of course I closed them only partially, and while being dragged away by the new guard I could see that we were headed for a staircase on the outside, Lebanese-style, of a building in front of us. As we climbed the steps to the second floor, I could hear loud music coming from some room in this building, and my immediate thought was, "Must be students here." Such is conditioned response.

7   Into Chains

It was up the stairs this time to an apartment, first into a sort of living room where several men seemed to be relaxing, so far as I could determine from behind a new blindfold, a towel. As I entered, one of them came to me and said, "Ahlen wa sahlen," "Ahlen wa sahlen," "Ahlen wa Sahlen." "My house is your house," the Arabic expression for "Welcome." The man kept on "welcoming" me over and over. He had small, pudgy hands and kept squeezing mine, which I felt were much more powerful than his, not that it made any difference in the situation. His companions also offered several "Ahlens," but he was obviously the boss here. Afterward, I thought a lot about the change from the Raouche apartment to this one. I never saw the first "boss man," Bassam, Jameel, or the cell block again. John McCarthy and Brian Keenan would underscore that they too had been held in the Raouche area when first kidnapped and then changed over. Had I been "handed over," or even "sold" perhaps, by some group specialized in kidnapping, but less prepared for long-term detentions?

A minute or two and I was led across the hall by this same boss with another somewhat younger man as interpreter to meet "new friends." My escorts stood behind me now and removed my blindfold. In front of me were two men with long, flowing, white beards and long white hair, Old Father Time and His Brother in boxer shorts and T-shirts. They introduced themselves. "My name is Benjamin Weir," said the first, the slighter of the two, whose blindfold was a pair of ski goggles covered with black tape. "Good God!" I thought, "the Presbyterian minister. Kidnapped over a year ago; no one's heard a word in all that time." The second, more heavyset man, now chimed in with, "My name is Father Martin, Lawrence Jenco"—a name I immediately recognized also as that of the Catholic priest who had arrived in November of 1984 to administer all the millions of dollars the Catholic Church was pouring into Lebanon, destined mainly for the Shia of the south of Lebanon. Kidnapped for his pains.

I began to realize that I was about to be locked up with two "Men of the Cloth," I who had hardly been in a church in 15 years, not even paying the second half of my pledge in 1970 because I was so disillusioned and angry with the minister. In my mild panic now, I immediately wondered if the good Lord was maybe telling me something about my past behavior. I told them who I was, and *how* I had been kidnapped, and *where* I had been held, so far as I knew. Our conversation in front of the guards, one of whom spoke fairly fluent English, was necessarily constrained and superficial. After about five minutes, the English speaker surprisingly asked me if I had any questions. "Yes," I replied, "do you know anything of my friend David Jacobsen?" This was a real shot in the dark, for it had been rumored that David, the director of the AUH, had been kidnapped by Palestinians, and that his boss, the dean of medicine, had leads to get him released in short order. For all I knew he might even be free now. But, "Yes," they replied, "would you like to speak to him?" "Good God!" I thought, "These characters seem to have *everyone!*" Aloud I said, "Of course!"

They replaced my blindfold: "Okay, come." They led me out of this bedroom cell and into the very next room. "David, you have a friend." "Who is it?" asked David. "It's Tom Sutherland," I replied. "Tom," exclaimed David, "it's good to see ... no it's not good to see you. That means you're kidnapped too!" I agreed. Both of us were of course blindfolded, but we conversed for several minutes at a slow pace, for the English-speaking guard, whose name turned out to be Sayeed—a man with whom we were to have much contact over the coming months and years—insisted on translating each sentence for his boss, who was being called by my newfound friends "Hajj," a term of respect normally reserved for those who have undertaken a pilgrimage to Mecca, but fairly loosely used these days among friends, it appears.

I explained to David how I had been picked up—I knew all about his case of course—and how I had been treated in the previous month, while David gave me a brief account of his recent experiences. Finally he said, "I want you to meet my friend, Terry Anderson." "Hi, Terry." "Hello, Tom." (A sepulchral reply—I don't think he was in a good mood.) Thus my first words with the man with whom I was to spend many months, 70, in fact, and was to exchange many millions of words in the ensuing years. I told them that it looked as though I were about to be chained up to the same wall as Father Martin. Terry, also Catholic, knew all about Father, having written about him when he'd been kidnapped in January. Immediately he picked up on the fact that Father was here, for as it transpired,

Terry had lots on his mind and his conscience that he wanted to confess. This was his opportunity at last.

A few seconds more and I was being led back next door to have my worst fears realized—*chains!* It was now my turn to be "fitted." I was instructed by the new guard, Sayeed, to sit down on a very skimpy one-inch thick foam pad covered with dark blue plastic that was ranged alongside that of Father Martin— My God! I thought. *This* close to a Catholic priest?!—and heard the clinking of a very hard piece of chain. Lots of discussion in Arabic between Sayeed and his boss, Hajj, and lots of chain clanking, and finally it was ready to put around my left ankle. Both of them fumbled around trying to decide which link it should be in, finally selecting one that made the chain uncomfortably tight. I tried to get into the act, protesting and pushing my finger inside the chain to show them just how tight it was ... Whap! a heavy slap on the back of my hand along with unceremonious rebuke to tell me that I had *no* say in the matter whatsoever. The slap on the hand, just as though I were a bad child, shocked me almost beyond description! I had not been hit like that since I was a boy and by this stage in my life—I was after all "a *dean* at a prestigious university," I had come to expect some respect, and for the previous month had received a reasonable amount of it, even in captivity. Little did I know that this was to be only the first of many similar insults. But that first smart rap from a powerful hand still stings in my memory. It was another lesson in humility in the school of captivity—you can be a dean in one context and a three year old in another with no problem.

The job done, Sayeed and the Hajj withdrew from our bedroom cell. Now I could raise my blindfold and examine my bonds. I had been given roughly five feet of fairly heavy staff, about the weight of tire chains, and case-hardened. "Ye gods," I said to Father, "They don't believe in half measures when it comes to chains." "No," agreed Father, "nor in lots of other things. They are paranoid about security." My chain was attached to Father's near the wall; his disappeared through a one-inch hole that had been drilled clear through the wall. Later, by peeking on the way to the bathroom, I discovered that his chain was secured on the other side in the hallway by a padlock through one of the links—simple and expedient. No shortage of padlocks here. The one around my ankle was made in China, a "Circle 3 Brand," much larger than was necessary to hold a man. In fact it could no doubt have held a wild horse, especially since it too was case-hardened—at least it said so on the lock.

We began to converse in earnest. I recounted first my conversation with David and then my having met Terry Anderson. Neither Father nor Ben had known either of our next-door neighbors, so I had to explain who they were, how and when they had been kidnapped, etc. I gave them an "update" on the world's happenings for the last six months since Father had been abducted. He of course had already given Ben a briefing on what had happened from May 1984 until January 1985, and they were fascinated to hear the next installment.

In turn, I found out all about captivity from these two "old hands." They had both recently come back from the Bekaa, where Ben had spent most of his year and a quarter. Father too had been taken over there immediately upon his capture and had been with a bunch of fairly laid-back guards, chained to the wall in a kitchen, in which he could stand up now and again, reach into the refrigerator, and even look out of the window, from which he had something of a panoramic view, including, in the near distance, the ancient town of Baalbek. At times he wasn't even blindfolded and was able to interact with his guards in fairly relaxed fashion. He told me all about his kidnapping, and how he had had to stand in an outdoor toilet for most of the first day, with very little clothing on—they had stolen virtually everything he was wearing, including a nice new pair of shoes—and about how he had been transported more or less right away into the Bekaa, taped from the tip of his toes to the top of his head with brown plastic strapping tape, and pushed into the space under the bed of a truck where the spare tire is normally carried. Ben Weir had been similarly bound and carted over and back. I was horrified, to say the least. I could hardly imagine anything so cruel, and I was glad that by bringing these two back from the valley, they were evidently preparing to release all of us. I wouldn't have to go through *that* kind of nightmare. Little did I know.

We talked far into the night. Frequently Ben warned me to keep my voice down; I wasn't used to having to pay any attention to voice level, for in my previous cell the guards were hardly ever there, and in any case with the whirr of the air exchanger in that place, it was hard to hear anything at all. But Ben insisted that the guards didn't like to hear us speaking, and would surely reprimand us. I had never had that happen to me up to this point, and wondered why both he and Father were so "gun-shy" of the guards. Father later confessed to me that he and Ben had been amused and not a little shocked at my behavior; I had arrived like some creature from outer space, wound up and ready to explode. "Where did *this thing* come from?" they had wondered. I was oblivious to this reaction, and they were being so kind to me that I was feeling almost human again despite the chain on my ankle. But finally, "Tom, time to sleep." I didn't feel at all like sleeping and would happily have talked on all night. But, "Tom, it's got to be after four in the morning!" So we slept.

Conditions in this room were much better than the others I had been in. There were even a couple of fans in the outside wall, one pulling air into the room while its twin was exhausting it, both of them through holes that had been neatly chopped through the concrete block put in where the windows had been. And here the electricity was running more or less night and day, for the militia-men had hooked themselves into all three zones established by the government's Electricity Board. These were three systems of distribution whereby each house-hold was supposed to get approximately eight hours of current per day, but in reality no one was getting that much; they simply couldn't generate enough juice per day to keep up with the demand. But our Islamic Jihad (or I. J. as we dubbed them) chaps had short-circuited the system for themselves—as I am sure many others were also doing, judging by the number of wires strung everywhere all over Beirut when we went back in 1993. They were thus literally stealing current from each set of wires, so that they (and we) had almost 24 hours of power. The room even got cold by early morning, and we had to pull up blankets around us by dawn. I didn't realize until later what relative luxury we were in.

Next morning, another guard came in fairly early. He examined me all over, rather like a rancher might a new bull. He was especially puzzled by my lack of facial hair and exclaimed, "You not have hair! You like little boy, no grow!" as he stroked my fuzzy beginnings of a beard. Ben explained to him in Arabic that I had been allowed to shave fairly regularly in my previous place, and that indeed I could grow hair. This guard introduced himself as Badr and was one of three guards in charge of us. The second was Sayeed, whom I had met the previous night. He seemed to have a genuine sense of humor, and spoke fairly good En-glish, and fast. The third was Michel, who claimed to be a boxer, and *was*, so far as we could determine, a fairly powerfully built man. Now Badr, in very broken English, gave me a long lecture on how I must behave. He was far from fluent, and seemed to me to be a bit unstable emotionally. This proved to be an under-statement, for the guy turned out to be bordering on completely crazy. He wanted no trouble. "I'm not here to cause trouble," I assured him. "I'm happy with my new friends."

As with my kidnapping a month earlier, this state of being chained was so far out of my experience, so unlikely ever to happen to me, that it seemed like an adventure, something that I could relate to my grandchildren in the years to come. Only as the days wore on did the massiveness of this experience begin to im-press itself upon me. The chain became inexorable. Not only were we locked in a roughly 12- by 14-foot bedroom whose windows had been cinder-blocked off, but we were now incredibly restrained, restricted nearly 24 hours a day to the vicinity of our small foam mattresses. At first my chain felt like a kind of umbili-cal cord to Father, who was taking all of this, like Ben in the far corner of the room on his own, like a real stoic. "It shouldn't be too bad," said Ben. "The Hajj has given orders to the guards to let us off the chains for half the day." So much for normal belief. These orders were just routinely disregarded, and Badr in particular told us menacingly that we could complain to the Hajj if we liked, but *he* was going to do things *his* way, and would let us off the chain for a brief period prior to our bathroom trip, then it was clank, clank as the chains were again secured to our ankles, sometimes tightly, sometimes much too tightly, seldom unobtrusively comfortable—if that's even possible—around one's ankle. At times, the third guard, Michel, who turned out to be a *real nasty* would refuse to take the chains off for even the brief 30 minutes we were generally allowed for exercise and would insist that we "run in place" with ankles chained; quite a trick to avoid stepping on the chain with bare feet—and that hurt! Michel had another particularly disgusting "trick." He would burst into the room trying to catch us with blindfolds up, then "shower" us with a mouthful of water.

Ben, Father, and I spent the next month in this room. Every morning Father said mass, and in the evening Ben conducted a Presbyterian–like service. In common were the readings from the Bible, for each day, morning and evening, we read a chapter from both the Old and New Testaments plus a psalm or a proverb. Thus we got through the entire Bible in short order. Each time, they invited me to participate. At first I was very reluctant, preferring to maintain my antagonism toward the organized church, even though this was a long way from the kind of church that I had become alienated from. But as time went on, I felt an increasing urge to join them, with a parallel feeling of guilt if I didn't, and eventually did take a small part.

The food here too was considerably better. Sometimes we even had a dish of stew *loaded* with onions and diverse other vegetables. Licking his chops, Ben would say contentedly, "Well, that was most acceptable. Very good food." I was rather surprised at his level of appreciation, for to me, fresh into captivity after a lifetime of eating like a king, this stuff was at best a mediocre dish. Ben explained. "To these young men, food is bread, and bread is food. It is that simple. Anything they give you in addition to bread is a luxury. When they give you cheese with your pita bread, or beans and rice, they feel they are treating you extremely well." "Well, I have news for them, Ben," I rebutted. "I never did like either rice or beans!" Then one evening came a rare treat—kibbi nayye, which is rather like the French "steak tartare," raw meat with some seasoning added. The Lebanese love it. But Ben was very skeptical. "I don't think you ought to have this, fellows. You have no idea of the treatment this meat has had!" So we turned it down. Next door, however, Terry and David had no such wise counsel, and ate all of theirs, and ours too, as it turned out, for the guards simply took our share in to them. Result: Next day, both David and Terry had a very severe case of the trots and had to go to the toilet a dozen times a day for over three days. They told us later that they had been *extremely* ill.

Sayeed even gave us a running commentary on their illness and began to ask me questions about what could have happened. Out of an initial explanation of bacterial contamination of raw meat grew a series of light lectures on the physiology of digestion—the composition of proteins as a long chain of amino acids, the role of enzymes in breaking them down, and the crucial role of the liver in all of that. I am not sure exactly how much he understood, but he was fascinated by the whole thing and kept coming in for days for more lessons. Sayeed was without question far above the average "hamster" in intelligence.

The Hajj was a relatively frequent visitor during this period, obviously respected Ben a great deal, and since Ben was fluent in Arabic, could talk freely with him. In the first day or two, he tried having "fun" with me, asking, "Do you know who is holding you?" "I don't know, really," I answered, cautiously. He insisted, "But who do you *think* we are?" "Well, since I am now with Father and Ben, and since Terry and David are next door, and since Islamic Jihad has claimed to be holding these four, I assume that you are from Islamic Jihad?" Whereupon, he laughed heartily. Why would he consider this supposition funny? Seemed totally logical and simplistic to me! On the second or third morning, I slipped on the wet tile floor of the bathroom and fell on my hip bone. That hurt! All I needed on top of a skimpy mattress! Made sleeping even tougher. Ben had explained to the Hajj, who kept inquiring for days about the state of my hip bone. I began to think that he must be a kindly soul after all. Wrong! Again! The Hajj and I also had discussions about the AUB and the frequent threats against it. Again cautiously, I informed him that, as far as I knew, most of these had been attributed to Hizbollah, especially the one that forced the university to put, at considerable expense, a ring of "razor" wire, a kind of barbed wire around much of the north end of the campus. To this he took immediate exception, and to my amazement claimed instead that it was Hizbollah who had *warned* AUB. The threat, he asserted, had come from "the other side" (the Christians in East Beirut). Hard to believe? Maybe, maybe not.

Having been introduced to Terry and David, we were now allowed within a few days to communicate very briefly with them as each one of us walked past their cell and into the *hammam* or bathroom. "Good morning, David. Good morning, Terry," we would say. They would reply in bright voices, "Good morning, Tom," … "Good morning, Father," … "Good morning, Ben." The guards were still a little suspicious of allowing us this kind of communication, but didn't forbid us, so long as we kept our voices low. A short time after my arrival, Terry requested permission to say confession to Father. Amazingly, this was granted. Father was unlocked and led into Terry's room next door. Father was gone a long time. When he finally reappeared, he gave a little rundown on what had transpired, without of course breaking the confidentiality of Terry's confession. There had been lots of tears of happiness between the two of them, Catholics united in prayer and confession. Weeks later, I was to discover firsthand from Terry the confessional details just as he would afterward give to the world in his *Den of Lions*.

A few days later, Ben requested that we be allowed to join Terry and David for a religious service. Again, to my amazement, this too was granted. Came the day, and we were escorted into the adjoining room. Father and Ben got the service under way with some very intense prayer, reading from both the Old and New Testaments, and a very short sermon. We even sang some hymns, though at very low voice—outside, we could hear very plainly some children playing and laughing and screaming, and I realized why the guards were so paranoid. If we could hear the kids outside, then surely if we were heard we would be immediately recognized as strangers and cause questions to be asked out there.

We had four or five visits next door for our services, which were reassuring and frustrating at the same time, for I especially wanted to ask lots of questions and get down to some real deep discussions about why we were here at all, and what Terry and David felt our chances were of being released in the foreseeable future. Ben and Father didn't seem to be much interested in discussing this, and seemed content to leave it to God and His time. I was in a much greater hurry. But we were never allowed to "stick around." Always when the service was over, we were escorted back to our cell with my questions unanswered.

We were still hoping to keep fit, and Ben Weir especially devoted himself to that as much as he possibly could. He always went strong on his mattress, running in place in the most professional way even to the detriment of his matress. I commented to him one day, "Boy, you are really serious about this exercise." "I sure am," replied Ben. "I'm determined not to let these bastards beat us." I was mildly surprised at his determination. He was such a gentle and caring man, but it was soon clear that his gentle demeanor hid a great determination, for which I admired him. "This guy is tough." And indeed, the more I got to know Ben, the tougher and more determined he seemed. "Take it one day at a time," he kept advising me. "Don't ever let yourself think that this may go on for months or years, or you will get very discouraged." Right. For his part, Father Martin also had a tough determination but little interest in exercise.

One day, Father Martin recounted a sad tale. In the place before this one, he had been in a large room where several hostages were being held. He had had no idea who they were, except for one who had become rather ill, and his name was being bandied around—William Buckley. Father recounted how the man had become more and more ill, and finally delirious. He would ask for all sorts of exotic things for breakfast, like pancakes and maple syrup. Later he was in desperate need of water: "Water, water," he would moan, and then the guards would reprimand him and tell him he should not have water when he was ill. Unbelievable. There was some disagreement among those who were present in that place as to just what happened thereafter—David Jacobsen felt that Buckley was hit over the head and carried out of the room; Terry Anderson felt that the big thump they heard was Buckley kicking the wall. The only sure conclusion was that Buckley died in captivity. I listened, but it seemed a faraway story—I didn't realize how soon and how closely I would come into contact with William Buckley through his "confession."

One evening toward the end of July 1985 the Hajj came into our room and began speaking to Ben in Arabic. "Tom," said Ben, "the Hajj is wondering where you got the article on Islam that was in your briefcase." "An article on Islam in *my* briefcase?" I asked him. I thought hard. It was well over a month now since I had been kidnapped, and in all that time I hadn't even seen my briefcase. Was I forgetting some article or other? I recalled that I had borrowed some papers on the Middle East from some of our faculty and had taken them with me to the United States to use in preparing my paper at the meeting in Santa Monica on the African famine, but I had no recollection of having anything on Islam. "I'm fairly sure, Ben, that there wasn't any paper on Islam in my briefcase." Ben relayed this claim to the Hajj in Arabic. Back came the reply. "Hajj says there *was* a paper in your case." "Ben, there couldn't have been. I have absolutely zero recollection of anything like that—only papers on agriculture and water in the Middle East, surely." Again Ben relayed my answer. Back came the affirmation with claim that it had to have been typed in America, and could not have been done in Lebanon since it was all right-justified and there were no machines here that could do that. I assured him there were, and that we even had machines to do it at AUB. He insisted it had to be from the United States. I began to get angry at his allegations, which I felt were decidedly unfair. "Ben, you tell Hajj that if there was a paper on Islam in my case *they damn well put it there!*"

Wow! Did the shit hit the fan! The Hajj was livid. He *had* found a paper. I was obviously lying, and must be CIA to do such a blatant thing. I was in for it—"Kizzab,

kizzab!" ("Liar, liar!") they screamed at me. And then there was *interrogation*. The Hajj kept coming in and harassing me and harassing me about the paper, insisting that I must have known about it. He was simply unwilling to believe that anyone could possibly have a paper like that in his briefcase without knowing it. I told him that I dealt with hundreds of papers every week, reading and signing them, and that it was entirely possible that it *had* been in there, without my knowing. But he made all kinds of dire threats, and by this time he and the others were sure that it was a CIA paper I'd been carrying. And that gave me the chills.

Not long after, early in August, the Hajj and Sayeed came in one evening and announced (through Sayeed the interpreter) that I was to be taken "to join William Buckley—in a very bad place." Immediate for Ben and Father was the worry about me, not to mention how I was feeling. But by this time I had sort of given up, and hardly cared what they did to me. I started to get dressed, and to put on my shoes, my "Freefoams by Freeman" of which I was pretty fond. Sayeed said, "No worry about shoes. Yella!" This seemed strange to me, but I went out the cell door barefooted. Sayeed then laughed and confessed that I was only going to a *new place in this building!* I hardly knew what to make of this; they had been making such a fuss in front of Ben and Father, and insisting that I was "for the high jump." But sure enough, I was taken downstairs to the basement, into a new room about 12 by 15 feet with no windows, terribly rough bare floor, a mattress and new sheets and blankets, and wonder of wonders, the mattress was brand new and much thicker than anything I had had so far. I lay down in a kind of a daze, wondering, "Why? Why am I now in semiluxury after such an amazing display of hostility and threats?" Is this the last luxury? The dinner before the execution?

Time passed, and I wasn't able to go to sleep anyway. Soon, commotion at the door, and voices speaking in English, discussing where they might be. "There's someone here already," said one voice. "By gosh, it's Tom Sutherland!" It was David's voice. "It sure is, David," I said. "What on earth are you guys doing down here?"

The Hajj and Sayeed had apparently withdrawn immediately and left us right away on our own. And wonder of wonders, *no chains*. Terry and David too had been given new and plush mattresses. Sleep was gone now, at least for some hours; I had two wonderful new companions to talk things over with, guys who were— I must admit—much more my speed and kind than Father and Ben. Now we could get into the "nitty-gritty" of things. We seemed to be entirely alone in this basement room.

First, of course, we "compared notes" on our respective experiences, which we had never been allowed to do during the religious services. They had been going at the exercise business with much more gusto even than Ben; they were used to running around the room at almost full pelt, which explained the thumps that I had heard "coming from somewhere." I found that in cinder-block construction, sounds carry fairly loudly, but that it was difficult to decipher from which direction—whether one side or other, from overhead or underneath. Strange sensation. I got the details on Terry's first three months, prior to his move to this building. He had been treated abominably, chained by both ankles and one wrist so that he could scarcely turn, teased and taunted, and threatened constantly—worse even than I had been getting in the past two weeks, until he was sure he was losing his mind. David had been in that same room for the six weeks prior to arriving in this place, but had not had such severe treatment. The guards knew that Terry had been a Marine, and evidently convinced that Marines chew nails and chains for amusement, they were taking no chances. But for me, bliss—to sleep in blessed comfort—even the abominable pillows were tolerable.

· Next morning, breakfast was shoved under the door, through a gap of nearly a foot at the bottom. Since we were no longer chained to the wall, the door was opened only when we went to the toilet. To Terry's disgust, the bread and cheese were pushed over the floor along with three cups of tea. The floor, partially concreted, was extremely rough, in the Lebanese pre-tiling stage, with thousands of small holes filled with dust, and numerous sharp, ugly, and dangerous protrusions of concrete. Extremely hard to walk, let alone run, on. But run we did, around and around that room, in bare feet. Soon I gave up. I was, by exactly two days over David, the old man of the group, but my colleagues kept on, each trying to outdo the other. David loped along with his long, skinny legs, dragging his feet behind him in the same peculiar gait that I recalled from watching him from our balcony as he ran on AUB Green Field track. He had run there some six miles daily and was very proud of his fitness and stamina. Ex-Marine Terry ran straight and hard as he had presumably run on the hard pavement of the Corniche for two to three miles daily with his Rhodesian Ridgeback dog, scaring the daylights out of any Lebanese who saw it even from a distance, for they all have the Arab severe dislike, even fear, of dogs of any kind. With his short legs, he was determinedly stomping around the room, each foot connecting with the rough concrete with a great thump. Two incredibly different styles—neither one pretty. These were no Olympic athletes, there was no grace, no symphony of movement. But I was watching a real drama of determination; each man vying to outlast the other in a competition that had been going on now for over a month. I was fascinated.

After the exercise, a shower—two new bathrooms downstairs, this time with Arabic toilets (again) and reasonable water pressure. We were to have daily showers.

Back in the room, we surveyed the scene, with the dust in every crack and hole. Terry's total aversion to dust and dirt began to manifest itself and he requested a broom from the guards—Sayeed, Michel, and Badr were still around. He was given a short-handled job and with great gusto proceeded to attack every particle. Whisk, whisk, whisk he went, and soon disappeared in a great cloud of dust. David and I watched in horror as the cloud grew and grew and soon filled the whole room—I could hardly see David beside me, and our nostrils and mouths and lungs and eyes filled with fine cement dust! "Soon he will give up," we thought. But no—Terry's fervor only grew. The cure was certainly much worse than the disease! "Help, Terry!" we pleaded. "Please, please quit!" To no avail. He was determined to move every grit. But to where? Obviously back to where it came from—and meantime we were choking to death.

For days, the routine was repeated until David and I could stand it no longer. Arguing bitterly, we finally persuaded Terry of the futility of his efforts, and he compromised by asking for a bucket of water and a cloth. Thereupon began a new regime of wetting down the floor, then wiping up the water. In no time at all the bucket was a concentrated solution of cement dust and the rag was in shreds from scraping the rough floor. Then Sayeed brought in a couple of large straw mats that made running a little easier. Not to be deterred, Terry conscientiously wetted these and wiped them daily ... soon *they* began to disintegrate. Sayeed was angry—his mats were melting under Terry's overzealous care. Reluctantly, Terry agreed not to wet them anymore, but kept wiping the concrete under them. What blessed relief to have no more dust filling the air.

We began to recount our life histories to each other. My new buddies had fascinating stories and were excellent "raconteurs." David relived his family trip from California to New York City, taken when his children were fairly young, and he proved to have the most incredible memory. He recalled every stopping place from coast to coast, the motels they stayed in, tourist spots they visited, the landscape, the people he met—all described in minute detail. I listened for hours in amazement—parts of his route I was familiar with myself so I could verify the accuracy of his story. What a memory! Somewhat selective, though, for we never were told how many hospitals he'd directed or how long he'd been in a place. Terry, too, I concluded, must have some kind of photographic yet also selective memory, for he could remember everything he had read—and yet for *experience*, he couldn't remember how we had met in captivity nor the date of my birthday.

Terry gave me a complete account of his work and his office in Beirut, and I began to appreciate for the first time the importance of the job done by a foreign correspondent. He described their equipment in the Beirut office, and the need for "dedicated lines" on the telephone system so they could instantly send photos of high-resolution, high-speed text on their telex lines (faxes were not in the picture at that time), and their use of computers to speed up the writing and transmission of their breaking news stories. I was fascinated. But I was still not sleeping well at night, was not terribly well rested, and at one point I drifted off into a sleepy trance. Terry was insulted and thought *he* had put me to sleep; it took quite a bit of persuasion to get him to resume his story.

All this—a brief honeymoon for me from Hajj's harassment about the paper on Islam in my briefcase. A few days later, I was taken out of our new basement room and led right across the hall into another room that yielded, with peeking, a blackboard on the wall; it must have been some kind of classroom. In came my new interrogator who spoke only French in addition to his Arabic: "Pourquoi vous mentez concernant votre valise?" ("Why are you lying about your briefcase?") "Je ne ments pas, monsieur." ("I don't lie, sir.") "Ah si, vous êtes très menteur." ("Ah, yes, you are a big liar.") Here we go again, with only a slight variation on "kizzab" (liar)—French this time. And not good French at that. His accent was atrocious and I could hardly understand what he was driving at. "No sir. I do not lie," I insisted. "Then why do you open these letters?" he demanded furiously, sticking one of the letters from my briefcase forcefully against my nose until it hurt. This particular letter had been given to me in Kennedy Airport by Dr. Raja Tannous to be hand-delivered to four of his department members. He showed me the others. "Why do you open?" he redemanded. "It wasn't I," I insisted. To me it was obvious that it was they who had done this, probably looking for money, or for some clue as to what I was all about. But they were now trying to pin the blame on me. I was getting deeper than ever into the shit, it seemed. "I haven't even seen my briefcase for a long time," I insisted again. "It must have been your group who have opened all these letters. I could never do that. These are letters for my colleagues, and in the West one would *never* do that." Wow! Mad? He promptly slapped me all over my shoulders, grabbed my now-bearded chin, screamed, and threatened me with dire punishments. I honestly can't say that I understood a tenth of what he was raving about, but he was *furious*. He called on some other guard, and instructed him to put me downstairs somewhere.

That guard turned out to be Badr, who escorted me down a short flight of stairs, turned to the right, marched a few yards, and opened a door. I was pushed unceremoniously into a small cage or covered stall in which a mattress had already been placed. The mattress took up the entire space, so it was roughly six feet by two and a half feet. Badr left after locking the door, and I looked around me—this cage was roughly the size of a horse box, and barely high enough for me to stand. The roof was made of a very heavy mesh, the kind that was used during the war to make temporary airport runways, and the side walls were made of steel. Several stalls in a row. I could make out perhaps two others to the left of me, but many more off to the right. Soon Badr was back, with a piece of really rusty chain, the weight of a good strong dog chain, and proceeded to padlock my ankle to one of the bars in the bottom of the gate to my stall. Amazing. Why on earth would it be necessary to chain me to the gate in a steel stall with barely enough room for me to lie down in? My God, I thought. What kind of powers of reason do these fellows have anyway? Badr muttered a few words of warning, "You good, okay?" and was gone.

I reflected on this turn of events, and the total injustice of their accusation about the letters, which seemed to be the cause of my banishment to this dungeon. But at least it was cool—blessed relief from the infernal heat that was building up in the upstairs room. Suddenly there was a new noise; someone else was being brought in, and was duly chained as I had been, in the stall two to the left of me. After the guards departed, I asked, "Who is there?" "Quietly, Tom," came the answer. It was Terry. "What on earth have you done to cause them to put you down here too?" I asked. "Shush," he answered, "We'll talk later." At least I had some company, but at a distance. Terry was adamant about keeping quiet until he was sure the coast was clear. I was eager to talk, as usual, and tell him all about the latest trouble I was into. Eventually he was satisfied, and we talked in a very low whisper. Our stalls were a small part of a huge basement room, well over 100 feet long and over 30 feet wide. We could barely see the end off to the right because of the constriction of the cage, but in the dim light, we could make out some piles of stuff lying around in the most helter-skelter fashion: steel bars, sheet rock, lumber, electrical wire, piping, bags of cement.

Terry had no idea why *he* had been put down here. He had had no arguments with them, had not even known what had happened to me until I spoke to him from my cage. Soon the guards brought the evening sandwich and tea. At least we were not to starve down here. But the concrete wall at the back of the cages had recently been "whitewashed" with the same kind of stuff my father used to use for the calf pens on our farm. Touch your bare skin to it, you burned. And difficult to stay completely away from the stuff, hard as I tried. I lay down to sleep, and even felt cold for the first time in weeks.

Morning came, and with it, guards who took Terry back upstairs to join David again. I was left alone until breakfast came, but in the meantime several workers arrived and began to weld and cut and do all sorts of noisy things with the mass of matériel lying around in this enormous warehouse-like place. It was obviously a busy operation for construction in the neighborhood. The workers paid no attention to me, but the guards came around from time to time during the morning to ask me in leering fashion, "You like this place?" "Not at all," I replied, and I certainly didn't. It was noisy, cold, and extremely uncomfortable with that old rusty chain bound tightly around my ankle and the whitewash still burning me. When the workers had gone to lunch, I was finally taken upstairs to the regular toilet, then brought down again. My lunch came and was passed through a kind of trapdoor in the main door in the most humiliating way. It was definitely in a place that seemed made specifically for prisoners. Finally, all the workers went home and I was alone in the quiet again, and soon had a visit from Sayeed. "Okay, now you can go up again," he said and led me back up to the room. Terry and David were overjoyed and gave profuse thanks to Sayeed for allowing me back. "I took *fatwa* [the Islamic religious ruling obtained from the Koran] and it was good," replied Sayeed.

Once he left, Terry said, "Boy, are we relieved to have you back again." "Not half as relieved as *I* am to get out of that place," surely the worst by far of the places I'd experienced. David in the meantime had christened them "the horse stalls" based on Terry's description of them. "We really had to argue with Sayeed to get him to do it." Terry immediately gathered the three of us into a tight hugging circle and started to pray, offering profuse thanks to God for my delivery from that hellhole, and reciting several psalms that had passages appropriate to our situation. I was astonished that Terry could come up with so much intense prayer. But this was only my first introduction to the awesome power of Terry's mind and memory. I was to have many more evidences of it in the years to come.

Next day, I had another grilling from my "French-speaking buddy." This time he was a little less abusive, and seemed almost ready to buy my contention that I really had known nothing about the article in my briefcase. When I returned to our room, I found that Terry and David had persuaded Sayeed to bring in the copy of the infamous article, and there they were huddled on their mattresses, already busy reading it. I peered over their shoulders as Terry flipped the pages but was so nervous by this time that I was scarcely able to read it. I did get the general gist of it before Sayeed returned and insisted on taking it back. By then Terry with his speed-reading had completely digested the thing, and was able to convince Sayeed that it had nothing to do with anything that the CIA would have produced, and was simply a harmless paper produced probably for some club meeting—well done in fact, and not at all even critical of Islam. They were still not completely satisfied, though, and kept harassing me about the fact that I had lied to them. They insisted that I swear to the fact that my wife had put the paper in my briefcase, and when I began to equivocate on that since I didn't know for *sure*, Terry jumped on me furiously and said, "Dammit, tell 'em your wife put it there. They can't stand hedged statements." So I swore to it, without any proof whatsoever that Jean had done it. As it turned out, when Jean gave me the whole story six years later in Wiesbaden, the paper had been written by a friend of hers in Syracuse, New York, and when Jean had read it, she had been so impressed that she thought that I ought to read it too. She had just stuck it in my case on the evening before my departure for Beirut without bothering to tell me it was there. Entitled *Islam Today*, it was a comparison of Islam in the various Islamic countries—Egypt, Saudi Arabia, Morocco, Iran, Kuwait, etc.—and how the people varied in their practices of the religion. Interesting, yes. And certainly all published material, nothing remotely confidential. But at the end was a picture of Khomeini and in bold print his words: "Death to America." Would raise the hair on your head—glad it didn't cost me mine.

A week or so later, must have been around the middle of August, Sayeed brought Father and Ben down to see us before they were put in the room across the hall. We three had been wondering what had become of them, but were fairly sure that they were still up above us, despite the denials of the guards, for we had continued to exchange the Bible every day. Terry insisted that he just had to have it, and would get it for several hours, after which a guard would reclaim it. When Sayeed came back to take the two across the hall, both Terry and David argued that they should stay with us; I was opposed to the idea, not only because we were already steaming hot in this room, but also because I was still mildly uncomfortable in the presence of these two religious fellows. Terry and David had no such reservations, and wanted to get our religious services renewed. They prevailed and we got my two former companions back. Now five in the room, and it got *really* hot! But I must admit that it *was* more comforting to have such a large group of Americans around, all with such diverse and interesting backgrounds. David named our services "The Church of the Locked Door," and truth to tell, the guards seemed much happier when we held these formal services; they themselves were still rigorously praying to Allah five times a day.

Sayeed loved to argue with Terry about religion. While no match for Terry, his mind was quick and nimble, and he could carry on a good discussion even in English. "You realize your God is the same as ours," asserted Terry. "No! No same God! You three God—we one God!" These Shia Moslems were having difficulty with the concept of the Trinity. "Okay. Jesus prophet, like Isaiah. We too, they prophets for Islam too. And Abraham and Joseph—okay. But no Jesus God. Koran more true than your Bible!" "No way," retorted Terry. "You can never convince me of that, Sayeed. We believe our Bible!" Sayeed gave Terry quite a rundown on the origins of Shiism, and Twelve Imams, the differences between the "Twelvers," who believe in all 12, and the Seveners, mainly the Ismailis, who believe only in the first 7 Imams. Terry loved it. Meantime, since I too had trouble with the Trinity concept, I took the opportunity while the subject was hot to bug Father Martin about it. After all, he had two master's degrees in theology, and had spent five or more years at the very seat of Catholicism—the Vatican. He should know. "Father, how would you explain the concept of the Trinity? When Jesus was down here on earth, did that mean that God had taken on another form only, and that there was no one left tending the store, so to speak, up in heaven? Or were there literally two Gods in existence at that time? Or now, for that matter? And how about the Holy Ghost? Can there really be three versions of one God floating around all at the same time?" I was being partly facetious, of course, but genuinely interested in an authoritative explanation. Father smiled his most gentle smile. "Tom, it's a *mystery!*" Well, I didn't need to feel so badly after all.

Besides the services, we began a routine of exercise, which included walking around and around the room where Terry and David had been running, and at times we even ran with five in a row, but Father Martin didn't like the running bit at all, and so everyone else deferred to his wishes, and we walked. Father insisted on leading the pack, or rather he inherited that place every morning—he walked more slowly than the rest, who soon all caught up with him, no matter where he started in the lineup. And no one wanted David behind him, for David kept walking faster and faster until he was pushing right up the butt of the guy ahead, who could not speed up—Father was in the lead keeping his own leisurely pace, as though he were walking around a monastery garden. So it became my lot to have David pushing up behind me—I was the only guy willing to put up with it. The funny thing was that after everyone had dropped out except David, he noticeably relaxed his pace. This total scenario lasted until finally Father was released nearly a year later, and we were moved into "The Prison," a place where walking became impossible.

In late August, a visit from the Hajj, who was in a very good mood—"You want radio," he asked. "Of course," we all chanted. "I give you *my* radio." Pronouncing "radio" to rhyme with "daddy-oh," he soon had us too calling it a "raddy-oh." It duly appeared. We were to have it only for two hours a day, but we were to decide which hours. Followed much discussion as to which two hours exactly would be the best time to pick up the Voice of America (VOA) and BBC (the beeb to Beirut journalists) both in tandem, or where we could switch back and forth. All of us had been avid listeners of the radio as it turned out, and we all had strong opinions on the best hours. Finally we settled on 11:00 P.M. to 1:00 A.M., yielding back-to-back news broadcasts from first the BBC then the VOA.

The "raddy-oh" was a nice one, almost identical to but slightly newer than the one I had had for some years, a Sony with seven shortwave bands, and medium wave (AM) and FM thrown in. We were in seventh heaven, for at least we could now catch up on some of the things that had been happening since I was kidnapped. But the real irony to this great generosity on the part of the Hajj was that it was not his "raddy-oh" at all, but actually, as I was to find out later, one that had belonged to Michel Seurat, one of the French hostages who were also being held in this same building, though we were not much aware of them at that time.

The Hajj was in such a good mood that he also asked, "You want watches?" Wow! What generosity! Of course we wanted our watches back. And we got them. All that is except Father, whose watch and all his clothes were missing; he had apparently been picked up by some other bunch and subsequently sold to the Islamic Jihad. But Father was not supposed to be into "things," and no matter. We could listen to news and have the time of day on four separate watches.

New guards joined us. Mahmoud, Abu Ali, and Fadl were, I figured, in their mid-twenties, and reasonably mature young men. As time went on, we were to learn quite a lot about them—we got to know these three fellows rather well—for they were with us more or less to the end. In fact, it was Mahmoud and Abu Ali who would help me dress on the evening of my liberation. Mahmoud told us that he was 26 and married, which no doubt accounted for his relative maturity. He was the biggest guard we ever had, six feet or more, big-boned, and powerful. But he never laid a hand on any of us—I guess he didn't need to prove his manhood. Abu Ali was 24, married, moderately built, rather a gentle person, softspoken, eager to learn English, but not yet very proficient, and, it should be said, not very bright. Fadl completed the trio; he was also in his mid-twenties, unmarried, tall and skinny, but also powerful. Initially he was kind and thoughtful—when it got hot and the power went out, he would come in with a large sheet of cardboard and fan us. But as time went on, he tired of this and ultimately became one of the most vindictive of all the guards. This somehow turned out to be a fairly standard behavior pattern. When a guard first arrived on the scene and saw fellow human beings locked up, and even chained to the wall, they were very sympathetic, and to ease our situation, tried to do what they could—bringing us coffee, candy, lots of Kleenex, water on request, longer periods in the toilet, etc. After a few weeks, however, they all became hardened to the situation, and much more hostile to us, even though we had done nothing to antagonize them. It was then that Ben Weir recounted his story of the American university experiment in which a random group of students was assigned as "guards," and another random group assigned as "prisoners." After a matter of a mere week or two, the guards became so oppressive that the experiment had to be abandoned. Wish we could have abandoned *this* "experiment"!

Both Mahmoud and Abu Ali had children, so were perforce more thoughtful and less irrational about our situation. Mahmoud seemed fairly intelligent, was interested in politics and world affairs, and interested in discussing the American role in the Middle East. His English was passable, though still a little halting and unsure at that time, but he sincerely wanted to improve on it. On the very first evening with us, he confronted us right away with the American support of Israel, and how they had really hurt the Shia during their Israeli invasion of South Lebanon. I had heard this complaint many times from our students at AUB, but this was the first time to hear it from one who had *really* and personally suffered from that massive Israeli assault on the south. "You really killed us," he said in his gutteral English. "Why you support them so much?" We tried to explain to him the realities of American politics, and the Western feeling of extreme guilt for our lack of action during the Holocaust. But he somehow didn't appreciate how people persecuted in one age had the right to persecute others in another, or how American feelings of guilt made supporting persecution a right thing. He was obviously still traumatized from the invasion, now some three years in the past; but the south was still occupied, and that was uppermost in his mind, as it was with most of the tens of thousands of displaced Shia who were crowding into the southern suburbs of Beirut. It was to be a running debate through the next six years. The third new man, Fadl, was very frustrated by his lack of English—he too genuinely wanted to learn, but his base was so far behind that of Mahmoud that he had little hope of ever catching up with him.

Ben also alarmed at least me, with a tale of prisoners locked in the same room for an extended period, who became very hostile to each other. I was very glad that we were not, thought I naively, going to be in there for a very long period. Our experiences again fairly well substantiated the theoretical findings; some of our group became very hostile to each other, notably Terry and David, who at one point appeared as though they might well kill each other. The two religious men did their best to calm things down, but the disagreements between Terry and David were so fundamental that they could never truly be reconciled. David was a far-right-wing-conservative Republican from Orange County, California, while Terry was a far-left-liberal Democrat from upstate New York.

Politically, as well as geographically, the two could not have been further apart. I do believe that even the guards had recognized the differences between the two, which was what led them to bring the three of us together in the basement cell, and then subsequently to move Father and Ben in with us when I was not able to maintain the peace.

David kept talking about "pecking order." "In every species," he would claim, "there is a natural 'pecking order' and in this group I aim to be at the top!" I was totally familiar with the concept—it was an Australian poultry geneticist friend of mine, Glenorchy McBride, who had done the definitive studies of the genetic basis of this phenomenon in chickens, in which it is most pronounced and from where the name is derived. My reaction—why in hell do we need to worry about who is "at the top" in this god-awful mess we're in? Father and Ben agreed. "We just need to survive, David! Let's all try to get along together!" But David apparently felt compelled to keep vying with Terry for the "top of the order." Unfortunately for David, whose idea it was, he wasn't able to best Terry in almost anything. For my part, I was in no shape to even begin to compete, since by that time I was having so many problems of my own I could hardly cope with those of the others.

In fact, I couldn't seem even to cope with the simplest mental activities and began to despair of my mind. To help pass the time, day after nothing day, we frequently played games, and I remember two incidents most graphically. In one, we were having a contest on place-names, and Terry beat me (as usual), and capped it with, "Gee, it's like shooting fish in a barrel." Right. The other occurred during one of our daily walks around the room when we were playing "Twenty Questions" and taking turns at specifying the unknown object. For this game, "Casper the Friendly Ghost" was our object. We got all the way to "a friendly ghost," and it was my turn to nail it down. Years of our children watching that show, yet I simply could *not* recall who the friendly ghost had been. I attempted to pass. But the group wouldn't let me—it was so simple after all. I struggled and struggled in my head to recall the name "Casper" but I could not *for the life of me* bring it up. "Gee," said Terry, with loathing in his voice, "you are *so* dumb!" I was absolutely shocked. I was being called *dumb*. I couldn't recall *ever* having been called that in my entire life, not in earnest and with such genuine feeling, anyway. Had there been anywhere to hide, I would certainly have run for it. But where can one hide in a 14- by 12-foot room with four pairs of eyes bearing on one? The ultimate in humiliation. And yet, why should such a simple thing worry me? It wasn't as though I'd failed to bring up an equation for figuring multiple regression, or to understand the complexities of the AUB budget deficit, or anything even remotely profound. Could I have come to this in less than three months of captivity? Not at this time but afterward I would get consolation from Victor Frankl who, writing out of his Nazi concentration camp experience said, "An abnormal reaction to an abnormal situation is normal behavior."

Terry's ridicule in this instance was typical. It seemed that everything I said was dumb, my opinions worthless. I found myself hating his guts, fell into extreme depression, and began seriously to believe that I was losing my mind and my sanity. It didn't go away. We began getting a few books, mostly of a religious nature at that time, which of course pleased Father and Ben, and Terry also. Some of these were veritable tomes. I remember especially two volumes on Shiism written by Professor Nikki Keddie of the University of California at Los Angeles, considered, so said the flyleaf, to be the West's greatest authority on Shiite Islam. Even David was plowing manfully through them, and the four of them got into some good, even heated, discussions. I too tried to read these books. But in contrast to my colleagues, when I got to the end of a page, I would stop and ask myself, "What have I just read? What did it say?" To my horror, I could remember *not a single thing* of what I had just read *word-by-word* in the previous five minutes! I truly feared that my mind was disintegrating and that I would never again be right. The end of my intellectual life? I was in panic! How I'd come to this point I couldn't say—whether due to the harassment from the Hajj and the guards or from the very fact of being in captivity, I couldn't have said nor did it matter at that time; all I knew for sure was that I was in deep psychological trouble.

I tried to avoid getting into any kind of debate or argument with Terry, avoided him as much as possible, and clung more to David, who was happy to have a buddy to whom he could also complain about Terry, for he too, even in much better psychological state than I, routinely came off second-best in their arguments—of which the really vicious ones were yet to come. David must have had in his professional life some rather unpleasant run-ins with journalists, for he had a really bad impression of the entire profession, calling them pushy, aggressive, shallow know-it-alls, who were the scourge of a hospital administrator's life. He had similar sorts of loathing for lawyers—as he told us, he had come off second-best in court when he was going through his divorce proceedings, and talked disparagingly about how it was so easy to become qualified as a lawyer. It didn't help him that he was losing most of his arguments with Terry, and the atmosphere of the cell was certainly "charged."

At this time, even in my state of despair, I was still naively convinced that it would all be over in a very short time. David was contributing to this feeling, for he kept saying, "I'm going home on Sunday, guys." Sunday would come, and of course there he was, still with us. Terry didn't like this approach at all, and kept deriding it, preferring not to get on this kind of roller coaster. But it was David's way of keeping his hopes up. To alleviate my own depression, I began to try it myself, and indeed it gave me a bit of a lift for the last half of the week. Then came Sunday and the Great Letdown. We had to brace ourselves to face it for a day or two, until we could get back to the "Sunday I go home" again. Father and Ben just kept on stoically, praying and reading the Bible.

One day the ceiling light went out. Like all their electrical work, it was a real Rube Goldberg arrangement. I was designated the fix-it guy, and to reach it had to stand on Terry's shoulders while being steadied by David. I had only a crude form of screwdriver to work with, and it took forever to get the repair done, especially when I fell at one point and pulled the whole fixture from the wire. That proved to be a sort of blessing in disguise, though, for on the ground we could study the makeup of the thing much more easily. I *did* get it working, which did a lot for my self-confidence and mildly improved my standing.

Late one night, two guards came in and took Father out of the cell. What's up now, we wondered? Father was gone for some time, and then came back in shaking like a leaf. "What happened?" we asked. "They took me up onto the roof, stuck a gun at my head, and told me to say my last prayers. I did, and told them I was ready. Then they just screamed with laughter, and told me, 'You no die. Look, see moon,' as they took off my blindfold. In the moonlight, I could see lying out in front of me the runway of the airport." We had known that we were on the north edge of the airport, from the way the planes were landing and taking off; now we knew we were in a two-story building and exactly our location—but at Father's expense. He hadn't seen *anything* to laugh about in that episode, and had really believed them when they told him he was going to die. One more evidence of their warped sense of humor, of their determination, especially in the early days, to keep us on edge and to taunt us as Americans.

We spent just one month down in the basement before they moved us back up into the room where Father and Ben and I had been. This was a relief, for the fans were still working there. With five of us, they were more than ever necessary too. The old routine continued—breakfast, toilet, exercise by walking, games, lunch, reading, napping, supper, then back to sleep. A new twist, however. Terry decided he wanted Ben to teach him Arabic, so Ben wrote out all the letters for him. To Ben's complete amazement, Terry had mastered the lot in a few hours and was ready to go on to words. In next to no time he had a fair vocabulary built up. Ben, in all his experience, had never met anyone who could handle stuff like Terry, and kept exclaiming, "My goodness, young man, you are incredibly quick!"

And he was right—Terry *was!* I began to study the alphabet too, but couldn't keep up with Terry.

The Hajj reappeared on about September 13 and told us, through Sayeed as usual, "One of you go home very soon now. You will choose. But," he added, "can't be Tom. He go home last." My heart sank, but I realized that in all honesty, in my mental state, I would be far from the best candidate to go home and plead with the president. In any case, this was real news, and seemed to be the result of much prodding on the part of both David and Terry, who had kept telling Hajj, "The only way to get your brothers released in Kuwait is to release one of us"— preferably one of themselves of course—"who could then go to the White House and plead your case for you with President Reagan." It seemed that the Hajj had finally seen the light, and we all had visions that soon now all of us would be going home.

We set about choosing the delegate. Each man has his version of this, but I think I can say that mine is the official version, since I was the teller, appointed because I was the only one who could not be the "winner." As teller, I recall the episode clearly:

Terry cut a sheet of paper into little pieces and gave one to each of us. We all voted, and I tallied. Two votes for Ben, two for Terry, and one for David. I knew everyone's handwriting by this time, so could easily see the way things were going. Terry and I had voted for Ben, Ben and Father had voted for Terry, and David had voted for himself. Next round. Still two for each and one for David. Once again. One for Father, for I switched my vote for a change, two for Terry, one for Ben, one for David, still determined to keep his chances alive. Next round, I decided to vote for David to see what would happen. Three for Terry, two for David this time. Terry had voted for himself this time, along with Ben and Father, while David was still for himself. Another round, and I now switched to Terry, who had four to David's one. But we had agreed it had to be unanimous, so it went for several more rounds with always the same result. Finally, Terry decided to vote for David, suspecting that David was determinedly continuing to vote for himself. Only this time David had given up, and had finally decided to vote for Terry and make it unanimous. The result was unchanged, but made Terry, David, and me all laugh—each of us knew exactly what had happened. Final round, and it was unanimous for Terry.

Terry immediately began his preparations for going home and representing us. He asked for suggestions on how he should proceed, and especially for names of our families and acquaintances who might have been able to help him in his mission. I gave him the name of Bill Murray, Jean's father, who had run twice for the governorship of Iowa and who was politically well connected. Also Najeeb Halaby, chairman of the Board of Trustees, who had actually hired me for AUB. And of course Jean, who would undoubtedly have some connections from her stay in Beirut. Each of the others gave him a list of those they knew back home who might be of most help to him in getting to the president, complete with addresses and phone numbers. Terry was indeed getting off to a fast start. I was relieved that we had chosen the strongest man to do the job; after all, this was somewhat like a journalistic assignment, duck soup for him. He was used to getting interviews with political figures and other important people.

Later in the day, the Hajj came in and we told him that Terry was the winner. "Very sorry, but no Terry either. We make decision. Must be Benjamin, for he longest here. Time for him to go home." Thus a victory for Islamic dictatorship over American democracy. And a terrible and cruel blow to Terry, who promptly broke down and wept openly in genuine grief. I felt sorry for him, but as it turned out over the coming years, that decision was a lifesaver and a sanity-saver for me, in keeping my companion in chains beside me.

In retrospect, however, that whole episode was one more cruelty inflicted on us; they were simply playing with us, as they had been all along in pretending to be listening to Terry and David advising them to send one of us home. We had no idea whatsoever at that time of the efforts of Ollie North, but as it transpired, our efforts, and the subsequent efforts of Terry Waite, had nothing whatever to do with Ben being the one released at that time. Our captors had their own agenda, and though most of our guards merited the designation of "hamsters" as given them by the Beirut journalists, the "bosses" were a shrewd lot who knew exactly what they wanted and how they were going about it. And at this time, they were having high success with the French, and mild success with Ollie North and President Reagan.

In the evening, the Hajj returned to get Ben. He sat down on his mat and proceeded to give Ben a strong and angry lecture in Arabic—we listened in awe to the tirade, feeling sorry for Ben. Finally finished, he rose and went out. Ben, still visibly shaken from the experience, for, like me, he was not used to this kind of talk and approach, translated it for us. He simply *must* tell President Reagan that the 17 Shia in Kuwait *had* to be freed before *we* would all get out—and if Ben did not succeed, "your friends are all going to be in here for a long, long time, with all the consequent dangers for their health." There, without equivocation, was the *demand*, the demand that had been there in the spring, the demand they would hold to until August 1990 when Saddam Hussein would accomplish it for them. It is still hard for me to believe that it was not until that evening that

I really learned why they were holding us! One other good thing came out of this session—Hajj had told Ben we could write letters home to our families for him to take out with him, so we all set out to write as fast as we could.

In came the barber, and what was to become the obligatory "departing haircut" was administered to Ben. Next a shower, then a track suit appeared, dark blue and reasonably smart compared to the rags we had been running around in, and Ben was off—without his glasses. We pounded and pounded on the door, but it was a long time before anyone came around, by which time, they said, Ben was gone. Maybe. But hope so—with a letter for Jean and the girls in his pocket— how long ago seemed June 8 when I had last seen Jean.

8 "We Should Have Talked"

It's June 9, 1994, as I write this—nine years to the day that Tom was kidnapped. Like that day, I am at our cabin in the Rocky Mountains where I look out on the same trees, only taller; the same wildlife, only different generations of them; and I sit at the same table typing. Granted that today a laptop computer has taken the place of the typewriter; granted that the words I write are for *At Your Own Risk* instead of *Shakespeare and Seneca: A Symbolic Language for Tragedy;* granted that Tom is in Fort Collins instead of somewhere in Lebanon; granted that the phone here is for some reason *out* today instead of very much *in* that day. Granted these differences, all is still so much the same on this Colorado morning that the memories and the feelings of nine years ago come sharply and vividly.

June 9, 1985—the call came Sunday about noon from AUB president Cal Plimpton: "They picked up Tom on the way back to the campus … he's been taken … we should have talked." There it was, what we had feared, what we hadn't thought would happen or could happen, had happened.

The rest of the day and evening flew by with calls to daughters Ann, Kit, and Joan, brothers Dave and John, Tom's brothers and sisters in Scotland, trying to reach my dad and stepmother Alice who were away on a trip, and then reaching some close friends who must know. With the girls these were big, important conversations. And then came that long first night. I recorded it in the morning simply as "A Sad, Lonesome, Scary Night Thinking Strength to Tom." I didn't sleep much. Somehow, though, it never occurred to me to cry. In fact, I never cried that summer but once one evening in July. Alone at the cabin, I picked up my autoharp, sat in front of the fire, and started to sing my favorite folk song: "When cockle shells turn silver bells, Then will my love return to me." I dissolved, and it was enough. When I picked up my autoharp again in Beirut the next winter, this time with my English as a Second Language (ESL) students, I could sing any-thing, and we did very strong renditions together of all the old folk songs, including their favorite "Bring Back My Bonnie to Me." That day, that night, however, there was no knowledge of the months and years to come, just the present agon.

June 10 started at 4:00 A.M.—calls coming in to the other Thomas M. Sutherland in Fort Collins (including the call from the State Department in-forming them in place of me of Tom's abduction) finally got relayed to me at the cabin. The news was out. The media in their inevitable way all inquired in the brouhaha that followed that day: "How did you feel when you heard?" And I can honestly say that I was numb, at first unbelieving, then believing, but calm. It was as though somehow the preparation for this day, that call, had been taking place unseen, unbidden, since we had arrived at AUB, especially since Malcolm's death. I remembered well that day not long before Tom went back to Beirut when he had asked me, "What would you do if I were kidnapped?" I knew of Sis Levin's and Carol Weir's efforts for their husbands, and I answered Tom without really thinking, "I don't know. What the other wives are doing, I guess."

But now the situation was in its very reality for me, and somehow what oth-ers had done or were doing was not for me. It was as if my own personal mode and code was there waiting and the principles for action were written and non-negotiable if I were going to do and be for Tom, and for us all, the best I could do and be. So while I answered call after call, nonstop those first two days, and put through telexes to AUB and talked with the family, it was as though a refrain was running at the back of my conscious mind:

> ... Strength, spirit, naturalness, calmness, normalcy—these are the keys. If we want and expect Tom to keep mind and spirit strong, we can do no less than that. Ann, Kit, and Joan have lives to keep going and they must keep them going, progress-ing—we must have a calm solidarity of purpose and mutual support—for them, for Tom, for me—we must ... .

> ... Emotionalism must give way to logic, to a sound mind, to a clear judg-ment, if we are to be effective at all in any way. Pity—either self-pity or pity from others—is not a prerogative ... not a prerogative ... .

> ... Our lives are forfeit. We chose AUB and Beirut as our workplace and stayed there against all warnings from the Islamic Jihad and the State Department. If that choice is to keep its integrity, we can neither plead with kidnappers nor expect nor ask the American government or anyone to help. We knew well the risks and must accept the responsibility even if that is to give our lives. If we had decided to climb a mountain or go to Antarctica or sail the Atlantic on a raft and gotten into trouble, there could be no cry for help. So not now. We can only have zero expectation and

always the highest hope and faith ... zero expectation, highest hope and faith ... zero expectation, highest hope and faith ... .

... I must get back to Beirut and keep on with the work begun at AUB, keep the continuity of all our lives going; ... carry out the plans Tom and I had made together for the coming year ... get back to Beirut ... get back to Beirut ... .

And then the irony of it—I had let both my passport and visa for Lebanon lapse. I put through urgent applications, but the situation in Beirut escalated beyond returnability before the best hopes for my passport could materialize. June 11 brought the call with the news: A Jordanian plane has been hijacked— with our AUB colleague and friend, Landry Slade, and his son William on it! More scare and fright and the thing didn't end until that airliner had been blown up at Beirut Airport, thankfully with all on board released, and then the second plane that Landry and William boarded got hijacked on its arrival in Larnaca, Cyprus. We watched the TV assiduously and saw our friends, the "two Americans aboard," safe and sound finally in Cyprus when it was all over. For the Slades, however, stories don't have early endings—Landry would be called up to testify against one of the hijackers on trial in 1991 at the very time that his older son Larry was a downed American airman being held prisoner in Iraq. All kept low-profile. Landry testified, Larry came home. Tough people, the Slades. AUB-bred.

Our thankfulness over Landry and William on June 12, 1985, turned to dismay once again on June 14 when the news broke: "TWA Plane Hijacked! Islamic Jihad Believed Responsible!" I had no idea then who had Tom, but every one of us including him and the others kidnapped were caught up in this one—especially those people on the plane. The calls from the media came thick and heavy again: "How did you feel when you heard the news?" "How do you feel now?" "What do you think about the hijacking?" "Is the government doing all it can in this crisis?" I had never talked to journalists much before Tom's kidnapping, and I couldn't understand why they would have any interest in my opinion about a world event over which I had absolutely no control or input. But as the TWA crisis unfolded day by day, with Robert Stethem the Navy diver murdered and thrown out on the tarmac (*Oh, my God!*) and the plane finally landed at Beirut International Airport the hostages, Nabih Berri, American government, and Shiite hijackers played out their amazing drama. There was President Reagan hitting his fists against the wall (*now why would a president do that? we surely need strength and objectivity and calm capability at the top?*) and then entering into negotiations with Amal leader Nabih Berri over the 39 passengers now captive somewhere in the southern suburbs. Suddenly it became a chance for a "Forgotten

Seven" with Tom as one of them and I was glad for every media person who called. I was still at the cabin in the mountains and amazingly no media people had physically found me except for Perry Patrick, the very nice reporter from the *Estes Park Trail Gazette* who scoured the mountains and made it to the door. But at this point it wasn't I that was important to them, it was they who were important to us, and when the number of Americans under negotiation went to 46, it seemed a victory and Tom might have a chance. Then came the press conference hullabaloo over the TWA hostages in Beirut. Allyn Conroy was the spokesperson who came forward for the hostages for which he paid a big price. For the demands of the kidnappers were to get the Shiite prisoners out of Atleet Prison in South Lebanon where they were being held by the Israelis contrary to international law under UN Resolution 242. *(But where had the demand for the 17 in Kuwait gone? Had Islamic Jihad given over to Amal to press for a "reasonable" demand?)* Certainly to the hijackers and even to the hostages the demand seemed reasonable, but it wasn't at all easy. Conroy voiced their opinion and it got reported in the papers as "Hostages Sympathetic to Hostage Takers." From this, "Stockholm Syndrome" became the cry. Conroy, a very fine man who was doing his best for his fellow hostages and the situation and understanding the way things were in the Middle East (that Israel and Islamic Jihad and the American government could be both right and wrong at the same time), became the scapegoat for the release and the sense of helplessness and outrage the American people had over the whole thing. True shades of Vietnam. And then came June 30. The TWA hostages were released and on their way, and at the finish the number of Americans arriving in Damascus was 39. No "Forgotten Seven," William Buckley, Peter Kilburn, Ben Weir, Father Martin, Terry Anderson, David Jacobsen, Tom Sutherland, nor, for that matter, any Frenchmen. Did Islamic Jihad want insurance against retribution for the hijacking? Was that why they kept them? Were they angry that the demand had changed from the freeing of their 17 brothers from Kuwait? Maybe both? I only knew that my motto "Zero Expectation, Highest Hope and Faith" was there and served me well—the first of a thousand times to come.

In the meantime, I was in touch on a continuing basis with AUB and Beirut and also with Washington, where it turned out there were caring people for me. My brother Dave's oldest son, Chris Murray, a foreign service officer then assigned to the State Department there, immediately took on our case as he could, telling me how things worked and what could be expected in Washington. Joel Kassiday too, top aide to our U.S. Congressman Hank Brown, was on the phone the first day and nearly every day after that to give support and information and guidance. From the start their collective support was continuous. Until they went to Belgium, Chris and his wife Joan were mainstays in Washington, making their Bethesda home a home to me when I was there. Chris introduced me over the years to pertinent people—Bob Oakley and David Long of the Office of Counter Terrorism; Jim McVerry on the Lebanon desk; and Steve Grummon, a Middle East analyst who shared with me so thoughtfully his insights on hostages and the evolving politics of the region. Hank Brown for his part was truly personal— taking me to breakfast in the Capitol dining room, giving me time in his office when I came through, being at every commemoration and event for Tom when he could during all the time to come, and giving us Joel Kassiday's time and energy. Joel was indefatigable throughout in coming up with ideas. He introduced me to Harry Newstein of New York who knew all the Organization of Petroleum Exporting Countries (OPEC) people and important Iranians. Joel was so personally concerned, keeping us constantly informed of developments, receiving me and giving me his friendship, updates, and pep talks on my visits to Washington, and going with me to pertinent meetings with people in the State Department. Thus, through Chris and Joan and Hank and Joel was Washington positively personalized for me from the start.

Kit's birthday on June 18 was honored but subsumed by her dad's kidnap-ping and the TWA crisis. But on July 2 it was Joan's 21st birthday and she was to have a special party. Especially since Tom had planned to make the trip back from Beirut for it and we kept faith up to the day that a miracle might happen. Ann and Ray came on their motorcycles from California, my brother John and children came from Lubbock, Texas, friends Dorcas and John Murray came from Boulder, but Tom came not. Joan was great and didn't show outwardly her dis-appointment although it was there: ... *During the party, I kept looking and hop-ing that he would peek his head around that corner, saying that he had been re-leased for my birthday!! Such silly thoughts, but in times like those, anything helped, even big wishful thinking* ... . Nevertheless we made a real celebration for Joan and generated double the spirit at the Loveland dog kennel where Kit was work-ing and she and Joan were staying, and the day was special for us all. The prin-ciple was set that day that we would celebrate fully all family occasions to be-come part of the Big Celebration when Tom came home. As it turned out, each event brought us closer together and affirmed our family spirit.

My passport duly arrived and the AUB New York office expedited my visa, but the Beirut International Airport was still closed—President Reagan was talk-ing retaliation. A blockade? An air strike? By this time I was very glad I was being asked for my opinion! It seemed that anything we could put in to calm the situation was a plus. I remember saying to one reporter who called—"We just need the clearest minds and soundest judgments now to work through to a positive resolution." She came back sharply, "What do you mean, 'positive resolution'?" Amazed that there wasn't instant perception, I answered, "That there is a positive resolution of the total conflict so that all the men there can come out and no more go in." Then I thought through what I had said and realized what it meant: I couldn't hope only that Tom would get out, I couldn't pray only that Tom would get out, I couldn't work only to get Tom out. I had to hope, pray, and work to resolve the conflict so all hostages could be voluntarily set free and no more taken. It had to be and so be it.

I was lucky. My brother John was a conflict resolutionist. He gave me a solid introduction before he had to leave Colorado that first week of July, and then the next two weeks, while I typed steadily to finish my dissertation, John and I went into telephone consultation. I learned everything he could tell me about "getting to yes" and the new theories, strategies, and techniques of conflict resolution. "It isn't anymore the rhetoric of one side giving up and the other side winning, or even of compromise where both sides feel they have lost. We work at 'enlarging the frame' to find a solution where both sides feel that they come away from a settlement with more than they thought they would get … . And we always negotiate on the basis of being 'solution-centered' not 'problem-centered' … positive, not negative." John was soon to become president of the Conflict Clinic at George Mason University in Fairfax, Virginia. A few years earlier he had helped to establish this negotiation-mediation clinic at Harvard with Roger Fisher, the well-known figure in conflict resolution and international negotiation and the author of the acclaimed *Getting to Yes: How to Negotiate without Giving In.* John consulted with Roger, Jim Laue (then president of the clinic), and other colleagues, and out of it all came the suggestion that I should get in touch with Jill Townsend, one of Roger's former students who was now working with an international conciliation organization out of Geneva with offices in Windsor, England. By this time, my dissertation on Shakespeare and Seneca was ready to deposit at the University of Colorado, the Beirut Airport was to reopen, and my ticket was in hand for the trip back. I called Jill and we set up to meet when I reached London.

I left the cabin July 23 and stayed overnight in Denver with our friends, Roger and Leslie Sherman. It was the next morning as I dressed, packed, and left the guest room for the breakfast table that I really looked at the framed sampler hanging over the bed where I'd slept. It was a poem in meticulous cross-stitch:

I said to the man who stood
at the gate of the year, 'Give me
a Light that I may tread safely
into the unknown,' and he replied,
'Go out into the darkness and put
your hand into the hand of God ... .
That shall be to you better than
light and safer than a known way.'

I asked Leslie at breakfast, "Where did you get the sampler in the bedroom?" and she said, "A good friend of my mother's made it and gave it to her in the 1940s and I inherited it." Well, the sampler stayed on her wall until Tom's release when Leslie gave it to me as a treasured gift for our wall. The poem, however, went with me in my mind and heart as a talisman for a way of life during Tom's captivity. Later in Beirut, I wondered who had written the poem and where it had come from, and I stopped at the British Council Library one day on my way to Smith's Grocery, consulted the *Oxford Book of Quotations,* and there it was. Written by Minnie Louise Haskins in 1908, it was given fame and meaning by King George VI who quoted it during his Christmas Eve broadcast of 1939 just before the Battle of Britain of World War II.

I caught the plane at Stapleton that morning of July 24, stayed for a day in New York to touch base with the AUB people there, and then took off for London and ultimately Beirut. It was a fantastic trip and I kept a notebook of the happenings:

JULY 26—Met at Heathrow by Andrew [aide to Michael Davis, the director of the Foundation for International Conciliation—it also turned out that he was the one who had gone to Libya with Terry Waite to bring back the hostages there] ... . Met Davis and Jill Townsend at Windsor Hotel about 9 A.M.—and went to their office in Windsor for full discussion re facts and people and events ... .

JULY 27—A day in Scotland with all of Tom's family [brothers Peter and Willie and families, sisters Elizabeth, Margaret, and Lena and families—all live within five miles of the home farm near Falkirk where the fields go down to the Forth River]. We talked and talked of Tom ... .

JULY 28—to Beirut—Met at the airport by Hussein Husseini, Speaker of Lebanese Parliament, his sister Selma [a good friend of Tom's in his faculty at AUB], and Adib Saad [Tom's associate dean, now acting dean, such a good man, good friend]; ... they had a patrol car with 2 soldiers; ... had a long talk with Adib who detailed all the efforts they'd made—said he felt uncomfortable about two things—1) at the Board of Deans meeting the Thursday before Tom's kidnapping he had asked if Tom shouldn't be informed about the seriousness of the situation and the chairman Raja Khouri had passed it off, saying, "The New York office will inform him"; ... and 2) that a directive to "stop Beirut/AUB efforts to free Tom" had come down from AUB administration a week after his kidnapping .... But by that time he had seen Berri, the Mufti, Jumblatt headquarters, etc. and students and faculty had been great and done all they could .... Afterwards I had a wonderful get together with good good friends at Heinekens; ... love and support was nonstop from everyone .... [Frits and Elien Heineken walked me home through campus that night as they would do many times in the years to come as they became brother and sister to me. Simply beautiful Dutch people who had made their lives at AUB since the 1950s, they had known early what hardship was. Frits, born in Indonesia, had spent a teenage year in a Japanese prison camp, and Elien in Holland had known the privation there of those World War II years—especially 1944–1945 when there was literally nothing to have or to eat. She had had Dutch friends who had given their lives to protect Jewish friends; she was grappling now with the fact of Jews in Israel committing Nazi-like atrocities against Shia and Palestinians. It wasn't easy.]

MONDAY, JULY 29—Talked to everyone .... [Joana came running into the house early in the morning to talk and talk and share all her feelings. She told me, "Mom, I had a dream just before Dad went away—he came to the house with many men and they all had hair on their faces ..." "Did you tell Tom about your dream, Joana?" "Oh, no, Mom—you think if I had, he wouldn't have been kidnapped?" "No, Joana— if he wasn't to be kidnapped you wouldn't have had that dream, would you?" She always told me her dreams after that. Sharif, Tom's driver, that small man with such a large heart, also came first-off, so full of emotion about the kidnapping—he told me all the details and said he would take me to the place where it happened and "Anything I can do for you, Mrs. Sutherland, anything, anything at all ..." and I reassured him that I was fine and would be wanting him to drive me places and take care of me and "Call on me, Mrs. Sutherland, for anything, anytime ... ." And I thanked him and told him it would all be okay. And all the six and a half years he would drive me and care lovingly for me—but not until Tom came out would he truly smile and be happy again.] Meeting with Advisory Committee of Tom's faculty (Bekaa Shiite advice—"Ask for complete release, be firm, delicate business, stay out of Lebanese politics.") ... Then talked to Radwan Mawlawi [head of Department of Information and a good friend of Tom's and all the years afterwards of mine]—he underscored Alumni Pressure Group that appears to be functioning not under AUB aegis and working for increased security—they've seen all official representatives—Hoss, Gemayel, Husseini—now to see political leaders Berri, Jumblatt, and Iranian ambassador; ... date for their Berri appointment set for Saturday, August 2—at first Radwan suggested I go with them—I gathered from telephone conversation that others not too much in accord with this so didn't ... .

TUESDAY, JULY 30—Picked up application blanks for job at AUB; ... addressed Tom's faculty and students at 12:30; ... talked with Muin and Nahla [colleagues and friends of Tom's in FAFS] about seeing Mrs. Berri ... . 6:30 talked with Alumni Pressure Group—felt they accepted me but were leery of including me in efforts—saw Ayashes who were in car in front of Tom when kidnapped—they were most affected and upset; ... "all happened extremely fast; ... won't forget Tom's face as he was taken away and looked at me ... . Our daughter most upset: Will he have enough to eat??

WEDNESDAY, JULY 31—Got application into English Department for job next year ... . Spent afternoon in garden pulling weeds—yard a mess ... .

FRIDAY, AUG. 2—12 noon meeting with Mrs. Berri. Sharif drove Nahla and me to Berri house—interesting ease of access, up elevator to apartment—beautiful but not ostentatious, had good visit with cold drink followed by coffee. Little girl of three years old in attendance. Mrs. B. was gracious, intelligent, spoke good English. She said to me: "We're very sorry about Tom ... . At first we all thought the 'other side' must have done it, we could not believe the group that has him because Dr. S. working for the people ... ."

She spoke long about the crisis of TWA hijacking and Nabih Berri's mediation; ... they got little sleep ... . She talked about the TWA plane still being at the airport and that some insurance company had offered 2 million pounds in return for plane, the money to be used for children hurt in War of the South—reply from Nabih Berri and group is that the plane is free for crew to come and get; ... they don't need money that way ... (what a great culture gap there is!) .

... Home to hear from head of English Department that Board of Trustees at Cyprus meeting had determined "no foreign contracts" so it looks like no AUB contract in the works for me ... .

SUNDAY, AUG. 4—Nice quiet family lunch with Saghirs [head of Tom's FAFS Crop Production and Protection department] ... . 4 P.M. Bernard Haunch from the Hariri Program called; ... he was the man who sought and identified Dennis Hill [the English teacher murdered just before Tom's abduction]—Bernard's an interesting, sensitive person—took Dennis's ashes back to England—finds no real efforts being made to seek killers—offered to take Tom's place in captivity ... .

Monday to Saturday—National unity front announced, Moroccan Summit; ... dinners and lunches with Hajjes, Solhs, Mawlawis, Ellises, Heinekens; ... wonderful, supportive friends here.

SUNDAY, AUG. 11—4 P.M. A shell from nowhere (an angry rumor says the East of course) hit campus—it was a direct hit on a Moslem boy, a Hariri student called "the gentle giant" because of his size and loving, helpful personality—body parts were everywhere—others near him were hurt … . Spent the next morning at the hospital with parents of Zena Tadmouri, an AUB student critically injured in the bomb blast [she so tragically died soon after] … .

AUG. 13—Important meeting; … lunch with Dr. Hallab and his right-hand man Tony Kassab, Hariri Program administrator … . Asked them if they needed an English teacher and they said "yes"; … also needed interviewer for applicants in Britain last part of September and could use administrative help in the program '85–'86 … . Meeting with Fadlallah was scuttled after AUB alumni met with him—"don't want to see any more AUB people—they accuse me of withholding the people …" Effort in Bekaa—to Moussawis—wall of silence, no go … . Talked with Husni Serhal [from the airport who had offered Tom—and been turned down—bodyguards June 9]; … discussed TWA crisis and told of great efforts of Middle East Airlines and others at the airport to help—had done much for treatment of passengers with food and clothes, etc. which American public didn't seem to appreciate … . TWA plane still there—why? "Guess they don't care about it"—consensus is that it is waiting for a crew to come and get it … .

AUG. 12–14—Noon meeting with Nabih Berri … strong, sharp, listened, responded well, but angry about TWA episode—"I'm now known as chief of kidnappers and terrorists"—felt he'd been betrayed by Reagan—said he had seen telex with own eyes: "Atleet prisoners released soon" and below was "one week" [full release of prisoners didn't come until September] … . Berri made these points: 1) condemned abduction, against Islamic law, 2) no negotiation possible until last prisoners out of Atleet, 3) big distrust of American government, 4) big trust of Tom—asked for him during the hijack, 5) Hizbollah—Bekaa—locked in—he can't secure release but will bend all efforts … . Consensus was that it was a good meeting … .

THURSDAY, AUG. 15—10:15 A.M. Went with Aref AbdelBaki and 3 students of AUB to Jumblatt headquarters Beirut—met with Akram Shuhayyib (second in command for Beirut area, a low-key, intelligent, and sensitive man) and Jihad Zihari; … talked of Bekaa and Hizbollah—said release would take three things: 1) TIME, 2) Prisoners out of Atleet, 3) Syria … . They offered protection anytime; … very positive meeting; … strong, independent, sharp people … . I caught MEA plane for London at 1:30 … .

SUMMARY OF TRIP:
1) Positive
2) Time important as well as Atleet prisoners released and Syrian involvement—

resolution out of individual hands

3) Seems ready for negotiation when situation conducive enough to justify—appears that Atleet's enough—will not press Kuwait ... (why is this?)

4) Why not get some U.S. positive action afterwards??

5) Americans should go to Lebanon—we definitely should return and carry on ...

I reached Fort Collins August 16, and the next day was graduation day. A gorgeous morning full of sunshine—my dad and stepmother Alice had come from Iowa to be there along with Colorado daughters Kit and Joan, and California daughter Ann, in spirit. The ceremony was outdoors at the University of Colorado, on the central lawn up and behind Norlin Library and before one of the oldest buildings on campus where I'd had classes. Informal in the sunshine and the shade of old trees, the degrees were granted—I received my hood and walked across the stage to receive the handshakes and the Ph.D. that meant so much. And then back to Fort Collins for a complete surprise party—a pig roast at Johnsons' with scores of friends. How I wished Tom could have been there! But just as at Joan's 21st we made a wonderful celebration and put it in our memory banks to be relived with Tom when we were all together again. And so the day was special and specially enjoyed.

Youngest daughters Kit and Joan were at crossroads in their lives and seeking actively their respective ways. Joan had been accepted for airline school in Vancouver, Washington, so on August 28 we left for the West Coast, the orange Honda Civic packed to the gunnels with her and her effects, Kit and me too. A night in Salt Lake, another in Reno, and then to oldest daughter Ann and Ray's house in Albany, California. What a delight to be all together again as Tom's family! We celebrated not only with a curry dinner and a toast to Tom but also by changing the wheels of Ann's Honda to Joan's Honda, "because Dad wants to save the 13-inch wheels and I have a buyer for my car" said Ann. The last day of August was up the coast to Oregon and then a settling-in for Joan for her three-month program. She was to do extremely well and finish up with a job in late fall with Continental Airlines in Los Angeles.

With hearts full, Kit and I left Joan with her new studies, prospective new friends, and the old orange Civic, and we flew back to Fort Collins to begin creating a new life for Kit, who, with her shiny B.A. in psychology in hand and a love for animals that even a summer living and working at a dog kennel couldn't quell, was ready for a *career*. She had decided to try the East and had written to six pharmaceutical companies to set up interviews, so she and I packed up her Toyota and took off for Pennsylvania and the wonderful home of the Panepintos called Montebello not far from Philadelphia. The first night on the road we spent with

Dad and Alice in Des Moines, Iowa, at the new Living History Farms Solar Home dedicated to Dad, the Farms' founding father. The second night we met up with my brother John in Columbus, Ohio, where he was doing a semester as a visiting professor, and the third night was a reunion with the Trachs and Georges, my Lancaster, Pennsylvania, cousins of Mother's family. Then on to a real Panepinto welcome and a week of interviews and apartment hunting for Kit. It wasn't long until both of us knew it wasn't going to work—the pharmaceutical labs wanted a permanent address for her and the apartment complexes wanted confirmation of job and salary so it was a catch-22 without a niche or feeling of belonging there. But we had a lovely weekend outing with the Panepintos' daughter Nina to Cape May—a trip back in time for me to the place where over 50 years ago in the summers just before World War II our family would drive east from Iowa and go with Mother's whole Furniss clan from Lancaster to have special beach vacations.

And then the phone rang. It was John Weir to say that his father was released and home and would be having a press conference at the National Presbyterian Church in Washington, D.C., on September 19. Could we be there? Yes, absolutely! Into the Toyota and down to Washington, D.C., Kit and I went.

A great church, filled for Ben Weir's release press conference. And it was there, September 1985, that Kit and I represented our family as we became "official" members of that growing group called "Hostage Families." Sitting at the end of a pew along with the others, we were mercifully bypassed by the TV cameras, which knew and focused on the Jencos, the Says, and the Levins, but knew us not by sight. I heard, as in a dream, Ben Weir say to the world and to us for the first time, "I was with Tom Sutherland … ." And in the private meeting afterward, a warm hug for us and a letter from Tom out of Ben's pocket. How the reporters wanted a look at that letter, but it was too new, too precious to share with anyone except the family. We read it over the phone to Ann and Joan and sent them copies—the letter itself went with me back to Beirut as a touchstone. Even now as I write, I pass my hand lovingly over those pages of the kind of notebook paper I would have my students writing on in our language program for the next six years, and I relive the emotion of the first reading:

SATURDAY, SEPT. 14, 1985—My Dearest Jean, Ann, Kit, and Joan … Greetings and my love to all of you. I hope all of you are well and getting along without me. I am hanging in there, and making the best of things in "captivity." We are being treated pretty well and we keep hoping for a quick release—but one day rolls into the next and we are still being held. Hard to believe that it is now over 3 months since I was picked up! I wonder what is happening at AUB? Adib Saad is presumably still acting dean—but I seriously doubt if we will get advice to return to campus. Then the question will be—what do we do? Have you Jean planned to come to Beirut? I have thought about you all so much and wondered how things have gone for you all—your thesis and graduation Jean—did Dad come? Your "word processor"? Did you buy one? And especially I have worried about our financial condition and your need to sell the house to meet all the bills ... . Joan, sorry I missed your 21st birthday—I had planned to be there as you know. Did it go well? And have you gone on to Airline School? And what is Kit doing now that her summer job is over (I presume?). And did Ann make a safe trip to Missouri on her motorcycle and take in your birthday, Joan? Gosh, I miss you all so badly—it is terribly boring to have so little to do and no freedom to come and go as we please. Five of us are together now and are being treated thoughtfully, by and large. Whoever is released and carries this letter can give you more details of the conditions of our treatment and captivity, as he will to each family. He will be released to stir up some faster action on negotiations for our release—the person may be Terry Anderson, but that decision has not been taken yet. He will call on you to help all you can too, Jean.

Ever since I was kidnapped I have been terribly worried about the impact of this whole thing on my career and on yours, Jean. We had planned a good year together at AUB. But now that seems remote from where I sit! ... So many problems to solve, and at this point, all by yourself. I am sorry this happened, Jean—I hope you have not let it shake you up too badly. You are strong and resourceful. Keep up your courage and one of these days we will be reunited. Our captors promise that we will come to no harm, and will be released safe when negotiations on the Kuwait-held prisoners are completed, which is the key to our release apparently. We are exercising daily and eating pretty well though the meals are high on bread and in general low on vegetables and fruit. But we are all seeming to be surviving pretty well on the diet. I don't know what will be the long-term effects on our health. I have broken one of my molar teeth on an olive pit ... otherwise I have been doing OK but not sleeping very well on foam mattresses on the tile floor—on top of my worrying about you all and about AUB and my career there! ... Here we now have a radio and can hear the BBC, Voice of America; and Ben Weir speaks fluent Arabic so he can pick up local news, so we are now well-informed on what is going on around the world. The first month was a complete blackout however, though I did hear about the TWA hijacking ... . I must close this section—Ben Weir has just been selected to go out tonight, and I have written another note with the group's ultimatum and details. Meantime I send all my love to all of you—... As always darling—Tom.

Dearest Jean—... Ben Weir will carry this letter—it is imperative that every effort be made under his coordination to secure the release of the prisoners in Kuwait. Please do all you can to effect this by whatever means you can devise—the consequences will be severe if that is not achieved. The group holding us claim to be able to kidnap other Americans still. They will not respond to pressures from the Syrians, Nabih Berri, or any other quarter; they insist on the release of the prisoners in Kuwait—all 17 of them. If this is not done, they may then kill the rest of us left here. So it looks like a serious turn of events in their decisions here—

Ben will give you other instructions, and your dad and John will also be able to advise you on how to influence the State Department, I am sure. Good luck on your efforts, darling … .

I send my deepest love to you and Ann and Kit and Joan, and to all the rest of the family wherever they may be.

With Tom's letter in our hearts and as part of "the group," Kit and I went to a meeting with Vice President George Bush, with Robert McFarlane and company present on the periphery. The other families had started out angry because Bush had opted the Levins and the Weirs out of the meeting; they fought to have the Weirs there especially, and so it worked out. There was lots of anger and frustration on the part of the family members and defensiveness on the part of Bush whose final word was, "The president is taking personal charge of the hostage situation." Kit and I, as hostage family neophytes, kept quiet. Later I would pass on to Jackie Ratner, the State Department liaison, that it surely seemed that they needed to work more closely with the families, keep in touch, and defuse anger.

Taking our leave of Vice President Bush and coming out of the meeting we faced more media, more microphones. "Do you think the government is doing all it should do for you?" I can't remember what we answered, but I know that my opinion about government was pretty much solid by that time—no matter how much we tell them what they should do or what we want them to do, "governments do what they do do" as some notable at some previous time said. And in our case I never expected our government to do anything for us and felt quite strongly that national security and foreign policy weren't to be made and changed over individuals—no matter that I also felt very strongly that our Middle East policy of complete and uncritical support of Israeli policy must definitely be changed to an objective if supportive policy. Instead of acting on the principle that "It is in Israel's best interests to annihilate Palestinians and carry on war with its Arab neighbors," we should act on the principle that "It is in Israel's best interests to recognize human rights and to make peace, even to giving back occupied land to make peace." Seemed clearly logical and right to me. But whatever my opinion, the American government for now, however it acted, was just a phenomenon in our situation—a player like Islamic Jihad, Iran, Syria, Israel, Lebanon; and it was up to us to be objective and work toward resolution with what was there.

Whatever Kit and I said, at any rate, the media took it and went away as it always does and at last the two of us got our private, rather disquieting time with Ben Weir. He told us of the awful conditions ameliorated only by the fact that the Americans were able to be together, "which helps a lot ... but I'm concerned about Tom—he's extremely depressed and they've been giving him hard interrogation over a paper they found in his briefcase ... ." We had to relay this also to Ann and Joan, but we resolved all together not to let this affect our spirits. But it didn't mean that we didn't privately worry. Ann got a chance later to have her own personal conversation by phone with Ben, and she talked to me about it afterward:

> You remember, Mom, when we were at the cabin after Kit's graduation, and we had that movie about the policeman who got raped and held captive and they were talking about what his greatest fears were and it was about being powerless .... Dad was asleep on the couch and you said, "Well, your dad's greatest fear is of being held captive and having people dictate to him ... ." So, this was right before his kidnapping, and now he was there and he didn't have the things that Ben Weir had—a very strong religious background with a faith in God .... I remember with Ben, talking to him, and telling him "I'm really worried .... I know my dad's not very religious and doesn't have that to fall back on"; ... and Ben was so comforting. He said, "Well, you know people have different things that give them strength"—it was so good to talk to him because it gave me more confidence about how Dad would actually react ... .

On the last day in Washington, the hostage families gathered once more quietly before they dispersed to their respective courses and causes. We talked— the first priority was to get a meeting with President Reagan. Next, other ways and means. Was it then that I first heard the name Terry Waite? Or was it afterward when I'd gone to Britain to start my job for AUB that I heard on the radio or read in a newspaper how he had accepted the request and pledged himself to negotiate the release of the rest of the Islamic Jihad hostages? I do remember that it was wonder and thankfulness that I felt, and his name was as magic to me as to others. He was a humanitarian, outside the adversarial warfare, representing a country also outside, and maybe there was a hope. He was, from the very first, as he recognizes with the title of his book, to be *Taken on Trust* by us.

On our drive back to Pennsylvania, Kit told me her decision was made to give up the search for a new job and place in the impersonal, suburbanized East and return home to Fort Collins to make her new life there for now. What a relief she felt—and I too for her; my problem was that it was time for me to get to London and start my interviewing job for the AUB Hariri English Training

Program. "Don't worry," she said, and saw me off on the train to New York and thence on the plane from JFK to Heathrow. For her part, she drove herself and her belongings all alone the 2,000 miles back home to Fort Collins, barely reaching it through a blinding blizzard that hit on an October day, as we had known it on past Christmas drives to Iowa to do, at Ogalala, Nebraska. I was blissfully unaware of this until later when she was fine, in a new job raising miniature pigs for the oldest Panepinto daughter, Linda, at Colorado State University's Charles River Lab in Fort Collins, and well settled into a new apartment. *Tough lady, our daughter Kit, Tom. Tough ladies also, Ann and Joan. You'd be most proud of them, Sweetheart.*

9   The Penthouse

Ben was gone. I had lost my Presbyterian buddy. I wondered what it would feel like to be going home, but it was difficult to put myself into that frame of mind. They had been treating me very badly, and the Hajj kept telling us, "Tom home last. He bad man." I had to be more or less resigned to a long residence.

Terry had also lost in Ben his teacher of Arabic, just when he was starting to make real progress. A few days later he asked, "Hey, man, you speak French, right?" "Yep," I replied, unenthusiastically. "How about teaching me to speak and read French?" he pursued. "Man, no grammar or dictionary. How can we?" Was I subconsciously afraid that my mind would let me down—that I would not be able to deliver for Terry, who still intimidated me terribly? "Well, let's try it. See how much you remember. We'll make up our own grammar as we go along." So began our famous French lessons.

First thing was to teach him all the tenses of the two basic verbs, "to be" and "to have." I went back into my memory to Miss Minty's class in seventh grade when I was starting out in French. I could still visualize these two verbs on the pages of our grammar; the future tense, the conditional, the imperfect, the perfect, the present, and finally the past definite. Wow, I hadn't thought of that lot in a whee of years. And there they all were. For the first time ever, I wondered why they were organized in that particular order. We concluded jointly that it must be because of the principal parts of the verb and the order in which they are generally given. Next, some basic vocabulary—we had paper and pencil in those days, so Terry began his own little dictionary. In next to no time he had well over a hundred words, then two, then three, and by the end of our lessons, he had in excess of two thousand words under his belt. Success. My pleasure in it was as much for me as for Terry, for surely this was a sign that my mind was still functioning.

Came a mild crisis of shelling, so the guards moved us downstairs again, to a room right next door to where we had been, and what did we find but two copies of *L'Orient le Jour*, the French-language newspaper published in Beirut. A genuine treasure trove. Just what we needed for our French lessons. Terry latched onto them to take back upstairs with him, and we translated every single word in those two papers. Every word, that is, that I *could* translate. French journalists are like English-speaking ones; they use lots of words that most of us don't. This "find" gave us fairly concrete proof that there must be French hostages held in this same building. We had suspected as much, for Terry was sure he had heard some French spoken from time to time. My ears were not that good.

Another consequence of Ben's departure: We had lost our evening minister. So Father assigned the three of us to do that. I joined in, but with little enthusiasm. I was still antagonistic to any form of religion. Terry and David were happy to serve; in fact, Terry embarked on a study of the parallel gospels on top of his French. He evaluated each section where two gospels were the same and itemized all the segments where there were discrepancies. He worked like a beaver—limitless energy and determination. Periodically, he came over to Father's mattress and held long discussions with him on his findings. For my part, I was discovering for the first time that Matthew, Mark, Luke, and John were all basically the same story, told in different words and sequence. I had always assumed that all four had different aspects of the total gospel, and that all four were necessary for the total picture, and in some respects this is true. I think now as I write this, that in a way our "hostage books" follow this model in trying to get to a "Truth" from our different perspectives, our different renderings.

We missed Ben as the days dragged by. But we were glad for him. At least he was now home. Strange thing though—not a word about him on the radio. We had assumed it would be big news. In a few days, the Hajj was back, angry that nothing was coming out of America on their "humanitarian gesture." And what could we do about it, for God's sake? Finally, news. President Reagan talked to Ben from Air Force One, the presidential jet, en route to New England, and claimed, "Today, we were able to bring home one of the hostages from Lebanon; but we will not rest until we have all of them home," or something to this effect. Almost four more weeks of daily routine passed, and the radio now brought us the news that the Syrians were going to comb the southern suburbs for hostages. The immediate reaction of Islamic Jihad was to move us out of the suburbs. Early in the morning, they took out everything except our pee bottles, and we were left in a *really* bare room—I had thought that our circumstances were about as barren as they could be—but when these mattresses and our few meager belongings went, things were even worse. Our very voices echoed around the room.

We exercised, knowing that soon we would be gone from this building. But we reckoned without the normal Jihad efficiency—didn't move until late in the evening! Lunch and dinner came—sandwiches, since our bowls and utensils were all gone. Finally, we were ordered to follow the guards downstairs, out of a funny door arrangement and into a waiting van. We had all to sit on the floor, with a number of guards accompanying us. In a following van, it appeared that the French hostages were also being transported. Badr was our driver and was in contact with the Hajj via two-way radio. We drove a little, then stopped. All sorts of booms and bangs were going on up ahead, and we had to wait until it died down before proceeding. A few more minutes, however, and we were unloaded, entered a doorway, and climbed several flights of stairs. I was soon out of puff. So was Father; this after only a few months of confinement. Even Terry and David, for all their vehement exercise routine, were not too good at this stair-climbing bit. After what seemed like an eternity, we resumed our climbing. We were passing apartment doors on every floor as I saw peeking under my blindfold! The guards were *very* nervous, and kept whispering among themselves and exhorting us, "Be quiet, no speak, okay?" We obeyed, more or less, but tried to keep track of who was where. No idea where we were going—must be the bloody Eiffel Tower, with a climb like this! Finally at the top, out into the open, where we could breathe cool, wonderful fresh air, and then instructed to climb up on a wall. Two guards grabbed my arms and assisted me in a jump onto another wall, then over an open flat surface, through a glass door, into a room, through that one, into a hallway, and finally into another room where we were "deposited." Must have been one or two in the morning.

Left alone, we took stock. "Did you see how high we were when we crossed from that other building into this one?" asked Terry. "Yeah," said Father and David simultaneously, "must have been well over a hundred feet down to the ground!" I gasped in amazement. "How in the hell did you see *that?*" "Easy," they said. "All you had to do was to look down under your blindfold, and you would have seen." They had brought us up the stair in one building, clear up to the roof, then had us jump *blindfolded* from that building to the one we were now in, leading us across the roof to a sort of "penthouse" apartment. This apartment, we later calculated (from timing the elevator when it was running: one-one thousand, two-one thousand), was on top of a 12-story apartment building, so that our "jump" was at 12 stories up. Shades of Dirty Harry chasing his prey over the rooftops of San Francisco; God, I was glad I hadn't peeked at that point!

Our new room was large, square, bare, and cold. It was almost the middle of October, and nights were getting chilly in Beirut. Terry was hungry and asked the guards for something to eat. What an optimist. Islamic Jihad never planned that far ahead. But wonders never cease; they did have something—a box of *halawi*—almost pure sugar with some flavor and spices added, which all Middle Easterners love. In the two years prior to my kidnapping, I had tried most things Lebanese, but somehow had never tasted *halawi*. Incredibly sweet! Right in line with Lebanese tastes; they put up to five or six spoonfuls of sugar in a single cup of coffee, and their "Lebanese sweets" are so sweet, they are almost poisonous! But this tasted good in the middle of the night, after all that adventure and energy expenditure coming up the stairs. We spooned away at it, and soon scraped bottom. My first introduction to the product, but not my last taste—we had lots of it in the years to come, even to *halawi* sandwiches. Reminded me of my childhood when we sometimes fixed ourselves "sugar sandwiches."

Blessedly, still no chains—but no central heating either. And in this big room, about 20 by 20 feet, we were too few for our bodies to heat it. After complaining to the guards—Terry especially, who turned out to be really cold-blooded, always needing lots of blankets—we were given a room at the other end of the hallway from the bathroom, much smaller and "easier to heat." This, of course, was a mixed blessing, for it also stank more easily. Much higher humidity as well; our faces were greasy again, our clothes wouldn't dry, our mattresses got wet underneath (I never could understand why the mattresses always absorbed the moisture on the underside—something to do with the cold of the tile floor?). So there was a price to pay for our warmth.

Even in this room, though, we needed more clothes than we had now. We asked the guards if they had any warmer clothing. In an hour or two, Fadl appeared with a big sack of sweaters and assorted clothing—sweatshirts, pants, etc. Terry took charge of distributing them around, and threw one to each of us. I got a beautiful wool sweater, soft and warm, and pulled it over my head, really happy with how I had come out. Then, "Hey! That's my sweater you have!" cried Father Martin. I looked at him in disbelief. "It's what?" I asked. "That's the sweater I was wearing when I was kidnapped," exclaimed Father. So I had no choice but to give up this nice soft cashmere one for the one Terry had tossed to him at random. That one turned out to be Shetland wool, a wool that's warm all right, but almost like steel wool, scratchy and decidedly uncomfortable next to the skin. No matter that Father had continually exhorted us—"You can't cling to *things*," Father was surely delighted to see his sweater, the only thing he ever recovered from what he was wearing on the day of his capture.

A week in this room brought Terry's birthday, October 27. One *enormous* chocolate cake, well-decorated—the Lebanese have wonderful patisseries, a legacy from the French mandate—and we *gorged*. The guards then ate what was left. Next day a video, very special one, of Terry's family. The guards stayed around and they ran it only once. It came at us much too fast for most of us, peering under our blindfolds, to sort out any of Terry's folks at all. But he did, and was extremely moved. There for the first time he was seeing his daughter, now four months old, born three months after his abduction. He cried quietly, as we all did for him.

In this place, the guards were much more nervous and ill at ease. Whenever anything untoward took place, which they did not completely understand, they would line us up against the wall and two or three of them would click the magazines out of their guns, pull the trigger, and then click the magazines back into them, all the while ordering us. "No speak, okay? No make any noise!" So nervous. But what really bothered me much more was the habit they adopted here when they thought we were talking too loudly, which might be heard outside of our "Penthouse." They hissed at us like a snake in the most insulting fashion. Somehow that "Hisssssssssss" really got to me, to all of us for that matter, as though we were a pack of dogs or cattle.

The Hajj visited us frequently these days, standing just outside the door while talking to us—Terry and David, still competing to be "the top of the pecking order," were almost comical to observe (or rather *hear* for we were always under blindfolds on these occasions) in their efforts to grab the attention of the Hajj—reminded me of a couple of first-graders vying for the teacher's attention. On one visit the Hajj told us, "You are in nice place here. Remember, we could be treating you *much* worse. Our brothers in Israeli jails are suffering much worse than you are. You should be happy here." Happy I wasn't, and to make matters worse, when he wasn't arguing with David, Terry was still picking on me, so that one day when walking around the room, I burst out at him, "Terry, for God's sake, you are being harder on me than the guards!" He stopped walking, and looked genuinely shocked, and even hurt. "Do you really mean that, Tom?" "Yes I do!" Whereupon he apologized, promising not to do it anymore. And in large measure he kept his promise for the next six years.

They always removed the key after locking the door so it was easily possible to peer through the keyhole. Father and I frequently did, to Terry's constant admonishment, "You guys will get caught, and then you'll pay for it." But we never were, thank goodness! We could see right down the hall and were able to follow the movements of all six guards. In this room too, on November 7, we first met

"Ali." He breezed in with a "Hi guys," in an almost impeccable American accent. "I am not one of the Islamic Jihad," he explained, "I am just helping them out as a 'liaison'." He didn't elaborate on who he was liaising with. But we came to the conclusion that it must be the Iranian government. He brought with him several bags of fruit and was most friendly. His visit, he said, was to have us write a letter to President Reagan, and if we were willing to do that, we could also write one to our families, or to anyone else that we thought might help out. We accepted that bargain, and the four of us put our heads together to decide what we should say. Ultimately it was Terry who had the most input. After all, this was his métier. He sat for a few moments, organized the whole thing in his head, then put it straight down on paper without hesitation.

We decided to write also to the Archbishop of Canterbury, and once again Terry's skills worked. This one was to be confidential to give the church the freedom to take it on if it wished. We had no idea at that time, or at least I didn't, that the Presbyterian Church U.S.A. had already contracted with Lambeth Palace for the services of Terry Waite to help get Ben Weir freed, on the strength of Waite's having "negotiated the release" of British hostages being held in both Libya and Iran.

We set about writing personal letters, each to his own family. The letters were given to a taxi driver, Ali told us, to be delivered to Associated Press. Terry had suggested that that would be the most efficient way of getting them back to the United States in a hurry. They *were* delivered on this occasion, for the next day Ali appeared with one of the Beirut newspapers and told us there was a photo of my wife in the Beirut office of the Associated Press, reading my letter to her— my first indication that Jean was back in Beirut. Ali said, "Steady, Tom. Don't be upset. Do you think you can stand this, to see your wife?" "Of course I can," I assured him. He apparently expected me to break down at the sight of my wife— Ben Weir *had,* in fact, broken down on reading about his family some time before, but I don't think that Ali would have known about that. It was indeed quite an emotional experience to see Jean. I realized that she had done what she had promised many months before—that if I were kidnapped, she would come to Beirut to show solidarity with me. I was proud of her. But what was she *doing* in Beirut, I wondered? The article said nothing about that, he told me, and it was all in Arabic, so I had to rely on his translation; and Ali, we discovered, could lie even *better* than any of the others! I knew that Jean's intention had been to come back to Beirut and apply for a position in the English Department and put her newly won Ph.D. to work. Had she? I'd have given anything for real information!

The "old guard" had now been complemented by a new bunch of young fellows all in their late teens whom we christened "The Junior Jihad." A mental cut or two above the average of the group—more alert, more fluent in English. They, like all new guards, began by showing us lots of attention, and loved to come in and discuss things with us and also to play backgammon or "tric-trac," a Lebanese form of checkers, but more complicated. We all took turns at playing them, and they were surprisingly good. But not good enough for Terry, who as an excellent chess player, had control of the board in all his games with them. They were, thus, always eager to play him in a continuing effort to beat him.

November brought some very heavy periods of shelling, one so bad that we were moved "into a safer room," the one at the other end of the hallway, immediately next door to the bathroom, through the wall from the big one where we were first held. "No touch anything, okay?" we were warned. And we didn't, for about five minutes, till we were fairly sure the coast was clear. Then we went to work—found all kinds of medical supplies, bottles, syringes, papers, etc., and by the window on a crude wire hook was a jacket. Terry immediately began searching the pockets and found three long handwritten letters in French, and I was ordered to translate. The letters were by a Jewish doctor, who seemingly had been kidnapped some time ago and held in a place different from this but later moved here in order to look after one of the French hostages, Michel Seurat, who was very ill. The doctor was lamenting the fact that he had no instruments or any aids with which really to diagnose Michel's illness. "If only I had access to the AUB Hospital and its equipment, I could do so much more." It took hours to translate them. All were long letters, and the French-style handwriting was difficult to read; besides, we were doing it by candlelight, and all the while leery of the guards who might appear any minute and find us reading these letters. The doctor had also commented about some Lebanese doctor, a heart specialist, who was supposed to have come from France to see Michel Seurat and who had given to the media back home some details of his visit and Michel's condition. The writer was able to dismiss this story completely, since he himself had been in constant contact with Michel and knew that the other had never seen him at all. The doctor also claimed to have given all six guards some lessons in cooking, particularly rice, and the technique of adding some linguini to it for variety and added taste. A strong preoccupation of his was his son, who it appeared had been for some time having mental problems (not surprising, given the state of affairs in Lebanon!). At that time, the boy was supposed to be out in the country on the East Side, where the writer was himself longing to join his family.

Next morning back in our own room at the far end of the hall, we found that the guards themselves had occupied it, to get *themselves* out of the line of fire. Their explanation, that the room we had been in was dangerous, had been the usual pack of lies. We reorganized our affairs and settled back into the "danger-ous room," also called the "keyhole room."

These days, with the news full of Terry Waite and his arrival in Beirut to free us, his pronouncements were full of optimism, and our spirits soared at the thought of being home for Christmas. But Christmas Eve arrived, and we were moved, but not home—only from one end of the hall to the other—to the very room where we had read the doctor's letters! To compound our agony, on the radio just before midnight, we heard the shocking news that Terry Waite had already arrived back in England, was giving a press conference at Heathrow, and was talking about how delicate the situation was for the hostages. *We* certainly didn't feel that things were in any way threatening, and didn't feel that there was any danger for us at that point—at least any more than usual. Why was he dra-matizing things so much? Did he know something that we didn't? But in truth our hopes were sadly dashed; we had had such high hopes of something hap-pening, engineered by Waite—we had been following his movements as well as we could on the BBC. And now here he was, back in England, and we were still cooped up in this damn cell, and now no hope of being home for New Year's, let alone Christmas. Father said mass at midnight, and we all prayed our own prayers, but with little expectation of a quick answer.

10 Teachers and Terry Waite

September 30, 1985—I duly arrived at Heathrow Airport from Pennsylvania, Washington, and New York, with Ben Weir, Tom, the hostage families, and our family close in my heart and mind. But there wasn't time to look backward or flail aimlessly—there was a job to do for AUB. Finding a small bed-and-breakfast with a Philippine couple in West Hounslow, I went actively to work in London for the month of October, screening and interviewing some one hundred British and Irish applicants for teaching positions at the AUB-Hariri English Training Program that I would be working for on my return to Beirut in November. Dr. Hallab and Tony Kassab in charge of the program were unsure how many men would apply because of the kidnapping of Brits, Americans, and Frenchmen in Beirut, but they thought they might hope for women who wouldn't feel targeted—"some Irish colleens would be nice." Soon after I arrived in London, however, I was eating in a small pub-restaurant in Piccadilly and on came the news: "Two women kidnapped in Beirut!" "So there it goes!" I thought.

But the screening and interviewing proceeded in England, Scotland, and Ireland, and the applicants were mostly men, many not qualified but hoping, I suppose, that Beirut would be desperate. Although the women in Beirut were released from what appeared to be a personally motivated abduction, bad news kept coming. Graphic in my mind is an image of me in my room at the top of the stairs of my Hounslow "home," hearing from the radio on successive days after October 7: "The *Achille Lauro* cruise ship hijacked in the Mediterranean … . Leon Klinghoffer has been killed … . The hostage William Buckley has been executed … ." Still the interviews continued, and I think my truest asset to AUB as an interviewer was that I exemplified in my person as Tom's wife the reality of Beirut and the region. I told each person who I was and said—"I can't recruit you or ask you to come—I can only tell you the dangers at the same time I tell you about the job that is there. No guarantee of anything—contracts are self-terminating 11-month-only contracts ... ." It was thus made manifestly clear to them as it had been to us two years before: *If you come, you come at your own risk.* But this was the month of October, English as a Second Language people in Britain were looking for jobs, optimism springs eternal, and they, like us, presumably thought, "It may happen to others but it won't happen to me." We thus ended up at the end of October, when Shehadeh Abboud, the program director, came to London to complete the selections, with 14 men and 1 Englishwoman—no Irish colleens. They, as it turned out, were either too savvy or perhaps had "the sight."

Those days in London, I renewed contact with the Foundation for International Conciliation in Windsor, and Jill and Andrew responded so sensitively—they would indeed become close friends, confidants, advisers over the next two years, interpreting and personalizing a process for me that would become my rationale for action in the Middle East and in America. It was through them that my first meeting with Terry Waite took place at Lambeth Palace, for Andrew, in having previously worked at the palace and gone to Libya, knew the archbishop and Terry Waite, and it was he who made the appointment for October 9 and took me to the 4:00 P.M. meeting.

My visit to that most special historic seat of the Archbishop of Canterbury is another of those graphic images to be forever in my memory. We parked and went through the gates, stopping a moment to view the palace. Then we walked up the steps and were ushered into the narrow reception hall where we met Archbishop Runcie as he came down the staircase from above. All was most, most impressive. Then I was taken into a beautiful old room where I saw for the first time Terry Waite, the concerned, genial but serious, bearded giant, the object of our hopes. We sat side by side in high-backed chairs before a great old fireplace; he spoke seriously of hopes and cares and his dedication to the cause of the hostages, and the setback caused by the *Achille Lauro* incident, while I spoke of going to Beirut and being at AUB. Afterward, Andrew took me to see the "Great Hall" at one end of the palace "where Sir Thomas More was tried." I was steeped in Thomas More because my major professor at the University of Colorado was Richard Schoeck, a More scholar. And there I was, all things coalescing for me in that moment, in that room—religion, politics, the state, and one's own life being the price of one's moral conviction at a certain place/time in history.

By November 3 I was back in Beirut and the next day hard at work scheduling 750 students and 56 teachers in the Hariri Program that was just starting up for the semester. Dr. Hallab had worked out the same 11-month contract for me as he had for the other foreign hirees. Without any benefits or assumption of liability, this contract didn't conflict with the Board of Trustees' freeze on regular AUB contracts for Americans. How lucky I was! And how lucky I was to have good friends already at the Hariri English Program on November 7, the day when the caller said the hostages were already killed and bodies dumped. All day my colleagues kept me occupied and away from the radio and then invited me for dinner so that it was 9:00 P.M. when I got home and heard the news: "The police search of the area reported by the caller turned up no corpses." In Fort Collins, Los Angeles, and San Francisco, daughters were not so fortunate and dealt on their own with the news of execution—Ann described it later to me as the most graphic day during the whole six and a half years for her:

> I guess it was at that point that I realized that I'd never considered the fact that Dad might be killed in captivity—that he could die and I'd never see him again and I hadn't said a proper goodbye ... . I just felt like "Oh, man, there was just so much that I wanted to say and now I'll never get a chance"; ... it was sort of a watershed thing .... All summer we'd thought "He'll be out anytime ... ."

Then it was November 8 and the Associated Press was on the phone and wanted me to come there "to get a letter for you from your husband." Excited, I went to their office across from the Commodore Hotel to pick up my second letter from Tom, enclosed in the packet containing the open letter to President Reagan, a letter to Archbishop Runcie, and letters for all the families from their men. I read Tom's letter right away there, with the press snapping photos of me reading:

> My Dearest Jean, Ann, Kit, and Joan—Greetings once again ... . We have no news of any of you, except a brief report that all the families had representatives meet with President Reagan. Were you in on that meeting, Jean? You therefore will know more of the present state of any negotiations that have been conducted or may still be ongoing—but whatever they are, they have not succeeded in releasing us. The conditions of our release so far as we know are still the same as articulated by Ben Weir. But President Reagan seems determined not to negotiate with people he perceives as terrorists. Yet such negotiations have been done frequently by Israel, by El Salvador most recently, and by the U.S. in the TWA hijacking—plus others—Thus, the president has it in his power to have us released quickly—and our captors are eager to bring the whole matter to a successful conclusion.
>
> You will know best what further action might be helpful at your end—in any case you could release pertinent details from this letter to the *Denver Post* or to the A.P. or both—our feeling is that "quiet diplomacy" has not worked in almost 2 years;

William Buckley is reportedly dead; and we four have now been held between 5 and 10 months so far. We wonder how far the patience of our captors will extend. So we have opted for pressing for more publicity for our case—

The whole experience seems like a nightmare—being kept in a locked room 12 by 15 feet, 24 hours a day, one trip of 15 minutes to the bathroom to accomplish everything (but only 2 showers in 4 wks); ... in the last month too, the diet has become much more unbalanced .... The boredom at times has been overwhelming but the four of us are trying to hang on—with God's help we may make it. Father Jenco says mass for us every day, plus evening "vespers"—takes most of 1 1/2 to 2 hours per day! But we do pray hard for a miracle and a quick release so that we can beat any health catastrophes which would surely be fatal under these circumstances now—

To some personal points .... 1. Joan's brakes were adjusted to the maximum in June—by now she will have had them done? .... 2. What is Kit doing these days? 3. What are you doing? Where are you all living??! 4. May be too late but some antifreeze in dishwasher at cabin would save pump .... 5. Have you made any decision about our Beirut possessions? ...

—Your loving father and husband, Tom

This time, for the first time, I "went public" as the hostage family vernacular put it. As I said in my next letter home:

NOV. 12—It was "the time" to go on TV to let them know I was here and let you all know the news! Hope you saw me and I did all right. We're back to September now and will see what can happen with Terry Waite. The letter from Tom was 7 pages and full of detail and questions—I felt his outlook was strong and the tone of the letter altogether more like natural Tom .... What a blessing to get the letter—but we're in for a long tough one even so ....

NOV. 14—Things are moving at last here with Terry Waite in Beirut and talking at long last. How wonderful it was that I had the chance to meet him in London that day—he knows all about me, what I'm doing etc. ... I even had written him the day before I left London and gave him my phone number so I may have information from him on top of Tom getting news of us and the fact that I'm in Beirut if he sees them all along with the captors. NBC and BBC have been great about keeping in touch with me and giving me the news personally—I did an interview yesterday again on campus about Waite's visit just before they left to meet him at the airport—I didn't feel terrific about how I did because I wasn't sure how to answer the questions. For instance, "What has this thing done to you?" I haven't even thought about it, much less try to make a meaningful statement .... I could have made the snappy comeback they like with a real answer like "I don't know—I haven't thought about it—my mind's on Tom, not myself ... ." Oh, well, the important thing was the publicity here at this time: showing America and the families there that someone is here working for them, and showing Shiite kidnappers that the hostage families are still to the fore pressing for action. It all comes into a day's work somehow—I got the call from Keith Graves from BBC at 1:00 to meet him at the gate to set up and do a short interview—did it and met Sharif at 1:45 to go to look at a flat for Hariri teachers at 2:00 when Graves was out meeting Terry Waite with a thousand other journalists (Maggie Fox heard him transferring a note from Mrs. Sutherland to Terry Waite)—then back to continue scheduling the rest of 750 students and 56 teachers into a workable arrangement of classes and deal with ashtrays for students on the second floor and mailboxes without names on them—then home for a quick supper and an evening of scheduling, punctuated with a visit from John Munro of the English Department who had a horrendous story of kidnapping of his own which involved a gun to the neck at 2 in the afternoon ending happily when a stone leaped up and broke the crankcase and leaked the oil, stopping the car and dispersing the kidnappers (I told him I knew why Middle Easterners believed in Allah!) and asking for an interview for the *Middle East Times* ... . The feeling here is positive—with great reservation—all think the show's on the road for Tom and the others and we're putting all the power of positive thinking into it ... . I must say I'm glad I'm here.

I was fortunate in reaching Terry Waite by phone at the Commodore Hotel where he was making headlines by getting caught in the street war (the Forbidden Impossible War—Forbidden because it was between allies and Impossible because that's what it was that anyone should or could win it!) and getting his concern for us all but nothing of substance about what he was doing (it was his trademark with us hostage wives). I had gotten caught at the Hariri Building with a few other teachers when the "war" started and knew for half an hour what Tom was going through. A gun-toting militiaman ushered us into a downstairs office while his colleagues in arms "swept" the building, making us all sit on the floor next to the walls while he sat on a desk brandishing his Kalashnikov and making angry and threatening gestures and shouting in Arabic. He then "gave us a lesson" by interrogating and kicking a Lebanese employee. When his fellows assured him we were all that were in the building, he, with great "alarums and excursions" of stopping at corners and swinging his rifle around (had to be learned from Sly Stallone in *Rambo*), conducted us finally out of the building in completely new and relaxed style, bantering and laughing with Clive Winbow, a British teacher, I suppose to have us think well of them in the end. Afterward, I walked home across campus, past an art student sitting in front of Marquand House engrossed in capturing a most peaceful garden and sea scene, which couldn't be further from the scene I'd just left—"No question about it, it's all relative," I thought. Our family must have seen Terry Waite in the news as he was caught in the cross fire a few blocks away—I didn't worry them, however, with my very minor "captivity" when I wrote:

It's been a very long weekend with the eruption of militia fighting on Thursday in the early afternoon and great shelling and gun battles about which you will have heard on the news but which had largely died down by Friday evening. People had not expected this one which is the reason for so many casualties; ... even with cease-fire no one believed in it and rightly so for fighting kept breaking out in various places—even now people are only gingerly out getting food and assessing the situation. Fortunately, Terry Waite was able to get out on Sunday and make his trip to the States ... and we're still hanging on and waiting for Waite to do whatever it is he is doing to generate his optimism. The journalists here in their inimitable way have dubbed it "Waite-watching." The campus did not receive any shells or bullets apart from a few on the buildings on the Bliss Street periphery—we even had an early Thanksgiving dinner at an English faculty member's apartment on Friday held on the razor's edge between two large plate glass windows with the noise of battle surrounding. Right now we have signs of peace to come outside with a soccer game commencing on the Green Field, the sun out after the rain with a rainbow out of God's heaven having just left (however, not knowing the extent of the promise of a covenant of God by the evidence in hand we are hoping only for a militia covenant, the one that never seems to get signed). AUB hasn't started up again since last Thursday, having had a Friday off for Independence Day and a Monday for The Prophet's Birthday and now a Tuesday and a Wednesday for Distrust of Cease-Fire Days. Thursday we will be in full swing again but people will still be looking over their shoulders. And I'm still sick in the pit of my stomach over Malta [the Egyptian airliner hijacking with 60 killed when commandos stormed the plane] and the Weirs' tragedy with their daughter Ann's death in Egypt [Ann Weir and a friend were in the back seat of a bus going from Alexandria to Cairo when it was hit by a train; she had just said goodbye to her parents] and can only hope that good news can come for us out of this time of such terrible news for so many others.

Perhaps also tomorrow the teachers talked to in October in Britain will appear in Lebanon to start teaching in our program and they'll need accommodations and help to get oriented which will give me another big job to do ... . The whole job of the program is enormous but tremendously rewarding with a big new building with 40 classrooms and such nice staff and students all trying hard to make things work well. I had just put up notices on Thursday about putting trash in the wastebaskets to "Help us keep classrooms and halls clear" when the militia war between Amal and PSP broke out ... .

About 14 Americans here at AUB and the staff in toto spread so thin that it's wonderful. And AUB keeps going which is also wonderful. Appearance is reality and that should keep us going if we're lucky until better days if they come. People here don't believe, however, in the sects coming together at all and Syria seems not to want to get involved to the extent of taking military control which would seem to be called for, so on it goes. And on Tom and I go, waiting. Terry Waite told me Friday things were "fine" and we have to hold with that ... .

Thursday, Thanksgiving Day—School opened again with half the students and teachers there—much disorganization and shuffling of classes and workmen still painting in the halls and rumors of a strike tomorrow evidently called by someone sitting in a cafe in Paris and negated by the Mufti here, which means a hard day tomorrow with us trying to hold classes for some students while others are trying to break up the classes probably with a bit of intimidation of students and teachers; ... and then our week is over. Today a tank and militiamen had formed a checkpoint at the corner across from the AUB Medical Gate opposite us—this was the peacekeeping force made up of Druze, Amal, and Syrian Party people all with white carnations in their gun barrels. Still a lot of tension though. I said to one of the teachers, "We're being peacekept—look at the flowers in the guns," and he said, "Yes, I've seen the flowers many times—they're 'death-dealing flowers'!" All quiet, however. Terry Waite was to be here today?? I've had no direct word since Monday and try not to wait hanging over the telephone which doesn't ring with good news ... . Always wishing there were something active I could do—wish I could be in Waite's pocket! And snatch Tom away! People do give me cheer and optimism out of their heavy lives here and I realize that at least I'm a reminding presence. My Ghanaian maid Joana has just come in and told me that she had her coffee grounds read last evening and "the tall man is to come soon by the road and I'll see him," and I told her that Tom isn't tall but she said "he's tall to me" and so he is and to us too! ...

A student came to me today and showed me his I-20 for Texas with all his friends around and it was wild and wonderful to discuss U.S. geography with them— "Isn't it near Florida?" ... Someone parlayed a rumor to me about Hariri students getting into trouble at Boston University for trying to buy term papers—I told him it couldn't possibly be true that they'd gotten culturally oriented so fast! ... [The irony might have been lost, but, in all truth, the cultural semantic difference between "cheating" and "getting an education" was another of those we dealt with as on another plane and in another context, the difference between "terrorists" and "freedom fighters." AUB fought with all it had to keep its American standards of "do your own work," etc., etc. against the force of the culturally acceptable Middle Eastern imperative to use *wasta* (influence) or the ability of another to get admission or grades. In the times of anarchy and militia rule to come, that the *wasta* at times took the form of out-and-out threat was a further challenge. We were extremely lucky that in our English program it was not a matter of grades but of quite manifest performance—we had only to make sure that the writing and the test-taking were individually correct, a universal problem.]

In the midst of everything I was very concerned about Tom's "papers"—his Lebanese residency and work permit needed renewal and somehow it just seemed terribly important that these be in order for him. So I applied through Hanna Haddad in the personnel office who handled all such matters for AUB and in due course they came. It would be the last time. The next time I applied, in January of 1987, Hanna came back from the Sûreté saying, "There's a problem. Come with me next week and apply in person and see if we can get them." What an episode that was! Just past the museum and over the Green Line in East Beirut was the Sûreté, the interior presenting a truly Dickensian scene—harsh, gray, cold, cubicled, and peopled by drab clerks and arrogant, officious bureaucrats. We waited for two hours in the middle of everything with people coming and going past us for "our man," a tall, thin, cadaverous person with, of all things, a long scarf wound round his neck and sitting in an office behind a metal desk. Our determined time finally came, he talked with Hanna, hemmed and hawed to give me time to come forward with the *baksheesh* I was determined not to pay, and then "La!" ("No!"). Throwing my application for Tom contemptuously into the top left-hand drawer, he clanged that drawer shut with finality and dismissed us. Never will I forget the clanging of that drawer—so graphic in its denial and symbolic "imprisonment" of Tom. If Tom's body was in a cell in West Beirut with Shiite fundamentalists, his spirit and his mission and his work were just as much in a metal "cell" in East Beirut with the Christians. Hanna told me afterward that the reason for denial was given as "We have no proof that he's in Lebanon." Thus from that day in 1987 on, Tom was "A Man without a Country." Angry at the time, I was glad later when the Lebanese government could not claim income tax from Tom's AUB salary. They lost tens of thousands—served them right.

Terry Waite duly arrived back in Beirut early in December to carry on pre-Christmas negotiations. With highest hope of its getting delivered, I wrote a letter to Tom and enclosed it with a note:

> Terry—I hope Husni is able to deliver this—I wanted there to be a letter for Tom available in case there is any possibility of delivery to him. Maybe it's not in accord with "the issue at hand" and if not, dispose of as you will. Tom said in his last letter delivered out that they were going to try to get the captors' agreement to allowing an intermediary such as a wife in Beirut to coordinate getting news into them. If there is any possible way I could do this, I'm ready and so willing. The moral support both ways during this time would be tremendous. I am trying not to bother you during your days of devoted effort for us, but if there is any way I could see you for any few minutes of time I'd go anywhere anytime—residence, airport, wher-

ever. And if there is anything in the world I or hostage families can do for this cause please let us know and use us. Always with thanks ... .

As it happened, although he was hardly able to achieve anything else, Terry was able to get letters delivered that trip and no matter how things ultimately turned out, he has a place in my heart for delivering that letter along with notes he was carrying from our daughters. For these were the only personal letters that would ever reach Tom from us during all of the six and a half years. He received them on Valentine's Day of 1986.

Intimations of problems for Terry and the "negotiation" process were not long in coming that December. The journalists of course were being very active during this time, coming to me when "Big Events" occurred or news came out on the wire about the hostages or about Terry Waite. Reporters by definition as well as by profession, they liked to catch me unprepared and get a "true reaction"—so it was one morning when a journalist cornered me in the school hall: "I have bad news for you." I found a chair in a nearby classroom and sat down. "Terry Waite's been denied a visa into Kuwait; how do you feel about that?" "I don't know, I don't know" was all I could say blankly, trying to juggle our differing definitions of "bad news." Tom was still alive! Although I didn't see the resulting story, I was presumably reported to be in shock over the fact that Terry Waite was denied a visa to Kuwait. As it turned out, it *was* bad news for Terry in spelling the end of his positive interaction with Islamic Jihad and the process to resolve the hostage situation. As he confirms in his memoir *Taken on Trust*, Islamic Jihad called and threatened him, telling him he had 48 hours to leave Lebanon; if not he'd be killed. He did leave and would not return to West Beirut until January 1987.

Since none of this story did I know until I read his book years later, what wonderful hopes I had for that Christmas of 1985! Somehow Terry Waite personified that hope—it would be a Christmas gift beyond all Christmas gifts! Christmas Eve I sat glued to the radio on the kitchen table. It came. "Terry Waite has returned home—there will be no release of hostages." That was all. Not even the vital information that his role was finished. Nevertheless, Christmas. A quiet day by myself in our AUB home with felt love from friends nearby, and somehow spirit and hope strengthened with a closeness to Tom. I wrote a note to him:

At Christmas with Love and Hope ... Dearest Tom, ... I am sitting at the kitchen table this Christmas morning, writing in hopes this message can reach you and bring my love and Christmas wishes to you. You will know how much your two letters have meant to us, and I can just pray that you have received at least some that we have written to know that Ann, Kit, Joan, and I are well and keeping strong for you. Joan called early morning to say that Dad had had his hip operation and was starting to walk again and that Ann and her Ray were planning to go to Fort Collins for the week after Christmas to be with Kit and go to the cabin (where I didn't forget the antifreeze for the Volvo) … . Joan has only Christmas Day off from her airlines job (you were right, she spends her day at the end of an 800 line and had handled two hundred calls that day). All of them along with me were wishing so hard for plans to get to change and we to have an all together time but the plans will carry us through to that time to come. They all send their love and thoughts to you. So does Fort Collins where the Larimer County Chorale sang a Robert Burns medley for you and have the yellow ribbons out (they even changed Fort Collins law so that institutions such as Home Federal could display them). The faculty and students here too had gatherings including me and expressing their care and concern and the students will put their greetings to you into the newspaper in hopes you see it. I trimmed the Christmas tree and the lights shine out the window over the Green Field and put up the Crèche and lighted candles last evening which I'll keep lighted until Twelfth Night for your coming. Christmas Eve I spent quietly at home focusing on us and Peter called to send all their love and greetings from Scotland and some friends dropped by to do the same. I may go for an hour to Heinekens today for dinner and then be home before going to use the president's line to call the family. If only the line could go to you. But know there is a continual line, mental and spiritual if it cannot be physical, and it cannot falter. It will be a good New Year for us when we are together.

People were wonderful that Christmas season and touched my heart. Tom's agriculture students did publish their letter to him in the leftist newspaper *As-Safir* just before New Year's:

On the occasion of the glorified holidays, and just before leaving to spend the winter vacation with our families and friends, we send you this message to express our deep feelings toward your person and to say we miss in you the father and teacher who has been detained and forced to be absent for seven months.

We want to reassure you that our main wish, faculty, students, and staff of the Faculty of Agricultural and Food Sciences, is to have you safely back among us and to see you resume the mission which you have devoted yourself to serve, the mission of science and knowledge, so that our life will be enlightened and our spirits enriched, and we carry the torch along the road to the future.

11 From Penthouse to the Marseillaise

January 1986. We now faced a long period of waiting. We walked, we talked, we argued, we read. Anything to pass the time. Terry took to making crossword puzzles, and I tried to solve them. My conclusion: He was making them far too difficult. He disagreed. They are not nearly as complex or as abstruse as the *London Times,* he claimed. "So?" I countered. "Aren't those the toughest in the whole world?" "No," he came back, "lots are tougher than those." "I'm glad I'm not doing those, for heaven's sakes!" Terry smiled and went about making up another.

Our mattresses were still getting wet every night, and we got a couple of electric heaters to help dry them out; we stacked them up on edge and let the heaters blare on them, both of them plugged into one extension cord. In a few minutes we had firsthand evidence of why there are electrical codes—the cord melted before our very eyes! We got a stern lecture from Mahmoud, who was something of an amateur electrician, he thought. But he did bring us another cord, and ordered us, as if we hadn't learned it already, to use only one heater at a time. Slowly, each day, the mattresses dried.

In this place, the bathroom window was not sealed, and at first some of us (guess who?) were given to peeking outside. The hamsters cottoned on and no longer allowed us to close the door. Instead, they put up a curtain to cover the bottom half of the door—Terry had complained bitterly about the lack of privacy, hence the curtain—and a guard was posted every day, sitting on a chair with a gun resting on his lap, to watch that we didn't go near the window. But over the top of the curtain, we could see down the hall a little, if we were careful not to let the guard see us; *that* invariably led to a furious outburst.

Father was the first to notice that the door to our old room at the far end of the hall—the one from which we had peeked at the guards through the keyhole—was now closed every day. Must be someone in that room, we decided, and we were right. While the rest of the Frenchmen, Jean-Paul Kauffmann, Marcel Carton, and Marcel Fontaine, were in our other old room, the big one into which we had arrived some two months ago, Michel Seurat had been moved into the "keyhole room." In fact, we could also hear him trudging down the hall, scuff, scuff, scuff, after everyone had been to the toilet. His footsteps became weaker and weaker, and sometime after Christmas, they ceased. Jean-Paul Kauffmann was fairly sure that Michel had actually succumbed at that time, though his death was not announced until March. The photo they sent out in March had no doubt been taken at the time of his demise, but not used until it suited their purpose later. He was shown in a crude wooden coffin, with the bullet hole clearly visible. The accompanying message was a threat to the French government that they would kill all of the French hostages if the French did not give in to all the demands of the Islamic Jihad. The truth about Islamic Jihad was that they wanted to *appear* totally ruthless even when they had not been, but make no mistake, they *could* be when they wished. For example, why did they not let Michel go free when they realized that his illness was terminal? The Jewish doctor had evidently told them that it was most probably cancer of the pancreas. And his family was appealing for his release. But they kept him in there, and allowed him to die in ignominy, with no one by his side, not even Kauffmann and Carton. These two told me later that it was when he got really ill that he was moved into the "keyhole room" by himself.

On February 14, Ali came in bearing letters from our families. One for David, a long one, with all kinds of news of his children. His sister had also baked a cake and they were saving some until he came home. Another long one for Father, from his family. A short one from Peggy for Terry, which began: "I gave you all the news in the last letter, so I won't repeat it." And of course Terry had never received the previous one. Was he pissed! "There are none for Tom," said Ali smugly, "for he is a bad man." What a bummer. But my friends stood by me, and they refused to take theirs unless he brought one for me. That was a long argument, and Ali didn't at all like this organized rebellion. He fussed and fumed, but the other three wouldn't budge. That was a real risk, for he could easily have taken away all the letters, and *no one* would have had news. Finally, however, he gave in, went outside, and returned with one short page from Jean, plus two brief telegrams from the girls saying they loved me. Well, I sort of knew *that*, and thought it would have been nice to have some *news!* The letter from Jean did have some news, but was written in her dashing hand, so that there wasn't nearly as much news on the sheet as I wanted. Of course ten legal sheets would still not have held all I wanted to know right then. But that letter and the telegrams were precious, to say the least. Ali took them all back soon after, and we had nothing but the memories of them. This little episode showed me very clearly the American way—of sticking together with your buddies in the time of crisis. All our squabbling was forgotten in that incident.

A cold day it was in late February and each of us thinking his own thoughts. Ali came in with a proposition for me. "I have these two documents, but I can't read them very well. If you will rewrite them for us, we will give you more letters, and also something very nice for you." "What documents, Ali?" I asked him. "These two," says he, and handed me two sheafs of paper, about 20 pages apiece. I perused them, and suddenly realized from their nature in even the first page of each that they were the "confessions" of William Buckley. Chills went down my spine. Here we go again with the CIA bit, I thought. And the handwriting was frankly much better than mine—my dad used to describe my hand as "like a chicken scratching in the dirt." I protested—"My writing is much worse than what you have on the page, Ali." "Let me see your writing," he asked. So I gave him a demonstration of my cursive and my printing, both of which he wanted to look at. "Oh," he lied, "I can read yours much better than this one. And we will do something very nice for you, remember." "Like what?" I asked him. "You will see." I was very skeptical, and still hesitated. "You know that we can *make* you do it, don't you?" he menaced. After a few seconds' reflection, I felt that the safest course of action was to agree to do it. I did, and he took me down to the "keyhole room." It was *really cold* in there, for the window was no longer covered, and the guards lolling around in there were all pretty well clothed (I peeked!).

Ali first warned me that I was on no account to discuss this request with my friends in the cell, on pain of very severe punishment, gave me paper, and left me to it. After a couple of hours, I was more apprehensive than ever about this project. Why on earth was he having me transcribe the confessions of William Buckley? The more I wrote, the more it was obvious that it was written by none other than Buckley. Though his name was nowhere on the papers, he was describing his role as the embassy station chief of the CIA, no holds barred; his daily duties in reading all the telegrams, telexes, and mail, followed by a briefing of the ambassador; how he had taken the chief of Lebanese Intelligence to Langley for some intensive training; his interactions with the secretaries and attachés at the embassy (military, commerce, agriculture, etc.); and on and on. Despite Ali's threat about talking with my colleagues, I felt that I just had to get some counsel from them. This whole bit might be getting me in a pile of trouble. Maybe, I thought, they will use all of this stuff, and say it is all mine, and that therefore I really was CIA. At the end of two hours, I suddenly began tearing up all the half dozen sheets that I had written, to the horror of the guards. "Why you do this?" they demanded angrily. I lied. "I have made many mistakes; I am not used to writing, and I am cold; my hands are very cold," which *last* was the truth. They hustled me back to my room.

Once there, I couldn't wait to tell the guys about my task, and all about Buckley's confessions. They were fascinated, especially Terry, who grilled me about all that was in them. I recounted as much as I could from having read through all of it rather quickly. "So what do you think it all means?" I asked. "Well, Tom," ventured Terry, "I can think of many reasons for them to have asked you, and *none of them are very good for you.*" We debated several strategies, mainly to prevent them from ever being able to pin the document on me, and settled on writing at the top of every page "Transcribed from the original by T. M. Sutherland," and subsequently, I added into the text every half page or so "Original text not legible, but I think it said the following."

The second "document" was a description of the general workings of the embassy, the names of all the personnel, their addresses as far as he, Buckley, had been able to remember them. Nothing of what I read in either document could ever have been labeled "highly confidential," and indeed I marveled at how well Buckley had been able to say so much (nearly 50 legal-size sheets, closely written) and yet give away so little of any consequence.

With cold hands, and an unwilling spirit, it took me several days to get through the two documents, and each day after my return from the "keyhole room," we all discussed what Buckley had written, and agreed that he had done a great job. I waited for the consequences of the whole affair, but none ever came; neither, incidentally did my "special favor," nor did I ever get any more letters from my family. Neither Terry nor I could ever arrive at a decent conclusion as to why they had wanted me to undertake the job at all.

In March, one of the Junior Jihad came in and sat himself down on my mattress in front of me. With my blindfold on, I couldn't tell which one this was, though I had seen all of them many times through the keyhole. "Tom," he said, "I know your wife." I was completely astonished. "You do?" I exclaimed. "How do you know my wife?" "I am in her class," he replied, quite calmly. I thought quickly. "Then will you take a message to her?" "Oh no, I am sorry. I have not the order." "Then please bring a message from her to me," I pleaded. "I am sorry, I have not the order," he repeated. Then the full realization of what he had said began to sink in for him as well as for me and he suddenly became distraught, stammered a little, and left quickly. Neither he nor I ever mentioned the episode again. But he must have had anxious moments afterward visualizing his identifying himself to Jean and she putting the finger on him, the subsequent tracing of all his buddies, and the giving away of the whole game for Islamic Jihad, that midnight, secret, shadowy organization. They were all scared spitless of the CIA, and one of the new Junior guys, Ahab (whom we had christened "Ayhab the Ayrab," and with whom we were to have much more contact in the years to come), told me that the CIA had $50,000 on each of their heads. "Fifty thousand dollars," I exclaimed. "The CIA wouldn't give fifty cents for any one of you guys!" "Oh yes," he protested, somewhat insulted. "They would. We know everything. CIA very bad men."

During this period, Ali became a frequent visitor, and for the first few times brought more bags of fruit. Then these tapered off, but we didn't care too much because he did seem to have power, and we had visions of all going home soon. By April, he alerted us to the possibility of going home any day. We were measured up for clothes by Fadl, who a couple of days later brought us in some really cheap pants and shirts. The legs were much too long for any of us, but seamster Terry got some thread and a needle from Fadl and set about fitting them to each of us. We were ecstatic. I went over to the wall and began tapping out the rhythm of "La Marseillaise," and in no time the Frenchmen on the other side, in the big bedroom, were responding and tapping along with me. They were in a similar euphoria. From then on, that apartment became known as the "Marseillaise Apartment."

For some days we kept at the ready. No release. Then in came Ali on April 14 with the news of the American raid on Libya, which he felt had been such an insult to the Arab world that it had probably knocked our release on the head. Renewed agony, anger, despair. Every time anything promising came along, something intervened to kibosh it. The new clothes lay around unused. And eventually we moved from that place wearing them, but not to go home.

In early June, the temperature was getting really hot, and the discomfort level was mounting. The Islamic Jihad solution? Huge steel gates installed on the outside of our door, and also of the Frenchmen's door, so that the doors could be left open day and night in complete security. Those gates would easily have contained elephants. In a few days, we were moved again, this time back into the original big room, in an exchange with the French hostages, who were now only three and we still four in a much smaller room. First though, we had to paint the walls with a really cheap paint. What a lark that was! Without a doubt, the most frustrating job of painting I have ever done! Four blindfolded hostages taking turns at climbing up on a high stepladder, for the walls in that place were the typical Lebanese ten-foot-high jobs, big buckets of watery paint, and drips everywhere. The guards of course could not come near the ladder, for the guy up there would have been able to peek at them from under his blindfold. What a mess, but we did get it done, got the paint washed off our hands, and subsequently moved our things into the new room—back where we started, in the Big Room. Definitely more space in there, and a bit cooler for the four of us.

In a few days, the books began to multiply, good ones, and our conditions improved. They even brought us a small table and four folding chairs—we were able to sit down and eat like civilized human beings for the first time in over a year. Nice—to be able to sit in a chair with our feet on the ground instead of sitting on our mattresses with our knees up in the air. But haircuts were scarce as hen's teeth. To get rid of some of my surplus hair, which only took added time to wash on shower days, I took to chopping away at mine with the nail clippers, which occasioned the remark from Father, "You look like the rats have been chewing on you, Tom!" We had no mirror, so I couldn't check the accuracy of his assessment! But it did help in the heat of summer.

Months earlier, in the airport apartment, Terry had given us hours of card games by cutting up with the nail clippers the cardboard from the box of Kleenex and marking them. These were small and hard to shuffle but then we weren't short of time! The guards, however, said "gambling bad" and kept taking away the makeshift cards. This, of course, set Terry to work again.

Terry now made a new deck of cards, and thus followed some really serious games of Hearts. I had never played that game, but the other three were pros, all of them. I soon caught on, being an academic after all, and entered into the spirit of the game. David had learned it while working in the parts department of an aircraft maintenance shed in Los Angeles, on the night shift, when there were few calls on the parts people. Father had learned the game as all priests do, apparently, with no wives to bother them. Father accused Terry of laying "Dirty Gerty," the queen of spades, on him unfairly. But when Terry kept count, it was just the reverse. It passed lots of time, but we had to be very much on the alert in case the guards discovered that we had cards again.

Early one afternoon, Abu Ali and Mahmoud brought us "sheeps feet soup," *complete with the feet!* Sheep are routinely slaughtered on the sidewalks, and one can pick up all kinds of parts for a song, or nothing at all. I wondered if they were serious, for it looked awful to me—and to David, so we both refused it. But both Terry and Father were game to try it and supped up a fair quantity, admittedly with their noses a bit screwed up. And through the afternoon neither one felt very well at all. But the pièce de résistance was yet to come. Abu Ali returned in the evening with the sheep's *head,* nicely boiled and served up on a plate, which he placed in front of Father for dinner and retreated. Father lifted his blindfold to discover a pair of sheep's eyes staring up at him out of the head, and *never* will I forget the look of horror on his face! Abu Ali returned to encourage him to try it, but Father was looking more and more sick by the moment—evidently there are *some* things that even a Catholic priest can't stomach! We teased Father for a long time about his refusing a sacrificial offering.

June 23, my 30th wedding anniversary, not at all a routine day. Sayeed and the Hajj arrived with a camera crew. We were instructed to write scripts for making a TV tape to send to President Reagan, and if we did well we might be allowed to send one to our families. They left us with plenty of paper and a pen, and we caucused on this request. We were convinced that they were trying to use us. But at the same time, we would be getting a message out to our families, who would see how we were getting along. We were reluctant, however, to give them too much publicity, and decided to keep our scripts very low-key. We traded our drafts, all except David, who apparently did not want anyone reading what he had just written. "I'm not finished yet, fellows." The recording began. First Terry, then Father, then me. "Greetings Jean and family ... I'm recording this on our wedding anniversary"—sudden interruption from Sayeed behind, "You shall have *kak* (cake) tonight!" Thrown completely off, I wheeled to stare at him. Dire consequences. Gone was my concentration, all further video opportunities, and anniversary cake to boot. The final presenter was David. To our amazement, David was waxing eloquent to President Reagan and the American people: "Will we be like General Custer, Mr. President? Will aid come to us too late also?" On and on he went, doing exactly what we had all four agreed *not* to do! We were shocked and dismayed. But evidently the Jihaders loved it, for henceforth until his release, they used David for all their taped messages to the United States.

July 25 arrived, and so did Ali. "You are all going far away. Maybe three, four hours. Do you know where it might be?" "The Bekaa," we all ventured. "No, further, much further." "How about Syria?" "No." "How about Iran?" "No. But you must all go down to a van, which is waiting for you downstairs, and go very quickly. We don't want anyone to recognize you." Seemed mighty strange to me. It was only about 5:00 in the afternoon, and the sun was high in the sky. These guys never moved anybody at this time of the day. "Line up, please. David, you go first; then Tom, then Terry, then Father." I knew exactly where the elevator was, so I made for there blindfolded. But the guard who was leading me forced me to go past it. "Don't you want to use the elevator?" I asked. "No speak, okay?" came the terse reply. I was hustled straight into the "keyhole room" at the end of the hall. The steel sheets were all removed from the window, and the daylight was blinding, even through my blindfold. I was told to sit down on the floor facing the wall. The air was fresh, not stinking like our room.

Someone came and sat right by me. Terry—by this time I knew his breathing and noises by heart. We weren't allowed to speak. There was an intensity in the air—I could feel it. Mustn't make one false move, or we are in for it.

An hour or more passed, and we still weren't going down to the waiting van. Two hours, three hours; couldn't be sure, but it seemed like an eternity. Then great commotion. Something was being brought in and set up. Lots of whispering and scurrying around. Suddenly David's voice broke out loud and clear, telling everyone that Father had just been released. He went on with a long message to President Reagan and to the American people, including his Custer's last stand line and condolences to Mrs. Buckley. Why was he saying that? In any case, it was clearly a videotape to be sent home with Father.

What a deception. Father had been the last in line and had never left the room until David had his script written and the tape made. Then Father was taken out to go home carrying the tape. By this time it was long ago dark, almost 11:00, and Terry and I were famished. Supper was brought in and finally, around midnight, we were back in the room we had left some seven hours earlier.

Number two gone. Our only remaining and direct pipeline to God. Only sinners left now to tough it out! This was like a bereavement to us, for Father had truly been a pillar of strength, even for David, who was steeped in his own southern California Chuck Swindoll brand of Protestantism and had no real love for Catholics. David had been all these months practically driving Terry up the wall with his righteous protestations: "I have made my peace with my God. I feel very comfortable in my relationship to Him. I *know* that *I* am going to heaven. And I feel sorry for you who are still searching and lost." "But David," Terry would reply, "isn't that what life is all about, a constant lifelong struggle to *find* your God and finally to arrive at the end of your life into a relationship with Him?" "No," said David, "I have already made my peace with Him." And so it would go on. Neither one willing to give in, and no argument so far as I recall ever ended amicably with a handshake and an agreement to "hang it up until we get out of here." Most ended up with Terry winning and David completely frustrated, and exploding, "Well, *fuck* you anyway, Terry!" "Okay," Terry would shrug, and that would end the "session," but the atmosphere was charged and hostile.

So Father went home and David's tape was duly shown to the world. It was evidently played on Lebanese television and taped by the Islamic Jihad, for Sayeed brought in a copy to show us. We watched in horror at the part where David expressed his condolences to *Mrs.* Buckley because NBC had added the three words: "Secret coded message?" *There was no Mrs. Buckley*—he had not ever been married. But David had not known that, and his remark was made in all innocence. We wondered if Islamic Jihad would react to this. They didn't, at least not right away. But five days later, Friday night, in came friend Ali and the Hajj. The interrogation started out mildly enough, but soon David and I were led outside; I was first into the "keyhole room" and seated right against the wall, facing it. "When did you first learn about Mrs. Buckley?" I racked my memory. "I think it was Father who had first brought her to our attention some months ago, but I am not sure." They didn't like that kind of hedging—shades of the article on Islam. "You are university professor, right? So how you not remember?" I tried to be modest. "I forget many things, you know, and especially now, my head is not good." So now I was making excuses, and they didn't like that either. "Maybe we saw an article about her in *Time* magazine some months ago?" I ventured. "You are lying!" Here we go again. Kizzab! ... The questions got more vicious, their anger was mounting. The questions were all being posed by Ali, but there were several other men in the circle behind me, and whispering instructions and questions to Ali. Frankly, I didn't see why *I* was being involved at all. I had had nothing to do with the tape in any way. Finally, I was let go outside. Two of the guards rather brutally stuck rubber earplugs into my ears, and I was made to stand just outside of the room while David was interrogated.

He too was getting the third degree about Mrs. Buckley. Now you are onto the right guy, I thought. Find out from him. I could hear everything despite the earplugs, and although I don't remember now his answers, I do recall that he whined a lot. I felt a little sorry for David, though, for they were really giving him a going over. But it was his own fault, if anyone's. Next they moved into our room, and started giving Terry the treatment. He was much more self-assured than David, but he was really getting it. I was made to stand just outside the door, with my hands raised up high over my head and leaning against the wall. Must have been there over half an hour before we got back to the relative security of "our cell." But things just got worse in a hurry. "Friend" Ali came in with the Hajj, and under the Hajj's instructions proceeded to give us the biggest dressing down yet. "You are all spies," he shouted. "You are liars. Why you lie? We are going to make you pay. You are American pigs. You're all CIA!" His voice was getting louder and louder, and the hatred in it more violent. Is this the same fellow who came in with, "Hi guys!"? Now an entirely different side of old Ali. After ten minutes of the tirade, they left. We tried to make sense out of their anger. Why on earth would they think (or NBC either, for that matter) that we would want to send out a "secret coded message" when Father was going home, and could tell anyone everything about our conditions? It all seemed so irrational. But then these were irrational creatures—just don't use our logic. We went to bed.

Next morning, in came Fadl and proceeded to take out every single book. In this room, we had read lots of books over the months, many of them still there. No longer! Everything went. We were to be punished for sure. But that was by no means the end of it yet.

12 Books, Brits, and an Anniversary

January 1986, Beirut. "Twice-warmed" I was with the clipping the AUB students brought me of their New Year's message for Tom and with the subsequent news that came from Colorado. As I wrote Dad and Alice:

> Kit called night before last with the story of a most moving tribute to Tom each night opening the National Western Stock Show in Denver that draws hundreds of thousands from all over the States and world—Kit was there one night and she described how the master of ceremonies opened the rodeo by leading a saddled but riderless palomino into the ring and spotlighted gave a 5-minute tribute to Tom and his work for agriculture and the livestock industry, calling for a moment of remembrance and a plea for freedom. I was just thrilled—and you know how Tom will feel—I've tried to send a message ....

Those who organized the ceremony were Chuck Sylvester and Mike Cervi, two former students of Tom's at CSU, and I thought how blessed Tom was in all his wonderful students there, here, and across the world.

Having no indication or knowledge that Terry Waite had been put out of the picture by order of the captors, we continued to take him "on trust." I sent him more letters to Tom just in case he had the chance to get them in, and all that next year we would think that he was truly involved in a continuing mission. He seemed to keep the idea going with significant others also, since letters from the Reverend Wilson of the Presbyterian Church, later that year, included mention of him:

> JUNE 3—Terry is one of the authentic saints of our generation. He not only is built on heroic proportions but his grace and guts in pursuit of this thankless, incredibly complex task defies understanding. He owes us nothing. The hostages aren't even

Anglicans much less Britons! ... We had expected him to be with us this week for a few days of intensive dialogue with Ben and Carol and a few others; ... the meeting is postponed because he is able in these days to engage in some direct dialogue relevant to all of us and that is clearly the first priority ... .

Because I felt that we as a family had a personal responsibility for Terry's travels on our behalf, I sent a check just after New Year's for $2,000 to the Archbishop of Canterbury to help pay for Terry's air trips in and out and about. The check was duly returned with a letter signed with Terry's name, thanking me very much but saying his expenses were being met by church funds. What these were I didn't then know, but I was later able to make this contribution and another to Terry's expenses by sending checks to the Presbyterian Church U.S.A., for at the end of February I received a letter from our minister Bob Martz in Fort Collins:

> I just returned last week from one of the three meetings this year of the Program Agency Board of the denomination, of which I am a member. At each board meeting I receive an update from the Reverend Dr. Fred Wilson ... . Fred assured me that Terry Waite is continuing to do all that he can for Tom's release and the others and that it was likely he is in Beirut this week [this may have been the trip with Ollie North that Terry talks about in *Taken on Trust* involving a wait in an East Beirut apartment for five days with no result]. Fred ... indicated that he knows Terry's whereabouts because the Presbyterian denomination, through the Program Agency, continues to keep our commitment to the hostages by providing financial support for Terry Waite's travels and all of the travel vouchers go across Fred Wilson's desk at 475 Riverside Drive, New York.
>
> So we shall continue to work and hope and pray with you and Tom for a "GOOD NEW 1986!"

Although for many it would not turn out to be a "GOOD 1986," it was certainly a "NEW 1986," and my letters sent always my continuing hope and faith along with the news of Beirut:

> JAN. 18—Dear Family and Friends ... The Season of Christmas Hope has given way to the Season of New Year Hope and we continue to work/wait for Tom. Rumors of the imminent return of Terry Waite which came out on Thursday were parried by the news in Friday's Beirut French newspaper that it would not be as soon as that, reaffirming Waite's "profil bas" and his "restant prudemment optimiste." We do the same, wishing we could do more to help in the long, hard task he's undertaken for us. To all of you I must say how much it has meant throughout this whole season to hear from you and to feel so much love and support along

with wonderful details of American life such as "we had 12 inches of snow" and "the hostage families are going to Washington January 20." Thank you from the bottom of my heart ... .

Things are quiet this weekend pending a new state of affairs coming out of the Battle of East Beirut which brought the defeat of Hobeika on Wednesday. Militias seem to be lining up at the Green Line and there's been sporadic shelling along with rather dire prognostications of new interfactional fighting. The ordinary people pessimistically talk about "Square One." Out in Hamra, however, life goes on as "normal" with shopping and traffic, at AUB the tennis players and basketballers are on their respective courts, and in our building on Friday we gave our midterm exam with scarcely a student absent. The palm trees blow in the wind, the sea turns shades of green and blue beneath the lowering January rain clouds (the course of this letter has turned them into a downpour), and look out still on blooming poinsettias in the bottom garden along with ripening grapefruit fallen from our trees for breakfast. It's a day-to-day life, just as schizophrenic as ever as I teach students from the Bekaa the difference between "raincoat" and "wrinkled" (which sound absolutely alike to them) while dealing with the Middle East concepts of time and battle and the international system of political power. Insh'Allah all will come together for the Moment of Release. I plan for Tom a gathering to celebrate Burns Night—we will be together in spirit if not in person because I am sure that Father Jenco's mass will be shorter that evening of the 25th of January so that even without the Scotch or the Haggis, "Our Rabbie" will also be praised with every bit of poetry Tom has in his memory.

To Auld Lang Syne and to the Future—

Joan was our woman-of-the-month family member who went to Washington January 20. Having moved to Los Angeles after airline school, she was living with friends in a town home in Redondo Beach and working for Continental Airlines. Thus it was she that was able to get leave and a ticket to go—she jumped at the chance. In due course pictures and her report of the trip came to me:

Other hostage family members were there such as Father Jenco's sisters, Peggy Say, and Eric Jacobsen. We met with various senators' aides and congressmen, all of whom looked at us with a blank stare asking what do you think WE can do about it? We finally got a meeting with Admiral Poindexter and Oliver North in the Situation Room at the White House. Poindexter and North repeatedly assured us that all was being done to get the hostages out and that President Reagan was briefed on the situation daily. I have to say that I really felt when I walked out of that room that for the first time since I had gotten to Washington, someone in the government really cared and was doing something about it ... . I met Carmella LaSpada there too. What a great woman!! The founder of the nonprofit organization No Greater Love, she organized a lot of events in Washington for us all and I stayed with her in her beautiful apartment in the Watergate Towers. I felt so important ... and I found out for the first time about Brie cheese—Carmella brought out the biggest wheel of it that I'd ever seen and after the first bite I was hooked ... .

For my part, I threw myself into the work at the school—no time just to "sit and wait" those beginning months of the new year. There were a thousand wonderful students there to learn English and no matter if a goodly proportion of the young men were militiamen, learning English five hours a day and then, if the situation warranted, going home and getting on uniforms and pulling the Kalashnikovs from under the beds and taking to the street fights or, as I discovered from Tom later, going off to guard hostages. It was vital to me to keep an absolute purity of purpose in what I was doing at AUB: I was not there as a female Rambo to get Tom out (however tempting that idea was) nor a spy to gather hostage information—I was there to share with Tom in carrying on the work of education that we'd gone there to do, to teach young people, to give them a chance at a life, and to make positive input into a very negative environment so that conflict could be resolved and captives released with no more being abducted.

I had no trouble with this, only bent over backward to fulfill a teacher's mission and responsibility—*never* to put students in jeopardy, just love and care and nurture them. And it certainly wasn't difficult to do that with the students in that program—they were like sponges, soaking up all the love and care and nurture it was possible to give. Suppose there *was* a small group of young men that hung fascinated around me, even saying one day, "You have a *very big problem,* Mrs. Sutherland!" I never asked who anyone was or what party he belonged to, I just alphabetized the family names mooted to be connected with Hizbollah and the kidnappings along with all the others, served the students no matter what their names were or where they came from, and filled the time with the myriad of things there were to do. As I wrote friends:

> I'm a sort-of general factotum/assistant to the director which means a job description comprising more or less "building superintendent, ID cardmaker, personnel director (we have about 80 teachers now including the 13 new ones I interviewed in Britain in October who have come needing reception, apartments, financial advances, orientation, etc.), scheduler, and replacement teacher." Students and teachers are great and I love the job. In between times I get the chance to keep our home fires burning, to interact with Tom's faculty and students ("Do you

have any news of our dean?"), and to just exchange friendship daily with people everywhere at AUB—they all care too ... . What can I tell you of these days? ... They move in a pattern of up at 6:00 with BBC (perhaps preceded by a midnight call from a daughter should she be able to get through), breakfast and cat-feeding, off to school at 7:15 to do the anything-but-routine school job—"Can we have some chalk, please?" ... "Where's our teacher?" ... "We need proctors for the exam" ... . "How can I get a visa for the U.S.?" ... "What's Colorado like?" ... "What does 'blips' mean?" ... "Help! There's a fight in the hall!" ... "High Elementary D needs a teacher!" ... "We need the complete list of students by tomorrow!" ... "I've lost my ID!" ... Then a visit to someone who might have advice about Tom and then home to ad-mire the garden with Rachid the gardener and the house with Joana the maid, and then a drop-in friend and perhaps a call from Tom's former associate dean and now Acting Dean of Agriculture Adib Saad, the evening news and a vain read at the French newspaper for some word that might cheer, a two-hour session with "The Complete List of Students" which turns out never to jell somehow, and then to bed with a book to fall asleep over. Around and over the ever-present concern for Tom ... .

But there's nothing routine about the daily round ... . I've been taking classes for teachers who have been sick and gotten to know a lot of students through that and through just doing administrative things personally for them like getting them their IDs to enter AUB and delivering messages from the career guidance people and talking to them in the halls, etc., etc. They are neat kids and love attention and rapport—some of them call me Mrs. Summerland because that's easier to say and a word they know, of course, it being the beach resort/restaurant (where the Ameri-can TWA hostages were taken for dinner if you remember) and the students get a real kick out of it. One boy always laughs with me in the morning when he comes in—he said one day I was the sun because I smiled all the time, so yes-terday when he came in he bowed and said "Good Morning, Morning Star" and we both laughed ... . A sweet girl who feels like I'm her mother made a beautiful butterfly for me—silver thread around nails on a board covered with black velvet (beautiful—it shimmers!) and they almost all think I'm great be-cause I'm not the director and can do things for them—they have most of them never experienced the American educational way where teachers care and do things for individual students and they lap it up; so you know who is busy. At least with all the Ahmads, Abdallahs, and Mohammads there one feels that a little progress is being made against future terrorism—probably if the truth is told, it is a lot more than the Sixth Fleet is doing. I just can't help really liking the kids and caring for them ... .

In early February came the buildup of the American military exercises off Libya and I had a strange brushing of acquaintance with two very different women, both of whom I mentally labeled as "Spy Ladies"—one who entertained me for lunch at her apartment near Smith's Grocery and then sent me to the American ambassador in East Beirut, Reginald Bartholomew, to put the squeeze on Nabih Berri; the other who said as she passed by me on the steps next to our home, "It is pleasant to walk in Schweifat [a village south of the airport] on St. Almond Street on a Saturday or a Sunday—things are blooming there .... I have signed a document for ownership of you ... St. Almond Street." I did go to the American ambassador, gave him half the information, and waited for him to extract the other half (the gender of the "spies" and the street in Schweifat I was to walk). Neither he nor his political advisers seemed to want more information. Bartholomew just said instead that their collective opinion was that it was a trap, assigned a man to entertain me for lunch since the crossing was closed at that point, and then got me an escort back to AUB.

My realization was that the embassy, even though they cared, probably did not have a high opinion of the worth of hostage wives (the best course was to give them a cup of coffee with a metaphoric pat on the head and send them on their way); but more than that, the embassy was not in a position to do anything anyway about the hostage situation on the ground—their hands were truly tied. I didn't trouble them again but had a very nice social relationship with the succeeding ambassadors, going to their very nice Fourth of July and Thanksgiving celebrations. The Thanksgiving of 1988 stands out especially in my memory because since embassy dependents weren't allowed in Beirut, about the only women present were the six of us hostage wives. They placed one of us at each table to, I imagine, spread the female company out in rather older and darker shades of Tom's female AUB students and the Sixth Fleet sailors. Ironic indeed, and I couldn't resist saying to Ambassador McCarthy, "Aren't you lucky you have us?!" April Glaspie mentioned the "Schweifat Walk" incident in my meeting with the State Department the following October, so evidently it had been reported back home. The upshot seemed to be that I was damned with faint praise as a brave woman who considered going, but that was the last I heard of it.

As far as the "Spy Lady" contacts were concerned, I decided that right or wrong I would trust to my own intuition that I was being used in the PSP/Amal militia confrontation and thus stayed home. I did check with a Druze friend who said that St. Almond Street was in the "wrong part of town," whatever that could mean (he probably didn't want to be connected to anything I might be considering doing), and subsequently in September 1993 I tried in vain to get someone connected with the NBC *Now* team to take me there. Actually, to this day I have neither discovered St. Almond Street in Schweifat nor whether I would have gotten any information about Tom had I walked there on that first weekend of February 1986—certainly I wouldn't have met him there for he'd been moved the last week of January to the place he calls the Blindfold Apartment somewhere near the Corniche Mazraa in Beirut. At any rate, I was never "contacted" in that way by strange women again, although the second woman frequented the AUB campus off and on for the next years, asking me once where the deputy president lived. I hope he's happy to know that I didn't tell her, but she was so blatantly a "spy" that it was most ludicrous. Joana said that her accent was Palestinian but that probably would not mean too much because she could get money from anyone at a time when assassins could be hired for $10—people said that Israeli spies before the invasion of 1982 were quite obvious in the same way, either "crazies on Hamra Street" or cart vendors.

If the American embassy had its hands tied, surely AUB didn't? I decided to press the issue with the AUB administration. On February 13 I wrote a letter to the Board of Trustees in care of Dr. Frederic Herter, chairman, presented it first to the Board of Deans on the campus and then sent it to reach Dr. Herter in Cyprus:

> I would like to make an urgent appeal to you right now to consider efforts being made for Tom, Dave, and Peter as AUB hostages. Please re-ask the questions of what have we done, what are we doing, what can we do at this particular time using the power of AUB to effect release for them. It may be as they say an international matter completely, but I don't think so. Even with strong faith and hope in Terry Waite's and others' efforts at that level, I have still, and more now than before, the pressing feeling that a personal and Lebanese avenue could open for AUB if we push to find it. We know timing is important, but maybe instead of waiting for that timing we can find or effect it by using creative strategy …. I would appeal to you to make the strength, resource, and prestige of AUB act on its own behalf.

Dr. Herter replied in his characteristically warm yet straightforward manner, telling me that he was moved by my letter, assuring me that we were in their thoughts, that the hostage problem was "foremost in the deliberations of the board," that there was nothing concrete at the moment in spite of their efforts at home and in the Middle East, and that if I had further specific suggestions on how "the university could use its influence more effectively, [he] would be most grateful to hear of them." Given this encouragement, I followed up with a long letter suggesting strongly that AUB:

> … appoint a special coordination team for hostage release who would focus on that and that only and who would be charged with the following:

1) to put together knowledge of all that's being done ... .

2) to actively solicit input from all possible sources ... .

3) to brainstorm, generate ideas, come up with creative strategy for an AUB effort to get its hostages back. AUB has the power and prestige to apply pressure where it could count, if not directly with the captors, then with those as tough as or tougher than they; ... try to separate from the American/international issue and make it a personal, local issue to get action from those who want very much for AUB to stay in West Beirut and their children to get that degree; ... clang shut, really shut, the doors of the hospital and the university ... . Add on no new registrations accepted until further notice and termination notices perhaps to shock people awake ... .

AUB President Plimpton answered this letter and these ideas, saying again that "everything possible is being done" and that "I don't honestly think there is very much more we can do." As for "creative strategy," he said that he'd suggested these things last summer, they were talked about in great detail, and the decision was that they wouldn't work. So much for my ideas and AUB effort. But how right the administration was about this was made clear soon after when a Lebanese political science professor, Nabil Matar, was kidnapped and the university did go on strike and march and protest and "shut the doors." Back came an answer in a communiqué, from the kidnappers: "Open the university or Nabil Matar will be killed." Simple as that. And clear that AUB's hands also were tied in Lebanon.

Brian Keenan was one of the Irish applicants I'd interviewed in Dublin for the AUB/Hariri English teaching positions; he came to Beirut soon after I myself arrived and took a place with four other Brits in a "bad area" that they had found for themselves—we'd been slow in getting housing and, although troubled by their choice, we were relieved at their being settled. But things were bad in Beirut that winter/spring, their place was burglarized, and Philip Padfield of the Hamra Street Language School and Leigh Douglas of AUB were kidnapped late one night on their way home from the Backstreet Bar. So we hunted and found another apartment in a "good area" in Ain el Mreisse for them. That was a Sunday. Brian decided against it on the following Tuesday because it was too expensive for him alone and if he moved he didn't want to live with others. On Thursday we had a meeting of all our westerners about the precautions to take against kidnapping, and on Friday morning, April 11, in direct and beautifully Irish opposition to the consensus we'd reached about precautions, he left the house alone early in the morning without telling the others and disappeared. So "they" got Brian instead of John, the older Englishman who usually left first for the school in the morning, whatever meaning that might ultimately have. In John's case, he was soon evacuated back to Britain where he had tragedy in his life. In Brian's case, his things were brought to our house by good colleagues and friends Omar and Jackie and Mick where they stayed safe until his release. I carried both Brian and John in my mind and heart with all the others for the next years. Somewhere underneath, always, the question—"Was I responsible?"

SUNDAY, APRIL 13—Hi Joan, Ann, Kit, and Others .... A quick note again .... I wanted especially to tell you I'm fine throughout this last round of kidnapping of professors and English teachers—you may have heard that one of my Irishmen, Brian Keenan, was taken on his way to school on Friday morning and the school has been in a bit of turmoil since. We brought all the foreign teachers onto campus—I had a couple (the Winbows) in your bedroom and an Englishman (Mr. Downes) ... in the study, and another Englishman (Mr. Evans) in the upstairs room—we've been all carrying on together since Friday night so that none of them have to go outside the campus. Monday the AUB administration goes to work in earnest, I trust, to find them all places (there are about 20—some stayed behind locked doors at home over this weekend and others came in and stayed in Marquand House and in other people's apartments) so there are going to have to be quite a lot of housing arrangements made! Brian's kidnapping made the fourth teacher/professor in two weeks—one, the Frenchman, you'll have seen got away in the Bekaa— how I wish your dad could do it!! I see by the paper today that finally the Lebanese community is getting worked up about the situation—there will be a general strike of the Education Ministry along with all of the schools of West Beirut including AUB and the bigwigs of parties and ministries are having meetings daily to decide on ways to stop the thing. Doesn't seem much way unless they can control the streets. The British Embassy has told all Britishers to go and the man from the Irish Embassy who came over on Friday night told me that unless the Irish could get housing on campus, they'd have to be notified to go also—if all of them left, a quarter of the English faculty of both our school and the AUB English Department would be gone! So it is a crisis finally—a year after Dave and your dad were taken, and we'll see if there's any way something can be done to include them in an effort to disengage from the general American political situation. I think most people say no, but it's worth a try. I have gotten more reassurance from roundabout here that your dad is being well-treated and is in good health—I judge these assurances to be not just idle or wishful thinking ones but rather more knowledgeable ones so please take good heart and keep up good spirit. In general, however, things seem poised for more disaster and calamity, with the war of the camps ... between the Amal militia and the Palestinians—it appears that Arafat has infiltrated a bunch more of his bunch into Lebanon since 1982 and these are fights for control. On all other fronts there are car

bombs and shellings on a sporadic basis but no all-out resumption of warfare yet
.... What Reagan and his Sixth Fleet are going to stir up in the Mediterranean again,
time will, I guess, tell ... .

And just four days after my letter went off to the States came the Libyan
raid—Joan called at 4:00 A.M. with the news and then it came out of the radio
that morning and it was like a blow to my stomach and a message to my mind:
"We'll see the answer to this in Lebanon." Next day, in the school halls, the students came rushing up with their radios in hand—"Dr. Sutherland! Three bodies being brought down from the mountains, two British, one American." Was it
three or four hours that we waited in the teachers' room in our campus building
for the identifications—round and round like a refrain in my head, "Which
American would they choose? Which American?"

It was nadir for me.

The bodies duly came to the AUH morgue and mercifully I wasn't called to
make identification. The news was confirmed next morning: "Philip Padfield, Leigh
Douglas, Peter Kilburn." Rumors abounded about how much Muammar Gadhafi
had paid for Lebanese hostages to kill in retaliation for the Libyan raid, and I was
enlightened about Islamic Jihad and its hatred for Libya: I ought to have known that
Tom would be safe. As a friend said to me afterward, "They would never have sold
any of their hostages to Gadhafi—they blame him for the disappearance of their
Imam Musa Sadr." Beloved Musa Sadr, the founder of the Amal movement who had
gone to Libya in 1978 and never been heard of again. Thus my education about
Tom's captors continued, we grieved for colleagues, and I inherited Crystal, Leigh
Douglas's Siamese cat, who joined our household along with Tibby and Nabby, the
Dodges' cats. Crystal would be my companion until I left Beirut—and she would
climb on my shoulder when I visited her in her new home on our return to Beirut in
September 1993. But that was still far in the future.

One thing the Libyan raid with American planes taking off from Great Britain clearly meant—Britishers were not from an "outside country" now. Their
embassy called for evacuation and our teachers, just arrived four months ago,
complied. For a week until all could be arranged there were 13 in our home at
AUB, using beds, couches, floor—no choice now, everyone was to be "on campus." And when the day came that they boarded the bus for East Beirut and we
held our breath until we knew they were safe, not one of the Brits wanted to
leave. Beirut had exerted its special hold on them—two even kept their apartments there for some years, hoping against hope they could come back. Still in
touch eight years later, they write of continuing correspondence with their

landlady, or the fact that they've had two children and gone to Oman and are keeping a bottle of champagne to open for Tom and me, or that they've worked in Tunis, or "seen Linda," or "Enclosed is an article about 'your poem,' *The Man at the Gate of the Year*." They were, and are still wherever they are, a great lot.

It was after the Brits left that spring that I had my brush with "an armed element." My friend Kay, an AUB English teacher, a single American woman, had left her apartment in Manara situated just across the hall from that of Leigh Douglas and been accorded the basement apartment in the Hajj house at AUB opening out at the back in the hillside wooded area just above our house. She frankly didn't feel at all comfortable in it and one night she called about 9:00 P.M.—"I feel like someone's out there looking in at me .... I'm just really nervous." I didn't think—"Hold on, I'll come up. I'm sure it's all right." Ready for bed, I flung on my robe and went barefoot the few steps up our walk, through the gate and right to her door. She met me and we talked and then I went ahead back out through the front door to meet a short, slim, curly-headed young man walking purposefully around the edge of the house. "I'm security," he said. "May I be of help here?" Brushing past me, he proceeded to start through the door. It didn't occur to me to think, I just knew there was something wrong about him and that he couldn't be allowed inside that apartment with Kay. I grabbed him from behind, pulled him out, shouted to Kay to call security, and hung on for dear life. Struggle and crash on the head and arm with the butt of a gun he'd pulled from somewhere and then he pulled away and ran while I shouted for help. Between my noise and Kay's call, men appeared from everywhere, aghast at me in a robe with blood streaming down all over. Upshot was a change of clothing, a trip to the AUH to get stitches and X rays along with the nightly contingent of diverse bleeding and groaning militiamen in so much worse shape than I, and then back to give the story with Kay to AUB security and administrators, all still aghast about the happening. For men to attack women in an Arab country is not common—our daughters had felt safer on the streets of Beirut than they had in the United States—and that I should be involved was, I knew, an extreme embarrassment for the campus men. For my part, I would never have confronted a "real" armed element, tall, bearded, and with a Kalashnikov, but a voyeur was after all a known quantity where I came from. For his part, he didn't want to hurt me, he only wanted to get away. Whether he did for good, we were never told. They moved Kay to the faculty apartments and moved a man into the basement apartment. I wore long sleeves and my hair carefully combed over to cover the few stitches for a week and the incident was absorbed into "Beirut Normal" and the informal annals of AUB as "the night Jean Sutherland floated around campus in her nightgown." At least, President Plimpton told it that way the next time I saw him.

It was nothing, for my concern that spring was much bigger than myself. The fallout from the Libyan raid continued even beyond the terrible deaths of our friends and colleagues, and we tried in vain to find a chink in the captivity armor. From somewhere deep within me I could feel a capped anger surfacing and I vented on the family and close friends:

Not even I can find now any shred of rationale for anyone here to release Americans, nor even to appear to be on the side of Americans, and the hostages now have added value as "anti-Libyan raid" insurance—their golden worth has increased to be hoarded carefully. It's still the same long, tough road ahead and more. So we re-evaluate and say, "What now?" I consider all the ways tried—I even consider the conventional "writing to Reagan" and I can't stomach writing—am I wrong?? So much in our foreign policy has been ugly and biased, with such dire consequences for individuals—I've experienced the blast at the Marine barracks with 250 killed and the *New Jersey* shelling and the Awkar embassy explosion and the Libyan raid with more killed in retaliation and Tom still somewhere out there. I don't see why we as Americans shouldn't be honest enough to face squarely what we're doing: If peacekeeping Marines die, is it because of terrorism or because of a government policy that takes sides when it shouldn't and leaves them defenseless? If seven die in a Challenger are they sacrificed to "space exploration" or NASA bureaucratic ineptitude? If six hostages are sacrificed in Lebanon, is it to Middle East terrorism or to an Israeli dictation of American foreign policy? I'm not a political person, nor is Tom .... We've just gotten caught in it and have to face it ourselves .... I think too of all the yellow ribbons and prayer services and letters and appeals from the United States—in truth it's meaningless exercise while the government continues its policy—Where are our statesmen and where is a balanced, positive, meaningful foreign policy?? Reagan cries over an 11-year-old girl killed in the Rome airport, while women and children killed by the score in Israeli raids in South Lebanon (or I should say American-Israeli raids which is what they're called here because the bombs are bought with our money) go uncried for by him .... BUT, through it all, we do try to keep strong positive optimism and a balanced mentality here—I've got a good American friend, Al, who keeps coming by to laugh cynically at American policy and bureaucrats—this morning he brought me back to normal with his analysis of the BBC news of Reagan's arming of the rebels of the world—on my suggestion that we might slip in the Southern Lebanese Shiites for consideration for missiles he said they were too straightforward, it was better to nominate the Mourabitoun (Sunni fanatics/PLO-Libyan sympathizers) for their democratic principles .... The nice thing is that all these people keep dropping by to bring me things or talk and I know they are looking out for me and giving me good company and their friendship in their own way. Just before Al came this morning, John Evans (one of the teachers I brought from Britain) came by with chocolate Easter eggs and a nice Easter card, and he brought tales from an after-Easter service British embassy luncheon where he'd tangled with another Englishman whom he considers "frightfully aristocratic and old-fashioned" and whom he'd advised to get his "hands dirty a little" so that he wouldn't be recognized—he's good fun and also passed on to me that the British ambassador was "furious" because they'd come to Beirut to work in the Hariri Program—John had of course replied that if the government could come up with teaching jobs for them in the U.K. with half-decent pay they wouldn't have come …. So there we go on.

... I spent a lot of time over our four-day Easter holiday thinking about Tom and what I should and could be doing in the coming days … . When things ease internationally I will plan perhaps for a trip to Damascus and to Jumblatt and Berri here again. I've pushed the American ambassador and AUB and found I won't find help there unless they're doing something they won't tell me about—so now I'm going alone. It's going to take lots of thought and effort … . Amazing how people here have told me of having dreams of seeing Tom released … .

MAY 3—Tom's birthday—surely wish we could celebrate it! When I get home to be with you for June 9th … . Right now we're being very careful and don't go outside of campus—to work and home again, and thank goodness for plenty of work! We do gather for meals on campus quite regularly and the weather is beautiful along with the flowers and the sea and we ride the tension until something worse or better comes; … it's one day at a time and life does go on—they even had the habitual spring football match between Arts & Sciences and Engineering, but it ended before the end when a student (reportedly) hit a policeman with a water balloon and a fight broke out and shooting started which canceled the game. In the meantime I'd left in the middle and gone to the Faure Requiem with the AUB Chorus in the Chapel which was wonderful so got the best part of the game in addition to wonderful music … . It's a fight to keep going, but still worth it.

My cousin Margaret Shepherd, a renowned calligrapher living in Boston, had offered to do for our birthdays this year a rendering of a quotation. I chose from Shakespeare's sonnets to match the feelings in my heart for Tom and it arrived soon after May 3 in all its poignant beauty:

> How like a winter hath my absence been
> From thee, the pleasure of the fleeting year!
> What freezings have I felt, what dark days seen!
> What old December's bareness every where!

From you have I been absent in the spring,
When proud-pied April (dress'd in all his trim)
Hath put a spirit of youth in every thing,
That heavy Saturn laugh'd and leapt with him.

Yet seem'd it winter still, and, you away,
As with your shadow I with these did play.

I was never quite sure during that month of May whether I'd be able to get home to Fort Collins for Tom's "First Anniversary Observance" and the ambivalence I felt about leaving Beirut was in my letters that month, an ambivalence that would be replayed over and over in the next years each time an important trip home came up. But that day did come toward the end of May when my mind felt right about leaving and right about planning—for AUB as well as for the States. I wrote to AUB's Acting President Lutfy Diab:

> As you are aware, I plan now to go to the States to take part in a two-day demonstration of support for Tom and the other hostages to take place in Fort Collins, Colorado, on June 8 and 9, the anniversary of Tom's abduction. I spoke about this to the Faculty of Agriculture here this morning which was planning its means of expression about the same event, because I will go to the States in advocacy for Tom which means also his beliefs, his life, and his love for his Faculty and AUB and I want very strongly to represent AUB, agriculture, and Lebanon in the most positive way possible. They have proposed a convocation here for FAFS and all others who wish to attend on Tuesday morning, June 3, "Peace Day" for Lebanon, to be held in the Agriculture Building and have received the gracious offer of Mr. Jarrah of education/Hariri to do a videotape of the proceedings as well as campus and agriculture activities, life, and people. They also plan to prepare a statement for me to carry home to read and to be printed in the newspapers here for Tom ....

I look back now on it all and realize how absolutely driven I was always to lift Tom's situation to the highest possible plane of educational mission—and I realize now as then that in both Beirut and the States this would be only dimly if at all understood by people over the years. Was I being too serious and lofty? Was I getting 'preachy' and overly righteous? Was it my Iowa heritage with Grandfather's dictum to "Do what you know to be right"? Or as my childhood friend, Sarah Hall Maney, wrote in her poem, "Iowa Child":

I am an Iowa child
Part and product of the land on which I grew

And I know my Iowa child must live
And come to terms with the part of me
That is controlled, precise, yearning
to be perfect—
Like the squared-off, ruler-straight rows
of hybrid seed corn[5]

Was I trying somehow, in my individual way, to "straighten" Reagan's foreign policy by saying "Look—there are terribly big principles here ... "? Or was I merely grasping at a survival strategy for Tom and our family that would say, "Look—this captivity is not for nothing; there is a big purpose here." I truly don't know, even yet, but I do know that that June 3/9 "happened" just as I hoped it would with bridged observances in the FAFS Building at AUB in Beirut and on the Oval at CSU in Colorado. And we were able to tie AUB to CSU as frontier universities struggling together to overcome prejudice, hatred, and conflict with education. That it involved sacrifice was a given. Tom and the others were not to be pitied or considered victims, they were to be honored and respected for the *work* they were doing. It was lofty, it was serious, it was "ruler-straight."

And it just seemed so terribly important to me.

June 3 was an extremely bad day war-wise in Beirut (probably because it had been designated as "Peace Day"), but it was such a nice day at AUB. The man with the video appeared about 9:00 A.M. and we had a lovely hour touring the greenhouses behind the Chemistry Building, the Mini-AREC, talking with Selma Husseini and with Tom's friend and first bodyguard, Hassan, and taking pictures of all the research and horticultural areas. We then came down to the Agriculture Building and toured the dean's office, which Adib Saad had kept just as Tom had had it. I wanted so much for people in the States to have a graphic idea of what Tom had been all about and the people he'd worked among. The hour for the gathering came and it was truly touching with the signing of the Remembrance for Tom and the speeches by faculty and students. The young woman who spoke, a graduate student in agriculture, gave me a copy of her words:

Kahlil Gibran once said: Remembrance is a form of meeting. It is. As a student of agriculture, I remember Dr. Sutherland. I "meet" him everyday in every improvement that was achieved since he took over his job as dean of agriculture. I never remembered him as someone who "was" with us but who "is" ... .

Dr. Thomas Sutherland was kidnapped on his way back from the States. One flash news and everything collapsed. Everything didn't matter any more: the expectation, the waiting, the joy of graduating, the future—everything. They were replaced by a sense of void. A gap in our thinking. A question: why?! Why to go on struggling against impossible odds and for what?! Why was Dr. Sutherland kidnapped?! He never bothered himself in any political conflict. The kind our country had for "ages" now.

Dr. Sutherland was too busy making friends with us his students to care for politics or political concepts and illusions. He was too busy preparing for the sock-hop party and the Saturday lunch with us ... . At the same time he was too busy organizing whatever measures necessary for the improvement of the faculty. However, he was never too busy to indulge in his casual chats with the students whom he knows by name ... .

We miss you, Dr. Sutherland. Your coming to the faculty encouraged us all. You gave us hope in the future in times all we could hope for was to get through the day and see the tomorrow alive, barely! Your optimistic enthusiasm made us feel ashamed not to hope for a better future instead of hoping for the present moment only. Your sense of devotion to your job as dean, teacher, father, and friend set new hopes and dreams in our thinking. We survived one year with you being away from us in body but never in thoughts and hopes and ideal. But we need your friendly encouragement and advice. We need you to go on. We are waiting for you, Dr. Sutherland ... .

And then a young man, a senior, came to the podium to speak out and to conclude with: ... *Sir, we need your presence and we're praying for your safe return. May our wishes and prayers be heard to see you soon among us.*

The speeches by themselves cannot convey the commitment and the bravery of these young students who walked purposefully to the front of the crowded agriculture lecture hall to speak out these words, not knowing who in the audience was watching and hearing and targeting for reprisal a person voicing a "wrong" sentiment. Especially would a young man be vulnerable. After a later observance a graduate student would walk me home and with tears in her eyes say to me, "I wish we could speak out more for Dr. Sutherland. But it isn't safe, it isn't safe." Tom and I knew well the pitfalls of speaking out, and I no longer said anything to anyone about anything. But these students testified and I honor them. Tom had tears when he read these speeches after his release and our hearts are forever touched. There is a meaning, and it is important.

After the ceremony, we hurried up to the Near East School of Theology (NEST) to get the videotape edited for me to take to the States the next day. The students had lined up still photographs of Tom in action with them over the two years he'd been there and they wanted them incorporated along with the events of the day. NEST had a great audiovisual department in their basement and offered their services free of charge—how wonderful people are! And that evening as I was packing the doorbell rang, and there was Tom's good friend and faculty colleague, Mahmoud Solh, with a letter for me:

> Dear Mrs. Sutherland … In a few days it will be one year since the inhuman abduction of Dean Sutherland. As a Lebanese I am ashamed of what has happened to a man who was helping Lebanon during the most difficult time in its modern history. AUB has been the light-house for the Middle East and we hope it will continue to be. People like Tom provided the energy for this light-house. To me and many others, Tom presents a symbol of dedication and determination of a devoted university professor.
>
> I met Tom first in February 1981, when, as a member of the Dean's Search Committee, I escorted him to AUB-farm as a candidate for the deanship position. On the way we stopped at the O'Berge Restaurant in Shtaura to have lunch. Tom asked me about the weakness and strength of our faculty. When proposing possible means and ways to bridge gaps in the faculty, I could feel his determination and devotion. For him the poor security situation and political instability were irrelevant. Tom believed in destiny: "misfortunes may happen to you wherever you are." …

So I carried tape, letters, good wishes, and love along with me on the plane to Colorado, arriving the evening of June 4. What joy to see the girls and friends and get in on the planning and preparation for June 9 that Tom's good friends Bill West, Frank Vattano, Bill Griswold, Jim Oxley, Gerry Ward, Jim Johnson, and so many dedicated others had put in motion with the help of President Austin and his right-hand woman Myra Powers. On June 7 I flew to Minneapolis and the General Assembly meetings of the Presbyterian Church where Ben Weir was taking over as moderator for 1986–1987. A special privilege to be there with Ben and Carol and Fred Wilson and to have the chance to address the assembly from the podium:

> Right away I asked, "What can I do for my Tom?" And they told me—"Go to the people with power." And either personally or through relevant others the visits have been made to Assad, Hoss, Husseini, Berri, Jumblatt, Bush, Reagan … . But tonight as I talk to you, I feel that I in truth address the people with power—the power of the Church, the power of prayer, and the power of willing commitment to action to free our men in Lebanon—and that feeling means the release not only of their physical bodies but of their creative energies which have been and still are committed to finding truth, relieving the needy, and seeking ways to peace in the Middle East and

our world. We know that because we have seen Ben Weir—I know it also because I know Tom and the excitement he felt last year in going back to Beirut and AUB ... .

It is in this spirit that tonight I appeal to you for a commitment to action for these men—we don't have time for helpless waiting nor do we need to do it—each day the men are there is a symbol that something somewhere is wrong—we can send a resolution along with letters to Washington to urge redoubled effort for alternatives to deadlock—we can also work personally to find alternatives to future violence even if it's just in small ways—for me it is in my return to AUB where 1,000 Lebanese young people between the ages of 18 and 22 can learn to speak English as they get to know and interact with one American. This must be a more powerful way to combat terrorism than air strikes—at least we have to hope so ... .

And then it was back to Colorado where Governor Lamm had pronounced June 9 as Tom Sutherland Day. That morning brought yellow-ribbon–tying around the great elms lining the walk in the old CSU Oval and around the great columns of the Administration Building facing down the central walk. On the steps a stage had been built and when evening came, a wonderful crowd gathered. Every one was a special person there for Tom—Ann, Kit, Joan, Dad and Alice, Representative Hank Brown, the Jenco sisters and the Jacobsen sons, the Northern Colorado Pipe Band, the Presbyterian Church with Bob Martz and friends, the CSU administration, students and faculty and alumni, the press and the TV media people, and the people of Fort Collins, the children, and dogs. Paul Jacobsen played and sang his song, "When the Word Comes," and Hank Brown spoke, and I spoke too:

> It is with a full heart that I have come from AUB to join you, my family and friends, in this Oval which has meant so much to Tom and me the last 28 years. Here Tom established and followed his career of teaching and research in animal science— and here he committed himself to the university ideal and made his decision to go to work in international agriculture as dean of agriculture at the American University of Beirut.
>
> Tonight we gather all together to send the power of our collective wills from this Oval to that prison wherever it may be to give comfort, strength, and support to those men we care so much for, to send the power of our collective wills to the captors in our appeal for release, the power of our collective wills to Terry Waite to offer thanks and support for his unflagging quest for solution, the power of our collective wills to Washington to urge again redoubled effort for a positive and creative strategy to make that release happen for individual Americans who represent in the largest and ideal sense America's quest for freedom in our world.

I have in a sense brought Tom with me from Beirut as I have brought in this videotape the Tom Sutherland Day held in his faculty of agriculture last Tuesday, the worst day of fighting Beirut had seen in six months. Although the campus was nearly empty of other students and faculty, all from agriculture who could make it gathered in convocation to support and remember Tom and they created in that day the videotape of their projects, their classes, their labs, their greenhouses, and their appeal for Tom's release. They and I want us here to see the importance of Tom's mission and to understand why he is where he is. It is the reason he kept remaking that decision to go back, and you must be as moved as I was when you go with the students from the empty chair at the desk in the dean's office to the convocation and the voices of those students ... .

Very much is this Oval at the historic and real center of the CSU campus tied to that other "Oval" in Ras Beirut which is in truth a last outpost where objective dialog between Christian and Moslem, East and West, can take place. There it is an Oval of 70 acres ringed around by bombings, shellings, assassinations, and by the sites of the kidnappings of David Dodge, Terry Anderson, Ben Weir, Father Jenco, Dave Jacobsen. These men are, as Tom is, bound to the Oval that is AUB and they symbolize the American way of going out into the world to serve. Instead of helpless waiting, may we commit ourselves to productive activity in the university spirit—to seek for truth and report it like Terry Anderson, to give aid to those who need it like Father Jenco and Ben Weir, to administer medical services like David Jacobsen, to strive for knowledge, apply it, and teach it like Tom Sutherland. I'm trying to do that for Tom so that as I work and wait for him I have a feeling that I'm working for a future for our children no matter what their sect or nationality. The way will not be easy—it will have to go straight through the circles of violence to get to the other side—but it will be worth it. On behalf of Tom and his family, thank you dear friends.

Saying good-bye to daughters, other family, and friends, I flew back to Beirut and AUB for the eventful July to come. There indeed, the Green Line still held—and indeed it held tragedy for AUB commuters that very week when their bus was hit with a rain of machine gun fire from a passing car on the East Side just after the evening crossing. Of the persons killed, one was a student in Tom's faculty of agriculture, Nellie Khairallah. We truly mourned.

Bittersweet Lebanon: The sadness for one family was followed by gladness for another as the Jenco family the next week got the wonderful news that their Father Martin was released. How we followed the news and the pictures! There was Terry Waite on the spot with his ambiguous "It's no coincidence that I'm in the area" and Peggy Say there for Father as well. I was in Beirut instead of Damascus, but I got a telex to Peggy and heard the news of Tom from Father Martin—what a high!

JULY 30, 1986—Dear People I Love Over There ... The eventful weekend is past and what will happen next still in the future balance .... What a blessing to hear of Tom after all these months and know he is fine and well even if still there for more tough days to come. Complete joy for Father Jenco—he looked well as did Dave Jacobsen which somehow gives added assurance .... By the time the news came through to me about the release and I'd gotten through to the embassy here who didn't seem to know much, it didn't seem practicable to try to get a taxi through questionable areas to try to make Damascus when I didn't know what their timing was going to be. Wish I had, though. It would have been wonderful to be able to see Father Jenco and talk to him personally. The embassy called me at 11 P.M. to give me his message about Tom and I was thrilled with that. Sunday evening they played the videotape on Beirut TV .... People really do all seem to be optimistic even though the message through Dave Jacobsen was direly worded—hope and faith can't falter. In the meantime here horrendous car bombs compound the dreadfulness which in its most recent manifestation started with the bus massacre of the weekend before last when four of our people were killed crossing the line. One of the students was a third-year foods and nutrition student of Tom's faculty—a lovely friendly girl who almost missed the bus that day. So in place of being in Damascus last Saturday evening I was visiting her family who were so shattered and that had to be the way things went. The bus has since been parked in front of our school building getting fixed up—a very grim reminder—today with the windows out to be replaced, it was loaded with people to make the crossing again. Oh, Lebanon! says my Ghanaian maid.

How right I was not to have agonized over being in Damascus for Father Martin proved itself the next day when Kit's telex came telling me of our chance to meet him—"Come, it's important," she said. And so I did, with stops enroute in London and Washington to see and talk to people. Then Ann, Kit, Joan, and I gathered ourselves together, and we all flew to Chicago where we were met by Father Martin. What a splendid man! All the way through that airport, in the concourse, on the escalator, and into the special lounge, people recognized him and called "Welcome home!" and we received a foretaste of the reception to come for Tom, if and when. Father Martin had made all special arrangements for the four of us to be visitors to the House of the Servite Fathers next to the cathedral—we ate at the refectory tables with them and went after dinner to see the newly renovated cathedral building with the man who was giving the last months of his life to oversee the project. Awe-inspiring it was, and especially so to us who had just had a wonderful afternoon with Father Martin, hearing in that soft voice of his about Tom—all the day-to-day details, living images, and stories to fill the voids of our minds and hearts. As Ann put it afterward: "... it was so good to talk to Marty, it was like Dad was a real person again—like he has farts and he has laughs and he's reciting poetry and telling jokes, and has his Dial soap." In its way, however, it tore us apart as it put us together with Tom in those cells. For Father Martin didn't mince words about either the conditions or Tom's situation: "They think he is CIA because of a paper in his briefcase and they're giving him a really hard time." So we agonized, but we wouldn't for the world have missed that day with Father Martin. What a gift he gave us with his sense of humor ("Whenever I go out now to get in a car, I automatically walk around to the trunk!") and with his martini and with his "Good on You!" He didn't know it yet but he was to become a godfather to our Joan while she was in Los Angeles and again in Portland, Oregon, where he was over the next 5-plus years—to the rest of us, well, we just loved him. Thank you and bless you, Father Martin.

How reluctantly Ann, Kit, Joan, and I parted to go our separate ways but how great were the memories I took back with me to Beirut. As I wrote Dad and Alice on my return:

> Such a fast but important trip for me—soaked up the girls all to myself and then the chance to talk to the people so important to our lives—in London, Washington, and in Chicago—I've come back with knowledge of the outside and international parameters as well as the inside—I'm feeling my way cautiously into this new limbo with the strong feeling it's now my time for action and it must be right action—the "dilemmas" are real and ever-present. Someday we will be talking all these things out face-to-face and somehow I don't think even then a clear answer of what should and shouldn't have been done will emerge. We can only act with faith and integrity ... .

13 Nadir

Sunday night, August 2, 1986. Terry, David, and I were taken gruffly from our nice cell, hustled down the stairs, all 12 flights of them, into a waiting van, and we were off to Ouzai, a run-down neighborhood just west of the airport, between that and the Mediterranean Sea. All six guards accompanied us, but this was the last time we "saw" the three Junior Jihaders. Was this location too far away from their AUB English classes? Or were they needed for some other job requiring more intelligence? No way to know. But without question, a couple of those who replaced them, especially one named Hadi, were none too long on brainpower. I was now at location number four for me. Into a garage, by the empty sounds, down a spiral staircase, through a very low door, and into a real prison again. A huge basement under the garage, with individual cells like the first place I had been held. No Hilton, this. Heavy steel doors, tiled floors, cinder-block walls on the inside, poured concrete on the outside wall, damp even on the second of August. Each door had a fan built right into it, and interestingly, a button rigged up that we were instructed to push anytime we wanted. Hard to believe this would last long. It didn't.

One of the Junior Jihad who had accompanied us out here gave us instructions on how we were to behave in this place. Openings at the top of each door, about eight inches high, with steel bars about four inches apart, we were not ever to look out of. "And," said Jr. J., "we have TV in each room so we see if you look. It very bad for you, you look!" I couldn't see any TV cameras around, but couldn't be sure. The buzzers were to request anything, but mainly to go to the toilet, for now they had decided that pee bottles in our cells were "not healthy." By God, there were lots of things about this place that were much less healthy than pee bottles.

The buttons were wired to an elaborate system of buzzers in their guard room, one for each cell, so that they could tell right away who was buzzing. Theoretically this would have been a nice arrangement, but it took no account of the laziness of the guards. "And how about in the night?" I asked. "No problem," they said. "Buzz anytime. Someone always awake," which was true of course, and always had been. One of them was always on duty. Much too good to be true. Sure enough, it took only a few days until they were being less than punctual in responding to our buzz. So I began to argue with Abu Ali to give us back our bottles. And he did. Amazement all around. We still had the buzzers, of course, which were handy. Ten cells in all, and we had two of them, number two and number three. The separating wall had been bashed down rather crudely so that the three of us could get into one single space. The other cells appeared to be still "as built." But the wall separating the two banks of cells had also been broken down in the middle of the prison, so that we could see across to at least some of the cells on the other side. A few days after our arrival, we were aware of two other men in the cell almost straight across from ours, number eight. We assumed it was the Frenchmen, or at least a couple of them. But a week or two later, we looked out of our window, and a heavily bearded man was holding up a sign which read, "*I am Irish. My Friend is English.*" Ye Gads. It wasn't the Frenchies after all! Who could these characters be, who had so boldly "hung out their shingle"? We began to sign to them, using our fingers in a crude letter-forming code, and soon had the information that they were Brian Keenan and John McCarthy.

This method of communication was obviously not very efficient at all, but they told us that they had a pen and a little paper; since we were still being punished, we had none of that kind of luxury at that time. Terry asked them to leave a note in the bathroom. Sure was a lark trying to tell them where to leave the letter but we finally got through to them. They were to leave it stuck high up behind the water heater. That was the beginning of some hilarious correspondence, during which I learned that Brian had been interviewed in Dublin by none other than Jean. He gave me lots of detail about her life, and especially that she was the assistant administrator in the program funded by Rafiq Hariri and run at AUB to give English-speaking capability to roughly a thousand young Lebanese men and women a year. I was familiar with this program in its inception, and had, on one occasion when I was acting president of AUB, welcomed an arriving group of new teachers. So an interesting turn of events for me; for the first time, now 14 months into my captivity, I had some information about Jean's circumstances. Brian had already been in captivity for nearly six months, meeting the same fate as I after only five months at Hariri. We found out a little about John McCarthy too. An employee of World Television Network, he had been sent to relieve the Beirut station chief for a month, had completed his assignment, but on the way to the airport he and all his luggage had been seized by Islamic Jihad, who were even at that moment wearing around the prison some of his very favorite clothes, including a special jacket given to him by his fiancée prior to his departure! Galling for him, to say the least. The two of them professed to be very surprised that we were in such good shape after our long captivity so far! A whole 14 months, by Jove! They took hope from that.

Out of the blue, Terry suggested that we should learn the deaf and dumb alphabet. I was less than enthusiastic. But he insisted, and I began for the first time in my life to get the hang of how deaf people communicate. He couldn't remember every single letter, having learned it in his high school days; but in true Terry fashion, he improvised where he was unsure, so we had 26 letters to use. Resourceful guy. Terry told John and Brian in a letter on paper that he was going to go through the entire alphabet a couple of times, then give them a short "letter" to try it out. They turned out to be very quick, and picked it up immediately.

About mid-September, Terry returned from his trip to the toilet with some discouraging news. He was sure he had just heard that two more Americans had been kidnapped, one of them Joseph Cicippio, the deputy comptroller at AUB. David was in shock and almost disbelief, for Joe had been a good friend of his during his brief stay at the university. And besides, Joe had married a Sunni Moslem woman, and had had to convert to Islam first, which David thought would be enough of a shield to prevent him from being targeted. Eventually we had confirmation that it was indeed Joe, and his "conversion" had been no shield at all.

The other man turned up in our prison within the next day or so, in one of the cells across the way, and began pacing in the small area and talking to himself. We were not sure whether he was addressing us or not, but he kept talking in a very deep bass voice, "There are hundreds of this kind of prison all over Beirut; I know all about them." Again, "I am a personal friend of Prime Minister Karami. He'll have me out of here in no time." We were impressed! When he went to the toilet, he walked with a nice springy step, and spoke Arabic words to Mahmoud, so we immediately christened him "the Arab." He seemed to be getting away with lots of talking that we did not feel free to indulge in. Soon after, he established contact with us—he was no Arab but an American by the name of Frank Reed, the director and owner of a private school, which he said would soon put International College (IC) out of business. That seemed to me to be an unlikely claim, for IC had a history and reputation almost matching that of the AUB, and had long been the "feeder school" for the AUB. Within a week or two, Frank began to hallucinate even more and to offer wild prayers to God. "Don't you know, God, that I am the world's greatest educator?" and similar pleas to the Almighty.

David was called out by friend Ali to write a letter to the United States, and returned all full of how he had really duped them this time, because he had made it full of spelling and grammatical mistakes. "I wouldn't have done that, David," counseled Terry. "They'll find that out and give you hell." And sure enough, the news media in the United States concluded that this could not have been written by Jacobsen, for he would never have made mistakes like those in the letter; and of course it hit the headlines in Beirut, as did everything about Islamic Jihad, and in a few hours, they had David on the carpet and were grilling him mercilessly. David denied having done it deliberately. We could hear the whole session. I was quite surprised that he took this tack, for the "bosses" were far from stupid, and David was certainly underestimating their intelligence.

Mahmoud arrived and ordered us to bring our things—we were moving to cell 11, right off the guards' room. Filthy! Really filthy. So bad that after looking it over and starting to clean it, Terry was completely discouraged and broke down in tears. Mahmoud came back in. "Why don't you just shoot me, Mahmoud?" he bawled. "Go ahead, God damnit. Shoot me!" "I have not the order," came back the Big M, calmly apologetic.

By late September, Ali was back again. "We want you all to make a videotape. Your government has done a negotiate with Soviet Union for the release of an American journalist named Nicholas Daniloff. They have exchanged a Russian spy for him. Why they will not deal with Islamic Jihad? Why they not exchange our 17 brothers in Kuwait for you? Are you less valuable than Mr. Daniloff?" He wanted us to get mad! "You must include those points very clearly in your message." David and Terry and I were then separated and told to write our individual scripts; the rest was up to us, whatever we wanted to say. I wrote mine, and was brought before his lordship, Ali, who read it. "Is this the best you can do?" he asked. "Well, that is more or less what you asked us to put in, right?" I felt that it was in all honesty not a bad script, but of course Ali was not going to miss any chance to humiliate me. "Ach." He dismissed me in disgust. Soon I heard both Terry and David making their tapes in front of the camera. Both were put back into their cells, David where he had been in isolation for some weeks now, and Terry now in cell number one. In the double cell, I was alone.

Confused at again not being allowed to make a tape, I requested one of the guards, "Please I must speak to Ali." To my surprise, the great man deigned to see me—a brief audience. "Why are you not allowing me to make a tape, Ali?" "We don't trust you," said "Trust-Me Ali." "You're a liar!" The ultimate insult from Terry's "Lying-Piece-of-Dog-Shit." Thus I never was allowed to make a tape for showing over American TV. I was never quite sure whether they really didn't trust me, or whether my showing on the day that we had all been "screen-tested" had been so bad that they didn't think I could make a worthwhile tape. I learned later that at no time did they ever publicly release either a photograph or a videotape of me, which caused many of my friends to wonder whether I was still alive. But perhaps this was one more reverberation from the incident over the article on Islam, now 14 months in the past? These new insults from Ali and his guards did nothing to restore my self-confidence, and kept me in a state of uncertainty and psychological misery— and I was now all alone to endure it. No "community" support. My head was more than ever in a semipermanent state of shock.

Next day we were all three assembled into the guards' room and allowed to watch both tapes being shown over American network TV, including the reactions of President Reagan. Each time Reagan made a comment, the Jihad would shout, "Liar, liar. You bastard, Reagan. Fucking liar." Then they would all scream with laughter. I wondered if they really knew what they were saying exactly, or knew the ugliness of the swear words they were using. Swearing in a foreign language never really seems like swearing.

Alone in a double cell. Mahmoud told me that I was to be exchanged with Brian and John, but that they were refusing to clean their cell; Brian was being stubborn again. But as usual, it was depriving them of something, this time a double cell, so I stayed in cell two/three for several weeks, and used our sign language almost daily to keep up on what was going on. Each of us had his own perspective on what each little happening in our very confined world meant, and it was interesting and reassuring to get and compare in clandestine fashion what the guards were saying to each of us. John and Brian were still communicating with Terry via letters left in the toilet; they had long ago settled on a very neat arrangement—rolling up the letter into a small tight roll, tying a thread around it, and pushing it into the left-hand pipe that supported the sink. Only a short piece of thread was left outside of the pipe, just enough to see and to grasp to pull out the letter. I could see those in there when I was in the toilet, but I was frankly afraid to indulge in this "game," for I was still under suspicion by all of the guards, who were still calling me *kizzab*. But I was getting all the news anyway by our sign language, including what Terry was writing. He was through the wall from me, and once in a while I would tap on the cinder blocks. At first he would reply briefly, but soon gave up and wouldn't respond. Resentful that he would ignore me like that, I wondered what could be going through his head.

The end of October brought a new development. I was taken out of my cell and stuck in the one off the guards' room, the cell Mahmoud had tried to change us to some time before. Abu Ali and Fadl were going back and forth from the two toilets that were just off their room, with buckets of water. I could see easily through the fan hole, which was just about head high, and in the few hours I spent in this place, I was able to see all kinds of comings and goings by their friends. They would come in, stay a few minutes and chat and laugh, then disappear up the spiral staircase, all of which I could clearly see from my temporary home. It turned out that Fadl and Abu Ali had decided to clean the double cell themselves. A few hours later, I was taken back to cell eight and told to clean it with the bucket of water and a scrubber and a cloth. I was not averse to doing this. It gave me some exercise, for one thing, and I knew that my farm background of cleaning out the cow barns and chicken sheds would let me do a much more thorough job than the hamsters would any day. So I gave it a good going over. Brian and John were already into the double cell, and very happy about that. We could still see each other of course from our reversed positions, and could still communicate. They were now through the wall from Terry, and still exchanging letters.

November 2. Late at night amidst a lot of activity, which I could plainly hear, Sayeed came into the cell block, past mine to David's cell, and took him out. I could hear David's voice, "Am I going home, Sayeed?" "Quiet. No speak, okay?!" From behind the bars of the little window in my door, I could see Sayeed leading David, over the little dividing wall and down the other side past cell two/three and Terry's cell one, and he was gone. One more hostage released.

Several days later, we had breakfast, then lunch, then waited and waited and waited. No toilet run, and my pee bottle was full. I started to bang on the door but no one came. So I kept banging away, and eventually Fadl appeared. "We eating now. You must wait!" I waited. Fadl returned to take me to the toilet. Arrived at the door of the *hammam,* he instructed me, "Give me bottle." "I must empty it," I protested. "Give me," he insisted and snarled a few words in Arabic—I didn't understand them at all, but the meaning was clear. He was pissed. Once inside the toilet, I began to realize the significance, but hoped against hope that I was wrong. I was not. When I came out and asked him for my bottle, he simply snarled again in Arabic and pushed me toward my cell. "Oh, my God," I thought. "Surely they can't do this to us?" But they did. Next day I discovered that everyone had lost their bottles. The hamsters were now going to decide when we could urinate, and settled on four times per 24 hours. At age 55, I was in trouble. Even the young guys, John and Brian, suffered. But for the next two months, we were at their mercy. For me, surely these months were the low point in the whole experience. After a few weeks, they were getting lazier and lazier, though it was hard to believe that they could! One afternoon, they took us at about 4:00 P.M., and we didn't hear from them again until well after midnight. Finally Fadl appeared. I could see him by standing back from the window and hiding in the shadow of the cell. He took John then Brian, and since we were not allowed to talk, I pulled down my blindfold and stood right by the window where he couldn't miss me. A few minutes later, all went quiet. "Oh, no" I thought. "Surely they aren't going to leave me in this state?" I was desperate. Slowly I lifted my blindfold to see what the hell was going on, and carefully looked over toward the double cell where they had been some minutes before. "Ya-Eeeeeh." A great blood-curdling scream came from my left, and Fadl came charging toward my cell. The bastard had tricked me. He had slithered quietly over to the end of the cell block to my left, and waited to see what I might do. Sure enough I fell for it and had looked out of the window, a big, big no-no. He came into my cell and proceeded to cuff me all over my ribs, and to scream in his best English, "Why you looking? Why you looking, huh?" "I have to urinate." He wouldn't listen and kept screaming and cuffing me. But soon he gave up and left. It hadn't hurt that badly, and I was thanking my stars that I had got off so lightly for such a heinous crime as looking out of the little window. Suddenly he was back, and led me out to the door of the cell block, where he made me sit on the ground. Several men began to pray urgently while I sat there. Then they were ready. They took me into cell 11 and laid me on my back. One of them held up my feet while another began to beat on the insoles with some kind of rubber truncheon. *Whap, whap, whap, whap.* God, I couldn't stand it any longer and began to scream. "No scream," Fadl shouted. But I was beyond it, and Fadl kept going. *Whap, whap, whap, whap,* until finally one of his buddies called "Khalas! Khalas!" ("Stop! Enough!"). Quitting my insoles, he switched to my calves, thighs, ribs, shoulders, and by the time he was done, I was black and blue from my neck to my feet. Then Fadl began to hustle me back to my cell without even allowing me to go to the toilet, the original cause of all this misery. I pleaded with them, and good old Mahmoud took pity on me and led me into the small bathroom—surely a misnomer, for these men didn't know what a bath is—with the usual, "Okay. But queeckly, okay?" Quickly? How could I possibly urinate quickly after such a beating? I tried, and sure enough, I was desperate enough by this time that I managed to "go queeckly."

Back in my cell, I reflected on this kind of justice. Fadl had been convinced that I had been trying to see him. If only he had known; I had seen him dozens of times, and certainly didn't need to see him any more to be able to recognize him with no problem! All I wanted was to go to the toilet—for which I was now black and blue all over. I hadn't been beaten like that in my life. Frankly I hadn't been in any kind of violent situation since I was about 12 and picked a fight with a boy much bigger than myself. Everybody was picking on him and deciding that he'd had enough of that nonsense, he decided to fight back for the first time. My bad luck, for he beat the dickens out of me. I decided there and then that fighting was not my game. Next morning, Sayeed came in and innocently asked in a feigned shocked voice as he examined my blotched skin, "What happened?" I was determined not to give him the satisfaction of knowing they had really hurt me, so I replied, "I don't know. Some people came to my room and beat on me for a while then left." He rubbed my legs a little, then left, and the incident was never brought up again. He was the boss of the scene at that time, and I wondered if he had chewed out the others—he sometimes did when he thought they'd gotten out of line.

But my problems weren't over yet. The guards apparently decided I was even more dangerous to their anonymity than they had thought, and that I really was a CIA agent who would stop at nothing to get a good look at them! So they promptly blocked off my little barred window with a steel shutter, and I was more than ever in the dark. I got no outside light, no candle, and underground like that, it is really dark! When they brought in my food, they had a candle, dished the food out, and left me in that darkness, not knowing what on earth was now in my bowl or how I was supposed to eat it. Experimentation by feeling usually led to messy fingers, and with no Kleenex and no trip to the toilet in the offing, this was not a good scene.

It lasted for several weeks, during which time I had no contact whatsoever with my companions. I was thoroughly on my own, in the dark, and "licking my wounds." I became more and more angry, and more and more discouraged, until finally I convinced myself that I simply couldn't put up with this nonsense any longer. I was damned if I was going to let other men treat a fellow human being in this inhuman fashion. I determined to end it all and commit suicide. We had read not too long before in *Time* magazine about a Korean prisoner in the United States or somewhere who had committed suicide by pulling a plastic bag over his head until he suffocated. So when the guards brought me a new clean plastic garbage sack, I set my plan in motion. I pulled it over my head and pulled it close in to my throat. But that wasn't tight enough—enough air was leaking into the sack that nothing drastic was happening. I then tied my sock tightly around my neck, and that did it—soon I began to feel the shortage of oxygen. Gradually it began to hurt more and more, until it really hurt. Finally, when I was getting desperate, a vision appeared before my eyes in my semistupor: Jean and

Ann and Kit and Joan were there, all four, clear as could be. "God," I thought desperately. "God. I can't." It was there in my head, clearly. "I can't do this to them. Not fair!" So I grabbed the plastic bag and hauled it off my head, gasping desperately. I had really been right on the verge of going. Three times I tried it, with three times the same result; I simply couldn't bring myself to go through with it all the way. Maybe I wasn't brave enough, or desperate enough, or determined enough. In any case, I am here today, and very glad to be here. *A day at a time, just get through a day at a time.*

By December, the guards had relented somewhat and had taken away my shutter, so that I had communication again with John and Brian, and amazingly, with Terry Anderson who had now been moved into cell number four, next door to them. Previously, that had been occupied by an old Frenchman named Sontag, who was rather deaf, and had always spoken much too loudly for the guards' taste. "My name is Sontag," he had said often in the early days, in a very loud voice. He had a distinctly French accent, with some German overtones thrown in, which made sense with a name like Sontag, German for Sunday. Some weeks ago, he had dropped his false teeth and could no longer eat, so the kindly Islamic Jihad had seen fit to release *him* at least. Why they had even kept around a man in his eighties had always puzzled us. Many things Islamic Jihad did puzzled us over the years. Anyway, here was my buddy Terry within eyesight again, and the two Brits beside him. I was now the "go between," for I could see both their cells and could take their messages, while they couldn't see each other. I became a real "signer."

In this most awful of all the places we were held, the next "big event" came a little later in December. I was awakened roughly by two of the guards, who began to search every nook and cranny of my cell. Everything we ever had in there had been brought in by them, so what they were looking for was always a puzzlement in these sorts of searches. I was hauled out into the hallway and frisked all over, easy to do for I had on only a set of boxer shorts and a T-shirt; even in December, it didn't get very cold down there. They began to interrogate me in the most hostile way. What had I done in the night? Who had I seen? I was puzzled, and told them honestly that I had seen no one, and had only been asleep until not long before their arrival. After breakfast, John filled me in. In the middle of the night, Frank had escaped from his cell, and had made the rounds speaking to them and some of the others in the place. I had slept through it all, and was quite unaware of his venture. The story was this: Frank had managed to reach down far enough to pull open the bolt keeping the door shut on the outside, and got out. Once out though he couldn't get through the main steel door, and returning to his cell, he wasn't able to get the bolt shoved back into place, since the door opened outwards and he couldn't pull it toward himself and push the bolt home at the same time. So the guards had discovered all this in the morning and had given him a severe talk. A little later, however, the talking degenerated into a rather severe beating, followed by isolation in cell six. A few hours later and he was taken out again, beaten some more, then put back into cell six. This routine went on for two days or so, in the course of which Frank sank into a catatonic state. Meantime, a whole team of "bigwigs" had arrived, and they now began to interrogate each one of us separately, asking us all kinds of leading questions, suggesting, for example, that I had no doubt talked with someone in the night. I answered them truthfully as usual, and this time they seemed to be satisfied, much to my relief. I was genuinely afraid that I was going to get the CIA bit again, especially since Sayeed was in the group and put in several facetious comments about my being a friend of Mr. William Casey, then director of the CIA. Each of us had much the same experience in that interview, and apparently the bigwigs were satisfied that no real breach of security had occurred, but the consequence was that the guards from then on sytematically locked the padlocks on every door.

Two days after Frank's escape attempt, Terry Anderson and I were "called up" by Fadl to talk to Frank and to try to get him to speak. He was lying in his cell like a cat that had been run over by a Mack truck, and refused to say a word to either of us, despite our assurances that we were American and friendly. Eventually, Fadl gave up and led us back to our respective cells. We were feeling, of course, very sorry indeed for Frank, but confused as to why he had even attempted to get out of his cell.

Christmas Day arrived, our second in captivity, and Terry and I were talking by sign language. For some reason he took off his glasses, the substitutes the Hajj had given him in August 1985 since he'd only been wearing sunglasses the day he was kidnapped. Somehow they dropped on the solid tile floor and went into a thousand bits. That ended our "conversation," for Terry could not see five feet without glasses. He almost cried, and may even have done so, for as he later told me, that was the lowest day in what he has described as the worst of all the places we were held. And our troubles were even compounded, for although Sayeed or Ali agreed to get his glasses fixed, and did a day or two later with the same prescription as before, they were not at all Terry's real needs in lenses. Still, they were better than nothing and all that he had for six years.

Confronted by Fadl and Sayeed again. One of the other guards was claiming that Terry and I had been speaking, and I could hear Terry vehemently denying this charge. I was wondering if they meant actual talking, or if one of the guards had actually seen us signing to each other, despite our extreme care to be sure that none of them were around when we were "talking." But when Sayeed said, "One of our friends heard you talking," I knew that I was on safe grounds to deny the accusation as forcefully and truthfully as I wanted, for we had not ever talked by voice across the cell block since Frank had first arrived. That was still a real no-no. They tried nevertheless to get me to "confess," and good old Fadl was at it again, slapping me on the ribs and pushing me, and squeezing my face in his hand until it hurt. Still I denied it, and finally Sayeed's sense prevailed. Terry found out that it was the new guard, a young fellow who until now had been rather kind and helpful, who was claiming that he had heard us. Using the name of Abed, this young man spoke rather fluent French, but little English, and seemed altogether a different sort of fellow. He was obviously much more intelligent than all the other guards, and told us that he was the son of a teacher in a high school. He claimed to have spent much of his life outside of Lebanon, and seemed to have a better perspective on world affairs than the "average" guard. But like all of them, he soon tired of his compassion and began to treat us perhaps even worse than the rest, and was more sly about it. He would sneak around the cell block ever so quietly, and we had really to beware of his presence before we began to sign to one another. That he would get off on making trouble for us when we were already on the edge of despair said a lot about him.

14   The Fall
of '86

September 1986—Frank Reed, Joe Cicippio, and Edward Tracy kidnapped one after the other and menacing videos released by Islamic Jihad of Dave Jacobsen and Terry Anderson amidst the international brouhaha over the U.S. exchange of a Russian spy for Nick Daniloff. Crisis. I got a quick letter off on September 18:

Hope you don't mind a general letter tonight—I've been really busy and have had lots of people coming by … . So far nothing is really changed for me yet although Joe's kidnapping from Faculty 2 Apartments inside of campus was a definite blow—even if we have always known AUB wasn't "safe" in any sense of the word, still the complete ease of the abduction under the noses of Syrians, Lebanese Army, AUB security, whatever, was unexpectedly horrendous. So far nothing indicates pressure on women, but if the situation deteriorates I'll get out, so don't worry. Meanwhile, I gave an interview and photo session to Reuters and talked to journalists, and "sat in" for Joe yesterday … .

The *Newsweek* man brought me a copy of the letter from the Jihad through Dave Jacobsen two days ago … . It was Dave's handwriting but dictated—this does mean a message that they want to deal (on their terms) and the basis is the Daniloff case. [In Islamic Jihad's eyes there was perfect equation: if the United States could exchange a Russian they held as a spy for their journalist Daniloff being held prisoner in Moscow, then they could work an exchange of 17 Dawa prisoners from Kuwait for American hostages held in Lebanon. Pure "logical" reasoning.] It was clear that they had seen Peggy Say's appeal in addition to accounts of the Weir-Jenco-Levin meeting in Washington. Somehow I think that every time Washington says "No" the voice gets louder and the accents harder—the French experience and her awful situation now with terrorists setting off bombs in downtown Paris I think presages a particularly hard line approach—in effect, the other extremists of the very nastiest kind are undermining the Jihad's position. (It's come to the point of "choice" among abductors—everyone had "hoped" if it had to happen to Joe that it was the Jihad that had taken him ... . What a state of affairs ... !!) Where it all leads we don't, of course, know. I'm staying cool (as I can) and trying everything and everybody (that I can) ... . And I work at the school—between sessions right now I'm cleaning and arranging offices, inventorying, and riding herd on secretaries and hired help, getting equipment and furniture repaired, doing a feasibility study on computerizing the program ... . I won't say I'm not schizophrenic because then you might worry ... . Please think strong thoughts for all of us but don't worry about me because I'm all right, doing what I have to do and want to do ... .

I think about you all ... . I'm set up for return on October 15 to give the speech at World Food Day in Fort Collins on the 16th—my ticket will probably be at least a 2-week one and if I can get a run-around ticket again this time I'll try to do just that ... .

The political situation vis-à-vis the hostages got worse instead of better as deadlocks and menaces continued. By the first week of October I knew I had to do something. Even given our belief in Terry Waite, I couldn't stand by. It seemed that Peggy Say and I were on the same wavelength because her mediation offer appeared in the U.S. press on October 8 and mine in Beirut on October 9. With the help of my wonderful friend Radwan Mawlawi in the AUB communications/ publications office so that it would go out in proper Arabic, I put an ad in the Beirut leftist newspaper *As-Safir* that the captors would read. Addressed to Islamic Jihad, the message offered my best offices to help effect dialogue between them and the American government—as the AUB press summary of October 9, 1986, reported:

Newspapers today published a statement by Mrs. Jean Sutherland (prepared by the Director of Information) whereby she offers to serve as a mediator between the U.S. administration and the Islamic Jihad Organization holding her husband, FAFS Dean Thomas Sutherland, hostage for the past sixteen months.

Mrs. Sutherland, who still resides in Lebanon after her husband's abduction, explained that the principal motive behind her decision was the continuation of efforts to release him and the other hostages. Her impression, she said, after carefully reading communiques and statements made by the U.S. administration and the Islamic Jihad Organization, was that both sides are clearly willing to discuss the demands and conditions, particularly after the American administration expressed a desire to conduct a dialogue directly or indirectly with the abductors.

Mrs. Sutherland concluded her statement by affirming her understanding for both the abductors' stand regarding their imprisoned comrades and the position of the U.S. government, but concentrated efforts she said were needed to surmount obstacles and reach a fair and honest basis for discussion and consequently secure the safety and the release of all the hostages.

Finally, Mrs. Sutherland asserted that she was taking this initiative individually, not on anyone's request and was at the disposition of leaders of the Islamic Jihad Organization if they decide to meet her, including in the statement her telephone numbers: 353081 and 340740 (ext. 2514), and her P.O. Box: 11/236.

The weekend that followed I sat on our balcony and waited for Islamic Jihad to call (at least, as I told Tom afterward, that's the story I could tell our grandchildren). The call never came of course—not that I truly expected it because it wasn't their style. What I hoped had happened was that the message had attracted their attention and they would wait and watch. My trip was set to go to the United States the next week—not only was I to speak at World Food Day, but Ann and Ray had set their wedding for October 18 in Berkeley so I could attend. I thought and thought about it and decided that the timing and the travel opportunity had to be "meant." Words weren't enough—actions had to be there to convince Islamic Jihad I could make good my offer to be of service to effect dialogue between them and the American government. Therefore, I would state publicly in Beirut that I was going back to the States to see President Reagan and then I would do it, and maybe when I came back they would use me as an avenue for dialogue. It was well worth the chance taken.

All worked out as planned with much publicity in Beirut on my leave-taking. I really couldn't have asked for better coverage and dissemination of my "going to the United States to see President Reagan." Eighteen hours later, the plane came into Dulles International Airport and I remember being absolutely struck by the beauty of the trees that October day of 1986— how glorious those East Coast colors are, and mingled with the sense of being *home*, unforgettable! While in Washington, I made contact with our State Department liaison, that wonderful man John Adams, who set up appointments for me—first with Undersecretary Richard Murphy and attendant people, and secondly with President Reagan for the end of the month when he would be signing the Rivers Bill out in Colorado.

The meeting with Undersecretary Murphy was most interesting. April Glaspie was there, and I had a warm feeling toward her because she seemed sincerely happy that I had not gone "walking in Schweifat on a Saturday or Sunday" that February weekend eight months ago while the PSP and Amal were at loggerheads. My overriding impression from the meeting, however, which amazed me because it was a decidedly new attitude, was the anger this State Department group as a whole felt toward what was happening with the hostage situation. Their words to me were something like an icy "If you want to know what's going on, you'll have to check with Colonel North, he's handling everything." I checked to see if it was possible to see Colonel North, but he was gone from Washington. I have not to this day met North, in fact, nor would I know what to say to him if I did, our visions of what constitutes "a neat idea" turning out to be poles apart. It was later that day in Washington that a State Department friend took me out for a walk around the block to give me the information about an arms-for-hostages deal that was going on through White House channels and bypassing the Department of State. I was further amazed.

Off I went to Fort Collins for my World Food Day speech on Thursday night, then Friday morning I flew to Berkeley for Ann and Ray's wedding, an ever so much more wonderful occasion than we could possibly have planned. It was a most special, beautiful ceremony in a friend's garden overlooking San Francisco Bay and then home for a reception with all their friends and Kit and Joan and me. I'll never forget Ann getting up on her wedding morning to make banana cream pies for the reception, "... because Ray loves banana cream pie!" Ann had asked me if I thought she and Ray should wait to be married until her dad came home; I told her for sure not—we had agreed that our lives should go forward in the most natural and productive way even while he was gone, and it would be the best gift she could give him when he returned. That a beautiful daughter, Simone, would arrive the next year, that I was in the States and could fly out to arrive at 2:00 A.M. to welcome her, that she would come to Fort Collins with Ann and Ray to be in a 1987 Christmas photograph of the whole family that would be published in *As-Safir* and delivered to Tom by one of his guards on Valentine's Day of 1988—all that was the icing-to-be on the wedding cake that day!

Another day with Ann and Ray and then it was on to Los Angeles with Joan who was living in Long Beach and working with United Airlines now, still taking reservations at the end of an 800 number. Such a treat for me to meet her friends and see their apartment and just talk and talk. Joan had earlier in the month appeared on the *Phil Donahue Show* and now told me the story:

> It was a panel with Peggy Say, Father Jenco, Eric Jacobsen, one of Frank Reed's daughters, me, and a few other family members, and it came right after Nicholas Daniloff had been released and the *Phil Donahue Show* thought he and his boss, Mortimer Zuckerman, should also be on the show. Biggest mistake ever! The audience turned out to be very sympathetic to the hostage families and very ugly to Mr. Daniloff. They couldn't understand why the government would deal for him and not for our people and they blamed Mr. Daniloff. The problem was that the two situations were

TOTALLY different and Mr. Daniloff should never have been on that stage with us. But more than that, we ourselves found out what ugliness was because by the end while the whole audience was in tears for us, everyone who had called in on the telephone was extremely antagonistic to us .... .

Fortunately for our family things were still positive and CBS came out and took pictures of Joan and me walking on the beach—a mother-daughter profile—and set up with me for in-depth interviews when I got back to Washington and "A Day in My Life" when I got back to Beirut. All materialized on their film, but never on TV, which was just as well I guess. (It was Juan-Carlos in Beirut who did the filming there and I'll never forget his horror when the result of his asking for a few students from a class at our English program was a horde of 750 students in the hall to be filmed with me. It was true microcosmic proof of how fast news travels in Beirut!)

Father Martin was at this time living in a Servite Fathers' house in Irvine, California, and invited Joan and me there with Eric Jacobsen to have breakfast and a nice get-together one morning. We did lots of catching up and brainstorming. Then it was for me back to Fort Collins and my trip to Colorado Springs and the Broadmoor Hotel where President Reagan and his entourage were staying. Such a fine October day to drive down to the Springs—I was met and taken up to the top of the Broadmoor to meet the president. No media circus, although I did meet the press quietly afterward for interviews, which I hoped would be picked up and mentioned in *As-Safir* or on the TV or radio in Beirut. An elegant room, a picture as I shook hands with President Reagan, then we sat together on a leather couch at one end of the room with a semicircle of "the President's Men" around us—I can only remember Donald Regan and Admiral Poindexter, the others were people I didn't think I knew. President Reagan was kindly and I didn't mince words to tell him that I'd given my name and phone number to Islamic Jihad, that I hoped a bridge could be formed to have dialogue with them, that I offered myself to him, since I would be in Beirut, to perform any service that would be helpful at any time to resolve this conflict situation. I also gave him the name of my brother's conflict resolution clinic and asked if he could designate someone to liaise with it. He kindly accepted all from me, and then he told me in turn that someone would be released within the next few days—he couldn't say at all that it would be my husband, however. I accepted this and we ended the meeting. I shook hands all around and Admiral Poindexter showed me to the door with, "Are you going back to Beirut?" "Yes." "Well, be careful." "Yes, sir, I always am." I said to Tom afterward that two months later I was working normally in Beirut and Admiral Poindexter had been fired as a part of the Iran-

Contra Affair and was out of a job—"I should have told *him* to be careful!"
How amazing!

David Jacobsen was the one to be released in the midst of Terry Waite's "Keep
Your Eye on Beirut" and Ollie North's jet-setting and helicoptering. I was in New
York by that time at the home of our AUB friends the Slades when the call got
put through in the middle of the night from Wiesbaden and I talked with David
about Tom. He gave me messages for the AUB New York office and next morning
I toyed with the idea of going to Washington for David's homecoming. But Terry
Waite was again/still in the news with his "24 hours" to know if the chance for
Anderson and Sutherland to come out would materialize—he was "on alert." No
question in my mind what I should do—I must be in personal touch with Terry
and be back on my way to Beirut. I made the contact through the State Department to Terry in Wiesbaden (I didn't often "command" help, but this time I said
I *had* to speak to Terry Waite), Terry confirmed that "24 hours should tell," so I
got on the first plane back, and I was in Beirut to receive the news: No Deal. And
then *As-Sharaa* broke the news of the arms-for-hostages deal with all the attendant scandal. We were into "Irangate."

The first week of December brought the first of the post–Irangate exposé
independent negotiators to Beirut—Americans Mohammad Mehdi, president
of the Committee for American-Arab relations, and Dale Shaheen, vice president of the National Council for Islamic Affairs. Mehdi, according to the Associated Press release, "hoped to open talks within a week with groups holding hostages, and to return with at least one freed kidnap victim before Christmas ... .
We appeal to the hostage-holders in the name of the Koran, humanity, and the
cause of peace to release the hostages ... ." Rather amazing rhetoric at this point
in time, especially for one who stated publicly: "We understand the language of
the people. We understand the pattern of their thinking." Surely those of us on
the scene had long ago recognized that humanity, peace, and holy books had no
relevancy for either the language or pattern of thinking of hostage holders. That
Mr. Mehdi had come with perhaps mixed motives on his "self-styled mission"
was signaled by the attendant publicity he was quite clearly enjoying, a phenomenon to be replayed a month later when Terry Waite would reappear as his own
independent negotiator. Without our knowledge or consent, Elham, Joe Cicippio's
wife, and I were made a part of the Mehdi media play, much to our dismay. A
former AUB employee turned Western journalists' helper, a man also named
Mehdi, told me that Mohammad Mehdi would like to meet privately with the
two of us to express his great concern and desire to help—he suggested our home
at AUB. I agreed, invited Elham to come, and then opened the door not only to

Mehdi and Mehdi, but also to a sea of reporters following in their wake. Nothing to do but be hospitable and photographed, duly appearing in a picture with M. Mehdi in a magazine afterward. At the finish-up, this first of the independent negotiators left early, without a released hostage and without a billfold, his hotel room having been burgled. He didn't come back.

Meantime, Terry Waite had also figured in the same first of December news release:

> Mr. Waite said in London Sunday he had resumed contacts aimed at winning the release of hostages in Lebanon, although recent political developments had made the task difficult. Speaking in a British Broadcasting Corp. radio interview, Waite said he did not think his work had been undermined by the news about U.S. arms sales to Iran, with the proceeds being used to fund Nicaraguan rebels. "I know my own motives and my own intents," he said. "I'm totally clear and independent of any Government, American, British, or any other." But he said some of his contacts in Lebanon's Shiite Moslem community had been "a little frayed by all the political mish-mash of the last weeks."
>
> He said in some cases it may be difficult for him to have continuing contact with them for those political reasons. "However, I'm glad to say that in the last few days I have resumed contact with a number of Lebanese friends, and I'm fairly confident that it's going to be possible to continue what is a purely humanitarian and right thing to do in seeking the release of these people," Waite said.

It might well be a "humanitarian and right thing to do" to seek for release according to our nice Western philosophy, but it was scarcely a realistic or viable concept with which to try to deal with Islamic Jihad at any time, much less this Irangate time. I kept going back to my brother John's conflict resolution theory and putting the results of the "no" and "yes" response to the demand for "unconditional release for humanitarian reasons." It came out the same as with M. Mehdi, the same as June 9, 1985, for that matter. Just no way that Islamic Jihad was going to even think of giving up Western hostages on a humanitarian basis because someone was "seeking the release of these people." Just no way. And I could accept it—for it was not being pessimistic against Terry Waite's being optimistic. It was being purely realistic, and the only way to go.

On the way home to the States for Christmas, I had a stopover in London and called Terry Waite. I caught him at one of the numbers he had given me and he came in his MG to my hotel near the airport and we talked. He wanted to know what Beirut was like and I told him the truth: "Kidnapping is rampant— young Lebanese men are being picked up for ransom—there have been dozens and the streets are very bad." Terry seemed hyped up, almost childishly excited— I'd never seen him like that. He suddenly and impressively pulled out his electronic address book, dialed a number on the phone and proceeded to talk to someone—"One of my contacts for the captors." He told me he was contemplating going back to Beirut before Christmas. Knowing I had to be in Beirut if he were there, I changed plans and stayed over in London for an extra day or two. When I called him back, he told me he had decided not to go then but later, so I hopped the plane and got my family Christmas. Everyone came from California to Fort Collins—Ann and Ray from Berkeley (Ann happily pregnant) and Joan from Los Angeles (unhappily strep-throated)—and what a wonderful time we all had together in Kit's one-bedroom apartment across from the Foothills Fashion Mall, even though Kit had to work at her pig lab on Christmas Day. On New Year's Eve when all the Californians had departed, my brother John came in with his two children, Peter and Allison—we celebrated the evening with back-to-back videos: *Indiana Jones and the Temple of Doom* and *Ghostbusters*.

And Tom, facing nadir 10,000 miles away in his black hole, was for us all that Christmas season a constant presence in his absence.

15 Up to the Blindfold Apartment ... Down to the Dungeon

January 25, 1987, and I was still alone. No big Burns Supper celebration this year for sure. No one around to listen to my praises for "Oor Rabbie!" So I had to do it all on my own. All during this isolation, recalling as many and as much of Burns's poems had all occupied *hundreds* of hours and helped immeasurably to keep me sane in that most trying of times ... reciting them over and over, trying to get into proper sequence the couplets of "Tam o' Shanter," trying to recall as much as I could of other long poems, "The Twa Dogs" and "The Cotter's Saturday Night," and almost endlessly repeating the many that I knew by heart: "To a Mouse," with its "The best laid schemes o' mice and men, gang aft agley"; "To a Louse," and its "O wad some power the gift tae gie us, to see oursels as others see us"; "My Luve Is Like a Red, Red Rose"; "John Anderson My Jo"; "Flow Gently Sweet Afton"; "Holy Willie's Prayer"; and on and on. I mused on Burns's genius and his wonderful words. And the bravery he had shown in times of tribulation, handling the overwhelming odds he was facing much of his life from the aftereffect of his rheumatic fever, eventually dying so young at 37. Two hundred nine years were as nothing—he was there in the cell that night with the poem Jean and I both loved so much:

> O, my luve is like a red, red rose, that's newly sprung in June,
> O, my luve is like the melodie, that's sweetly played in tune.
> As fair art thou, my bonie lass, so deep in luve am I,
> And I will luve thee still my Dear, till a' the seas gang dry.

I wept.

A few days later, another midnight visit from Sayeed. "Come. Bring your things." "Am I going home?" "Maybe. I don't know. Come quickly; no speak, okay?" The usual. I had suspected that something was afoot, for there was lots of activity around the cell block prior to Sayeed's arrival at my "suite." I was led into the guards' room, where two of them hauled me bodily up the little circular stair that we had descended some six months before. Thank God we were leaving this hellhole. We had dubbed it "The Prison" with good reason—the worst of all the 14 places over six and a half years.

Upstairs was the huge garage; sounds echoed around it as in a barn. They pushed me into some kind of truck where Terry was already installed, but between us was a skinny kind of fellow, whom I didn't recognize at all by his grunts and excited pokings into my ribs. It didn't seem like anything that Brian or John, either one, would do. Who on earth *could* this guy be? The guards warned him sternly. Then one of them spotted him still trying to make contact with us, promptly beat on him, took him out of the truck, and we had no further contact with him. To this day, I have no idea who it could have been. Next in his place came Frank Reed, who sat very quietly. The truck took off, but soon stopped. Terry and I were transferred into the back of a car, and even in the pitch black of the middle of the night pushed down out of sight. A short drive of ten minutes, and we were hustled out and marched up several flights of stairs into a room with no mattresses, no blankets, nothing. It was *cold*. We had come from the underground "cozy warmth" of "The Prison," and in the cool air of the night, we really felt the difference. But my overriding feeling was that this must be some sort of halfway house—probably we would be here for a few hours, or perhaps a day or so, then on our way home. This room was totally unprepared as a prison cell—simply had to be temporary. Ah, sweet delusions. Now in my *fifth* "cell," the "Blindfold Apartment," where I was to spend the next month.

This new location proved to be a nightmare of a different sort. The temporary nature meant that the two windows had not been covered in any way, and the apartment building across the way was many stories higher, so that even lying on the floor, we could be seen by the occupants of the high floors. So we were sternly instructed to keep ourselves well back into the nether reaches of the room. Soon, Frank arrived with little idea of how he had been brought and zero idea of where we were. Terry figured we had to be somewhere in the region of the Corniche Mazra, more or less on the very north edge of the southern suburbs. By midday, some blankets appeared, but it was a couple more days before we had mattresses between us and the hard tile floor.

The guards too had to be omnipresent, otherwise we would have been able to look out of the windows, so day and night we wore those damn blindfolds. At night one of the guards slept with us, or rather was supposed to be on duty, but most of them ended up falling asleep. The night guard would come in, lock the door from the inside, and take the key over by his mattress. When he fell asleep, there was his gun by his side as well as the key, so there was again a remote chance of escape here. But, we reasoned, no point in risking anything in this "halfway house" when we were about to be given to the Syrians or whomever any day. But it was a bit of a temptation, for all the rest of the young men were in another room, sound asleep.

The days were awful, for all three of the guards shared our room, and it meant 24 hours a day under blindfolds. They became filthy and began to bother our eyes. And no real opportunity to wash them out, for trips to the toilet were four a day and brief as usual. The consideration of the guards extended at this time to deciding when these four toilet trips would be *exactly*. They had nothing to do here, the toilet was right at the door of our room, it took zero effort to allow us to go, for we weren't even chained, and it was just a question of allowing us to crawl to the door, stand up, and enter the toilet. No matter: *Four times in 24 hours was it.*

No reading in this place. We hadn't, of course, been reading in "The Prison," either, for all privileges had been taken away as punishment for our behavior in the "Marseillaise apartment." So it was Frank lying right alongside me on one side and Terry on the other—three prone "corpses," almost. We were allowed to talk quietly after a few days, but Frank was still semicatatonic and not talking, so only Terry and I communicated. "Say, Sutherland, you were a college prof, right?" "Yep." "Well, teach me your courses." "Man, are you crazy? I don't have any notes. No college prof can teach without his notes!" "Well, just teach me what you can remember," he insisted. "Oh, God," I thought, "I became a dean partly to get away from all that, and now this character wants me to do it with no notes, lying on the floor, blindfolded, guards a-go-go tripping over us." I was less than enthusiastic. Terry insisted still, and pointed out that it would pass the time until we went home. So I agreed. "We'll start with the 'Introductory Animal Science' course, AN 100. That was fairly elementary, and I think I can recall most of it." So we got going. The course was an overview of the main subject areas: breeding, nutrition, reproduction, meats, management, marketing, etc. It turned out to be rather fun, and it did pass the time. The guards even understood what we were doing, and approved, for they wanted us to be happy, and not morose and bitter. Terry was a fantastic student, for, without taking any notes either, he was into everything, asking very penetrating questions and remembering virtually every word I said.

In two or three days, we were done with the introductory course—it was what would be called in academe a solid block course! "Now, how about your animal breeding course?" "Man, that was for juniors and seniors, at a pretty high level," I countered. "I don't know if you could follow that." Only a little trace of arrogance in my reply. "Okay. But let's have a shot at it and see how much I *can* follow. Got anything else urgent to do?" he replied. So off we went into the intricacies of selection theory and heritability, inbreeding and crossbreeding. I had forgotten that Terry had taken some statistics courses, and had also been heavily into dogs, including some breeding and showing. So he was in fact well placed to follow much of what I was telling him. And he did. Again, he would have been an A+ student, no question, and I had some of the same sensations as Ben Weir had had when he was teaching him Arabic, or again as I had had in teaching him French, though there the concepts were not nearly so abstract. It took quite a few lessons to get through the animal breeding stuff, and as soon as we were done, he came up with more requests. "Statistics. I never understood sampling theory," he said. "And that's what is most useful to us in journalism." Ouch. I had never studied sampling theory either, but I taught him what little I knew about it. This evoked long arguments, for Terry had an innate suspicion of statistics, and was convinced that the primary purpose in using them was to lie. He is not alone in that belief, of course. But I had a dickens of a time persuading him that statistics don't lie at all, and it is only when they are misused that they breed confusion. In animal breeding theory, statistical techniques have wrought wonders, leading to incredible improvements in animal performance—milk production, growth rates, back-fat thickness in pigs, tenderness of beef, and on and on. So we did the Socratic thing with blindfolds and a tile floor in place of a log.

Armed with all this new knowledge of agriculture, Terry had an idea. He would develop a dairy farm in upstate New York for boys potentially in trouble with the law—the boys would live on the farm and do all the work, while getting about a half day of schooling each day from resident teachers specially selected for the job. The questions began to flow. How much for an acre of land near Rochester? How many acres will we need? How much for a cow? How many should we keep? How much does a cow eat? How much milk does she give? How do you raise calves? What about vet bills? The wholesale price of milk? What is a milking parlor? Bulls or artificial insemination? We talked about the design of the dorms, the number of teachers, the age of the boys, the possibilities of their going on to college. We discussed getting a big grant from Ford or some other foundation to buy the farm and get it all under way. It all took weeks and months at a time and kept our minds very occupied—all the while talking from behind blindfolds with no pencil or paper. All done at this stage in our minds. In subsequent cells, we had paper again and talked of revising the project, the size, the nature (we talked of introducing pigs into the scheme), and of honing the budget. Endless hours of discussion and planning. But time we had.

All this time Mahmoud was treating us fairly well, so we took the chance to bug him for fruit. "If you're going to keep us around here, Mahmoud, on a very limited diet, you've got to keep giving us fruit—we must have vitamins or we will be very ill." We had been getting some in previous locations. Came back an astonishing reply—"We have talked to doctor, and he say you must have *halawi*. That good for you." *Halawi!?* Almost pure sugar—surely the last thing we needed while lying flat on our backs 24 hours a day! In the main, the diet was passable. Rice and beans, very "third world" to be sure—but rice has 16 percent protein, and beans anywhere from 20–40 percent, depending on the variety. And we surely were having variety—I never realized there were so many kinds of beans in the world! Which was good, for each would have a different balance of amino acids. As for the rice, another startling admission from Mahmoud—"Best rice Uncle Ben's. We all like it much more than Egypt rice!" "But Mahmoud, that is American rice!" "I know." Well, well! It took a while, but we eventually won the fruit battle again, and got one piece every day until our release—an orange, an apple, a peach, some apricots, some tangerines, a bunch of grapes, a pomegranate, a banana, fresh figs. Beirut and Lebanon are covered with fruit stands of all kinds, so that was an easy battle, relatively speaking!

"The Big M," as we frequently called Mahmoud, was, however, giving us other news of various kinds, presumably more reliable than his advice on health matters—such as what was really going on in the Iran-Iraq war. We could rather easily tell who was winning by the mood of the guards, particularly Fadl and Hadi, who were so pro-Iran that we chuckled about it. Mahmoud also gave us a few comments on Terry Waite, who had apparently arrived back in Beirut. And Sayeed came in once in a while, reporting one day that Waite had disappeared. "Nobody know where he is," chuckled Sayeed. "Maybe he go America. I don't know!" Then he would laugh roisterously, as though it were some great joke. We were worried, for our spirits had been uplifted somewhat when Mahmoud had told us that Waite had at last reappeared after leaving Beirut on Christmas Eve over a year ago. On the radio, the guards were listening to the reports in Arabic, and we heard frequent references to Waite and Anderson and Sutherland, though they would never interpret for us. For many days this went on, without ever any mention of Frank Reed. Terry remarked that it must be discouraging for Frank to hear so many references to us two, without *any* mention of *his* name. Mahmoud informed us that Nabih Berri was angry about Waite's disappearance, but that Walid Jumblatt was absolutely furious, for he had undertaken to protect Waite, and this was an affront to the efficiency and competence of his militia. Islamic Jihad of course had no love whatever for either of these two gentlemen, so this whole episode was a cause of great amusement for them.

After three and a half weeks, a crew of workmen arrived and worked around and over us. They were at last putting up the steel shutters on the windows. My heart sank. Gone was the illusion that this was a temporary place. Visions of more and more months appeared. It took a whole day to finish, and out they all went, guards and all. *Blessed relief.* At least we could lift our blindfolds. *And walk around!* For we were still not chained. After three and a half weeks of hardly moving we were getting really stiff. What a blessing this new freedom was, even if it did leave us in the dark much of the day. And we could sleep in peace.

The steel shutters were this time not a good fit, and we had a few glimpses of what lay outside for almost the first time in our captivity. It was almost eerie, looking outside and seeing people in the daytime, and tall high-rise apartment buildings all around us and, at night, brightly lit at times, when the power was on. But even Terry, fairly familiar with much of Beirut, wasn't able to recognize any of the buildings—they were all nondescript apartment buildings, like hundreds of others in the southern suburbs. The guards had taken the key out of the lock, too, so we could again peek across the hall. Even Terry had a go at it this time. Lo and behold, who appeared in the room directly across from us but John and Brian. We were fairly sure that they had not been there before, for no one else had been using the toilet.

Five weeks passed, and we were just beginning to get used to the exercise, which was feeling better and better as our muscles adapted. Then, one middle of the night, in came the Ghost and told us to get dressed as warmly as we could. Now where, we wondered? As usual, great stress for us in the change, leaving what we knew, bad as it was, for what we knew not. Several other guards joined the fray and nervously (as usual the stress for them was as great as for us) escorted us down the five or six flights of stairs, this time on foot. Into a big van, all three of us. I was first, and heard the tape being pulled off the roll. Just what Father and Ben had told me about; now it was my turn. I begged them not to do it. I wouldn't make a sound or try to escape—"Promise." To no avail. *Chrrruch. Chrrruch.* Roll after roll came off, and was wrapped around my head, leaving only a small opening for my nose, around my neck, my shoulders, my midriff, my thighs, my knees, my calves, and finally my feet. Long ago I could no longer stand alone, and they were propping me up, and by the end I was wrapped exactly like an Egyptian mummy—couldn't move a muscle. They lowered me out of the truck while they started on the next guy—Terry by the sound of things—and carried me like a log across the street and began to push me into a very confined space—the space where the spare tire normally goes under the bed of a truck. Soon we were off. En route to location number *six*. So much for our "halfway house"—the cell between #4 and #6.

It must have been about dawn by this time, for traffic was now beginning to roll. With numerous stops for huge holes in the road and for militia checkpoints, we must have been about three hours en route—that truck didn't go very fast—it too sounded as though its differential was about to fall out. At checkpoints, I could hear the guards talking with the militiamen on duty, and I wondered if they knew the kind of cargo my escorts really had aboard, despite the way they had camouflaged the truckload. It was raining and the road was wet. The air was cool, even cold, and fresh, and I gulped in great gulps of the stuff. But "my space" had lots of leaks around, so that when the truck stopped, I got the fumes instead of the fresh air. While we were running, the rain would splash up into my space; at least the tape was waterproof. Good God!

Up the hill a little and we stopped. I was dragged out of my tire well, stood up, and released from my "plastic bandages" by the Ghost cutting through layer after layer. Whew. What a relief! I hoped never to go through that again. I was the first to arrive, and was led into what turned out to be a kitchen. The owner sounded like an older fellow, and quite relaxed about things. He had me lie down on a blanket; no mattresses of course. Soon Terry, then Frank, arrived, both of them in trauma. They had each been transported in a Volkswagen van, in the wheel well inside. That was much more confined than I had been, by far, and Terry had even been too big for it, so that they had had to sit on the cover to get it to shut. It had also leaked like a sieve, as had Frank's, so both of them were soaked to the skin despite their plastic coverings. Terry was complaining bitterly about how they had treated him, and the guards didn't raise any fuss. They apparently realized just how bad it had been. But neither did they apologize.

Soon breakfast and hot tea, better stuff than we were used to. The old boy produced some "Mana-eesh," a rather tasty sort of semileavened bread. By lunchtime, Terry and Frank were beginning to dry out and to warm up a little. Terry gave me an account of his journey, and I began to feel better about mine, for he had fared much worse than I. By evening, we had an early supper and were on our way again. It was already dark, still raining, and the roads were muddy. A few miles up a hill we got stuck and had to wait for a long time until another van came to pick us up. We had driven only a few miles up the hill, and now were parked on the road somewhere, waiting for God-knows-what. Despite having dressed as warmly as we could before leaving the Blindfold Apartment that morning, we began to get cold, but worse was to come. For hours we sat there, and now got *really* cold! I began to shiver seriously, until it even made the van shake, and Hadi and the Ghost kept hissing at me. Terry's true humanity showed itself here, too, for he insisted that I have his jacket to keep me a little warmer—he who was almost always cold himself! I refused—he insisted, and I did wear it for a while. Must have been close to midnight when finally we started up again for a few hundred yards, then stopped. We were ordered to get out, and could walk this time, for we were neither taped nor bound. Over some fairly rough ground—hard on our soft bare feet—into a building and down through a hole in the floor of what seemed like a closet.

It was some kind of basement, with a dirt floor that was not even level. And horror upon horrors—we were again chained, this time by the wrist, with a piece of case-hardened dog chain to a hook set into the wall by some new concrete that was not even properly set yet. It would have been easy to pull them out, and even the guards realized that, so we were warned not to do it. This was a worse disaster than the uneven dirt floor, and it was to presage our condition until the day of our release, for never again in our captivity were we to be free of chains.

As usual, I was desperate to urinate. Wonder of wonders, the Ghost produced a huge plastic bottle and promised that we could keep it—he would even get one for each of us. The reason became obvious the next day, for the journey to the toilet in this place was tortuous: up the two huge steps hewn roughly out of the dirt and difficult for us to negotiate, through the closet, through the guards' room, down a hallway, into a pre-toilet where there was even a wash-hand basin—hadn't seen one of *those* in a coon's age (but we were not allowed to use it anyway)—then finally into the toilet, on newspaper all the way, so that we "unclean" infidels wouldn't soil their floor. (I never did get culturally oriented to being considered "unclean" and have people wash their hands after touching me—I learned well what it was to be an outcaste.)

In a day or two we came to the conclusion that we were in some kind of Husseiniyeh, a kind of meeting place generally associated with the local mosque. In this place, the guards were never very relaxed except late at night, for people were coming and going over our head all day long, and we were generally forbidden even to whisper. We were given Arabic names by the Ghost, so that they could address us without anyone hearing Western names. The first suggestions were Dalaal, Talaal, and Bilaal. We complained that we couldn't distinguish among the three, especially since they were speaking now more softly than ever. So they modified them somewhat, but we refused to cooperate. After all, to lose one's own name would be the last straw. They soon gave up. We'd found that perseverance was not one of their strong points.

"The Dungeon," as we soon dubbed it, was indeed on a slope. The wall opposite to the one we had entered by opened to the outside and was made of extremely poor quality cinder blocks that were broken and uneven, so that there were lots of holes to the "outside." This "outside" was a garage, where a car was kept; it left periodically, but the holes into the garage were not big enough to let us see the driver. They were certainly big enough, however, to let in the mosquitoes. At night, the light from either our electric lightbulb or from our candle attracted them by the thousand, and they were soon buzzing around our heads. The Ghost took pity on us and brought in some green coils, which he said would kill them. Wrong! These coils are meant for use on a lawn and generate a stink that drives the mosquitoes away. In our dungeon at night, however, the insects couldn't find any way out since it was *dark* on the other side of the wall, so they just became angry and buzzed ever more furiously until we had a veritable air force of fighters, determined to attack *something* or *anything!* Terry and I argued about whether these coils really would kill them. Eventually I won that one, and even he agreed that the coils were useless, and were only making things worse for us. Sleep was impossible—absolute torture. I can hear them now, and thank God that nightmare's over.

Here we had only two guards, the same both day and night. No relief for them, nor for us, for they were the worst—Hadi and the Ghost—and they were still after Frank. They made him lie right under the trapdoor into the closet, so that when they were hovering over the door, Frank was looking right at them if he so much as raised his face. He was still paranoid about seeing them, stemming right back to his escape attempt, and this was about the last straw. Terry therefore asked to change places with Frank, but they refused. "Frank stay there. No possible move, okay?" The Ghost also got on my case. He brought in a radio, set on a station with music, and gave us specific instructions not to touch it in any way. An hour or so later, he came storming down into the dungeon, dropping the entire depth of the steps in one leap, and accused me of tampering with it. "I see you change it," he screamed at me. "Why you touch it?" I was furious. "I did not touch it in any way," I replied coldly and with determination in my voice. This time the little bastard was not going to get away with it. "Tell him, Terry, whether I touched it or not." "He did *not* touch it in any way," agreed Terry. "You quiet, okay Terry?" screamed the Ghost. But Terry also was determined, and insisted that I had not touched it, to the extreme frustration of the little guard. It was the most coldly calculated setup one could ever imagine, and in retrospect we should have told him from the outset *not* to leave the God-damned radio down there at all, thus giving him no chance to set me up. But we were so starved for any kind of entertainment. From what pettiness is such great issue generated in a captive situation.

Frequently during an evening, people would come into the building upstairs and conduct some kind of meeting. During the entire time both guards came into our dungeon and sat with us. We were not allowed to speak, whisper, cough, move for three, four hours at a time. Finally, when all the people had gone, we were allowed to make a slight noise. Sometimes this must have been past midnight, and it was our first time to go to the toilet all day. We had the distinct impression that no one knew that anyone else was in the building at all, neither hostages nor guards. We were to be a well-kept secret in this evidently public place.

Having a haircut meant removing the blindfold. To protect the "barber," a second guard would sit on the ground directly in front of the hostage and stare relentlessly at his closed eyes. Even the suggestion of a peek brought forth harsh threats. On one occasion, I got a haircut during the day, this time from Hadi. Dexterity was not one of Hadi's strong suits—in fact he had relatively few if any of these—and after more than an hour, I said to the Ghost, the asssistant on this occasion, "Tell Hadi that he wouldn't make a very good living at this." Wrong move again, Sutherland! Hadi's sense of humor didn't stretch that far—he snarled some reply in Arabic. Maybe just as well that I didn't understand! It didn't sound like a compliment.

A little field mouse joined us and became quite friendly. Terry fed it with a little of his bread, and it would carry it into the nether regions of the wall. I surely longed to be that mouse and crawl through that concrete block wall. I had conducted selection experiments with mice at CSU, and at times had had as many as 10,000 mice in my lab, so I was rather familiar with the little fellows. Terry christened this one Mehitabel (I think after Marquis's classic cockroach and cat story, although Mehitabel was the cat; no matter). After a few more days, we had the dubious pleasure of sitting through and watching a great event—the guards mixing cement and building an entirely new wall inside the existing one. The holes were now all covered up—no more Mehitabel and fewer mosquitoes, but much less fresh air. Had we been able to vote? Then came a load of tiles for the floor. They lay there for a few days, but we were gone before they even began to lay them.

It happened without warning, as usual. The Ghost began to pack up blankets and sheets and bowls. "What's happening?" I asked. "I don't know"—the standard reply. But soon we were being hauled up the dirt steps (these had never been improved in any way) and were held in the upstairs room for an hour or so while the two young men loaded everything into a Volkswagen van, into which we too were pushed after everything else was stuffed in higgledy-piggledy. A short trip and we were back to the kitchen in which we had been held for a day some five weeks before. Location seven.

This time we were chained to the refrigerator, all three of us, and we had our mattresses, which amazingly had accompanied us in the van. The toilet was right off the kitchen, and it was all very convenient, except that we were once again under the constant surveillance of the guards. A few days of this and we were moved into a room down the hall from the kitchen, a big room, but it did us little good, for after a single day of "freedom," we were once again chained to the wall following the arrival of Terry's "friend" Abu Janzir, "father of the chains." Completely sick in the head about chains was that guy, and he drove Terry up the wall with his insistence on tightening them to an extreme. He spoke little or no English, at least with us, and had a sinister demeanor that came through to us even without our seeing his face or hearing more than a few words in Arabic.

We had two visitors here. One was obviously a boss man, who listened to our complaints and suggestions in a sympathetic and almost rational way—his English was even fairly good. He promised us lots of things: no chains on our legs or wrists, better food, opportunity to write letters home; sounded like a really nice man, but unfortunately, none of his promises materialized. A day or two later came a young fellow bearing a questionnaire for each of us. Terry's was by far the longest and most detailed, with questions that made him fairly guffaw with laughter:

"In your organization, who attends the secret meetings?"

"Which part of the government controls your organization?"

For an AP man, that would have been the last straw. Terry tried to give them sensible answers to ridiculous questions, but by the end he gave up and just wrote down garbage. Frank and I had simple forms, nothing either challenging or difficult, not even ridiculous, so that I have even forgotten what the questions were. Methinks they were only doing a token thing with Frank and me. Terry was their objective.

The temperature was rising—we were into April.

16   Taking Action

January 1987. Back from Christmas in Colorado to Beirut Normal:

JAN. 9—Ann, Kit, Joan … wanted you to know I got here safely and am back in the swim again—it's been busy. I discovered that Crystal my cat has ringworm—hope I don't get it—I got her to the vet today and she's on medication so hope she'll get rid of it … . The trip home was long but uneventful except that my bags did not make the shift of planes either at JFK or Heathrow so I'm without all my clothes and am scrounging. Mostly wearing your dad's sweaters … . If I arrived without bags, I arrived with the flu that laid me up for two and a half days in bed—I was unable to move I was so full of cold and chills and fever—but now I'm feeling good so am back into the fray … .

Our Christmas greeting to your dad was in the papers—I'll get and send a copy—also two French wives carried the publicity ball by coming over the holidays. My maid Joana is getting ready to leave for Ghana to take her son Patrick to stay—she's taking a picture of your dad with his full name and birthday and birthplace on the back to take to her "Prince" who works white magic.

Had a day of street fighting—heavy stuff—on Bliss St. and Hamra—Amal vs. pro-Syrian party I guess—and I stayed home as did everyone else until they reached some kind of "solution" … . A shell landed in Marquand House garden, Barbara Sayers got a bullet through her living room window and couch, and the poor Baasiris on the top of Penrose Dorm had eight bullets … . No one at AUB hurt but it was quite a fright for a few hours.

Looking forward to a quiet weekend to catch up … . The Lebanese pound has dropped to 85/$.

The "quiet weekend" was instead a change in my life. This out of the fact that tucked into the range of events of my October 1986 trip to the States had been a breakfast meeting with a man, his name and number given to me (and as it turned out, mine to him) by a person I especially respected. It might have seemed at the time a small event, yet it was destined to become the most significant happening for me in Tom's hostage years—a watershed. I don't know even now what behind-the-scenes process brought us together at that meeting—I know only that when I reached Washington, D.C., the last week of October, I simply called the number given me and we made an appointment to have continental breakfast together at the Mayflower Hotel. We met and we spoke, and somewhere in that hour and a half he made up his mind to work with me to try to get a resolution of the conflict that was keeping hostages so tightly held in Lebanon. Was this meeting the outcome of my *As-Safir* ad for Islamic Jihad? I don't know for sure, but I think yes. The important thing, however, was that a course of action for the next five years was initiated that morning. M (he still prefers anonymity in order to serve an ongoing Middle East peace process) is a quiet, knowledgeable man, a man totally dedicated to his business, a man who, because he is apolitical and respected by people in a sum of countries, can go across boundaries, travel freely, and get audiences in high places. His motives were then, and are now, open and clear—for mutual understanding, for peace. He told me that he would be in Beirut after Christmas and he would take me to see Sheikh Fadlallah.

That "quiet" weekend in January, M called. He set up a meeting for me with Sheikh Fadlallah for the next week and the day came. Taking an early lunch hour from the school, I was picked up by M and a driver at the AUB gate and driven to Fadlallah's heavily guarded residence in Bir al-Abed, passing quite easily through the checkpoints and gates. M went in through the "men's way" and I, with a beret on for a head covering, went in through the "women's way." We came together in the meeting room where Fadlallah meets the public and the press and hears petitions from his "parish." Sayeed (the term of respect for a Shiite religious leader) came in, a man in brown and black robes, of medium height, bearded, and with strong piercing eyes (I was very aware of and struck by them although by Islamic custom I as a woman could not *meet* them), and we sat and met together with M doing the interpreting from English to Arabic and back again so that there could be a "conversation." A glass of tea was served, but we met alone, the three of us, which M said was significant—usually at least one other man is present for security purposes. Quite formal it was, but not at all a formality.

I think back now over those years when Fadlallah and I would meet or would communicate indirectly through M and I try to analyze my feelings about Fadlallah—the man that personified evil for Mary Seurat and for the CIA who held him responsible for the bombings of the American embassy and the Marines. There is nothing for it but to say I respected him. And it was not just adversarial respect; although knowing the power he had in the fundamentalist Shiite community whose militia was held responsible for the kidnappings and terrorist activities, the aura of adversary would have to be there. The aura of adversary, however, was also necessarily in our situation with the American government, and I was to come to know and respect greatly people in the highest offices there. But Fadlallah was like a modern-day Sitting Bull to me in the power of his personality, the power of his office as spiritual leader of his people measured in the utter respect of his people for him and his for them, the power of his intellect and political astuteness—all were felt things and I gave him the respect I would give to Sitting Bull as a Native American leader. For I knew certainly at some level of consciousness in our talk that morning over tea instead of a peace pipe that here was a man of power, a man to work with, and *the* man to get into dialogue as an equal with the leaders of our government. There was no issue of like or dislike involved—our concerted goal was resolution of the conflict between the fundamentalist Shiite community/Iran and America/Israel—for Islamic Jihad it was war, for America it was terrorism, and for all it was conflict at the highest international level with zero trust and understanding among parties. Throughout the years to come, my relationship with Fadlallah through M would be conducted in always an objective, professional, most formal, and restrained, yet somehow cordial manner. M himself set the tone through his obvious and genuine respect for this man he addressed as Sayeed—a respect for his writings, his scholarship, his influence, his leadership. And M, though an Arab, was not a Shiite, nor even a Moslem. M had clearly developed his own relationship with Fadlallah through mutual efforts toward resolution of the Lebanese conflict in years gone by. As much as it was possible for trust to exist between two men, it was there, and when M wished to see Fadlallah he told me that he was admitted without question or wait or, most importantly perhaps in indicating the extent of the trust, without security or body search.

The next week brought Terry Waite back to Beirut, and it was an absolute media bonanza. Terry was staying at the Riviera Hotel just down the Corniche from AUB, and he was under the protection of the Druze PSP militia, a fact that seemed unbelievable to us there because the PSP and the Shiite Hizbollah militias were at war with each other. For a week Terry with attendant publicity went the rounds calling on all the important leaders in Lebanon. Writing a daughter, I put him in my overall Beirut context:

… Crystal's ringworm is clearing up with the medication, Terry Waite is in town, and I'm dodging reporters while he holds court. I'm working hard at all kinds of student problems and situations, having some meals and drinks out (last night at Buckleys' to say goodbye to Suzy who leaves tomorrow and takes this letter)—to-morrow at Jean-Marie Cook's with Munros including KC who's been here and had an operation … .

Terry Waite ended up his week of "visits" on Friday afternoon with one to Fadlallah. Why Fadlallah *last?* M wondered that too. And why be making those formality calls anyway like we all did at the beginning, years ago? Done once, it is done. But it seemed that this was Terry's "purely humanitarian and right thing to do"; that he was making the attempt to start all over again and establish himself as a genuine, independent negotiator, to distance himself from the Iran-Contra scandal, and carry on his work, whatever it might be now, for the release of West-ern hostages. I couldn't fathom how it would work in such a media blitz or what he could possibly have that could possibly interest Islamic Jihad, but I called him at the Riviera Hotel and he said he would meet Saturday with Elham Cicippio, Fifi Reed, and me, the Beirut hostage wives.

Saturday morning arrived and with it M at the Faculty Gate and subsequently our balcony to talk of events. He was not feeling at all good about things; he had picked up in the southern suburbs the fundamentalist weekly *Al Ahd* with clear and direct warnings for Terry Waite: *You're no longer of use … . You're no longer welcome … . Leave before it is too late … .* I remember it clearly. But Elham drove Fifi and me that evening to the Riviera Hotel and the three of us duly fought our way through ranks of journalists and TV cameramen and met up with Terry in his hotel room. He had thought he would be leaving, but said that it now looked like there was a good possibility of getting Tom and Terry out—not any of the others, he was sorry. I encouraged, the others let down, we left, again wading through a sea of journalists in the Riviera lobby.

I didn't discuss with Terry the warnings in *Al Ahd.* It really troubled me af-terward—should I have made a strong point of it? Surely he must have been aware and have made his decisions accordingly. I was still taking him "on trust." And yet there seemed such naïveté in his actions. What was right? I was too newly in the know to know. Had I been given the warning to pass on definitively? Must I be responsible again? I'll take on what I have to, and yet from today's vantage point, there's his responsibility for his actions too. He had had definitive warn-ing as we now know. Tom and I have talked and talked it over, and we've read Gavin Hewett's book, *Terry Waite: Why He Was Kidnapped,* and Con Coughlin's,

Hostage, and the truth seems to be that somehow, somewhere, Terry had not gotten the message that it was not *his* power that had released hostages in the past, it had been governmental power behind him. It was clearly not there now. Was it his fault he didn't know? Who's to know? Rising unbidden to the front of my mind were graphic scenes from two movies out of a nebulous black-and-white movie past: one about a French (I think) magician who had spellbound his crowd with a flying act on an "invisible" high wire and said one night, "I have the power to fly—leave off the wire," and then "flew" out of the window and crashed. The other was with a woman singer whose microphone was cut off and she said, "Don't worry, I'll go on; they love my voice," and was booed off the stage because they couldn't hear her beyond the first row. It just seems that Terry had not been made aware of, or he had not realized, or he had forgotten, that the true power behind his hostage negotiations in Iran, Libya, and Beirut was a British or American government for which he was the covering humanitarian front. In the case of Iranian and Libyan hostages, he was covering for his own government; in Beirut he was covering unconstitutional actions of a foreign government, and a government at odds with itself in addition—George Shultz presumably putting pressure on Kuwait to keep prisoners *in* while Ollie North was carrying out his extremely dubious arms deals with Iran to get hostages *out,* among other things. But it was government that had the power respected and sought by the Arabs and Iranians. A humanitarian had none. Thus when Terry tried that January of 1987 to "fly" on his own or to "sing" on his own, he had to fail. And just as it was for the rest of us, his learning would come through a deal of suffering. After it was all over, and I was reading Rivkah Scharf Kluger's *The Archetypal Significance of Gilgamesh,* I was struck by her statement:

> Increasing knowledge is paid for by painful experiences, but maybe we would not learn otherwise. Jung once said that the deep meaning of the very cruel initiation rites among primitives is that without pain there is no learning. After having been initiated, the youngster can say: "here, where I have this burn or scar, he said such and such to me," referring to the sacred history of the tribe which was told during the painful initiation. The story was literally burned into their flesh. And I think that even without a formal ritual, that often the real things we have to know are also burned into us, because we do not learn otherwise.[6]

Would that governments also could learn through the suffering. But it's individuals who pay, not governments, *per se.* If Reagan, Poindexter, McFarlane, and North got burned, the Clinton administration will still go its way in the Middle East without the history and its lessons being "sacred," and perhaps it's someone else or our children who get the burn. It appears to be the price we pay for democracy, but surely the price can be changed. Tom was criticized on his return from Lebanon for his criticism of Terry Waite. Not apropos for a hostage to challenge another fellow hostage. He mostly desisted. But the issues are too important to put aside even if America does not wish to sacrifice a President Reagan or Britain an Archbishop of Canterbury or his Terry Waite. Perhaps it is the nature of things political, governmental, international, to "understand" what the truth is without spelling it out and let persons and countries save face. On the other hand, perhaps it is crucial that we citizens of democracies take the responsibility for what is the truth of our governmental actions abroad and demand a continuing accountability. Especially when our citizen lives are at stake.

The whole issue of dealing for hostages or prisoners—of getting some out with the result of others going in—was one that Terry Waite had to carry on his conscience as well as did Oliver North the next year. After his release, Tom received a long and fascinating letter from Jim Abra, a British subject taken by Gadhafi in Libya following Terry Waite's trip to that country in 1985 to "negotiate" the freeing of four British prisoners being held there against Libyans in prison in England. In this, Waite was successful, but the freed Britons didn't result in freed Libyans from British prisons. Said Jim, "Gadhafi had expected; ... of course there was no possibility of Margaret Thatcher agreeing to this," but they did seem to result in Abra's being taken in retaliation—"Waite must have known that Gadhafi would be enraged by what he considered was trickery and it was inevitable that he would retaliate ... . My interrogators openly conceded to me that this was the purpose in capturing me." Twelve days before Jim's trial in March 1986 resulting in the commutation of a death sentence to life imprisonment, Abra's MP wrote to Terry Waite to ask for his help. The reply came back from Waite's personal secretary: "Mr. Waite asked me to write to say he is still so deeply involved in his Middle East mission that he dare not take on any further cases at the moment. He was sure you will understand. Very many people are writing to him on behalf of those who are in difficulty and in sad situations, and Mr. Waite regrets that it is quite impossible for him to take up each case individually at this time." Abra was subsequently released after 998 days in a Libyan prison.[7]

M came to see me at AUB on Monday morning and we discussed my going to see President Reagan and working out a bridge for dialogue. "Yes, of course, I'm willing to do that," I said, "but Terry Waite is here and he seems optimistic about Tom and Terry at least and wouldn't it be worthwhile to wait and see what he can do?" So we left it up in the air and arranged to meet again. Wednesday morning and the papers were full of it: "TERRY WAITE DISAPPEARED." *Oh, my God!* On Thursday, M came back again to me to say, "The word is that Terry Waite is kidnapped and there is no way to say or know what his fate will be. It's so important that there be a link, a genuine and authentic link between here and the American government. Dialogue is vital. Will you go to President Reagan?" My answer of course was "Yes." My conclusion could only be that Terry Waite had been kidnapped to get him out of the way—whatever his role had been or he hoped now it *could be,* it was obviously over. His time, along with North's, was past. So be it.

I left right away and again made my way to London and to the same Heathrow hotel where a month ago I had seen Terry Waite. This time I put through a call to our State Department liaison: "I'm on my way to Washington from Beirut—it's extremely important—I need to talk to Secretary of State George Shultz." A call came back through to me and I made an appointment for two days later. The next day found me in Washington in late afternoon in unnatural and dreadful cold and snow walking the streets to find a cheap hotel M had told me about from his experience in Washington (since this was my third trip to the States in three months, my salary was used up, I was into Tom's, and I felt I needed to economize somewhere). So even though a Holiday Inn was in the area, I stuck it out, stopping and querying passersby who seemingly had no more idea than I about either the hotel or the street it was on, or for that matter what street we were on right now. I finally got to that hotel by guess and frozen feet only to find that it was a dilapidated residential hotel that didn't take credit cards. Prayer or blasphemy or awful wonder, the words were there as I turned away from the desk: *Jeesus Chrrist!* And I hobbled straight to the Holiday Inn, gave them my credit card as I winged my thanks to Tom and AUB, still and always paying his salary, and sat for an hour in a steaming hot tub, thawing my feet and drinking a glass of wine—the most absolute and unforgettable luxury.

Next day, I dressed carefully for the meeting—and warmly for the weather—and took a taxi to the State Department building. At the desk I gave my name, a security person came soon to meet me, and up we went to the famous seventh floor where I stepped off the elevator directly into the wood-paneled, elegant, historic rooms of the U.S. secretary of state. Only a few minutes waiting in an anteroom looking at a historic painting, and then I was ushered into the office and was greeted by Secretary Shultz with a handshake. Welcoming, hospitable, but professional, he gestured me to a seat on the couch and took a chair opposite (a standard practice of diplomats, I was learning, to put visitors at ease and per-haps at disadvantage) and asked my business. I told it straight: "I have come from Beirut to see President Reagan. It is most important and essential that I see him. I have been in communication with Sheikh Fadlallah in Beirut, and I have a proposal for dialogue. Could you help me?" We discussed around the subject, he asked some questions to find out something about me, then all of a sudden the decision was made—I could see it reflected in his face: "Yes." He went to the phone and put in a call to General Colin Powell, asking for an appointment with President Reagan.

The day and the hour came, and I was picked up and taken to the back door of the White House. Our meeting was downstairs in the informal but beautiful Map Room and the president met me in the hall—his most cordial self again. Then he and Secretary Shultz and General Powell and I went into the room and took our seats for the meeting. "I so appreciate your seeing me again, Mr. President, and I hope you know that I wouldn't bother you for anything not of the utmost importance." We discussed the hostage situation, and wonder of wonders he said, "You know that I sent them a Bible with an inscription? They told me to do that—that it would help." I looked at him in amazement. Who all were "they" that he depended on for knowledge? Did they misinform and thereby betray the president willfully? And did he not know that Iranian fundamentalists were *people*? Did he not realize that a Bible, for all its meaning to Christians, and given as a gift, didn't have a shred of meaning as opposed to a genuine offer to *discuss* the situation honestly and meaningfully? I voiced none of this but told him that what I had come to him for was to set up an avenue for dialogue. I talked about M—who he was, what kind of man he was, and my confidence in him. "M and I will form a bridge for this dialogue with Sheikh Fadlallah in Beirut. This will be conducted with the utmost confidentiality and there will be no risk for you or for him because we will be the ones walking that bridge and crossing that minefield out there. You can use it or not when and how you please—if you accept that it be there. Will you accept it?" It had to be *his* decision, it just couldn't work without his knowledge, his involvement, his agreement. On the U.S. end, the hostage buck always stopped with the president; on the Beirut end, the symbolic significance of dialoguing with The Top was critical. The president turned to Secretary Shultz—"It couldn't hurt, I suppose." And Shultz took it: "We'll handle it in our office," and General Powell, as new National Security Adviser in these Iran-Contra scandal times, said nothing as he took the notes of the meeting. We said good-byes, Secretary Shultz set up a follow-up meeting for later in his office, and that was that. Even given my naïveté and the basic rationale for acceptance of the avenue for dialogue with the spiritual leader of Hizbollah being "It couldn't hurt …," it was nonetheless clear to me that the meeting was symbolic in a process of formally giving back the handling of the hostage situation to the Department of State where in our country it perhaps belonged, or at least where Secretary Shultz felt it should be. In his recent book, *Turmoil and Triumph,* George Shultz confirms this.

One last meeting with Secretary Shultz to hand me over to Charlie Hill, his top aide, who had authorized a statement for me to present to Fadlallah, a formal statement of greeting from President Reagan and an agreement to conduct dialogue. I sincerely thanked them. So simple yet so momentous a start to five years of "talk" between our secretary of state and Muhammad Hussein Fadlallah, the spiritual leader of his "nation" of Shiite peoples. Both of these persons had within their "constituencies" murderers and kidnappers as well as multitudes of people of goodwill, both had the weight of their respective powers and their politics and ultimate goals, both were persons to be respected. One had the enormous power at his back of the number one country on earth and the other had his Islamic religious ideology, a zealous following willing to die, and a handful of Western hostages somewhere on hold by a clandestine group called Islamic Jihad. It was more than enough for "talk." I kept thinking about Sitting Bull and the American government. Same but different.

I flew back to Cyprus with the message close in hand and took the boat to Beirut, the airport being in one of its by-now-customary closures. On the way I got the news that the secretary of state was putting on a passport ban for Lebanon, exempting, however, the immediate family members of the hostages. This meant me. How lucky! Or, perhaps, how State Department providential! First thing on my return, I was in touch with M, he came and picked me up as before, and again we entered the Bir al-Abed villa in our separate ways to meet with Fadlallah—just the three of us as before with my presenting through M as translator the message approved for me by Charlie Hill on behalf of the president and the secretary of state:

> I have just returned from Washington. I met with Secretary of State Shultz in the Department of State on January 29. Later that same day I met with President Reagan in the White House. Secretary Shultz was also present. Our meeting lasted for an hour.
>
> I told the President about my contact with you and I gave him my views on the current situation in Lebanon. The reaction I received from the President was serious and positive. He has a humanitarian concern for all the people affected by the troubled situation here.
>
> The President was interested to hear that I had met with you and that I would be meeting with you again. The President welcomes this kind of exchange of ideas and views.

The President authorized me to say to you what I have just said.

I believe that further exchanges along this line possibly could be of value. I would appreciate your advice about this.

—I know that if [M] goes to Washington this week, he will be able to meet with Secretary Shultz.

—After my meetings in Washington I feel that a mutual sense of respect and fairness might be achieved.

—I also feel that some form of dialogue at closer range might be possible.

This was accepted and discussed and we parted. M then set up with me to go back again to Washington, D.C., not the next week but the next month, this time to go together to the secretary of state's office and formally introduce him to Charlie Hill and Secretary Shultz as well as bring to them the reply from Fadlallah. Thus was the "bridge" being built, carefully, meticulously.

Before this next trip, however, I got back to work and back to letter writing—a quick note to the family who knew I'd been in the States although not what for, according to the pact of confidentiality M and I had taken about "the avenue":

> I got back to AUB in good form—unfortunately the boat to Jounieh [in East Beirut] didn't go overnight so I had to spend a night in a hotel in Larnaca and another in East Beirut (got in at 7 P.M. after a very good boat ride this time and it was raining so I stayed over with a nice Armenian family I met on the boat)—they were expecting me at the embassy—Thanks! Kit, for calling for me—and I got royal treatment and a safe jeep ride home ... . Back to work—people so glad and amazed to see me. Strikes, etc. delayed registration for a week—this next week will be busy! Keep good hope and cheer and don't worry—I love you much ... .

And a new start February 15 on my interrupted New Year's letter to "Everyone I Love Over There":

> It is a warm, sunny, breezy spring Sunday afternoon that I look out on from my Beirut balcony—not-so-distant shelling and shooting has caused many families to vacate the AUB playing field and the seaside road in front of me, but two groups of avid basketballers tell me that the situation is still on the side of the weather and AUB security. It's the fine edge of knowledge that's been perfected over years so that normal life can continue as much as possible under the impossible circumstances of war, death, anarchy, kidnapping, shells, assassination, starvation under siege, theft, betrayal, poverty from the fall of the Lebanese pound, the imminent catastrophe of complete cutoff of electricity and water ... . I haven't written in months to you all and I can only say that the belatedness of this letter is in direct proportion to the

size of my gratitude for your understanding support, thoughts, prayers, letters, just "being there" as a lifeline. Somehow I haven't been able to speak it or write it—just feel it and absorb it and tell you now: Thanks ... .

February 9th I felt as I could with Tom the 20 months—somehow the last few months have compounded the complexities of all the long time for him—the Iran arms sales enormity, Terry Waite's appearance and disappearance, the TWA hijacking again with the Hamadehs' arrests, passport invalidations, more kidnapping of Americans from BUC [Beirut University College] and threats of execution, a meandering, menacing Mediterranean fleet, harsh rhetorical exchanges—all circulating around Tom and the others in their prisons wherever he and they are ... . There will be new initiatives because there must be—my Ghanaian maid, Joana, does her best to keep me optimistic with her "God's Time—Victory!" and I love her for it because her faith in God is invincible and she is completely convinced that His Millennia will be compressed for our sake ... .

Joana, indeed, practiced her belief during her trip back to Ghana to take her son to live with her family and go to school in Accra. There she saw her "Prince," participated in a midnight cemetery ceremony, held a 40-day fast for Tom, and returned in March much thinner and with a consecrated white prayer handkerchief for me, which I still treasure. She also delivered assurance of ongoing intercessory prayer in Ghana through her Spiritualist Church, and the information given her by her Prince that "seven men were responsible for Tom's kidnapping—three from inside AUB, four from outside—two said kill him, five said let him live." What a person, Joana. I thanked her from my heart for all she had done so lovingly and sincerely and wrote her reverend my thanks also.

February brought momentous events with the Syrian Army finally coming down from the mountains where it had been on menacing hold for weeks. We had come to know by that time Assad's patient and deliberate wielding of power as over and over for weeks the litany was repeated: "*When* are they going to come? *When?*" He had waited and waited with his tanks and 40,000 soldiers until the militia warfare and chaos in Beirut had pushed everyone beyond the point of endurance. Lebanese Moslem leaders (and so it's said the Christian government too) issued an invitation—then did Syria move, and fast. Within 48 hours the tanks and soldiers had taken on the militia strongholds in West Beirut, finally cleaning them out and "disarming" them (meaning, of course, that a lot of arms left Beirut to be put on hold until some future time). The February War of 1987. Hizbollah? The Syrians did not go into the southern suburbs but gave Hizbollah its "lesson"—attacking the Hizbollah headquarters/barracks at

Basta and killing 23 Hizbollah militiamen. Carefully calculated not to break completely the Syrian-Iranian alliance, but definitely to "send a message," the act raised a storm of Islamic protest manifesting itself in the usual way with thousands on the streets marching and chanting "Death to the Assassins, Death to the U.S.," the United States this time held responsible for green-lighting Syria's action. Fadlallah took a firm position not to retaliate. But later when Syrian shelling was bombarding his home in support of Amal's fighting Hizbollah, there was crisis. M crossed the line and made his way to Fadlallah in his bunker, "I just felt I had to go, but it was the worst I've been through," the journey a hair-raising one through the falling, exploding shells and deadly streets. Fadlallah by this time could only be speculating himself whether America had teamed up with Syria to get him. But M had been able to get through by phone to Charlie and get the definitive word of American noninvolvement to relay."Knowledge made productive." Fadlallah waited it out, and consequently envoys and committees worked out peaceable agreements. M felt that the hostages had come at this time the closest to ultimate reprisal that they could come although that was just speculation. For the crisis was defused, our channel tested and proved. Three years later, in another crisis, knowledge would be shared in the other direction. It was good.

On March 9, I made my second trip back to Washington, meeting M who had gone on ahead and going with him to Secretary Shultz's office. We met first with Charlie Hill and then with Secretary Shultz. Charlie was the man with whom M would be in contact on a regular basis, and that morning they got to know each other. I don't think I know a finer man than Charlie, such a gentleman and diplomat—M was extremely impressed also and would over the next two years develop an unshakable respect for him. M's respect for Shultz was very great too; "even though he's hard, he's straight." Shultz of course was hard as nails and angry through and through about terrorism—when we talked of the demands of the captors for the 17 in Kuwait, Shultz's eyes flashed and his voice rose:"We will have nothing to do with that." Fadlallah, however, was quite probably correct when he said publicly in Beirut that it was not a matter of America refusing to put pressure on Kuwait to let the 17 prisoners *out,* it was instead a matter of Shultz putting pressure on Kuwait to keep the 17 *in.* Shultz was not willing then or ever to be party to leaving Kuwait free to entertain *anyone's* negotiation to release the 17 embassy bombers being held in the jails there. Not under any circumstance—surely not to effect the release of American hostages. It was hard, it was clear, it was transmitted to Fadlallah—the message exact in words, tone, and manner.

We discussed that morning the manner and form that the "channel" would take. It was to be a line for dialogue—we were not mediators but transmitters in pure form of whatever Fadlallah on his end and George Shultz on his end had to say. It would be informational in pure form also with M and Charlie and M and Fadlallah spending many hours in wide-ranging discussions of the Middle East. M in his travels and his abilities to interact with all parties everywhere had invaluable knowledge to impart, and I could see him being "used" in the best sense of the word to provide genuine channels of dialogue between parties who needed it. In a world where there is no trust, enemies everywhere, rumors and disinformation rife, a person like M with an open agenda for mutual understanding and no personal axe to grind or power to defend or get was an incredible asset—more than that, a miracle. In a world where there is no trust, he was "trusted." Absolutely amazing. And absolutely amazing the happenings that attended or resulted from the "dialogues" between enemies. People got to know each other indirectly, to interact genuinely and authentically with each other—even when the dialogue was hard and negative as it was almost all the time—through M as third party. I saw it happen.

George Shultz, afterward, in his book *Turmoil and Triumph*, mentioned our channel in a footnote on page 868:

> *Jean Sutherland, wife of hostage Tom Sutherland, called on me and presented what she regarded as an opportunity: the possibility of an indirect dialogue with Sheikh Hussein Fadlallah, the spiritual leader of Hizbollah. During eighteen months of exchanges through a third party, Fadlallah's view seemed to shift from advocate to opponent of hostage taking. Nevertheless, in the end, so far as we could tell, he could do nothing to bring about the hostages' release. The hostage holders continued to demand the release of the Dawa prisoners held in Kuwait in exchange for the hostages' freedom. Such a swap was totally unacceptable to us. When the Dawa prisoners became "free" after the Iraqi invasion of Kuwait in August 1990, I felt that our hostages would finally somehow be released as well. In fact, all were out before the end of 1991, the last being Terry Anderson.*[8]

One thing about Shultz was his consistency. It was always and ever essential to him that there be no "negotiation" for hostages; it was at the same time, however, always and ever his goal to secure the release of hostages. *Our* goal was not the release of hostages per se, but resolution of the overall conflict that was putting them there and keeping them there. I would say, in looking back over five years of the dialogue channel from the start of 1987 to the end of 1991, that neither Shultz/Hill nor their successors James Baker/Dennis Ross would ever acknowledge the fact that there was a conflict to be resolved or that our channel was for that purpose—always it was "get the hostages released unconditionally." Over the two years of cold storage for hostages from 1987–1989 and perpetuation of the conflict at the end of the Reagan/Shultz era, the channel was the vehicle for the "No" and intransigence from both ends, but while that was being said, the channel was being used and tested, providing information and personalizing the conflict and its issues as well as defusing crises and tensions when they arose.

M said one day after all was over and we sat and reflected on the channel: "There was a sense of security about the channel, a sense of order at a time of disorder … . We served to keep 'the damage' to a minimum, to keep things on track instead of deteriorating and getting out of control … . It was, in the end, not for solution but when that time came to ensure that it came forward right, … it was a line of communication that never existed before … both sides were determined not to be on record as doing business or compromising on principle and although it was an ongoing search with both sides making a genuine effort to find a way to each other, they never could come to accept or live with each other or find a common ground." The principles summed up in the concept of "freedom fighters" as opposed to "terrorists" were and are still unyielding.

When, finally, our great hope was realized and the "resolution" of the conflict came with release of live hostages and bodies at the end of 1991, it was only a step on the way to a full resolution of the conflict. Even so, as a result of great shifts of world realities in the fall of the Soviet Union, the death of Khomeini, the invasion of Kuwait and the resulting release of "the 17," the Gulf War, the empowering of the United Nations, and a critical new objectivity in the U.S. relationship to Israel, it was as if a giant kaleidoscope had shifted and rearranged the pieces into a new world pattern where individual objectives on all sides in this particular issue could be met and faces could be "saved." It was indeed, in my brother John's conflict resolution parlance, the "enlarged frame" and new environment where a "win-win situation" for our two parties could be achieved. If there is one regret that both M and I would have, it is that it was not possible for Fadlallah and Charlie Hill or Dennis Ross to meet personally or to understand each other. One time we thought a meeting on Cyprus might be able to happen for Charlie and Fadlallah. But it was not to be. The two sides ended as they began—poles apart. And the Clinton administration has gone back on Baker's objectivity in relation to Israel, and Fadlallah's name now resides along with that of a man like Abu Nidal on America's terrorist list. Are the five years of dialogue down the drain? Is there no discrimination that can fine-tune foreign relations and work with a noted, powerful, extremely intelligent religious leader for the betterment of relations and the possible finding in a proactive way of productive avenues for peoples in a region rather than the declaration of open season on him? Was no real progress made during all those years? If nothing else, let us hope that the process was established for dialogue between enemies and will not be given up. It's so important.

For if our channel did not "result" in the release of hostages, it was nevertheless a continuous factor in the hostage-release process as well as continuing as we hope it will through M's efforts in the overall process for peace in the Middle East today. How strongly can we say, "Keep talking"? How strongly can we say, "Use genuine and authentic avenues—"M's," not Ghorbanifars or Ollie Norths"? How strongly can we say, "Commit positively to peace"? These are bases for constructive resolution of conflict and one can just hope that America is a Statesman. I guess, in all reality, when the world situation decrees a resolution, the right avenues with the objective of "making knowledge productive" will eventually be found and used. I know that in our situation it was the American people's holding strong throughout the years, throughout the Iran–Contra Affair and all its revelations, holding strong and saying, "Resolve this thing and resolve it in the right way" that made a difference. Since Tom's release, we have had the very great privilege to meet and get to know John Mroz, founder and president of the Institute for East-West Studies in New York, who is a channel, catalyst, and adviser for American-Russian/East European relations, a man, who in his own words serves, as M does, the objective of "making knowledge productive." In a world where the prevailing idea reigns that "knowledge is power" and therefore to be hoarded and used for self-interest, it can only be most reassuring to us as Americans that there are these people devoted to the opposite, people who so positively "bridge" the gaps between national and self-interests to make good things happen for people. Now that the old and deadly Cold War lines are erased, the possibilities for right interaction come naturally into being. May that same thing happen when the old bitter lines are erased in the Middle East and new paradigms come into being there too.

M and I returned to Beirut on the same plane and boat from Cyprus. With his meetings this time with Fadlallah, the channel for dialogue was set up. A process, informal and versatile, it could be used in whatever way was necessary: M came and went, his business carrying him back and forth, and each time in Washington, D.C., or Beirut there were face-to-face meetings. The telephone reached back and forth also—whenever it worked. Each time M was in Beirut he would come or call and I would meet him—up for a coffee at Movenpicks on Abdul Azziz Street or at a sweet shop on Hamra Street, in various hotel lobbies in West Beirut or across the Green Line if he happened to be in East Beirut to lunch at a special fish restaurant he knew. We talked, he told me all that had gone on and was happening, we discussed, we brainstormed. Sometimes two months would go by without word, but then the telephone would ring or a note would be left on the door—"I'm back, I'll be in touch." I never doubted or questioned and he never disappointed. Consistent and dedicated, personal yet always professional. I never questioned or doubted the process for dialogue either—it was strong, it was authentic and genuine, it was *right*.

The one requirement we insisted on with the channel was that it be conducted with absolute confidentiality—it was a given with Fadlallah, and we asked that on the American side only the president, secretary of state and his aide, and the national security adviser know of it. This pledge was given and as far as we could ever tell, it was kept. Frankly, I think they didn't feel it was important enough to talk of it, and that's okay. I certainly found that in the Middle East to be discounted was a plus—no one was threatened or afraid and lots could be done in just straight human doings. On our side, we also respected this absolute confidentiality—my father went to his grave never knowing a thing of what I was doing in Washington or Beirut nor did our children until afterward. To their everlasting credit, they never asked, just supported. Blessings on them. I always called them when I was in the United States—this time in March 1987 when I returned to Beirut I wrote them:

> MARCH 25—Just a note to say I love you and that I'm back safe and sound as I'm sure you gathered by now … with help crossing the line from the embassy here. Hard at work at Hariri again … . All is going well and the city is quiet and Syrian-orderly. AUB has a new American president—Dr. Fred Herter—son of Christian Herter and past chairman of our Board of Trustees—a wonderful man! Now we'll see what they can do about on-the-terrain leadership … .
>
> Much later … April 13—Last weekend I decided to take time off and go to the East Side with Lou Lou, a friend of mine—her husband had been kidnapped in September 1985 (after her husband's brother's whole family was kidnapped, including the dog, disappearing with the other thousands of Lebanese kidnapped)— and she is a great person who keeps her life and family going. She'd wanted me to come so I mounted the AUB bus and found it easy to melt into the anonymity of the 400 who cross every weekend—we bus to the crossing and then walk across to the other side with checks and rechecks and hopefully no snipers, and then mount another bus which takes us into the heart of East Beirut—from there a service taxi which takes us up to her village. She played squash in a sports club that evening while I watched (thank goodness!), and then the next morning she went horseback riding while I watched (again thank goodness), and then we went striding across the mountains to see a shepherd with goats who lived in a deserted 100-year-old convent and gave me goat cheese, and the next day another hike over more

mountains to a most wonderful restaurant with great food overlooking a big canyon—it was all simply lovely except that it was so COLD (42 degrees) and I froze but loved it. We came back to AUB on the bus again Monday morning with a fight on the back of the bus with me in the middle but it wasn't serious and I was still anonymous and since it was 6 A.M. no one was particularly interested and here we are into the next week before midterms and spring vacation which I will work—Happy Easter to you and I'll be thinking about you as always ... .

APRIL 23—A quick note again in case the mail goes out today—it's a bit problematical this week because there is supposed to be a three-day strike because of the economy and maybe the courier won't go. It's a belated Happy Easter to you— I thought of you all very much on Sunday and imagined what everyone was doing. I was invited by a teacher friend, Huda Balah, to join her family at the golf club for a Lebanese buffet which was very nice and relaxing although the weather was quite cold and windy—there was first a cold buffet with all the dishes of hummus, tabouli, baba ghanoush, olives, kibbe, etc., and then a hot buffet with couscous Lebanese-style and a type of shish kebab. The club is located next to Shatila and other assorted southern suburbs and after the meal Huda and I walked down the lane by the golf course on the way to the tennis courts and on the other side was a rough field where the southern suburbanites were playing ball and picnicking and it was a very interesting juxtaposition of societies; frankly, it looked to me as though the poor were having every bit as good a time as—if not better than—the rich ... .

There doesn't seem to be a lot of hope for quick opening of the airport—they're still locked over terms East and West with the latest charge by Berri that the U.S. is pressuring to keep it closed ... . I just got a call from Dr. Salti, whom I've never met who is as of today our new deputy president. He and his wife are coming to call at 5:00 this afternoon—how very nice to be on the first day's agenda! He's just back from New York ... .

Weather here these last two days has been gorgeous—in some ways it helps, in others it makes the heart ache a little more. No news anyway from anywhere these days so keep hanging in there ... . Love you.

APRIL 29—Monday was my birthday and friends here just came around me in such a warm way! Wishes and cards at the school with presents—a book of wildflowers of Lebanon and a plaque showing Jonathan Livingston at the gate of a dark cave and the inscription "Even in darkness, light dawns for those who believe," a handmade vase covered in shells, ... a tiny vase with balloons on it for my desk, and a silver plate with chocolates. At 11:00 the coordinators of the various levels of English learning gathered and presented me with a beautiful mirror framed in an intricate wood inlay and we had coffee together. Nighttime and other friends gathered for a progressive party starting here—drinks and presents—a wine holder from the Buckleys, a Lebanese cookbook from the Heinekens, Arak from the Munros, champagne from Julie Flint, and dinner out from Marilyn Raschka and Jean-Marie Cook—we went to Le Grenier, one of the fine restaurants from the old days (down by St. George Hotel). We were the only ones there (you feel good just giving them business these days) and we had Lebanese food and a great time, ending up singing. Julie Flint and three friends including a Bulgarian journalist and his wife who are really nice joined us and we ended up at the Bulgarian journalist's apartment in Raouche up from Nasr's Restaurant and he played the guitar and we sang until midnight. It was lovely from first to last and filled the gap of my not being there and your not being here.

Such wonderful Beirut friends they were that became over the years family—they made AUB and Beirut as much home to me as America. They loved and cared, and though I was alone I was never lonely. I'll never forget them with their hearts as big as the sky: Elien and Frits Heineken, the last foreign couple on the AUB faculty who dispensed love and quiet financial aid to needy students and the mentally handicapped as well as total dedication to the highest ideals of AUB and to me; Al and Lou Buckley, whose hospitality in their wonderful apartment complex on the edge of the campus was legendary as was Al's tall white-haired hauteur and cynicism, which overlay a true gentilesse and kindness that looked after me; Jean-Marie Cook, head of the English Department who had her passport confiscated at passport control at Dulles on a trip back to the States after the passport ban and spent a semester documenting her Irish grandparents so that she could return to Lebanon on an Irish passport ("Our State Department doesn't really care about our bodies being here, just their passports") and who owned a sailboat; Marilyn Raschka, the tall, wonderful, lean, and blond American freelance journalist who spoke Arabic and was absolutely fearless in trekking anywhere in Beirut or hitchhiking through Lebanon in search of fascinating characters, places, history, events, and who loved holidays and made us dress up at Halloween and go caroling at Christmas for the coterie of elderly foreign women she looked after and who frequented the Turkish baths; Elaine Larwood, who produced the *AJME* (Americans for Justice in the Middle East) *News* with Marilyn, quiet, thoughtful, reserved, nice; Julie Flint, the pixielike British journalist who worked first for ABC and then for the *Guardian,* who introduced me to the Druze surgeon whose work we could help with supplies and took me to see the mountain hospitals and who was also intrepid in going after stories and cats—it was she who rescued the tiny abandoned tiger kitten during a shelling in the Palestinian camps, naming him Mahmoud after a good mutual Palestinian friend/philosophy graduate student/Hariri teacher (pleasing the cat, which she gave to me, but hardly our Palestinian friend Mahmoud who felt that it was taking the alternate name for Muhammed in vain); all my wonderful colleagues at the Hariri English Program including Omar Djezzini who looked very fierce but was most gentle in his love for the spiritual and for Indian philosophy; Nada Haddad who mourned the loss of cultural things from AUB and the Beirut life; Jackie and Hayat and Dina and Yusr and all the others; and my AUB colleagues—Lou Lou Khoury who took me to the East Side and yearned to be a writer and loved her Club Med trip into the Tunisian desert on a camel; Radwan Mawlawi of the AUB Information Office, who helped me with all my media and Arabic and newspaper needs ("Tom was like my brother"); Abdul Hallab and Tony Kassab and Adib Saad, Tom's associate dean who became dean in 1989 and with his wife Ahida cared so much and kept faith with Tom throughout in the Faculty of Agricultural and Food Sciences; and on and on and on. Hundreds I know and love who made all the difference to my being in Lebanon.

As a birthday gift for Tom and me, Cousin Margaret had again offered this year to put a special poem into her beautiful calligraphy. And I chose for 1987 John Donne's "A Valediction Forbidding Mourning" because the compass—or "pair of compasses"—image seemed so meaningful:

> Our two souls therefore which are one,
> Though I must go, endure not yet
> A breach, but an expansion,
> Like gold to airy thinness beat.
>
> If they be two, they are two so
> As stiff twin compasses are two,
> Thy soul, the fixed foot, makes no show
> To move, but doth, if the other do;
>
> And though it in the center sit,
> Yet when the other far doth roam,
> It leans, and hearkens after it,
> And grows erect, as that comes home.
>
> Such wilt thou be to me, who must,
> Like the other foot, obliquely run;
> Thy firmness makes my circle just,
> And makes me end where I begun.

Thus as I prepared in May for the second anniversary of Tom's kidnapping, I sent by letter to our whole circle of friends worldwide the compass image with its concentric circles around the fixed center point:

MAY 7–13, 1987—Dear Everyone There … I've just been out on the balcony with my morning cup of coffee—it's Thursday and the first day of summer weather which means warm and humid with a fog over the sea so that from there I could just barely make out the forms of the mountains to the east and two small fishing boats on the close horizon to the north. A few joggers on the Green Field below, Mounir giving tennis lessons on the court at the side, students walking up the road and the steps to class at AUB, an administrator picking up two doctors to drive up the hill to go to work in respective places, geraniums, nasturtiums, snapdragons, cabbage roses in my garden, banks of oleander, honeysuckle, rhododendron bushes on the hillside in front of Marquand House—that's the scene on this Thursday morning as I sit down at my typewriter to make sure that a letter goes to you by way of the president's office courier this week.

How do I put it all down for you—our center static with no change for Tom but at the same time so much happening around that fixed center. Since Christmas: Terry Waite's disappearance, the BUC professors taken, threats of execution, invalidation of American passports creating a great stir for a while of American passport holders leaving, staying, writing letters for exemption, the February war that took militias out and brought the Syrian Army in, and some trips out plus the daily for me in the Hariri English Program at AUB here with its 850 students and 65 teachers generating as much work as possible. My life—days are 7:30 to 5:45 at the school and my duties as assistant administrator include coordinating all the writing, giving out chalk, tutoring for the TOEFL [Teachers of English as a Foreign Language], substituting for sick teachers, being the native speaker resource person (yesterday's issue was whether the instrument that draws circles is called a compass or a pair of compasses and I disagreed with Webster alas), answering the phone when Abir is out somewhere, photocopying, making sure the teachers have coffee, talking to everyone, proctoring exams, giving folk-song classes with the autoharp (I wish you could hear a class of 20 render "Bring Back My Bonnie to Me" because it's wonderful) … . This is my small circle inside the larger one of AUB where we now have a new president there and here, and where I live and move, having friends everywhere who ask me for dinner or who drop by, or just keep asking, "Have you had any good news?" … And these circles lie within the larger one of Lebanon with Ras Beirut where I go out to shop or to the bank (the Syrian soldiers have established with the Lebanese Army firm control of the streets although people are still a bit wary because of the explosions which have punctuated the last two months), the southern suburbs where I went to a Ramadan dinner with 600 war orphans along with a Hariri teacher who teaches also there and some of our students (it was a lovely evening—great kids with caring people—I go back Saturday with the autoharp for a day with the English classes), the East Side where I can go because of my lovely Lebanese friend Lou Lou who gives me a place to stay on her mountain and I was able to visit a wonderful priest, Father Labaki, who came out of the massacre of Damour in '76 [a massacre of Christians by Palestinians] and established an orphanage, wrote books, became director of a college whose students bring 300 sandwiches a day for refugee children who don't have food, formed a choir which sings for peace, and started work for the handicapped who are so desperately many, and then the Bekaa Valley where I just went to visit the AUB farm and had the grand tour and hope to go back, and then finally, these circles within the largest circle of the world that includes all of you from Lebanon to France, Germany to Australia, Africa to England, Scotland to America. I guess I need more than "a pair of compasses."

I sat on that mountainside in east Lebanon last Sunday, Tom's birthday, thinking about him and us all and June 9th with our constant hope yet no expectation coming again and what to do for him that's most meaningful given the situation and the circumstances of this time. And I knew what he'd want me to do. First—to try to do the impossible and say enough thank yous to you all who have been our lifeline of support, offering it so freely and generously—love, prayers, letters, thoughts, trips, wishes, yellow ribbons, appearances, talks, special activities of all kinds, Running for Tom, Playing Soccer for Tom, keeping Vigil, the letters to Washington, newspaper and magazine articles, TV and radio programs, ... and just-plain-being-there. There is no way to express our feelings truly or to dream of repaying. Second—to try to make it possible to "release" and "activate" him in a positive way—to show that "stone walls do not a prison make" and that he can still have presence and effect and a vocation at AUB and in Lebanon where he chose to come and come back and still is—to assert that he's alive and that these two years have not been lost but on the contrary have a powerful meaning, his work continuing and captivity part of that work. Hence this letter. And I'll tell you in it what he and I together are doing. We're creating with initial contributions two funds: the Tom Sutherland Fund for AUB and the Tom Sutherland Fund for Lebanon; the first to go to AUB to affirm our commitment to her in her struggle to be viable here, the second to go to educate young war orphans and handicapped East and West—just because they're there, innocent-caught, needing, and part of Lebanon's future. Knowledge is deep that if we can't break the cycles of hatred and violence, we can still enter them with love and with ourselves and work as we can for conciliation, and we must. I'm hoping there might be a special project at the AUB farm or in the faculty of agriculture to present to the AUB Fund; the Lebanon Fund will go to Father Labaki's orphanage, Foyer Notre-Dame-de-Joie at Ain Saade, to his and

Dr. Khaddaj's work with the handicapped, and to the 600 at Mabarat al-Imam al-Khoey at Doha. We're sending these contributions to four places in Colorado, Iowa, and Scotland with matching funds because they're part of Tom's meaning—and I'll include the addresses in case you care to join us at one of them and truly show that he and we together can, as John Donne said, make "a little room an everywhere" … . The funds, although anonymous, will be personally given by me … . I'm finishing this after the school day and a dinner out with a British journalist, a British professor-journalist-writer and his wife, an American woman journalist, an American woman English professor, a Lebanese French professor, and me. We talked of compasses and lo and behold the Britishers to a man said, "a pair of compasses." So I came home and reread John Donne's "Valediction …" with its "twin compasses … Thy soul, the fixed foot, makes no show/To move, but doth, if the other do" and I thought of Tom and us and Colorado and Beirut and it is true. But first this afternoon, in another context, Mahmoud, my good Palestinian teacher friend at the school, gave me a copy of one of Einstein's letters of 1929. I didn't mean at the start of this letter to load you, my friends, down with quotations, but the last line of the letter struck me forcefully as it must have been meant to do: "In the service of life sacrifice becomes grace." It is what we want Tom and all the ones who are there and who have been there to know.

This letter I sent to Kit with our Christmas list of people plus friends and supporters for her to send as our "second anniversary" letter. And a wonderful thing happened. Over the next years of Tom's captivity, people sent in contributions to the funds—from $1 up, whatever they wanted or could give—and many people bought a poster designed and donated by Bob Coonts, a graphic artist in Fort Collins, with the money going into the funds. By 1989 the funds totaled $20,000, the voluntary contributions coming from over 600 people in 35 different states in the United States, ten different countries, and all seven continents. It was decided that the Tom Sutherland Fund for AUB would be an endowed annual prize of $250 each to the outstanding graduating senior from Tom's Faculty of Agricultural and Food Sciences and to the master's degree student with the most outstanding thesis. I would present the first awards at the 1988 graduation, Tom and I underwriting them ourselves until the proceeds from the fund grew enough and became available. The money that collected at the Presbyterian churches for the orphans and handicapped was deposited in a special account—I would split it three ways and give interval checks to Father Mansour Labaki to dispense to his Christian orphanage, to the man in charge of the Shiite orphanage at Dahiye, and to Dr. Khaddaj for his Druze handicapped children in the Shouf Mountains. The thank-you letters came back and were touching—I kept sending them with a letter to all who participated in the fund effort.

Dad, never questioning my motives or decisions, never flagging in his dedication to us, took upon himself the Iowa effort for the funds and set up, with the Collegiate Presbyterian Church in Ames, the special account to receive both Tom's and my contribution and those of others who wished to give. We were in touch as always:

MAY 28, 1987—Dear Dad and Alice ... A quickie note sent from a lovely hotel called Byblos-sur-Mer. It was Ramadan feast weekend with Thursday–Friday off so I came across to East Beirut to see people and relax a little. Byblos is supposed to be the oldest continuously inhabited city in the world and it has great ruins by the side of this hotel. Last night I ate out on the terrace and had fish kebab that was delicious and this morning after a great night's sleep I'm writing letters and watching people sunning, swimming, and fishing. It's nice! Tonight I'm going down to Jounieh (just above East Beirut), will stop enroute to see George Nader, a journalist friend, and then go on to stay overnight with Jean-Marie Cook, my English professor friend, who has a boat in Kaslik Harbor. We'll sleep and eat and sun on the boat and relax. Friday I hope to see Father Labaki and then I'll go back to AUB. I must work hard for Hariri this next week and also for Tom's Day June 9—I'm trying to help them generate a very positive day—a commemoration of Tom in "A Focus on Agriculture Day" with seminars, discussions, and special events. Hope it works! Also hoping and praying that messages can get in to Tom—pray with me for that ... .

[Later, June 1] How wonderful to get that call from America and hear your voices. My spirits soared! I hadn't realized quite how much I'd missed hearing from and being in touch with you all. And to know that people there are willing to stick in there with us and support this project really touches my heart ... . Please be sure that there is never the suggestion that the funds are in any way meant to have any other motivation than the right and only one—to give from our hearts to those in need whose lives and bodies have been shattered by a war that there but for the grace of God go we—it is being done in Tom's name in order to symbolize the release of his creative energy over here—it is what we would do if he were released. It is so essential now that Irangate has become Irongate for us that motivations are kept very pure—not only there but here. One thing I've found through these two years is that if you never do anything artificial but keep always true to yourself and your beliefs that you can't lose or be caught in a false position. And I feel that it's so exceptionally important to bring the true American spirit and basic ideals back to this part of the world—the belief in justice and fairness and the right to life, liberty, and the pursuit of happiness. All the things that have become clichéd somehow gain over here the strength of their original meaning—like "where there's life there's hope" ... .

And thus came the time of commemoration and we had for June 9 our Focus on Agriculture Day. I spent the morning with the faculty at the Mini-AREC and going the rounds in the building followed by TV cameras. At noon a nice group gathered in the lecture room. The students put on a great slide show, Associate Dean Adib Saad spoke, and then it was my turn. Instead of a standard speech, I read to the assembled crowd "A Letter from Tom Sutherland" written by his "other half" Jean Sutherland. Interestingly, several people missed the fact that I had written it—"How did you get a letter from Dr. Sutherland?" "When did it come?" "Isn't it wonderful that you could have heard from him?" "Could I have a copy?" I clarified for them: "Tom and I came as a team and we are as one person—I wrote, but it was Tom's words as he would have spoken them." I truly felt that the response showed that the letter had brought his presence dynamically into the room that day, and I was so pleased:

JUNE 9, 1987 [From Tom Sutherland, by Jean Sutherland]—To my Family, Students, Faculty, Staff, and Friends at AUB and Everywhere Around the World ... Today I send you greetings and deep thanks for being there—for your remembrance and support that means everything. I am with you today as every day in my mind's eye, seeing you in many places—Colorado, California, Iowa, Texas, New York, Scotland, France, Australia ... and there at AUB where I picture you in agriculture and food sciences classes, at AREC, in and out of the dean's office, on the campus, at the Green Field, up the long steps, even upper campus, College Hall, Main Gate, Ras Beirut ... .

I am well, and I want you to have this message from me on this day, the day that marks in agricultural terms the end of a second bad season with the ever-present hope of a good new one to come. Amen to that. But the time when things are the toughest is not the time we give up our beliefs—it is instead the time we reaffirm them and this I want to do with you:

I believe in myself, my family, my friends, my countries, and my profession.

I believe in the university and all that concept means—for me represented by CSU and AUB for whom I work. And I dedicate myself again to FAFS and AUB— her students, staff, and faculty—today as I did two years ago and four years ago when we first came for Malcolm Kerr to do the job of dean of agriculture. I do this not because AUB is perfect but because she is not. She is as every university is absolutely of this human world with its worst of self-seeking, betrayal, and violence— and yet as every university is also with the very best in the belief in the power of knowledge in the service of good for mankind. The work to erase the first and serve the other is what we are all about.

I believe in one world and that we are all together in our work; that what I do is a work as a human being and as dean of agriculture at AUB. Every day I am here says to that world that there is the basic human problem that we must continue working to solve. It is bound into whatever we do to further knowledge in the universities of this world and it is bound into the great challenge of feeding its people who are hungry. I believe my effort here is your effort and your effort there is mine.

I believe that if together we do the jobs we're called to do the very best way we can, we will win through.

All my very best to all of you and thanks for giving me presence out there on this day, for letting me participate through Jean in building a greenhouse, attending class, seeing your labs and offices and buildings and campus again, and just being with all of you family and friends around the world wherever you are as we think of each other. I hope you'll accept as a tangible sign the funds I give—for the Dean's Revolving Fund for FAFS Affairs, and a Fund for AUB and Lebanon. These are meaningful because they are there for you to share in if you wish and we can do them together.

And also as a tangible symbol of our togetherness this day this telex:

TO OUR FAMILY ALL, KIT, JOAN, ANN, RAY, ALEX, SIMONE, MURRAYS AND SUTHERLANDS, AND FRIENDS IN THE CSU, FORT COLLINS, COLO-RADO, AMERICAN, SCOTTISH, AND WORLD COMMUNITIES: JUNE 9, 1987 ... .

MAY THIS TELEX LINK US ACROSS THE WORLD TODAY AS TOGETHER WE CELEBRATE THE LIFE, HOPE, FAITH, AND SPIRIT SUSTAINING US. OUR HEARTS ARE FULL AS WE THANK YOU FOR YOUR GIFT OF LOVE AND SUPPORT HELPING US TO REAFFIRM OUR COMMITMENT TO AUB, TO THE DAYS AHEAD, AND TO CONTINUING BELIEF IN "THE POWER OF OUR COLLECTIVE WILL" TO EFFECT "PEACE AND RELEASE."

IN LOVE—
TOM AND JEAN SUTHERLAND,
WITH STUDENTS, FRIENDS, AND COLLEAGUES IN THE AUB COMMUNITY, BEIRUT.

We sent the telex to CSU in Fort Collins—it was read to the people assembled there on the Oval for Tom, bringing our presence to them. They had their wonderful commemoration on June 9 attended by Father Martin Jenco and David

Jacobsen, and the First Presbyterian Church held a 24-hour prayer vigil. In the course of time I received the full account with pictures, but best of all, the next evening on Lebanese TV News, there was American film footage for me and all in Beirut to see and I wrote the family with joy in my heart:

Just saw a wonderful film clip from the CBS coverage of Tom Sutherland Day—yellow ribbons, Father Jenco praying for release, a rodeo shot, even me saying for the umpteenth time (but this time with the agriculture greenhouse tractor behind me) "all hope and no expectation carry us through" and Dave Jacobsen defending any means to freedom and THEN—the pièce de résistance—KIT in gorgeous full face answering question on arms to Iran … .

How I picture you at the cabin together … . You know I can just taste it and it's going to be about the hardest one to miss—but you know I'm just not going to miss it really because I can just feel and see every minute—you're going to raise a glass of something every night after sitting on the deck in the sun after a bit of wood chopping and food—and just lots of talk. What can I tell you? I'm submerged in schedules and new and old students … . And a nice thing—Hariri basketball team beat engineering for the intramural championship and gave me a bouquet of roses beforehand in center court—"To the greatest friend of them all—Hariri Students"—so it was awfully nice. The other thing that was wonderful was the way the agriculture students came through for your dad. They did handsprings to get a wonderful slide show produced (did any of it come over on the CBS program?)—of all the years of your dad—even the great shot of his goal as International Soccer Star in his youth. But amidst all the inhibitions and reticences of faculty—the students really made an impression and Adib Saad did a great speech too.

… I'm going to the East Side this weekend and will spend Sunday with Father Labaki—10:30 A.M. Mass and then dinner and the day with him seeing all he does … . A great telex from Americares says they're sending the medical supplies for Dr. Khaddaj, the mountain surgeon—you just have no idea the absolute joy in his voice when I told him over the phone—he couldn't believe it was true. Could you call your Uncle Dave and just tell him he effected a morale miracle for a good man over here who will save lives with it?! I'll send you the pictures and results as they come—we're going to visit in the mountains weekend after next … .

Things still "quiet"—contained—but tense here after Karami's death [Rashid Karami, Lebanon's Sunni Prime Minister, was killed when his helicopter exploded after takeoff from Tripoli].

The next week brought a letter from Dad about the ceremony for Tom in Ames, Iowa. Dad never spoke or showed his feelings—he just stayed calm and true and positive and worked for Tom at Iowa State University, Tom's and my alma mater (as well as Terry Anderson's), galvanizing the state of Iowa as well:

JUNE 11/15—Dear Jean ... You will be getting lots of news stories from the ceremonies honoring Tom on June 9 .... The ceremony and vigil for Tom here at ISU was touching and impressive .... The *Des Moines Register* front page on June 10th was a colorful story in itself. Bagpiper Robbie Stinson came 150 miles at no charge to salute Tom with his pipes and did a beautiful job. Dick Willham brought tears with his personal comments on the friendship he and Tom enjoy .... Mike Warren made it clear how important it is to give of our time, effort, and resource to the Middle East and to Africa.

We have as of today $2,350 in the two funds at our Collegiate Presbyterian Church ... .

Love, Dad

Large donations had come not only from Dad and Alice but also from Dad's sister and her husband, Win and Robb Kelley of Des Moines. I was just so touched that I wrote them right away:

When the letter came from Dad with the contributions for Tom's fund it touched my heart and brought tears to my eyes. That you could be so sensitive and so generous—it was as though you were right here close sharing and helping. I wish I could show you all that it means; ... at the base is the intangible that is Tom's feeling when he comes out that he was active and useful and positive—Dr. Khaddaj came over one night for some medical supplies and he said when we talked about it all—"I can't think of anything that would mean more to a man than to have his work carried on for him." It's so humbling to us that people would hang in for over two years supporting us to get *out of* this place, but it's something beyond when special people understand and support our staying *in* this place. There aren't words to say except we love you. And there will be children's books in English for the kindergartners at the Ain Saade and Al-Mabarat orphanages, and perhaps a scholarship for Bassam who is so good at soccer and biology, a wheelchair for a paraplegic in the Shouf, and at AUB something that means Tom in agriculture. There is a young man from the faculty going to CSU for irrigation engineering next week and he carries an application from another for horticulture to join two others who are trying to get funding to go—they're great kids and I think in choosing CSU for graduate work they are paying their homage to Tom ... .

17   Cold Storage

April 6, 1987. In the evening. A miracle. We're given a TV to watch *live* the Sugar Ray Leonard–Marvelous Marvin Hagler fight. But then the reverse of miracle. In came the Ghost and Hadi and told us to bring our things—we were on the move again, to location number eight. Another short trip, and we entered a huge garagelike place, with an absolutely *fierce* wind blowing. Up a stair *inside* this place, through a couple of doors, and into a small utility room, all three of us jammed in like sardines. The place, barely finished, had no doors hung, but it did have washer-dryer hookups. Some of them were just lying outside in the kitchen area—still to be there when we left months later.

Next morning, besides Hadi and the Ghost, some new guards. There was Bilaal, a very heavyset fellow with extremely muscular arms, as heavy as any farmer's I ever saw. But he was about the most gentle of any of the guards, never threatened any of us, and was, if anything, more rational in his thinking even than Mahmoud. He spoke in such a soft voice that I had difficulty hearing him, but he didn't mind repeating. His shift companion, Mazzin, we never got to know very well in this location—but he eventually proved the nastiest of the bunch. They asked, "Can you stay in this room?" "No way," we chorused. "Impossible. We need more space—here we're on top of each other." "Okay. We put you in another room, after some times." (They always translated from the French *temps,* keeping the "s" for good measure.) Followed lots of activity in another part of the apartment, and sure enough, we were led into another really large room that had been fitted with an elaborate system of blankets hanging from wires strung from one wall to the opposite side, and we were curtained off from both the large window and the doorway, up to the height of a blanket. After "some times more," the window got the usual treatment, only this time in spades. Two huge steel doors were mounted on a rail and could be slid to each side of the window.

We counted seven padlocks. The doors had reinforced edges, with a U-shape crimp in the steel, making them *incredibly* strong. What excess, we agreed. Zero hope of ever busting these down, for sure. Then came the *chains*. This time they buried the rings in the floor. Terry's one began at the steel door, round his ankle, to a ring in the floor, on to me, round my ankle, into a ring in the floor, then on to Frank. All linked together now, in the coziest of fashions.

A man named Shafic came in to talk to us after a day or two: "This is my apartment, but I am going to sell it soon. I leave Lebanon to go to Africa—maybe to the Ivory Coast. Lebanon finished. I don't want to stay here now. Everyone fighting, fighting, and the economy finished. For me is a much better life and make more money in Africa." "But," I asked him, "I thought that the Shia are having a hard time getting a visa for anywhere these days." "Yes, but I have relatives in Africa. I already have visa, so not a problem," he asserted.

"You can look at me," invited Shafic. "For me, not a problem if you seeing me." This was a new twist—we were tempted, but decided it was a bit risky. What if the other guards came in and caught us with our blindfolds up? Anyway, we couldn't be sure that Shafic really meant it. It soon became obvious though that he really did mean it, but we never took him up on it. He was possibly the most thoughtful and kind of all our guards—but in fact, he was not really a *guard*— only lending or renting them his place. He also did all the shopping for the others, driving a long way to do it—clear up to Chtoura, he told us, which is on the main Beirut-Damascus highway. We were at that time fairly far south in the Bekaa, so it must have been a journey of some 20–30 miles clear up to Chtoura. We concluded that this was another security arrangement—first, having a local fellow do the buying for the guards, who were not from the local village, and second, to shop in a distant village so that large quantities of bread and cheese, and rice and beans would not arouse any suspicion. One consequence was that he only bought bread perhaps twice a week. Pita bread is tasty when fresh, but when stale, it's brittle, loses its flavor, and is even hard to chew and swallow. Impossible too to make a sandwich with the cheese rolled inside of the hard bread, so that they would just give us the two separately, and let *us* fight with it.

A couple of weeks brought new arrivals—John and Brian again. No mistaking John's distinctively aristocratic English accent. From the sound of things, they were in the little utility room that we had occupied on the first night in the place. True, it could take the two of them better than us three, but they told us later that it really *was* incredibly cramped, and also terrible living right in the pockets of the guards working in the kitchen although they were honestly able to interact with them more easily than we did. Terry was still going into tantrums and deep huffs, arguing vehemently with our guards, and generally ending up by putting his face down in the pillow in complete frustration. No way to win an argument with these fellows— they had all the guns, literally. They tolerated this kind of behavior from Terry more readily than from the rest of us, but they really didn't like it at all. Always tension in the air—an atmosphere of constant confrontation. Hardly ever would they come and joke or play a game with us now.

Somebody decided to give us a TV set. Programs here were being broadcast many hours a day, and we were allowed to watch everything, *except the news*, which came on every night at seven and lasted for well over an hour. We soon discovered that this was all courtesy of Pat Robertson's Christian Broadcasting Network and every afternoon there was a full rendition of the *700 Club*. This program sparked lots of arguments about God and miracles and the nature of the deity, a continuing theme until then, now taking on renewed vigor and meaning. We found out years later that it was broadcast from Israel, by arrangement with the Israeli government.

A woman from a Chicago station led us in 30 minutes of calisthenics every day at 12:30—difficult for us to follow her exactly while chained to the floor. After her came a soap opera, *Another Life*, heavily Christian, which meant that there was much less sex, lechery, and treachery than in your average American soap. But it was well done, and we found ourselves thoroughly caught up in it, and were sad when our "thoughtful" guards would forget to bring in the TV in time for us to watch it. Many old movies, mostly classics starring Gregory Peck, or the Marx brothers, or Jimmy Stewart. We couldn't always see these, for we were sharing the box with the two Brits in the utility room. Generally we had first choice of afternoon or evening, and they got it the other period—and when we finally met them many months later, they gave us a royal roasting for having deprived them of their favorite programs from time to time. "These bloody Yanks get preferential treatment in everything," they had said. "Of course," we riposted, "we're far more important than you God-damned Brits!"

The guards' favorite shows in this era were *The A-Team, All in World Class Championship Wrestling* out of Texas (reputed to be the most popular program in the whole Middle East), and *McGyver*. These were completely improbable—especially *McGyver*. A piece of pipe, some chewing gum, some baking soda, and some soil out of the graveyard at midnight, and *ka-whoom:* He had blown to smithereens whatever it was that needed blowing up, and sometimes things that didn't. *The A-Team* was the guards' absolute favorite—all that shooting with machine guns, and the daredevil stuff gave them a real thrill. Nobody ever seemed to get killed, though, despite all the bullets whizzing around everywhere. I decided it had to have been conceived by the National Rifle Association who also believe that "guns don't kill people!" Things unfortunately were not quite like that in Beirut, or in all of Lebanon (or even in the United States), where reality prevailed and people died from real bullets. Our good friend John Pratt, an ex-Air Force colonel, had given me a poem prior to our departure from Fort Collins, of which a recurrent line went: "*A-root-a-toot-toot, they shoot guns in Beirut.*" How right he was, and not only guns, but cannons and RPGs and bombs and anything else that would explode—all of it great fun for our guards and their "brothers."

In this place, we had the feeling for the first time of being definitely in "cold storage." We had fewer visits than ever from anyone "important" such as a "boss man" from Beirut; even their "junior lieutenants" were seldom around anymore. Shafic was our main "connection" and although he knew about the Dawa 17 in Kuwait, he obviously had little idea of what was really going on. Why this cold storage? The guards kept telling us that "everything is good and very good. Soon and very soon, you go home." But they had told us that before, many times, and we hadn't believed them then either. Only now, it sounded more hollow than ever. It would still be a year until I would hear the word "Irangate" and suddenly our situation would be clarified.

Terry became extremely frustrated over the lack of movement. He would fuss and fume at the stupidity and incompetence of the Islamic Jihad. "These God-damned hamsters are *so dumb!* They can't negotiate *anything!* If they would just let me have a telephone conversation for half an hour with the American ambassador, I could have it all solved, and we would be on our way home in no time." He was still under the delusion that it was David and he who had brought about Ben's release, then Father's, and finally David's.

We were clearly out in the country here. Every day we could hear birds chirping and the bleating of a goat or two, which the guards told us were chained to stakes; in fact, they were amused by this kind of noise, so rural to kids raised for the last few years in Beirut where rifle fire and cannon blasts were much more common than goat noises. The only traffic was a lonely motorbike that passed once in a while.

One afternoon, we were aware of strange sounds, and one of the guards went rushing into the kitchen; strong thuds began that sounded ominously like a bat hitting human flesh, but no one was crying, and it went on for far too long for someone being beaten. But sure enough, in a short time, there was the Ghost in our room: "Do you want to fight, Terry?" he asked in a voice full of fury and even derangement; he was out of breath, obviously spoiling for more of a fight. "No thank you," replied Terry coldly. "You want to fight, Tom?" He was now challenging me.

"No way," I replied. "I don't like fighting." "Okay, Frank. *You* want to fight?" "No," replied Frank tersely. "American meat no good. British meat good," vaunted the Ghost cockily. "British meat much stronger than American meat," he repeated, strutting around the room. It was an extremely tense situation, and all three of us realized it instinctively. One of those occasions when the wrong move might easily result in one or all of us being shot, even. No time for valor. Some nine months later when we finally met the two Brits face-to-face when they were moved into our cell, we learned that Brian had opened the little window in the utility room and had incurred the wrath of the Ghost, who had hit him. Brian charged at the Ghost, and this led to the scurrying of Bilaal to the aid of the Ghost, and Bilaal had held Brian down while the Ghost laid into him with his broom handle, or perhaps a baseball bat. *Brave little shit.*

Some days later, the Ghost came back into our cell and examined the steel doors covering the window. He found a small space along the edge where the fit was not perfect and through which sunlight was streaming in simply because the sun was beating full strength right into that crack; they had never seen the sun hit it just right like that. "Terry, why you bend this door?" he demanded. "What?" said Terry in complete amazement. "What do you mean bend this door? I never touched the door let alone bent it!" *No* man could ever have bent that door even with a crowbar, let alone with his bare hands. "Yes, you bend this door. Not like this before. See much light now coming in here? Why you do this?" "Sure there is light coming in now. It comes like that every day when the sun is just right. In a few moments, it will not be like this," explained Terry rationally. The argument continued, and the Ghost was again working himself into a state, spoiling for a fight again. Terry stood his ground, so finally, "Tom, you see Terry bend this door?" "No way, man," I responded. "No man could bend that door with his bare hands." "Yes, Terry do it," he insisted. "No. I was here all day every day, and I know that Terry never has even been near that door." "Okay, Frank. You see Terry bend door?" He now appealed to Frank. "I don't know," replied Frank weakly. He didn't want to get involved in this stupid argument any more than any of the rest of us. After a minute or two more, the Ghost retreated, with dire threats about what was going to happen to all of us. "Thanks for standing up for me Tom," said Terry.

We all breathed a deep sigh of relief. The Ghost was small, more intelligent than the others, rather younger, and more immature than most of them, but with a dangerous and malicious spitefulness to him. He had taken to extremes the condition that guards fall into, according to Ben's story. And we had no guarantee of how deranged any one of them could become, and how much damage—

despite the orders from their superiors—they were capable of doing to us before any of their friends could intervene. The personalities of the guards, however, were schizoid, for after all his threats and accusations, the Ghost was soon in with herbal tea in which he professed implicit faith as a sure cure for colds or whatever ailed us. Strange how many bizarre beliefs they held about health matters.

In this place, Terry's ingenuity once again showed itself. He asked for a big piece of cardboard and a pen from Bilaal, and in no time had made a Monopoly board. I had never played Monopoly in my life. In fact, I had seldom played *any* of these sorts of games, having been much too busy on the farm in my youth in Scotland, and later with my studies as a graduate student, to have the time for games. But Terry knew them all by heart, having grown up in an American town with more time on his hands and in a family that was "into" games. He remembered all the parts of the board, and proceeded to draw in "Boardwalk," "Park Place," the four "Railroads," "Vermont Avenue," the lot. Little pieces of paper he transformed into "money." We had no hope of course of getting any dice from these vehemently antigambling fundamentalists. But Terry struck again. He concocted an arrowlike spinner from a piece of cardboard, used a toothpick to pivot it around in the center of the board, and drew in numbers 2 to 12 to equate to a throw of the dice. Houses and hotels, and we were in business.

We spent hours every morning becoming capitalists, and quickly became addicted. It taught tons about use of money and the value of investing it. Frank had had many jobs in the business world—some 17 or 18 different jobs in the past 23 years. But he was the least venturesome—Terry was always willing to trade properties, and even made Frank some ridiculously good offers. But Frank wouldn't budge! So I frequently won, for Terry had been *too* venturesome and lost his shirt, while Frank stuck to his little properties and seldom came out ahead. Valuable lessons here, perhaps, about *taking a risk,* but not *too much* of a one.

Terry's favorite game was Scrabble. Another big sheet of cardboard, and Terry's memory, and there was the board—he recalled where you get double scores, triple scores, and how much each letter is worth and in next to no time, we were playing. A journalist, he was not only keen on the game, but very good at it. Frank had been a teacher, so he too fancied himself at the game. But he hardly ever beat Terry. Nor did I. But we had some wonderful arguments about which words really were words, and listed in the dictionary—of which we had none of course, so all we could do was to agree to "hang it up until we get out of here." A disputed word was "biomass." Frank had never heard of it, and refused it, but Terry was claiming it! I *had* heard of it hundreds of times, especially from the Natural Resource Ecology Laboratory at CSU, where they routinely measured the biomass produced on the plains of eastern Colorado. Still Frank wouldn't accept it, so Terry, to keep the peace, agreed to "forget it."

In Shafic's apartment, Frank made a reasonable recovery from his beating and proved a wonderful storyteller—he had us in stitches for hours on end. He had organized a tour to both poles, with stops in Alaska, Japan, Australia, and New Zealand. He regaled us with accounts of each stop, the bars they had visited, the women he had succeeded in picking up along the way, the interesting characters on the tour (most of them rich as Croesus), the time when their chartered plane broke down and they had to wait around until it was fixed, which never happened so they had to get another flown in. Frank also had an obsession with Italian shoes, and bought them on every possible occasion. Fifty or more pairs he said he had in his closet, and believed in never wearing a pair more than once a month. All very fine light shoes, but not the kind that any self-respecting Scotsman, who needs a heavy pair of brogues to walk like Rob Roy through the bracken and the heather, would ever wear. So we nicknamed him "Frankie the Shoe," or "the Shoe" for short, a name that stuck throughout the rest of his captivity.

Occasionally the guards were nice to us by opening the doors to let in some wonderful fresh air, even daylight, which was bright enough to blind us. "It sure is amazing how bright God's light is" we remarked to each other—and it was. After months of incarceration with a candle, or a 100-watt bulb, it always amazed us to be exposed to daylight. We were forbidden to look out of the French doors, but we disobeyed and were rewarded with a view of South Lebanon. I had never seen this part of the country so it was interesting to see the low, rolling hills and the rock outcrops, despite our very limited view from back in the room. I was seeing *nature* for the first time in years, and I felt an intense longing and a severe frustration with present conditions.

November 2 arrived, and so did Ahab, bearing the nice clothes Terry had been given on departure from that terrible "Prison" nine months before. "Okay, Terry, you go home now," said Ahab, who was proving rapidly to be almost as good a liar as Ali. I tried to talk to Terry—all kinds of things I wanted him to do for me. But, "No speak, Tom. Okay?" came the eternal injunction. Terry sat around for several hours, and at last was taken out of the room. It was still daytime, but down here the guards were fairly relaxed, so maybe he left right away. Finally somebody else going home. Cold storage over?

Frank and I were alone and things were *much* more tranquil. It was a huge relief to be done with Terry's nervous energy and questing brain, his demanding personality, and confrontational tactics. Then, in three weeks, Frank was gone too. I was alone with Bilaal as my only guard, who was, in fact, fairly civilized. He treated me very gently, asking what I would like to eat and drink, and whether there was anything he could do for me. As usual, I replied, "How about a taxi to Beirut Airport, Bilaal?" "Okay," he would reply, "I think that will happen soon." My hopes were up, for I thought it was at least possible that both Terry and Frank had gone home. I might just follow them soon? But somehow, things didn't feel quite right yet.

November 26, 1987, the day after Thanksgiving, I too was on my way, but not to freedom. First I was taped up unceremoniously, not as badly as for under the truck, but still pretty tightly, especially around my mouth and nose. A very rough character had arrived who spoke a few words of English and gave me a very stern lecture: "In car, no speak, okay? You speak, I shoot you." Well, that sounded tough enough. Outside we went, down the stairs through the huge garage that I had entered early in the morning of April 7. Eight months Shafic had hosted us. Now he was maybe on his own way, to Africa? Could that be the reason for this move? I was instructed gruffly to get into the car. But I was partially bound, and totally blind from my wrappings. I had no idea where the car was, let alone the door. My new friend pushed me roughly toward the car and said, "Get in, queeckly." I still had no idea of how to bend down to get through a door, but made some attempt. "You stupid like donkey," commented my friend, pushing my head down and partially lifting me. Finally in, a guard by my side, and off we went, slowly down the road. The car sounded powerful, probably a Mercedes. In ten minutes, I could hardly breathe and began to protest. The guard began to tell me to hush, and as soon as the tough guy heard the sounds from the back, he pulled up sharply. "I tell you no speak. Why you make noise, huh?" He was furious and began to punch my face very hard. First time they had ever hit me directly in the face, but this guy sounded like a real hard-liner who would stop at nothing. Our drive resumed. No idea of where we were going or how long it would take but this was one of my shorter journeys. A few minutes more, we stopped, I was handed over to another guy, who sounded *much* less threatening, up one flight of stairs, and I was seated on the floor while my tape bindings were ripped off.

Location number nine. Instructions: "You have two friends, but you no telling them your name. Your name now Sammy. Okay?" What an insult. I was brought up with the Scottish belief that calling anyone "Sammy" indicated a certain lacking somewhere. That was not all, though. "You not telling them *anything* about you. You country. Where you with us. You family. You age ... nothing. Nothing, understand?"

I got the picture. "You friends' names Labeeb and Habeeb," he informed me. At least we will all have names. But how about that; the same old story—Labeeb and Habeeb. Wonderful. How in hell am I going to tell the difference between two names like that?! He wasn't finished. "You not ask *any* questions you friends, understand? Nothing. No speak their country." The whole thing struck me as rather bizarre, to put me in with two new guys but not allowing me to speak freely—at least they weren't *forbidding* me to *speak* entirely. "You speak them French only. Okay?"

Through a door and into the bedroom where I was to spend the next three months. I greeted my new companions in my best French, and they replied in the most fluent French I had heard in a long time. It took me only seconds to decide that they *had* to be French, though one of them had a strong trace of Lebanese-type French. Few of us can *ever* learn to speak French quite like the French do it. At first we hewed to the instructions and talked only pleasantries, for we could easily deduce that we were being watched and listened to very carefully.

But soon it becomes impossible for intelligent people to abide by such nonsense when thrown together in an environment like that, and I soon divulged my identity to them, and in the ensuing days told them about my experiences. Labeeb—bearded, slight, medium height, ready smile in sweatpants and shirt and wearing his own glasses—turned out to be none other than Jean-Paul Kauffmann, the French journalist in his early forties who had been kidnapped a few days before me, along with Michel Seurat, en route from the airport to the city, exactly as I had been. Jean-Paul had been on his way to an assignment in Tripoli for *L'Evenement de Jeudi,* the weekly that he had just joined a few months before he was kidnapped, after a long and distinguished career with *Le Matin,* one of the major dailies in Paris. My other colleague in the room, Habeeb, was Marcel Carton, a man in his mid-sixties with gray beard and dressed also in a sweat suit. When picked up, he was chief of protocol at the French embassy in Beirut, aged almost 65. The son of a Syrian woman and a French soldier, Marcel had grown up in Beirut and spoke fluent Arabic as well as Lebanese-French.

It was interesting about the pseudonyms. Where some months before, we three Americans refused to accept Bilaal, Dalaal, and Talaal, here with the French we were willing to accept these names and to keep up the pretense of anonymity to gain the freedom to speak to each other. We used the names routinely, careful never to divulge to the guards that we knew all about each other. To this day when we call each other on the telephone, it is always: "Allo! Habeeb/Labeeb. C'est moi, Sammy!"

The guards were all new to me. It was immediately obvious that these two Frenchmen knew a lot more about how to get along with Islamic Jihad than we Americans. They had a working relationship with the guards such as we had never had, due mainly to Marcel's long acquaintance with Arabs. But even Jean-Paul was much more astute than Terry in his dealings with them. He maintained his dignity, and never gave in to them, but *insisted* on fairness in treatment. Amazingly, he seemed to get it, almost as though he had some kind of invisible barrier around him through which Islamic Jihad dared not penetrate, and within which Jean-Paul maintained his dignity and demanded his "rights," rights that were never accorded the rest of us, except as I later learned, John McCarthy. From these two men, I learned a lot about behavior in captivity, and especially dealing with young kidnappers.

Jean-Paul had given them all nicknames, the most peculiar *Le Rat Musqué*, French for muskrat, reserved for a nasty character who called himself Mazzin and who was to stay with me for many months, even after Jean-Paul was long home. I never did know the logic of his getting this particular name. Jean-Paul just felt that it fitted him!

In French (all our conversations were in French, for neither of my companions spoke more than a word or two of English) I told them that I was fairly sure that Terry Anderson had gone home, but Jean-Paul challenged me on that. "How do you know he has gone home? I don't think he is home. It is not in the air. We would have had some input from the guards here. They get excited about every little happening, and we have had no scent of anything. Furthermore, our colleague Marcel Fontaine was taken from here the day you arrived, and the guards have not given any indication that he is now home. You are on his bed now, and we are very happy to have you here in his place, for he was always upsetting the peace with the guards. He made lots of mischief," confided Jean-Paul. "My Lord, did he make mischief!" agreed Carton. It was obvious that the two embassy employees had not gotten along, perhaps because Fontaine, a native of La Reunion, a French colony, had been a kind of vice consul who, although much younger than Carton, had outranked him.

Speaking of Terry, I related to the Frenchmen how he had been so critical of Islamic Jihad, insisting that they were *so* dumb, could not negotiate *anything*, and that if only they would let *him* have 30 minutes with the American ambassador, *he* could have it all solved. "Don't you believe it," retorted Jean-Paul. "We are in a very complex international situation. There is no easy solution like that. Besides, these people are extremely intelligent and are very astute in their negotiations! They are getting everything they want so far." This struck me, and I began to realize that Terry was indeed fallible, that his arrogant attitude was in no way justified, and that I probably should have been much more assertive in dealing with him. And so I was from this time on and our relationship would normalize. To Jean-Paul, really, I owed the start of my psychological rehabilitation.

I brought to the two Frenchmen a new outlook and background, new knowledge and experience, and therefore lots of new discussion material. After two and a half years of captivity with the same group, they had experienced much the same as Terry and I had, almost running out of topics to talk about. Jean-Paul and I immediately struck up a very close friendship. The year I had spent in France on sabbatical leave had given me a fairly thorough acquaintance with La belle France, which pleased both of them, particularly Jean-Paul. He knew his country like the back of his hand, or as they say in French, "comme ma poche" ("like my pocket"), and when I would make a mistake about some region or its produce, he would correct me, "Je connais mon pays!" ("I know my country!") and he *did!*

A native of Brittany who had only migrated to Paris to attend college, then stayed, he had traveled widely in his career, and had a memory at least as good as Terry Anderson's, and was obviously more intellectually talented but without any pretense at knowing a single thing about practical things, as opposed to Terry who was extremely talented with his hands as well as his head. Here we had French books, some of them bound in the most beautiful fashion. "Where on earth did they get such beautiful books?" I asked Jean-Paul. "These are the books of Michel Seurat! He was allowed to go home under tight guard and picked up a mass of books, some of which you see still here with me. I have read them several times by now, so that I almost know them by heart. He also brought back a radio, a Sony shortwave, which we used to have part of the day. But recently they took it away from us." So *that* was where that radio had come from two years ago, the one the Hajj had claimed was his personal radio that he was lending us so magnanimously. Jean-Paul wanted to improve his English, which at that point was rather rudimentary. He chose a book in English to read because of the cover photo of the author—Liv Ullmann—who he thought must be one of the most beautiful women in the world. I agreed! A full-page photo on the front and back cover brought us inspiration every time we picked it up. Her autobiography *Changing* was a tender tale, which transported us from our dreary damp cell to the glittering world of stardom in Europe and the United States. Fascinating to read about her reactions to her fellow stars, especially Charles Bronson—definitely not one of her favorite people. Jean-Paul read a few pages a day, and made considerable progress in the three months we spent together. More importantly for me, he did not have any ambition to be "the leader" and to put me down as

Terry had constantly felt the need to do, so that my self-confidence rapidly came back. Once again some pride in myself, my knowledge, and my background. I began to feel at peace with myself for the first time in well over two years and, looking back, date my progress forward toward "normality" from this point.

Each day, to "spin out" the books a little, Jean-Paul would recount the plot of some book he had read long ago (and he had read just about everything there was to read) and passed hours speaking in a very soft voice—we were not allowed ever to speak "à haute voix." What a memory! He included wonderful detail from each book, as I listened in amazement. A somewhat different kind of memory from Terry Anderson's, but just as incredible—gentle, soothing accounts delivered in his beautiful French. I found him comforting as a companion, and gradually my head began to straighten itself out, my memory began to work ever more efficiently. The power of community, and I was finding it more strongly with Frenchmen than I had with my fellow Americans.

Jean-Paul, for all his knowledge of "mon pays," had not heard of the research station where I had spent my sabbatical leave, at Jouy-en-Josas, one of the most renowned in the world with a group of "jeunes chercheurs" with few equals in the field of animal science—especially reproduction physiology, but also genetics and breeding, nutrition, microbiology, and even such areas exotic to animal science as audiology, which was being investigated to scare off crows and other birds, always a big pest for grain farmers. He was delighted to have such positive reports about the strength of his fellow Frenchmen in a field unfamiliar to him. I suggested that he ought to pay Jouy a visit, and gave him names to contact. This, in fact, would happen after his release and then mine, and we have had wonderful get-togethers *en famille* in Paris!

Mid-December brought taped radio messages from the wives of both Jean-Paul and Marcel, duly recorded by the powers that be of Islamic Jihad. Surely couldn't have been the guards, for they had never had that kind of responsibility or authorization. Among us Americans, only Terry Anderson had ever been given this kind of treatment. The illusion of anonymity was still being pursued, so I was taken out into the guards' room, while the two listened to the tape recorder. But we were not long back together before I had received a rather complete report of the message. It was extremely encouraging, and Joelle Kauffmann had been more optimistic than ever before. Things were finally looking up for the French, and she had been requested by the government not to "rock the boat," for things were still somewhat delicate, but definitely and finally more positive than she had ever been able to report. What a good tone this set for the three of us, as we came to Christmas 1987.

18 Getting to Christmas

The last week of June this year of 1987 was special with a Cyprus brainstorming workshop for the AUB-Hariri Special English Training Program. For some months we had been talking and looking for ways to improve and promote our intensive language school—make it modern and up-to-date with the latest in ESL expertise, strategy, and techniques. I had suggested perhaps getting a review team in from outside—I knew Joy Reid from CSU who was very good, very dynamic, and very up-to-snuff. But it had not been pursued, probably because Americans couldn't really come to Lebanon. But in June, all of a sudden, there was a planning session in the works—four days in Cyprus to brainstorm a possible workshop for selected administrators and teachers in the program, bringing a cadre of distinguished ESL people from the United States. We went and brainstormed and came up with a list of seven names of top-flight people in the United States in the field and decided that the first workshop would be a week-long seminar in Larnaca, Cyprus, at the Sandy Beach Hotel for the level coordinators and administrators and senior resource people. It was now the end of June. Dr. Hallab said that it was probably too late to get such noted and busy people to come for a workshop in September. But all of the rest of us said, "Try it! Tell them about our program, stress Beirut and our need, and then describe Cyprus and the Sandy Beach Hotel. Bet they'll take you up on it."

And so they did—three of them, including Joy Reid from Fort Collins, said "Yes." What a coup! Through the summer we planned, we organized, and the last week of September held the workshop, days of 8:00–5:00 intensive sessions (with extracurricular swimming, eating out at fish restaurants, informal brainstorming and talking, and beachcombing) of learning about the latest in ESL teaching: the natural approach for beginners, "bins" for articles on all and sundry subjects like medicine, psychology, the sexual revolution—you name it, individualizing, networking, planning. We talked, we role-played, we interacted, and despite the prognostications of the U.S. experts who said that a study showed that only 5 percent of any academic workshop went back to the workplace, we returned to the AUB campus and the Hariri School with 95 percent integration of what we had learned. We held in-service workshops for all of our teachers and even shared with the AUB English Department group—what a tremendous success! Most of all was the vitalization of our administrative personnel in "getting out" and "getting with" the best in the profession from the United States. Did these American ESL experts appreciate how great was the gift they gave? I think yes, and I think they received a lot in their turn. Joy and I walked the beach and picked up smooth white stones; I sent one back to each daughter with "Love from Cyprus—Mom" written on it. Since then it's become a tradition, and each has a collection of special stones from every beach I've visited since.

The workshops were held annually for a time—the next year the top-level teachers participated. After the third year, I didn't attend and I don't know what they have done since, the Hariri English Program dwindling and dwindling these past years and my being out of it. But what I know from the start is that the result was incalculable. With those ultrabright Lebanese teachers, it produced a cadre of trained ESL "specialists" and afterward they formed a team themselves, going out as an extension program into other parts of Lebanon doing workshops for English teachers in the government and private school systems. One of the teachers who participated in a summer ESL course in England came back saying she had more up-to-date knowledge and experience than most in the course she took there—including professors—and ended up doing some of the teaching herself. We put together a presentation of our program with videotapes of the school and classroom scenes and three of us took it to the National ESL Association meetings in Chicago in the spring of 1988, just after Tom's 1,000-days observance, and we and the program were well received in America. Joy Reid was in charge of the conference that year and it meant a lot.

We had no way of knowing at that first planning session at the end of June 1987 in Cyprus how truly successful the workshops would be—just had a good and "right" feeling about it. We also loved the R and R that Cyprus gave us and the chance to call the United States on telephones that worked! I wrote home after I got back:

JULY 4—Dear Guys ... It was wonderful to speak to you from Cyprus—I tried to call you from here after I got back but absolutely no luck—I didn't want you worried over the news again about the hostages being moved in coffins to Iran. It didn't sound like a very nice journey to say the least, but it's just news and we can't believe it any more than the opposite. There's just no sure knowledge right now about anything so the best is just to march straight ahead through the news without changing style . . . . The rumors about the move of hostages seem to flow in and out of rumor systems about Glass [Charles Glass, former ABC bureau chief in Beirut, who was kidnapped on June 17, 1987, and released on August 18, 1987] as a spy, Terry Waite as dead of a heart attack, and Ollie North as the new Super Star . . . . It doesn't seem that probably anything has changed but then we don't know anything—except that in the boiling down of Ollie North's stardom there hasn't been any result except two wars still going on while three hostages out were exchanged for seven more in—probably worth a decoration?? ... All is still quiet in Beirut except for the intermittent explosions—one day before yesterday in Hamra area near a Syrian checkpoint—they keep trying to challenge Syrian order this way they say ... .

The summer days progressed, hot and humid as usual for Beirut—I could understand the old missionary families moving up to Shemlan, Aitat, or Ainab in the mountains to escape, and I blessed David and Doris Dodge for putting air conditioners in three rooms of our house. When Elien came over for coffee and a chat, we'd hole up in the study or the bedroom and enjoy the coolness. One evening in August during the Feast of Adha (when Moslems celebrate God's sparing of Abraham's son Isaac from sacrifice on the mountain), the wind changed and brought God's coolness to us. I was mulling over a question that Dr. Hallab had put to me—"Why AUB? Think about it and tell me"—and I climbed the stairs to our open rooftop balcony. Coming down a half hour later I recorded the experience for him:

So Abdul Hamid, I told you I'd take my coffee out on the balcony and think about "Why AUB?" and it was tonight. And it was the top balcony because there was for the first time in weeks a fresh breeze blowing off the sea from the north and I had letters to write to people who had given to Tom's funds and a thesis to read for a girl in PSPA [Political Science and Public Administration]—so I stepped out on that balcony with my cup in my hand and the breeze hit me like I was on a prow of a ship and I looked toward the sea and there was a ship's light way out to the left and the complex light of Jounieh off to the right and near at hand the Corniche lights with the Adha throngs moving up and down, up and down (are they thinking about that complex interaction between willingness to sacrifice and the ability to give mercy??)—then coming backward onto AUB, the quiet darkness over the Green Field, the lights of Architecture on as always to the right as students work through the night, a couple, arm in arm with white shirts, walking slowly down toward the beach area—I turned around and all that I had seen was behind me and there in front of me was the sight that means Lebanon and my home to me—the three-quarter moon behind the waving dark palm tree in the garden and to the left this time the lighted clocktower of AUB ... . And turning around again there was the ancient symbol brought from the East/West—the Great Bear pointing to the North Star—Shakespeare's "ever-fixed mark/That looks on tempests and is unshaken/A guide to every wandering bark/Whose worth's unknown although his height be taken" that symbolizes TRUTH as it symbolizes POWER—it was dim but visible about three-quarters up from the horizon 60 degrees up, "that light to the Phoenicians" ... . Why AUB? And I came down to start reading and helping the girl on her thesis ... . And the LBC TV had many film clips from the U.S. tonight—Gulf ships everywhere with helicopters flying and Iranian suicide boats (canned shots) dodging about, and the shots again of the riots in Mecca as Saudis clash with Iranian Shiites during the Hajj—they say 200 killed. Tomorrow it's again a problematic day at the Hariri Program because many want to stretch the holiday to the whole week and the Level 4s are bored and only maybe the change in the weather will help ... . No summer school classes in agriculture this summer—only the farm—but the girl who won the Penrose Award and graduated with distinction told me, "I can't wait to start on my master's—if there were no AUB I'd have to leave."

So why AUB? I guess it's somewhere in all of that ... .

Work was a salvation and there was plenty of it. And with the airport open and planes flying, the mail came in, another salvation. A delivery in late July brought a letter from the secretary-general of the European Association for Animal Production to tell me of the resolutions taken at their meetings on Tom's behalf. How touched I was for Tom! As I told Professor Boyazoglu in an August thank-you letter to him:

I hope I can express personally and adequately through you to each of Tom's colleagues at those meetings and in the countries represented how much this meant to me—doubly, because I felt it for Tom and know what it will mean to him when he returns. His work is his life and he has especially valued the opportunities to carry this out internationally with the firm friendships that have come from the mutual respect animal scientists have for each other in their profession no matter what country or culture ... . We have no new direct word of Tom and the events on the World/Middle Eastern scene seem to indicate "lock" on top of "deadlock." ... Sometimes it seems as if the price of international commitment is too high, yet when Father Jenco and David Jacobsen both told me on their release that Tom wanted still "to get back to his work at AUB" I knew that he hadn't changed in his commitment and I was glad ... .

A letter came also from the American Society of Animal Sciences with their annual resolution and a copy of their letters to Washington and I put all together with the other wonderful notes and letters of support from friends everywhere to be there for Tom when he got out—a box of treasures. How warm his heart would be—and it was!

Along with the Saudi-Iranian conflict at Mecca and the U.S. ships entering the Persian Gulf to become involved in the Iran-Iraq War, there came another hijacking, this time in Geneva. Threats naturally resulted with the arresting of the hijacker, and we felt it in Beirut when we went to the Swiss embassy fete for their National Day through ranks of guards, M-16s, and rocket launchers. We could but hold on and hope for no repercussions. In the meantime, 17 boxes of medical supplies had come from that great organization AMCARES (Americares Foundation for Emergency Relief) for Dr. Khaddaj, and he was ecstatic. My brother Dave, an orthopedic surgeon in Syracuse, had asked around for me and finally gotten in contact with AMCARES who came through in the most wonderful way in response to Dr. Khaddaj's need. I suggested to AMCARES that they "adopt a surgeon" so that he could operate and treat people in the Shouf field hospitals and his clinic in Beirut without worrying about payment from people who couldn't pay—they did this also and it meant a lot. One of his cases was a Ghanaian young man who had been shot on the East Side in a drive-by shooting as he played soccer—a bullet had lodged in his knee and he couldn't walk. The smile on his face when he came back from Bhamdoun after the operation by Dr. Khaddaj was pure joy.

September came with its trip home for me—Joan had decided to give up the Los Angeles rat race and come back to Fort Collins, so she and Kit moved in together into a two-bedroom apartment that, along with the cabin, would be our Colorado home for the next two years. The three weeks went by much too fast as always and then I was back to the Cyprus English workshop and my work at AUB.

This year, for the first time, all teachers at the Hariri Program were on Lebanese pound salaries. I looked at that and knew that I couldn't again take an American dollar salary and be treated so differently and so much better than anyone else. I told Dr. Hallab, "You must give me payment in Lebanese pounds this year." "You can't do that," he said. "Yes, I can—I must. I'm here to share, to serve. What do the words mean if I take dollars that others can't have?" He capitulated and my salary went from about $1,200 a month take-home to $80. *(Sorry, Tom, but there's no other way. You'll have to support me and those trips to the States.)* But I was able to add an AUB overtime class in Renaissance literature for a little extra money and teach in my field for the first time. What a joy that was going to be! I even planned to bring the students to our house sometimes and sit around the living room with coffee and cookies and open discussion Renaissance-style. It would be wonderful to be back in the world of ideas! By November I was organized and well into the fall session and writing again to all our friends:

The sun is shining brightly for the second day since an absolute deluge of rain on Friday—it's now noon because I went down to the Faculty 2 apartment building to have coffee with my dear Dutch friend Elien whose husband is head of physics and associate dean of arts and sciences. They're the only foreign couple left on campus (a Canadian philosophy professor, a Lebanese-American English professor, and a handful of single American women along with an English woman at Hariri complete the foreign roster) and they are wonderful people. They came over last Wednesday evening for dinner with some off-campus friends and we socialized over Burgundy beef and crepes—I redid the evening the next night with three young couples from Tom's faculty who are staunch friends and the food was appreciated by all of us because the country went on open strike Thursday to protest the collapse of the Lebanese pound and none of us knows when the grocery stores will open again (it looks like Tuesday when MEA says its planes will fly again and the airport will reopen although a massive demonstration is scheduled for tomorrow and we'll have to see). People are just "fed-up" as they put it—they see the economic situation as another form of political warfare and it seems worse somehow than the shells and bullets because for most of the middle-class and poor on Lebanese currency there is no way for anyone to escape. One of my teacher-colleagues said that she and her husband together were scarcely bringing in $80 per month equivalent. One can see and feel the desperation as savings are used up for food and medicines. Outside money has kept things going, relatives sending hard currency from other countries, aid programs dispensing lentils, rice, and oil though the mosques and churches and political parties. But an especially hard year is seen by all and while the pound now is 500 something to the dollar, the prediction is for up to 3,000 to the dollar next year.

But, the sun is shining brightly and even though my typewriter is faltering under the severe influence of the sea air I can tell you that there are joggers, running children, and a basketball game going on the Green Field below and tennis players on all the courts next door although most of the students are gone home for the long strike weekend. And I will go from this letter to you to very normal preparations for the next busy week—testing and placing the last group of students for the Hariri English Program of 750 and getting lectures and class sessions ready for my English Renaissance course Tuesday-Wednesday-Thursday ... . We're reading Sir Thomas More's *Utopia* now in this course and it's wonderful—just about 12 students, mostly English majors, and we're into all the classical and Renaissance treasures of the world. The Wednesday class is from 1:00–2:00 (to avoid a Saturday class) and they come to our home for a symposium where we discuss love, art, reality, the Ideal State, Reformation, beheading, the meaning of Pygmalion, and such things (we'll do poetry in December and *The Faerie Queene* in January) and it's New Learning for them as it was in the Renaissance—when I found out last week that they hadn't done the assignment I asked why and one student said they hadn't had electricity and all appreciated the point when I said that the Renaissance scholars hadn't had electricity either …. So you see that there are great people here to share with and work to do to keep busy.

For all those who had given to the funds I enclosed a special letter of thanks and update on what was happening to their contributions:

I had my meetings with people to give your money to them …. Our love and thanks are wrapped around this letter because you've helped give Tom a presence in this place and meaningful work at a time when all else is deadlock and "No News."

Father Labaki sent a wonderful letter of thanks to the churches, detailing the recipients of the monies: "the orphans of Our Lady of Joy, 135 kids in the area of Sid el Bauchrieh, for a daily breakfast sandwich operation, the poor students of Rosary College, university students, the old age home in Antelias, the poor students of the Infant Jesus Institution, and to various orphans in homes." How far those dollars went! The director of Al-Mabarat was also sincerely appreciative—we discussed specific things to do but I left it that the funds were theirs for their needs with no strings attached. My teacher friend, Ghada, from the Hariri Program who worked with the English program at Al-Mabarat introduced me to several of the upper-class boys, deserving and needy, and we found some more money to buy them school supplies and backpacks. The boys' thank-you letters came December 10 enclosed in a card saying "Happy Birthday to a Son"— their understanding of Christmas. The composite expression touched my heart:

By the Name of Allah
Dear Mrs. Jean—Thank you for your gift and letter that you send them to me …. The gift is very nice and wonderful and it's good for our school and our luggage …. I don't forget that your present came to help me or let me say that to help us because you know the situation in Lebanon is very hard …. I hope that my God will help you in your life …. I wish for you and for your family and for all the world a new year filled with love and peace.
    Marry christmas and happy new year. Yours sincerely, Bassam, Houssam, Bassam, Kassem, Jamal

We certainly had a "marry" Christmas, Ann and Ray and tiny Simone coming through snowstorms in their car from California to Fort Collins, I from Beirut, Kit and Joan hosting us all in their new apartment with a fireplace. Snowy and cold, the weather only closed us in with Christmas tree and gifts and turkey dinner and increased our feeling of togetherness. What joy, what happiness that we caught in a photo one day. It was the one I took back to put in the *As-Safir* newspaper with hopes Tom would be allowed to see it. Much later, our complete joy that he did on Valentine's Day in 1988 and saw his first son-in-law and new granddaughter.

I returned to Beirut for the New Year 1988, but with a lot of my heart left still with the family.

19   En Français

January 25, 1988—A special challenge for me this evening. Not only to transform old pita bread and bad tea into haggis and whisky, but to translate Robert Burns into French for Jean-Paul. Even most Englishmen have a hard time understanding Burns and the emotions that he conveys in his poems, so it was going to be doubly difficult to do it in French! But I reckoned without my Jean-Paul and the powers of his imagination. He had heard vaguely about our Scottish Bard, and now launched himself into the spirit of the celebration of his birthday with unbridled enthusiasm as I recounted the themes of the poems and the nature of his life—especially his wild escapades. The fact that Burns had had some half dozen illegitimate children prior to his marriage to Jean Armour really appealed to his French concept of the supreme lover! And of course the tales of Burns's riotous drinking and debauchery filled Jean-Paul with renewed glee. Chained to a wall in the south of Lebanon, the two of us were nevertheless roaming free over the fields of Ayrshire or eavesdropping in the withdrawing rooms of Edinburgh where Burns was holding forth to the literati of that great city, having finally been accepted as the genius that he truly was. What a night that was.

But a day or two afterward, I was sick—God, how sick! Raging fever, vomiting, diarrhea, black urine, and white feces. The vomit went into the garbage bag; the guards took me to the toilet for the diarrhea. I showed my urine bottle to Jean-Paul. "Oh," said he in his French language and manner, "This is exactly what happened to Michel Seurat just before he died." I could only look at him—frankly so ill that at that moment I simply didn't care whether I lived or died. We told the guards, and when Ahab appeared, he brought in a juice bottle from the kitchen to take a sample back to Beirut with him. Some days later he reappeared with a true medical sample bottle duly sterilized for a new sample—the juice bottle not having been acceptable for some reason—and he stood looking at me in most un-Shiite fashion while I tried to produce a sample for him. A week later he was back with the strange diagnosis—we needed more protein in our diet. We enjoyed a few days of chicken and lamb for lunch, but by this time, my health had come back more or less to normal by itself without *any* medication. So the novelty soon wore off, and we were back to good old pita bread and processed cheese, with the usual rice and beans and only pleasant memories of the meat.

February 13, the day before Valentine's Day—both Labeeb and Habeeb received written messages from their wives, brought from Beirut by Ahab. "Ahab," I said, "I simply don't believe that there have been no messages from my wife in all this time. It has now been two years since I had a single thing from her, and I am sure that she must have sent something for me too." "No, no. Beleef me, beleef me. There is nothing. If there is something, trust me, I will bring." "Ha," I thought. "Trust this dude? He's got a hope." Imagine my surprise when the very next day, Valentine's Day, he announced, "Tom, there is a message for you in the paper today!" "Can I have it please?" "Yes, yes, after some times." My patience stretched to the limits, it was late afternoon before he finally brought it in, with a strict injunction to my French colleagues, delivered to Habeeb in Arabic, not to look, under penalty of severe retribution. A clipping from the *As-Safir* with a photograph of my family seated all together and a brief message underneath:

> "A Christmas Picture with Valentine Love, Loyalty, Strength, Perseverance, and Steadfast Hope and Faith. Beirut—Jean, Fort Collins—Joan and Kit, Berkeley—Ann Ph.D., Ray and Simone."

A brief note, but full of news. Ann had finished her Ph.D., as I suspected she would have. But there was "Simone!" Who could she be? Gradually it dawned on me that Ray and Ann must have married and had a daughter. *My granddaughter!* What an incredible sensation. All kinds of emotions were coursing through my head. Suddenly I was brought back to reality by an angry roar from Ahab at Habeeb, who had been leaning over my shoulder in the most obvious way to see what my message was all about. Ahab, peeking through the crack at the hinged end of the partially open door, had seen him. "Why you looking, Habeeb? I tell you no looking," roared Ahab in English this time, and proceeded to give him a severe dressing down. Soon he calmed down and withdrew to the guards' room, while Labeeb reciprocated his verbal lambasting in French. I was oblivious to all but my "message," surely one of the most precious pieces of paper I have ever received. I kept that photo for a long time before they reclaimed it.

After this brief interlude in the routine, it was back to the books. A new batch had arrived, some in English this time—several Mills and Boone volumes: British, brief, skinny, miserable excuses for literature, reportedly written by a "stable" of women who write to a formula: A woman goes off from England on holiday to Spain/Greece/Portugal/South of France/Italy, always warm, somewhat exotic, meets handsome rich male, falls in love despite all her resolves after many false starts and misleading clues about who is really in love with whom. But amazingly, these sorts of adventures—when one is chained to the wall (by the wrist here) in a cold, miserable place, no wine, no women, no travel, no treats—give a vicarious sense of pleasure even allowing for the routine of the plots. I discovered the real meaning of "escapist literature." I could be back once again in the real warmth and magic of the Mediterranean, instead of engulfed in the present horrors of its eastern shores. What would I have given for just one evening among these belles and beaux! The other kind of book in the new delivery was exactly the opposite. *Blue, blue, blue!!* Sex-a-go-go, sadomasochism, prostitution, perversions of all kinds. Where on earth could they have picked up such stuff? If only these prudish Shia could have known what they had brought, they would have been *horrified*. Or maybe they knew.

In came a small black-and-white 13-inch TV and a VCR to be put on a cardboard box at the foot of our beds. They showed us a couple of videotapes called "This Is America," which surely did no favors for the image of America. A collection of the *most* bizarre aspects of American life—a demolition derby where contestants bash each other in junk cars until only one is left running; a family that grew huge worms and ate them live for protein, with a strange relish of course for the camera; a retirement home where an old codger was seducing an old lady into his bedroom and winking at the camera in the most leering way as he closed the door; a nightclub where all sorts of sordid scenes were being played out— prostitutes being picked up on the streets of some big city—and on and on. I insisted with them that this was *not* America—that my daughters would be absolutely shocked to see this, more than the guards themselves were. They were not convinced; they *wanted* to believe all that junk about the United States. But of course, both Habeeb and Labeeb supported me in my contentions, so we perhaps instilled *some* doubt into their minds.

Toward the end of February it was obvious that we were about to move again—things were being packed up by the sounds emanating from the guards' room next door. Sure enough, Jean-Paul (Labeeb) was on his way to God knows where, as usual, on the 28th. Next day it was Carton (Habeeb). For four days, I was alone with one of the nicer guards, and got to know him fairly well. He claimed to have a master's degree. But the most amazing thing was his request of me. He knew that I wanted to come back to Beirut to take up my old job, so "Tom, after you are free, when you come back to Beirut to the AUB, will you help me get a green card?" Here was a man who had been chaining me to the wall by the wrist for some three months now, who supposedly had all these bad impressions of the United States, and who was now asking me to help him to get residence with the Great Satan. It was not the last time that I was to receive this request.

March 4 it was my turn to go. About 4:00 or 5:00 A.M., they taped me up again, with once again the eternal promise: "You going home. Soon you with your family," with a nice jovial sound to their voices to convince me of their sincerity. They more or less did. Out of the "French apartment" and over to some kind of big barn again, and out of the trunk of the car into the spare tire space of the same old truck in which I had arrived a year ago. I recognized the sounds of the old jalopy ready to fall apart. Two hours later, we were in Beirut, beside the airport, again in some kind of garage in Ouzai. Must have been anyway, for planes were landing one after the other—the airport must have become much busier since my kidnapping. The driver and another man pulled me out of the wheel well and stood me up against the side of the truck, where I leaned helplessly for about 15 minutes before another truck arrived, this one a V-8 with a very smooth engine and transmission. The man in the garage now came back, spun me around, and stuck a gun very forcibly against my throat. "You no speak when we in car, okay?" he menaced. "You speak, I blow your head off. Then we not getting what we want for you, but okay—no problem. I kill you. Understand?" The tone was deadly menacing. "Don't worry, I'll give you no trouble." I sensed that I was facing the door of the garage for I could feel the rays of the early morning sun and see the light from under my blindfold. It must have been around 6:30 or 7:00 A.M. judging by the airport noise; most of the flights for the day arrived about then— by late morning they were off to safety where shells couldn't reach them. No time to wonder. Pushed into the spare tire space of the new truck, I was joined by a guard, the kindly one from the French apartment, who whispered, "No speak, Tom, okay?" I assured him I would cause no problems, some "camouflage" was installed (impossible to discern what or how!) over our heads, and we were off. In a few minutes we were out of town, and by the feel of it beginning to climb the west side of the Lebanon Mountains that rise over 11,000 feet straight out of the sea. This truck had no problems with the slopes, even though we were taking the back roads with their frightening curves and gradients with the main Beirut-Damascus road presumably still closed. Smoothly it climbed while my ears popped. On the way to the Bekaa. Well, no problem with that, I thought—they

are going to hand me over to the Syrians somewhere in the valley, standard pro-
cedure. To pass the time and keep down the anxiety level, I began to count the
seconds, using our well-tried system— one-one thousand, two-one thousand,
three-one thousand—and keeping track of the minutes on my fingers.

Downhill on the eastern slope now, and my ears began to "de-pop." Down
and down and down into the Bekaa Valley. I had done it several times as a free
man sitting in the comfort of a Chrysler belonging to the minister of agriculture,
Mr. Adel Osseiran—"ubi sunt" those days?—by my counting, must be about 10:00
A.M. by now. Into a garage of some sort again, and down through a trapdoor into
a basement with a dirt floor. "Hungry?" asked the kindly guard, who had come
down into the basement with me. "A little. What time is it," I asked. "Ten o'clock,"—
I hadn't been far off. He soon produced a sandwich of french-type bread with a
filling of pâté, not very good, but I was hungry enough to devour it, swilling it
down with a can of Pepsi ... mmm. We were alongside a very busy highway, and
the cars kept roaring by all day—a long, boring day, lying on a cold dirt floor,
mummified by tape.

By late in the day, friend Ahab appeared on the scene. I had to go again, so
asked his permission. "Can you wait six minutes?" he asked. "Six minutes? Are
you sure it will be only six minutes?" "Yes, yes. We go another place, and in six
minutes you can go to real toilet." "Okay, Ahab, but please not longer—I'm getting desperate!" "Beleef me, beleef me." Believe him? One more time? Boy, if this
is only six minutes, it will be the first time they have *ever* told the truth, or been
remotely accurate in their estimate of time and distance. Back into the spare tire
well, camouflage into place, and we were off. I counted. One-one thousand, two-
one thousand, three-one thousand. Wonder of wonders, after almost exactly six
minutes, we stopped, I was pulled out again into the cool air, and was supported
upright while the tape was completely cut off. I walked, still blindfolded, over a
piece of wet concrete, which soaked the soles of my socks, into a house, through
another trapdoor in the floor (these characters surely know all about trapdoors!),
and down some crude and enormous steps cut into the clay, and I arrived in
another basement. Surely this was not the kind of place where I would be exchanged to the Syrians? Where on earth am I now? "Here is toilet. You go in
here," allowed Ahab, obviously very much in charge of things again. Taking off
my blindfold, I found this to be a small toilet with a vitreous unit over the hole in
the floor, in some respects the usual—pipe coming out of the wall for a faucet
and a pipe coming out about head height for a shower head controlled by hot
and cold valves. But in one all-important respect, this toilet was special—it was

inside our room! Finally, a toilet to which we had free access. Wrong again. I came out and joined the small crowd of guards, one of whom (Ahab?) promptly attached a chain to my leg. "You have friend here too," volunteered Ahab. "Who is it." "C'est moi. Habeeb," came the voice of Marcel Carton. He hadn't gone home either, after all. My heart sank, for I had been convinced that he was home. The French wives had both been so positive, things more hopeful than ever. Everything had pointed to this being finally the time. And now here we were back together again in a damp, smelly hole-in-the-ground. *Shit, shit, shit.*

The guards left, and we took up where we had left off four days before. "How long have you been here?" I asked him. "Only since yesterday evening." He explained that he had been carted around all over the country, presumably to disorient him, and had been forced to sleep in the seat of a van for the past three nights since he had left me. They had succeeded. "Do you know where we are?" I asked him. He was convinced that we were on the edge of the Beirut-Sidon road! That was the only road that carried as much traffic as he had heard while he was in the exact same waiting place where I had been held all day. "No, no," I assured him. "We are in the Bekaa." "Not possible," he countered. "There is only one road in all of Lebanon which carries this much traffic." So I had to explain to him that they had not seen the necessity to carry *me* all over Lebanon to disorient me, since I had not grown up in the country as he had—I had come straight over the mountains in about two hours, had passed through several towns, and had been held in the same place he had yesterday.

I won the argument. Two days later, we got a sack for our garbage that was a plastic bread sack from a bakery in Baalbek. He still was reluctant to give in, though, arguing that some of the bread from the valley was so good that it was sold in Beirut. He was only finally convinced when a few days later, we were given a TV and a video, with strict instructions that we were not to touch the TV or change the channels in any way, the same old routine. The film over, Habeeb promptly began quietly to search around the channels, and what did he come up with but a channel from Syria. Impossible to get *that* in Beirut, he knew! "Okay. You were right. We really are in the Bekaa." What a blessing—a sense of orientation and direction! It was vital to our sanity.

Cockroaches were everywhere in this, our 9- by 17-foot room, tile floor, rough plaster on the walls. This whole basement had just been completed immediately prior to our arrival, specially for us, no doubt, and the plaster on the walls was still wet. With so little air exchange too, it was taking much longer than it should to dry out. So the environment was just right for our flat-bodied, antennae-bearing, long-legged, fast-moving, nocturnal friends of the family

Blattidae! The walls were covered with them, even in the day. Apparently, they felt no need to hide in the dim light of this Roach Hilton, though hiding places abounded. So on our return from the toilet, we held our daily roach hunt, whapping them with our plastic slipper. Ugh—but necessary.

Nights were very long and very dark here. But quiet. And wonder of wonders, I began to experience sexual urges, the first in almost three years! Could I really be recovering?!

The guards were mostly new here again. The fellow in charge of looking after us called himself Bilal—not the one from the Shafic apartment, though—this man was younger, also quiet and considerate, but tall and almost skinny, especially in comparison to Big Bilaal. One was the owner of the building, he claimed, and gave us his name as Younis, which may just possibly have been his real name. He explained in fairly good English, "My wife is a student at the AUB. She has many books. You can have some of them." Sure enough—next day he brought in *Jane Eyre* by Charlotte Brontë. My parents had never possessed many books at all, but they *did have* a copy of *Jane Eyre* in their small bookcase and I had looked at that cover thousands of times as a young boy, but had *never* opened it. So I began with relish. After a few chapters, Habeeb's curiosity was aroused. "What is she doing, this girl?" he asked. I recounted the plot as far as I had gone. He was fascinated. And he kept asking every few hours as to what was going on now! I found it very interesting and challenging to describe the scene in French for him, and it surely helped pass the time. Younis also brought down *Les Fourmis Rouge*—a French translation of the American novel *Sarkhan* by Burdick and Lederer—a fascinating treatise on the follies of American involvement in the Far East. Many of the French words in this were unfamiliar to me, and I kept asking Habeeb for a translation, or at least an interpretation of the phrase in which they were used. "I am praying," he would mumble. "After prayers, I will help you." But there never was any "after the prayers" for he was completely engrossed all day every day. Same story with several other French books. He in turn was doing no reading at all—still "counting his beads." How *could* he spend so much time in prayer? Those sessions with Father Martin kept coming back to me—each of us to keep up the praying for two hours at a stretch. I had invariably found my mind wandering off in all directions. *Why* was I not more of a religious person?

By mid-April, we were getting more time off the chain, and I began to really work out, jogging in place and lifting my body up on tiptoes to strengthen my calf muscles; it was really bothering me that my calves, of which I had always been so proud, seemed almost to have disappeared. I worked feverishly on them—Habeeb became a bit worried that I was overdoing it. But it got him started on the routine too, and soon we were both in better shape. Amazing how fast the body responds if given half a chance. Meantime, I was still relaying the plots of the English books we were given, which occupied time and kept our minds busy.

Toward the end of April, Ahab arrived with questions about some "Exalted Personage" of the Order of the Cross of Malta, whom Habeeb had met at some time in the past in the conduct of his duties. This man was apparently interceding on his behalf, which was not only reassuring to him, but very flattering as well. Habeeb was very much caught up in the French system of honors and medals, had received one or two, and was extremely proud of them. Ahab took many photos of him (*none* of me), which left him very excited and encouraged.

May 3 came—my birthday again and Islamic Jihad gave me chocolates.

Whether the Order of the Cross of Malta had any influence on his case, I don't know. But early in the morning on May 4, in came the guards with their haircutters and did the job on Habeeb while informing him that he was going home. All of them were chatting away very happily to Habeeb, who, naturally, was beside himself with joy. After his shower, they left us together for some hours. Sleep was impossible, so we talked and talked. I told him how to get in touch with Jean. Then he was gone. I was alone in this dank, smelly, roach-infested dungeon somewhere in the Bekaa Valley.

20   A Brand New Year

1988—Election Year. Ever since the Iran-Contra Affair, everyone had said, "It will take an election and a new administration to get the hostages out." Indeed, the fact of "cold storage" had been a felt thing all year—now it was as though there was just one more year to get through.

Back in Beirut once more, I reentered the fray, struggling with colds, flu, and a virus infection as well as three jobs and no news about Tom. Nothing to do but keep in there with a strong heart. The first anniversaries of the kidnappings of Terry Waite and the four BUC professors came with their attendant pain. I wrote to the girls:

> Virginia Steen, who's taking these letters to the States will be there two weeks and has given me her parents' address where she'll be in case you want to send anything or call to give any verbal message … . She leaves Detroit February 20 to come back to start teaching second semester at BUC. She's such a nice person—her husband Alann Steen is one of the kidnapped BUC professors and she's just been through a particularly rough week at the anniversary of the kidnapping. They released a picture of him—so thin and tired-looking—with a letter saying "no solution in sight as long as Palestinians are in jail"—Oh dear, it's so tough. I'm glad somehow they don't release pictures of your dad. It has to make it hurt more … .

And then the telephone rang. It was Ann from Berkeley to let me know that she had become Dr. Ann Sutherland. How proud I was and her dad would be too! I went right away and included her new title after her name under the Christmas picture to be put in *As-Safir* for Valentine's Day so Tom could know too if the guards showed him my message. I celebrated with the rest of the family:

> —just a small note to send you my love and a big hug at the same time I'm writing to Ann to say Congratulations!!! It was wonderful to get her call to say she is

"Phinished" with her Ph.D.—and in high style with another year or two guaranteed .... Now we must try to make the ceremony in June—that will be finals and the start of the summer session here—nice time to be gone but it won't be easy! I'll start saving now for the ticket—

Money was tighter with only a small salary coming to me, and I know my dad was worried:

> FEB. 4—Dad and Alice ... Your offer and Win's of financial assistance touched my heart, but don't worry! We'll make everything work! AUB is funding my trip back in March for the TESOL [Teachers of English to Speakers of Other Languages] conference in Chicago which will give me the chance to be "repatriated" and in telephone touch with everyone if not there in person .... Ann will be graduating at UCSF in June, so I'm going to try for a trip then. But no money from anyone unless an emergency or error in check deposits ... but this shouldn't happen and AUB has been meticulous with Tom's salary which is surely high enough to carry all. And guess what? I lived on my Lebanese pound salary this month! Went to work, came home, paid newspapers, Joana, and the gardener, and that was it! So see, we'll endure and do it with your love and support that is more important than money!

AUB was indeed wonderful to us, not only in paying Tom's salary but in keeping him as dean of the Faculty of Agricultural and Food Sciences for a full five years after his kidnapping. Even when Tom's associate dean and acting dean in his absence, Adib Saad, was named full dean in 1990, he left Tom's name on the faculty listing in the main hall of the Agriculture Building as dean. "It will stay that way until he returns." It is difficult to pay the kind of tribute one would wish to loyalty like that. And I found it both in America and in Lebanon. The American president of AUB, Dr. Fred Herter, never wavered in his goodwill, his caring, his loyalty to all those who had given their lives to AUB. He was a gentleman of the first order as well as a personal friend as well as a president of the university and he supported my efforts wherever possible. I wrote him in February 1988:

> My Season's Greetings come to you long after Christmas and well started on a New Year and a New Season of more hope and faith—may it be a good year for us all. Elham Cicippio brought back a warm feeling from her time with you in New York as did my brother John from the earlier meeting in the fall. Thank you for receiving him and making it possible for his presence at the next meeting [of the National Committee on Counter Terrorism]—he was asked for his reactions and sent a long letter which you may have seen. John will work away, and this issue is so enormous *it can use all possible lateral strategies* ... .

A short closing vignette from on the way home after celebrating a colleague's birthday tonight: Fadi, driving Yusr and me, drew up to a Syrian checkpoint and an interchange took place in Arabic with Fadi saying "Jamia Amerikiyya" [American university] to which the soldier responded and Yusr answered and all laughed and we were waved on. They translated for me: Fadi said, "I told him I teach at the American university and he said, 'You teachers don't carry guns.'" Said Yusr, "I told him 'Education is our weapon,'" and I said, "You mean you didn't say 'The Pen Is Mightier Than the Sword?'" and we all laughed again .... the whole a lovely moment of international camaraderie in the larger circle of Irony that is this place.

If I hoped at the time that Tom could "celebrate" Valentine's Day with a picture of his family, my heart ached that he would probably not be aware until much later of the Valentine love that winged its way to him from the students at CSU. The valentines turned up all over the place—boxes of them on the balcony of *As-Safir,* boxes on our balcony at AUB, packages of them sent back from the State Department to Kit and Joan. I was overwhelmed by the student caring and just had to write back:

> To the Associated Students of CSU, To All Students—
> I wish I could tell you what the Valentines meant to us—they're still coming into *As-Safir* newspaper ... while they've filled boxes in our home .... You truly showed a heart and filled mine, and there it is in hundreds for Tom when he gets to see them, and you've done it without knowing him personally but just simply giving freely love from student to professor—all of you individually from Karen, Janet, Victoria, Katie, Jim, Jeff to all the sororities, fraternities, and independents—Everyone. You just came to us when we needed you to tell us it was worth it to keep on going. Tom and I have never forgotten attending a University of Chicago conference in 1967 which broke down over the issue of the university's role—is it an Ivory Tower or a Human Welfare Organization?? Why the either-or ... ?? Somewhere, transcending these "issues" there's a Truth that forces us to go for more than we are for Something—you've shown us that you're with us and we can only thank you and hope we don't fail you .... .

In March, Rima, Kassem, and I duly went to the TESOL conference in Chicago and had a super time, meeting some who had been AUB colleagues in earlier years and hundreds of others. We even had a lovely show of loyalty with a good group attending our session.

In addition, I got my blessed telephone time with the family and friends and participated vicariously and after the fact in the observance in Fort

Collins on March 4 for Tom's 1,000 days. Father Martin was there, Joan broke down in tears, the former AUB Lebanese students at CSU gave Tom a plaque with "We Remember, We Appreciate, We Hope" engraved on it, and Kit told the assembled—Congressman Hank Brown, townspeople, CSU students, faculty, administration, children, and all—Thank You from Us. So many people took the opportunity the anniversary gave to give to the funds. Touched, I wrote a letter to all of them and sent with it "a collage of response" from the recipients of the monies.

Then I went back to Beirut. Easter came. With it, a note from M in the door said, "I have just arrived. Need to see you; urgent message. Call me .... I will try to come back soon again. All my best. Happy Easter." I called and we met in brainstorming sessions, and in and around our meetings there was life as usual with work, friends, and letters home:

> Easter—Dearest Kit and Joan ... I'm thinking of you so specially today—I'm just home and writing letters after playing tennis with Jean-Marie, having coffee with the Heinekens, and having Al Buckley for a drink and a chat—the real Easter for me has been a concentrated ESP on your Dad and you all and wishing you spirit at Easter with lots of love ... .
>
> Had good trip back—Sharif met me—the weather is absolutely gorgeous—working double time to catch up at Hariri but we have next week as vacation so I'm saved! I saw the videotape you sent of the 1,000th Day at the school on Good Friday—just sat all by myself and don't think there were dry eyes ... . You and the program/vigil were perfect—Joan—don't worry about breaking down—it set the thing for Kit and the two of you together were a unit of meaning—because you broke down and Kit said all that should be said through tears, you had full impact—you two were the ones shown on LBC [Lebanese Broadcasting Corporation] here and so many people saw and told me when I got back—"It was so touching," "We were thrilled to see your daughters," "You mean the Lebanese students were Tom's students?" "I missed it at 8:00 and stayed up till 11:00 to see it." ... Your efforts have been really appreciated, and your dad will be so touched and proud when he comes back this year, to say nothing of my feelings which I guess you must know. You are doing an enormous effort for him—you're facing and dealing with what I couldn't and I want you to know that. And it's with Ann and Ray, Simone and Alex too—because everyone is facing and not only facing their individual challenges—they're somehow creating an entity of triumph which will enfold your dad when he returns and give him such strength and base to make up for years—years not lost but years meaningful. How do I send our love and pride to you—each of you personally for the individual effort you have made and have to keep on making—we're a family team, sweethearts, that can't fail ... .

I wrote to the CSU and Fort Collins communities—and to Tom's Lebanese students as well, now graduate students at CSU—Basil Hamdan and the others who had given the plaque at the ceremony:

> I can't find words to tell you what it meant to us and to many more—your coming out for Tom on that 1,000th Day. I talked to the girls from London and they told me of the day and the ceremony—and Joan said, "It was Basil's talk, the Lebanese students doing what they did, that made me break down—to think that after all this time I broke down!" And Kit said, "In five minutes Basil and the other students did what we've tried for three years to do—to make people understand why Dad was there at AUB and stayed."
>
> I can tell you for sure that Tom will never forget what you've done for him—if ever it could happen that he could return to the dean's office, the central spot in the plaques on his wall would hold your's. When that release does come, you can know that you have had a very special part in it.

And then Islamic Jihad went directly after Kuwait, hijacking the Kuwaiti airliner, ending up in Algeria:

> Today, April 10, is Greek Orthodox Easter and my balcony this perfect Beirut spring afternoon looks out on a lovely Mediterranean and on a full AUB Green Field activity—two half-court basketball games in juxtaposition to full-court volleyball and an official soccer match presided over by a referee in combat fatigues—while inside, the radio has just given the latest update from Larnaca Airport and the Kuwaiti airliner that circled and circled here Friday night—each time clutching my heart as it headed in over the Green Field and our house to the Beirut Airport before it finally turned away to Cyprus ... .

Ending up in Algeria, the hijackers negotiated and thought they had a deal for Kuwaiti royal family members in exchange for their 17 prisoners. The royal family got back to Kuwait, but none of the 17 appeared in exchange. No way to know what hand George Shultz played in all of this—I was not privy to knowledge of the details—but I would have bet on his pressure on Kuwait not to release, if they needed any after that hijacking. But somehow the whole deal seemed an echo of the British Libyan negotiation Terry Waite had been involved in three years earlier where Gadhafi gave up four Britons and didn't get any Libyans back, and I trembled for the wrath of Islamic Jihad when their "brothers in Kuwait" didn't materialize.

Our birthdays came and went this year, Tom's being celebrated with the release of the three French hostages—Jean-Paul Kauffmann, Marcel Carton, and

Marcel Fontaine—and the eruption of desperate street fighting in the southern suburbs. Wonders for us, Jean-Paul and Marcel Carton had been held with Tom, Marcel having been taken from the same cell to be released. They were in touch with us—Carton spoke with Ann about Tom, Ann being quite fluent in French after a senior year in high school at the American School in Paris and a summer as a telephone receptionist at a Neuilly hospital. Jean-Paul reached me through the American embassy in Beirut, which set up the call for Fifi Reed and me and escorted us across the line to Awkar. How I wished I could speak and understand French like Ann and Tom! Jean-Paul was wonderful but his French was overpowering. I got well his "Tom est mon frere, mon cher ami—mon cher ami!" ("Tom is my brother, my dear friend"), but then I had to speak through Fifi who was fluent in the language. Jean-Paul gave so much of himself after his release— he and Joelle went to Scotland to visit Tom's family there and made a video at the farm with his brothers and sisters for Scottish television news saying how great Tom's French was—"even the swear words"—and "All the English I know he taught me." Though Tom and Jean-Paul were only three months together, they forged a truly deep and lasting bond—Jean-Paul spoke truth for Tom too when he said "mon frere." It isn't, in the last analysis, a matter of time or forced togetherness—it is a spiritual and mental "meeting." For these two, a truly serendipitous meeting.

Along with it all, Joana and I were dreaming:

MAY 4—Hi Guys ... . Joana had a second dream in a week which seemed a good omen—she said, "We must pray hard this month." The first dream was seeing our door wide open when she came and she asked me about it—I told her it was closed and she said "No, I came right through—it's wide open." Joana said she asked her friend Regina who evidently is a dream interpreter she trusts and Regina said, "It's good, it's lucky." The second dream was different: "There were plenty plenty men coming out and getting in a car, and you said 'Can you see him, Joana?' and I pushed people aside and looked and looked and I saw him and put out my hand and took hold of his and he put his other hand on mine." So now if all our old dreams come true with these new ones we'll be there together this summer! Speaking of which I go to MEA this morning and make reservations for the trip home to The Graduation ... .

I spent last weekend on my friend Jean-Marie's sailboat in Kaslik Harbor Yacht Club on the East Side—Soaked up the sun, worked, drank gins and tonics and talked to boat owners here and there and imagined what fun it would be to take off and sail off to Cyprus steering by the stars which she has done several times. She's trying to get a crew to do it later this summer—if I spend June reading sailing books I might be able to go ... .

Then came a letter from Dad and I wrote again to the girls:

Did your Grandpa let you know that his cancer has flared up again—this time not contained but through the bones of his back? He underwent surgery in April and I didn't get any word until his letter yesterday. I'd love it if you could all call him to give him our best together and personally … . I'm going to try and call today—don't know if I'll get through.

The fighting in the southern suburbs has really raged but last night's paper said Hizbollah was still holding the great part of the area—but that's OK because we'd like release to come from them out of strength not weakness. Maybe Ramadan (May 16th) holds something, maybe not. The three Frenchmen can tell us only that your dad and Terry Anderson are separated—no direct word or glimpse of your dad.

All set for me to arrive Washington May 30. Love you … .

But, after all, I didn't get there.

21 Back to Five

I had exactly three days to reflect on what Habeeb's leaving really meant and to evaluate *my* chances of following in his footsteps. Fat chance. Down the stairs in the middle of the night came another hostage with a very familiar New England accent—none other than Frankie the Shoe. Hadn't heard of him since the end of November, five months ago. Still the same Frank—lanky, bearded, boxer-shorted and T-shirted, and diffident. And a couple of days later, another guest arrived, none other than staff sergeant formerly of the U.S. Marine Corps Anderson himself, his same dark-bearded, sturdy asserted self. I quickly learned what had happened to them. When he left us in November of 1987, Terry had been taken straight to Beirut from the south, then held with the third Frenchman, Marcel Fontaine, whose place alongside of Habeeb I had taken. They had spent the entire five months together in Beirut. So Labeeb's intuition was solid—neither Terry nor Fontaine had been released in November. But Terry was convinced that Fontaine had now gone home. The Hajj had been on the scene, and given all kinds of hope to Terry about impending releases—even promising him that he would be gone home soon. And this time even Terry was inclined to believe him.

Frank, meantime, had left me in Shafic's apartment that same November of 1987 and been transferred just down the road to the same place as John and Brian, but had not been allowed to interact with them in any way (as I learned shortly, this apartment had been christened by John and Brian "the Pigsty"— *not* a very nice place at all). After about three months—Frank was never very sure of the time or the date—he too had been transferred back up to Beirut and put in the same cell with Jean-Paul Kauffmann, my buddy Labeeb. Frank did in fact speak rudimentary French, and said he had used it a little for Jean-Paul, but he said they had not communicated much. Jean-Paul as usual was reading up a storm, while Frank had refused to read anything. Must have been a quiet scene.

By contrast, the scene in this dungeon was now anything but quiet! First of all—the cockroaches. Fastidious Terry was appalled but I assured him, "These are just the friendly ones left, Terry—you should have seen the place a month ago!" Secondly, I had regained much of my former cockiness, since Jean-Paul had shown me the flaws in Terry's self-assuredness, so I was all set to hold my own much more aggressively than in the past three years. The sparks flew. I now disagreed with Terry just as often as he did with me—all the time! It was fun to feel my old confidence in arguing, and, frankly, Terry appreciated it. One thing he simply could not stand was a wimp—and I realized how much of one I'd been! No more.

We argued about airplane flaps—I said they were down while the plane took off as well as when it landed. "No," said Terry. "If the flaps were down when the plane took off, it would never get off the ground, for it would tip the nose down all the time." "Not at all," I rebutted. "It's like throwing a Frisbee. The downturned edges give it buoyancy, and the wing flaps give the plane extra lift. I've seen them many times, as a plane took off." "Bullshit," retorted Terry. "Not like that at all. The flaps are turned lightly up on takeoff, and that turns the nose up, and off it goes." "Nonsense," I insisted, and so it went. No way to resolve these arguments in any definitive way, so we had simply to agree "to hang it up until we get out of here." Flying from Wiesbaden back to the United States after my release, I posed that argument to the captain—"You were both wrong," he told me! "The flaps have nothing to do with the takeoff. It's the shape of the wing, and what we do in the tail section that causes liftoff!" Well, one that Anderson *didn't* win, even if I didn't either.

From airplane flaps, we went on to inner-city problems. A staunch Democrat, Terry felt strongly that the government had an obligation to "solve" the problems of the inner cities around the country. "Nope. I disagree, Terry. The folks in the inner cities don't vote, and politicians listen only to people who vote. You've gotta be realistic. Inner-city people are heavily on welfare and pay no taxes. Do you think that politicians are gonna spend taxpayers' money to solve problems for folks who don't pay taxes? That is the surest way known to lose a seat in the Congress," I pontificated. "I don't care about that," said Terry. "It's still the responsibility of the government to cure that running sore on society." I had to admit that the inner cities do present a terrible dilemma for the nation. "Something has to be done, I agree. But how?" And so on went that argument too without solution.

Next came the nature of God. *That* was an ongoing one, and of course no solution known to man at all, so we had faint hope of ever solving *that* one in captivity. But it surely made great material to argue over—and it got even hotter when we met up with Terry Waite a couple of years later.

Our threesome was augmented in a little over two weeks. Bilaal came in and began, from the sound of things, to lay down some extra mattresses. "Are we going to have some more friends in here, Bilaal?" I asked. "Maybe. I don't know!" Where had we heard that before? We pushed him. He was rearranging us three, separating us to put two new mattresses up against the other wall—one staggered between Frank and me, the other between Frank and Terry— so there had to be *something* going on. Eventually, he admitted that there were two more men coming, "but only for short time," he asserted. Who? The mystery was solved later that evening. Down the crude steps came two more "unfortunates," one with a very pukka English accent, the other with a strong Irish brogue—none other than our old friends from the "Prison" in Ouzai, John McCarthy and Brian Keenan. This was the first time that we had seen their bodies below the face and actually heard them speak out loud, for in the Prison we had done all our communicating by signal through the bars at the top of the doors. So here was John— young, slender, dark-haired, sparkling smile and wit; and Brian—short, stocky, broad-chested, full-bearded, Irish through and through. Soon the guards left us alone, and down here there was very little restriction on how we could speak. So the stories flowed like a torrent. New companions with new backgrounds, new experiences—some of it we knew from signaling, but in a few minutes we could exchange more of our life history than we did in hours and days in the Prison— one of our first conference decisions was to christen this hole "the Pit."

What fun! These two had a legion of tales to tell. They had a sparkling sense of humor, and were constantly teasing each other. Even though McCarthy is a solid Irish name, and John's ancestors had indeed come across the Irish sea, he was by now pretty solidly into the English gentry, with an accent that all upper-class Englishmen aspire to as a definite symbol of class identification. Entry to clubs, colleges, and cricket grounds is predicated upon accent. Although Brian was a Protestant from Belfast, he was virulently anti-English, with an equally recognizable accent from the other end of the scale; definitely a barrier to admission to almost anything or anyplace in England, especially when backed up by Brian's Irish Republican Army (IRA) sympathies. And yet, here were the two of them getting along like a house afire despite these ancient enmities, hostilities, and class differences— laughing and joking and insulting each other a mile a minute. This was obviously how they had survived and kept their sanity during their 25 months of captivity.

Everything they treated more or less as a joke. So when they heard Terry and me going to it in violent bouts of argument, they were aghast, and admitted later that they were shocked at how hostile we seemed to be with each other, themselves very reluctant to get into our arguments or even our milder sounding "debates." We were only doing, however, what Terry and I had both grown up with—arguing. We were both from families of six children, and in both of these, vehement argument had been the rule—only within the family, however, for with outsiders, each family had sprung to the defense of their own. So, now that I was somewhat "rehabilitated," we were both "doing what came naturally."

Next idea of Terry's was that I give some lectures to the other four on the latest concepts in genetics—"Advanced Genetics for Beginners," I labeled it. So we spent quite a few hours explaining and debating the basic structure of DNA, the nature of the gene, the role of amino acids in the genetic code, the reasons for and nature of mutations. But soon John and Brian had had enough, and they were never motivated sufficiently to take it back up. So with half the class having dropped it, our Genetics 101 was abandoned.

Frank and I locked horns on several occasions too, bickering across the bottom of Brian's mattress. By this time, Terry no longer paid much attention to Frank, finding him much too stubborn to argue with at all. But I took up the fray on the subject of the density of oil and water. Frank maintained that crude oil is more dense than water, so I of course challenged him on that score. Here even Terry could not resist *that* challenge. "How do you reckon that one, Frank?" I asked him. "Haven't you seen gasoline or oil floating on the surface of rain puddles around any gas station?" "Okay," agreed Frank. "That is true for *refined* oil. But *crude* oil is different. *That* is heavier." "Then how do you explain the use of water in pumping out oil from wells? They pump down water and the oil floats to the surface." "Nonsense," insisted Frank. "Look, I taught chemistry in high school for years, for God's sake. I know what I am talking about. The trouble is that you both forget the difference between specific gravity and density." Together, Terry and I could not convince him of his fallacy.

Then there was the case of the direction of the revolution of an intake fan that sometime ran in this hole, at the end of a piece of four-inch plastic pipe. Frank insisted it was an exhaust fan despite the shape of the blades and the direction in which they were rotating. I invited him to watch the direction with me when the electricity went off (which it frequently did) and then to study the shape of the blades. We did this, and he still maintained it was an exhaust fan. This one Terry refused even to comment on. And I finally blew my stack at Frank and told him he was the most stubborn bastard that I had ever met. Meantime, John and Brian were horrified at my brutal treatment of Frank, and suggested that it would be a good thing if I did not speak to Frank at all. (Later they both admitted that they too had become totally frustrated by the Shoe when they spent many months in his company just prior to his release.) Truth to tell, I did feel a modicum of shame at my own behavior, and could not help but look back at my feelings when Terry had been so harsh with me when I was psychologically "under the weather."

Soon after the arrival of the Brits, out of the blue a radio appeared. A beige plastic case about nine inches by five inches by two inches thick, the works inside had both AM and FM, though FM was of little use to us there in the Bekaa— all stations playing Arabic music of a religious bent. But we were still able to get fairly clearly on AM (medium wave) the BBC World Service, even over the Lebanon Mountains, while at night we were able to pick up the Voice of America from the relay out of Turkey. That was much farther away than Cyprus, so that the signal carried only at night. We were finally able to catch up with the world, especially the United States and the United Kingdom, the primary interests of our little group. The Olympics were going on, and the Koreans were doing a bang-up job of it, despite the fears of some people concerning the terrorist acts that had badly affected the overall reservations and attendance. We heard all about Jackie Joyner-Kersee and her spectacular performance for the U.S. women's team, and even got a *Time* magazine that gave us some details of her successes, along with those of her sister-in-law, Florence Griffith-Joyner. We also got a kick out of the Voice of Lebanon, whose news broadcasts were read by young women who obviously didn't know English very well, and mispronounced every other word— expressions such as "There appears to be a crack in the door to a window of opportunity for peace" left us roaring with laughter.

But we listened in horror to the news of the *U.S.S. Vincennes* shooting down an Iranian Airbus and killing hundreds of innocent Iranian citizens, men, women, and children, and *Time* showed gory photos of bodies floating in the sea. A disaster. Would it have any repercussions on us? How could such a thing happen, given all the modern technology aboard one of the most modern ships in the world? The guards predictably said it was deliberate, and were not at all persuaded by our protestations that American sailors could never even think of doing such a thing; their attitude was that this was just exactly what Americans of any kind *would* do.

Late in the summer I began to reflect on a discussion I had had with one of our young American faculty members at AUB, Bob Rice. He was furious at "the system" in the United States, which practiced age discrimination, at least in Ohio where his father lived. In his early fifties, his father had been refused several positions solely on account of his age. Bob felt that his father was every bit as active and talented as he had been in his thirties and forties, and that age should not play a role in hiring, at least not at that early age. I had agreed. Now here was I halfway through my 58th year. Who on earth is going to want a 58-year-old, I began to wonder? The thought discouraged me terribly, and I raised the question with Terry and John. Both of them pooh-poohed the idea. "You will have dozens of offers of jobs when you get out of here," they kept assuring me. I am not sure if they really *did* feel that way—but it did my morale a world of good to hear them say it in such a positive fashion. For them of course, age was no problem—John was barely embarked on a career, while Terry was just in midstream. They could well afford to be optimistic for themselves.

I was not alone in my despondency. Even little Hadi came down to visit with us from time to time, and struggling greatly with his English, said very philosophically: "Lebanon finish. No good. Everyone now going. Maybe America, maybe Canada, maybe Brazeel. Don't know." He genuinely seemed to want to interact with us.

The elections were coming up in the United States and we were engrossed in the campaign as it progressed. George Bush had been selected as the Republican candidate and looked like a winner. Then came some ominous reports. Islamic Jihad had issued a statement, along with a photo of Terry for authenticity, threatening to harm two American hostages it was holding— "America, the criminal, should know that it will not get away with what it is doing, especially in relation to the fate of the hostages in our custody. This aggression will not pass without punishment." This threat was incited by yet another Israeli air strike on South Lebanon, the 12th this year, this one "on clinics, killing nurses and patients." The group asserted that the United States had backed the raids. Of course, this strike was itself in retaliation for one by Hizbollah on Israeli troops in which seven Israeli soldiers had been killed, but Hizbollah was as usual careful to make the distinction that they had attacked only *military targets,* while the Israeli retaliation had been against innocent civilians.

Terry and I were unmoved—we simply didn't believe these threats. Dead hostages are of little value to kidnappers, so we simply brushed them off. Then in came Hadi. "Give me raddy-o." We tried to dissuade him. "Look, Hadi. We heard all these threats on the radio, and we don't believe you're serious. Anyway, if you are going to kill us, go ahead; but don't take the radio. We know *everything* that is going on. Don't worry. *We* are not at all worried about these news reports." "Give me raddy-o," insisted Hadi. "No, please, don't take away the radio. We are not worried about the news!" We were trying to hide the radio, hoping that he might give in and go away. "Give me raddy-o," he repeated in his extremely gutteral English. Nothing to do but surrender it. Damn, we thought, now we can't even follow the election. Nor anything else, for that matter! We were really discouraged— that radio was a real lifeline for us. And God only knew when we might be able to get it back again, if *ever.*

Two days later, in came Ahab again. "Frank, you go home." Well, we had expected that something might be evolving, and clearly neither Terry nor I were in line for release. We would be the last to go home for sure. So we were not surprised that it was old Frank. By now Terry had had lots more recent kidnaps precede him home, and we were glad that Frank could finally go back to his seven-year-old son whom he was so proud of and whom he obviously loved very dearly. A big scene followed, and we gave Frank our requests of what we wanted him to do on our behalf when he got home. Then he was gone. Down to four!

Here in this dank, smelly basement, however, we had more books, many of them most memorable. Homer's *Iliad* and *The Odyssey* I had heard of all my life but never read. Now here was my chance to study these classics. In the *Iliad*, I attended the siege of Troy with Odysseus, to which he had gone to participate; then meandered with him in *The Odyssey* all the way home, sharing his adventures, while he even resisted the Sirens en route. Strong man. Set in the Mediterranean basin, it is a wonderful tale, and I wondered how the eastern shores had come so far into the pit, though even in those times, it was far from peaceful. I found an interesting coincidence with my own case, for at the opening of *The Odyssey*, Odysseus had already been gone from his home in Ithaca for over ten years, and in several places had been detained against his will. I had by then been gone over three years, and though I had not gone deliberately to participate in any Middle Eastern war, nonetheless I *had* gone to a war *zone!* And Odysseus's wife had been in the meantime beset by suitors. But loyal.

The Cardinal was another favorite with John and Brian and especially with Terry, our resident Catholic. So too was Thackeray's *Vanity Fair* on which Jean had done her master's thesis in English (*The Levels of Irony in Thackeray's Vanity Fair*), and I was especially looking forward to reading both of these volumes. In came Fadl one day in November, totally unannounced, and began to rummage around with our book supply. When he left, I examined the concrete shelf on which we kept them, and what had he done but pick up several, including both *The Cardinal* and *Vanity Fair*. Nothing to do then but hope that each would reappear some day, but they never did.

Some months before, Terry had finally decided that his "Farm Project" was in as good a shape as he could put it while in captivity, and to avoid losing it like everything else every time we moved, he had decided to conceal it and keep it with him. He wrote it all out, every detail, in the smallest handwriting I have ever seen. It was completely illegible to me, and I have seen some pretty weird handwriting in 30 years of grading exams. He wrapped the pages, perhaps eight to ten of them, in plastic, and hid them in the one place where the guards, given their extreme prudishness, never ventured—in his crotch. He had carried that with him now for many months, and always had been able to keep it securely concealed. But one morning, the guards came in for one of their routine searches. What they were hoping to find always puzzled us, for they brought us *everything* that we ever got in every location! On this occasion, however, they lost their prudishness and decided to search even in our crotches. Terry was first, since he was the closest to the door. A great commotion broke out. What on earth had they uncovered? Having heard Terry protest fiercely—"Don't you dare touch me there!" I began to suspect that they were indeed "going all the way" in their search this time. They had. Total chaos and frenzy. They gave Terry the fifth degree in interrogation, demanding to know if this was meant for the CIA, and why was he doing this deceitful thing. In vain Terry protested that Mahmoud knew all about it and had given him the paper and pen to do the project. They wouldn't hear of it and continued the rounds, demanding to know if we too were hiding anything in our crotches! They turned the entire place upside down, clothes, beds, bottles, blankets, the lot, leaving it piled high in the middle of the room, and departed in a whirlwind, taking with them every scrap of paper and every piece of pencil or pen that we had had. We never saw paper or pen again until the day of my departure when Terry was allowed to write out his poems and a letter for me to take home.

Christmas Eve, 1988, was memorialized for us all by The Beating. It happened this way: The guard Mazzin took Brian to the toilet, and when he was locking him back up again, gave the chain a hard tug. "Don't do that again," came Brian's voice in a bass and threatening tone delivered in Brian's best Belfast accent. "Wha'?" asked the guard in a most surprised voice, "Wha' you say, huh?" "Don't do that again," repeated Brian in ominous tones. So guess what … ? *Tug* went the defiant guard, upon which Brian leapt at him to the end of his chain. The guard took off like a scared rabbit, for in truth none of them were very brave fellows at all; they could fake a brave stance as long as they had guns with plenty of their buddies around, but I was always convinced that if we were to meet them face-to-face when we were alone with no guns on either side, every last one of them would take off running. Mazzin did take off in a hurry. But in two or three minutes, he was back with Bilaal, and a stick and a leather belt, both. *Thump, thump, thump, thump, thump*—all over Brian's body, as hard as Mazzin could draw both his weapons, one after the other. Horrible! What to do? Lift my blindfold and attack Mazzin? That was a sore temptation, but surely would have been viewed as full-scale rebellion, and might have resulted in one or even all of us being summarily shot—we always felt that the guards had been warned to use restraint so long as we "behaved," but that if we were seriously to rebel, they most likely had permission to do us in. Simply can't be sure of that, but it was our strong belief. And there was Bilaal in the doorway certainly with a gun. Meantime, the longer Mazzin went on, the more frenzied and furious he became, and God only knows when he might have stopped but for the intervention of Bilaal—*Khalas! Khalas!* (Finish!) he called from the doorway, then repeated his injunction several times, until finally Mazzin heeded him and stopped, breathing hard and grunting. They withdrew and we raised our blindfolds to survey the scene. Brian had never even whimpered all that time, but there he was now, quivering like a leaf and black and blue from neck to toe; Mazzin had really done a job on him.

We were all four of us furious at this unnecessary treatment. Once again the punishment was far and away too severe to fit "the crime," if indeed any crime had really been committed. Yet another reaffirmation of the results of the college experiment with student guards and prisoners. We vowed to stick together in our reactions. We would refuse to eat. And we didn't for the rest of the day, and on Christmas morning. By lunchtime, when nearly everyone in the West would be sitting down to turkey and dressing, the guards were determined that they would force us to give up this brief strike. "You must eat. You not eating, very bad for you. Maybe we kill you." They even took Terry out and up the clay stair into their own toilet and held a mock execution, with a cap gun no less! We were not fooled, knowing the sound of a real bullet! They returned. "Tom next, okay?" "Okay. But I am not going to eat. Go ahead and kill me!" They didn't even take me out of the room, but they *did* tighten the chain on my leg, tied my hands behind my back and forced me to lie on my face. Not nice. We still refused, believing correctly that they were now playing games, though in fact, there was still an element of deadly seriousness in the atmosphere, and we all realized that they were indeed capable of getting very angry, very quickly once again. We held out nonetheless, and eventually they brought Terry back into the room with us, and warned us again. "You have one hour to decide—no eating, everything getting *very* bad."

We held a council of war, and decided that this confrontation had gone on long enough. But we demanded to see Mahmoud, who did appear from somewhere, and we told him that we would cooperate only if they would withdraw Mazzin from his guard duties. Mahmoud promised us that they would do that, and we ate lunch—not turkey, but rice and beans. Mazzin did indeed disappear for a few days, but eventually they restored him to the crew. Once again they had won their victory in the ultimate power struggle. They still had the guns, they outnumbered us, and they had us chained to the wall! And they had succeeded in giving us yet one more Christmas, our fourth in captivity, memorable for all the wrong reasons.

22 Two Seasons in Beirut

The Reagan-Gorbachev Summit in Moscow was set for the first week of June 1988 following the War of the Suburbs in Beirut in May. M was in constant contact with me through that time and at the end of May when I told him of my plans to go to the States he said, "We must get together just before you leave—things are very fluid—it may be necessary for you to be here. I'm going to Helsinki to meet with Secretary Shultz and Charlie Hill when they're there before the Moscow Summit and we may need connection in Beirut." So we set up that on my way to the airport to catch the plane for home, I'd stop for a last meeting with him at the Sweet Shop on Hamra. How could I forget that morning—Sharif picked me up with my bags at AUB and we drove up to the shop and we met, M and I. "They may call—it is essential you be here to take it and relay the message to me in Helsinki." What could I say but: "Yes." I went back out to the green Caprice, "Sharif, I can't go—you need to take me back to the house." Sharif never questioned, just drove me home and brought my bags back inside. And that is how I took the call from Islamic Jihad instead of celebrating with Ann at her graduation June 2 with *People* magazine taking pictures, instead of observing Tom's kidnap anniversary in Fort Collins, instead of celebrating with Kit and Joan at their birthdays on June 18 and July 2, and instead of being with everyone in Ames, Iowa, for Dad's 85th birthday celebration and reunion on July 15. I got the stories and the pictures from the United States, and although I didn't get Tom, it couldn't have been expected, only hoped for and prayed for while the process went ahead.

The call from Islamic Jihad came in Beirut on the evening of Ann's graduation day in San Francisco: "Jean Sutherland speaking ..." "Hello, I am calling for those who hold your husband." "Yes, how may I help ..." A sharp, impatient, angry voice: "Don't talk, just listen. Send message. The Algerian government.

Start from Algeria for solution." "Yes. I understand. How else may I help ... ?" *Click*. That was it. M called about an hour later from Helsinki and I transmitted the message to him and Charlie. Maybe there was a chance that under the Summit umbrella something could go forward with a neutral mediator such as Algeria—I didn't know but it didn't seem auspicious to me. And in the great "Wait and See" of course, nothing came to fruition out of it all.

But I had to be content even though I was desolate about missing Ann's graduation and couldn't even tell her the details of why. Later, after Tom was home and she and I could talk it out, I told her how guilty and sad I felt that June even though I felt I could say to her: "We did it all together for the cause. It didn't matter if my being in Beirut wasn't any solution. Even if they were only testing the channel, it was enough. They knew I was serious in really being there, that I could be reached by telephone and transmit messages—if that's all it was, it had to be enough that I was there. It was part of the job we undertook. And the bottom line was always of course: "How much are you willing to give up?" And Ann being Ann, she took away the remembered pain by telling me her understanding:

> ... your not being at my graduation? I just felt like there was too much sentiment about that kind of thing anyway—your life wasn't all that fun and I wasn't going to add and give you grief about not being here for this or not being here for that. So what if it didn't coincide with what we wanted you to do? We would have loved having you there for every Christmas too, having you live in Fort Collins where we had complete access to you instead of getting one letter per week or maybe once a month, but that was fantasy land. There were a lot of other things that had to be done and we understood that. It wasn't our place to be telling you what to do .... At graduation, Kit and Joan and I had a really good time and after all it was for me to feel good that I had got through all this and managed to write a thesis and they accepted it and liked it and I've been able to go on from there—really it's an internal thing— I just felt very strongly about it—and I just felt like whatever you felt you should do was fine with me—that's why that song of Tracy Chapman's, "She's Got Her Ticket," spoke to me: we knew that we couldn't and shouldn't try to persuade you to do anything you felt you couldn't do—your decision was it ... I felt like it was your song, that you knew what you had to do. It's all OK.

So I was in Beirut instead of Colorado for June 9, 1988, and it meant that we had an observance in the Agriculture Building at AUB again for the third year. And I held forth with my usual zeal:

> It is something so special and so much appreciated that you're here today for Tom— that together we can make it an occasion of spirit and hope with the knowledge he

knows we're here and gets strength and heart from the warmth of friendship ... . In a sense he's here with us in your presence and mine—we came as a team to join your team and the effort is complete by being shared. In the world today the university is defined by the jobs it's called on to do and serving it is not just in textbooks and laboratories, but is in the full sense of service to the larger human community ... .

But as always the students stole the day—Salman Abbas who would win the Sutherland Award next month spoke out for Tom:

Three years ago he was here working, caring, organizing, and helping us in every way he can, changing things for the best; ... we have not forgotten and we can never forget. Instead we feel it is our duty as senior students to tell the new agriculture students about our dean ... . I am sure that Dean Sutherland even in his capture still thinks about us and we should in return not forget him ... .

And the summer went on.

JUNE 26, 1988—Dear Dad and Alice ... A tough letter to write, but I've thought so long and hard about what I must do and it's clear to me—if Tom and I cannot come to your birthday reunion together next month, neither of us can be there. I just can't leave him, Dad—not in these culminating days, weeks, months, whatever it takes. Since the War of the Suburbs in May, things have settled into a new pattern—and it looks to most everyone a matter of time and probably hard behind-the-scenes negotiation. The timing can't be estimated, nor can the ways and means, and I just know that I must be here with Tom as my only priority. He deserves and needs all we have this summer.

Dad's birthday was celebrated with great festivity—Ann and Simone, Kit, and Joan went to Iowa to be part of the big reunion. On our side of the Atlantic, there was tragedy with the Iranian Airbus disaster, the *Vincennes* shooting it out of the sky. A horror. Repercussions were felt and feared. *People* magazine did their story on the hostage families July 18: "Caught in the Crossfire ... . The Iranian air tragedy threatened to make them pawns in a deadly game of retribution. Here's how their families endure." And in our story was the wonderful picture of Ray, Simone, Ann, Kit, and Joan taken at Ann's graduation. Brought a lump to my throat when I saw it. There was nothing to be done but to wait out the time of repercussion, and in the end it was not, this time, hostages who paid with their lives but the hundreds in Pan Am 103 over Lockerbie, Scotland.

Such a long, hot summer. And all the air conditioners but one had folded on me. So I sat down at my poor sea-worn typewriter and wrote the "Guys I Love over There" on August 21:

I'm just back from having a coffee on the Corniche with two teacher friends—we were working on the school newspaper this morning and gave it up as too much to do to finish it by final exam day tomorrow so reset the deadline for October 20 and went to sit under an umbrella next to the sea and watch the fishers and the bathers who have returned now that the toxic waste scare from Chernobyl seems to be over. This summer has been something for people here—no electricity, water, money, sea, or fish and steady hot, humid weather—can't believe how they make it. Fortunately, I have electricity and water, a very little money, I don't need to swim to enjoy the sea nor do I need fish—but I could surely do with less of this sticky weather. Anyway, I'm back in the school building upstairs in the secretary's office and using the typewriter which works and will photocopy this for you since I owe all of you letters and I have time to write only one before I go for lunch at Jean-Marie Cook's place in Ain el Mreisse—she's leaving tomorrow for the States and will take these with her and I hope they reach you because she's the one who had the problem with her passport and got back here on an Irish passport she could get because of her Irish grandmother .... She's now taken on the headship of the English Department at AUB, however, so we've got to have her back. The other woman to be there for lunch today is Marilyn Raschka who works for the *Chicago Tribune* going all over Lebanon, hitchhiking and story-writing—she spent last Thursday morning in the Villa Mansour in the middle of the Green Line waiting for the Parliament to convene and elect the new president for Lebanon which they didn't do because they couldn't get a quorum (some stayed home, others were detained on the way by the Christian Lebanese Forces who seemingly didn't like the guy they figured would get elected) and maybe I'll find out today when the election might try to take place again—I stay so out of politics that I'm woefully ignorant.

I haven't written anyone in so long I don't know what to say—my life this summer has been just go to work and stay until 6 P.M., lock up, and come home. Perhaps then someone comes by to sit on the balcony and talk or I read or watch a video, then to bed in the one air-conditioned room in the house. I've been helping students with their master's theses (one of the effects of the Thomas M. Sutherland Awards we gave last month has been an influx of theses for help with the English— a lot of work but it's progress). Jean-Marie has asked me every weekend to come sailing on her boat, and Marilyn has also asked me to join her at her chalet in the Cedars, but I just haven't felt like going anywhere nor that I'm really here to enjoy myself. Not that I'm getting morbid about it—I'd just rather wait to do those things when Tom's out .... I still can't find myself going away from here. I thought about coming to the cabin for September, but it didn't feel right—so I've decided to stay right here and keep in and REST and RELAX in our own house looking over the Green Field and the sea. I'll give Joana the maid the month off and do everything my way—get up when I want to, not have to be anywhere at any particular time, read all the books I haven't had a chance to, sit on the balcony, and not work or think about work! And I'll take up correspondence again, and go through things, and get on top of the paper war—that is, if I feel like it ... .

I've made a decision to make a change for fall—my contract wih Hariri runs out the end of August and I'm not going to take a new one. I've been offered a course in the English Department which Jean-Marie says she can guarantee to teach if I should have to leave for any reason and that should give me eating money. For the rest of the time I'm going back to take up my fledgling career—do the reading and research necessary to turn my dissertation into a book and get going on it. I feel the time is right for change and I need to do what I want—the Hariri Program has been truly wonderful for these three years—I've learned a lot and met great people and students—but it's not my field and ... I want to get back to ideas and creative thinking again. So we'll see how it works out ... .

Well, it worked out that the Hariri Program "needed me" and how could I turn that down? So all my selfish plans went for nought and I signed up again—including another great workshop in teaching English as a foreign language on Cyprus:

SEPT. 21—Dad and Alice ... I'm mailing this from Cyprus where I'm at the Golden Bay Hotel for the English workshop ... . I've had vacation and relaxation as well as the work of the conference and it's been great. Also got a chance to get calls from Kit, Joan, and Ann, and it was nice to feel close again by phone; ... they said this A.M. when they called that you had made some day trips to the cabin when you were in Colorado on vacation—was it lovely?? This is just my favorite time there with the leaves turning and the crisp weather ... . I've so enjoyed the pictures from the July 15th birthday celebration and reunion—I even brought them to Cyprus so you'd all be close—I'm glad to know you're doing so well, Dad—I keep thinking about you a lot ... .

Every new season somehow had its new revival of hope—even missing the golden change of the aspens in the mountains of Colorado, I could "feel" fall in the air in Beirut. And this fall there would be the U.S. elections, the elections we hoped would make the difference for us all. Back in Beirut from Cyprus, I thus took a certain pleasure in a new surface lifestyle of half-time employment, albeit with the old concerns, continuing back-of-the-scenes work and meetings with M, the old "zero expectations," and, of course, the familiar "Beirut Normal."

Oct. 10, 1988—Dear Guys I Love ... A quick note as always, this time early Monday morning before I go to work—I'm up to do a workshop for teachers at 9:00 on one of the aspects of our Cyprus conference ... . Right now it's 7:00 and I'm still not dressed—went out on the balcony and sat with a cup of coffee, smelling the night-blooming jasmine in the corner and enjoying the softness of the air—joggers were out on the Green Field as usual and two people were playing tennis. It was foggy over East Beirut and Jounieh so couldn't see the other shore but the sun was coming up in the haze over the Lebanon Mountains and it was beautiful. The other reason I'm not dressed yet is that when I went to take my shower there was a cockroach in the bathtub which I wasn't ready to deal with [only afterward did I know about and deal with the irony that Tom at this time was dealing with hundreds of cockroaches zipping in and out of their hole in the floor toilet] ... .

I had a quiet and wonderfully relaxing 10 days after coming back from Cyprus—I still had Agriculture's VCR on loan so I watched a lot of films I should have seen years ago—Steve McQueen and Clint Eastwood and Robert Redford and Barbra Streisand. Also read lots of books and didn't do anything at any specified time. It was so good, in fact, that I've had quite a job getting back to work ... .

You will have probably heard about our presidential elections here which didn't take place and still haven't, resulting in two prime ministers and governments each declaring the other illegal (Al Buckley declares it's a case of 1 plus 1 = 0)—no one yet seems to know what will happen and there's a lot of uncertainty and tension not to mention threats against two of our hostages at the same time that Dr. Singh was released. Until there is an election here and there, it doesn't look probable for any Americans to get out although the British may make it. All is extremely fluid, though, so we stay on standby and keep hoping as always.

I got the book *Best Laid Plans*, the history of America's war against terrorism in the Reagan administration, and am finding it heavy-going. It's by two journalists and has excerpts from Weir-Jenco-Jacobsen reports about captivity—I'm too involved I guess to read objectively such a doomed and wretched story and seeing Tom's name in the index with page numbers after it seemed incredible. Dr. Khaddaj also brought me back from France Marie Seurat's book *Les Corbeaux d'Alep* and I'm glad I can at least read French—it was an extremely compelling book—an experience really which also got to me—what an awful time they had with his coming back to get books and things and then being taken away again in front of her eyes and her having breakdowns as well as the Armenian persecution experience and her uncle's captivity death in her background—it does put things in perspective and make you realize those who are worse off. He also gave me another book— *Beyrouth, ou la fascination de la mort (Beirut, or the Fascination of Death)*—but I haven't started it yet. I think I'll try something light-hearted first ... .

I must go—if I'm lucky the cockroach will be gone by now ... .

And so the American election day came and George Bush was elected. At least I'd met him once. And it looked as if Jim Baker would be secretary of state. Unknown yet to me but M was impressed with him.

And then a beautiful Thanksgiving week came. By this time the tradition had been established that we gathered at our AUB home, I doing the turkey (Smith's had them imported from Virginia this year), Buckleys bringing drinks, and everyone else bringing a dish as well as a guest if they wished. I invited our AUB neighbors—the Mishalanis (head of the physical plant) who lived in the former house of the agriculture dean below us, the Hajj family (dean of students on the hill right above us), the Diabs (dean of arts and sciences on the hill next to the Hajj house), the Nassars (head of the AUB infirmary living below the Diabs), and of course the Saads. I had by this time gotten into a niche of nonentertainment, as not being quite apropos for our situation, but "a Gathering" for Thanksgiving was "recognized" as well as "felt" by all as being "right." What a feast as well as a celebration of friendship, goodwill, and hope! They let me do the blessing as we all stood with crossed arms and clasped hands around the walls of the dining room, so I had full scope for expressions of togetherness, thanks, and international peace. I did as usual two turkeys and along with the food gifts of our friends the table "groaned" in a most American-International-Lebanese wonderfulness.

And then it was Christmas all of a sudden again. I took off for Washington and Colorado, knowing that I would not return until I had attached President-Elect Bush and Secretary of State-Elect Baker for M and our channel. Continuation of talk was a priority—the job was not finished, and it was essential, if the American election was to mean anything to our work in the Middle East, that the channel must continue. I stopped in Washington on my way West and talked with Charlie and Secretary Shultz and we set up for January meetings to "hand over." But Christmas and family first. As always, we made it beautiful to give as a gift to Tom.

23   Meeting 1989 Head-On

Waiting for Godot had almost nothing on "Waiting for Bush" in the first three months of 1989. I went to Fairfax, Virginia, where I was extremely lucky again that my brother John was beginning his new position as chairman and CEO of the Conflict Clinic of George Mason University and had a two-bedroom apartment. I started as a guest in one of those bedrooms and ended up renting from John, I stayed so long. But I had the final meetings with Secretary Shultz and Charlie Hill, and got my introduction to Dennis Ross, the new first-in-command to Secretary of State Baker to come in the new administration. I remember that meeting—Secretary Shultz came through to Charlie and me in the adjoining office in his informal Norwegian blue-and-white sweater and was so relaxed, friendly, and congenial. He and Charlie were "going out," and M and I and the hostages were "still in." Dennis Ross came into the office and Charlie introduced us. I remember being pleased to meet him although I had no idea who he was or how things would go in the future. I was impressed with him—he was then, and is so now, a man of substance and a gentleman. He would never show M or me in the years to come other than a calm and confident demeanor, even when he was exasperated with Sheikh Fadlallah or with the Islamic Jihad's refusal to release hostages. Nice to know that a man of his caliber out of a Republican administration is still being allowed to be integrally effective in the Middle East peace process in a Democratic administration—reassures one somehow about our own democratic process. Power to him and to both processes.

Bush entered his presidency by taking down Reagan's yellow ribbon on the presidential office door and it caused a brouhaha of sorts for a time. I stayed quiet about it but my opinion was very positive about Bush's action, which I felt quite symbolic in marking a change from wrong and ineffective emotionalism on the part of our head of government to right and tough objectivism. Where the yellow ribbons on the part of American people were so right and so meaningful, a yellow ribbon on the presidential office door was not and sent a wrong message out to the world. A president has "two persons" just as in a monarchy a king has "two bodies"—one that is personal and one that is official. A president can thus be very personal and personable and even emotionally involved with individuals in his private person, but he makes national and international policy for an entire nation in his entirely separate and objective official person. I feel very strongly about this and had no patience with those who "blamed" the hostage families for Reagan's problems in the Iran-Contra Affair. No matter how he empathized with the hostages and their families, the responsibility for his presidential actions was his alone. The other factor in the yellow ribbon episode that bothered me because it touched another basic principle of mine was that evidently this particular ribbon had been ceremoniously presented to him by a hostage family effort in Washington. That should not have been. Never did I, nor anyone in our family, *make* anyone—even another family member or a neighbor or *anyone*—wear a yellow ribbon or do anything else for that matter for Tom. For unless the external symbolic gestures came spontaneously and meaningfully from the individual heart, they were artificial or forced and thus denigrating. I was adamant about this in our case because I felt it touched on the integrity of the choice we had made to stay in Lebanon.

I somehow was not to know that the next two months would be such a "Waiting for Bush." Dennis Ross stayed in touch and pushed for my meeting with the president. But after the inauguration there were a million and one things for President Bush to do—in all reality, I don't think he really wanted to see me, hostage wives, I'm sure, not being his favorite people. At any rate, I was low priority and understood that. But our avenue was too important and I wasn't going to give up. So I got leave from Vice President Hallab at AUB and waited, and while I waited, I set into the task of making up a New Year's letter to send out to all our personal friends and all the other people who had been in touch and caring. Composing, photocopying, writing notes to each, signing, addressing, and mailing the 850 letters gave me purposeful occupation for over a month. In the meantime, Dennis was able to make a preliminary appointment for me with Secretary of State Baker.

What I knew about Jim Baker was limited to the *Time* magazine article of February 13, 1989, showing him in combat fatigues on a turkey shoot—"Whether stalking turkeys or talking turkey, Jim Baker says, 'the trick is in getting them where you want them, on your terms.'" So he got me in his office on his terms and I went thankfully, prepared for a tough man, no expectations, and if shot down so be it. I had nothing to lose I hadn't already given up. Dennis Ross accompanied me and made the introductions. Secretary Baker greeted me with a smile, and then, interestingly he gestured *me* to the chair while *he* sat on the couch, Dennis to the side taking notes. I told him about the channel, about M, about what I felt had been accomplished—from dialogue to personalization to "defusing" a crisis, and said that I must see President Bush. I had a place to stay and I was waiting until that was accomplished—otherwise it was no go. He was pleasant and receptive, but reserved, neither his face nor his manner giving anything away. Then his question, "Why are you involved in this?" And then he answered himself—sharply, directly, shrewdly, "... because you can get to the president." I didn't answer, I didn't have to. So we finished the meeting and parted and I went to the reception room on my way out, thanking the secretary there. Suddenly Dennis appeared at my side—"He'd like to know: What crisis was defused?" I told him of the bombardment of Fadlallah's residence and the conclusion drawn that the Americans had teamed with the Syrians to "get" him, not a far-out conclusion seeing that the CIA was held "responsible" by most everyone including fundamentalist Shiites for the car bomb outside Fadlallah's residence that didn't kill him but killed 90 or so civilians. I told Dennis how M had gone through the shelling to Fadlallah to make contact and to get the official version of "the truth" to him. "Thank you," said Dennis, and he saw me out with, "I'll be back in touch." And he was. Twice he thought something could be set up and then it had to be postponed, and I kept reading in the *Washington Post* about all the things on the presidential front burner—budget and read-my-lips tax issues, gun control, Soviets, savings and loan bailout problems, the John Tower appointment and nonconfirmation, off to Tokyo-China-Korea-Canada—obviously, patience would have to be the name of my game, but then it had been for nearly four years by this time.

My letters mailed, I started on brother John's bookshelf of Louis L'Amour books. I had known a Warrant Officer Webb in Addis Ababa who had the whole collection and who was addicted to Louis L'Amour. For my part, I'd read Zane Grey in my youth but had never taken up the Sackett Saga. Waiting for Bush seemed like a good time to start, and once started, I read everything on John's shelves, one after another after another. They appealed to me. First there was the idea of the simplicity of good guy vs. bad guy, solved by the righteous gun, hard yet easy. Then there was the lawless frontier with the whole body of books telling the complex story of how the West was won with its rape, pillage, kidnap, burning, massacre—about the only thing Beirut had over it were shells and car bombs. And then there were the epigrams, little nuggets of truth in small bites that spoke to me:

"One fights one's battles alone, not asking mercy nor expecting help." (To the Far Blue Mountains)

"It is the willingness to accept responsibility, I think, that is the measure of a man." (Bendigo Shafter)

"No man is lost while yet he lives." (The Walking Drum)

"Women are neither weaklings nor fools, and they, too, must plan for what is to come. He who does not prepare his woman for disaster is a fool." (The Walking Drum)

"Most men do not give a woman credit for intelligence ... And that may be an advantage." (The Lonesome Gods)

"A year? What is a year? All time is relative. One day may be a lifetime, a year can be forever." (The Warrior's Path)

"I would not sit waiting for some vague tomorrow, nor for something to happen .... I would begin here, I would make something happen." (Sackett's Land)

"Out on the frontier we do not have heroes, only people doing what is necessary at the time." (The Lonesome Gods)

"Often ... I find it best to do what must be done without going through the usual channels." (The Warrior's Path)

"Be wary ... of trusting too much. Men change and times change, but wars and revolutions are always with us." (To the Far Blue Mountains)

"The way to stay out of trouble was to avoid the places where trouble was." (Lonely on the Mountain)[9]

How privileged I was to meet Louis's wife Kathy L'Amour and their children Beau and Angelique in Las Vegas with Tom after his release. Angelique had gathered her father's aphorisms into a special volume, and I've savored her volume as well as continued Louis's Saga—a mighty American story in so many individual stories. Each time I pick up a Louis L'Amour book these days I remember with warmth those other days in 1989 when I read while I waited for Bush, comparing the situations from one century to another and one country to another and finding not much difference.

February brought Salman Rushdie's *Satanic Verses* and the consequent death sentence from Khomeini. Furor on all sides about it. The issue couldn't help but touch me especially. For all that I believed in authorial freedom and freedom from censorship with all my being, I could only appreciate that these were hard-fought, hard-won Western values just as I could appreciate the absolutism of the Koran to Moslems and that Khomeini had almost no other choice given the circumstances, his religion, and his character. Empathizing strongly with Rushdie, I still would have respected him so much more as a person and an author and felt he'd have had so much more effect if he'd taken his sentence in steadfast silence, neither apologizing nor asking for quarter. Filling my mind was another man of my Renaissance studies, the Italian Giordano Bruno, who disbelieved in Aristotle and believed in the new Copernican theory that the earth revolved about the sun instead of vice versa—he spoke it and wrote it. In essence, the pope in Rome sentenced him to death. On his return to Italy, Bruno was convicted of heresy by a Catholic tribunal and was burned at the stake in 1600. Maybe I was too much into risk and responsibility by this time, but I truly felt that the mark of a great author was that he was willing to risk and take the consequences for writing what he saw as the truth. I got *Satanic Verses* and read it—a great book, a rhetorical tour de force, worth the risk.

The month of March came and I told Dennis Ross that I would be setting my departure for Beirut for Friday, March 10; was it possible that the meeting with the president could be set by then? Seems it couldn't, but Dennis called and said it was going to be possible at the first of the week after and General Scowcroft would be handling it. I was so glad and set back my departure. And sure enough the day of the meeting materialized, and the car came for me, and I was taken into a small room at the White House where General Scowcroft was waiting for me. He accompanied me to the Oval Office. President Bush greeted me and we took our seats in two chairs toward the back part of the room facing down an "aisle" between two couches leading to his desk. Millie the dog lay down on the rug between our chairs and General Scowcroft sat on the couch nearby. A few pleasantries, including talk about Millie who was due to have her puppies (it happened the next week). I was definitely not there for a social visit, however, and I began to speak in earnest: "Mr. President, I'm not here to take up your time unnecessarily, nor to ask you for anything. If it weren't extremely important, I wouldn't be here. A man called M and I have for two years now effected a dialogue between the American administration and Muhammad Hussein Fadlallah, the one they call the spiritual guide of Hizbollah in Lebanon, the group mooted to be in charge of the hostage-taking." At this point, a door to the back and side of the Oval Office opened and a security man came part way in, Millie got restless, and I stopped speaking to look at the man intruding. It would be the president's choice whether we went on or whether, by what was clear to me a prearranged interruption, our meeting would be terminated with "I'm very sorry, but something has come up." I was lucky. President Bush called the man in and told him to let Millie out—as we waited patiently, he walked to the garden doors, did this for what I was sure was a happy Millie, and then he left by the same way he had entered, turning and pulling the door closed. President Bush turned back to me, and I went on with the description of the channel that was there for him, the channel that had been used and tested and retested and proved its worth in so many ways if not yet in hostage release. But it was for him to decide if he wanted it—it could be dropped, it could be set aside to be used only if and when there was a necessity, it could be a positive thing for helping to bring resolution.

President Bush then turned to General Scowcroft and said, "I don't suppose it could hurt." *Deja vu.* Scowcroft appeared to agree and there was a short exchange. "I think that Dennis Ross would be the one to handle this," said the president. I interjected, "It couldn't be General Scowcroft in charge?" It never occurred to me not to say it. When you are willing to die, you are free, I guess. More than that, and, what I'm sure President Bush didn't realize at the time, was that I was relaying to him the opinion and request from the other end of the channel relayed to me by M—Ross was down on the totem pole and unknown, the General was way up, known, and respected. He was, however, also, as we all knew, the national security adviser and military—the counterpart of Poindexter in the former years and therefore "inappropriate" after Iran-Contra. The president probably thought I was either presumptuous in suggesting anything to him or that I was testing whether he would go the way of Reagan, and he flashed me a glance so full of—I don't know what, suppressed irritation? scorn? contempt?—that it was a palpable thing. I suppose it was what would be called in a novel a "withering look," but in this game one can't afford to be withered. I sat quietly. Bush turned back to Scowcroft and said, "It will be Dennis Ross." And there it was and had to be. And it turned out in the long run to be very right and very good.

We stood up, shook hands as I thanked him, and then I left the Oval Office to return to the small anteroom with Brent Scowcroft. He helped me on with my old green suede coat, gave me a private number to call and report back, and then I turned to him as I went out. "It will take *months.*" I don't think he even answered—his countenance was confirmation.

I was in touch with Dennis Ross and gave him the word that the meeting had taken place (which of course he would have known, but symbolic action was absolutely essential), and let M know the outcome. And that evening at 9:00 P.M. I phoned the private number of the general and he answered. I said, "All is accepted and will go ahead. But will we have your good general's mind on this?" "Yes."

It wouldn't take just "months," it would take almost three years. Almost three years of continuing dialogues between Fadlallah and Baker/Ross effected through M's shuttling, telephoning, meeting face-to-face, and exchanging information and ideas for resolution of issues in Lebanon and the region. Meanwhile, the Soviet Union fell, the Berlin Wall fell, Kuwait was invaded, the Gulf War happened, and Jim Baker catalyzed the Arab-Israeli peace process. M and I met continuously through the years, at the Sweet Shop, on the East side, on the West side, in hotel lobbies, at AUB, in restaurants, walking on the Corniche, at the Summerland, in Washington. We brainstormed, we discussed, we visited Fadlallah, we visited Dennis Ross and Secretary of State Baker. I remember so well our trying without success to come up with some intermediary in 1990—the pope? the UN? Japan? Algeria again? Timing was all and it wasn't to be until 1991. But the start with Ross and Baker was that March of 1989 when M and I went together for him to be introduced and for them to meet for the first time. I stood aside and watched and listened to them talk—about everything. It was good. And we had plenty of time that spring for American meetings—I had set my return to Beirut for March 18 and on March 14 General Aoun's "War of Liberation" against Syria started. The airport closed the next day, and I would not return to Lebanon until the following October. AUB was suspended while the war raged. *(Tom, I don't know where you are—and I can't get back—please be safe ... be safe ... be safe ... .)*

Thus in April my return was to Fort Collins and house hunting. Kit and Joan had spent the winter scraping ice off the windows of frozen cars and cooped up in an apartment, and we all longed for a house where we could spread out and have a garage and yard. Not wanting to disturb the rental arrangement for our own house on Garfield Street, we scoured the town for a condo or small house that would be "right" for our present circumstances. Nothing. At almost complete discouragement, we got a call from good friend Bobbie Cook, a realtor. "Wes Miller's son and daughter-in-law are off to Belgium for a year or two and he wants someone nice in their house." What a piece of good luck for us. This house on Gatlin Street was perfect—a trilevel with two bedrooms up, two down, and a full floor front to back of living-dining-kitchen area. Plus garage and yard and wonderful landlord. We moved in—everyone with a bedroom—and celebrated with a backyard barbecue on a new gas grill that good friends Jim Johnson and Butch Roelle put together for us. For the next two years, that house gave us happiness and made a difference in our lives.

24 The Toufeili Apartment

Mid-January, the 12th or 13th I believe, Terry was loaded up and taken off. This time there were no promises that I could detect. He just left, and my "opponent" was gone. With only John and Brian left, I immediately felt again a lowering of the tension level in the room, just as Frank and I had felt in November of 1987. I wanted them to join in a Burns birthday celebration on the 25th but they showed little enthusiasm this year. So I had to celebrate alone that momentous day.

February 2 arrived, lunch came, and we began to eat. A minute or two later, in came Ahab. "You don't need to eat this stuff, Tom. Soon you will be home with your family, and you can eat good food, not this bad stuff you have now! Come quickly, Tom. We must hurry. You don't have to eat this stuff," he repeated. "But I am hungry now, and it will be a while before I get together with my family. I want to eat *something* at least," I rebutted. "Okay. But queeckly. We must go." I was amazed, for it could only have been around 3:30 or 4:00, and most likely broad daylight outside. How could they think of moving me to wherever in *daylight?* They had *never* done that before. I gulped down some food, and declared myself ready. "Okay. You must give Brian and John a hug before you go." I dutifully complied in spite of the strong odor of the great unwashed. "I'll call Jill for you John, and tell her you are okay. I must warn her about you too, you bastard! I'll get in touch with your family, Brian, and give *them* the truth about you too!" I assured them. Then we were on our way upstairs, the same dirt stairs that I had descended on March 4, 1988. I hadn't been out of that hole for 11 months. Seemed hardly possible. Aside from the earlier generations of cockroaches, I had been the longest tenant.

Upstairs, I got a milder form of taping; not the "mummy" job, but just enough to hobble me, and back under the bed of the same truck I had come over in, with the smooth engine and suspension. In two to three hours, we were back in Beirut, and I was transferred to the trunk of a car and left there for several hours with little Hadi and the Ghost. We seemed to be in a big garage, but people were coming and going for a few hours. "You no make any noise, Tom, okay?" after which they kept hissing at me every time I cleared my throat or coughed, and once in a while would even threaten, "No noise or we shoot you." Not an enjoyable evening. Eventually we were on our way. Out of the trunk some minutes later—we had been parked all these hours somewhere close to our destination.

This still did not feel like an imminent release to me. Up more stairs, maybe ten flights, and into a room where they finally cut off my tape. "Do you want anything to eat?" Ahab was evidently here again. "Yes, please!" I answered. "It's been a long time since that lunch that you wouldn't let me finish, Ahab!" The inevitable "sandwich" arrived, with a cup of tea, and I was on my own to eat. Or I thought I was, because as soon as I lifted my blindfold with blessed relief after all the hours, I perceived another body lying on a mattress against the other wall! Who? "Hello," I said softly, "My name is Tom Sutherland." "I know. I recognized your voice right away." It was Frankie the Shoe! "God, Frank, I thought you had gone home long ago." I replied. "No. I've been here ever since I left you all down in the Bekaa. They were lying again when they said I was going home." No shit!

I spent seven days with Frank. He had a book lying beside his bed, but was paying no attention to it, so I picked it up and looked it over. It was one I had read before, *The Return of the Native* by Thomas Hardy. Wonderful book. I enjoyed reading it a second time. Frank told me, "I refuse to read any of that stuff they are bringing me. I will read when I get home again." The atmosphere in this place was intense with constant "activity." There were obviously more hostages in the apartment than just Frank and me. Through the wall from me was the bathroom, and I could hear people in there for a long time each morning. By the flushings, I counted at least two others. Sometimes it sounded as though there may have been three or even four. For me, it was almost like being in isolation, for Frankie the Shoe just lay with his blindfold on all day and all night. This was the place we would call the Fadlallah Mosque Apartment because we were close to the mosque where he delivered his Friday sermons. It was also the place where you had to put your foot on the metal cap of the toilet to keep it from backing up.

Then things changed. Ahab was back in the middle of the night— "Bring your things." What now? Was I *finally* going home? I was bundled into a huge sack—the norm for a trip inside Beirut. But they left me lying by the door of the apartment for well over half an hour, during which time I became convinced that there was at least one other guy lying alongside of me. Down the stairs with four guards carrying me, panting and puffing as usual, and into the trunk again.

Another body was thrown in on top of me, and we were off. "Who is it?" I asked when the motor was running and we might whisper unheard. "Shush. It's me, Terry." So he hadn't gone home after all. Ugh and ouch! Five minutes later, out of the trunk and carried (even more fierce puffing and panting!) upstairs, just two or three this time, down a long hallway into a room with an area curtained off just for us.

Close quarters here. Ahab set to work with the chains, and this was his finest work yet. We were between the wall and a filing cabinet on which were piled huge heavy cartons of ceramic floor tiles. Ahab chained my left leg to the filing cabinet, my left leg to my right one, my right one to Terry's left one, and also to his left wrist. Then his left leg was chained with a very short piece to my right wrist. I had five padlocks securing me, while Terry had four. Only my left arm, Terry's right arm, and his right leg were unchained. Morning came, and so did breakfast. Lots of noise outside—must be teeming masses of Shia out there. Toilet time—Ahab started to unlock us. He brought in a bunch of at least 20 keys, all unmarked, and proceeded to try each one in turn on each padlock. After the best part of half an hour he finally had me free, and off I went to a modern Western-style bathroom, complete with bidet, and all nicely tiled. I was even given paper to wipe with, but sternly instructed *not* to put it down the toilet. Our hosts were always paranoid about any paper of any kind going down the toilet, for they knew that it would choke the thing for sure. Several men had been there before me, as the paper already in the bidet informed me.

Ten days in here, and each day gave the same evidence. We could hear other people going into the bathroom—it sounded not too far away. But we were never able to get any kind of clue on who it might have been. We speculated that it might be John and Brian. John told us much later that they had not been in any place like this. We thought of the rest of the American hostages, the Beirut University College quartet, but they too later (after liberation) told us it did not sound remotely familiar. A blank here. But without doubt, there *were* others.

Ahab was our lone guard in this room, and even slept in the room with us in another corner. It seemed to be an office of some kind, for we stood up on occasion and surveyed the scene to our left over by where Ahab slept. There was a desk and a chair, but more importantly a window. It wasn't covered in steel, hence their precautions with the chains, the curtains, and the nocturnal companion. We slept with difficulty, for every time either one of us moved, it disturbed the other because of the chains running ankle to wrist. The whole scene was ridiculous, but we were powerless as usual to influence them in any way. Ahab was by this time apparently quite high in the organization and had much more responsibility than any of the other guards, despite having started as a very young wet-behind-the-ears kid back in the "Marseillaise Apartment" in the fall of 1985 when we had christened him "Ayhab the Ayrab." And in that time, he had gone from being quite gentle and sympathetic to extremely authoritarian and ruthless—the typical psychological evolution of a guard, alas.

After those ten days, another move, this time just down the hall to a strange room—about 18 feet long and only 8 or 9 feet wide, no electrical outlets, and with the only access through the kitchen. Usual bare walls, 100-watt bulb in the ceiling, tile floor, two wooden-shuttered windows, and new foam pads on the floor to sleep on. I didn't know it then, but Terry and I were to spend the next 18 months in this place. At first, Ahab was our sole host and continued sleeping with us, but the chaining was less severe. We had dog chain on the wrist, but at night he added an enormously heavy piece from my right ankle again to Terry's left ankle, passing through a ring set into the concrete floor. The chain was of the kind designed to lie flat, so that each link had a fancy shape; in a normal chain, each link lies at right angles to both the preceeding and the succeeding links. The problem with our new "fancy" chain, and God only knows where they came up with it, was that if the links were deliberately twisted, it did anything but lie flat and *hurt like hell* on our ankles! Furthermore, it was only long enough to reach from the edge of my mattress to the edge of Terry's, so that our feet were constrained to the edge of the mattress all night long, and it was impossible to turn over. I'll never forget it.

After a few weeks, relief came. Mahmoud showed up again, along with a new man who spoke no English and no French. He refused to tell us any name, so I christened him "Jameel," after the first guard I'd had. I never did set eyes on *him*, so knew not whether he qualified for my compliment, but at least we had a means of addressing him. Our pidgin Arabic got a good workout too. The two men switched every second day, and each was on his own, the only time we ever had a single fellow on duty. It was very clear, however, that this building housed a nest of Islamic Jihad types, for they were always quite relaxed, even though we were only on the second floor. Fadl was in the wings too, and occasionally took over for a day or two for the others. Even Ali, the "Lying-Piece-of-Dog-Shit," showed up again, and we had a chance to bug him again for the radio. "No. You will be unhappy if I give you the raddy-o and you hear bad news like before." "Come on," countered Terry, "I am a journalist, remember, Ali. I can take all the bad news you can dish up to me. That's my job!" "No, no," rejoined Ali. "No raddy-o. Pray to your God!" "Well, we are praying, but 24 hours a day is a bit thick, Ali. Come on. Give us the radio?" "Okay. I will take a *fatwa* and see what happens." We could only hope that the holy book would be kind to us this time. But later, Ali reappeared with the news that, "The *fatwa* was bad. You cannot have the raddy-o." "How about trying another one, Ali?" I asked him. "Okay. I will try." I had no idea at that time, but a *fatwa* is supposed to be irrevocable. Surely Khomeini's *fatwa* of the death sentence on Salman Rushdie was declared irrevocable by the fundamentalists, and it will hang over his head until someone kills him or he dies of natural causes. In any case, Ali returned a few hours later. "This time the *fatwa* was good," says he. "Here is the raddy-o." Wow, we thought, what a piece of good luck—we were ecstatic. It was exactly the one we had had in the Bekaa some eight months ago, and amazingly it was still in reasonable shape. Even the batteries were good in it, so we lost no time in tuning into the World Service of the BBC. Reception was fantastic, much better than in the Bekaa. Wonder of wonders. So from March 1989 until our release, we were never without our little gem, except for a day or two when Terry would get obstreperous and they would take it away to punish us. We reveled in catching up on world and American events.

On the Lebanese war front, things sounded very quiet when first we moved in, and we could hear hundreds of children laughing and shouting and playing outside. Terry lost no time in reminding Mahmoud and Jameel that we were now hearing *all* the news from wherever, and that they might as well let us now watch TV and *see* it as well. And lo, what did they do but bring in the TV for Terry to operate on his own, the usual Phillips model that could operate on either 110 volts or 12 volts (i.e., on a car battery), a handy feature in Beirut, a city with so little power. They also gave us a battery charger, so that Terry could keep the battery charged up whenever there was power.

The quiet in the city was reflected in the TV schedule; the LBC began transmitting as early as 2:00 P.M., then noon, then even by 10:00 A.M., something that I at least had never heard of in my time in Lebanon. They went even further, and began transmitting on UHF, channel 33. That now meant four channels in all, since the national station, Tele-Liban, was split into a West Beirut branch for the mainly Moslem audience there and one on the East Side for the Christians. Those two frequently carried the same material, but not by any means always, so for a time we had choice, and more than 12 hours of TV. The highlight of the day was the evening news, beginning about 8:00 P.M. and lasting an hour or more. Most of this was from American networks—ABC, NBC, and CBS—but also frequent clips from CNN. LBC also used a fair amount of the telecasts from BBC-TV as well as from Tele-France. In the A.M. hours there was even a half hour of CNN

Headline News. Wonderful. But it was frustrating to get only the quick-and-dirty treatment of the news; we wanted the full treatment with all the details. Even so, this was a miracle, to be able *finally* to *watch* what was going on in the world.

Most of their programming was of course still coming from the United States and Europe. Soap operas were still popular with the Lebanese, and we had a great variety of those. *Dallas* reruns gave me in fact my first viewing of that most famous of them all—I had never had the J. R. fever and had stolidly refused ever to watch it in its heyday when he had been shot. We also saw Julie Harris in many episodes of *Knots Landing*. Fabulous actress whom I was to meet years later at the University of Connecticut. But perhaps the soap that proved most nostalgic of all to me, which again I had never watched as a free man, was *Dynasty*. Set in Denver, every episode opened with shots of the Denver skyline, *so* familiar to me, and it set up in me such intense longing to be there again. I could hardly stand to watch those shots—or the barrage of scenes through the episodes likewise familiar—but I could almost forgive Joan Collins her bitchy role for bringing me "home" even if only for an hour at a time!

On the radio, a detailed treatment of the news by the BBC World Service. At night the Voice of America from faraway Turkey—it was all a dream come true. We quickly became some of the world's best-informed citizens, listening to every single news broadcast in the hopes that there might be something relevant to the hostage situation, and were surprised at the amount of coverage. Much of it was pure speculation. One broadcast, for example, had Terry and me in the southern Bekaa and a possible rescue attempt being contemplated, an exercise in futility, for at that time we were right beside Sheikh Toufeili's mosque in the southern suburbs of Beirut. This we discovered during one quiet period, on one night of which there erupted a horrendous clatter of machine guns, rocket-propelled grenades, and rifle fire—a pitched battle par excellence. Next morning on the Voice of Lebanon we learned that there had been an attempt to assassinate Sheikh Toufeili right by his residence/mosque, without a doubt what we had heard the night before. The attempt had failed, though several of his guards had been killed in the fray. At least we knew where we were and our cell was duly christened "The Toufeili Apartment."

Terry lost no time in demanding books, his usual cry wherever we were, and this time too we got them. The guards brought in a huge box full of books—well over 50 of them—set the box in the corner by the door well out of our reach, and gave us a dozen or so volumes out of it. Terry devoured them at three times my rate and soon had read all of them, many a second time around. Losing patience with me, he began to sort out the various volumes. "This one is very good; read it for sure. This one is shit; let's give it back to them. You won't want to read *this*, no way." So I took his advice. To this day, I have no idea as to the correctness of his judgment, but it allowed him to trade in many more books and get a new supply much faster. We read several hundred books in the space of those 18 months, going through many big boxes.

It wasn't that I'd never been a reader. In grade school in Scotland I learned to read early and loved it. I rode into town from our dairy farm every evening with my father, and while he took the milk to the retailer, I exchanged my book in the public library. I knew then what it was to knock off a book a night, and by the time I entered junior high I had consumed a fair percentage of the children's section. But then I hit puberty and discovered sports and girls, in that order. I had no time, and "outside" reading went into oblivion. In high school, my English teacher asked, "How much are you reading, Tom?" Shamefacedly, I confessed that except for what was required, I had not opened a book. "I suspected as much from the state of your writing skills!" It was the first inkling I'd had that writing and reading were related. But needless to say, I didn't turn over much of a new leaf, and when I went on to university and then into a scientific and academic career, there was never enough time even for the scientific journals or the grading of papers, much less the "luxury" of reading "literature."

But here I was, in captivity, with nothing *but* time and no other luxuries, and housed with Terry Anderson, a journalist, political scientist, and a real biblioholic. Without books to read, he was like a caged lion—with them, it was good-bye to Terry until he had devoured the lot! No thought of rationing them, making them spin out over a given period. Zip. Right through them with his speed-reading skills, with his photographic memory, recalling everything with perfect accuracy, even to the page whereon he'd read a certain fact or phrase. What a super combination, I thought—I could surely have used *those* talents in my academic days! As it was, in these days it made Terry's mind a veritable encyclopedia, an unbelievable resource for us.

So Terry would never let the matter of reading material rest, and the books we got through his badgering were an incredible mélange—books acquired, so we learned, through the guards' visits to West Beirut bookshops where departing westerners had dumped their libraries to lighten their loads going home. It became a library "lending" of sorts, where the guards would, by some means or other, take a bookcase at a time, 60 to a 100 books in a box, and then when we'd finished and the box had made the rounds to other hostages, there was a return for another box of 100. There was no order—either alphabetical or subject-wise. We had everything from John Adams to John Updike, from Thomas Paine to

Thomas Hardy, from *The Federalist Papers* to *Fanny Hill*. We roamed the moors of Yorkshire in *Wuthering Heights;* we tramped the roads of Devon in *Tess of the d'Urbervilles;* we attended school in early Iowa in Hamlin Garland's *Life on the Prairie;* we suffered with Abe's Mary Todd Lincoln in *Love Is Eternal;* we waded through tomes of *The Complete Transcripts of the Watergate Hearings* (I defy anyone to make coherent meaning out of Richard Nixon's statements) and marveled at the modern political machinations of the CIA in Bob Woodward's *Veil;* we explored the floor of the ocean in *The Blue of the Pacific;* we quested religion in the pages of the Bible and Koran and the ways of man in *The Works of Shakespeare*. And we had thus, almost literally, freedom in captivity. If Islamic Jihad could chain our bodies to the wall, they couldn't imprison our minds. Our imaginations ran free. And my education expanded daily. I was, in fact, getting the liberal education that my scientific agricultural studies had not given me.

We had also a biography of Henry Kissinger, but he had definitely alienated me rather completely in the early stages of our captivity by saying in public that it was the responsibility of the hostages to get *themselves* out! We had all wondered what ideas he would have had for getting himself out, were he in our circumstances. His biographers, however, were obviously great fans, and in their view he could do no wrong—they praised him to the sky.

We read Solzhenitsyn, and he said in his *First Circle,* "Thank God for prison. It gave me time to think." Now, while I don't remember actually *thanking* God for *my* prison experience, I do know that the reading we did was the impetus for our thinking, more deeply than ever before, about life, its pleasures, its traumas, and its meanings. And perhaps more importantly, we *argued* about all the ideas set free from the pages we read—argued and argued, honing and activating hourly our minds, interacting strongly and stridently and stimulating each other.

People ask me—"What was the key to your survival?" And I struggle with that question. Could there be *one* thing most essential? Surely it was a complex that can hardly be analyzed—a mind kept active, wonderful family, mutual support, the luck of relative good health, perhaps sheer Scottish-American cussedness on my part, or the lack of an acceptable alternative? But one thing I know for certain is that reading ran like a powerful thread through those years keeping me in the world, stimulated and going. To read was to live, and even today as a free man I live a fuller life with that reading done in captivity and all it meant as a part of my total experience. For I have forever in my mental bank the Old Testament wars, the Yorkshire moors, the banks of the Seine, the Russian prison, the dark halls of Glamis Castle, the intrigues of Casey's CIA, and all the rest that I can pull out at will to contemplate. For whatever it's worth, I feel somehow more of a man now than when that steel door clanged shut on me that June evening of 1985. And much of that evolution took place in the darkest southern suburbs of Beirut in a part of Sheikh Toufeili's mosque that I never saw from the outside until our return to Beirut in 1993.

Fadl came in fairly regularly for a spell to get lessons in English. He brought in one of the BBC books with which lots of non-English speakers out in the world get their basic language. Of all the guards, he had been perhaps the most conscientious, though even he was far from diligent. All of the others had given up after one, or sometimes perhaps two, days, and never came back again for their lessons. And after each lesson, we would remind him that now it was his turn to teach us some Arabic; the reply was always the same—"Bukra," tomorrow, which as in the song, never came. I am still waiting for my Arabic lessons. Of course, they didn't at all want us to learn the language, for then we could have listened in on what was going on, as we had been able to do when Ben Weir and Marcel Carton were with us.

Our peace and quiet and all-day TV didn't last long. From the Voice of Lebanon, we had learned that no elections had been possible to select a successor to President Amin Gemayel, who had appointed his military commander, General Michel Aoun, as temporary prime minister. This infuriated the Moslems, for by agreement long ago, the prime minister is supposed to come from the Sunni community, the president from among the Christians, and the speaker of the house from the Shia; Druzes, described to me by one of my Moslem friends as "Protestant Moslems," got various lesser posts in this sort of confessional government. So the mainly Moslem western part of the city elected its own prime minister, making two separate governments in a country the size of Colorado's Weld County (i.e., about 4,000 square miles or, as the Lebanese always referred to it, 10,400 km^2). Aoun, it turned out, had grandiose ideas for Lebanon, even more so for himself. After alienating all of the militias by trying unsuccessfully to regain control of the port, he decided it was time to get rid of the Syrian army from Beirut, so he started the "War of Liberation" by shelling the western half of the city. For the following months, we had the most unholy bombardment all around our location. Shells were falling several a minute for hours on end, day after day. These things, 155 millimeters or 6 inches, make one heck of a racket, and do an awful lot of damage in a few milliseconds. Early on, Fadl came in to reassure us after one had scored a direct hit on our building. "Don't afraid, okay? No problem here. Don't afraid." "No, no. We're not afraid. Don't worry." We were lying! Anyone who *isn't* afraid for his life under conditions like that is either completely stupid or one hell of a liar! The shells were falling on my side of the building, and I was crouching behind one of the poured concrete pillars that make the backbone of these cheaply constructed high-rise apartment buildings in Beirut, thinking that it would give me a *little* more protection at least than the cinder-block part of the wall. Terry was a little removed, and alongside an interior wall. But if a shell had indeed scored a direct hit on our room, we would both have bought it there and then.

The shelling continued all the way from about mid-March to nearly the end of September, and the consensus seems to be that it was the worst in all the 14 years of civil war so far. It certainly sounded pretty bad to me, and even to Terry, who had much more experience than I with shells and gunfire. The children playing outside disappeared and the sounds became less and less, until finally we concluded that our guards must be about the only Lebanese left in the whole area. Everyone had evacuated—no children shouting, no motorbikes roaring around, no horns honking, no elevators running. Dead silence between each blast. What kind of commander was Aoun anyway? Even I, who had never been in the military, knew that to dislodge an army from a city, it has to be done house by house, block by block, street by street; it is impossible to sit and shell it out. The troops just go underground and wait it out. Which the Syrians did, coming out now and again to return the fire, more ferociously than even Aoun was sending over our way, with the sound of outgoing rockets and shells adding to our misery. Finally, the shelling ended and the conflict was taken to the conference table in Taif, Saudi Arabia, to work out a solution. The "solution" would bring more war. We would listen to it on our radios for another year.

25 Odyssey

Time rolled toward June 9—this time, the fourth time. The first week of May, when I was again back in Washington, D.C., there was in Fort Collins a "Thomas Sutherland—Ride for Freedom" event at the CSU Oval. One of the senior students, Scott Armstrong, had said, "I've been four years at this institution and it's been a lifetime—that's Tom's captivity. I can't leave CSU without doing *something*." And he did a "something," which was really special, organizing a bike-a-thon of 100 bicyclists (including Joan and Kit) doing in four hours 3,900 laps of the Oval, with pledges going to Tom's funds. A great event. And thereby a relationship was created between Scott and our family, and he kept in touch. Into the military, to Alaska, to Texas, and then to Germany where he was based when Tom was released at the end of 1991. Scott called into the hospital at Wiesbaden and then came with his wife for a visit—an extraordinary and touching meeting of two men who had never before met and who were separated in ages but not in spirit.

For me—what to do for June 9 for the fourth time? Almost without conscious decision, I went on an "Odyssey," visiting the places most important in Tom's life. Home to Scotland to see his family—Peter and Jane, Margaret, Elizabeth, Willie, Lena and Dunc, and all their families. The planting long done and the crops up and beautiful, the Sunday service at Bothkennar Church, shopping in Falkirk, seeing neighbors; we talked and talked of Tom. They had done so many things for him, even though technically he was an American hostage because of his naturalization in 1963. While the British government disowned him as its responsibility since he was after all an American citizen, with the Archbishop of Canterbury declining as well to add his name to his public prayer, the Scottish people and media began to "re-own" him. Once a Scot, always a Scot. It was a thing that touched my heart and, more importantly, touched Tom's most profoundly on his release.

Back then to Ames, Iowa, and to Iowa State where Tom and I shared so many memories of classes and graduate student friends and Murray family doings. Iowa State along with Dad had organized a remembrance ceremony for him on June 3—it was "Alumni Days" and people from all over drifted to the lawn in front of the Campanile to see and hear. Most powerful was the carillon at the end tolling the months of Tom's captivity—48 times those bells of Iowa State rang out for him bringing a lump in the throat and tears to the eyes. The newspapers did a beautiful write-up, and the strength and feeling generated that day I soaked up on Tom's behalf as well as mine.

On to Fort Collins with the death of Khomeini the big news as preparations went forward for another anniversary observance of June 9. Speculation about whether Khomeini's passing would make a difference was rife but we could only go on the assumption that there would be no change for us. But lots of media attention this anniversary because of it and I got to get up at 3:00 A.M. to talk to CBS, NBC, and ABC one after the other in the CSU Oval. The *Fort Collins Coloradoan* did a wonderful front page for Tom, also printing "A Letter to the Community" I'd written:

> As we mark today the start of Tom's fifth year of captivity in the Middle East, I want to share with you something of what's in our minds and hearts. Coming to be here on this day has been in a very real sense a personal odyssey I have made for Tom, to touch into his sources in Scotland, Iowa, and Colorado. What has come to me in these places amid family, friends, and precious memories has been truly A Happening that I will take back with me to Beirut to get somehow to Tom wherever he is—that he can draw the renewed strength to endure.
>
> Today in Colorado is a special day in this journey. As the clan of family and friends gather for Tom on the Oval of Colorado State University "our collective will" is once again expressed for him in yellow ribbons, the bagpipes, and the joined hands of friendship. And it is expressed for his mission also, for his commitment draws from this vitality of Scottish roots, the university idea, a belief in world community, and you. May this go from the heart of one frontier university to that of another—the American University of Beirut—and make a difference. And may this day mark not only the day of abduction but also the day of positive reaffirmation of our hope and faith in resolution of conflict, release, and reconciliation.
>
> To you, our continuing community, we can only say from the deep gratitude of our hearts, thank you for being here for us and extending without fail the lifeline of your support through these years.

On the evening of the ninth there was again that special occasion on the CSU Oval with its continuing beribboning of the old elm trees and the gathering of friends and family. This year we formed a circle around the Oval to sing "Auld Lang Syne" and then gathered at the podium for our observance. More collective will—how great people are.

And then I was off to the mountains to finish up for the summer where we'd begun four years before—it was as if it had been yesterday. Ann, who was out from California for the ceremony, went with me and saw a "For Sale" sign on the property next to ours. Nothing to do but call Ray her husband—"I want it." They bought it and started dreaming of the cabin they would build. For my part, I soaked up the mountains, the trees, the wildlife, and saw one day another "For Sale" sign on nearby mountain property. Maybe Ann's enthusiasm sparked mine, but I had to see that land. So I called the agent and there it was—the top of a mountain, wild, free, jeep-trailed, primitive, and with a site at the very top that looked hundreds of miles north and south and west onto Longs Peak and east onto Twin Sisters Mountain. It was like a religious experience when I climbed on those glacier-piled boulders with the wind-twisted pines and the view hit me. "I want it." It was to be Tom's Land—not knowing what he would want or be like after captivity, I saw this land as a working and healing place for him. I bought it with his "captivity money"—the Lebanese income tax that couldn't be claimed— and it became "Tom's Land."

Meanwhile, in Lebanon, Aoun's "War of Liberation" continued through the summer with AUB not exempt. In an August letter to Dad and Alice I wrote: *Talked with close, close friend Elien Heineken just out of AUB Beirut and she said our house took a shell the night before they left—not nice but Joana okay and cleaning up … .* There were indeed many shells falling at AUB—one in the middle of the Green Field that Joana told me afterward had hit while she was in the house. "Flash and terrible bang … ." Another hit the front of the Mishalanis' house just below. By the end of the war in September nearly 100 shells had hit the campus. All still there on the hill were living in the basement of Nicely Hall on the drive above our house.

Late July—more crisis on the hostage front. Sheik Obeid kidnapped by the Israelis; in retaliation, Colonel Higgins hanged and shown hanging by the neck on TV *(God!),* and Joe Cicippio now to be executed by the Islamic fundamentalists. I knew M was in Lebanon and was assured that he would be in touch with Secretary of State Baker and that the avenue would operate to defuse the crisis. Elham Cicippio went on the TV in Beirut, pleading for leniency, a beautiful person doing a beautiful job. Then my telephone rang. "This is Dennis Ross's office." Dennis came on—"Can you get hold of M for us?" I was absolutely nonplused. Why had I not been contacted before this if M hadn't been on the phone from

Lebanon? The president had cut short his speaking tour and I was so sure that they would have been in touch and in dialogue. Worry. Could something have happened to M out there? He was always walking such fine lines in that minefield that maybe this time in the midst of that terrible war ... ? "I'll do what I can from here," I said, and dialed the number I had of a mutual friend who was in contact. He was away from Beirut. I left a message to have M call me if he could, as soon as he could. Deadline for Joe Cicippio was to be at midnight the next day. Two hours later, about noon, the telephone rang again. It was M: "I couldn't get to a phone that worked until now—I've just been in touch with Dennis to relay assurance that Joe would not be killed ... . No, I didn't get your phone message. Everything will be okay with hostages but it's just not a good situation at all." What a tenuous thread it was that put people in touch, but how powerful it was. The captors ended the crisis 24 hours later, saving face in not carrying through on their death threat by "yielding to the pleas of Mrs. Cicippio." It seemed to me that Sheikh Fadlallah had shown his mind and his hand. And M certainly—the knowledge with its power had brought a needed assurance to defuse a crisis.

I began to think that Aoun's war with West Beirut and Syria would go on and on, and I started to get in wood and contemplate wintering over at the cabin. Somehow, the more primitive and more simply I lived, the better I liked it. I don't think I was actually trying to re-create for myself a situation close to Tom's, I think rather that my priorities were simplifying and distilling out in the basics. Nature healed and stimulated; the birds, raccoons, deer, and elk were uncomplicated friends; food on the cookstove, fires in the fireplace, and water from the stream were all that was needed, along with the telephone to talk to family. If winter posed any problems, I could cross-country ski to the road and go live with Kit and Joan. I began to look forward to such a life.

Then I talked to a friend in Beirut who had talked early on to someone close to the Syrians who said that they would let the war go on through September and then end it. Amazing. And that was what happened. The war ended with a truce brokered in Saudi Arabia called by all the Taif Accords after the town of its birth. It was supported by the Arab League and signed by both Christian and Moslem members of the Lebanese Parliament. The airport reopened, AUB resumed classes, and I flew back to Beirut on October 20. All seemed unchanged at AUB, the damage from the 100 shells had been repaired—including our windows and the great crater in the middle of the Green Field. And Sharif, Joana, and Rashid the gardener were all smiles for me on my return. Only Crystal, the cat, showed visibly the enormous strain of the spring and summer of blasts and loneliness and I couldn't believe how she could still move, so thin and straggly she was. I took her on my shoulder as I caught up with Joana on all the months away. And then I got caught quickly into the Beirut life again:

NOV. 3—Dearest Ann, Ray, Alex, Simone … I'm on the balcony basking in a beautiful sun, a relaxed morning because I don't work till 9:00, and a peaceful scene with joggers on the Green Field and a couple of fishing boats on the sea. In fact, everything is so "Beirut Normal" and like it was before that only the stories everyone has told me make me believe in the dreadful interim.

I hope Kit and Joan have let you know of my safe and sound return—such a warm welcome from all and a delight to find everything as it was. Work just sprang at me and I needn't have worried about being busy. The English Club will meet at my house Wednesday afternoons, I am employed for one course at AUB in the Education Department finishing up two master's students, and then the full teaching load at Hariri plus some volunteer hours … .

Islamic Jihad is against the Lebanese peace accord along with all else—but I'm not going to give up hope on our all being together for Christmas—it's just such a warm, wonderful thought … .

On the political front, a new president of Lebanon, René Moawad, was elected November 5 according to the terms of the Taif Accords. He seemed a good man and I remember the euphoria that greeted his election. Finally we had hope to go forward with. My writing students at the school all did an essay on what this day meant to them and to Lebanon and they were all so positive about everything. Seventeen days later as President Moawad drove in a motorcade he was blown to pieces (some even said that the explosion was so enormous that they never even found pieces). Again, *who?* Could it be Michel Aoun with his claim to leadership and absolute rejection of the new government as well as the Taif Accords that didn't spell out the departure of Syria and its 40,000 soldiers? The *New York Times* on November 23 and 24 reported: "… the questions echoed everywhere tonight after the news of the assassination: who did it, who suffers most from it and who stands to gain? … . Political analysts have noted that many of the groups in Lebanon—Christian, Muslim, Israeli—might have some motive for wanting to kill the new president." They didn't mention the Syrians, but rumor was also abroad that Syria had perhaps wanted him out of the way because he was too independently Lebanese for them. Joana's phrase "Oh, Lebanon!" seemed to sum it up. The parliament met in Shtaura in the Bekaa under heavy Syrian guard to elect Syria's man Elias Hraoui who is still alive at this writing and president of Lebanon. But there wasn't to be peace at that time, with General Aoun still in the picture:

NOV. 30—Things here a bit tense and uncertain with the assassination of Moawad, the election of a new president, and the standoff now between the new administration and General Aoun. Most feel that there won't be a military solution—rather a diplomatic something for all to save face and forge ahead .... But then it's always wait and see here. The French deputies came beflagged with the tricolor for France to give big support for Aoun yesterday—saw on TV last night all the demonstrations, speeches, etc. The Syrian Army is reported to be massing support in strategic areas—but somehow they've got to make the country work again. Meanwhile, school and daily life continues for me as usual—and we had a very nice Thanksgiving Day gathering here—50 people, two turkeys (from Wisconsin), lots of food, gorgeous weather with on-the-balcony eating and remembering of "all those near and dear to us."

Christmas Eve and Day I'll be here with a fire, videos, and beautiful solitude to be with your dad and you all in spirit if not in reality .... Hope Springs Eternal.

26   Outside In

In early June 1989, mournful and dismal music began to pour out over the loudspeakers of the mosque. "Fadl, what is this all about?" He even told us the truth for once! "Ayatollah Khomeini dead. All people sad." The entire Shiite community was obviously thrown into mourning, the grief was resounding everywhere: the radio, the TV, and mosques all over the southern suburbs. But Terry and I felt no grief—only jubilation, at least on my part, for I was and am convinced that here had been truly an evil man. Terry called him "an old man ... full of hatred and venom." If anyone was to blame for all of this bombing, hijacking, and kidnapping of westerners, it was the old man himself, for he hated westerners, particularly Americans, with a passion. So I *celebrated*. We saw the scenes on TV of his funeral, and were absolutely amazed at the depth of feeling the Shiites had for this man. Hundreds of thousands of young men were going absolutely crazy over in Iran, and even though by this time we were thoroughly accustomed to such rites as the head cutting to make themselves bleed at Ashura (a festival to commemorate the death in A.D. 680 of the Imam Hussein, one of the original leaders of the Shia), this was out of all comparison even with Ashura—astonishing scenes. And of course the mourning went on for days on end, as is the Islamic custom.

By way of cultural contrast, we also saw on TV in June a dramatic appeal by John McCarthy's mother for his release. She looked very ill indeed, even though she had obviously been well groomed so as not to disturb John, were he to see her. We had no idea whether John and Brian might have been given a TV like us, and perhaps might have seen it if perchance they were up in Beirut; or they might have heard the appeal on the radio, as we also did. But in early July came another desperate appeal by Pat McCarthy for John's release since his mother was *desperately* ill. This too was ignored, and in a few days, her death was announced. How sad. A story similar in some ways to that of Michel Seurat. These men had no sympathy in their veins. But if we leave it to Heaven to sort out, we still have to wonder how, in the Great Scheme of Things, John's mother and Michel Seurat will equate or compare to Khomeini. No way for us to know I guess.

Toward the end of July, the TV news gave us a gruesome sight. Colonel William Higgins was shown hanging by his neck, swinging lifelessly. *God.* Fadl came and hastily unplugged the TV. We told him we wanted to keep on seeing it—he didn't even reply. By radio, we got the news that he had been hanged in retribution for the Israelis having kidnapped Sheikh Obeid, a powerful young Shiite leader in South Lebanon. The Israelis had wanted a hostage of their own to pressure the Shia to release their own airmen prisoners of war, who by this time had been held for about seven years, having been shot down over Lebanon during the 1982 Israeli invasion. Naturally we wondered whether the repercussions would descend eventually on us, especially since the next news was that Joseph Cicippio would be the next to be killed if Obeid was not released promptly. Joe's wife Elham also appeared on our TV with a heartrending appeal for his release— that he not be killed; an ultimatum with a very short time limit was given to the U.S. government, prompting President Bush to fly back from the western United States in a big hurry to handle this latest crisis. In the end, Joe was not killed. And in the meantime our own treatment did not vary a whit from day to day. The immediate impact on us was thus zero. But who knows what it *might* have evolved into. We were never given any warning of *anything* pending.

All this time my ear was glued to the radio, listening to the BBC World Service, and at night, the VOA—25 hours a day, it seemed. I let Terry handle the TV, for he was much more a child of the TV generation than I, who had grown up with radio as my constant companion. My younger brother Willie and I had bought crystal sets in the thirties and forties, and had fallen asleep many a night with the headset stuck to our ears. In captivity now, my favorite program was BBC's "Outlook," with hosts Barbara Myers and John Tidmarsh. Barbara in particular had such a gentle way of handling interviews, and was always so courteous with her guests, while evidencing a piercingly sharp intelligence that always got the most out of them, and kept the show moving so refreshingly. I loved her for all she was bringing into our cells, the reassurance she gave us that out there in the real world, there were still rational, sane, and intelligent people who cared about improving the world and broadening people's intellects. Thank you, Barbara, John, and all at BBC.

"Music Review" came every Friday morning. Done by real musicians who knew their classical music, it too was a highlight of the week. I had become, in

the years of marriage to Jean, and of singing in the church choir, fairly knowledgeable on the subject, but far from an expert—just enough to allow me to
appreciate good music and to know when critics really knew what they were
talking about. So I had an hour of ecstasy every Friday. Thank you again, BBC!
How many times did I say that to myself? Countless. Then there was Paddy Feeney
and his Saturday sportscasts. What a guy. I marveled at how he kept everything
going on that show, for hours on end every Saturday, embracing all kinds of sports.
Admittedly he had lots of help, and lots of experts also by his side—but he was
the king. He kept it going. On the days when he was off, the show didn't have at
all the same sparkle. Thank you, Paddy! And thank you, Bob Holness for "Anything Goes"; and thank you, Malcolm Billings for "Seven Seas"; and thank you,
Religion Staff for your weekly "Focus on Faith" and daily "Words of Faith"; and
thank you, Science Staff for your "Science in Action."

We were also getting a wonderful flavor of the United States from the VOA,
but could only get it late at night during the hours of darkness. Coming from
Turkey, on medium wave, the signals carry that distance only in the darkness—
a fact that I have long known but never understood completely. My favorite program was the "Magazine Show," hosted by Barbara Klein, and I can still hear her
wonderful voice, "Hi, I'm Barbara Klein. Welcome to the 'Magazine Show.' " After which she would take us all over the U S of A: to the state fair in Ohio, to hear
about the record number of entries that year, and a nice discussion of the various classes of livestock; to a frog-jumping contest up in Oregon, an annual event
up there apparently, which occasioned lots of interest and merriment; and to the
Tattered Cover Book Store in Denver, for a guided tour of that famous Denver
landmark. (I went back to buy books first thing after release.) Then on to Powell's
Bookstore in Portland, Oregon. I couldn't know that at that very moment, my
daughter Joan was working up in Portland and had bought many used books
and a few new ones at Powell's. Like Kit, she had developed into an avid reader.
Jean and Ann have always been bookaholics since childhood. So many other
excellent programs on the VOA, including news, brought us America.

Then there was Radio France Internationale (RFI), which we could catch
for an hour every morning from 6:00 to 7:00 A.M., during which time they borrowed the frequency used all day and evening by Radio Monte Carlo (RMC), a
station broadcasting in French also, and very much respected by the entire Arab
world. Most of my friends at the AUB were regular listeners to RMC, from which
they felt they could trust the news much better than any of their own national
radio stations, which were heavily propagandistic. In Lebanon, none of the broadcasters were free to say their opinions or to tell the whole truth—that invited a

fast trip to the bridge and into the river, or even more quickly, a bullet out of the blue into the head. Both RFI and RMC therefore played an extremely important role in the Middle East in keeping the people properly informed. They had correspondents all over the region who understood the culture, and they were, if anything, more insightful even than the BBC; though that may be disputed by ardent beeb-o-philes. Certainly the French have always had a more clear perspective of and a greater sympathy for the region than the average Brit. But for me, the real advantage of the RFI was the chance to listen to pure and beautiful French accents and to brush up on my French again. Terry too was interested in improving his spoken accent, but that was a bit early in the morning for him.

Early one morning, Terry still asleep, I was listening to a discussion of the hostage situation on the VOA and was chilled to hear, "It has now been a very long time for Terry Anderson, and he probably has no idea that both his father and his brother have passed away during his captivity." No mention of the reason for the passing of each of them. I knew that his oldest brother had had a bout with a form of cancer when he was in high school, but that after treatment, he had amazed the doctors by his recovery—a medical miracle, they called it. So I wasn't sure that it was his oldest and favorite brother. Could have been Bruce, who had led a rather wild life, and might have even caused his own demise. But my dilemma was whether to tell Terry in these grim circumstances and give him more grief than he was already being called on to bear. I resolved not to say a word to him, at least not for now. Perhaps there would be a more opportune occasion in the future.

October 27 brought Terry's annual birthday greeting from Madeleine and Sulome. LBC was very good about transmitting messages for him from his two women, and Madeleine had generally cut a tape showing Sulome playing around the house and talking to her dad. "Happy Birthday, Daddy. Please come home soon. We all miss you." That crystal clear voice of an obviously very intelligent little girl conveying meaning far beyond her years. We watched, both of us with tears streaming down our cheeks, our hearts wrenched almost beyond tolerance levels.

Christmas came. Our fifth in captivity, this one the "best." It was between Aoun's two wars—the "War of Liberation" and the "Militia War" in the East, and the LBC was back in business in nearly full swing. We marveled at the resilience of the people who ran the TV stations and the radio station, keeping them going through the most hellish of bombardments. From the Christian side, Christmas was celebrated more fully than I had ever seen it done anywhere I had ever lived. Masses were said, musical programs were broadcast, specials were put on. There was John Denver and Placido Domingo in their Christmas special from John's home in Aspen, Colorado. Two wonderful voices that brought us real Christmas cheer. Surely that couldn't be beat, we thought, when lo they broadcast another, with a youth choir accompanying a soprano I had never heard of, but who brought tears to my eyes the moment she began to sing—the most glorious voice one could even imagine. *Jessye Norman*, they announced. Where had I been all this time that I had never heard this woman? And to make things even more majestic, she was singing in a cathedral with fantastic acoustics. I sat mesmerized on my mattress, with my left arm chained to the wall, and let the tears flow freely. Oh, Jessye, if you could only have known that day the joy you brought to me! How wonderful that I could tell you in person two and a half years later!

27   *Pity the Nation* and World Cup Soccer

The New Year—1990—duly arrived. Into the nineties. Almost half a decade chained to the wall and cut off from civilization, family, and friends. Will *this* be the year of our liberation? Still reading, still arguing, still watching TV: *The A-Team* was still on, and *McGyver*, and *The Wonder Years*—the young star of junior high has just entered Harvard as I write. We also watched lots of old movies, which, if I'd only known, Jean was also watching—on videos rented from Smith's Grocery. Ali, the "Lying-Piece-of-Dog-Shit," arrived again, full of news of a new book that had just appeared, *Pity the Nation,* by Terry's journalist buddy, Robert Fisk. Terry had an enormous respect for "Fisky," as he called him, and could hardly stand not getting the book immediately. It was being serialized in one of the Beirut newspapers, Ali told us, and he was most interested in it. He took great delight in the fact that one of the characters, nay, one of the stars even, was our Terry, and gave us a daily summary for some time. Terry worked on him to the best of his ability to get the book, but Ali never did buy it for us.

Terry had no illusions about the nature of the book. It would be excellent, for Fisky had written the definitive work on Northern Ireland, for which work he had received not only a Ph.D., but critical acclaim from the experts. Terry had read that, and stood in awe of Fisky's abilities. Again, I could not know it, but Jean had become a friend of Fisky and his friend Lara, and had frequent conversations with both of them at our place on campus and at theirs, above where Terry had lived. Fisky had given Jean an inscribed copy of his book, which Jean and I both treasure. A special treat for me to meet them afterward in a Paris cafe.

Having failed with the Syrian Army, Aoun's next venture, in the springtime, was to try to destroy Samir Geagea's own Christian militia, the so-called Lebanese Forces, and get himself totally in charge of the East Side with his somewhat more legitimate army. Although the battles took place on the East Side, we in the West got some of the spillover, and so had several more weeks of hell. It was a standoff, the army not quite able to knock off the militia. All Aoun succeeded in doing was to destroy even the city's East Side, which until then had escaped serious desecration, and also in splitting the Christian community into two bitterly divided factions. Watching him on TV at his palace giving interviews and pronouncements, and during his speeches, which tended to be sessions of ranting and raving, I couldn't help thinking how much he reminded me of Adolf Hitler.

Our guards here were beginning to treat us almost humanely, and we were getting to know them rather well. Mahmoud and Jameel were our constant companions and bringing us everything we had—which wasn't much, of course—and they were among the most rational of all the guards we had had. Mahmoud brought us a chess set, much to Terry's delight. He was eager to teach me how to play, but he was so much better than I, who had only played a few games in all my life, that it was once again discouraging for me to be beaten so consistently. So I gave up trying the impossible. They brought us an Exercycle, and let us pedal it for five to ten minutes a day—not nearly enough to make any real difference to our physical condition, but better than nothing. A dilemma—whether to use it prior to going to the toilet while we were sometimes desperate to get there, or to use it on our return and work up a sweat on the hot Beirut mornings of spring and summer just after having had the chance to wash, and occasionally to shower.

Only one hostage had been released since the three Frenchmen had gone home on May 4, 1988—Dr. Singh, an Indian man holding a green card and who had been teaching at the BUC. Suddenly there seemed to be movement. The *Tehran Times* was predicting that the Islamic Jihad for the Liberation of Palestine was going to release another hostage, and indeed in late April, Robert Polhill was on his way home. We saw him on TV, throwing a football for the journalists and joking with them. This guy must have a great sense of humor, we thought. And he does. He received a grand welcome from President Bush at the White House. Hot on his heels came Frank Reed. In sharp contrast to Polhill, however, Frank still seemed to be at least partially catatonic, still harking back perhaps to his massive beating in "The Prison" in the fall of 1986, three and a half years before. Frank seemed to have gone downhill since the last time I had seen him, for he was mumbling during his brief press conference in Damascus. I resolved there and then that when I got out, I was not going to act like that in any way. I would give the press a story that they might feel was worth their while coming to Damascus for. Two more gone home. When would our turn come?

The World Cup soccer tournament was coming in June. "Italy 90" was to be an extravaganza, especially on Lebanese television, for the Lebanese are about as soccer-daft as any Scotsman. LBC kept announcing that they would broadcast *all 52 games!* That would take up the whole evening every day for a month, one of the games being shown on time-delay. I made my jubilation very clear to Terry, who was no soccer fan. "Okay, Sutherland. You can watch the damn soccer games, but we are not going to watch them all evening for a whole god-damned month. I insist that we watch something else for *some* of the time at least." "Okay," I compromised readily. "But I want to see the good ones at least. Scotland for sure. And England. And Germany, and Brazil, and Italy, and Argentina. These will all be good games, man. Even you should appreciate a great game like soccer, fellow, Leaves your basketball in the shade any day!"

The great day arrived, and we watched the opening ceremonies on LBC. Then Terry changed channels. Tele-Liban, both East and West Sides—the World Cup. Channel 33—the World Cup! All four channels were carrying all 52 games, so that there was scarcely anything else on for a whole month, save the odd news broadcast. Like it or not, Terry was stuck. And was furious! But after a few games and some explanation from me on the finer points, he began to get quite enthused about the nonstop action. He shared my disdain of Maradona of Argentina, a great player but not a good sportsman—always faking a foul, and groaning at the referee. He cheered with me for Scotland—in vain, for they didn't make it through to the final rounds. England did, though, so I kept on hoping that the United Kingdom could come through with flying colors. So did Ireland. Game boys, the Irish! Fought the good fight. In the end, it was the Germans who put the kibosh on Maradona and his mates. Worthy winners. "Never count out the Germans or the Italians," says my younger brother, a keen fan—"they'll always be there or thereabouts at the final game." He's right. The Germans *were* worthy winners. The guards too were all glued to their sets, and were fascinated that I knew so much about the game. I had to inform them that soccer had been my life at age 17, when I played for the Scottish Youth International team and was signed by the Glasgow Rangers. They came in every evening to discuss the day's events—then shut off the light.

Soccer wasn't the only exciting event on our TV. The Berlin Wall had fallen before our very eyes in November of 1989. Who would ever have believed it? I certainly never thought *I* would live long enough to see the sights we did—East Berliners pouring through the gate in their clunker Trabant cars, the champagne corks popping, the wall torn down in chunks, young men scrambling over it and scribbling on it—such euphoria comes once in a lifetime. And here we were, chained to the wall, not able to do it real justice. No champagne for us—only the usual horrid tea. But wait until we get out of here, *then* we'll celebrate! As though that weren't enough, there came all the happenings in the Soviet Union, and communism had fallen on top of the wall. *The whole damn world is going to be topsy-turvy by the time we get out of here.*

Even that wasn't the end of the fantastic—Saddam Hussein, president of Iraq, lined up his troops on the border of Kuwait, and though we knew that he was smarter than to go in and invade it, he wasn't. I got the news early on the second of August of 1990. "You'll never guess what happened this morning while you were snoring it out, Anderson." "What?" asked he. "Saddam went into Kuwait!" "No way," rebutted Terry. "He is smarter than that. The United States would never stand for that!" Whatever the truth of it all, for us the most significant immediate act in Saddam's invasion was the emptying of all the jails in Kuwait City, including, said both the BBC and the VOA, the one holding the 17 who had tried to bomb the U.S. embassy and the French embassy in Kuwait. *God!* When the guard came in with breakfast that day, I asked him right off, "Where are my shoes?" "Shoes?" he asked. "What shoes?" "*My* shoes," I repeated. "I need them to go home. You told us when your brothers in Kuwait are free, we go home next day. I want to go home today." "Oh, *that*," replied the guard. "That Saddam Hussein. No America free our brothers. Okay. You go home soon and very soon, but not now." *No Shit.*

28   A War in the East

New Year, 1990—Dearest Ann, Ray, and All … Happy New Year! Got the beautiful telex from everyone and our thoughts crossed mid-Atlantic on Christmas Day! I could picture everything and really participate vicariously but I'm looking for real pictures! … I have high faith and hope for the next three months—somehow I came through the Christmas–New Year week with renewed spirit. Maybe it was communing with your dad and you all and having a lovely retreat at home—I put up the tree and the crèche and bunches of candles and I made fudge and shortbread and a puzzle and listened to tapes and watched movies on my new VCR—saw *The Mission*—remember you recommended it to me—and it was powerful and good if a trifle close to home … . Weather here was gorgeous the whole time with just enough chill in the air at night to enjoy the fire.

Jan. 18—I tried the phone last Friday to you all but AUB operator said she couldn't even get through to the city operator … . I'm getting through the days here in not bad fashion but praying hard for the next two months—just no news, but that's as it has to be now. Meanwhile plenty to do while the political game keeps playing between Aoun and Hraoui and Arab countries—I'm still teaching, editing the manuscript for the collected *Studies in Honor of Malcolm H. Kerr,* overseeing two student master's degree projects, getting your dad's awards ready to present to students at graduation next week—we come up for semester break 1st of February. Will be nice … .

Jan. 25—Tonight is Burns Night and a small gathering of friends. Tomorrow the English Club meets—I've put together a tape of your dad reading Burns's poetry and speaking about Burns's life and then he and I singing together Burns's songs—"Rantin' Rovin' Robin," "Comin' Thru the Rye," "A Red Red Rose," etc … . So your dad's here! I told the senior English students that they couldn't graduate without knowing Robert Burns … . Keep praying—

And then the "political game" became "deadly combat." Five days after Burns's birthday, General Aoun was locked into factional warfare with his Christian rival, Geagea, head of the Lebanese Forces, over control of Christian East Beirut. Geagea, commander of 10,000 militia troops, had supported the election of Elias Hraoui according to the Taif Accords in November, while Aoun, commanding 15,000 army troops, was still in opposition, holing up in the Presidential Palace in Baabda and declaring himself the head of government. The battle was inevitable and reportedly started when a militiaman fired a rocket-propelled grenade at a public picture of Aoun. What transpired was intra-Maronite Christian carnage. I thought of my "keep praying." Even in wars between different religious groups, prayers to the same God for victory become ironic exercises. Surely in internecine warfare, as Shakespeare so wonderfully and dramatically epitomized it in "Richard III," the irony takes over as Christian prayers for victory become diametrically opposed. And somehow when brother fights brother it is the worst—I myself knew Christians who had held up strongly throughout the years of Christian-Moslem warfare only to become totally disillusioned and devastated by this war that raged for months that spring, shells raining down (at times at the rate of ten a minute), rifle and heavy artillery fire, tanks, armored personnel carriers and all, decimating neighborhoods, killing by the end of May over 1,000 people and wounding some 3,000 more. There were people who went into bomb shelters and basements who didn't emerge again for 18 days, others who had to see the bodies of family members in the streets lie day after day without a chance to go and get them. Electricity and water were cut off. In truth, as the Christian radio station Voice of Lebanon put it, the residents of East Beirut "had seen living hell." Those who could leave came to West Beirut to be safe—another irony—or left altogether for any place they could get to. I remember so well one evening when a small group of us went to the Smugglers' Inn on Makhoul Street close to AUB for dinner. A woman and her daughter from East Beirut were there and came to our table to talk and tell what it was like on the East Side and how they were leaving Lebanon the next day from the airport. It was her eyes more than anything that struck me and I thought—*Shell-shocked ... that's what they mean by shell-shocked.*

In West Beirut we mostly "escaped" this war, participating, however, through the agony of friends, the news, hearsay, and the distant crash of shells with the attendant black pall of smoke to be seen hanging over the East. "Mostly" because as always the war "spilled over" and the West took shells too (Aoun, of course, was not averse to putting pressure as well on Hraouwi and the Syrians, his external foes). A whole family of five was killed in a direct hit on their apartment and even Hamra, the shopping street five blocks up from AUB, did not escape one Saturday. That Aoun had taken the opportunity at the beginning to cut off water and electricity to the West Side was a given. Tension and apprehension ruled:

> FEB. 7—A quick note to get out with the courier this afternoon to let you know I'm okay and no matter what happens here with attendant dire reports on U.S. media I'll be fine—all contingencies prepared with safety valves and places—Do Not Worry or Be Uptight. It's a mess on the East Side—awfulness. Here on the West Side people are tense and unsure of what will happen—looks like perhaps a showdown—but then again maybe not. Elien Heineken and I went out shopping this A.M.—AUB and Hariri Program have suspended classes and operations until Monday—and shops, etc. were open but people purposeful about stocking up .... I got plenty of videos and important things like wine, scotch, turnips, leeks, lentils, milk, butter, and flour (for lentil soup and shortbread) and water and cat food. We're all cut off from water except a short time in the early A.M.—otherwise Rashid has gotten me in a big load of wood for wood fires and I've a bathtub full of water ....
>
> FEB. 15—Some shelling on the East Side started up again this morning—hope it doesn't mean more like before—people over there are about desperate .... (later A.M.) ... seems to have stopped—hope for truce. Must get this to the courier—

Thus true to form as always, we adapted (as those on the East Side had done when the war had been on the West Side) and lived accordingly, making the most of the life we had:

> Today's a lull in the fighting in the East—so we're taking our good American journalist friend Elaine Larwood out for lunch for her birthday and tonight Elien comes over for a glass of wine and Roquefort by a fire for her birthday—our social life does go on. I've been also doing some work—edited up a storm on the 1984–88 Research Report for AUB and Malcolm Kerr's Memorial Volume plus the work for the Hariri Program which is between semesters ....
>
> What did you hear over there about the bizarre story that the journalist Hala Jaber told of being at a Hizbollah wake and someone pointing out a building where "Sutherland and McCarthy were held"; ... seems an amazing story—but at least a positive one. Keep heart and hope—maybe after this round finishes in Lebanon it will be their turn for something good ....
>
> Feb. 14—Hi Sweethearts! I didn't think anywhere near soon enough to get a beautiful card to you arriving today—but I want you to know I'm thinking of all of you and sending special Valentine love to you as well as Tom. The Christmas pictures didn't arrive so I went ahead and put into *As-Safir* "The Harem Picture" of us

all from last June for your dad—hope you think the message okay—their layout meant we bought a lot of space for Tom, but maybe that's a nice concept. The paper goes to everyone in West Lebanon ... hope that doesn't scare you?? I just have a feeling it will get to him for Valentine's Day like the other one two years ago—the story about Tom and McCarthy said they treated them well and gave them magazines, etc. ... I truly think this is a way to reach him, and Ann, don't worry about the fact we're smiling—it's normality and cheer that must go into him ... . When I finish this letter I'll go up and buy a copy or two and see if it appeared as we sent it in. Radwan Mawlawi, the director of information at AUB, does the Arabic for me and gets it into the paper—a true friend. [Breaks of the game—this time the picture did not reach Tom.]

I've been thinking I owed you a longer letter for a much longer time—since we're presently on hold with classes suspended both at AUB and Hariri, this is the time ... . I'm in the kitchen with sheets in the doorways and the oven on because it's been raining and chilly—we have no heat and water is cold but we still get it an hour every morning which is a blessing and we do have electricity from AUB so I can heat water and take sink baths and work in a warm room with my space heater. This is the second week we've been off work and I must say I'm luxuriating in being at home—it is, however, a bit of a hotel since no one outside AUB has any water still and I'm at least able to provide friends with the odd wash, ironing, water bottle fill-ups, ice from the freezer, etc. Also since Rashid has kept me supplied with wood (even if most of it is green) people usually drop in around six for a drink in front of the fire.

This weekend 11 faculty members from AUB leave for Cyprus for your Uncle John's workshop on conflict resolution—it seems to be a big deal and much looked-forward-to ... . I am hoping all works for me to fly over and get a weekend there also Feb. 24–26. Just relax, see John, and get perhaps a trip to somewhere like Paphos and be a tourist. But most of all to be at a phone that works and I'll call ... .

My latest adventure was last Sunday with my journalist friend, Marilyn Raschka [*Chicago Sun Times*], when the two of us got into my newly rejuvenated car (Tom's '71 Peugeot 204) and set off for Sidon to buy fish and see the sights (I've never been there and it's only 20 miles south!) ... . Everything went wonderfully at the start—got there about 9:30 A.M. and went out on the sea road and parked and went to see the castle—it was closed (people were "misbehaving" there evidently—seemed very normal) and we "could go somewhere and talk to someone and get them to open it" but we didn't since we could see almost all we needed to see and it wasn't ancient, only 13th century crusader—then we went to the Suks and spent a lovely hour watching them make pastries and quilts and seeing everyone selling everything—then we went to the fish market and bought fresh fish and talked with the men there who wanted to know all about us and were interested in talking about America—then a little more sightseeing (an old hotel with a great courtyard now a militia headquarters—they welcomed us as Americans but said "no pictures" and then we drove by an old mosque and down the main street of Sidon) .... Then we started home and got only halfway there when the clutch went out on the car. I jammed it into first since it was raining and we were on open highway and we drove the rest of the way in first gear, 20 miles an hour, checkpoints every mile—had to stop completely only about four times all the way back to AUB although it was a bit hairy through Ouzai [we didn't know, of course, but we were stopped as it turned out just outside the garage facades behind and under which Tom was held from August 1986 to the end of January 1987] and the Beirut Corniche and checkpoints—stopping was our trouble though in first gear because it wouldn't start again easily and three times Marilyn had to get out and push and then run and jump in the door I was holding open on her side ... you wouldn't believe it! But the greatest thing was how nice everyone was—they helped her push—one policeman at the Corniche Mazraa [a right-turn intersection for Tom when he was kidnapped] in Beirut came to help push which was not so helpful since all the traffic went every which way when he left his post. But all's well that ends well (Lebanon always reactivates old clichés) and we got back and parked the car [it never left that parking place again until after Tom came back and we gave the car to a friend from the East Side who took it away—I think for parts] and came in and had a FISH FRY par excellence. We'd also bought fresh lettuce from the wonderful truck gardens along the road before the clutch disaster so we had fresh salad along with the fish ... .

Last week two friends had birthdays so we celebrated—a lunch out at the Istambouly Restaurant above Hamra with delicious Lebanese food and a gathering at Heinekens' in the faculty apartments with ten friends—nice. So you know that we continue to lead a somewhat normal life even in the midst of the Eastern shoot-out and AUB suspension and the water and electricity cutoff. It's still tense and people seem to be waiting for what comes next—the scenarios vary between optimism (cautious) and extreme pessimism. No one seems willing to even venture an opinion about what will be the outcome or the next day's events—we all wait together and do what we can for each other. Next Saturday people are going to gather here for a potluck in front of the fire—unless Hell is breaking loose and then it's understood all's off and everyone goes to wherever they're safe. Just want you to know that you're not to worry about me no matter what the news—I've got places to hole up and I will stay safe ... .

News came from Kit and Joan that Coloradans were signing petitions to be sent to the United Nations on behalf of their dad and others. A University of Denver International Law School professor Ved Nanda and some of his students had drafted the petition, Tom's good friend Wil Huett, a Fort Collins radio personality, was leading the drive, and people were signing everywhere—at basketball games, conferences, malls, and stores. Kit and Joan were to take the petitions personally and present them to Javier Pérez de Cuéllar. They called to let me know, and wonder of wonders got through! "They've gotten 18,015 signatures, Mom! And Pérez de Cuéllar is scheduling us in for 15 minutes between negotiations with Greek and Turkish Cyprus!" What a time they had in New York! Joan wrote about it:

> Kit and I flew into New York with the petition for Javier Pérez de Cuéllar which informed him that the people of Colorado were behind any efforts he made to free all of the hostages being held in Lebanon. We stayed with our cousin Bruce and his wife Mary for three days and just had a ball. We saw the Broadway play *Cats*, went out for lunches, and really got to know our cousin again. We got a late meeting with the secretary general the day before we left which went really well. I could tell that he was genuinely concerned for the well-being of the hostages and really wanted a resolution, something I think he was working on with his assistant Johnny Picco, the best-looking man that I think I have ever seen up close .... .

Indeed, as it came out afterward, Giandomenico Picco was interfacing with Iran at this time, a year and a half before he would come to Beirut. I was not aware of this but I surely appreciated the mental picture of Kit and Joan as the international dividing line so to speak between the Greeks and Turks, and I could imagine Pérez de Cuéllar finding two lovely girls a welcome interlude in the course of his efforts at Cypriot conflict resolution. Most of all, however, what a wonderful harbinger of Picco's diplomacy and omen of the American hostage resolution in Lebanon to happen through the UN at the end of 1991!

April came in with the release of Frank Reed who pleased the girls with a call about Tom. And the start of a new semester at AUB on the 23rd was the reuniting of Christian and Moslem students on Main Campus in Ras Beirut as the East Beirut Christians fled their war zone and were welcomed in the West. I could hear the new voices going up the Main Gate steps—counting as they went in French, "*Un, deux, trois ...* ." The *AUB Bulletin* reported this historic event:

> 612 OCP students ... were warmly greeted by University staff, faculty, and students as they moved to the main campus. It was like a family reunion, with many old friends meeting and embracing after years of separation. "It was more than just renewing old friendships," says Dean of Students Fawzi Hajj. "Many students vacated their rooms to allow for housing the newcomers. It was a gesture that shows the real feelings of brotherhood among students." ... To the question "Are you staying on the

main campus even if the situation in East Beirut improves," the answer was a unanimous "yes" from the newcomers. "I wouldn't trade it for any place in the world," one student exclaimed.

Amazing the ironies AUB can generate. What was impossible in 1985 was a blessed given in 1990. The "Eastern Establishment" had thus "lost," having done it to themselves, but the young people, the students both East and West, became the ultimate winners. The Green Line was starting to fall like the Berlin Wall and had set them free to know each other. For a short time, the East Beirut students kept together, making their gathering the Main Gate steps and College Hall area, while the West Beirut students maintained their territory in front of West Hall. But before we all knew it, there was integration.

April also brought a time of decision for me—at least that was the way I figured it. For the last nearly five years of Tom's captivity, the AUB Board of Trustees and Administration had retained him as dean of AUB's Faculty of Agricultural and Food Sciences, Adib Saad serving as acting dean for him. But the Faculty was going downhill without a real dean in the office—I knew it, everyone knew it—and the time came when the new dean had to be named. I was so pleased, and I knew Tom would also be, that Adib Saad was appointed. Adib and Tom had been in accord on what was best for the Faculty on the ongoing basis from 1983 on. I felt keenly that with the naming of Adib Saad as full dean that Tom and I were without real "occupational" places at the university. So what was right to do now that fit in with our integrity and our mission at AUB? No indication when or even if Tom would be back. Joe Cicippio, comptroller of AUB at the time he was kidnapped in September 1986, had told me after Tom's abduction that AUB insurance would support Tom for four years and nine months. This time was now up. I thought about it all very long and very hard. There seemed no other course but that we should resign when Tom's contract was up May 31, and that I should not only release AUB of obligation but also release our on-campus home.

I wrote to Ann and Ray, Kit, and Joan about it all and received a telex right back:

APRIL 12, 1990—RECEIVED YOUR LETTER. THE FAMILY IS BEHIND YOU WITH LOVE, STRENGTH AND SUPPORT FOR YOUR DECISIONS. HOW CAN WE HELP? WE LOVE YOU ... .

With this I proceeded to resign. I had Tom's power of attorney so I wrote April 16 a letter to Dr. Herter, the American president of AUB, Dr. Goheen, chairman of the Board of Trustees, and the Board of Trustees, signing it in both our names:

It is important to us as we reach the end of our contractual affiliation with AUB to show our recognition and appreciation of the honor and respect you have paid us in giving us both the opportunity to have presence on campus and share in AUB's mission for the past seven years. This you have done with genuine and warm concern and our thanks goes beyond words as your support has gone beyond obligation. We can only trust you feel as we do that the total has been a mutual work, a Shakespearean work as it were … "Whose worth's unknown although his height be taken."

We wish this letter also to be official and say unequivocally that we release the American University of Beirut from any further obligation to us—contractual, financial, or otherwise. It is time. And as we enter a new relationship based on our mutual concern for AUB, know well that you can count on us for whatever we can do in new capacities to help ensure that her vital work continues.

Again, to you all, our heartfelt appreciation for the past and our equally heartfelt hope for the future … . Most sincerely, … .

In addition to personal, heartfelt letters of appreciation to President Herter and Vice President Hallab, I also wrote to others who would be involved in the finishing-up details of our contract and stay in Beirut, ending with a letter to David and Doris Dodge, who after his release from captivity in July of 1983 had left their AUB home with furnishings intact for us to use during our time there. Such generosity had made all the difference to us over the years:

Dear David and Doris … How can we thank you enough for all your things that you so kindly surrounded us with: the dining room table alone saw the Marines for Thanksgiving '83, the big Christmas Party of '83 when the Kerrs came, FAFS parties, especially the graduation of '84, and all the other things through the years— Hariri Program potlucks and student parties and this year the English Club for Burns Night and next week a lunch after the English Conflict Resolution Workshop. The four of us know well that "things" aren't important—and yet things somehow absorb and transmit the emotional investment and thus have a wonderful worth. Through your things you gave us the comfort of a home here and allowed us to continue and share work with you here—something perhaps too special for words … .

To you and yours, all the best from our mutual Beirut where tragedy is so fully integrated with the surrounding beauty of campus and people … .

My letters brought instant response from President Herter who sent word to have me come to Cyprus to see him at the board meeting just coming up there. I went and we met and he spoke strongly: "You must know that the Board of Trustees is adamant about this—they have passed a resolution of support for our hostages until the time that they come out. There is no question of it. Tom will be supported fully and you must not consider staying anywhere but in your home on campus until he is released." He would take no demurring from me, and I of course capitulated completely before such graciousness and concern. But our offer of resignation was there, straightforward and serious and duly registered with the AUB Board of Trustees as it had to be, and I was glad of that. There are never half-measures for "At Your Own Risk." For their part, it seemed that there were no half-measures either.

The war in the East continued through a sea blockade and the obligatory intermittent cease-fires: The *New York Times* of May 27, 1990, told the story in a nutshell:

PAPAL ENVOY TELLS OF LEBANESE TRUCE
But Christian Rivals Continue Fighting in East Beirut
Snipers Kill 3 People

... The latest fighting raised the casualty toll to about 1,000 killed and 2,750 wounded since the power struggle between the rival commanders broke out on Jan. 30 ... .

The conflict wasn't just in the East. In the usual fascinating juxtaposition that happens always in Lebanon, this *New York Times* article went on to say:

In a separate incident, Israeli-backed militiamen killed four Arab guerrillas during a clash today in south Lebanon ... and Syrian troops armed with automatic weapons and rocket-propelled grenade launchers moved into the south Beirut slum quarters of Hajjaj and Haymadi before dawn to stop the fighting there.

Beirut's Muslim sectors remained tense, with fighters of the fundamentalist pro-Iranian Hizbollah, or Party of God, and the Syrian-backed Amal movement still on combat footing.

The factions have been battling for dominance of Lebanon's 1.2 million Shiites, the country's largest sect, for two and a half years. By police count at least 1,049 have been killed and 3,136 wounded in that feud ... . Hundreds of Muslim families used the lull to evacuate the slums and head for the relative safety of villages in predominantly Shiite south Lebanon, where the Party of God and Amal frequently clash ... .

One is compelled to think, "So that is what it means to be 'between a rock and a hard place,'" as one tries to come to terms with internecine warfare, or any kind of warfare for that matter. "War in the Name of God" surely manifests its true nature as "War in the Name of Earthly Power," not that thinking people haven't always known that.

Keeping our residence in "Dodge House," I did, however, pack up our things into boxes for easy negotiability. Keeping at the same time to my resignation from the Hariri Program, I went home for the summer. I had taken out an ad in *As-Safir* on May 3, Tom's birthday, in which I "sent" him Burns's love poem and "told him" where I'd be, just in case:

> I send you the best gift I have, My Dear, "a red red rose" of Love. May it touch your heart and spirit in a special way on this your Special Day. Come June I go to our mountains where we parted, in hopes that we can come together there again soon.

(He got this one! Brian Keenan told me in August that he'd seen it just before his release in a book in the room where Tom and Terry had been held.)

Dr. Hallab hadn't wanted me to resign—he told me that—but I also knew that the program was having to cut 25 Lebanese teachers from the ranks the next year due to big cutbacks from the Hariri Foundation. We had been coming down rather steadily in student enrollment each year from the 1,000 of 1985–1986, and the number projected for 1990–1991 was some 375–400 as I remember. Hariri had not been finding it practicable to send his students to the States and Canada for undergraduate study and was placing them at BUC and the AUB instead. There could only be so much space each year. What I knew was that I couldn't take the place of a Lebanese English teacher who needed the job so badly. And I was finding that there was lots of work at the Publications Office in editing and proofreading manuscripts. I could always volunteer my time, have enough to do, and be free to come and go as the situation dictated. As it turned out to do.

So I made it back to the States and was there for Tom's Fifth Anniversary Observance on June 9. How people kept in with us and kept coming to these things never ceased to amaze me. It was the year also that Kit turned 30 on June 18 and she and Joan had a *party* at the house on Gatlin Street. Joan's birthday came soon on July 2 and Dad's on July 15, and it seemed like celebration summer. I came and went to the cabin and up to the top of Tom's mountain land, breaking an axle on the Honda Civic on the jeep trail there. August 2 came. "Iraq has invaded Kuwait!" *(God, what will this mean? Will "the 17" be released?! But what then? What more?)* But American life went on as usual of course, and that next week as Kuwaitis died and suffered and we heard definitive news that indeed "the 17" Dawa prisoners held in Kuwait jails had been released, the annual

Scottish Highland Festival in Denver put on by the St. Andrew Society was celebrated with bagpipes, a fair, dog shows, food, clan tents, dancers, and the traditional athletic contests—caber tossing, shot put, and all. Kit, Joan, and I put on
our "Sutherland Ales" T-shirts and jeans and went down with visiting brother
John and children to participate. I had been asked to say a few words, and never
loath I gave them "an address," which cheek by jowl with a letter of greetings
from President Bush they printed in their next newsletter:

> To All at the Highland Games ... It is a wonderful pleasure for us to be able to be
> here at the Highland Games this year—for there's something important about these
> games that makes them special to us. For the tradition they represent is one of con-
> test, perseverance, mental and physical strength, determination, loyalty, honor, and
> survival—the finest values of Scotland in fact that her people, her tartan, and her
> pipes have taken throughout the world. Tom would have us as his family tell you
> that this is as current and real as the contest he's engaged in, and I know that he's
> reaching deep into his native heritage of Scotland and his chosen heritage of America
> for the strength to carry on and come through. This strength comes from commu-
> nity—Tom knows he's not alone, and he would have us also express somehow to
> you as extended family his heartfelt thanks for the continuing care, concern, and
> support you have given through these years. You're wonderful—we love you—and
> may Tom be here next year to say these things to you in person. Here's tae him and
> here's tae ye.

29   Back to the Bekaa

Late August 1990. The *Tehran Times* struck again—forecasting the imminent release of Brian Keenan. Finally, Brian back to his beloved Ireland. He must have convinced Islamic Jihad that the Irish could never give them anything for him. Joy for us too—one more Islamic Jihad guest going home. But for several days, there was no announcement—we began to wonder if this time they had made a mistake in Tehran. But no—in the middle of the night again, Abu Ali, back on the scene from long ago, and Mahmoud arrived and told us to get ready. In a few minutes, we were back in the company of John McCarthy, first time since "the Pit" over in the Bekaa. And we were back in the very room where I had spent a week with Frank Reed. The Fadlallah Mosque Apartment again. Terry's mattress and chain were just inside the right of the door. Mine were end to end with John's to the left.

"You just missed Brian!" said John, in greeting us. "I think he has gone home. At least I hope so." "I know," said Terry. "They have been talking all about it on the radio, and the *Tehran Times* has been predicting his release for days now. In fact, this is the second time they have called it." "On the radio?" asked John, a little incredulous. "You mean you bloody Yanks have had a radio all this time? You bastards have had it a lot better than us Brits. And we clearly deserve much more than you do, you buggars!" "They just recognize quality, John-Boy," Terry rebutted. "The Islamic Jihad has its priorities straight, old boy." We had a lot of catching up to do.

Brian and John hadn't come back to Beirut until October 10, 1989, eight full months after Terry and me. They too had been stuck into this same room with Frank, and had spent seven months as a threesome until the Shoe's release on April 29—then a further three months here for John alone with Brian. But the most exciting news John had for us was that Terry Waite was in a room on the other side of the wall to which Terry Anderson was now chained. Brian had discovered this while exercising one day. He had tapped his name on the wall, and back came the name "Terry Waite!" That was all he had dared to do. But it was enough, for now Brian, if indeed he had gone home, would be able to give the wonderful news to his family. As we had heard many times on the radio, no one knew a thing about Waite—he had simply disappeared off the face of the earth.

We had more news for John. He had almost no idea about the Gulf War, the collapse of communism in the Soviet Union, the fall of the Berlin Wall. Mahmoud had given him a vague idea that momentous things had happened, but had been, as always, nonspecific. John was astonished to get the "rest of the story," and at first almost thought we were pulling his leg. But when we asked Abu Ali to be sure and bring the radio, and got an immediate promise that he would, *bukra*, John began to believe us. Abu Ali promised also to bring over the Exercycle, which further astonished John for *they* had been asking for one for months!

Terry lost little time in establishing contact with Waite, who had been in a *total* blackout for his entire three and a half years. He too was absolutely astonished at what Terry, slowly tapping away over the course of several mornings before the guards were up from their postprayer sleep, had to tell him. Terry advised him, "Ask for a radio, TW. You never know. Maybe they will give you one. We've had ours for well over a year now." Next morning, he told us that he had been promised one "after some times," which he took for a polite refusal. A couple of days later he was elated to receive a little transistor that was picking up the BBC World Service perfectly. We began exchanging views on the news. I would relay to Terry what I had just heard on the early morning programs, VOA and RFI, and Waite would give us his latest stuff. So began our dual monitoring of stations, which lasted until our release.

This place was much better than anything we had had so far. There was even a Toshiba washing machine in the bathroom, with the guards doing all our laundry—such as that was, undershorts, boxer shorts, T-shirts. What a vast improvement over the old stripping-the-water-method that Father had taught us that had *never* gotten things very clean! Now they came back fresh and clean. The guards even dried things for us in the sun up on the roof. Great advance. The food was *much* better too—lots of french fries, even some steak once in a while, and a cup of coffee from time to time. We all soon became addicted to *mana-eesh*, an Arabic specialty bread lightly leavened and laced with olive oil and sesame seeds that we got once or twice a week for breakfast—a welcome change from dry pita bread and cheese. Candy came more frequently—Mars Bars, Snickers, and Milky Ways were their favorites—and we always got what *they* liked. Our pleas for straight chocolate—a bar of Cadbury's or Nestlé's—were never heeded, but never mind.

Exercise improved—each person on returning from the toilet was allowed to stay off the chain until the next fellow returned. We walked around the room (thank God, no David here!) and rode the Exercycle along with the guards. *They* competed with each other and rode it *extremely* hard until it came partially apart. It still worked, but not well, so Terry and I set to, found out exactly which piece was broken, and asked them to get it in one of the stores in Beirut. Mistake. They never did get the part and lost the original part off the bike, so it was useless from that day until we left. Live and learn.

John gave us an update on Frank Reed. It appeared that Frank had reverted just about all the way to his semicatatonic state, and had lain most of the day with his blindfold down, thinking about goodness knows what. Had not talked much, except when John or Brian had spoken to him, and in general, had thrown a rather depressing aura all over the room. John still thought that I had been far too hard on old Franky, but by now had a much clearer view of why. Frank had had all kinds of hallucinations and even told them that he knew that both Terry and I had been released, and that I was already dead! Of cancer. Fortunately, "the news of my demise had been rather premature!" John thus confirmed what we felt about Frank when we had seen him at his release.

When Terry was in the bathroom one day, I told John about Terry's father and brother, and about how I had refrained from telling him. "I think we should, however," said John. "It will give him some time to get used to the fact, and won't be such a shock when he is going through the euphoria of his release and freedom." So after the "toilet run," I broke the news to Terry. As I suspected, he took it very calmly, and said that he was not too surprised at either one. Rich had had a much longer lease on life than the medical profession had predicted; but they had all known the end could come anytime. His father's health too had been wobbly for some time, as a result of emphysema, evidently caused by a lifetime of driving a cement truck.

Terry continued to develop a very close relationship with John, being, I suppose, glad to have someone other than me to talk to. I felt somewhat the same way. We had known John for months in the Bekaa, so it was like meeting a long-lost buddy. John's and Terry's mattresses had been adjacent there, and they had been a matched pair of journalists, while my mattress was alongside of Brian's, and he and I had the AUB-university experience in common, so we had seemed a little more compatible. The Scots and the Irish have always been united against the English in any case. But John's aristocratic background also intrigued Terry a great deal, and he had been and was now very interested in "Public School Life" and all that it had done for John. John now showed a nice interest in learning chess, which I had never done even though we had had a chess set for many months over in the Toufeili Apartment. Terry found him an excellent pupil, and they spent hour after hour quietly poring over the chessboard. John made fast progress and soon was a mild challenge to Terry, to the delight of both. I sat quietly reading and catching up on some of the books that Terry had already digested. John read at about the same speed as myself, or perhaps even a little slower, so was much more normal.

Our companion next door began to cough rather badly, especially at night. Terry and John both thought we should attempt to get him moved in beside us, and began to agitate for this. I held back, not wanting to destroy in any way the rather remarkable calm and easy relationship that we three had with each other. Each seemed to "read" the others, and to know what they wanted in terms of speaking, sleeping, reading, comfort, debating. The ambience was special.

But Terry kept on. "Abu Ali. There is a man next door. We can hear him coughing, and he sounds very ill. We would like to invite him to come in with us, please?" Terry did not dare tell him just how much we knew about the man next door! But Abu Ali had a story. "Terry, the man next door is Lebanese. He very bad man. You no like this man. Not good for you, he moving here with you. Better he stay his place!" Terry even asked the Hajj who had appeared briefly, but again to no avail.

Meanwhile, the Lebanese situation continued outside. The news had been predicting an invasion by the Syrian Army, and General Aoun was daily strutting his stuff on LBC. There were impressive scenes of thousands of young Christian men and women, all of them clustered around the Presidential Palace, occupied for now by the brave general, the self-proclaimed president and savior of Lebanon. He would *never* leave, he vowed. Daily my recollections of Adolf Hitler were strengthened. The resemblance from my youthful memories was striking. And all of these young people would make a human shield that would never yield. Now came the supreme test. On October 12, all hell broke loose in Beirut. I monitored the whole thing all morning, and gave Terry and John a running commentary. We were moved immediately into a different room, on the sheltered side of the building, for shells were raining in—it was another Holy Hell. And all these young supporters did exactly what I had suspected they would, and certainly what *I* would have done in the face of a terrible bombardment from the powerful air force and army of Hafiz al-Assad of Syria—they fled instantly. Only a total idiot would stick around in a hail of *real bombs*, more powerful by far than even 155-millimeter shells. But the most pathetic of all was the behavior of Aoun. Within three hours, the radio was reporting that Aoun had fled from the Palace down to the French embassy, where he was granted asylum. He remained there for many weeks, to the consternation and great anger of the "legitimate government" of Lebanon. They wanted him very badly, and intended to make him pay for all the evils he had perpetrated on the country and the destruction he had wrought. But they could not invade the sanctity of an embassy, so it was a standoff, with a very strained diplomatic relationship between the two governments. The French government was showing solidarity with its Catholic brethren in Lebanon, who had also received considerable moral support during all this time from Pope John Paul. We ourselves had seen on TV several delegations of French deputies visiting the East Side, assuring them support for the Christian cause.

By noon that day, however, it was all over, and we moved back to our own room. The Syrians systematically disarmed all the militias in Beirut, and I was convinced that *now* we must *surely* go home; no way were they going to drag us all the way back to the Bekaa, another real stronghold of Hizbollah. Surely this was the perfect time for them to call a halt to all this nonsense. *Wrong!* We were soon on our way, but not home. This time we were not so badly taped; only a light job on each of us, then into the sacks used inside the city. And this time into the trunk of a car, not the spare tire spot on the truck normally used for transmountain shipment of hostages. The problem this time was a leaky exhaust system pouring fumes into the trunk—nearly gassed us to death. We were both sick as dogs by the time we got into the northern Bekaa, even though the midnight journey took only a little over an hour. The main Beirut-Damascus highway was now open, the long Christian-Druze feud that had closed the road for years finally over.

Out of the trunk and onto the floor of our new room, ground level of a house built on a hillside. I was very close to vomiting, and only supreme willpower had kept us from throwing up all over ourselves in the sacks. I was even worse than Terry, and desperately pleaded with Mahmoud—fortunately the man in charge of this move—to bring me a bucket. This he did and I told him, "Never do that to us again ... just kill us."

John arrived shortly afterward and told us that he had been in another trunk with Terry Waite. Waite was stuck in the room next door, across a sort of hallway that led to the outside. Our room was a drafty place, the doors not a good fit at all, and the windows not much better. But we had *fresh air!* Hallelujah. Next morning, Mahmoud took us to a toilet in the kitchen area, adjoining our room. Then he brought Terry Waite through our room to the toilet: "Good morning, gentlemen," sang out

Mr. Waite, cheerily as could be. "Good morning, Terry," we chorused—no snarls of prohibition from Mahmoud. It apparently didn't occur to him to question how on earth we knew that it was Terry Waite who was talking! The next move was to ask Mahmoud if we could have a conversation with Terry Waite. "I don't know. But I will ask. Maybe it is possible."

Another miracle. That evening, TW, as we christened him to differentiate between the two Terrys, was led in and sat down on our mattresses to talk to us. Mahmoud insisted on attending the whole session, so that it was not as relaxed and open as it might have been. But it was a start. John said hardly a word, and Terry and I kept urging him: "John, it's your turn to speak. After all, he's your countryman. Go ahead." But he demurred. "I will have a chance later on. Don't worry about me." It sounded strange to me, somehow. Terry and I tried to outdo each other, and we got many of the superficial preliminaries out of the way. Next day, the Hajj arrived out of the blue, and came in to check on us. "Hajj," said Terry, "we know that Terry Waite is next door. You know that we know that Terry Waite is next door. We know that you know that we know that Terry Waite is next door. So why don't you let him come in and join us?" Mahmoud was translating, for the Hajj spoke little English. Soon he was chuckling, as the humor of what Terry had just said to him dawned on him. "Okay," he agreed. "Soon, but not now. You must wait some days. Then he can come with you."

A couple of weeks passed before it happened, and we all moved upstairs by an outside stair up the hillside to a room that we had heard them preparing. Lots of hammering and sawing, and though we were not sure why it was going on, it all became apparent when we were put into a room now outfitted with a stove to keep us warm in the winter of the Bekaa. The floor of the valley is at about 3,000 feet (1,000 meters) and winters get cold. Even the early summer mornings when I had visited in the good old times had been quite fresh, so we were very glad to see the stove, with a long pipe crossing over our head and through the wall as a chimney. A strange kind of stove it was too; the fuel oil was allowed to drip onto a flat surface, where it burned without any wick or jet; the faster the drip, the more the heat. Very simple. I had never seen a contraption like this. But later, we had water heaters that worked in the same primitive way. The only problem was that they were difficult to light, and they went out fairly often. Setting them just right was perhaps a bit above the abilities of the average Islamic Jihad warrior.

Still at ground level in this room and next to a—wonder of wonders—*modern* bathroom. Here we were arranged four across the room: McCarthy, Anderson, Sutherland, and Waite. The two Englishmen were as far apart as they could get! But we were organized by age group into two pairs. Terry and John took up their chess games again, and spent more hours than ever in total absorption, the kind that only chess players experience. This threw TW and me into long conversations, mainly on my part. I saw clearly that after three and half years of isolation, TW's attention span was extremely short, a minute or two at best. He saw it and reports it that I bored on interminably. However that may be, I tried to get him to concentrate, but his mind would wander, and he would pop another question clear out of the blue. I kept working on him though, and little by little, his mind was stretched, and we could have longer and longer discussions on a wide range of topics. We had much in common: fairly close in age; both had owned an MG, and indeed he still had his; both loved music, especially classical, though he knew music much better than I; both radio addicts, and neither of us cared much about TV; both spent time in East Africa, he in Uganda with the Church of England, I next door in Ethiopia with the International Livestock Center for Africa; on and on went the list of common interests.

It was fun to have a new mind in our midst again, who could bring us interests and information that none of us had. He reintroduced a religious presence among all of us sinners, and began to offer "services" on Sunday evening. Even sitting, at six feet eight inches he dominated, and he gave his thoughts each week. Of the four of us, I was the least enthused about this, but went along with it. He seemed to love doing it, and had preached some in his free days. Soon, however, the other two grew even more tired of his sermons than I did, and began to suggest diplomatically that we should not have them much longer. But he didn't take the hint, and kept on readying himself every Sunday evening. Finally, I was the one who rebelled outright and refused to participate any longer, but that was later.

Books? Both Terrys now raised the cry. In a few days, a dozen or more arrived—but all were by Barbara Cartland! TW balked—"I absolutely refuse to read that kind of nonsense!" "But TW," I said facetiously, "she is a relative of your friend the Queen. You have to pay her homage." "Only by marriage through Princess Di," he retorted. Terry chipped in. "Words on the page, man. Words on the page. Better than nothing." He read every one. Then twice. Then three times. Still no more books. Instead of books, we got magazines: *Time, Newsweek, U.S. News and World Report, L'Express* (the French equivalent of *Time*), *Business Week*, and best of all *The Economist*, perhaps the best magazine in the world. Sometimes we got newspapers too, including even the *Financial Times* out of London. One Sunday edition arrived, which to TW's glee carried a huge section of book reviews, which he devoured with relish. But despite his constant requests for more of the same, they never came. I got a bang out of his addiction to the book review sections of everything. He professed an addiction to books, and as for the rest of the *Financial Times,* he never even cast it a glance. Almost the same with *The Economist*—first part he read was the book review section. Then the section on the United Kingdom, understandably. The sections on finance, business, technology, etc. were left unread. As for *Business Week*, it was gross in his opinion. Much too concerned about making money. "But, TW," protested Terry, "that is what it is all about! Specialized in business matters, and how to make more money. That's why people buy it!" "Harrumph," snorted TW. Meantime, Terry and I were devouring both *Business Week* and *The Economist,* and trying to understand the complexities of finance and investment, subjects rather unfamiliar to both of us—neither of us had ever had much money to invest! We had great fun developing potential portfolios for when we were released, and relished getting our hands on all that money that was piling up for us on the outside!

For two or three months, we all got along famously. Waite had many experiences behind him as the special envoy of the Archbishop of Canterbury, and he regaled us with fascinating tales of his travels. Obviously he loved to travel, and was very proud of all the places he had been and all the people he had met. Admittedly, he was doing lots of name-dropping, but then we all liked to do that—Terry, too, as a journalist had met and interviewed many famous people in his shorter life. But Waite maybe had met more. Gradually, he revealed some of the more outstanding things he had done, such as negotiating the release of British hostages in both Libya and Iran, for which he received copious praise, and the distinction of being named by "Radio Four" Britain's "Outstanding Young Man for 1985," the same year that Margaret Thatcher had been named Britain's "Outstanding Woman." *We were impressed!* He knew Uganda, and indeed much of Africa, over which he had traveled extensively. He had also seen large chunks of India, where I had never been, though Terry Anderson had, and could discourse with him. I found his travel tales fascinating, and spent many hours listening to him. He was familiar with the United States and professed to have crossed the Atlantic so many times that he could not even begin to count the number of crossings he had made. He considered himself almost a native, so familiar was he with the North American continent. He didn't know Colorado very well, however, and was quite interested in my long tales about the Rockies and our cabin ten miles south of Estes Park. We dreamed of sitting on the deck and gazing at Longs Peak to the west and the Twin Sisters to the east while we sipped my favorite recipe for old-fashioneds. I told him too all about how I had done most of the work on the place: the wiring, the plumbing, the cabinets, the paneling, the floors, the ceilings, the whole works—Terry Anderson had already heard all of that, so he was content to play chess with John McCarthy who was improving at the game. Waite had done quite a bit of remodeling in his own home in London, south of the Thames in the area called Blackheath, though he was not at all mechanically minded and had very few practical skills, so far as I could tell. But he was proud of his home. He told me all about the layout. It had four floors, as I recall, which gave privacy for each member of his family.

Soon after he joined us, I began to ask Waite about the circumstances surrounding his efforts to get us free: Whom had he talked to of our captors? Where had he met with them? How often? What had he been offering them for our release? I was overflowing with curiosity. His response: "Now is not the time to be talking about those things, you know." I looked at him in amazement. "It's not!? Man, we'll *never* have more time to talk about them! I'm curious. Tell me about them. Tell me the whole story." "No. There are people listening outside the door, you know." "Good Lord," I said, "they won't understand your English accent, TW. No way, man!" The guards couldn't follow him at the best of times, let alone behind a closed door. "Well," he said, "someday we'll talk about it all when we are at your cabin in the Rockies, drinking an old-fashioned on the deck." Waite had been very intrigued by the idea of going up into the mountains after our release to recuperate and vacation. I had encouraged all of this, first of all because it gave us something pleasant to think and talk about, and also because it was something marvelous to look forward to. And I was fairly charmed by TW's suave manner and free-flowing conversation by this time.

Soon again, however, TW's asthma began to really get to him, and his wheezing and whistling became almost intolerable. During the day, he now wanted to be talking all the time to at least one of us—generally me, since I was right alongside of him—and he was becoming a little overbearing. But come "bedtime," his wheezing and whistling would begin in earnest, just when the rest of us wanted to get to sleep. He would begin to hyperventilate, and it appeared to me that he was *deliberately* doing this so that he could make even more noise and generate more sympathy from us. Terry Anderson rose to the occasion in true Christian fashion, and spent hours at a time trying to get him calmed down and to dissuade him from hyperventilating. Gad, it got old, listening to that horrendous noise. He is a huge man, and was practically making the roof shake—a solid concrete ceiling at that. I began to lose patience with him, and he proved ever more irritating to me.

We began to argue about religion. I accused the church of having promulgated over the centuries much too simple an image of God—a God who is a kindly old gentleman living somewhere up there over our heads in a place called

Heaven, listening to billions of prayers like some sort of supercomputer and deciding which ones should be approved today and which ones should not. "Nonsense," he exploded. "Of course we don't foster that kind of image." "That's surely the impression I've had in all the churches I've ever attended!" Came back a further snort. He was constantly boasting about all the traveling he had done, to everywhere in the world, it seemed, and always by first-class air. That seemed somehow out of keeping with the mission of a church, any church, and even a waste of good, hard-earned church money, so I challenged him on it. That *really* stung him. I soon learned that he could never stand to be on the defensive—on anything. In his life, he had obviously learned some really effective defensive mechanisms, and he would strike back vehemently at the least sign of attack with a fast offensive movement to ward it off; and I must say, it proved effective. His defensive posture frequently featured his explosive "*Nonsense!*" delivered with such force and conviction that it really did cause one to pause and reflect for a moment. But after dozens of such ripostes to *my* statements, I grew tired of hearing them and would reply coldly—"My friend, I *don't speak* nonsense. I *think* before I speak, and I *resent* your accusations. *Cut it out, dammit!*" These exchanges got more and more bitter, and once even ended in a wrestling match, half serious, half jesting, in which I finally managed to pin him. This was no real test of his or my ability, though, for he was still suffering severely from the asthma.

He was also incredibly insensitive to others and their needs—no compunctions about interrupting and posing questions or raising any kind of subject *he* wished to talk about. When he turned over in bed, it sounded as if a herd of elephants had just entered. When he blew his nose, he practically deafened all of us. When he snored, it made the walls shake in the night. His insensitivity revealed itself too in the way he treated the guards—he had the utmost contempt for them, and would make sarcastic and even grossly insulting comments about them in their hearing and presence, much to the discomfiture of Terry Anderson who kept warning him, "I wouldn't say these things, TW. They understand more than you think, and they will get after you." Frankly, I felt that they were always on the lookout for an excuse to give him a good beating as they had done frequently to Brian Keenan. We all realized that they didn't like TW, and made it obvious in so many ways—they always gave him a really short piece of chain allowing only a minimum of movement, despite our constantly asking them to please give him more. When he asked for Kleenex, they would bring him three or four pieces, whereas when John asked, they brought him a whole box! Same with Terry, whom they also liked and respected. Both of them had great long chains, much longer than mine, and infinitely longer than TW's; the "pecking order," I guess, had established itself from Islamic Jihad.

In the early days, Terry had taken on TW in debate in his usual aggressive fashion, and Waite was even less match for him than Jacobsen had been, or I. This led to a rather embarrassing situation for Waite, who was obviously not accustomed to anyone challenging his authority, so he made it rather plain that he didn't exactly love Terry. But an interesting accident changed all of that. The pointer on the dial of Waite's radio was sticking as it moved along the dial, and TW had already had evidence of Terry's manual dexterity, so he asked, "Terry, how about taking a look at my radio?" Terry was a little offhand with him. "Wait a bit, TW, I'll do it in the next while." But he didn't get to it, and finally after several days, TW, frustrated, took a shot at fixing it himself, and pulled the two halves of the radio apart so thoroughly that wires parted from their moorings— power lines, antenna wires, speaker connections all severed and sadly lying around the radio in all directions. No more BBC. TW was completely mortified and in total despair. In one pull, he had lost his lifeline. *Then* Terry came to the rescue! He took the radio and worked on it for hours, finally pulling in the BBC. But it was not right yet, so he wanted to work on it some more. TW was in favor of leaving well enough alone, since at least he had a weak signal from London. But Terry wanted to persevere, and in about two more days, with nothing more than a nail clipper and some superglue, he had it back almost as good as new. For my part, I thought that this whole episode was little short of a miracle. I have done my fair share of fixing things in my day, but *never* could I have pulled that one off. From that day forth, TW held Terry in the highest esteem, and even when Terry was hard on him, he felt that he had to take it in good spirits.

Every time "Sports Roundup" came on the BBC, TW would snort in disgust and very pointedly switch off his radio and slap it down on his bed. I myself enjoy sports of all kinds, and gradually began to applaud the arrival of the sports programs, to his annoyance. In our small cell, little antagonisms like this gradually assumed more importance and became growing sources of conflict, a fact not lost on either Terry or John, who tried to dissuade me from picking on him and keeping a constant tension in the air. I was, however, still less than kind to him, and the other two, regardless of their own feelings, soon tired of my constant bickering about TW and my complaining about how hard it was to be in the same cell with him. "Cut out your carping, Tom."

The stove had been proving a bigger blessing than I had thought, for in order to keep it burning, it needed lots of air, which it actively pulled in from the rest of the apartment and exhausted it through the chimney. For almost the first time in five and a half years, we had a constant circulation of relatively fresh air. But the stove also gave off fumes, and as TW began to feel that these were worsening his asthma, that set off another argument between the two of us. I wanted the warmth, but even more the fresh air. He wanted it shut off, since he was scarcely able to breathe at all, whether the air was fresh or not. He won, as of course he should. So the stove was shut off for a time. But TW's asthma didn't improve much at all. Terry got after the guards, especially Mahmoud; "You simply have to get this man to a doctor or he is going to die. He is very, very ill. Can't you see that?" They had to consult with their bosses, as usual. They had no authority to decide anything as major as a visit to or from a doctor. "I am sorry. I have not the order." The old refrain—but when they did consult with their boss, the order came pronto. And TW was taken late at night down into the town of Baalbek in the back of a station wagon, and was able to follow the direction taken. Down a steep hill, turn to the left, ten minutes up a road, over a bridge, a few more blocks in the town, and they were in the front hallway of a physician. After a brief examination, he diagnosed asthma all right, prescribed Ventalin pills and a couple of gooey medicines, and TW was on his way back into our midst. The gooey stuff was to be taken every four hours, and the guards followed that rigorously, along with his daily dose of pills.

It all helped very little. Terry told them, "You know guys, my father had emphysema for much of his later life, and his doctor prescribed a Ventalin inhaler for him, and it really worked wonders for him." "Terry, no speak. Doctor said Ventalin pills, okay?" "All right," agreed Terry. "I was only trying to help, for these pills don't seem to be doing very much good." "Quiet. No speak." TW went on more or less as before his medical attention—very ill, to say the least. Finally, out of the blue one day, Mahmoud walked in and threw something onto TW's bed. "Here, Terry Waite. Tek." It was an inhaler! TW took a deep breath and inhaled a huge quantity at the first gulp, and was almost instantly cured for the ensuing months, clear into summer, when he apparently didn't need the inhaler at all. We all felt very sorry for TW who had had to put up with all that agony for many months, when blessed relief was a simple inhaler away. And we could resume using the stove!

Then came Desert Shield. We watched the buildup of the Western forces in Saudi Arabia, and even Terry was amazed. "My God," I said, "with this kind of force, they will blow Saddam clear out of the water." We had long discussions with Mahmoud about the impending war. He was very curious about what we were hearing, and how it compared with their Arabic newscasts. They too were beginning to appreciate the might of the West, and in particular, the United States, and starting to evince just a little bit of doubt about their own situation.

Meantime, Terry and John were getting more serious about their chess. Terry thought that if only he had a second chessboard, just a little cheap thing, it would allow him to show so much more to John. He could leave the original board intact, while he showed John what all the alternative strategies might be for any given situation. Ask, and thou shalt receive. He did, and did. Now we had two complete sets, and TW and I began to take advantage of the periods when the second was not in use, and began to pick up the rudiments of the game. Neither of us would have caused much concern to Bobby Fischer, Anatoly Karpov, or Gary Kasparov. We never even presented any problem to Terry Anderson, who is, he explained, city championship caliber. I concluded that there must be one heck of a lot of good chess players, and that Waite and I were pretty far down the line.

Wonder of wonders, we also got a deck of cards, brand new, shiny, and slick—a vast improvement over Terry's homemade jobs. And we had a "foursome." "Who knows how to play bridge?" asked Terry. "I don't." "Nor do I," from John. "Nor I," chorused TW. That left me. Should I admit that I had at least played for several years long ago with the Animal Science Department at CSU? I wasn't sure that I could remember much about it anyway, but here we are, stuck in this hole. Why not? It would help pass the time, so: "Well, guys. I have to confess that I have played, but I never liked the damn game!" "Hi-ho," chortled Terry, "never mind about that. Teach us now!" I struggled with the rules, and brought out from the inner recesses of my mind what I could recall. We asked the guards for a Goren, the bible of bridge players. Result—same as always. But what I couldn't remember, we made up. The players soon sorted themselves out. Terry Anderson was a veritable card shark, and had even ventured out among the poker pirates of Beirut who played for big stakes—the Lebanese *love* to gamble! Terry Waite was at the other end of the scale, and had absolutely no "card sense" whatsoever. John and I were about the same level of mediocrity. So for a week or two, the two Terrys paired up. Despite Anderson's skill, he couldn't compensate for TW, and John and I won every hand day after day, to the point that even Terry got tired of losing. He decided he had had enough and demanded that we switch around. We now played 8 hands with each partner, a total of 24 hands of bridge every afternoon. I couldn't believe I was playing that much bridge, and asked the others never to tell my wife. We improved, especially in the *playing* of the hands, and even became quite expert in the defensive aspects although always frustrated that we didn't have the correct rules for bidding. But we did pass time!

30   Good-Bye to the Green Line

August 1990. Brian Keenan *out!* We got in touch by telephone while he was in the hospital in Dublin and talked several times. "How about coming up to Scotland in September when I'm on my way back to Beirut," I said. "It would be great for all Tom's family and me to get to see and talk to you in person—and you could see those farms you've heard about." So it was set up. He and his friend-bodyguard-manager Frank flew to Glasgow, I flew into Edinburgh, and we got together at Peter and Jane's house with the rest of the brothers and sisters—Elizabeth, Margaret, Willie and Ginny, Lena and Dunc—all gathered around. Having carried Brian on my conscience those many years, I was so glad to see him, now a softer, quieter, grayer, thinner Brian. We talked and talked and talked through dinner and the afternoon, keeping at bay the media hanging around outside. It was Willie's wife Ginny who went outside finally to tell them to go. I'm not sure what she said but they went! And then Peter and Willie took Brian on a tour around their farms and we all had a meal together, and then I remember Brian talking to me alone in the evening and giving me advice in his quiet, quiet voice on what to do for Tom when he came out. I listened, but when Tom came out I didn't do any of the things Brian told me because Tom was his own man and decided for himself what he wanted to do. I respected that.

Next day, Brian and Frank were off to Dublin and I soon after for London and Beirut, making sure that their trip to Scotland had been reimbursed as Tom's gift to his family and to Brian and that Brian's things that I had stored for him at AUB were sent back to him in Ireland through Dr. Hallab's office. What a joy that he was home! But now what of the others? The anti-Iraq rhetoric had fired up, Baker was shuttling from country to country and gathering momentum for a showdown, and how in this world could Americans be released? They couldn't.

We resigned ourselves to wait and see, to work and wait and see. M came and went, came and went again. The January 15 deadline for Saddam Hussein's capitulation was announced and Baker's shuttling and the rhetoric continued.

I took on a new project—the letters of Daniel Bliss, the founder of AUB, letters written home to his wife and children in Amherst during the year 1873–1874, the year that the construction on College Hall at the then Syrian Protestant College was begun. I was fascinated by those letters that the family had found in the old home on Bliss Street in 1956 before it was razed. They had been in manuscript form until the 1970s when Belle Dorman Rugh, a granddaughter of Dr. Bliss, had gotten them typed up and had started the process toward publication. Now Al Howell, chairman of the AUB Foundation, was engineering that publication, having himself done the work to write the quite voluminous notes on people, places, times, and events. I thought I would only proofread, but it turned out that there were pictures to find way up on the top floor of the AUB library, and pictures even to take—such as the old bell still in the bell tower. What an experience to climb up with the photographer into the tower and see the bell and the clock, the Seth Thomas four-sided clock that had been there since the turn of the century. The pictures would still be there in my mind a year later when the bomb brought it all down.

Among the old photos of the early AUB days that I found in the library were daguerreotypes of President Bliss and the first faculty members, the first graduating class, the Medical Building, and faded photos of groups of unknown people as well as the completed College Hall. These I collected to be used for the volume of letters. And then there was one that had presumably been used around the turn of the century to raise money in the United States for the college that at first made me angry and then grabbed my mind. It was a photo taken of a well-dressed society woman looking at a long, narrow placard in a glass case surrounded by pictures of the Syrian Protestant College and on it the words in large letters: "*Look What America Is Doing for the Middle East!*" My instant reaction was "What self-righteous, priggish, condescending piety!" But the next instant there it was suddenly in its historical context—it was those self-righteous, priggish, condescending, pious, anti-Catholic, Protestant, Arabic-speaking missionaries who went out to save the world who raised the money to build a medical college on a barren Mediterranean headland in what was then Greater Syria, which would become from 1919 onward the American University of Beirut with English as the medium of instruction and the place for which we were willing to give our lives in 1985. What an evolution of institution, what a tangled skein of motives that went into the ongoing creation of a university. To the medical college the adding of all the other colleges and then the cutting back as the war in Lebanon pressed in the 1970s and 1980s: the dropping of the fine arts program and the freezing of Ph.D. and M.S. programs and even undergraduate programs in psychology and others. Tenaciously, AUB had hung on while wars had come and gone around it, and not just "our" war. Uncle Edgar had written home years ago about an Italian-Turkish gunboat battle off Beirut in 1912, prelude to World War I, which he watched from the tower that I had just climbed in my turn:

> The Italian vessels were completely enveloped in smoke out of which came crimson flashes of fire and enormous detonations that shook the building. In the city everything was chaos; the exploding shells tore the buildings along the water front to pieces as if they were cracker boxes, spouting the water high into the air and throwing huge stones and wreckage about until it was impossible to estimate the amount of damage that was being done.

And Hazel Porter, mother of my childhood friend Lois, and whose husband, Howard, was acting dean of agriculture in 1958 during that revolution that brought in American Marines, wrote:

> We got a paper today that reports 10 killed and 50 injured here, with 11 killed in Tripoli and 150 injured. Trouble has spread into many sections and in the mountains. The Opposition insists that President Chamoun resign or they won't call off the strike. He says he will serve to the end of his term in late summer and then they can decide what to do about him .... . The American embassy is right on the job and so are AUB authorities. There is a whole emergency set-up .... .

And Al Buckley told us hair-raising stories of going out to find eggs for breakfast on the morning of the worst day of shelling in 1975.

But AUB endured and endures still. With its problems. We discovered almost the first day we arrived that AUB was a microcosm of the country as Ann Kerr also avers in her book, *Come with Me from Lebanon.* In a sense that was good because you could read the tenor of the country; in a sense it was hard because most of what was going on was warfare. When the Palestinians were "in" the others were "out" and pressured. When the Christians were "in" the Moslems were "out" and pressured. When the Moslems were in control, they called the shots and their sheikhs spoke in the Assembly Hall. The campus was ringed and invaded by kidnappings. Americans left under threats and then under passport ban, and the Lebanese took over the running of the campus albeit under the directive of the New York office. With a Christian as deputy president, the number of vice presidents climbed to six so that all sects could be represented in the senior administration. As Syria determines the president of Lebanon, so the new president of AUB since 1993 is of Syrian descent. Peace has not yet come to Lebanon—the south and the Syrian-Israeli issues are still to be resolved—so AUB will mirror and contend with the conflicts. And yet survive. We are sure of that and hope for that. And the greatest hope of all is that the American University of Beirut will go so far beyond not only self-righteousness, condescension, and yes, corruption, but also so far beyond the bitter and yes, deadly internal power struggles, that a true university, international in scope and faculty and student body and cross-fertilizing ideas and cultural exchange, can emerge to be a real "lighthouse" for the Middle East.

October 12—the Syrians moved against Aoun. Finally. Again we appreciated in full the infinite and strategic patience of Assad. As he had done in 1987 when he moved his troops into Beirut, he waited again and let Aoun rant and then he chose his timing. This time he just went into East Beirut with Hraoui's Lebanese Army and they stormed the Presidential Palace where Aoun was holed up and another war in the East was there but then it was over in six hours and Aoun was holed up instead in the French embassy. At the same time that Christians and Moslems embraced on the Green Line, anti-Syrian sentiment was rife and bitter in the Christian East, but the shortness of the war defused that as life at last "normalized" in the area (shades of the feelings to come with the Gulf War in terms of anti-American sentiment there). And then it was time to disarm all militias and reintegrate Beirut. The Lebanese forces moved their arms out of town and the Syrians moved into the southern suburbs and the Hizbollah militia moved their arms down south and their hostages to Baalbek in the Bekaa— I could actually "feel" Tom going away from me, "feel" that he was no longer close in my vicinity. But it was all "rational," power-imperatived, understandable. And Hrawi became in fact president of a Lebanon now divided into Syrian- and Israeli-controlled components—as though unwritten, unspoken even perhaps, agreements had allocated the south to Israeli control, the northern two-thirds to Syrian control. It made for security in the north, which included Beirut, but it continued the war zone in the south as Syria left Hizbollah there with arms to fight Israel and its Israeli-backed Christian army in Israel's so-called "security zone." At long last, however, Beirut's Green Line had fallen.

I worked at my work—AUH nurses' English program, editing the Bliss letters and Malcolm Kerr's memorial volume—and I settled into an almost withdrawn, ascetic lifestyle. Except that our small group of "internationals" kept working against the ascetic—going to movie theaters (we saw *The Bear* with three other persons one night in a theater built for 1,000), having music nights, happy hours, and as a matter of course the Halloween party at the Buckleys. I found, however, that I missed the daily interactions and stimulations of the Hariri Program, missed the young people, and missed the give-and-take with my wonderful Lebanese colleagues there.

For Thanksgiving, I celebrated twice. Jean-Marie and I as remaining AUB Americans from the West Side went over one day to the Salems' in Baabda on the East Side, a ghost of an echo of the old tradition that used to reign at AUB in the "good old days" when everyone on the American faculty brought food to someone's house for the feast at which the Lebanese could be guests for a day they did not by custom celebrate. Elie Salem had been the dean of arts and sciences in those days before he had left to become Amin Gemayel's foreign minister, American Phyllis Salem had long been and was still the director of AMIDEAST (America in the Middle East/Organization for Education and Training for Middle East Development) in the region with offices on both the East and West Sides. Just a month, this Thanksgiving, since the Syrian-Hraoui troops had put Beirut together again, and I was struck by the hard feelings and talk about it all by Lebanese East-Siders we met that day. But the party seemed to be part of a healing process and the special hospitality and food of the Salems helped to transcend and integrate the divisions. The next weekend, the traditional Ras Beirut gathering for Thanksgiving was once more at our home, for which occasion I even raided my boxes and got out silverware and we did turkeys and everyone brought food and we said the blessing and had our special brand of conviviality. A different group, a different ambience.

The end of November came right after with special thoughts of family—Ann's birthday and Christmas coming up when I wouldn't be home to see them all.

If days were for work, the evenings were largely for escape through the medium of my VCR. But I rationalized the indulgence as "catching up on my education in the American movie cultural phenomenon"—almost 30 years at least of nonmoviegoing had left me woefully ignorant and when people mentioned Rambo or Clint Eastwood I was out of it. The years of war in Lebanon had brought people largely away from the outside movie theaters and into the safety of the video theaters of their own homes—often making a social occasion of it with friends invited in for the evening. The entrepreneurial instinct being what it is in Lebanon, versions of almost every film for decades were available for rent—cheap. At Smith's, we could rent as many videotapes as we wanted for a week at 50 cents each, and thus the entertainment of my evenings at home was assured. It was, however, more than entertainment—it was America, and I reveled in it. From *Meet Me in St. Louis* with Judy Garland to *River of No Return* with Mitchum and Monroe to *High Noon* and Eastwood's "spaghetti westerns" and "Dirty Harrys" and Barbra Streisand's *On a Clear Day You Can See Forever* and Robert Redford and Jane Fonda in *The Electric Horseman* on to Stallone's "Rambos" and "Rockys" and on and on. And it was a sociological phenomenon indeed to see what Americans had been viewing for 40 years condensed into a time period of a year or so—from musical froth, Cary Grant romance, and detective fiction to frontier violence to sociopathic cops and murderers to *Every Which Way* blue-collar antiheroics to *Die Hard* "multiplosions" and assault weaponry.

I must say that deep within I responded as positively to Eastwood and Stallone as I did to Louis L'Amour—violence was met with violence and the "good" and the "bad" of the American frontier and the war in Vietnam blurred but was still decipherable in the mighty effort of the individual. At the same time, however, the contrast with my situation was clear—I could not be a female Rambo or American Western counterpart meeting violence with violence, nor could Tom—we were at the other end of the spectrum trying to meet violence with peace and education. Our lives, too, had to be forfeit although the chance for survival and making a difference was there. It all struck me forcibly as I thought about the "new hero" or even "antihero" as personified in Eastwood and Stallone being absorbed and desired by the American public—the individual going against mighty forces alone and all-but-dead or dishonored coming back to fight again. How did we fit into this? How did this reconcile with what we met in America with the prayers for Tom's return home to safety and a good life ever after? Or even the few who said, "They deserve it. Crazy to go there in the first place! They were warned!" I remember a friend saying to me two years after Tom's release when we went back to Lebanon in 1993: "I was angry that he went back. All that was done to bring him home safely and he went back. I was angry at him." Or the one who said, "How could you do this to your children?" when we went to Lebanon in the first place, and I just had to reply, "We did it *for* our children. Someone must go to dangerous places and try to solve problems, or where's the future for them?" It seemed to me almost as though Americans wanted the easy myth of good vs. evil and the continuing heroic challenge to it in the movies, but they didn't want in real life the complexity of good and evil all mixed up with human effort and sacrifice of ordinary people—the necessary ingredient—and "new frontiers" throughout the world as well as in our own country. Another thing that struck me forcibly with the recent far-out violent movies or the wackos and neo-Nazis was that the public is being prepared for disaster that can most easily come—and has in the World Trade Center and Oklahoma City bombings. This seems to be Hollywood's mission. I guess we wish that this were also more a myth than a reality.

But not all my video reactions were so "heavy"; very special and positive scenes stay up front in my memory. Like the thoroughbred running free in slow motion at the end of *The Electric Horseman,* which brought me vicariously the spirit of Tom free as I cried unashamedly, and the spectacular views of the great northwest to the song "The River of No Return," which brought me home to mountain country. I'll never forget. Nor will I ever forget Andrew Lloyd Webber's *Requiem,* which Elien gave me as a present in video and I heard for the first time "Pie Jesu." All are firmly woven into my Beirut experience.

Christmas 1990 came with as ever the special thoughts of family far away: Tom's brothers and sisters and families in Scotland; Dad and Alice in Sun City; my older brother Dave and wife Judy in Syracuse; younger brother John in Fairfax, Virginia; and Kit, Joan, Ann, Ray, and Simone all together in Berkeley, California, at Ann's where they would tape the whole morning's events around the Christmas tree for us. The students on campus were selling UNICEF cards and I found one with a beautiful mountain village—so typically Lebanese—with the great star shooting overhead and lights twinkling out from every window and door of every house built up the mountain among the snow-covered pines. Perfect. This one I sent to Berkeley:

> Sending you love and faith and hope and spirit from Lebanon with a card that expresses the eternal hope of the Lebanese—enough electricity to make all that light shown in the picture! I have candles in the windows every night to light your dad home and the house is warm and bright. All is ready—may Advent become Celebration! Be sure to know I'm with you along with your dad every minute picturing you and savoring the cheer, the camaraderie, the great food, and Christmas Eve and Morning. You're all wonderful! All Our Love, Mom and Dad.

It would be our last Christmas apart.

31 In and Out of Beirut

I'm not sure why I decided to leave Beirut and go back to the States on January 15, the day of the Bush/Baker/UN ultimatum for Saddam Hussein. It wasn't an "evacuation" because I couldn't see us being in the war zone nor if we were would that have scared me. But I always liked being able to move, and the Beirut Airport was ever a questionable proposition. And as it turned out, M was to have need of me in America. Anyway, I just got a ticket and went back to the United States, did my customary rounds in Washington, got together with our girls, watched CNN, did the needful for M, and then hit the air for Beirut again, arriving February 20:

FEB. 22—Hi Joan! Just a note to tell you I'm back here safe and sound—great trip and wonderful welcome waiting from friends. Saw Heinekens and Elham last night and got caught up on news ("Be aware—lots of anti-American feeling here because of the Gulf War!")—been out and around today to get money deposited and contact all my people in the workplace—tonight Marilyn and Jean-Marie take me to the Istambouli for dinner .... Cat and plants and house in beautiful shape thanks to Joana and weather is gorgeous—warm and sunny. People not happy about Bush's war I can tell you—and it will be worse if he draws it out ... but they are amazingly happy to see me! ... P.S. ... Hold tight for your dad—postwar. Maybe with Soviet peace plan it can be soon .... Now's the time to PRAY ....

And so the days of spring went by.

Happy Easter! ... I'm finishing up jobs and easing myself out of all responsibilities so I can come back soon with Tom. No news now but I feel just right being here and am hoping hard for the end of Ramadan in mid-April—Glorious weather this week—real springtime ....

I guess it was right to close out on responsibilities—M called me back to Washington on a personal matter and things were there for me to do. But so important to me, as it turned out, was the chance this trip to get to Iowa the first week of May and spend five days with my dad. He had fallen and hairline-fractured his pelvis. Confined for the first time in his workaholic life to a wheelchair, he gave me hours of time he'd never before given. He was in a "make sure all is taken care of and regularized" mood. Looking back I realize he knew his time was not long and wanted to be sure all was in order. He and I spent hours in his study together, talking and talking, collecting and boxing all the "hostage clippings" he had, drawers-full, and letters from 1956 onward in addition to my high school and college memorabilia to get back to Colorado. It would be the last time I'd see him and it had to be meant that we were given that last chance at time together. We didn't know it then—he told me that Aunt Win and Uncle Robb Kelley were having their 40th wedding anniversary celebration late June with all the family invited—it was to be a glorious reunion! I planned of course to come, but with all the usual reservations:

> Saturday evening, June 5, 1991—Joanie ... Sending you just wads of love by this note with the Heinekens who leave tomorrow. I've made the decision to stay until I see your dad, so I may not be there the end of June—but I'm fighting for that and praying and somehow hopeful ... .

32   From Gulf War to Pérez de Cuéllar

New Year 1991—Baalbek, Lebanon. Some things new. We still had the TV, but no longer got LBC over the 11,000-foot Lebanon Mountains. We were stuck with Baalbek TV, run by fundamentalist Shiites, whose programming left a lot to be desired, at least to us. The news was read no longer by glamorous young Christian beauties but by young women thoroughly wrapped up in their chadors. But we had gotten to see the buildup of General Schwartzkopf's forces in Saudi Arabia and now after January 15 saw the start of the air war with Saddam Hussein. From these incredible air attacks, and missiles going down chimneys, we realized how far things had come during our period of captivity. War was a completely new game. The nightly news never failed to astonish us. Nor any of the others watching it, no matter where, we soon discovered. Few people outside of the military had had any idea of what the might of America had become.

I seized the chance. "Mahmoud, when the real war begins after the air force is done, I bet you a hundred dollars it'll be over in six days." No idea where I could have found the hundred dollars, but I bet it anyway. "No," replied Mahmoud. "Long time. Okay, maybe America win, but many month." "No way," I insisted. "Six days maximum." "Okay. Saddam air force no good. But on the ground, he very tough. Okay maybe America win, but get bloody nose. On the ground, Saddam Hussein very tough. Many month." He was predicating his remarks on the Iran-Iraq war, which had dragged on for over eight years and ended in a standoff. The end of that story is well known. But I was wrong. It didn't take six days—only a hundred hours. Never again did we hear, "America scared Islamic Jihad," which had been thrown at us constantly over the years. Now *they* were running scared, realizing that the West, in half a day if it chose to, could knock off the whole of Lebanon, let alone the southern suburbs of Beirut. In fact, the whole Arab world seemed to be running scared, and believing that the Americans were about to replace the French and the British in an imperialist role, and once again have the whole Middle East under their control. So the war happened, but very wisely the West left Saddam to fill a potential vacuum and Mahmoud and I let the bet go.

In April, John had his fifth anniversary, and "Outlook" carried a special greeting to him from several of his friends. Jill participated and told Barbara Myers that she preferred to be known as "John's former girlfriend." John was devastated, and both Terry and I had to work hard to bring him any comfort. Terry was very rational, and told him that we were *all* going through the same kind of experience. How would we have changed, any of us, on release? How could we know?

May 2, the day before my birthday, we were on our way again. No warning, no explanation, no preparation; but this time, the guards seemed distinctly less nervous. The move was down the same route that TW had taken some months before to visit the doctor. Into Baalbek. And into a rather large room adjacent to the toilet. Same bare walls, same covered windows, same tiled floor, same 100-watt bulb, same door with no handle on the inside. Water bottles, pee bottles, and blankets. Here a TV—13-inch black-and-white Phillips with chadored maidens reading the news. Same guards—Mahmoud, Jameel, Abu Ali, Bilaal—Hadi and the Ghost thankfully had long ago disappeared, and we never did see them again. The news seemed to be constantly improving, and we were assured that the whole ordeal would be over by Christmas. Could we really believe them this time? The Israelis were trying to get into the picture too, to get their prisoners of war liberated; they felt that three or four of them might still be alive, but most of the reports seemed to indicate that only one, Ron Arad, could possibly be. We tried to get information out of Mahmoud, who was back to talking fairly freely. But he really didn't appear to know much at all about Arad. He was only hearing the same kinds of speculation and rumor on his Arabic stations that we were hearing on the BBC. The overriding feeling, though, was that Islamic Jihad wanted the Israelis to get no credit whatsoever for the release of hostages.

This new place had a good toilet and a shower in the tub, which we were now allowed to use about every third or fourth day. The water heater had the same drip arrangement as our stove up the hill, very effective, and gave all four of us plenty of hot water. In this place, though, the air too was *hot!* The May sun was beating on the roof, and on at least one of the walls all day. Mahmoud recognized this right away, and told us, "You will have an air conditioner very soon." "Ha," we thought. "Heard that one before!" Imagine our astonishment when we were told to hide ourselves for several hours while workmen were in our room—we went under our blankets—and when they were finished and we came out from under our blankets, there was a brand-new Japanese-made air conditioner fastened to the wall with an elaborate set of hoses going to the compressor, presumably on the roof. It worked like a dream—blessed comfort such as we hadn't known in six summers so far. The guards even came in from time to time, telling us that it was nicer in our room than in theirs. Possibly. But my feeling was that they had a large compressor and had several units connected to it. Surely they would not have given just us the benefits.

Our bridge games continued. TW sometimes went off the deep end and made crazy bids that would drive even his opponents up the wall. And his poor partner would explode when TW laid down his hand, "Good heavens, TW! How could you possibly bid with a hand like that?" "Well," he would reply flippantly, "I am tired of not being able to bid." His partner was left trying to play an impossibly overbid pair of hands. The chess games were still challenging, and Terry would give us lots of advice and help. TW and I were competing with each other, and I believe that I won roughly two out of three of our games. Occasionally I would make stupid mistakes and lose the game, and on one occasion I lost three in a row! I was absolutely furious with myself, and on the third loss, I took my hand and swept all the pieces off the board.

TW and I were still the primary radio monitors and kept passing on news items. Hostage news was becoming ever more frequent. Peggy Say had told Terry on his anniversary in March that she was more optimistic than ever before. We all took enormous solace from that. Could it be that their promises of pre-Christmas liberation might finally come true? We *knew* that much of what we were hearing was still, as always, speculation by journalists, broadcasters, and columnists. President Bush was a frequent commentator, but seemed, along with Jim Baker, to be maintaining a hard line, with vague promises of "goodwill" to Iran if only they would help. Rafsanjani was likewise coyly offering to help if the United States would release the funds that were being held in the United States—that was an enormously complex situation, and in *The Economist* we read a long treatise on what might be required. No one was even sure where the Iranian funds were. Most of the money had been paid by the former regime, under the Shah, for arms, spare parts, and repair of war materials. Most of it was believed now to be in the hands of private companies. The United States agreed that the matter should go to the World Court in Holland, which seemed like a fine idea to us. Our objective conclusion was that impounding all these funds was neither legal nor fair. It had really stung the Iranians as a matter of principle.

The United States was deliberately taunting the Iranians for their humiliating actions in taking embassy personnel hostage. The more we thought about all these international shenanigans, the more it resembled grade school politics, or at best junior high.

May 3 was my 60th birthday, and I had a fantastic surprise—my daughter Kit on VOA for the first time, speaking from Fort Collins and saying, "Happy Birthday, Dad." I was elated. It was the first time I had heard the voice of anyone close to me—really bucked me up—and soon I was thinking again about what I could do when I got out of here. Like a rider thrown off a horse, I wanted desperately to go back to the AUB and take up my position as dean again. I had *enjoyed* that job, and if worst came to worst and no one would hire me, at least I might get my old job back. My fellow hostages from Father Martin on had warned me that I would never be allowed to go back there for a long time. Father Martin had said long ago, "You will never be able to go back to Beirut! If you showed your nose back there, someone will *shoot* you for fear of being recognized!" Terry and John renewed their reassurances begun in "the Pit" and continued regularly—"Tom, you won't have to worry about a job! When you get out of here, there will be dozens of positions open for you!" Again they succeeded—made me feel much better.

So that I wouldn't run out of batteries in the middle of the night, I took to hoarding a few in my mattress; when the guards gave us new ones, they didn't always pick up the used ones, so I kept those until the next change of guard and got more new ones, offering them the dead ones of a day or two ago. It worked. For months I was able to keep a spare set, which TW too called on from time to time. His radio was harder on batteries than ours—when his got slightly low, his radio just quit. I could take his old batteries and run ours for at least another day. Terry didn't like my hoarding. "Look, Tom, they've never refused you yet in over two years—all you have to do is ask and you get them. If they find you hoarding batteries, they'll take away the whole damn radio. Quit it, man!" I felt a bit sheepish. A part of my personality was showing—my propensity for making provision for a rainy day. At the grocery store, I always buy two of everything. I keep a store of batteries of all kinds, pieces of wood and metal, screws and nails of all sizes, even to a spare car or two! I never did get caught by our hosts, but it sure kept Terry and John on tenterhooks! *Had* I been caught, there would have been no end to "I told you so, you dumb bastard." No illusions about that.

June 9—Sixth anniversary of my kidnapping and another super surprise! Early morning VOA—a bell tolling. "I am standing on the campus of Iowa State University," said the reporter, "where the bells of the Campanile on this beautiful campus are being tolled 72 times, once for each month of captivity of

Tom Sutherland, one of the Americans being held hostage in Beirut." I was stunned. Moved beyond description. Those bells, so sacred to generations of Iowa Staters, were ringing out all over the world, *for me*. A girl was not a true coed until she had been kissed under the Campanile—so it had very tender memories for tens of thousands of coeds. My memory went back. Walking across the campus for 8:00 classes, listening to Professor Ira Shroeder of the Music Department playing the carillon every morning—simply wonderful—was one of my most treasured memories from that great university. I broke down and cried.

Moments later, another VOA reporter. "I am on the campus of Colorado State University in Fort Collins, and have with me Professor Frank Vattano, the chairman of the Friends of Tom Sutherland." Good old Frank! At least *he* hasn't forgotten me. And what was this—"The Friends of Tom Sutherland? Never *heard* of *this* organization! "The Friends of Terry Anderson," and "The Friends of John McCarthy," sure. And what the Church of England was doing for TW. But "The Friends of Tom Sutherland"? *Well!* I hadn't been forgotten, after all! "Could you tell our listeners a little about this group, Professor Vattano?" "Well," replied Frank, "we just didn't want anyone to forget old Tom. You know, when a guy is gone for years like that, people begin to forget. We just wanted to keep him alive for the community here." Good old Frank! *You did it!* Exhilaration. My three colleagues awoke. "You'll never guess what I heard on VOA, fellows! My old buddy Frank Vattano has organized both of my Fort Collins friends into the "Friends of Tom Sutherland!" (Kit said afterward—"There were lots, Dad—Frank just held open bar.") They all chuckled at the thought, but realized how touched I was. Terry didn't know much about the Campanile, its significance. He was married when he attended Iowa State, and commuted from 30 miles away—participated little in any social life. I did, in spades! But he realized what this all meant for me.

So many reports and encouraging messages coming in—maybe the guards were right? Maybe we *would* all be home this year? We began seriously to plan for when we got home. Terry would be off to the sun first thing for a long vacation with Madeleine and Sulome—Gabrielle too if that could be arranged. TW thought he too would need a while in the sun, and had contacts all over the Bahamas and the Caribbean. If Terry got out before him, he should contact so-and-so on this or that island. I told them, "I don't need to go to the Caribbean for sun—we have over 300 days of sun every year in Fort Collins. If they just let me get back to our place in the mountains, that's fine!" I even suggested that they could all come out there and have a long vacation in God's Country for free. But I couldn't dissuade them from hotter climes. John wasn't as determined to seek sunshine. He just wanted to get back together with Jill.

Early August. The *Tehran Times* again. An American and a Brit would be released, and they would be carrying a message for the secretary general of the United Nations. A brilliant stroke. Islamic Jihad had finally decided to turn things over to Pérez de Cuéllar to end the hostage drama. We speculated on who would go. Joe Cicippio and Jackie Mann were both rumored to be having health problems. Given the increase in humanitarian concern that we had experienced of late, these two were the likely candidates. Surprise. Late in the afternoon of August 8, Mahmoud and Abu Ali came in and quickly unchained John—no explanation—"Come queeckly, John," and he was on his way out. Abu Ali stopped long enough to pick up both radios, provoking a chorus of protests from the two Terrys and me. To no avail. But John intervened outside, insisting that the radio was our lifeline, and incredibly, they brought them both back within a half hour. John was on his way home. The radio carried reports of his release, and we saw him first in Damascus and later at Lyneham Air Force Base in England. Happy. People were astonished to find him in such command of himself after five and a half years of captivity—smiling and articulate, self-confident. He said little on the air about us back in Baalbek. But we had long ago given each other detailed instructions—whom to call and what messages, regardless of who went out first. Everyone would be informed of everything.

Amazing thing. John was announcing to the world that he was carrying a message from Islamic Jihad to Pérez de Cuéllar—as Mahmoud had predicted following John's departure. So John was the envoy! And indeed, a day or so later, there was Pérez de Cuéllar himself, all the way from New York, meeting John on the tarmac of Lyneham Air Force Base. He immediately announced that he was assigning Giandomenico Picco to be his special envoy to deal with Islamic Jihad, and for weeks we followed the reports on Picco's progress—much in the news, but handling things quietly, discreetly. Picco is on his way to Tehran. Picco is in Geneva. Picco has gone to Beirut. Picco had just left Damascus. Boy, was he logging the miles. On our part, chained to the wall, we were moving 20 feet daily to the toilet and back.

Three days after John left us, the promised American was freed. Not Cicippio, but Edward Tracy, who, it transpired, had been held all along with Joe. Tracy's appearance was in stark contrast to John's. The man was obviously in very bad shape, and the embassy people allowed him only a minimum of time to talk in front of the cameras, during which time he came over as halting, incoherent, and thoroughly befuddled. There but for the grace of God go I, I thought, and quietly gave thanks.

A few days later, two new "boss men" came in to us—one evidently young, the interpreter, the other older with a deeper, authoritative voice. They wanted to talk to us Americans, and took Terry Waite outside. In several hours, they gave us a thorough rundown on their schedule of releases. "Soon one more American will go home," they said. "Then one more British. Then another American. Then another American. Then you Terry. You last." "Well, I always figured to be last," agreed Terry. "But that's okay with me. Just as long as you have me home for Christmas." "Of course," came the reply. "You home for Christmas. No problem!" How often we had heard that. "*No problem.*" Sure, for them, it was "no problem"—never had been. They weren't chained to the wall, either—we kept reminding them. This time though, it seemed different. These two fellows seemed to know what was going on—finally news straight from the horse's mouth. Then came the request. "Will you make a tape, Terry?" Why on earth would they want him to make a tape just days after John McCarthy had gone out, and had presumably told everyone who mattered everything? Puzzling. Terry reluctantly replied, a little wearily, "Okay. I'm willing if you think it will help." "All right. But we must wait some times. The camera is not here yet. We will come back." They left.

Terry Waite reappeared. He had been kept in the kitchen. "What was all that?" he asked, obviously very worried about what had been going on for the hours he was sitting on a hard, cold floor. Terry Anderson couldn't resist. "Oh, TW," he said. "Things don't look good for you. I'm glad I'm not in your shoes. I'm sorry." Waite became *really* worried! "Good heavens, Terry. What on earth is it?" His voice was strained. "Oh, I don't think I should tell you, TW. Let them tell you." "Oh my God. What on earth did they tell you?" His voice was so anxious that Terry couldn't keep it up any longer and broke into laughter. "No, I'm only kidding, TW. Everything is good and very good, beleef me, beleef me," he parodied the guards. "They have just been giving us a rundown on all that is going to happen in the coming months, and things do indeed look very good." TW was vastly relieved, and Terry was still laughing, as was I. It was a cruel thing to do, admittedly, but Terry couldn't resist.

In a few minutes, the boss and his interpreter returned. The interpreter started right in. "Mr. Waite. We are very sorry we kidnap you. Very sorry. Was not good. But Mr. Waite, why you come back Beirut?" The tone was distinctly more menacing now. "Why you come back, Mr. Waite?" he repeated. "We tell you, Mr. Waite, you come back Beirut, we kidnap you! So why you come back Beirut, Mr. Waite?" The tone was now very intense. I sat right beside this drama in disbelief. TW had never confessed this sort of thing in nine months of lying right alongside—despite my asking over and over for an accounting of his visits to Beirut, whom he met, and where. He had always refused any details. And here were the bosses now spilling the beans about him. What is he going to answer to that one? A few seconds of hesitation, then a lame, "I always like to finish any job that I start, you know?" My mind was racing, trying to fathom all the ramifications of what I had just heard. They had warned him not to come back. And he had come back despite the fact that more than 50 westerners had been kidnapped on the streets of Beirut. What kind of a rationale did he use? What did he think would have protected him? I was stunned, realizing that I was hearing for the first time the true story behind his kidnapping. No wonder he had been so worried all this time about what the people of the United Kingdom would say when he was released.

The camera crew arrived, set up their tripod and videocam as was customary, wrapped their heads in scarves, and Terry Anderson duly removed his blindfold and made his tape for America, not knowing any more than I did as to why they should even want a tape at that time.

With John gone, we no longer could play bridge, and Terry had lost his chess partner. He retreated into writing poetry, and got tired of my bitching about what a pain in the ass TW was, and made no bones about telling me. But frankly, my respect for TW's judgment had sunk to a new low. I simply couldn't reconcile myself to the man's obvious lack of sensitivity to what he had been dealing with in coming to Beirut, and to his lack of acumen about Moslems in general, despite his reputed skill as a negotiator. How could he possibly have gone to either Libya or Iran and accomplished *anything*? And now, with "the cat out of the bag," so to speak, TW was even more on the defensive, and even more reactive to my "attacks" on him. We still played chess from time to time, but ever more competitively, with the loser taking the loss as an extreme slight to his overall ability and credibility. Despite this, however, we all recognized that in a confined space such as we were in, we simply had to be *civilized* and not let our feelings get completely out of hand, otherwise the entire fabric of our "community," so important to our survival, would be destroyed.

We were still getting *The Economist* every week, and Terry and I were still wrestling with the intricacies of investment, dreaming of what we would do with all that money. Freedom seemed to be looming ever larger, a feeling backed up by the news. A month after Tracy went home, another "old-timer" was released— Jackie Mann, the British war hero and former MEA pilot, who was by then well into his seventies. A month later, Jesse Turner, the BUC professor who had also been held by the Islamic Jihad, went free. His release was marred at Wiesbaden by his father-in-law taking some video footage against Jesse's will. But he was soon back in Boise and on the steps of the state capitol late at night, being welcomed home by the governor of the state. Things were definitely swinging, and we were hanging on, waiting day by day.

Early on, I had suggested that whoever got out first should do the max to get messages to the others, especially about family affairs. I was the most eager for this, since I had heard almost nothing of my family and their doings. I suggested that the logical program for this was "Outlook," since it covered a wide range of subjects, with frequent guests on the show—a logical choice. No surprise then when the World Service began announcing one day that the next day's program on "Outlook" would consist heavily of messages for the hostages in Lebanon. Good old John, I thought. He remembered. But the entire program consisted of a long session devoted to Terry Waite, orchestrated by his cousin John, an employee of the BBC who substituted on the World Service—followed by a long session for Terry Anderson. Squeezed in was a very brief message from my brother Willie in Scotland, and *nothing* from Jean, Ann, Kit, or Joan! I was *furious*. It had all been my idea in the first place, and I was once again on the low end of the totem pole. I resolved to have it out with John when I was released—but to this day haven't even mentioned it to him. The hurt still remains, however.

33 Getting to November 18

My summer was after all destined to be spent in Beirut, even though I'd promised Kit that I'd be there mid-July to help them move back into our home on Garfield Street in Fort Collins. I'd thought hard about what to do about the house—if we kept on renting our home to others we'd have to redecorate and fix up for them and maybe get into a situation where Tom would come back to Fort Collins and his home would not be there for him. It was surely better to take it back and move everything of our own into it and fix it up for us—even if we couldn't "expect" him to be back. The moving job would be monumental—I knew that because I'd moved us out of it in 1983. But we lived by the day, and M said I should be in Beirut, things would break this summer, so Kit and her fiancée Scott did the entire move in July by themselves. True to family form, they didn't hold it against me that I was not there to share their trauma—they just did the work. What I know is that after all their labors they had a special place in their hearts for it all when, on December 1 to come, Kit accompanied her dad from that welcome home ceremony with 10,000 in Moby Gym and watched him walk through the door and into the home he'd left eight years before with everything as it had been, as though he'd never left. We could have made it without that of course, but to have the homecoming perfect and complete was beyond all.

M was also in Beirut almost all that summer and had been contacted directly by Islamic Jihad. He was thus now seeing the captors themselves in earnest as all sought to bring the hostage crisis to a "right" conclusion. He came often to discuss the issues with me and to see what we could bring to bear that would help, but I could be only in the background while he was the one on the line, meeting with Islamic Jihad representatives night after exhausted night. All angles were explored, all ideas probed for a right resolution.

Clearly, in the month of July, while the furor raged over "Land for Peace" in the Israeli-Palestinian peace process south of us, the "German Problem" in the hostage situation in Lebanon became critical. It was an issue, in fact, that went clear back to June 1985: the hijacking of the TWA airliner, the killing of Robert Stethem, and the subsequent capture and incarceration on January 13, 1987, in Germany of one of the men held responsible, 22-year-old Mohamad Ali Hamadi. He was charged with bringing explosive ingredients into Germany as well as with the TWA hijacking and murder, for which the United States was calling for extradition. Mohamad's older brother, Abbas, a German citizen, was also jailed in Germany, having been picked up as he came back into that country on January 27, 1987. Twenty-eight years old at the time, not involved in the hijacking, he was ostensibly being charged with involvement in the Beirut kidnapping, following Mohamad's arrest, of two German businessmen, Rudolf Cordes and Alfred Schmidt, to be held against his brother's well-being and probably most especially his extradition to America for trial. The death penalty was at issue. Cordes and Schmidt were subsequently released, Schmidt on September 8, 1987, and Cordes a year later on September 13, 1988, the kidnappers apparently having the idea that the Hamadis would come out in exchange (shades of Gadhafi and Britain in 1985). The German government, however, backed strongly by the American government, said *no*. So two more Germans, relief workers Heinrich Struebig and Thomas Kemptner, were kidnapped in Beirut in May 1989 (actually kidnapped twice that month, the first time held briefly and released to bring out the demands, the second time two weeks later to be held three years). Now in July 1991, the two were being used in another try to regain the freedom of the Hamadi brothers in Germany. On July 19, the news release from Islamic Jihad came to back up pressure on Germany with pressure on America—a photo of Terry Anderson along with the threat: There would be "dire consequences" if harm came to the Hamadis. Again on July 25 came another public communiqué with the threat of taking action against the German hostages held in Lebanon unless Germany would provide details on the Hamadis' condition. It was clear that the "German Problem" was not to be ignored in any settlement for other Western hostages.

August came, and John McCarthy was suddenly released on the eighth with the famous communiqué for Pérez de Cuéllar. So clear to me even now is the meeting M and I had on our balcony that day—"This is their decision," he said. "Almost it came to my being the one to handle it if the Americans had given sign of approval. But the Americans were suspicious and also adamant on their principle of no dealing, not even an appearance of dealing. So the captors have gone for the neutral avenue of the UN although the Americans won't be happy about that either—they would want complete capitulation and unconditional release of hostages without any face-saving for captors." But to us it was terribly important that the resolution of this years-long crisis and conflict be a positive one for all parties involved so that all could go forward for peace afterward. M said to me after McCarthy's release, "When I found out they had opted for UN resolution, I went to see them and suggested that they would not be wanting me anymore, but they hastened to assure me, 'Yes, you must stay involved.'" We talked it through, all the implications and meanings. And somehow, even with the tremendous reservations M had about the ultimate success of the thing, we agreed that this decision with John McCarthy and the UN had to be the start of the solution. The UN had been empowered enough by the Gulf War to carry the resolution of the hostage crisis. The decision not to have M as mediator of the final resolution was purposeful and symbolic and sent a very important message—that *fatwa* had been issued to end confrontation with the American government and instead to make an international resolution. Strong, shrewd move. Taking the ultimate decision on its own, Islamic Jihad empowered itself as it gained necessary face with equality in international negotiation. No matter that the American government was not pleased with this—it was essential that face be saved in the Middle East and that the environment in which to go forward be as positive as possible. And as M said, "Even though you and I were never and not now intended to be part of the solution, we must continue with our avenue to play a helpful role in making sure that all goes right in the release process—that's what's being said when they say 'It is important you still be involved.' Everyone's help is needed now."

The communiqué to Pérez de Cuéllar had offered to release Western hostages in exchange for some 400 Shiites still being held in Israeli prisons. This was immediately picked up both by the Israelis and the world media who urged that a deal be struck. The Israelis came back with an offer that included the Shiite prisoners plus Sheikh Obeid in return for their Israeli prisoners taken in Lebanon over the years since 1982—some of these were presumed dead, but their navigator Arad captured in 1986 was presumed still alive and they wanted him badly. Could this work? A total deal? A prominent and well-connected American businessman offered his help and did all he could. But Islamic Jihad could in no way deal with Israel, especially without a resolution to the war in South Lebanon, and to this day neither Arad nor Israeli bodies nor Shiite prisoners nor Sheikh Obeid have surfaced. Rather, Abbas Moussawi, the new leader of Hizbollah, and his family were assassinated in a personal air strike by Israel in 1992; and Mustafa al-Dirani, the Shiite guerilla leader considered the head of the detail that took Arad, was in 1994 taken as well by means of an Israeli raid into Lebanon. Thus does the war in South Lebanon go on—presumably until the day that Syria and Israel work out their peace accord.

It was obvious to everyone that even with the calling in of the UN there would be trouble in working out the details of the full release of the hostages. The Hamadi problem was still an enormous obstacle, because the family, a powerful Shiite family of the Bekaa Valley, was not at all in accord with a release. In fact, just after John McCarthy was released, a French medical worker, Jerome Leyraud, was kidnapped in retaliation and threatened with death if any more Western hostages were released. All hell and the Syrians broke loose with ultimatums. Door-to-door searches with 48 hours given—and the man was released, pushed out of a moving car. M told me that he had expressed his grave foreboding that things would fall apart, but he had been unequivocally assured, "There is no going back, no reverse, the decision has been made to close the file." *Fatwa.* Thus the die was cast by those in power and the release of Edward Tracy on August 11 underwrote that. But still the Hamadi problem rubbed. Pérez de Cuéllar and Picco would not under any circumstances touch the German issue, and this meant that the two German hostages being held in Lebanon would not be part of a resolution by the UN, if any such resolution could be reached. One day, soon after, I remember well M coming from having seen the top Hamadi, perhaps highest in the Islamic Jihad hierarchy and certainly holding up proceedings. Hamadi was adamant. Germany must release his brothers before the release of any more Western hostages. M said he had argued positively with the man with all he had for a "higher understanding"—give it time, see what would happen, let Germany handle it, don't "tie" one to the other. But no go. M went to Europe to consult with people he knew and see what could be done about the situation.

And I in my turn took off with my friend Marilyn in Jean-Marie's little British Mini to go to the Cedars, that fabled grove of historic Lebanese cedar trees in North Lebanon I'd never seen. Wonderful trip! We stopped enroute above Byblos on the sea and dabbled in the Mediterranean, gathering snails off the beach rocks for a feast to come when we got to the Cedars condo of a friend of hers. Lunch in a little seaside restaurant after which the little Mini took to the mountain roads and we reached the condo and those ancient trees in late afternoon. I wish there were words for feelings. The area of the stand of trees is small—you walk around and through it—but the effect is immense. And for me, steeped in the classical tradition and those ancient manuscripts and epics describing "The Cedars of Lebanon," the actual trees were symbols of historical continuity. Although separated from that most ancient epic-myth of *Gilgamesh* by 4,000 years, we stood before the Cedar Forest just like Gilgamesh and Enkidu, and the archaic lines on ancient tablets were absolutely current:

At the green mountain they arrived together;
Stilled into silence were their words, and they themselves stood still;
They stood still and looked at the forest.

They beheld the height of the cedar.
They beheld the entrance to the forest.
Where Humbaba was wont to walk there was a path;
Straight were the tracks and good was the passage.
They beheld the mountain of the cedar, the dwelling-place of the
*   gods, the throne-dais of Irnini.*
The cedar bore its wealth on the slope of the mountain
Fair was its shade and full of delight.[10]

That the ancient cedar forest was the dwelling of the fire-breathing giant Humbaba that Gilgamesh had come to destroy spoke also of this day of good and evil inextricably mixed. As the Jungian *Gilgamesh* scholar, Rivkah Scharf Kluger, put it: "The cedar as the tree of life blossoms in the land of death." This certainly described the Lebanon Tom and I were in.

Marilyn and I had our "snail feast" that evening and next day visited the Cedars ski area some little way beyond the trees, and Marilyn said I must come back and go over the mountain toward Baalbek at the time of the full moon— "Absolutely breathtaking"—and someday I will. But this day we would go back and around the mountain to the monastery built around the great Cave of Chains in the Holy Valley. From being the place of chained prisoners in former days, the cave was today the place of healing, and Marilyn and I stood back in that rock vault and watched the people come—particularly a crippled child who was placed by her mother and father on the stone altar built beneath the old, old chains suspended from the rock-vault ceiling, and blessed by the priest. We saw too in their adjoining museum the first printing press brought into Lebanon long ago. Amazing, all of it, with the juxtaposed ironies in our case manifest. Then we wound back up the mountain and stopped off to see the hermit whom Marilyn knew and had interviewed. He looked the image of a hermit—worked a small garden and had a tiny cell along with a lovely chapel, and ate one meal a day brought to him by someone from the monastery. But he was much of the world with all the people who came to see him. Marilyn had influence, however, and we got a chance to talk with him in the front pew of the chapel, and he blessed Tom and me. It was a lovely experience altogether. And then we had *meza*—that fabulous Lebanese mountain lunch with hummus, tabouli, baba ghanoush, kibbe, and all in an open-air restaurant in that famed restaurant village of Ehden before we headed back to Beirut with a stop-off and a hike into another cave with a stream that Marilyn knew about. Never forget.

Back to Beirut. Life continued apace with the sense of progress and my knowledge that Tom had a radio. On September 1, I wrote to Ann and Ray:

> …. Things are progressing—the process is sure this time, even if negotiations will take time and be back channel—in the meantime I've sent a request to BBC's "Anything Goes"—music 6:30–7:00 A.M. that your dad listens to—"Scotland the Brave" and "Westering Home" by his favorite Kenneth McKellar …. I was sorry VOA didn't interview you to tell about your December child to come—I told them to …. Don't worry that I'm not going to be there December–January—wild horses won't keep me away or situation because I have ESP instructions from your dad for this boy …. Love you all so much, Mom

Back to Beirut also meant back to world politics and the "German Problem." Somehow there had to be a "dealing with" it, even symbolically, if the rest of the hostage release was to be effected. There were some "hooks" on which to hang dialogue—"reports" that the Hamadis were being badly treated in Germany and that their family wanted to see them. I said to M when we met on his return from Europe without a breakthrough on that front: "Would it help if I went to Bonn and saw the German government?" "Yes," he said, "I think so."

I planned. M wanted me back in Washington on another matter the first week of October. On the way I could get together with John McCarthy in London—Tom's brothers Peter and Willie could come down too and get a firsthand account from him about Tom. Then it was on to Washington where I knew I must see Secretary Baker before I did anything about going to Germany. After that I would do what I needed to do about getting to see the right people in Germany and then I would go back to London and do the round-trip to Bonn.

It all worked. Basically. Peter and Willie and I got a wonderful meeting with John McCarthy in the Penta Hotel by Heathrow where I had just come in from Beirut and John had just come in from being with Brian Keenan in Ireland. In a mostly quiet island in the front lobby with big armchairs—Peter and Willie were there from Scotland before us—we all had nearly two hours together. The only problem was that, like Brian before him, John had come out of captivity with a whispering syndrome and Peter with his hearing problem heard almost nothing. But he touched him and saw him and it was reassurance. I, in my turn, did not press enough for what I could do to get to Tom. And John, in his turn, didn't give me the message from Tom I should have had: "Tell Jean to get on BBC 'Outlook.'" What John said on leaving me was "I'm going to be on BBC—is there anything I can do for you?" And I answered, "Yes—do urge them to put on my

'Anything Goes' request." So in the end I didn't get on "Outlook" but the songs did come through to Tom with my dedication. And it was good—but I regret, for both would have been wonderful. No way to redo. If only we had known that for two whole years we could have been getting through to him on radio—if only—what a difference to him. I should have pressed harder.

In Washington, M's business took a week and then I got my meeting with Secretary Baker. When I told him I was going to Bonn to try to talk with Chancellor Helmut Kohl about the Hamadi brothers, he came back angrily—"They are terrorists and murderers! It was one of them that killed our Robert Stethem in cold blood!" Right at that time, indeed, the Stethems were making a very vocal plea about not giving in and releasing the murderer of their son, and American opinion was solidly behind them. And rightly so. The Hamadis had been caught for a crime and been legally tried and imprisoned—just like the Dawa 17 in Kuwait. But behind his rhetoric, shrewd Secretary Baker would understand exactly why I was going to Germany, especially after two years of my being part of an avenue for dialogue between him and Fadlallah. Just as M and I had *never* come to him to try to talk the American government into giving anything for hostages, I was *not* going to the German government as a representative for the Hamadi family or for Shiite fundamentalists to try to get the Hamadi brothers out of jail in exchange for Western hostages. I was strictly an "avenue," an "action" as it were, to allow indirect but straight dialogue between two enemies, dialogue that could maybe put forward the resolution of the hostage crisis, even if the answer that came back was "No." I knew that our avenue's "No" would at least be accepted and respected and acted on as it had been all along and knew that Baker understood too. And I knew, too, that the totality of the trip, including the visit to Secretary Baker, would constitute the ultimate dialogue when M reported back to Hamadi and Islamic Jihad in Beirut the first week of November. It was what was left for us to do to support the UN's work. That all the living British and American hostages and the remains of Buckley and Higgins would be out by December and the German hostages held in Lebanon out the following June (attended by Picco) would be the vindication of the total process. But we didn't know the results then.

Still in Washington, D.C., I went from the State Department to the German embassy. I must say that I was now in very unfamiliar territory. But people there were extremely nice when I told them who I was and that I had just come from Beirut and that it was most important for me to see Chancellor Kohl. The woman who received me sent me off with the name and number of a counselor, Wolfgang Gaerte, in the foreign office, in addition to some other names and numbers for good measure and a friendly, caring smile and handshake.

I left for London on October 23, calling family from a Dulles Airport telephone. I spoke a while to Dad, and he told me he hadn't been well, was having a lot of pain in his neck area, and was wearing a brace. I said, "Get treated, Dad." "I'm going to," he said. "I love you." "I love you, too." So short the exchange in a lifetime of father-daughter exchanges but speaking volumes. We both knew it. From Heathrow I went to my favorite hotel and got oriented, making a call through to Bonn to Gaerte in the foreign office to set up an appointment. Chancellor Kohl was then out of the country but expected back, so we set up a time. I bought my ticket to Bonn and took off into what I knew not on October 30, finding when I got to Bonn the Hotel zum Adler, which was not close to where I was going to see government people, but was a lovely haven otherwise.

The next day I found the subway and Gaerte and kept to my initial request: "I'm Jean Sutherland, wife of the American hostage, Tom Sutherland. I've just come from Beirut and it is most important that I see Chancellor Kohl." "If you tell us what it is we can handle it." "I'm extremely sorry, but it's impossible to do that." Seeing that I was absolutely determined, he gave me a Mr. von Hoessle's name, a man higher up in another building. And that evening a call came through with the name of Dr. Ueberschaer, the director of Chancellor Kohl's office, along with an appointment to see him.

Next morning I took the subway again and found the building on the Bundes Kanzler Amt. and was met and taken to Dr. Ueberschaer. And there my standard request was handled in finality. "Mrs. Sutherland, I'm sure you will agree that we cannot put you into Chancellor Kohl without knowing what you are here for. That is our office. Do you think any wife of a German hostage would be given an appointment with your president without knowing what she was there for?" Touché, granted. I'd gotten as far as I was going to get, but it was as far as I needed to get to have the necessary credibility to serve the purpose in going at all. I told Dr. Ueberschaer first off that I had not come without informing Secretary Baker, that I was working with a most knowledgeable and credible man in providing an avenue between the secretary and Sheikh Fadlallah in Beirut, and that I had been doing this with American administrations for five years. Then I told him the whole story of the Hamadis, the holdup to the release process, and their demands. He listened attentively and then came back with straight answers, saying in effect: "The Hamadis were tried and jailed in accordance with German law. There is no question about their being released for any reason outside of German law nor by anyone's demand for any reason of their own. But I will say this—that they have been treated in accordance with our law for prisoners and we are in the process of working out visitation from their families. In respect of the German hostages being held in Lebanon, the kidnappers have not given us any signs of life in pictures or otherwise, nor have they given us information concerning the hostages' well-being. But as to those hostages—we told them not to go to Lebanon and they directly disobeyed. We have no responsibility to them." This of course would be conveyed back to Lebanon in the same tone that the rest would be conveyed—that signs of life—pictures—should be produced, and that visitation by the family was to be arranged so that they could see their sons and brothers and cousins directly and find out firsthand how they were being treated. Straight.

Dr. Ueberschaer then called for Dr. Peter Hartmann, General Scowcroft's counterpart in the German government, who came in to meet me and reiterate the German position. Dr. Hartmann was severe and careful and imposing, but not really scary to me since as always I had nothing to lose that I hadn't already given up. I suppose that in the last analysis I liked Dr. Ueberschaer better, but I could definitely appreciate Dr. Hartmann as a man in his position. The two were a complementary team. I certainly cannot comment on Chancellor Kohl, for as it turned out, I did not see him—he was saved the necessity of dealing with me. Interestingly, as I read between the lines, I understood that I'd been routed around Hans-Dietrich Genscher, the foreign minister, to get to Ueberschaer and Hartmann at all, and this seemed to be another National Security Council (NSC)/State Department situation German-style over who would deal with the hostages. Made me appreciate the similarities and differences between countries and people, adding Germany to France, Great Britain, and the United States in my cache of hostage-taking-and-holding and dealing-with experiences.

Dr. Hartmann left me with: "There's a direct line from General Scowcroft's office in case you should need to use it in the future," by which I understood that I was not to bother them again personally and that if the matter was important enough by General Scowcroft's standards it would be handled in the proper way between governments. I was satisfied. All was correct and accomplished. And somehow I was left to understand that without other words the total situation had been understood on both sides of the ocean and the way paved for my mission to be completed. I had then and still have now a real respect for Secretary Baker, General Scowcroft, Dr. Ueberschaer, and Dr. Hartmann. And for President Bush and Chancellor Kohl above and behind them. And a respect also for the mind behind the resolution in Lebanon that mandated an acceptable resolution for all parties there.

M had arranged with me that when I had had my appointment with the chancellor's office, I would come to Frankfurt by train and meet him there where he was meeting with other people on another matter. So I did, and enjoyed the train ride, not realizing that I'd be back in Frankfurt within three weeks to meet up with Tom in Wiesbaden. Amazing. M and I met in a hotel restaurant, had an hour together to discuss everything he would report back in Lebanon, and then he took me to the train station to return to Bonn while he would return to Beirut the next day. For my part, the next day I said good-bye to the Hotel zum Adler and was on my way back to Heathrow.

In London, since my mission was completed, I succumbed to temptation and decided to spend a day or two there, getting an inexpensive hotel in the Bloomsbury district, obtaining my library card for the British Museum Library, and restarting my research into Seneca and Shakespeare to see what it felt like. It was a simply wonderful two days. But that last night, back at the hotel, I was restless. *I must get back to Beirut, I must get back to Beirut.* And next day, Wednesday, November 6, I arranged my ticket with Middle East Airlines and caught the plane for Beirut, arriving at 5:00 P.M. as usual with Sharif there to meet me. It was right and good to be back. On November 7 I was to have a day of normality, then half a night of normality, and then *THE BLAST*.

It's hard to describe an instant—a flash, an enormity of sound, a waking, a putting out of the hand to the light switch, the light, the unfamiliarity of all around with broken glass and fallen plaster and window frames and door frames over the bed and floor, in the midst of no sound. The sound was gone with the tremendous force that had swept through our house just 50 yards from the detonation that brought down the clock and bell tower and the great facade of AUB's College Hall and sent the front axle and wheels of the explosive-laden Volkswagen bus 100 yards through the air to land on the roof of the Mishalanis' house below us. Devastation. But amazing—I had been sleeping on Tom's side of the bed and although the rest was covered in glass and heavy pieces of plaster, my/his side was absolutely clear. I could do no more than wonder, as tentatively I began to get on the phone and find out what had happened. It seemed impossible that AUB's venerable 128-year-old College Hall had been blown up, but it had. And thus was our time at AUB to be framed for all time—by the assassination of President Malcolm Kerr in 1984 and the destruction of College Hall in 1991.

The next days were traumatic—finding out that a man had been killed who had slept overnight in College Hall (against regulations, but many people had no homes), seeing the damage at College Hall, finding out that the front of the library had been destroyed but not the back part housing the collections (including the pictures gathered for the volume of President Bliss's letters I was working on), getting people's stories from all over the place of what had happened. Seemingly the Volkswagen bus had come in somehow through the Sea Gate off the Corniche at the bottom of the campus and been parked against College Hall on the library side. One studied all the facts and could hardly come to another conclusion than that a very professional job had once more been carried out by some persons or faction who didn't aim necessarily to kill anyone or destroy the library but did want to send a big message by destroying the symbolic center of AUB. Who could that be? Islamic Jihad? They categorically denied it instead of claiming responsibility as was their wont. The Israelis? The Christians on the East Side disgruntled at losing their "own" AUB, the Off-Campus Program that had been closed out? The news came out later that "they" had caught the three or four people "who did it" and they were each from different sects and parties. Thus does College Hall's demise go to rest in the same void as Malcolm Kerr's assassination. Thus Beirut Normal.

The next ten days I spent cleaning up the debris and moving all my things (which had been thankfully boxed up a year ago) into the dining room, the one room in the house farthest from College Hall that still had windows and a roof to keep out the rain. Since the administrative offices had been destroyed with College Hall, I offered the university administration the use of all the house but the dining room, kitchen, and upstairs maid's room that formed a still intact unit and could be closed off for me to use. They did store some things in the old bedrooms that next week, but found the rest of the place too devastated to use.

Also in those days between November 8 and 17, I called my father on the international line next to Smith's Grocery every other day. He wasn't well, was in the hospital, but it wasn't until Saturday morning, November 16, that I talked to Alice and she said, "The doctor tells me that if you want to see your dad again you must get here as soon as possible." Getting a ticket home on Saturday was not impossible but almost so. But it was an emergency, and with the help of friends I managed it for the early Sunday morning plane, and I got set up to leave. I also got through to M to tell him. Saturday night, my friend Marilyn made a special trip down from the AP office to let me know that according to the *Tehran Times* an American would be released with Terry Waite. I remember well Marilyn and I sitting that evening in the two chairs by a lamp in front of the TV that I had in the dining room of our devastated home, backdropped by all the boxed possessions Tom and I had brought to Lebanon or gathered there. She and I talked, but I was so used to zero expectations that never did I think "an American" would be Tom. So when I left early Sunday morning for Iowa, I had only the drive to see Dad.

That was not to be. I called his hospital room from Heathrow Airport when I arrived and there was no answer. I called Alice, and she confirmed. Dad had died Saturday night, for me just about the time I was getting up to make the plane. It was instantaneous, she said—"I heard his voice talking to the nurse as I came down the hall to his hospital room door and when I got to his bedside he was gone." I called Ann, Kit, Joan. We mourned together over the phone.

Alice had said the memorial service would be Wednesday or Thursday and I boarded the plane to finish my journey to Iowa. Arriving late into New York, I got into the Roosevelt Hotel so I would be ready the next morning to catch the plane to Chicago from Newark, New Jersey. I didn't listen to any news either then or the next morning when I got the bus to Newark Airport and checked in at the gate for Des Moines. Then I went to a phone to call Scotland and tell them there about Dad. Peter's daughter answered the phone: "Where are you? Uncle Tom's been released and Dad and Uncle Willie are off to Wiesbaden." I called Kit—same news. I called Alice and got my brother Dave. To everyone I gave the number of the airport telephone next to me so that I had an outgoing phone and an incoming phone. Then I thought about my luggage soon to be on its way to Iowa and went back to the gate counter and told them I'd have to cancel and why. United Airlines then took over. They found me a private room, recovered my luggage, set up my phone situation with a line into the State Department, and found a black-and-white TV as well.

I must have been in that room five hours before I saw Tom's face on the TV. I talked to daughters, to Dave and Alice who were handling media in Ames and had set the memorial service for Dad back to Friday for us, to United Airlines to fix up tickets to Wiesbaden for Kit and Joan and me—Ann wouldn't be able to fly and come because of Willie's imminent arrival. Meantime, Joan, out in Oregon, had told the media that I was in Newark Airport—"I thought you deserved your own back, Mom! You were never around other times and we had to handle the media." The upshot was that the journalists and TV cameras were all set up and clamoring for me through the afternoon. "Not till I see his face … Not till I've talked to him." And it happened: Our liaison Nick Rishutti in the State Department, beautiful now no matter what negatives in our previous lives, called me back and said, "Tom's on the line for you."

"Jean, is that you?"

"Tom, is that you?"

We talked on and on, interrupting each other, glorying in the other voice, and afterward I couldn't remember a thing we said.

But it surely could only have been yesterday that we parted.

The press conference in the outer lobby happened and I took off for Wiesbaden and the historical rest. I've been back to Newark Airport several times since that day and I always go back to the spot and back to those initial phones and back past the inner room door where Tom's release became manifest to me. It's as though all that too were just yesterday—all the feelings flood back each time: the ultimate grief for Dad inextricably mixed with the ultimate joy for Tom.

PART III

Freedom
1991–

Part III part page—The American Air Force Hospital balcony scene of Tom and Jean, joyously reunited in Wiesbaden, Germany, on November 19, 1991, after being apart for six and a half years (courtesy *Associated Press*/Peter DeJong).

Tom

34 "Good News Today"

By mid-November, the *Tehran Times* was at it again, predicting that "Terry Waite and one American will go home very soon." Fine. Bound to be Joe Cicippio. No way Terry or me. With John McCarthy gone from our room, and TW about to go, we couldn't be the "one American." Joe's health was still bad—had to be Joe. Imagine my amazement then at 3:00 P.M. on November 18, when the two men who had visited us in August came through the door. Down came the blindfolds. We were all very quiet. Sitting on the middle mattress, I had just begun to listen to the three o'clock news on the BBC. Terry was working on his poems quietly in his head and TW was relaxing on his mattress to my left. Suddenly, the words that I had been waiting six and a half years to hear. "We have some good news for you today," the interpreter announced. "Like *what?*" demanded Terry. "Today, Mr. Waite and Mr. Sutherland go home." "Yaba-daba-doo," I cheered. "*When*, today?" "At six o'clock," came back the reply. I could hardly believe my ears. But TW was arguing with them— "I don't want to go home. It must be Terry Anderson who goes. He has been here far longer than me, and I insist that it be he who is freed!" Such magnanimity. "Shut up, TW," ordered Terry. "That decision is made—you can't possibly change it." "No, no," continued TW. "I insist it has to be Terry. I won't go before him!" "Will you shut up, TW. This is all decided long ago by the big boys. Get going—don't argue!" Terry was really angry by this time, and even TW sensed the futility of further argument. The atmosphere relaxed. The two bosses began talking to us in very friendly terms. Terry asked for pen and paper to write a letter to his family, and began furiously to set down the poems he had been keeping in his head. They brought them, and told him to be quick—we had to leave. In fact, he got a good two hours in before we left, and managed almost 20 poems, plus a long letter to Maddy. I carried them all.

Soon Mahmoud, Jameel, and Abu Ali came in to join in the merriment and joke with us. They brought in their barber's outfit and cut our hair and TW's beard. Clean underwear. TW took his shower. My turn—I shaved and donned my underwear. Back into the room to find a complete wardrobe—pants, shirt, shoes, socks, cardigan. A belt of a kind I had never seen before and couldn't seem to get fastened, so Abu Ali helped me. It was a reversible one with a brown side and a black one—handy. I still wear it, but it's beginning to fall apart. Lots of laughter. "You will talk about me on TV?" asked Mahmoud. "Certainly, Mahmoud! You were our best guard. I'll talk about Jameel too!" "Are you sure?" he asked. "Absolutely. And when I come back to the AUB, I want you to come to dinner with my wife and me. And bring your wife and children. I'll fix you a better dinner than you have ever fixed for me, buddy!" "No, no. I come your house, you give me CIA!" "No sir. I won't do that. I just want to sit like two civilized human beings when you don't have me chained to the wall, and you don't have any guns. We'll be equals. Then we can argue, and see who is right in our arguments." "No," he insisted, "I not coming your house. Okay. Maybe I call you on the phone. But I not coming your house."

Must have been about 4:30 P.M. Baalbek time. "Okay. Now we go. You must talk with Terry, then we come to take you." TW blurted out in his finest English accent. "You know—you owe me a watch!" "Oh," replied the interpreter, a little taken aback. "You want watch?" "Yes," replied TW. "You stole my watch, you know!" Big deal. They stole *everybody's* watch. Why is he worrying about a stupid watch? We're going home after all. "Okay," replied the interpreter. "No problem. I get you watch." Then followed a brief discussion in Arabic, and they left. Ten minutes later Abu Ali was back and distributing *three* watches, one to each of us—Citizen watches, inexpensive—nice souvenir. I still have mine—quartz, and keeps perfect time!

Terry was still hard at work on his poems. One after the other, just as he had recited them to us. Five minutes to six—in came Mahmoud, Abu Ali, and Jameel, plus a host of others we couldn't identify. "Okay," said Mahmoud. "Now hug Terry and we go." "Get out of here," Terry chuckled. "I'm glad to see the back of both of you. Now I might be able to get some sleep!" We *did* give him a hug, and were hustled out of the room, poems in hand, down a long hallway—I vaguely remembered it from six months earlier. Out into really fresh air. We were bundled into the trunk of a car, first me, then TW on top of me, all 280 pounds of him. I didn't care. I was on my way to freedom.

Five minutes up the hill in the trunk of the car. The trunk opened. "Queeckly, queeckly. Out of the car," came the order. Good old Islamic Jihad! "Queeckly,

queeckly" right up to the last minute of these 2,354 days! "Now into this car. Queeckly, queeckly." But who wants to delay on the way to freedom? This time it was into the *backseat*. First time that had happened in a long time. *Zoom*. We were off. "Now you can take off blindfolds if you like," came a voice from the front seat. "It is okay now. No problem." Off came the blindfolds, carefully. Fat lot of good it did us. The backseat of the car had been curtained off all around by a black piece of cloth, so we were in almost pitch black. And of course it was after six o'clock in late November, long ago dark outside! "We not Islamic Jihad," explained our chauffeur. "We just helping them getting you free." We didn't argue. Didn't matter now—we were roaring south, toward Zahle and Shtaura, and in less than 30 minutes, we stopped, up a side road. One more time—"Queeckly. Out of the car." *Vroom*—it was gone, like a turkey through the corn, but not before I had a look at it in the light of the headlights. As I suspected—a huge Mercedes, probably a 600 series? Only a car like that would have that much room in the back—almost like a Checker cab.

Now what happens? Suddenly, out of the shadows a figure. "Welcome to *freedom*," came the friendly voice in well-nigh perfect English. "My name is General Baaloul of Syrian Intelligence. I have come to take you to freedom! Please come into my car." Whereupon he led us over to *his* car, which was no less impressive than the Mercedes. A BMW 700 series! TW in front in deference to his long legs, I in the backseat behind the driver to balance the weight a little. Half a mile down the quiet side road where we'd been traded and we joined the main Beirut-Damascus highway. Now we sped off in earnest, and General Baaloul was in fine form, telling us all about his son in medical school in Washington University in St. Louis. I could tell him that it was an excellent school by anybody's standards—my brother-in-law graduated there many years ago. Small world. His daughter also wanted to go to America to study, which obviously pleased the general very much—here was no anti-American Syrian. He knew all about the relative merits of the United States and the Soviet Union, and left little doubt as to where his allegiances lay!

He was driving with one hand, while his other contentedly caressed his pipe. God, I thought, we seem to be going awfully fast! I glanced over his shoulder, and sure enough, the speedometer said 95 miles per hour! Here was I, after six and a half years a hostage, and now in grave danger of dying in a car wreck! These were sharp curves we were taking on the roads through Lebanon's mountains! But the BMW negotiated them in great style, and I realized once again why my brother Peter had always been so attached to that breed of car. I had traveled this exact road several times prior to captivity, and knew that we were approaching the Syrian border. There we detoured a little, stopping outside a very impressive "villa" as the Lebanese like to call single residences. Inside, General Baaloul introduced me to yet another general, General Ghazi Kanaan, "the man in charge of Syrian Intelligence in Lebanon," General Baaloul explained. "Ahlen wa sahlen," said General K. He spoke no English. General B translated. They conversed a moment, and Kanaan excused himself while he put through a phone call. "He is calling headquarters, and telling them that you are free," explained Baaloul. Fine with me. Now my family will soon know. As it happened, the news had been broken much earlier than that moment. My friend Frank Vattano had been awakened by a phone call from the Denver press at 5:00 A.M. Colorado time, *an hour before I had any idea in Baalbek of my impending release!*

I asked to use the bathroom. It was a beautiful room, carpeted, clean, warm, and inviting. By far the nicest I had been in in six and a half years. And there on the shelf was a brand new "Water Pik," made in Fort Collins, Colorado, by Teledyne, the company started many years ago by John Mattingly, a professor at CSU who had the idea of a small pump irrigating the teeth and keeping them cleaner than a brush could ever do. I told the generals about my discovery in the bathroom—to their delight. On his table, there was the biggest display of flowers I had ever seen, or so it appeared to me, who had not seen the like in years. "You must have some," insisted the generals. And so I left with flowers in hand and one in my lapel.

Minutes later, we were entering Damascus between 8:30 and 9:00 P.M. Straight to the headquarters of Syrian Intelligence, where we met a bevy of generals, colonels, and other brass, all in a great mood, and all joking and laughing. We even started telling stories to each other, jokes that came out of the recesses of our minds. That's always difficult to do—to translate a joke into another language and have it still sound funny. We tried anyway, and the laughter was raucous. Terry Waite looked at himself in the mirror for the first time in years, and didn't like his beard at all. "Do you think it might be possible to visit a barber?" he asked. "Of course," they answered. An officer went out, and within *two minutes* there was a young man in the room complete with a kit and all the accoutrements. I never cease to wonder how they could possibly have produced a barber, obviously competent, in such a short time, at ten o'clock at night.

A few minutes later we were on our way again, this time a short hop across to the Foreign Ministry, to the scene that had become familiar to us on TV watching other hostages being released. *Finally,* I get to meet the Syrian foreign minister, Faruq al Shiraa. I had dreamed of meeting him for years now! Into the huge ministry building, and I was given over to the American ambassador, Chris Ross.

A scholarly and gentle man, he took me aside. "Your wife is not here to meet you," he said in kindly tones. "She is on her way to Iowa to attend her father's funeral." I was devastated. From being on cloud nine, I descended to the depths of depression. "Not Dad," I thought in disbelief. "He can't be gone! Not Dad." I had known full well, of course, that in six and a half years, lots of friends and acquaintances would die. Even relatives. I knew too that Dad had been fighting prostate cancer all these years—but he came from long-lived stock and he was one tough fellow. *Nothing* could touch *him*. I just *knew* there was no way *he* would be gone. I stood there, unable to speak, and wanting to weep for that wonderful man, but again not able to let the tears flow.

Ambasssador Ross asked if I could go into a small room and speak with the Syrian press, who had been promised a private session with Waite and me. I finally managed to blurt out a word. "Yes, of course. It will be okay." Two or three TV cameras were already set up, and Waite spoke first. Then came my turn. I struggled to get out a sentence or two, but I didn't feel that I had done a very good job—TW was much more articulate. The cameramen tried out their recording, and surprise, surprise, they didn't have their sound set properly, and had only silent tapes! They decided that rather than redo it, and lose the spontaneity, they would take the sound off the radio man's tape, who had recorded it all perfectly.

Into the main pressroom of the ministry. What a zoo! Dozens of journalists of all kinds, print, radio, TV—I had never seen so many TV cameras pointing at me. But no Minister al Shiraa in sight. Instead, we were to be introduced by his deputy, Nasser Kaddour, who spoke briefly in Arabic and introduced Andrew Green, the British ambassador to Syria. Green spoke very briefly, thanking the government of Syria, especially, for its role in our release. Then TW took over and spoke for five or ten minutes. Supreme irony here, however—his speech didn't make it over international TV, at least to America, for the sound wasn't working on their pickup either!

My turn. By this time, I had recovered my composure, and realizing that I would be talking to the entire world, I resolved to give it my best shot, even though I was still *devastated* inside about Dad. I too thanked a few people, especially the governments of Syria and Iran. As I had promised, I thanked also Mahmoud and Jameel for being kind to us, and for at least *trying* to help us from time to time, albeit not very extensively. I gave some details of our conditions, and how we had left Terry. I told the world that I owed my survival to Terry Anderson, for his constant support and encouragement. I joked about TW having come to get us out almost five years ago. "I think we will have to send some American technology over to the Church of England and improve their efficiency, for this fellow Waite came to get us released over five years ago, and only now are we getting out."

The ambassadors were clearly uncomfortable with my expansiveness, but I knew that these journalists had come a long way, halfway around the earth in some cases, and that they wanted a story. So I continued. I especially thanked Iowa State University for ringing the carillon bells on my anniversary: "I heard them," I told the world, "on VOA early on the morning of June 9, 1991, the sixth anniversary of my kidnapping. *Bong ... Bong ... Bong ... Bong* they rang out across the world. They gave me a tremendous lift, and helped incredibly to keep me going during these long last months. So," I concluded, "*Keep those bells ringing Iowa State, and we will all be happy.*" What I didn't know at all was that the bells of Iowa State had since been silenced. The Campanile was in such bad shape that Iowa State had shut it down as being potentially dangerous to the populace. What I also didn't realize was that my words on TV that day of release, sincere and earnest, would have such effect on people listening. An alum from Chicago called up President Martin Jishke and pledged $1,000,000 for the permanent upkeep of the bell tower. And right after, another family called from Des Moines and pledged $250,000 to endow permanently the chair of the carillon player, who was being let go for lack of funds. Various other groups got behind the campaign, and soon President Jishke had over $1.6 million pledged and renovation proceeded. The restoration of the Campanile and the hiring of a carillonneur has now been completed and celebrated with all appropriate pomp and circumstance. A truly amazing story of American networking somehow—that innocent and heartfelt words of gratitude for a gift of loyalty and concern can move people thousands of miles away and inspire them to such magnificent generosity!

I didn't get my "normal 50 minutes on my feet." After only 15 minutes, someone cut in on me and gave the podium back to Terry Waite, apparently feeling a little upstaged and wanting to get back into the limelight for yet another brief spell. This time the sound was working! He chastised our kidnappers, and appealed for the release of all prisoners being held in Lebanon and elsewhere, and we were ushered out.

Ambassador Ross's Cadillac soon had us at his beautiful home where I met his charming wife, Carol. She fixed me the best cup of tea I had had in at least the last six and a half years, if not ever, and we chatted amicably in one of the most comfortable rooms I have ever been in. Almost casually, Ambassador Ross asked, "Would you like to speak to your wife?" I looked at him in amazement. "How can I? She is on an airplane to Des Moines." "Oh no. We have her in Newark Airport!" "Of course—I want that more than anything in the world!" Without another word,

Mr. Ross picked up the phone on the end table by his side of the sofa, said a few words, and laid it down. In 30 seconds, it rang, he picked it up, spoke, and handed it to me. "It's your wife." Blessings on American efficiency! "Hello Jean! Is that you?" "Hi, Tom! Is that you?" We began a conversation as if we had parted just yesterday. That familiar voice—the calm but excited and rational discourse. "I won't go to Ames now. I'm going to turn around and come straight back to Wiesbaden—meet you there! Should be there by mid-morning!" Elation! We could have talked all night. But Mr. Ross was anxious to get the show on the road, and signaled time to go. Reluctantly—"I've got to go. The plane's already waiting for me at the airport." A hurried au revoir to Mrs. Ross, with profuse thanks for her hospitality, and we went outside, where to my surprise lots of reporters were hanging around. "We don't have time to talk to them," said the ambassador. "Gosh, surely I can take a couple of minutes with them? They've come a long way for a story—I don't mind giving them a quickie." And I did, to the delight of the small group—no idea who they were or from where!—answering a few questions, then told them, "There's a plane waiting for me at the airport," which I knew was some 40 miles east of Damascus.

Back into the Cadillac, and I couldn't resist teasing the ambassador a little. "Is this a foreign car, Mr. Ambassador?" He was downright insulted. "Not at all!" he retorted. "This is a *Cadillac!*" Of course I *knew* that all along, cars being one of my hobbies. But I got a quiet chuckle out of his retort! Apparently the ambassador didn't quite know how to handle a hostage with a sense of humor intact! And after all, a Cadillac in Damascus *is* a foreign car! All the way to the airport the chauffeur kept in touch with the plane by radio, which was already running and ready to take off. Four motorcycles ahead of us and four behind us, as I recall. Did I ever feel important. What a fuss over us ex-hostages! I didn't know quite how much until we got to the airport where we went straight through open gates onto the runway and there was the plane—an enormous C-130! Out of the car, hurried good-byes to Ambassador Ross, and I was going up the ramp with Jim Stejskal from the embassy who was to accompany me all the way to Rhein-Mein Air Base, then on to Wiesbaden and the hospital. Jim had a "care package" for me—pajamas, toothbrush, a shirt, underwear, all courtesy of the embassy.

Inside the plane was a crew of some 50 medical people of all stripes and denominations—all from Wiesbaden to look after *me!* Absolutely amazing! Nurses, orderlies, psychiatrists, cooks, heart specialists, internists—and a great cheer went up from the whole bunch as I entered! *Vroom*—we were off and in the air before I even had my bearings. Cameras flashing—I was having my picture taken with men and women in all kinds of uniforms. Euphoria. I was being shown the kind of attention and love I hadn't known in 77 months. No request too small—filled instantly. Finally I sat down, with Dr. Fohlmeister at my side. I looked at his uniform and saw the big bright eagle on his lapel—a full *colonel,* no less! He explained, "I'll be in charge of you for a few days. How do you feel? Is there anything you need now? *Anything.*" A true gentleman, I decided instantly. And the next week proved my initial diagnosis of my doctor to be absolutely correct. One of America's finest. I'll never forget him.

It was after 1:00 A.M. when we took off. An hour into the air I began to feel hungry—I hadn't eaten since about 1:30 in the afternoon of Monday, over 12 hours ago. What would I like? "I would love a real steak, medium rare, please!" I was soon gorging on a huge T-bone. *Mmmm!* Heaven. The first of a series of rediscoveries of what real food could taste like. On the heels of this super-fashionably late dinner came a couple of psychiatrists, both of them gentle and kind, and interested in how crazy I had become in captivity. A whole series of questions to elicit the details of my mental state, rephrased from time to time to test the truth of what I told them. I answered straight and truthfully, and after 15 minutes, each shook his head, pronounced me to be not *too* insane, and said, "I am going back to get some sleep." Most of these fellows were accustomed, even in the Air Force, I suppose, to having a solid night's sleep, and we were in the "wee sma' hours." I, on the other hand, was quite accustomed to having my sleep interrupted at any time, and damn few nights of blissful, uninterrupted rest. And I was still on a tremendous high, ecstatic and euphoric. I interacted with all comers—signed autographs, had photos taken with all combinations of personnel, and joked with them all. Even went for a walk around the back of the plane, big as a football field, as the huge props roared us toward Germany.

Tom

35   Wiesbaden

By 4:00 A.M. we were at Rhein-Mein being met by the American ambassador to Germany, Mr. Robert Kimmitt, and his wife. As Mrs. Kimmitt presented me with a huge, beautiful bouquet of flowers, she told me that her maiden name had been Sutherland! What a welcome! I was still ecstatic, and talked to the reporters on the scene in a pouring rain. Ambassador Kimmitt insisted that I stay under an umbrella, but I told him, "Mr. Ambassador, this is the first rain I've felt since 1985—I'm loving it!" They had a helicopter waiting to take me the 40 or 50 miles to Wiesbaden. But the weather was so atrocious it couldn't fly. Instead, we piled into the ambasssador's car, a regular limousine this time, half a block long. Forty-five minutes later we were at the American Hospital in Wiesbaden, and out of the limousine to another storm of cheers all around. The balcony on the second floor was crowded, people were waving and applauding like crazy. At 4:30 in the morning—crazy was the word! I was getting a reputation as a "talker" (which didn't surprise any of my friends), and the press were loving it. No hostage had ever given them more than a word or two before disappearing into obscurity—but none of them had *taught* as long as I had! Here were *more* press with *more* questions, and I obliged, but briefly, for Dr. Fohlmeister wanted me in his examining rooms where he could really get into my health. "You're in surprisingly good shape," he said. But when he asked me to walk a straight line, as drunk drivers are asked to do, I failed miserably. I was surprised, for I had been trying to keep my legs in shape for these last months in particular, anticipating freedom. Colonel Fohlmeister wasn't worried. "This is to be expected. In a few weeks, it'll come right again. Don't worry. You'll be walking straight and true in no time."

A bit of rest, then breakfast with Air Force waiters. "What would you like?" "Wow! Bacon and fried eggs! I haven't had any in over six years, guys! Half a dozen rashers, and two eggs sunny-side up!" My wish was their command, and in short order, there lay a huge plate of bacon and eggs. And all the coffee I wanted to drink, real American coffee, croissants French-style, and more orange juice than I could possibly get around. Heaven.

My suite was enormous and palatial. It was down "Freedom Hall," christened on the release of the American hostages held 444 days in the American embassy in Tehran, way back in 1979–1981. And every American hostage released in the Middle East since then had been brought to that hallowed hall. I was the latest, perhaps the most jubilant, and the longest-held up to that point. A huge living room, four times the size of any room I had been held in. A bedroom almost as large, with a *king-size* bed! A TV to match, tuned to the American Forces Network, color, perfectly tuned, and bringing in programs the like of which I had never seen in Lebanon. The color seemed too real to be true and on a 40-plus-inch screen—after our 13-inch black-and-white with Islamic Jihad, which had zigged and zagged until our eyes hurt. Heaven.

Must have been mid-morning by this time and I was standing in the living room by the coffee table. The door began to open slowly, hesitatingly, and I looked to it. There was Kit and there was Jean right behind her! *Just beautiful.* A tiny bit older, Kit more mature … but then impressions got lost in pure emotion. Ecstasy—here was the scene I had waited six and a half years for! We hugged, we kissed, and hugged some more, all three intertwined in loving embrace. Finally, we began to talk. We talked and talked. Jean told me "they" wouldn't let Ann fly. Nine months pregnant—with our second grandchild—"A boy this time!" I plied them with hundreds of questions. So much to catch on. I had had almost no news of Fort Collins, Denver, Colorado, Scotland, Iowa, California—*nothing* of any of my family. A couple of hours later, Joan arrived from Portland, Oregon, flying into my room and into my arms. Minutes after that, my two brothers, Peter and Willie from Scotland. They had known about my release before Jean did, and had booked seats on the first available plane. Added euphoria, with news flying in all directions. Joan had had difficulty getting a flight, but like Peter and Willie, made it in time for the "photo-op" the State Department had requested for the press. "No talking today, though," they suggested. "This session is for photos only. If you really would like to talk to them, we'll arrange a press conference for tomorrow." "Fine," I replied. "I won't say a word out there, but I'll be happy to talk to them all they want, and then some, tomorrow!" Out we went, onto the same second floor balcony that had been crowded a few hours earlier. Now we were the only occupants. Six of us in front of the cameras of the world. And of course, the press wanted to ask all kinds of questions, which we all persisted in refusing, until one reporter asked: "Mrs. Sutherland, can you tell us how it feels to be with your husband again?" With a great twinkle in her eye, Jean replied mischievously as she leaned over and gave me a huge hug: "No *words*. Just *body* language." The entire press crew roared approval and loved it. It was promptly dubbed the "Balcony Scene," although we were certainly no Romeo and Juliet, and the whole episode was replayed over the world's television screens for days and even weeks and months.

Jean was allowed to stay with me in Freedom Hall, while Kit and Joan were put up in the guest house next door and Peter and Willie found their own hotel. But we were all together every waking moment that I wasn't with the State Department debriefing team or the medical testing team, though, frankly, it wasn't enough for any of us even though I didn't sleep the first three days. We ate together in the special dining room in Freedom Hall, except one evening when Kit, Joan, and Jean accompanied the State Department team out into the town to a nice German restaurant. By that time I was in intensive care, but I wasn't allowed out of the hospital even at the best of times "for fear of being molested" by the press or "the people"! The State Department Overseas Emergency Services team were absolutely fantastic, like the whole hospital staff. The attention I was getting was a sharp contrast to that of the past six and a half years—almost overwhelming, but I was lapping it up.

The State Department had sent a surprisingly large debriefing team. They wanted as much time as I would give them, making it clear that they didn't want to interfere with our family reunion—I told them I was prepared to give them as much time as they wanted, within reason. I would have weeks, months, and years with my family. They had *thousands* of questions—I tried to answer every one fully and honestly. They wanted to know even the most minute details: How high was the wall around the last place we had been held in Baalbek? What kind of chains did they use? How could I know where I had been held? How had I really been treated? Who all had I been with at any given time? They were frankly surprised at how much I seemed to know, and how sure I was of what I had been telling them, despite the fact that I had told them that I would tell them candidly when I really didn't know the answers to their questions. And on top of that, they asked me to write out every single detail that I could think of.

They checked up on me in an interesting way: They gave me about 40 photos and asked, "Do you recognize any of these as your guards?" I looked long and hard at every one—they were all scruffy, bearded types, exactly like our guards. But, despite having seen quite a few of our guards over the years, I couldn't recognize a one of this lot. I apologized. "Sorry, fellows, but I can't *honestly* tell you that *any* of these guys were my guards." "That's all right," replied one of the team. "These are all American men—we just wanted to check up on you." I smiled. Some of my friends were surprised that they had done this to me. "Weren't you angry at them for trying to trick you?" "No," I replied, "they were only doing their job, and had to be sure about what I had been telling them." After all, they were getting much more than they ever had from a debriefing, or so they said. Were they genuinely from the State Department? Or from the CIA? I never asked. They were American. That was enough for me.

The second day, the press conference duly began at 2:00 P.M. I opened it, on the last minute suggestion of Jean, with a couple of stanzas of Robert Burns's "To a Mouse," which I felt was very appropriate to my case, ending with:

> The best laid schemes o' mice and men gang aft a-gley,
> and lea' us nought but grief and pain, for promised joy.

How the Scots in the TV audience loved that I was soon to discover. A brief statement from me led into a barrage of questions on all aspects of the hostage experience. I answered every single question as honestly and as fully as I could, to the expressed amazement of the mass of press people there. No hostage to that time had given more than a few perfunctory remarks in Damascus, and never a full press conference in Wiesbaden, so it was a gala occasion for all the attendant press. No question was too important, none too trivial. I did them all. One was: "What are you going to do when you get home?" I thought for a moment, then replied, "I am going to get out my old skis, wax them up, and go skiing in the best doggone skiing in the world. Colorado, U.S.A. Nothing like it anywhere, and I'm going to take it up again, in God's Country!" How much the Colorado ski areas loved that innocent and sincere reply I was also soon to discover. An hour and a quarter later, I got the message that the base dentist was ready for me, by which time I was ready to quit, and the journalists were convinced that I was a regular gasbag, no surprise to Kit or to Joan.

At Dr. Mandel's (a lieutenant colonel, no less), I got the news that my broken tooth was too far gone to do anything about, except extract. Six and a half years after the side had broken off it, three and a half after the filling had fallen out of it, and three years since that nut had fatally split it completely in two. Never had it hurt, but by this time it was all out of line because, as he told me, the gum had been trying to push the tooth out by itself for months and months. Out it came, and I now sport a bridge and a false tooth there. Amazingly, however, that was about the sole damage to my teeth. Everything else was salvageable, for which I was and am eternally grateful.

With a clean medical record and debriefing concluded, we were to be on our way home on Thursday in order to get to Jean's dad's memorial service. They had, in fact, rushed everything and pushed it solidly into my three days there so I could make it out by then. Thus, Wednesday night, I was invited to the USO to get a new outfit, head to toe. I got my first new suit in a long time and all the accoutrements to go with it. The Colorado TV crews wanted me to swing by their hotel, but the State Department people were strongly against it. Kit, however, told me how kind the crews had been to her and us all over all these years, how much they had all cared, so I said, "Okay, Kit. I'll go and meet them, and we'll not worry about the State Department." So we swung by and sure enough, there the TV crews were, all set up and ready to go, for as it turned out, Kit had told Roger Wolfe she'd do everything she could to get me there. Thus I met Roger and Bill, Lyn and Carl, Jim, and others who had come all the way to Wiesbaden for me, and with whom I have had many enjoyable encounters since my homecoming. I thought later that if I *hadn't* gone over to that hotel, I would never have forgiven myself. It was my first venture into the reality of what had been going on all the time I was in captivity. I discovered then just how much *Kit* had been doing on my behalf all these years; she knew all of these press folks by first name, and felt very comfortable in joking and teasing with them. The whole interview was relaxed and enjoyable to say the least, and Lyn and Carl got an Emmy for their coverage. And so I *didn't* after all get the kind of treatment that Terry Anderson had warned me about, and from which Brian Keenan, John McCarthy, and Jill Morrell have been running away for the past three years. All of the American press—print, radio, and TV men and women—have been thoughtful, kind, and considerate in the extreme. Perhaps the British media are less so? But, with one exception, I have not found that either, in any of my several visits back to Britain.

Arrived back at the hospital, I found a huge care package had been delivered for me from Colorado's "Ski the Summit." It contained a sweatshirt with "Ski the Summit" on the breast pocket area, four hats, a watch with their logo, and ski passes for the entire season for the whole family! When we finally got home to Colorado ten days later, similar packages from every single area in the state! Heaven.

Wednesday night, I got hold of Terry's sister, Peggy Say. The longest telephone conversation I have ever had! After three and a half hours, beginning at 1:00 A.M., Peg was still full of questions! I finally had to say, "Look, Peggy, I haven't been to sleep for the past two nights. This now makes three, and I'm supposed to be up by six o'clock to go to Ames, Iowa, for my father-in-law's funeral ... so I'd better get some sleep. I'll call you again when I get home." Reluctantly she let me go, and I crawled into the bed where Jean had been sleeping blissfully for hours. Seconds later, it seemed, the nurse was in the room taking blood samples, the last, I thought, that I would have taken there.

Wrong. Into the shower I went, promptly felt giddy and nauseated and had to get out in a hurry to throw up into the toilet! *Blood!* I told Jean, and she went for Dr. Fohlmeister, who came rushing in, very concerned. "Come into my room immediately," he ordered. I was in no shape to disobey, especially a Bird Colonel! He examined me. "No way are you getting onto an airplane today," he pronounced. "No way." He had the ring of authority in his tone. "Dr. Fohlmeister, I have to! I simply have to make it to my father-in-law's funeral. They have delayed it till today so we can get there just in time!" I was begging him. "No, sir. You are not leaving this hospital." "But Doctor, I haven't had any sleep since I arrived. That's probably the reason I vomited. I'm exhausted, but I can sleep on the plane all the way home. And I think the blood is coming from the tooth the doctor pulled. Please. I *have* to go." Without a word, he left the room, and in a few minutes he was back. "Your wife agrees with me. You can't leave." I was stunned. He had gotten Jean to go along with him, so that we would *both* miss her father's funeral! "I can't believe she would say that, Colonel!" "Well, she did. You're going right into intensive care for some tests for a bleeding ulcer. You may well have one, and there's no way in the world that I can let you go on an airplane with a bleeding ulcer, young man. No way." Into the emergency room I went—a huge comedown from Freedom Hall. Bustling with nurses and orderlies, and more tests galore. Here, for the first time, I felt as if I really must be a sick man. Dr. Fohlmeister announced that he was going to have one of his colleagues look down into my esophagus and stomach to determine for sure what was going on with the bleeding. The upshot of that test was "Only a mild little something up near the top of your esophagus. But no big ulcer problem." But just to be on the safe side, and to keep me under close scrutiny, they kept me in the intensive care ward. In a couple of days, I was pronounced well enough to go back to my king-size bed and see my family again, who hadn't been allowed to spend more than a few minutes with me in the past couple of days. Meantime, *they* had been having the time of their lives out in Wiesbaden, which they described as an absolutely marvelous place. But it was time to get home.

Tom

36   Homecoming

Departure time. By now, Jean's dad's funeral was long past. We had spent another four days beyond the Friday of the service, but Jean was quite reconciled. "This way, Dad had his day of tribute with us there very much in spirit and all the attention on him not on us." I had no idea of the reception for us that had tentatively been planned when it was thought we'd be there, but Jean had been in touch with her brother Dave and stepmother Alice and realized how the great hoopla of my return really would have overridden the memorial service for Dad that day. Bill Murray had given his life to Iowa State and to Iowa, had twice run for governor, and at the culmination of his life had founded the wonderful Living History Farms west of Des Moines. He deserved undivided respect and homage on that day celebrating his life and thankfully received it. I think Jean also heard afterward that on the Saturday when we would have been attending an Iowa State football game the temperature with windchill factor was -16 degrees. Dr. Fohlmeister would have had apoplexy even over the thought of that so she probably didn't tell him.

We were escorted back to the airport, stopping in a store en route to pick up a few presents for grandchildren and their parents—lots of fun in German stores—TV cameras omnipresent. But no problems at all. Soon we were at the airport, where our State Department escorts handled everything like the pros they were—we were in the Delta first-class cabin in no time. Off into the skies, lots of photos with a whole bevy of flight attendants, over the pole, and down through Canada. What a thrill to have the captain announce, "We are now crossing the border into Minnesota"—my first time over American soil since 1985. We were headed for Dallas, where we passed through customs and immigration, chatted briefly with the press and welcoming friends, then boarded for San Francisco. Arriving there, we were literally taken into custody and escorted to a private room where Ann, nine months pregnant and smiling radiantly, was waiting with Ray and Simone. I had never met either, but it was wonderful friendship instantly. Jean had given me many details about both of them, and I could see immediately why she was so happy with that marriage, and how fruitful already in producing such a little charmer as Simone. In the room too were lots of officials including the manager of the airport, who told me that outside waiting for me were more TV cameras than they had ever had at the airport, even for a visit from the president of the United States. The chief of police was already worrying about how they would ever get the press conference to finish. "Don't you worry about that, Chief," piped up Kit, with a knowing twinkle in her eye. "My dad will just keep talking on and on and on till the press all get tired and go home!" Laughter all around the room. And that was almost how it did end! I carried Simone out into the big hall, to Ann's surprise for, as she explained later, Simone had always been rather shy around strangers and wouldn't ever let them pick her up. Yet here she was, cuddling up to me and beaming all over her face as though she had known me all her life. Must be something to genetics after all! Another memorable press conference. Again, I tried to answer all questions fully and honestly; the journalists left satisfied— perhaps even satiated?!

Near the end of the conference, one journalist asked, "What are you going to have for Thanksgiving dinner?" I thought for a minute. It really wasn't my call, for we would be in the home of Ann and Ray. But I answered anyway—"We're going to have *turkey!* I haven't had any good juicy American turkey in six and a half years, and we'll have it this year!" "Ah," he came back, "and what for desert?" Without hesitation, I told him, "*Ice cream!* Haven't had any of that either, and nobody can make ice cream like the Americans. *Nobody!* We'll have ice cream." Again, the power of TV showed itself, for next morning early, a telegram arrived: *Greetings from the American Turkey Federation. We are sending you by Federal Express a 30-pound turkey. Have a Happy Thanksgiving.* And the delivery man was no sooner out of the driveway than a kindly gentleman came to the door wearing a colorful uniform, and below we saw the most beautiful antique ice cream van. He smiled and told me, "I am from the Dreyer's Ice Cream Company. We are giving you these two gallons of ice cream for Thanksgiving! And here are 52 coupons for a half-gallon of ice cream to give you one every week for the next year!" Heaven. And only the beginning of the American generosity to come.

I don't even recall whose car we rode in from San Francisco International Airport to Arch Street, Berkeley. But I recall clearly climbing the steps from the street to the front door with TV cameras and lights still playing on me, and still the questions coming—"How does it feel to ..." Of course, for me *everything* was euphoria. Next day phone calls, telegrams, letters, parcels. A deluge. And I was loving every moment of it. We were all together for days on end, with nothing to do but celebrate the most rapturous Thanksgiving ever for any of us. How much to be thankful for: more than words can express. Joan and Kit had each been given a month of vacation by their employers, and Joan had brought a video camera with her all the way from Oregon via Germany, so we even recorded much of the rapture for later. Heaven.

My friend, Frank Vattano, from Fort Collins was frequently on the phone, wondering when we were coming home, explaining that Bill West had arranged with Anheuser-Busch our transportation back to Fort Collins in their corporate jet. "Besides," said Frank, "we are planning a little homecoming for you in Fort Collins. Can you let me know?" We conferred at Arch Street. The temptation to stay until our grandson might arrive was great, but then babies tend to take their own sweet time. It could be a couple of weeks yet. So we decided to travel on Sunday, December 1, 1991.

On the day, we packed early and drove to the Oakland airport, just down the road. There was a gleaming jet, six-passenger, and we four piled in, cramming the other two seats with boxes, parcels, clothes, mail; and we were off at 600 miles an hour. The view of the Rockies was absolutely spectacular—for us this time a real John Denver "Rocky Mountain High." Swooping down to land at the Fort Collins–Loveland Airport in well under two hours, we could see a huge crowd of people gathered all around, who gave us a clamorous welcome, including sky divers with American flags, flyovers by Air Force jets (arranged I found out later by an old friend, Dr. Dallas Horton), hundreds of yellow signs carried by everyone saying "Welcome Home Tom"—the works. An enormous stretch limousine two blocks long, this too with a huge sign of welcome attached all along the side of the vehicle, awaited us, with my old friend Frank Vattano—and Bill West, a new one whom I had never met but who, I learned, had worked tirelessly for me for years and had been Frank's right-hand man in arranging everything that was to come for the next several hours. Thousands of well-wishers lined the road all 12 miles from the airport to the campus, all carrying the same yellow "Welcome Home Tom" signs. A short tour of downtown—complete with an escort of mounted police all around the limo and dozens of press (the whole thing was being carried live on *national* television) and police cars both ahead and following—before we entered the campus proper, where we were met by Senator Hank Brown, Representative Wayne Allard, and Governor Roy Romer. Then there was Mayor Susan Kirkpatrick, along with several others on the steps of the Administration Building. A few brief words with each, then over to "Moby

Gym," the 10,000-seat field house where after a quick bite of lunch, we were escorted by 80 pipers in full regalia into a packed arena. One of the pipers, the pipe major, told me afterward that he had never before heard a bagpipe band completely drowned out by cheering until that day. An absolutely incredible *Welcome Home.*

The proceedings were opened by Frank Vattano, and a prayer by the Reverend Rich McDermott, the new young minister of our Presbyterian church, after which Kit and Joan took the podium for five hilarious minutes of advice to me on "how to handle the media." Jean then spoke, reading some of the messages she had put into *As-Safir* for me that I hadn't gotten—and then truly stirring the crowd as she gave them her ovation for having brought me home: "You did it!" she said. "You did it! *You did it!*" And then with Kit and Joan joining her, she said, "And now, we all give you *Tom Sutherland.*"

It was indeed my turn. What an ovation! I'll never forget it as long as I live and it made up for all those years. And I took my 50 minutes and more describing the captivity and giving my reactions to everything: captivity, homecoming, the United States, my family, the lot. After that, the dignitaries on the platform were given two minutes each to speak. President Yates said in front of those 10,000 in the audience that, "We want you back at CSU, Tom. In any capacity that you want!" Kit, still and always a bit of a wag, leaned over to me and said perkily, "Tell him *president*, Dad!" We all laughed. The speeches over, the bagpipes skirled into "Amazing Grace," and then it was into the limo, which delivered us to our home. There it was—812 Garfield Street, our beautiful two-story green wood-and-brick house behind now-enormous trees, with the welcome lights shining, the place so often evoked in my memory over six and a half years—HOME. Home, too, in the next three days, came the last of the living hostages from Lebanon—Joe Cicippio, Alann Steen, and longest-held Terry Anderson. And to cap it all, on December 6 came the call from Ann—a grandson, William Thomas Sutherland Keller, was in our world and perfect. Pure Joy.

Tom & Jean

37 Professorial Heaven

Tom

So I write today on the third anniversary of my return to Fort Collins. And three glorious years they have been. I've been treated in every way like the hero I'm not. People go out of their way to do things for me, and everywhere I go, I still have greetings of "You are probably tired of hearing this, but *welcome home!*" And I assure them, "I will never tire of hearing these words!" We receive, Jean and I, invitations to concerts, banquets, receptions, anniversaries, and reunions of all kinds. The mail is still flowing in, with greetings and good wishes from everywhere. We have traveled all over the United States and even in Europe and the Middle East and met thousands of people—in truth, the exact opposite of captivity.

To be back home in the midst of a loving and faithful family has been the greatest gift of all. There is no substitute for the love of a family, so instrumental in allowing me to take up immediately "where I left off" as though nothing had ever happened to me. The family gatherings we have had have been joyful, rewarding, and healing in the extreme: Need a hug? You can have ten! Having a wonderful home with beds, bathrooms and basement, loads of room, oceans of water under high pressure for showers whenever I feel like it, coffee as often as I wish, delicious food at every meal, color TV in large screen, high-fidelity music on compact discs—all a dream come true. And then there was working in the yard and on my old cars and repairs to do on the house and symphony nights and dinners with good friends, and CSU, Broncos, and Nuggets games. And sunrises, fresh air, green leaves, rain, snow. All a heaven.

What luxury to have Fort Collins as a hometown. It had always been a wonderful place to live, rated among the best in the United States, with a fabulous climate and the glorious Rocky Mountains towering off to the west. It was

growing rapidly before I left for Lebanon, but on my return I found it tremendously changed—grown from 60,000 people to over 90,000 in eight years. But
the growth had been managed in a thoughtful way, with new parks and golf
courses, superb shopping malls, and dozens of new restaurants. The university
too had grown to over 21,000 students. Amazing phenomenon, however, was
that everyone in the community knew me and was a friend—store clerks, gas
station attendants, post office clerks, bank tellers, schoolchildren, faculty, students, old friends, and former acquaintances—all going out of their way to be
nice. What a change from Islamic Jihad!

I must admit that I have absorbed it all selfishly, opening to this community
warmth as a flower to the sun. I don't know that I've grown, but I've certainly
healed. I wanted to give back and become a real part of it and the opportunities
were there—honorary chairmanship for the United Way; an evening of Scottish
poetry and song as a fund-raiser for the One West Art Center; a weekly seminar
at CSU called "The United States in Global Affairs" with Frank Vattano and other
great CSU colleagues; and talks to schools, churches, community groups, and
service clubs. I have loved going to the schools to speak and I still try to do one a
month or so. The schools everywhere, but in Colorado especially for me, had
kept the memory of the hostages alive by sending letters and cards, tying yellow
ribbons, and releasing yellow balloons. I simply had to say thank you to as many
as I could, and they have been delightful as well as rewarding. The teachers have
taken pains to inform their classes about the whole hostage issue, for many of
them were too young to follow the saga. Shortly after my abduction, the sixth-
grade students of one school in Fort Collins wrote to Jean in Beirut. In her reply,
she promised them that I would come to their school when I was released, and
would be sure to "tell them a story." I did, but not to these students. By the time I
was released, the original sixth graders were already sophomores in college.

Truly I was home. And truly, I had not one home but many. For Scotland
took her own back and I, instead of being the one who "abandoned the native
soil for the fleshpots of America," became a native son again. My rendition of
Burns at the Wiesbaden press conference had been heard by Joe Campbell, general manager of the West Sound Radio Station in Ayr, and organizer of the world's
largest Burns Supper, held annually each January in Glasgow. Before I even left
the hospital in Wiesbaden, I had received an invitation to be there for the 1992
supper. Thus I was given a hero's welcome on my native soil with a flyover of
Scotland in a British Aerospace jet and a fantastic evening in Glasgow, with absolutely the greatest performers of Burns art that I had ever heard: Kenneth
McKellar, Scotland's best-loved tenor, who sang "My Love Is Like a Red Red Rose"

especially for Jean and me; Isobel Buchanan, world-famous operatic soprano; Tom Fleming, whose readings of Burns's poems are also world-renowned; Ian Powrie, without a doubt the doyen of Scottish fiddlers; Ian McFadyen, world championship piper; on and on it went, Scottish artistry par excellence! Jean and I were enraptured.

That was just the beginning. Later that year Bewick Films made the film *Burns in Beirut* to show in January 1993, and Jean-Paul Kauffmann came over and we did "Burns Country" together. He was so moving when he spoke on film of our celebrating Burns in captivity—"They could chain our bodies to the wall but not our spirits." And I also had such a memorable meeting with Professor David Daiches, a leading Burns scholar from the University of Edinburgh. He said about the power of Burns, "You proved it on the pulses." In 1994 Joe invited me to give "The Toast to the Immortal Memory" of Robert Burns, and I brought to my countrymen the stories of the Burns Suppers of the Beirut cells. And in 1995 when all the Glasgow performers brought their performance to the Denver Burns Supper, it was a happening. Once it gets started, there isn't an end to the network of beautiful and deeply meaningful shared experience among countrymen.

Home too was Iowa for both Jean and me as Iowans opened their arms and hearts to us. We came back to visit the grave of Jean's dad, to walk again through his beloved Living History Farms, and to be part of Iowa State University's spring celebrations and commemoration of the wonderful reconstruction of the bell tower and the sounding of the carillon. Home indeed. And in the years after, we would keep going back to the people of Iowa who kept proving with their reception and love that they were family.

And then there was France with my old friends and colleagues at Jouy-en-Josas and my new friend Jean-Paul Kauffmann. They gave us honor and welcome and a warmth of friendship that told me I was again back home.

Within two months of my return I found myself a professional speaker for the Washington Speakers Bureau. What a joy and privilege to address groups all over the country and to find myself at home everywhere I've gone. And the center of the speeches I've given has been my "lessons from captivity." It just seemed to crystallize the first time I spoke, and although every audience and speech is different, it is the essential message I brought back with me from my encounter with the Middle East and Islamic Jihad. It is important to me that Americans of all kinds and ages interact with it. For no matter how much I recount the negative in cell horrors or tales of chains or traveling taped up under the bed of a truck or dark holes or a terrible beating or three suicide attempts, the positive of the experience comes through in the end—for that is how it translated itself in me. Jean's brother John gave me a quotation from Walt Whitman's "Leaves of Grass" right when I got back that said it:

> Have you learned lessons only of those who admired you, and were tender with you, and stood aside for you? Have you not learned great lessons from those who reject you, and brace themselves against you? or who treat you with contempt, or dispute the passage with you?

I could only say *yes* to this, and when one *learns,* it's positive. I learned the value of freedom, of family, of simple pleasures such as color and fresh air, of education, and of the active mind that kept Terry and me going in endless debates and exchanges of information, of community—for isolation was a hell—of the American way of life with its volunteerism and people working together to make a better place for everyone to live in instead of pulling the place apart in their own self-interest. I learned how much more we can take than we think we can: When people ask as they do so often— "How did you survive? I couldn't have taken that kind of treatment," I can tell them, "Yes, you could." In truth, I came out of captivity a wiser and more educated man than when I went in, more educated about myself, about others, and about the life of the mind, and there isn't a place for bitterness in me about the whole thing. It was perhaps the biggest lesson of all—that a larger understanding can convert negative experience to positive experience.

So I ran and spoke, and many of my colleagues were astonished at the pace I kept up, and especially at the number of speaking engagements that I was accepting. Even the psychiatrists worried that some of the returned hostages were "doing too much," and that we might have a nervous breakdown. I participated in a memorable occasion at George Mason University in Fairfax, Virginia, on a panel of ex-hostages, organized by the Lebanese student contingent there. One student suggested to Robert Polhill that *he* had been doing too much, and that the psychiatrists were worried about the possible ill effects on us. Polhill grinned and gave a reply that I wish I could have thought of: "The trouble is that not enough psychiatrists have been held hostage! They need to get out and do their fieldwork!" The crowd exploded in laughter. Robert had indeed been keeping as hectic a schedule as I, speaking for diabetes and especially for cancer causes, having come home with cancer of the larynx and overcoming it with surgery and an artificial voice box. A good man, Robert.

Some of the hostages indeed felt the need for and the benefit of psychiatric counseling. John McCarthy was given counseling by a Royal Air Force team, and he appreciated it so much that he persuaded Terry Anderson to engage the same group. Somehow it never even occurred to me that I should need or want a psychiatrist—I had family, friends, freedom, and euphoria. But both John and Jill Morrell, when they came to Scotland for my brother Willie's sumptuous homecoming party, told me they were worried about me. John had even taken Jean aside by that time and confided to her his fears that even if I was on a high now, I might hit a terrible low, as I had admittedly done at times in captivity.

Maybe that's in my future. But no one can say what it could be or should be for another. Each hostage was and is his own man. Each had to find his own way back into the mainstream. And in truth, for those first two years of freedom I could no more have done as they did and gone off to a sunny beach or a secret destination or holed up from the press to write a book than fly to the moon. To each his own.

Jean

To speak frankly, Tom and I were on totally different need levels when his release came. He had had two and a half years of "halfway house" at the end of captivity with better treatment and radio, TV, and magazines bringing the world in, and he came out hyped to participate as fully as possible in that world he'd only heard and seen. You couldn't give him enough travel or people to meet and talk to or things to do. A "people person," he was ready to go and do. I, on the other hand, had already gone and done for years, and I could happily have gotten snowed in at the cabin and read books and fed birds for the winter—with Tom of course. For some reason that didn't appeal to him. So we compromised— we went and did, and it was indeed wonderful! What a joy to participate in Tom's joy and see America and France and Scotland again. Everywhere we went, people were absolutely beautiful to us both and they gave us such rare gifts of love and things and themselves that our home and hearts are full.

Ann and I spoke one day about her dad and his "professorial heaven" as we dubbed it and Ann gave her view of it:

> I think part of the meaning of Dad's going around and talking to people was that it helped him psychologically—I think most of the other hostages coming out had more trouble than he did—and part of the reconstruction of his soul was in talking to people and having people reach out to him. It was kind of like group therapy— instead of just small group therapy though, he did mass therapy—having thousands of people to talk to and talk it over and think about the meaning and figure out what good parts of it there can be after all.

If "therapy," I could see too that it was a mutual one. For Tom gave of himself to people everywhere he went, and they, who had felt helpless to do anything over those years and had wanted to do something, were able to see and touch him or give him a hug and kiss and know that he was all right and give a gift of presence or applause or tears or something tangible—a bracelet they'd worn for him, a chess set with a tinfoil chessman, a painting and a facsimile first edition of Burns's poetry, an honorary degree, a photograph with a famous person like Barbra Streisand or James Watson of the double helix discovery, a Broncos game ball, a set of cuff links, a letter, plaques of appreciation. These are not just "things," they are precious imbued mementos that adorn his memorabilia room or the walls or bookcases or mantelpiece of our home and have meaning far above "thingness." Indeed for Tom there was no better or more fulfilling way back into life than to interact with people everywhere. I don't think it was just "Applause the Best Medicine?" as *Time* magazine captioned a photo of him the spring after his return; it was a mutual happening, a mutual healing. And I think it was in the finest sense too that Tom naturally did it—the bringing back in a positive way his personal encounter with the Middle East.

What did this return ultimately mean? Tom and I have talked and talked about it. Was he a symbol of something—of American *victory* after a Vietnam *defeat*—of a coming back from death, beating odds … ? Was there a sense of vindication after keeping in for six and a half years? Or was it pure joy at life in place of death—somehow a confirmation that an individual can survive ordeal and that there *is* a merciful God? I guess Americans must come to grips with what the hostages are to them if they will make true meaning out of the total experience. What *we* know is that we feel the mutuality of commitment with the American people. And the Scottish people and the French people and the Lebanese people and all the others of goodwill in this world. There *is* a collective will, a collective goodwill that triumphs.

Jean

38   Family Talk

In between the going and doing and the tremendous gifts of extended community, the home and family was, as Tom said, "the greatest gift of all." For us, too. The house at 812 Garfield wrapped itself in love around us—the furniture with its old cat scratchings, the fireplace, the dining room table that had been Mom's and Dad's, the worn-out kitchen appliances, the garage with its tools in place, and the Volvo in the driveway. And although the days have been few that all our immediate family could get together at one time, we have made the most of them and cherished them. A week at home and at the cabin each August and Christmas, all nine of us together, talking, laughing, hiking, cross-country skiing, feasting, sitting around the table and the fire—in all "making celebration" for all the years' celebrations we had saved up. And we've looked back over the years and talked and talked and talked about everything, and, in the talking, made it all an integrated, shared experience.

In between Tom's cell stories the rest of us would interject the stories of our own "captivity years." Joan had tales of experiences from Los Angeles to New York, back to Colorado and on to Oregon, and told them with her unique verve and spirit—tales of Nancy Fontaine ("everything that Nancy did was in grandiose style") who organized observances and limos paid for by wonderful people in Los Angeles, including a Sunday at Crystal Cathedral and even a boat ride:

One time, after Father Jenco had been released, we went out on a replica of the Mayflower in December of 1986 and saw all the Christmas lights around San

Pedro Bay. The Jenco sisters and Dave Jacobsen I think were there too … . But one of the things I especially remember was that Nancy worked with nursing homes and had people there adopt hostages—it was the man who adopted Ben Weir that died the day he was released and it made such an enormous impression on us … .

Joan had spent three years in Fort Collins with Kit and they traded innumerable stories about the media with whom they were in almost constant contact over the years. It was "Do you remember … ?" and then a story about swapping their TV presence for a lunch or a beer or about Kit giving tit for tat to the New York press after seeing Pérez de Cuéllar. Kit, especially, being the hometown spokeswoman for the entire time, dealt the most with the media, and she put their experience and feelings into serious words:

> … the whole question of whether they did the wrong or right things as media people is in the same category of whether the government did, or we for that matter did. There's no use saying what any of them should or shouldn't do; everyone did what they had to do and it all became part of the phenomenon over the years.
>
> We came to know two different types of "media-folk." Those that were the blood-thirsty, big-city, get-the-bite-and-get-on-with-the-next-job hounds, the hard kind … . But then there were those—national and hometown—who lived with the story, grew with us, felt the emotion, and cared. This group— well, we went through a lot together, and we had many good times during the long, long years. Dealing with me, they found more willingness to do early morning interviews if they donated the Bloody Marys; that to get one good sound bite they had to wait out all of my bad jokes; if they wanted a picture, I wouldn't pose without a smile. For my part, I learned that even the most trivial rumor required a comment and then, if I didn't want to go before the camera, they would fish out their "Ugly Kit pictures" and put them on the screen; that they can, and will, show up at any time of day or night; and finally, that I had made some close friends in our shared situation that would remain important to me even after the story ended. I'd invite them to my wedding to share in it, not to report on it.
>
> I think of the people, the channels, the newspapers, the radio stations—so many of them. They had concern for the story and they cared about it, about us, about each other. They were people of integrity. And it wasn't just for us here, because you, Mom, had all those journalists in Beirut you told us about—they became true friends and supported you and wrote right things about you and told you what was going on … .

Ann's stories for her dad were different—becoming a motorcyclist, the struggle to get grants for her work at University of California–San Francisco, Ray's accident and the months of hospital, the making with Ray a home, a marriage, a family with his son Alex and their new daughter Simone, a new house in Berkeley and daily commutes to her lab, then graduation and the postdoc struggle to be a good supermom, and her happiness with it all. Hers was and had to be a different work not only for herself but also for her dad; it just wasn't easy for her to see that it *was* for her dad:

> I had so much work to do and so much to cope with that I kept trying to put your captivity, Dad, into the background and not think about it all the time but only at certain times when I had enough strength or energy to manage it; … and it was such a boon that Kit and Joan wanted to do all the publicity stuff because it would have sent me over the wall … . I felt totally guilty about not doing it like I was the bad daughter because I didn't do all that—I felt like you'd come out, Dad, and say "Why didn't you go on TV and press for my release? Why didn't you do this or that and be more proactive?" … I guess I couldn't see how much I could do for the cause—and yet at the same time I felt entirely guilty because there I was leading my life with a job and a family and a home and a bed and a shower and there you were … . And yet I couldn't give up on my graduate work because I felt if I did that and you came out, Dad, you'd say, "What the hell did you do that for?" I couldn't serve your commitment, Mom, because I hadn't had anything to do with it—I guess the only thing I did to serve the cause in the family was to be a center for Kit and Joan, to form a family.

And her dad, as thrilled and proud with all Ann had done as he was with the others, gave her the hug that affirmed: "You did just the right thing."

Tom was simply overwhelmed with what his friends and the larger community of Fort Collins had done for him. He had thought in captivity that he was a forgotten man because his name wasn't on international TV and radio like Terry's, TW's, and John's. But the treasures of community effort had built up for him over the years in Fort Collins as they had in America at large to be given him on release. Kit especially filled him in on the background of hometown effort:

> "The Friends of Tom Sutherland" in Fort Collins were just the greatest—hundreds of them, people you could count on. Working with them on all the things they came up with was a really great experience. As Sutherlands we didn't initiate anything, we didn't even do anything except start the Funds, but we didn't organize, they did. People just came forth … . It was like I told Reverend Martz when he said, "You just

tell your mother that when people ask here are five things they need to do …"
And I said, "You can tell me that, Reverend Martz, until you're blue in the face, but I am never never going to tell people that there are things they can do and here is a list." What we did when someone came up and said, "What can I do?" was to say, "Whatever feels right to you, whatever feels like it's coming from you is the right gift." "Can I bring the spaghetti to the luncheon?" "Can I organize a bike ride?" "Can we make T-shirts?" Tree plantings, spirit of the season, Christmas gatherings, a tree with yellow ribbons, crane-folding—all so unique because they were created by different people who wanted to be involved. One year the handicapped riders biked up through Estes Park and finished at the Sculpture Gardens bringing yellow flowers—they dedicated their ride to you, Dad.

How do you ever say thank you to people like that who just give so much? It's so great, Dad, that you're now able to do things with these people and be a friend back and it's right. The Friends—we'd sit in a meeting and Frank would say, "Now how about doing this?" and I'd think, "My God, that sounds impossible like such a headache to the police or to facilities or grounds, and yet the person in charge of that would say, "Oh well we could do this or that, it would work" … and then we'd work with it and it always worked. All they had to do was call Karl Brown, the bag-piper, and he'd say "How many pipers do you want?" And the culmination was your homecoming with all that happened and everyone came out including 80 bag-pipers. And every one of those thousands of people who came out to welcome you home gave you a special gift—as well as those you've met since all over the world who have said "We prayed for you … Welcome Home!" And you saw it and received it and it made you whole again.

Sometimes we got emotional and it was okay. Kit and Joan talked of their loneliness as they started new jobs, new lives, and Ann so uncharacteristically cried one day we talked. And then I found among all the papers of the years of Tom's captivity the message I'd put in *As-Safir* for him: "You'd be proud of your daughters for they are 'true, fair, and kind.'" I found also the letter I'd written Ann, Kit, and Joan on March 31, 1986, and gave it to him for the first time and to them for the second time:

I'm just so proud of all of you that I can hardly restrain crowing about you … . I hope you all realize that what you do by being so strong and independent and successful is to make it all possible for me to be here to be the same thing. And what else can we do for your dad that's so productive. We could be flailing around expending useless energy in public—what will count in the last day is what we've done to keep a tight family together and a strong ongoing individual effort for self so that he comes home to a support group that can't fail. Keep that wrapped up for the great day and know that you are doing everything that is just right for us all.

And God Bless You All ... .

Part III photo collage (clockwise from top left)—Tom's daughters register their emotions at news of their father's release from captivity, November 18, 1991: Kit (left) raises a bottle of champagne in the front yard of the family home in Fort Collins (courtesy *Fort Collins Coloradoan*/Michael Madrid); Joan (center) in her Gresham, Oregon, apartment holds up a joyous banner (courtesy Dennis Boyer); Ann (right), caught by reporters early in the morning in their Berkeley, California, home, awaits confirmation of the news (courtesy *Fort Collins Coloradoan*); Good friends in the Fort Collins and Colorado communities give Tom a big Colorado-style "WELCOME HOME" as a homecoming present December 1, 1991; Tom, Terry Anderson, and Alann Steen share a moment of humor with President Bush as he shakes the switchbox for the national Christmas tree after the lights fail to go on when Terry Anderson throws the switch (courtesy *Associated Press*); Tom and Denver Broncos quarterback John Elway exchange greetings on the sidelines during a Broncos–Phoenix Cardinals game, December 1991 (courtesy Dave Zalubowski); Tom meets granddaughter Simone Sutherland-Keller for the first time, shown here at the press conference at San Francisco Airport on his arrival, November 23, 1991; VICTORY!! Tom arrives at Fort Collins-Loveland Airport December 1, 1991 to the tumultuous community reception—"Welcome Home Tom!!"

Part IV photo collage (clockwise from top left)—Tom meets with Hajj Hasan Khalil, politburo chief of Hizbollah, Hizbollah Headquarters, southern suburbs, Beirut, during filming of his return to Lebanon for NBC *Now,* September 1993 (copyright National Broadcast Company); The famed six columns of the Temple to Jupiter in the Roman ruins at Baalbek, Lebanon, a special trip for the Sutherlands during their return, September 1993 (courtesy John Murray); The closed and guarded Medical Gate of AUB exemplifying the "no entry" for Tom and Jean on their return to Beirut and AUB, September 1993 (copyright National Broadcast Company); Tom and Jean together in the den of their Fort Collins home as they begin this book of their experiences, March 1993 (courtesy Ossie Abrams); Tom with his beloved 1966 Volvo in the driveway of their home in Fort Collins, November 1994; Tom shown in happy reunion with his friend and driver, Sharif Kanaan, September 1993, Beirut, for the first time since their shared kidnap experience eight years earlier on June 9, 1985 (courtesy Marilyn Raschka).

PART IV

Beirut Balcony Revisited
1993

Part IV part page—Tom at the base of the Roman columns of the Temple to Jupiter, Baalbek, Lebanon, on his return trip, September 1993. In the far background, seen through the space between the mighty columns, is the Sheikh Abdullah barracks of his captivity.

Tom

39 Abu Dhabi to Jerusalem

Sometime in 1992 the Young President's Organization (YPO) called: "We're having a "YPO University" in Cairo and Jerusalem .... Could you join us as part of the faculty?!" A whole week in each city in May of 1993 to learn and experience firsthand the Arab and Israeli cultures? *Yes!* We had been to Cairo several times and had loved it, but never to Jerusalem. It was a dream come true and we accepted immediately. But problems of security developed in Cairo; tourists were being assassinated by the fundamentalists there, with a view to ruining the tourist industry and thereby toppling the government regarded by them as much too close to the decadent, immoral, imperialist West. Thus, at the last minute, the YPO changed their Arab location—instead of Cairo, we would go to Abu Dhabi where things were peaceful as well as Islamic.

Thus our return to the Middle East, with our first stop Abu Dhabi on the Persian Gulf. We had never been there, and frankly we were both extremely impressed. Formerly a poor state, it now ranks among the wealthiest in the world, and where there were mud huts only 30 years before, now there were sumptuous houses and hotels. The Abu Dhabi Hilton in which we were lodged ranks among the most luxurious we have ever been in. Marvelous testimony to what can be done with oil wealth when it is used to better the lot of the people of a country, rather than to buy arms. Perhaps most amazing of all, the Abu Dhabi people had retained their gentleness and goodness. The Sultan Ahmed Sulayem, himself a member of YPO, spared no expense nor effort to prepare at such short notice a completely fantastic visit, including a desert overnight. A whole town of tents was raised for nearly 500 couples out in the dunes. The logistics must have been horrendous, but their tiny army pulled it off, with showers and camp beds and electricity—the works! Bedouin food and entertainment along with camel rides and authentic dune experience—fantastic.

If that was our Arab cultural experience, we also had a true learning experience in the Arab-Israeli-Western culture clash and we knew we were truly back in the Middle East. It came the first morning in Abu Dhabi's civic center with the keynote speech given by Dominique LaPierre, a Frenchman and the coauthor of *Is Paris Burning?* and *O Jerusalem*. Whether he was just insensitive, purposefully incendiary, or had as his objective the setting up of an experiential happening for the audience, he proceeded to give a speech extolling the Israelis and denigrating the Arabs, to the point that a row of Abu Dhabi dignitaries in their flowing white robes and head coverings rose and left the room. The woman member of the Egyptian parliament, Dr. Laila Takla, also participating in the conference, left after them. A minute later and the sound system was turned off. LaPierre, however, proceeded without amplification to the end, with his audience sitting stunned. The sound system back on, Madame Takla from Egypt came back in and went to the microphone. Quietly, calmly, but most forcefully, she made a statement on behalf of the Arab people, explaining the symbolic action that had been taken and why. All there understood the strength of the feelings of the Arab nationals and their knowledge of a grave discourtesy done them in their hallowed civic center in the midst of their most sincere and generous hospitality, by a guest from the West—and their knowledge as well of their reciprocation of a discourtesy done by them in return, a heavy penalty paid in respect of their cultural ethics. Without an apology offered on any side the university proceeded, Abu Dhabi hospitality impeccably maintained. But the shared experience made an indelible impression on all the participants, who left the small country with a sincere and augmented respect for its Arab people.

On May 1 we flew to Israel by way of Cyprus, landing at last in Tel Aviv. Security here was quite a bit tighter than it had been in Abu Dhabi, but the arrangements had been so carefully made that we were soon in buses for Jerusalem and our hotels. Hard to believe that we were finally in the Holy Land. We toured the city, old and new, and did a "Christian Pilgrimage" tour up the Jordan River, stopping at the spot where John had baptized, visiting Peter's home village, and sailing the Sea of Galilee. How much closer to the Christ of our belief we were in the countryside than in the Jerusalem edifices built over sacred spots and absolutely desecrating them. A symbol somehow, we felt, of the effect of institutionalization on a living truth, an underscoring of what we'd found in Lebanon. In Galilee, we looked across and up onto the Golan Heights, towering over the northeast corner of Israel, and could easily see the former strategic advantage to such a location; now, however, despite Israeli hawk rhetoric, the area was of doubtful value as a position of defense against modern missiles. Even the relatively unsophisticated missiles that Iraq tossed at Israel during the 1991 war had wreaked havoc in the country. Israel will, in any case, have to restore the heights to Syria before President Assad will ever come to terms. That canny dictator will wait it out—we saw him do it in Lebanon. And turning to the left, then, we looked north from the Sea of Galilee toward the notorious border with South Lebanon with its "self-proclaimed security zone" and turncoat army, and destruction of the lives and homes of its inhabitants. Indeed, we felt the complexity of our "Christian Pilgrimage."

Fascinating too were the presentations given by several key Israelis and Palestinians that provided the clash of viewpoints. Frankly, the impression was that in the panel discussion, the Palestinian spokespeople came out ahead, the Israelis defensive and rigid, the Palestinians intelligent and reasonable. In the separate sessions, Moshe Arens gave his usual hard-line approach to handling their "Palestinian problem." But he seemed like a dove compared to Benjamin Netanyahu, the new leader of the Likud party. His solution was to deport all Palestinians over the Jordan River into Jordan. "*There is a Palestine already,*" he avowed. "*It is called Jordan!*" Our immediate reaction to hearing the rhetoric of Netanyahu was that if he ever gets into power, it is good-bye to the peace process. Fortunately, the treaty between Israel and Jordan was signed before this could happen, and interestingly, the American participants listening in on this session gave only polite applause.

By absolute contrast, the final keynote speaker was brought in with a standing ovation. It was the statesman, Shimon Peres, insisting: "A million and a half Palestinians simply can't be ignored, and the present state of chaos and injustice has been going on long enough. We simply must trade land for peace." The entire speech was thoughtful, logical, and conciliatory, and when he finished, the room exploded in applause, and everyone rose to give him a five-minute standing ovation! It was one of the most moving experiences of our lives, and it was clear to us just how much the bright and thoughtful American-Jewish business leaders feel both about Peres and about the peace process. Our Abu Dhabi-Jerusalem YPO University thus ended on a high and optimistic note, with a wealth of experience and unsettling ideas jockeying for our attention.

During our days in the region, both the local people and the members of YPO kept asking me, "Doesn't it give you a bad feeling—aren't you a little scared being back here in the Middle East?" But in truth, I wasn't at all. Rather I was exhilarated and enjoying being back, and it was fun to be tasting pita bread that was fresh and soft, and hummus and baba ghanoush and all the delicious Arabic and Middle Eastern dishes. The whole atmosphere, both Islamic and Jewish, was seductive and exotic, and it began to inspire in us thoughts of going back to Lebanon, to revisit old haunts, meet our friends there again, and lay to rest any possible remaining ghosts, dragons, or demons that might be remaining from my captivity in that place. We could restore our positive image of Lebanon again, and it would make a right closure on our entire experience there.

We discussed such a trip on our TWA flight homeward from the Middle East, where incredibly we met and talked with one of the flight attendants who had been on the TWA liner that had been hijacked on June 14, 1985, so long ago. "I am the only member of that crew still flying," she said. Even with that murderous hijacking stark again at the front of our minds, we continued to think about a return trip to Lebanon. When, soon after, I was invited to a meeting by my French animal industry friends to be held in September of 1993 on the island of Sardinia, we began to plan an extension of that journey to go on to the eastern shore of the Mediterranean, "to see Lebanon again in the sunshine."

In June I got a phone call from John Siceloff, a producer with NBC inquiring as to whether we might be interested in going back to Lebanon to commemorate the tenth anniversary of the blowing up of the Marine barracks and the killing of 250 Marines while they slept. "Amazing that you should call, John, for just last month Jean and I had decided it was time for us to go back to Lebanon." "So you might consider going with us?" he asked excitedly. "Let us discuss it, John, and I will call you in the next day or two."

Jean and I did discuss it very seriously, weighing the pros and cons. A couple of phone calls to friends in Beirut, just to see how things were looking at that time, a call to M as well for his reaction ("That's wonderful," he said), and our minds were made up. But we had serious reservations about doing the program on the blowing up of the Marines. I called John back. "Why don't you think of doing a documentary on the American University of Beirut, John? That is a venerable old place, with an interesting history. And they are starting a campaign to raise many millions to rebuild College Hall, the original building on the campus destroyed by an enormous bomb just before I was released. That could be made into a very positive story about Lebanon. If you do the one on the Marines, you will surely rekindle old animosities and bitterness, which will greatly impede the patching up of relations between the United States and Lebanon at a time when the Lebanese are very discouraged about their country." "I guess you are right," replied John, a sensitive and thoughtful man. "Let me think about this. And I've got to do some clearing before I can commit to you. Send me a statement of your rationale for going and I'll put it to them. Somehow I think we can do it!"

A day in the composition, and the statement was off to John:

AUGUST 4, 1993, Revisiting Lebanon—A Rationale, Tom and Jean Sutherland—
Our commitment to Lebanon and the region has been a continuity from 1983–
1993 … . Captivity became a part of that commitment, the result of having taken
the risk of going to Lebanon and then staying to carry on a job at the American
University of Beirut, an institution caught also in the violence and sticking to its
commitment to education there. It is important in our view to act on our belief that
if something terrible happens to you on a mission you have undertaken you don't
give up on that mission. We see both the captivity for Tom and the work in Beirut
that Jean carried out through the six and a half years as a part of our total
"work" in Lebanon which doesn't stop with Tom's release and our return to
the United States. The message we take to the American people in our travels
and talks are an extension of this and the concept is central to the book we are
writing … . Our return is a sign of our continuing positive commitment to
Lebanon and the Middle East as well as America—for there are many American issues involved.

Since Tom's release we have thought of a return to Lebanon—a personal journey
to see people and places that meant a lot to us, to see what's different, what's the same,
what's the possibility for the future there. To go to AUB, to the farm in the Bekaa, to the
Faculty of Agriculture, up the streets into Ras Beirut, down into Ain el Mreisse, to
Smith's Grocery … . Jean has been back twice since the release but Tom's going is the
crux—it is a sign that he does not hold anger or bitterness toward either the place or
the people and that we care as we always did. To go back to AUB from the airport is the
journey that was interrupted in 1985 and will be an emotional moment as well as a
strongly symbolic one. It is an essential journey together we would make to reestablish
the so-important connections; … at either end they cannot be overemphasized.

Whatever return we make will be in a most positive way—in peace and for
peace. If the peace process is to go forward in the region, people will need to come
forth out of most terrible experiences to say no to continuing cycles of violence and
retaliation, and to say yes to resolving the conflict and setting the terms for a positive future of coexistence. It can't be done by talking from the outside, it must be
done by being there in Lebanon and the Middle East. There is so much work necessary to ensure American support that is just and impartial and it is our belief that
individuals can make a difference and thus have the responsibility to do so. We'd
like to discover and focus objectively on the possibilities for resolving such critical
human issues as South Lebanon, reconstruction, the economy, the refugee problems … . Perhaps there are ways to see and talk to such strong government and
industry people as Rafiq Hariri and George Frem.

It is for us and for Lebanon that we would go back—there are big issues that
cry out for bold and different action that speaks.

This done, I called Dr. Nancy Pyle Nichols, the vice president for development at the AUB. "Nancy. I want to talk very confidentially to you!" I explained all about the plan to go back to Lebanon to do a documentary on the university, which would be aired nationally on NBC. Nancy laughed in delight. "What a stroke of luck," she exclaimed. "Just what we need at this time to help with the fund-raising for rebuilding College Hall! National TV. Wow!" "But remember, we all want this trip to be kept a strict secret," I reminded her. "We don't want any booby traps greeting us on our arrival! I've had that happen once before! This time, I'll be a little more careful!" She agreed, and pledged all the help we would need. We hung up, both happy at the prospect of doing something really great for AUB. The plans evolved and were solidified.

The question of traveling to Lebanon when there was still a State Department ban on going there caused us some discussion. For Jean, it was no problem, for her passport was still stamped "Valid for travel in Lebanon." I was in the process of obtaining a British passport, since nowadays it is apparently no longer against the law to hold another passport like this, as is done by most Israeli and Lebanese-American citizens. "I could go on my British one, John?" "No," said John Siceloff, "we will travel on American passports. We are journalists, and you are our consultants. There won't be any problem. Besides," he continued, "one of our senior executives phoned the State Department for help in getting entry visas for Lebanon, and he was advised, 'Don't ask. If you ask us, we have to say *no*. But if you run into any problems, the telephone number for Secretary Christopher is such and such!' So," concluded John, "I think we have everything in hand. If not, I'll call you back." Jean called M and asked if we paid his way would he contemplate going over to be there in the background as personal security for us, "just in case," and he agreed.

Two days before our departure, Jean called Dr. Nichols back at the New York office: "Nancy, I've talked with Elien Heineken and she's been very hospitable about our staying in their AUB apartment while they're gone and we're there. But we'll get there late without notice—what do you suggest we do?" "Just roll up to the gate and ask for the deputy president," came the reply. "There'll be 50 people wanting you to stay with them .... Incidentally, I have to tell you that the new AUB president, Dr. Haddad, and I are not working things out together and tomorrow will be my last day with AUB. But I'll have letters delineating everything for everyone when I leave and the man acting in my position on Monday will be in charge of everything with the campus." Thereby, as they say, hangs part of our tale.

Tom & Jean

40   Beirut Diary

Tom

Thus it was that we set off for our second Beirut adventure, this time as "journalists" with the NBC *Now* production team, John Siceloff, producer, and Fred Francis, interviewer. I kept a diary of it all:

SATURDAY/SUNDAY, AUG. 28–29—Flew from Denver to Dulles and then to London. Lined up at 9 A.M. to board the MEA flight to Beirut … . Who should we see but Efat, one of my former students who had come to CSU for her Ph.D. and was now returning to take up a position with AUB. Happy Reunion! Such a nice young woman and it was somehow felt that we'd been through a lot together. We boarded and it was exactly the same flight I had taken on Sunday the 9th of June of 1985, arriving in Beirut around 5:00 P.M.

   5:00 P.M.—Our visas, stamped only on a piece of paper rather than in our passports, gave us no problem at the Beirut International Airport, and we were met by the drivers who were to escort us around the country for the next week, and by Gerald Butt of the BBC, whose voice I had heard reporting from Beirut dozens of times, before I was abducted, and again after we got the radio in captivity. It was fun to meet him in person, and as in all first encounters with radio personalities, he was nothing like I had imagined! Much younger than I had thought, much taller, and much more relaxed than possibly he had a right to be working in that part of the world. He too was a consultant, and turned out to be first-rate. He had studied Arabic and the Middle East in university, and was fluent in the former and an expert on the latter. With him in charge, I felt comfortable right away … . As we waited in the milling crowds to get our luggage, Jean spied M among the hundreds outside the immigration fence and had a chance to have a few moments of anonymous conversation with him … . She let him know our plans and who was handling our schedule and where we'd be contactable. He reciprocated with a number for him and a parting word of advice: "Just be cautious … . Fadlallah is gone from Beirut this week."

7:00 P.M.—Met our driver, dropped off the NBC crew at Summerland Hotel. They offered to have us stay there with them too, but we opted for AUB to be back on campus, just like old times … . Arrived happily and confidently at the gates of the university at about 7:30 P.M. But there our problems began. The guard at the gate had no idea who we were, and had not even heard of me. He began making phone calls to get authorization for us to enter the campus, but Deputy President Makdisi was out of the country and he had no luck in reaching anyone with authority for the longest time. This was a holiday for the prophet Muhammad's birthday as well as for Musa Sadr Day. The guards went across the Corniche and got us chairs as well as coffee from one of the vans and we sat at the gate for over half an hour talking with all who appeared while the guard called around. Amazingly, there were colleagues and friends … . One of the first was an AUH nurse, one of Jean's former students from the nursing English program, and they had a good talk about what he was doing … . Even one of the faculty from the Hariri Program, Omar Djezzini, ran up, all sweaty from his jogging on the Corniche but nevertheless folding Jean into a great bear hug! All were quite excited to see us. "Are you returning now to the university? We hope so! We need you!" "No, unfortunately," we replied, "this is just a short visit." Finally, the guard got someone whom he considered enough of an authority figure to let us on campus. An AUB driver in his Jeep took us up to the door of "Faculty 2" and delivered our baggage to the fourth floor. We picked up a key from mutual friends and soon were ensconced in the comfort of the Heineken apartment.

Jean's first priority was to get reacquainted with her cat, Crystal, the Heinekens' special acquisition since November 17, 1991 … . Jean scooped her up and laid her over her shoulder in a long-accustomed way and she and Crystal both purred! She was in good shape. A hot and humid August evening, and we were dripping sweat. I shed most of my clothes and fixed us both some eggs and a couple of vodka tonics, mentally keeping track so that we could reimburse.

10:00 P.M.—Surprise call from Haddadin (head of chemistry while I was there but now vice president for academic affairs, who it turns out is acting deputy president at this time in the absence of Deputy President Makdisi) and Vice President for Administration Tomey who wanted to come down and collect us to take us up to Marquand House to talk to the new president of AUB in New York, who had already heard that we were there on campus! How did that happen? Well, he must have called to welcome us to the campus! Drove up to Marquand House with Haddadin and Tomey almost without conversation. (Where is the welcome here? Why the officiousness? Why no friendly interested questions about what we're doing and going to do, etc., etc.?) Tomey went to the phone and while he was putting through the call, Jean and I understood that there was going to be a big problem. Haddadin said, "You know there are serious considerations here." We looked blank. "Your presence on campus, you know, is a risk for AUB; … any building you're in could be targeted." Jean challenged him a bit, not quite realizing how bad things really were: "But taking risks is what a university is all about, isn't it?" He wasn't seeing the big picture, however: "After all, we've had two attacks before this, as you well know." Since we and the Lebanese would know that I had been released on *fatwa*, which would guarantee my safety from attack from Islamic Jihad, we grappled with who would bomb a building I was in—the Christians, Palestinians, Druze, Sunnis, Amal, Israelis??? But the call to New York had gone through and I got on the line with AUB's new, and by us unknown, President Haddad, who, instead of a nice warm welcome or even a reasoned series of questions about why I was there, proceeded to give me a lecture on why I should not have come there as an American, "You are an embarrassment to AUB." He didn't seem, like the Christian Lebanese administrators, to be worrying so much about my putting AUB into danger as about the fact that USAID was one of their donors and the State Department might think we were welcomed by AUB in flagrant opposition to their passport ban and withdraw their support. But that didn't seem truly feasible as a reason, for no true university allows any government to dictate its actions and policy through its grants, nor in my case would the U.S. State Department make an issue of it. It did seem to be the passport issue with him ... . "Are you there on your American passport?" "Yes, as part of an American journalistic team." No way then to escape it, I received a thorough dressing down.

I was stunned. Needless to say, my tone changed dramatically from enthusiastic to cold and cautious. I proceeded to tell him that if he really felt that we were "an embarrassment," we would be very happy to get off the campus and have nothing to do with AUB on our visit, but that if he wanted in truth some positive publicity for AUB, we would be able and well placed to give it to him, and thus the die was cast for our No Entry to AUB henceforth. Although he said that he was sorry that our first encounter should have been like this, and he would get back to me, he didn't. Nor to NBC.

I told Haddadin and Tomey that we would move out of the Heineken apartment and off-campus right away, and Jean went off in the AUB security Jeep to find us a place to stay, straight to Al and Lou Buckley's whom she knew would welcome us with open arms. And they did—she walked the four flights of stairs in the darkness of no electricity and was back in a few minutes saying that Al Buckley was dumbfounded to see her in the flesh—so were Lou and Suzy—she told them about our "welcome" at AUB, which did not surprise Al in the least. So back to the apartment to collect our luggage after this very brief stay (but we had been on campus and in a residence!), and hightailed it down to Buckleys across the wall from AUB arriving about eleven at night. Al immediately poured some stiff gin and tonics and we visited till the wee sma' hours. What real and good friends, and what a lovely rest of the evening and overnight and breakfast ... .

MONDAY, AUG. 30—Called Nancy Nichols in New York and left her a firsthand report on her answering machine ... . A telephone call to Summerland to set up a meeting with the NBC team at the medical gate. Walked along the Corniche to the parking gate with Al and Susy—this time no problem in getting in through the gates with Al, who is used to coming and going freely—also different guard! Sauntered up quietly through AUB. Up the drive with the old Marine/AUB Faculty baseball field now a parking lot on one side with Agriculture beyond, the Green Field on the other, and then looking up—there were the familiar white Arabic arches of Our Balcony ... . But no faltering in our conversation or our stride, we turned and climbed the familiar great steps up to the left of our old home. And there it was like before but now different—so kind of desolate with no grass or garden, and probably our imagination but "feeling" empty. We didn't stop nor would there have been a way to get in. Nor did we tarry, looking in over the green gates. It was up the steps and over the spot where David Dodge had been abducted, past Marquand House with its memories of the Kerrs and long-ago deadly shells. And all of a sudden a very present and open arms joyful reunion with Marilyn Raschka and Elaine Larwood running to meet us ... . Marilyn: "I was at the Turkish bath with a friend who knows a stewardess. She said you had come in and I dashed to find you."

Then there we were, face-to-face with an open area that had once held College Hall. I just couldn't believe it ... . So many fond memories of interesting meetings in that venerable old building ... all gone now ... just a huge hole in the ground. Strolling down the road in front of the Assembly Hall—still there—and past the ancient Roman stone marking Malcolm's memorial—were some of his ashes there? Then down toward the medical gate past the building where Jean had taught a boy from one of the families they said had kidnapped me. Met up with the NBC crew at medical gate, under the big old banyan tree, and told Fred and John of my encounter with the president of AUB. They too were dumbfounded. They had been in touch with the director of information on campus and were waiting for permission to film in a customary way. "Can we call New York and get some support from the NBC office there?"

And thus I returned to AUB where I had been prevented from coming on June 9, 1985, so long ago. Nostalgia of days gone by met the filming needs of the present and since we couldn't film right away on campus as planned, we took off with NBC for our old shopping haunts of Hamra with a get-together at Buckleys for Wednesday half-planned with Marilyn. Meantime, John asked us if we would mind just moving in at the Summerland with them, which would ease the travel and communications logistics. He preferred to have us available at all times in case anything interesting came up. So later in the day, we moved down to that beautiful hotel. My last recollection of it had been speeding by it with Islamic Jihad on the 9th of June of 1985. What a change this time! But we said "Hello Summerland" with a very reluctant "Good-bye Buckley Manor!"

Meantime, the interviews and visits have been going wonderfully well, and my impression at least at this point is that John and Fred are both very happy with how things are going; ... we surely are. Our visit to Smith's Grocery was ecstatic, and

Patrick (the owner) received us with big smiles and open arms, and it was all on camera!! Then the meat man, Ibrahim, and the drink man, Aziz, and the cheese man, Youssef, were all blown away that we were there. The cameras got it all in its authentic and real Lebanese welcome. Jean saw and had nonstop exchange with one of her teaching companions, Nada Haddad; … amazing reunion.

After Smith's, we walked around the streets and saw the city again—much the same, really, but electric wires strung everywhere from everywhere as people tap into lines as they can for a bit of electricity. Saw the Four Steps Down bookstore that Terry and I had talked about so often … . It smelled awfully musty (no air conditioning) so we did not stay long there. Then off to lunch at a nice place across the street from Nasr, near the end of Bliss St. … . Wonderful Meza with perfect service and we perfectly appreciated it. Checked in to the hotel for a bit of a rest after that and then it was off to the southern suburbs; … they were fascinating to say the least … . We went to the place of my kidnapping on the cutoff road to the Corniche. Fred and I did an interview, and talked of the kidnap scene. Then to the north end of the NE-SW runway of the airport, and found a rooftop to look down it from, near to the spot where Father Martin had been told to say his last prayers with a gun at his head. Lo and behold, what did we find but the home of one of Jean's former students! What a fantastic coincidence … . He was an exceedingly nice fellow, with lots of the neighbor kids around all over the place, also very nice youngsters … . Fred and I did an interview looking down the runway which went well again … a shot of the setting sun … then back to the hotel, and cool air.

Had a call from a Mr. Vincent Battle, the chargé d'affaires at the American embassy, who had been informed by Undersecretary of State Ed Djerejian that we were here, and that they were very concerned about my presence here in Lebanon, but were, however, very willing to help us in any way they could. I thanked him for that and relayed to him Al Buckley's comment about safety in Beirut vs. D.C. and New York … . "Danger? Americans are a lot safer here than in D.C. or New York!" [Which indeed turned out to be true, for Jean's surgeon brother Dave told us after our return, "While you were being safe in Beirut, I was being mugged in downtown Syracuse and ended up unconscious in the hospital."] Battle and I had a very nice conversation in fact, and I told him about our experiences so far in Lebanon. He did his duty, however, and told us unequivocally, "It is still very dangerous here for Americans … . You know that the 'travel advisory' is still in force?" What he didn't say was either that I was an embarrassment or that I should leave immediately, or that I was here illegally.

TUESDAY, AUG. 31—Day 2. Slept well and were up by six, and down to breakfast with Fred and out to golf club to do another in-depth discussion for their film … good vibes all around. Up to Buckleys, and they said OK for Jean to do her interview there, which also was just great; … ecstasy all around, and we are all fired up about the big party planned for tomorrow night at the Buckleys. Everyone who wants to come is invited, so it will be a big celebration … .

Our biggest reaction up to now: the overriding paranoia about security. Rumor and misinterpretation must be as great or even greater than when I first came! Obviously Haddadin is still much affected by the syndrome, but perhaps there is still a bit of manipulation of the situation through fear as Jean found over the years, and also, perhaps, although I might be wrong, a bit of feeling of threat to the Lebanese hegemony over the AUB in a Returning American. If I can come, then everyone can come, and Americans will have top jobs. Not true, can't be in this "Mutual Concern" university, and yet the talk floats about that AUB Christian administrators are happy that "it's our university now" and see threat at the time "when the blue-eyes come back ... ."

WEDNESDAY, AUG. 31—Today we had another experience at the parking gate; the guard would not let us on campus and called Main Gate to get permission for us, which amazingly was again denied. Then when we went to the Medical Gate one of the security men who had known us from the good old days told us that Captain Chalak, head of security, wanted to talk to us, so we went along there, and met him. He's a very pleasant fellow in his mid-forties, and was obviously embarrassed on his part that he had had to turn us down on orders from New York. It was the traditional Lebanese hospitality and we assured him that we had no problem with his following orders ... . Left his office to find at least a dozen of my former security guards to give me heartfelt greetings, hugs, and even a tear or two of happiness that I am still alive ... . Very moving scene—the word of my presence must have gone out around the entire campus to bring that many to headquarters! Could it be that Captain Chalak had as a gentleman kept us there long enough for the news to make the rounds? At any rate, this was our "official welcome" to AUB and the genuine warmth in that security office touched my heart and made up for all else ... . Jean did her interview at the front, locked gate of the Hariri English Building, and then we went down to the gate which was open, down the hill a little, and were met by a very hostile woman who shooed us away in the most unceremonious way ... . Jeff arrived with camera rolling, much to their distress, and though Jean asked him to stop in deference to their wishes, Jeff simply said "tough shit" and kept it rolling—much too great a news story I guess. How that can be positive for AUB I don't know for it was really incredible that they were doing this to Jean, who had been in and out of these gates for six and a half years, and given her life as assistant director of the program. Seems, however, that AUB had circulated our photos to every gate with a notice saying that "these people are not to be admitted to AUB." We left the area not to return for we would not jeopardize the jobs of these people who needed them so desperately. We saw that in the eyes of the Hariri guard when I asked him, "Do you know her?" "Yes."

To Buckleys' for The Party; ... the cameras set up to record arrivals and reactions of our old friends ... but nicely and informally. The film crew were themselves set to join in the party. An absolutely wonderful evening. Sharif and Joana came. The deans we had invited didn't materialize but rumor had it that they had been warned not to attend, or to speak to us in case of cameras … . But Tony Kassab was there, and his greeting made up for the rest. It was genuine and sincere and warm as toast. [A year later as we transcribe this we mourn Tony who just died of a massive heart attack—maybe his heart was too big for Lebanon. Such a true and wonderful friend he was where friendship was on the line.]

THURSDAY, SEPT. 1—Baalbek Day! Had an early start, stopped for a great labneh sandwich at the Laiterie in Shtaura. Rolled on up to our long-sought destination Baalbek and right up to the Roman ruins … . How spectacular, how grand, how totally beyond words to describe … . We had a great tour by a great guide, and the cameras were rolling, including Jean's. Had noticed a car behind us all the way and, conspicuous by their nonchalance and absolute attendance and proximity, Lebanese Security made their presence known. Must be the result of the call I had last night from a major in Lebanese Security. Felt good somehow—perhaps especially since it felt sincerely meaningful. The Lebanese government wanted us for sure to stay safe, but we felt from these individual men a personal desire that we stay safe. Turns out that a picture of me and a news story finally made its way into the papers and they worry about me.

Workers were taking down the awnings for the Musa Sadr services of commemoration for his disappearance in Libya and Jean said, "Feels familiar." … Meanwhile Gerald Butt was phoning Hizbollah headquarters to set up a meeting with Hajj Hasan Khalil, political chief of Hizbollah. Tentatively set up. So we hightailed it from the Temple of Bacchus to Beirut and the "Lion's Den" in the southern suburbs … . Had frankly a dicey reception at first, with many questions put to us as to why we were here at all; … a lot of indecision, but finally they were satisfied and escorted us to a place a little down the road where we were received by Hajj Hasan … in a very ceremonial room with very fancy chairs and photos of Khomeini and of Khamenei, former president of Iran, on the walls. But our camera crew was not allowed to join us, despite Gerald's negotiating skills. Only Gerald and Jean and I were admitted. First, with Gerald translating all the way, we had from Hajj Hasan a long lecture on the evils of Israel, and how the U.S. should not be supporting them. He said at one point such an important thing I think—"You were a victim of the reaction to the policies of Israel and America, but that policy was as wrong as the American policy … but that is all in the past; … this is new times now." As close I guess to an apology as we will ever get out of Lebanon, I am sure. Interestingly enough, then, in came both their cameras and ours, and it became obvious that our NBC crew had not been allowed in until the Hizbollah TV station cameras were on location as well. With both sets in place, the real nitty-gritty began. We had a nice interchange in front of the cameras, theirs as well as ours, including a tape recorder that they wanted to put down somewhere, and to their surprise, I invited them to put it right in front of me … . I made my greetings anew, and then a few statements from Hajj, and then some pointed questions about the south, which I responded honestly to. "I have said everywhere in all the speeches I have given in America and even have I said it in Jerusalem—*Israel must get out of South Lebanon.*" That *really* surprised them, for sure, and from that moment on, the entire ambience changed and it all ended with cakes and puree of strawberry for everyone all around. Amazing, for the party menu was just like the treats in the good old days when Islamic Jihad wanted to be nice to us—only more of it and better this time!

FRIDAY, SEPT. 2—A beautiful vacation day at the Summerland while the NBC crew went their way getting pictures of the Ouzai area and other things they had in their minds for the documentary. Leisurely breakfast, writing, beaching, lounging, soaking up the Old Beirut ambience. At 11:30 P.M., we had a joyous reunion with my colleague, Dean of Agriculture Adib Saad and his wife Ahida, who happened to be at a wedding reception at the Summerland. What a coincidence to meet them there. We had a great long visit, including discussion of all our joint problems over the years and then all the good things that were happening and the hope for what was to come for the FAFS—a dialogue between true friends thus ending our visit to AUB, Beirut, and Lebanon.

Saturday morning, after saying au revoir to John and Fred and the marvelous camera crew, we were on our way to Zurich, thence to Washington and Denver. Lots of hours with lots of thoughts about what we had seen and experienced in Lebanon. It seemed to me that things were so much better in the country. The airport was infinitely busier than it had ever been while I had been there, the restaurants were going like gangbusters, the road over the mountains into the Bekaa was seething with traffic, and the Bekaa itself was raising its wonderful vegetables again instead of hashish. Back in Beirut buildings were beginning to be rebuilt all over the city, although there remains an incredible amount of destruction to be taken care of yet—those war years had wreaked an enormous amount of havoc on the place, far more than I had ever seen during my precaptivity days and that was enormous. I was frankly aghast. Shortly after my arrival in 1983, I recalled walking through Martyr's Square with visiting professor Dr. Owen Brough, an economist from Arizona. The whole area then was a no-man's-land—the desecration was unbelievable after nearly eight years of continuous bombardment—and Owen, the economist in him coming out, kept remarking, "I wonder just how much it cost to do this much damage?!" Now I was seeing the results of a further ten years of continuous, senseless bombardment. What men will do in an effort to get control of their fellow men and the land and institutions on which they reside. Then I thought again of Jean's stories of how the young people from the East had come back after the collapse of the Green Line and had hugged their brothers on the West Side of the city and talked nonstop, so excited were they to be back on the main campus, or in some cases places where they had never been all their lives, only a few miles from their homes! That the Green Line was gone had to be an omen of better times to come. That the Lebanese use the surface destruction as a chance to probe archaeologically into the lower, ancient layers of their city as they plan their new and renovated "City Center" as part of their ten-year rehabilitation and reconstruction program is also strongly positive as a sign that their historic and cultural pride is still intact. And that they have a ten-year rehabilitation and reconstruction program launched is indicative of determination and Lebanese go-gettiveness.

We saw people still cautious in their optimism, however, almost as though they were going to wait and see if something further would bring about another mayhem. They were so used to disappointment, and so many cease-fires that were always broken almost as soon as they were agreed to. But this one seems real, and if the Israelis will only pull out of the south and the Syrians then pull out their troops, the Lebanese will finally feel that peace has come at last. Then the Lebanese diaspora will begin to return, or if they decide not to come back, at least most of them will pour money into their beloved homeland to help in re-building it. So far, most of them are playing a very cautious game, and want proof positive that their money will not just go down a rat hole on the resumption of civil war. There isn't anyone better as an auger of fortunes in Lebanon than a Lebanese who could invest in the country if he or she wanted to do so. The time will come. And when the Lebanese themselves lead the way to investment in their own country, the world will follow suit.

And what of the American University of Beirut? The State Department travel ban means that no Americans can be hired to work on the campus, so the concept of "A Mutual Concern" on-site is a bit moot. But one gets attuned to "Arabic Time" and the patience required to deal with it. "What's impossible one year is a blessed given another" as we found with OCP and the war in the East. So hold on a few years, for a "true" AUB is worth it. We put this to the chairman of the Board of Trustees about our interaction with the university in the detailed report we sent him on our return:

> The true AUB was there for us, however, in one hour in a friend's apartment with a bed, eggs in the refrigerator, our cat in a new home, and air conditioning; in the peaceful stroll through the campus in the sunlight with friends in the morning be-fore the gates were fully barred; in the warmth of the sharing of hugs with friends, colleagues, former students we saw everywhere. It was all we wanted or needed in order to come home to AUB as we did to Beirut and Lebanon, to know it again and

feel complete and restored. Indeed we found that the true AUB is there to be touched and recognized—it cannot be kept inside the gates nor can it be kept outside the gates. And we'll never forget that experience, even as we would challenge both the decision of some to manipulate with fear and the manner in which the situation was handled and allowed to escalate in a most negative way. Jean and I are, after all, most reasonable people, we love AUB, and we would have responded positively to a calm, reasoned discussion of the issues and a consensus reached for the true good of the university. Before Dr. Haddadin and Mr. Tomey called President Haddad, they could have come to welcome us and then sit and talk with us to get the facts— that we were in an apartment by invitation; that we had checked through thoroughly the security situation in Lebanon with responsible people and made personal provision for it before coming; that we had also checked through our travel and plans with the vice president for development in New York; that we were part of a documentary to be filmed to give Americans a positive image of Lebanon and AUB; and that before any filming, NBC would be checking with Ibrahim Khouri who would by Monday morning have a fax from Richard Bannin in New York. Their subsequent call to Dr. Haddad could have been conducted in a true and rational manner and he and I too could have then had a meaningful dialogue. A definitive decision could have been reached the first day and everything handled quietly and with dignity—either a two-hour filming session on that holiday morning on the stroll through campus, a filming from the street going toward the gates, or even no filming or presence on campus at all. Whatever the decision, a most positive image would have gone out through the documentary to the American people. As it is, NBC does have negative footage, but we want you to know that we have spoken most seriously with John Siceloff and said that our sincere wish is that they put out as positive an image of AUB as they can in the final version of the program given all the circumstances. John said that his feeling for it was the same as ours—he is truly a sensitive person—he requested from us and is presumably making use of earlier film including Super 8 footage, stills, and slides of ours showing happy former times on campus with our students and faculty friends. It can thus be very positive at the same time that it shows no AUB involvement now, in line with Dr. Haddad's concern, with an American who has come as an American.

Trust that this comes to you in my hopes of serving, as I meant my return to serve, the greater interests of the AUB, for which I developed a lasting and genuine affection and a very sincere commitment—indeed I was willing to give my life for the place and still am—during my all too brief association with it. It was truly important for us to make this return to know and to show that six and a half years of captivity can dim neither our commitment nor our spirit. Jean is one with me and we continue devoted supporters of the true AUB in hopes that it too will be restored.

I tried in my mind to deal squarely with the fears the Christian vice presidents at AUB used to bar me from the campus, namely that my very presence there posed a threat to the university. The chairman of the board had answered my report to him with the response: "I think your return at the time that you made it (on the eve of the Prophet's birthdate and with a big general strike poised for the day after that) was ill-considered and potentially quite harmful." Would any building I was in be a target? In the Lebanon of 1993, the Shiite role seemed to me to have changed dramatically. Terry Anderson was told at the time of his release, "This was not a useful tactic. We will not do it again." And I was likewise informed by Hajj Hasan Khalil of Hizbollah, "These are new times." And indeed we had seen on footage NBC had taken one afternoon how Hizbollah, disarmed in Beirut, had turned its attention to the construction of hospitals and water systems in the southern suburbs, and in general, was becoming much more politically active. In the most recent parliamentary elections in 1992, the biggest gainers were the Shia, while by boycotting the elections, the Christians were the marked losers. It would appear that Hizbollah had found general and anti-American violence no longer productive and was trying other avenues. Certainly, we had known for years that the vast majority of the Lebanese, including the Shiite community, were sick and tired of the war and the fighting and the car bombs and the maiming and kidnapping of their young people. Our strong impression was that Hizbollah's focus would center fully now on its war in the south against Israeli occupation—where it began. Hajj Hasan made it plain to me in our meeting that Hizbollah had been formed to fight for their homeland taken from them by the Israelis in 1982, and they would continue until it was theirs again. They find their support, of course, in Syria.

It reminds us of the Soviet-American Cold War tactics of fighting the "big war" with "little wars," always of course with real people. The Syrians maintain their challenge to the Israelis by supporting the Shiite Hizbollah militia in the south who oppose the Israeli presence in every way possible—suicide car bombers, attacks on the South Lebanon Army, and attacks on the Israeli Army itself whenever it ventures into its self-proclaimed "security zone" in the south. This, the real war zone, is now localized on the Syrian-Israeli "red line" in marked contrast to the rest of Lebanon. It is obviously a part of the Syrian strategy to continue harassment of the Israelis to persuade them to leave Lebanon and allow Syria to resume its hegemony over that part of "Greater Syria," which it had never really recognized as truly independent. But the Taif Accords are on record with promised Syrian withdrawal, and Lebanon must and will be independent when peace is made among all. Peace *must* be made among all, and it is a long time coming. Anything involving Assad would be so.

But Syria with the Lebanese Army and its own army has effected security for the rest of Lebanon, and the threat to Americans there seemed to us to have diminished markedly with the State Department ban on travel to Lebanon appearing now after eight years to be a needless harassment of the Lebanese and of the Americans who want and need to travel there. It was, and is, regarded as totally unnecessary now by all the Lebanese to whom we talked. And the prime minister, Rafiq Hariri, is incensed that travel is still banned. The most severe impact is on American businesspeople, who are being denied the opportunity to participate in the rebuilding of Lebanon, a multibillion dollar project. The French, the Brits, the Germans, the Italians, and the Japanese are all already there and reaping the benefits, while American businesspeople become the losers from the State Department policies based on its perception of the dangers for Americans there and a resulting problem for them if an incident should occur. "Americans are marked and the information stored." That, we would say, is anywhere and everywhere—America does the same with Shiite fundamentalists also. It is the world we live in. At the same time, we need to recognize and seize the "new times."

But how does Lebanon relate to other parts of the Islamic world? Having been face to face with Islamic Jihad in Lebanon, I have found myself since caught in thinking, discussing, studying, and reading about the Islamic question today. The entire Middle East indeed still seems to resemble a cauldron, with crises springing up from time to time in diverse parts of it. Extremist fundamentalism seems definitely on the rise. And yet there are many varieties of this fundamentalism, and differing reasons for its appearing in each region. It is very important that we not develop general paranoia against all Islam or Islamic countries, but truly understand and discriminate. What is it that causes so many young men to espouse "Islamic fundamentalism," the return in extremist ways to a pure form of Islam, after decades or even centuries of suffering from modernization, change, and Western oppression? Certainly it is poverty and the denial of equal opportunity that make young people easy to recruit to a cause that offers them relief and restoration of their dignity. Political Islam certainly promises that and much more, but so far it has not shown itself able to deliver. The fundamentalists have been frequently, in their tirades and crusades against existing regimes, much more effective at diagnosing what is wrong with the government than coming up with viable alternatives based upon their fundamentalist tenets. Indeed, as Graham Fuller points out in a *Middle East Insight* article: "Islamist regimes in Iran and Sudan have demonstrated that in many respects they are patently worse—less effective, less capable, sometimes more violent—than some of their predecessors … and they have fallen into greater international isolation as a consequence of ill-considered policies."[11] In reality, most governments in the Islamic world are still heavily based upon Western paradigms, a fact that further adds to the frustrations and antagonisms of the extremists.

Young fundamentalists indeed, as I saw firsthand, suffer terrible frustration at trying to live in a modern age, in which many of them thoroughly enjoy TV, telephones, walkie-talkies, automobiles, Pepsi, and blue jeans, while at the same time they try to cling to their seventh-century Koran and Islamic traditions. In the West, it is easy for us to say that what they need in Islam is a reformation like the Christian one sparked by Luther. But the vast majority of Moslems, especially those who were holding us hostage, still believe absolutely in the infallability of the Koran, and would not countenance *any* attempt to reinterpret what they consider the absolute word of God. Supported by more moderate Moslems, an Islamic movement called the *ijtihad* is attempting just such a reinterpretation, but so far has had no impact on Islamic forms of governance—the conservatives continue to hew to the literal texts. These problems were certainly very obvious to me, and Terry and I used to argue at length about them. I was fairly convinced that fundamentalist Islam is wrongfully confining its adherents to the seventh century while Terry of course took the other viewpoint.

What then should be our reactions in the West? One thing is certain: No matter how much we fear it, no matter how much we rail against it, or even try to destroy it, no matter how much we try to ignore it—Islam is here to stay. On the other hand, Islam cannot possibly repeal the Western enlightenment, no matter how much its rational thought and its assault on revealed religion offends and infuriates Moslems. We must therefore learn to live with each other, learn much better how to understand each other and to tolerate each other. The dangers for us all if we don't were voiced in *The Economist* article, "Islam and the West": "One of the commonest prophecies of the mid-1990s is that the Muslim world is heading for a fight with the other parts of the world that do not share its religio-political opinions …. On current evidence, this is by no means impossible."[12] In his volume, *Target America*, Yossef Bodansky argues that the fundamentalist attack on us has already begun—the Trade Center bombing was only the tip of the iceberg, and they are hard at work forming cells all over Europe and America to carry out further terrorist attacks. I hope he's wrong. But a disturbing thing—everything I know about the hostage issue he has covered with accuracy. Perhaps he is right about *all?*

Whatever the projection of the future, the *extremely critical* thing for us right now, it seems to Jean and me, is to take the opportunity, in this time we have, to learn about and understand Islam, to seek out and dialogue with its responsible leaders, and be *proactive* in helping to combat the conditions of poverty and inequality in Islamic countries that breed militant and fanatic fundamentalism. *And* to remember that the bombs in the streets of Paris in September 1986 were apparently from Christian extremists, and the horror in Oklahoma City in April 1995 was apparently from American extremist militia. We need to understand and be proactive about all—that is, if we care about our children.

Jean

What a joy and a fascination to return to Beirut with Tom that first week of September 1993! I had realized how important it was for him to go back—to retake control of his total experience there, to regain his former images of Lebanon in this new time along with the people, the places, and the years so that it was current and positive for him. I hadn't, however, realized fully how much it would mean to me not only that he could give me the places of his life there, but also that I could give him *my* life there during the six and a half years—my friends, my work, my days, so that our "sharing" could be as complete as possible. I myself had been back twice since Tom's release—in January and April of 1992 to take the reality of his freedom personally to our friends there and to expedite the shipment of our things back to Fort Collins. But to be able to show him the Hariri Program building (no matter the cleaning woman and the guard so frightened and adamant that we not enter—we saw it together and I pointed out the windows of my office and the classrooms and the big entry doors where the thousands of students had gone in and out), and to show him Smith's Grocery and Hamra again, and the Heinekens' apartment with Crystal and the residue of so many happy occasions of friendship shared there, and the desolation of our home after the blast at College Hall, and Summerland Hotel, and the Corniche. In all this, my life was no longer disconnected from his. But as the week went along I came to realize something else so important, something I see again in reading Tom's diary of events—that in that week, we were forging together a new relationship with a Lebanon of 1993 and finding here the meanings of what we had done in the past that would work forward into a tomorrow for whoever would be there to carry on. I think it's contained best in four small stories or vignettes.

The first vignette became an NBC videocam shot—our walking to the Medical Gate of AUB with the bar down and the great "No Entry" signs on it. How much is contained in this picture of a thousand words?! Can a university be a university if there is "no entry"? Can a university be a true university without a cross-fertilization of the ideas of many nationalities instead of just one? Can it be that Tom poses a threat to this institution he loves? Is there anything due a man who has been willing to give his life for an institution and still is? Can it be that the image of the "Returning American" is anathema to administrators on both sides of "The Great Atlantic Gap" between New York where AUB is chartered and Beirut where the campus is—that the American administration makes policy according to State Department decree or that the Lebanese hegemony now in charge of the campus cannot accept a shared responsibility, "A Mutual Concern" as it were? Does this represent the American spirit or the sacred rite of Lebanese hospitality? When the State Department ban on American passports to Lebanon is lifted, the answers will, of course, be found. What struck us as we stood at the closed gates is again the frame of our AUB experience: Where we started with a Lebanese visa problem to get in, we now end ten years later with an American passport problem to stay out. This is the real and complex issue of "no entry." When a Lebanese hegemony says that control of a chartered foreign university must be in their hands, are they destroying that university? One can't help but ask: Should they not be honest and nationalize, put their own money where another's money is, and give up trying to have their university cake and eat it too? And on our side, when the State Department decrees that our passports are not valid for this country or any country, is it not denying Americans a basic freedom that is their absolute right? The State Department must be able to advise and warn us as citizens in the strongest terms, but it must also give us the freedom to travel—to any place, even space, that we want to go and must go. Was our country not founded and built on the fact that people came to a dangerous place? That is the definition of American. And Americans in our new global society must continue to go, and be able to go, to dangerous places, or where will our futures be? The corollary, however, is clear: Americans cannot hold any government, including their own, responsible for their safety, just as the pioneers could not hold any government responsible for their safety in that new continent we call North America. It was then and must be now "At Your Own Risk." Just as we must accept as adults the risks we take on our national highways, in our workplaces, and with a cup of hot coffee from a fast-food restaurant. We watched in December 1992 the furor over Aspen skiers in our state of Colorado— skiers who went out into bad weather not fully prepared, got lost in a blizzard, and put hundreds into search and concern for them. In all the hullabaloo following, we couldn't help but think that the issue here was not one of skiers being to blame for putting rescuers at undue trouble and risk—the issue was instead that this is America. People will, and must, be free to go into danger without expectation of help if they get into trouble. And people will, and must as Americans, go out to search and help and succor if they can those who are in trouble. If we lose *either* concept, we lose the best of what it is to be American.

The second vignette—we got to go to Baalbek! From the start it had called to us. I guess I was half-Roman anyway with the studies I'd made of Seneca. But we had also heard so much about the ancient ruins of the immense Roman temple complex of Heliopolis built in the great Bekaa Valley that the Romans had envisioned as the breadbasket of their empire—the Great Columns, that were all that was left of the Temple to Jupiter after the earthquake, and the Temple to Bacchus (which sort of puts it all together—heaven and earth—if you will) so portrayed by etching and then by photograph over the years, and the sound and light shows they had had there "in the old days" since World War II—*Romeo and Juliet, Antony and Cleopatra* as the Porters described in 1957. But once the Iranian Revolutionary Guards had by Syrian invitation become ensconced at Baalbek in the Sheikh Abdullah barracks in 1983, they had put the ruins off-limits. Many, many of my students had invited me to their homes in Baalbek during those long years of Tom's captivity, but I never went—maybe subconsciously I didn't want to go without Tom. So what a joy finally to go to those Roman ruins and climb the great stairs with him and to feel the ancient and the present merge, as off to one side I watched the NBC team film Tom standing dwarfed at the foot of those enormous Roman columns in between which all of us including the camera could see the hill in the distance with the Sheikh Abdullah barracks where had been the cells and the chains of Islamic Jihad. There was for me that tremendous overlay and telescoping of time and empires of power with the individual limned against it—*Plus ça change, plus c'est la même chose.* How many individuals over those centuries of Roman, Arab, Umayyad, Christian Crusade, Ottoman, French, Christian/Druze/Moslem power had felt the chains? Interestingly, God's earthquake had brought down all but six of the mighty columns of the Temple to Jupiter but left almost completely intact the lower Temple to Bacchus. Makes one think.

A third vignette—that first day on the second-floor roof of the family home of my former student in the general area of the place where Tom was held in 1986 by the airport. "Over there was the 'bad area,'" my young friend said. "And I remember years ago being awakened in the night by noise outside—I went to the door and it was the TWA hostages being taken down the street by the hard men with guns. They threatened and said, 'Go to bed. This is none of your business. Go!' And I went." And thus on Haytham's rooftop, while Tom and NBC's Fred Francis looked down the runway of the airport with Father Jenco's moon on the left side rising as the great sun sank down on the right side and they talked of captivity, I sat back with the young man I had known as a student eight years before and we talked and talked of old days and what had come for him since. He had gone to Beirut University College from the Hariri Program and had graduated in four years with a degree in computer science. Then he had gone back to his village, once outside in the countryside but now enclosed in the southern suburbs, to work and support his family. Proudly he told me of the good job he had gotten as a distributor of Pepsi-Cola for West Beirut: "And my best area is Ras Beirut with the universities—the students love to drink Pepsi-Cola," he laughed. By this time all the neighborhood children and half of the adult population of the area were gathered on the rooftop with us, excited by the action and the filming, the older men showing their nonchalance as well as their interest by getting out their tric-trac or backgammon board and indulging in their favorite pastime as they kept watch on the ensuing drama of the roof. A small boy came up with his plastic AK-47 to play, and Tom went over to talk through our interpreter to the group of children giggling and laughing. Some young men appeared, much more serious and inclined to be suspicious. But then Haytham, true to his tradition of hospitality and his current position in the community, dispensed Pepsis to one and all in paper cups and it was all at once a party atmosphere. If Tom and I had needed anything to tell us that we had made the right choice to stay and make whatever sacrifice was necessary, this was it. Clearly obvious in his dress and manner and in the regard of the children and the adults for him, this young Shiite, now a man, was a budding leader in his village and among his people. What a privilege to have been part of his education and his rite of passage into manhood—and to be able to multiply him by the several thousands of all persuasions that Tom and I personally knew. It was so clear, and we could be content that the barring or opening of gates—whether by Islamic Jihad or by AUB—had no real significance beside the genuine cultural and educational interchange that had taken place through them.

The fourth very moving vignette—in Hizbollah headquarters ("That AUB should exhibit less magnanimity than Hizbollah is ominous," said one former AUB board member). Scarved, reserved, quiet, yet very observant, I sat on a couch to the side and watched Tom and Hajj Hasan Khalil, the political chief of the fundamentalist Shiite organization presumed responsible for the kidnappings, interact in formal conversation. It was a wonder—to see these two men talk civilly, seated side by side: no guns, no chains, no captor, no captive. I looked to the back of the room as they drew to a close and saw the room absolutely full now of bearded men leaning in closely to see all this happening. Came the question about South Lebanon and Tom's strong straight answer, "Israel must get out of South Lebanon," and the tension dissolving into the party atmosphere. Same as with the young men on Haytham's rooftop. At the end, Tom and Hajj Hasan Khalil shook hands, and as Tom turned away to go, Hajj Hasan's hand went quite naturally up over his heart in the Arabic gesture of respect. The picture stays with me and I think often of that symbolic meeting and that symbolic handshake. It was echoed macrocosmically ten days later when back in the States we watched Rabin and Arafat shake hands on the White House lawn. In neither handshake was there a giving-in, a Stockholm Syndrome, a compromise, a question of forgiveness, a forging of trust. What there was instead was a civilized meeting of two men with history between them, two men who could say, "Time to stop violence and go forward in peace." Why should we Americans not be able to do this if we expect Arabs and Israelis with a thousand times six and a half years of mutual violence to do it? There can be the recognition of "new times." There must always be the opportunity seized for "new times."

Next day, the last in our revisit of Lebanon, I went down to the beach at the Summerland Hotel, looked north and west into the Mediterranean Sea, and thought over all these things and all those years. What we had done was good, was right. I just knew that. And I thought how it was the culmination of the letter of thanks to President Reagan I had drafted six and a half years ago at the end of January 1987 when he had received me and accepted our avenue for dialogue between the American government and Sayeed Fadlallah:

Dear President Reagan,

I would like to say a very personal Thank You to you for receiving me again yesterday and giving so much of your valuable time to listen and then to make that decision to give our bridge a chance as a new avenue toward solution of the hostage crisis. I pledge to you our dedicated effort to fulfill the trust you have placed in us and may we pray for success.

I thank you also for understanding and for telling me you understand why American educators are still in Lebanon against what seems like all reason and government warning. It is a vital shift in perspective to see us not as crazy people who deserve what we get but as committed teachers of valuable young people. Both "deserve to be saved" as you said, and I truly think you will do this in validating an avenue which can serve as a continuing and positive process toward conciliation, coexistence, and peace in Lebanon. I was warned, "The field is full of mines," and so it is, but I somehow feel that even the men who have taken the risks and paid the consequences will think that it was worth it if it has served as a step in the peace process. My conviction has never wavered—that the only true and lasting means to counter terrorism are the positive ones—showing our belief in the basic American values of fair play and the rights of the individual and educating the young people to them—not only those who are disposed toward us, but also those who are not—those taught to hate, to kidnap, or to kill. Again, the vital shift in perspective—as true Americans we must not run from danger but instead go into it with all the best that's in us to find the goodness and attach and cultivate it for the future. I can tell you from experience that there are thousands in Lebanon who want this America very much.

I feel it is symbolic that the day after your tribute to the *Challenger* crew, you would receive me to give recognition to the idea that the frontiers of resolving human conflict are as big and as worthwhile a challenge as space.

It has been my honor and very great pleasure to get to know you personally.

Again, With Respect and Appreciation,

Jean Sutherland

Epilogue

"These Are New Times ..."

We came home from Lebanon that September of 1993, having walked under old balconies and having found new ones. Refreshed and at peace, we understood that it wasn't for us to think of "going back again"—accomplished for the time was our mission at AUB and in Lebanon, "whose worth's unknown although his height be taken." And we understood too that we could make positive affirmation of the experiences we have had, always to be such a significant part of us, for we cannot regret a work undertaken and carried out by conscious choice, especially when it was a work shared with so many other people and part of a very large peace process. Accomplished too now is our book, ending in a new beginning as we look forward to what's next for us, for there is much to do in our global society. Perhaps it will come in another "There's a job for you, but if you take it, it's 'at your own risk.' Do you want the job?" "Yes." So we keep Cousin Margaret's new calendar for 1995 on the wall as a reminder, turned to June, the quotation from Henry James in her beautiful calligraphy opening out in the middle of the month as if to mark and make positive the tenth anniversary of abduction:

Appendix I

Abbreviations

ACS—American Community School

AJME—Americans for Justice in the Middle East

AMCARES—Americares Foundation for Emergency Relief

AMIDEAST—America in the Middle East/Organization for Education and Training for Middle East Development

AREC—Agricultural Research and Education Center, of the AUB in the Bekaa Valley

AUB—American University of Beirut

AUH—American University Hospital

BUC—Beirut University College

CSU—Colorado State University

ESL—English as a Second Language

FAFS—Faculty of Agricultural and Food Sciences at AUB

FAO—Food and Agriculture Organization

IC—International College, K–12 school next to AUB

IRA—Irish Republican Army

LBC—Lebanese Broadcasting Corporation

MEA—Middle East Airlines

NEST—Near East School of Theology

NSC—National Security Council

OCP—Off-Campus Program

OPEC—Organization of Petroleum Exporting Countries

PFLP—Popular Front for the Liberation of Palestine

PLO—Palestine Liberation Organization

PPS—Syrian Progressive Party

PSP—Progressive Socialist Party, Jumblatti Druze Party and Militia

PSPA— Political Science and Public Administration of the AUB

RFI—Radio France Internationale

RMC—Radio Monte Carlo

RPG—Rocket-Propelled Grenade

TESOL—Teachers of English to Speakers of Other Languages

TOEFL—Teachers of English as a Foreign Language

UN—United Nations

USAID—U.S. Agency for International Development

VOA—Voice of America

YPO—Young President's Organization

Appendix II

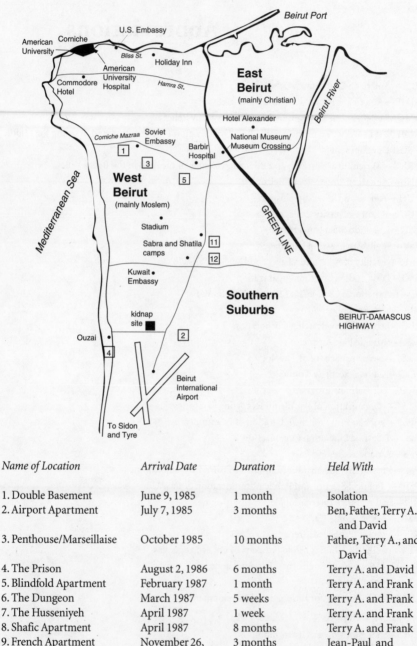

Name of Location	Arrival Date	Duration	Held With
1. Double Basement	June 9, 1985	1 month	Isolation
2. Airport Apartment	July 7, 1985	3 months	Ben, Father, Terry A., and David
3. Penthouse/Marseillaise	October 1985	10 months	Father, Terry A., and David
4. The Prison	August 2, 1986	6 months	Terry A. and David
5. Blindfold Apartment	February 1987	1 month	Terry A. and Frank
6. The Dungeon	March 1987	5 weeks	Terry A. and Frank
7. The Husseniyeh	April 1987	1 week	Terry A. and Frank
8. Shafic Apartment	April 1987	8 months	Terry A. and Frank
9. French Apartment	November 26, 1987	3 months	Jean-Paul and Marcel C.

General Locations Where Tom Was Held

Name of Location	Arrival Date	Duration	Held With
10. The Pit	March 4, 1988	2 months	Marcel C.
		9 months	Terry A., Frank, John, and Brian
11. Fadlallah Mosque	February 2, 1989	1 week	Frank
12. Toufeili Apartment	February 12, 1989	18 months	Terry A.
11. Fadlallah Mosque	August 23, 1990	3 months	Terry A. and John
13. Bekaa Mountain Marriot	November 2, 1990	6 months	Terry A., John, and Terry W.
14. Baalbek Hilton	May 2, 1991	6 months	Terry A., John, and Terry W.

Release: November 18, 1991, after 2,354 days (77 months) in captivity

Appendix III

Hostages

Hostage	Nationality	Date Abducted	Date Released
Terry Anderson	American	March 16, 1985	December 4, 1991
William Buckley	American	March 16, 1984	Killed in captivity in June 1985
Joseph Cicippio	American	September 12, 1986	December 1991
David Dodge	American	July 19, 1982	July 21, 1983
William Higgins	American	February 17, 1988	Killed in captivity in July 1989
David Jacobsen	American	May 28, 1985	November 2, 1986
Rev. Lawrence Jenko	American	January 8, 1985	July 26, 1986
Robert Polhill	American	January 24, 1987	April 22, 1990
Frank Reed	American	September 9, 1986	April 30, 1990
Frank Regier	American	February 10, 1984	April 15, 1984
Alann Steen	American	January 24, 1987	December 4, 1991
Thomas Sutherland	American	June 9, 1985	November 18, 1991
Edward Tracy	American	October 21, 1986	August 11, 1991
Jesse Turner	American	January 24, 1987	October 21, 1991
Ben Weir	American	May 8, 1984	September 14, 1985
Jan Cools	Belgian	May 21, 1988	June 15, 1989
Alec Collett	British	March 26, 1986	Killed in captivity in April 1986
Leigh Douglas	British	March 1986	Killed in captivity April 16, 1986
Brian Levick	British	Abducted and released in March 1985	
Jack Mann	British	May 12, 1989	September 1991
John McCarthy	British	April 17, 1986	August 1991
Geoffrey Nash	British	Abducted and released in March 1985	
Philip Padfield	British	March 1986	Killed in captivity April 16, 1986
Terry Waite	British	January 20, 1987	November 18, 1991
Jonathan Wright	British	August 1984	Escaped in September 1984

Hostage	Nationality	Date Abducted	Date Released
Nicholas Kluiters	Dutch	March 14, 1985	unknown
Roger Auque	French	January 1987	November 1987
Michael Brian	French	April 8, 1986	April 12, 1986
Marcel Carton	French	March 1985	May 4, 1988
Aurel Cornea	French	March 9, 1986	December 24, 1986
Marcel Coudari	French	February 2, 1986	November 10, 1986
Marcel Fontaine	French	March 1985	May 4, 1988
George Hansen	French	March 9, 1986	June 20, 1986
Christian Joubert	French	July 21, 1983	April 15, 1984
Jean-Paul Kauffmann	French	May 1985	May 4, 1988
Jean-Louis Normandin	French	March 1986	November 1987
Gilles Sidney Peyrolles	French	March 24, 1985	April 2, 1985
Michel Seurat	French	May 22, 1985	Died in captivity, date unknown
Camille Sontag	French	February 2, 1986	November 10, 1986
Rudolf Cordes	German	January 1987	September 7, 1988
Thomas Kemptner	German	May 16, 1989	June 1992
Alfred Schmidt	German	January 20, 1987	September 7, 1987
Ralph Schray	German	January 27, 1988	Five weeks later
Heinrich Struebig	German	May 16, 1989	June 1992
Mitheleshwar Singh	Indian	January 24, 2987	October 1988
Brian Keenan	Irish	April 11, 1986	August 24, 1990
Alberto Molinari	Italian	September 11, 1985	Killed, date unknown
William Jorgensen	Norwegian	February 5, 1988	One month later
Do Chae Sung	South Korean	January 31, 1986	October 26, 1987
Emmanuel Christen	Swiss	October 6, 1989	August 8, 1990
Elio Erriquez	Swiss	October 6, 1989	August 14, 1990
Jan Stening	Swiss	February 5, 1988	One month later
Eric Wehril	Swiss	January 3, 1985	Less than a week later
Peter Winkler	Swiss	November 17, 1988	One month later

Notes

1. (p. 20) From *The Moon and Sixpence* by W. Somerset Maugham (Doubleday, 1919), p. 276. Reprinted with permission.

2. (p. 22) From "Guerrilla U.," *Newsweek*, October 5, 1970, as quoted in *A Mutual Concern: The Story of the American University of Beirut* by John Munro (Caravan Books, 1977), p. 166. Reprinted with permission from Caravan Books and Newsweek, Inc. All rights reserved.

3. (p. 24) From *The Arabists: The Romance of an American Elite* by Robert D. Kaplan, p. 37. Copyright © 1993 by Robert D. Kaplan. Reprinted with permission of The Free Press, a division of Simon & Schuster.

4. (p. 25) From *Come with Me from Lebanon* by Ann Zwicker Kerr (Syracuse University Press, 1994), p. 234. Reprinted with permission from Syracuse University Press.

5. (p. 158) From "Iowa Child" in *Coloring Outside the Lines and Other Poems* by Sarah Hall Maney, 1982. Reprinted with permission from Sarah Hall Maney.

6. (p. 199) From *The Archetypal Significance of Gilgamesh: A Modern Ancient Hero* by Rivkah Schärf Kluger (Daimon Verlag, 1991), p. 44. Reprinted with permission from Daiman Verlag.

7. (p. 200) Personal Communication from Jim Abra, Isle of Wight. December 1991.

8. (p. 207) Reprinted with permission of Scribner, a Division of Simon & Schuster Inc. From *Turmoil and Triumph* by George P. Shultz. Copyright © 1993 George P. Shultz.

9. (pp. 275–276) From *A Trail of Memories: The Quotations of Louis L'Amour* compiled by Angelique L'Amour (Bantam Books, 1988). Reprinted with permission.

10. (p. 351) From Alexander Heidel (trans.), *The Gilgamesh Epic & Old Testament Parallels*, Tablet IV, column vi (p. 45) & Tablet V, column 1 (p. 45), University of Chicago Press, 1946. Reprinted with permission from the University of Chicago Press.

11. (p. 412–413) From Graham Fuller, "Has Political Islam Failed?" *Middle East Insight*, Jan./Feb. 1995, 8–11. Reprinted with permission from *Middle East Insight*.

12. (p. 413) From "Islam and the West," *The Economist*, August 6, 1994, p. 3. See also Yossef Bodansky, *Target America & The West: Terrorism Today* (S.P.I. Books, Shapulski Publishers, 1993).

Index

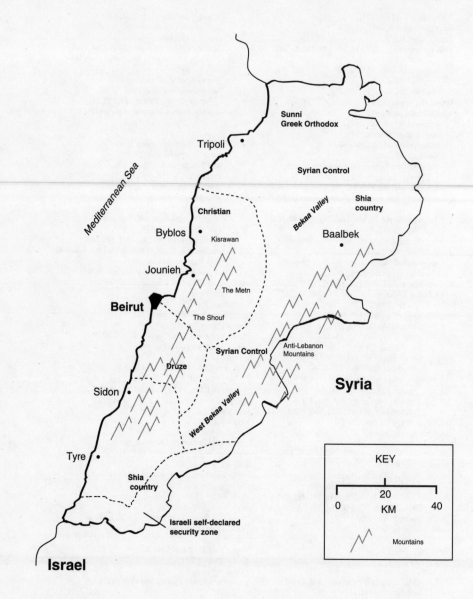

Sunni
Greek Orthodox

Tripoli

Mediterranean Sea

Syrian Control

Christian

Bekaa Valley

Shia
country

Byblos

Kisrawan

Baalbek

Jounieh

The Metn

Beirut

The Shouf

Anti-Lebanon
Mountains

Syrian Control

Syria

Druze

West Bekaa Valley

Sidon

Tyre

Shia
country

**Israel self-declared
security zone**

Israel

KEY

0   20   40
          KM

Mountains

Sectarian Lebanon